Encyclopedia of Rock, Pop & Folk Music in Canada

Encyclopedia
of
Rock, Pop & Folk Music
in
Canada

Rick Jackson

Second Edition
2.2

Hidden Brook Press
www.HiddenBrookPress.com
writers@HiddenBrookPress.com

Copyright © 2016 Hidden Brook Press
Copyright © 2016 Rick Jackson

All rights for content reverts to the author. All rights for book, layout and design remain with Hidden Brook Press. No part of this book may be reproduced except by a reviewer who may quote brief passages in a review. The use of any part of this publication reproduced, transmitted in any form or by any means, electronic, mechanical, photocopied, recorded or otherwise stored in a retrieval system without prior written consent of the publisher is an infringement of the copyright law.

Encyclopedia of Rock, Pop & Folk Music in Canada
by Rick Jackson

Cover Design – Richard M. Grove
Layout and Design – Richard M. Grove
Cover Images - Photographers unknown

Typeset in Garamond

Printed and bound in Canada

Library and Archives Canada Cataloguing in Publication

Jackson, Rick
[Encyclopedia of Canadian rock, pop & folk music]
    Encyclopedia of rock, pop & folk music in Canada / Rick Jackson. – Second edition.

Originally published in 1994 under title: Encyclopedia of Canadian rock,
   pop & folk music.
ISBN 978-1-927725-44-3

    1. Popular music--Canada--Encyclopedias. 2. Rock music--Canada--Encyclopedias. 3. Folk music--Canada--Encyclopedias. I. Title. II. Title: Encyclopedia of Canadian rock, pop & folk music.

ML102.P66J13 2016   781.640971   C2016-906501-4

Valdy

Allen Sisters

The Stampeders

The Emeralds

Encyclopedia of Rock, Pop & Folk Music in Canada

The Girlfriends

Hagood Hardy

The Checkerlads

The Mynah Birds

Rick Jackson

The Esquires

Contents:

Introduction by Rick Jackson – 1

Aarons and Ackley – 4
Abraham's Children – 4
Ronney Abramson – 5
Bryan Adams – 6
Susan Aglukark – 9
Chad Allan – 10
Allan Sisters – 11
Barry Allen – 11
Tommy Ambrose – 12
Bill Amesbury – 14
Paul Anka – 14
Peter Appleyard – 20
April Wine – 21
Jann Arden – 24
John Arpin – 25
The Arrows – 27

Bachman Turner Overdrive – 28
Randy Bachman – 30
The Band – 31
Barenaked Ladies – 34
The Barra Macneils – 36
Bearfoot – 37
Beau Dommage – 39
The Beau-Marks – 40
The Bells – 42
Willie P. Bennett – 43

Barney Bentall & The Legendary Hearts – 44
Bentwood Rocker – 55
Art Bergman – 46
Justin Bieber – 47
Big Sugar – 49
The Big Town Boys – 50
Bim – 51
Heather Bishop – 52
Terry Black – 53
Blue Rodeo – 54
The Blue Shadows – 56
Blvd – 57
Bond – 58
Mars Bonfire – 59
Ray Bonneville – 59
The Boomers – 60
Bootsauce – 61
The Bourbon Tabernacle Choir – 62
The Box – 64
Oscar Brand – 65
The British Modbeats – 67
Charity Brown – 68
The Brunswick Playboys – 68
Brussel Sprout – 69
Brutus – 70
Michael Buble – 71
Bundock – 72
John Burt – 73
Bush – 74
Edith Butler – 75
Marty Butler – 76

Meryn Cadell – 77
John Allan Cameron – 78
Canada Goose – 79

Cano – 80
The Carlton Showband – 81
Andrew Cash – 83
Cat – 84
Chalk Circle – 85
The Chantones – 86
Robert Charlebois – 87
The Checkerlads – 90
The Checkers – 91
The Chessmen – 91
Chester – 92
Rita Chiarelli – 92
Chilliwack – 93
Choya – 96
Christmas – 96
Les Classels – 98
David Clayton - Thomas – 99
Tom Cochrane – 101
Bruce Cockburn – 103
Leonard Cohen – 105
Holly Cole Trio – 107
Dorothy Collins – 108
The Collins/Pickell Project – 109
The Cooper Brothers – 109
Copper Penny – 110
Corbeau – 112
The Courriers – 113
Cowboy Junkies – 114
Johnny Cowell – 115
Deborah Cox – 116
Crack of Dawn – 117
Crash Test Dummies – 118
Crash Vegas – 119
Creemcheeze Good-Time Band – 121
The Crew Cuts – 121
Crosstown Bus – 123
Crowbar – 124

Susan Crowe – 126
Cub – 126
Burton Cummings – 127
Bobby Curtola – 128

Wes Dakus & The Rebels – 131
Lisa Dal Bello – 132
Daybreak – 133
Dee & The Yeomen – 134
Deja Vu – 134
Dewline – 135
The Diamonds – 135
Celine Dion – 137
Dionysos – 140
Melanie Doane – 141
Bonnie Dobson – 142
Rich Dodson – 143
Denny Doherty – 144
The Doughboys – 144
Doug and The Slugs – 145
Downchild Blues Band – 147
Drake – 148
Dr. Music – 150
Annette Ducharme – 150

Earth Boy – 151
Econoline Crush – 152
Edward Bear – 152
Cliff Edwards – 154
Shirley Eikhard – 155
The Emeralds – 156
Rik Emmett – 157

Eric's Trip – 158
Eritage – 159
The Esquires – 160
David Essig – 161
The Eternals – 162
Everyday People – 162

Eria Fachin – 163
Percy Faith – 164
Robert Farnon – 166
Stephen Fearing – 168
Ferron – 168
The Fifth – 169
54-40 – 170
Figgy Duff – 172
The Five D – 173
Fludd – 174
Flying Circus – 175
FM – 175
Peter Foldy – 177
49th Parallel – 177
David Foster – 178
Fosterchild – 179
The Four Lads – 180
Freedom – 182
Frozen Ghost – 182

Georgette Fry – 183
Nelly Furtado – 184
B.B. Gabor – 185
Andre Gagnon – 186
Gainsborough Gallery – 188

Lennie Gallant – 188
Patsy Gallant – 189
Garfield Band – 191
Gary and Dave – 192
Gary O – 193
The Gemtones – 194
Gettysybyrg Address – 195
Nick Gilder – 196
Bobby Gimby – 197
Ginger – 198
The Girlfriends – 199
Glass Tiger – 200
Goddo – 201
Gogh Van Gogh – 202
Matthew Good Band – 202
Lawrence Gowan – 203
Tommy Graham – 205
The Grapes of Wrath – 205
Greaseball Boogie Band – 207
Great Big Sea – 208
The Great Scots – 209
The Great Urban Band – 210
Lorne Greene – 210
Joey Gregorash – 211
Bobby G. Griffith – 212
The Guess Who – 213
Bruce Guthro – 216

H

The Halifax Three – 217
Hammersmith – 219
Keith Hampshire – 219
The Happy Feeling – 221
Hagood Hardy – 222
Harem Scarem – 223
Harlequin – 225

Harmonium – 226
Corey Hart – 227
Lisa Hartt Band – 228
Hart Rouge – 229
The Haunted – 230
Ronnie Hawkins – 232
Haywire – 234
The Headpins – 235
Jeff Healey Band – 236
Heart – 237
Helix – 239
Hemingway Corner – 241
Wade Hemsworth – 242
Pat Hervey – 242
The Hi-Fis – 243
Dan Hill – 244
Honeymoon Suite – 246
Gavin Hope – 247
Lorence Hud – 248
Huevos Rancheros – 249

Ian and Sylvia – 250
I Mother Earth – 251
The Inbreds – 252
The Infidels – 253
Influence – 254
The Irish Descendants – 254
The Irish Rovers – 255

Jackson Hawke – 258
J.B. and The Playboys – 259
Shawne Jackson – 260
Susan Jacks – 261
Terry Jacks – 261
Les Jaguars – 262
Jale – 264
Colin James – 264
Patti Jannetta – 266
Paul Janz – 267
Jarvis Street Revue – 268
Carly Rae Jepsen – 268
Jericho – 269
France Joli – 270
Jon and Lee and The Checkmates – 271
Debbie Johnson – 271
Marc Jordan – 272
Sass Jordan – 274
Juliette – 275
Junkhouse – 276
Diane Juster – 277
Justin Tyme – 278

Connie Kaldor – 278
Kashtin – 279
Christopher Kearney – 280
James Keelaghan – 281
Mart Kenney – 282
Kensington Market – 284
The Killjoys – 284
Kilowatt – 285
Andy Kim – 286
Tom Kines – 288
Bill King – 289
King Biscuit Boy – 289
The Kings – 290
Klaatu – 291
Ritchie Knight & The Mid-Knights – 293

Moe Koffman – 294
Tony Kosinec – 296
Wally Koster – 297
Chantel Kreviazuk – 297

Robbie Lane and The Disciples – 298
k.d. lang – 300
Penny Lang – 301
Daniel Lanois – 302
The Last Words – 303
The Lavender Hill Mob – 304
Leahy – 304
Avril Lavigne – 305
Brent Lee & The Outsiders – 306
Lee Aaron – 307
Leigh Ashford – 308
James Leroy – 309
Leslie Spit Treeo – 309
Monique Leyrac – 310
Life – 312
Gordon Lightfoot – 313
Lighthouse – 315
Little Caesar & The Consuls – 317
Colin Linden – 319
Little Daddy and The Bachelors – 320
Liverpool Set – 320
Lords of London – 321
Lost and Profound – 322
Loverboy – 323
The Lowest of The Low – 325
Luba – 326
Luke and The Apostles – 327
Doug Lycett – 328
Ray Lyell and The Storm – 328

Ashley MacIsaac – 329
Gisele MacKenzie – 330
Tara MacLean – 332
Gene MacLellan – 332
Natalie MacMaster – 333
Rita MacNeil – 334
Alan MacRae – 335
Bob McBride – 336
Bob McCord & The Vibrations – 337
John McDermott – 338
Kate and Anna McGarrigle – 339
McKenna Mendelson Mainline – 340
Loreena McKennitt – 341
Catherine McKinnon – 342
Patricia Anne McKinnon – 343
Sarah McLachlan – 344
Murray McLauchlan – 345
Ellis McLintock – 348
Ben McPeek – 349
Maestro – 350
The Magic Cycle – 351
Mahogany Rush – 351
The Majestics – 353
Major Hoople's Boarding House – 354
Malka and Joso – 355
Mandala – 356
Maneige – 357
Amanda Marshall – 358
The Marshmallow Soup Group – 359
Martha and The Muffins – 360
Mashmakhan – 361
Ray Materick – 362
Shirley Matthews – 363
Max Webster – 363
Carol Medina – 364
Sue Medley – 365

Shawn Mendes – 366
Men Without Hats – 367
Messenjah – 368
Megan Metcalfe – 369
Mighty Pope – 370
Lynn Miles – 370
Alan Mills – 371
Frank Mills – 373
Minglewood Band – 374
Joni Mitchell – 375
Kim Mitchell – 377
Mitsou – 378
Jackie Mittoo – 380
The Moffatts – 380
Moist – 381
The Mongrels – 382
Monkey House – 383
Mae Moore – 384
Moran – 385
Alanis Morissette – 386
Morse Code Transmission – 387
Motherlode – 388
Mother Tucker's Yellow Duck – 390
Moxy Fruvous – 390
Moxy – 391
Anne Murray – 392
Bruce Murray – 396
Alannah Myles – 396
Myles and Lenny – 397
The Mynah Birds – 399

Bif Naked – 399
Nash the Slash – 400
National Velvet – 401
Rick Neufeld – 402
Night Sun – 403

Noah – 403
The Nocturnals – 404
Don Norman and The Other Four – 405
Tom Northcott – 406
Northern Lights – 408
The Northern Pikes – 409
The Nylons – 410

Ocean – 412
Octavian – 413
The Odds – 414
Offenbach – 415
Mary Margaret O'hara – 417
One to One – 418
The Original Caste – 419

Our Lady Peace – 420
Michel Pagliaro – 421
Painter – 424
The Parachute Club – 425
Paradox – 426
Partland Brothers – 427
A Passing Fancy – 428
The Paupers – 429
The Payola$ – 430
Pear of Pied Pumkin – 431
Pepper Tree – 432
Percy and The Tearddrops – 433
Perth County Conspiracy – 434
Colleen Peterson – 434
Photograph – 435
Pinky – 436

Platinum Blonde – 437
The Pointed Sticks – 438
The Poppy Family – 438
Powder Blues Band – 440
Peter Pringle – 441
Prism – 442
The Prowlers – 443
Pukka Orchestra – 444
Pure – 444
The Pursuit of Happiness – 445

Rain – 447
The Rankins – 447
Gary Rasberry – 449
Rawlins Cross – 449
Ginette Reno – 451
The Rheostatics – 454
Riverson – 455
Robbie Robertson – 456
Alys Robi – 457
Garnet Rogers – 459
Stan Rogers – 460
Vladymir Rogov – 461
Rough Trade – 462
The Rover Boys – 463
Craig Ruhnke – 463
Rush – 464
Ryan's Fancy – 467

Saga – 468
Buffy Sainte-Marie – 470
The Sands of Time – 471

Satan and the D Men – 472
The Sceptres – 473
Eddie Schwartz – 474
Jack Scott – 474
Scrubbaloe Caine – 476
Shadowy Men on a Shadowy Planet – 477
Sheriff – 478
Jane Siberry – 479
Les Sinners – 480
Skydiggers – 481
Skylark – 483
Amy Sky – 484
Sloan – 485
Grant Smith and The Power – 486
Laura Smith – 487
The Smugglers – 488
Snow – 489
Gino Soccio – 489
Jack London and The Sparrow – 490
Spirit of the West – 492
The Spoons – 493
The Staccatos – 494
The Stampeders – 496
Steel River – 498
Suzanne Stevens – 499
Stitch in Tyme – 500
Kim Stockwood – 501
Stonebolt – 502
Strange Advance – 503
Streetheart – 504
Streetnoise – 505
Stringband – 505
Sugar n' Spice – 506
The Sugar Shoppe – 507
Sweet Blindness – 508
Syrinx – 509

Michael Tarry – 510
Bobby Taylor & The Vancouvers – 511
R. Dean Taylor – 511
The Tea Party – 512
Teaze – 513
Teenage Head – 514
Jay Telfer – 515
Diane Tell – 516
Thirteen Engines – 518
Ian Thomas – 519
Three's a Crowd – 520
Thundermug – 522
The Tierras – 523
Ken Tobias – 523
Toronto – 525
Jerry Toth – 526
Toulouse – 527
The Townsmen – 528
The Tragically Hip – 529
Tranquility Base – 531
The Travellers – 531
The Triumph – 533
Domenic Troiano – 534
Trooper – 535
Tsufit – 537
Shania Twain – 537

The Ugly Ducklings – 539
Shari Ulrich – 540

Valdy – 541
Gino Vannelli – 543
Denny Vaughan – 544
Roch Voisine – 545

The Waltons – 547
Christopher Ward – 548
The Watchmen – 548
Wednesday – 550
The Weeknd – 550
Weeping Tile – 551
Moxie Whitney – 552
Wide Mouth Mason – 553
David Wiffen – 554
David Wilcox – 555
Wild Strawberries – 556
Willie and The Walkers – 557
Jesse Winchester – 558
Witness Inc. – 559
Priscilla Wright – 560

Neil Young – 561
Yukon – 564

Zon – 565

Introduction

Canadian artists have dominated the Top Ten of Billboard's Hot 100 since October 2015. As I look back at the evolution of Canadian music from its humble beginnings, back in late 1940s when The Four Dukes were singing in Toronto, it was a time of great excitement when the vocal group was emerging as a force to be enjoyed. They later changed their name to The Four Lads. They had two major hits in a row: Somebody Loves Me in 1952 and Istanbul in 1953. The Crew Cuts followed their success with Canada's first number one hit, Sh-Boom which was number one for nine weeks from August 7, 1954.

They were also the first Canadian group to have a full cover story in Macleans's Magazine in its December 1, 1954 issue. The story by the late June Callwood was entitled "SH-BOOM!" The Crazy Career of The Crew Cuts. The first paragraph revealed how the public responded to Sh-Boom. It sold more than a million copies in the first four months of its release. It paid them $27,500 in royalties and their fee for nightclubs and theatre appearances vaulted from $500 to $1,000 a week. The record was also an international best seller in England, South America, Hawaii and Japan. A motorist driving from Syracuse to Buffalo, New York heard the song eleven times on the radio. Dinah Shore opened the new season of her TV show in October 1954 with a special new song, "Somebody Goofed," which contained the words, "We wanted to bring a ballad into your living room, but nowadays the rage is Sh-Boom! Stan Freberg, best known for satirizing Dragnet did a parody of Sh-Boom which impressed the Crew Cuts enough to buy four copies so they could play it and laugh.

CHUM was the first radio station to inaugurate a chart on May 27, 1957. It listed the top 50 songs of the week. On August 10, 1968 it became the CHUM 30 until the last chart was published on June 7, 1986. Other stations who implemented their own chart were CKLG and CFUN Vancouver, British Columbia; CKXL Calgary,and CHED in Edmonton, Alberta; CKRC Winnipeg, Manitoba, CKBB Barrie, Ontario; CKOC Hamilton and CFTR Toronto, Ontario,

CKLB, Oshawa, Ontario; CJBQ Belleville, Ontario; CKWS and CKLC, Kingston, Ontario; CFNB, Fredericton, New Brunswick and CHNS, Halifax, Nova Scotia.

The record chart flourished until the mid-1970s when radio formats had changed and FM started to make inroads. Some stations didn't feel the need to keep putting them out and they became a thing of the past. Few stations even bothered to keep copies of their charts, except for record collectors who recognized their value, The heyday of the 78 and, later, the 45 RPM or single was also the era of the chart.

Paul Anka was Canada's first teen idol. In 1957 his Diana was a number one hit and a million seller. The Diamonds who signed with Mercury Records joined The Crew Cuts as two of the most popular acts of the Rock and Roll Era. Canadian music received a boost in the United States when Anka, the Four Lads and The Diamonds appeared on American Bandstand. It would also help later acts in the late 1960s and early 1970s to help create a major explosion of Canadians who entered Billboard's Hot 100.

The early 1960s saw Bobby Curtola become our first home-grown pop idol cause a sensation and propel him to stardom. He was also the first to have songwriters Basil and Dyer Hurdon in his hometown of Fort William, Ontario (now Thunder Bay) write songs for him, the first to have a full-time manager, Maria Martell. His backup singers were named The Martells. He was the first Canadian artist to start his own record label, Tartan Records, and the first Canadian to record a commercial that sounded like a hit song. The commercial gwas for Coca-Cola.

On February 24, 1964 RPM, Canada's first trade weekly, published its first issue. During the beginning it looked at Canadian music in its Chart Action Across Canada. On September 1, 1984, RPM introduced "The Top 0 + 5" which later evolved to the first Top 100 Singles Chart On March 21, 1966. It later became Top 100 Hit Tracks And Where To Find Them on August 18, 1990.

The Record became Canada's second music trade weekly in 1981. RPM ceased publishing in 2000 and The Record in 2001. An on-line version failed to take off and by 2003 there was a bi-weekly trade magazine: Canadian Entertainment Network.

The Canadian Songwriter's Hall of Fame was established in 2003. On its website, it describes its mandate to honour and celebrate Canadian songwriters who have dedicated their lives to the legacy of music and works to educate the public about their achievements.

For this edition, I have added record labels and numbers in response to the demand from collectors. I would like to thank all those who wrote to me for their suggestions and comments.

I personally am indebted to many of the artists in the first edition who talked to me: Robbie Lane, Andy Kim, Rich Dodson, Rich Dodson (The Stampeders), Domenic Troiano, Pat Barrett (The Crew Cuts), Dave Somerville (The Diamonds), Frank Bussieri (The Four Lads), George Semkiw (Ritchie Knight & The Mid-Knights),Tyler William and Bill Ott (The Sceptres), Pat LaCroix (The Halifax Three), Martha Hardy (Mrs. Hagood Hardy), Keith Hampshire, Catherine McKinnon, Wayne Faulconer (Satan And The D Men), Maureen Murphy (Sugar And Spice), Gerry Mudry (The Happy Feeling), Lynn Miles, Bill Durst (Thundermug), Dave Bingham (The Ugly Ducklings), Priscilla Wright, Richard Patterson (The Esquires), Paul Huot (The Townsmen), Gavin Hope,Murray McLauchlan, Tsufit, Michael Fonfara (Jon and Lee & The Checkmates), Reid Diamond (Shadowy Men On A Shhadowy Planet), Joey Frechette (The Beau-Marks), Dougie Trineer, Dennis Abbott (49th Parallel), Terry Black, John Hayman (The Emeralds), Heidi Fleming, B. J. Cook and Donny Graves (Skylark), Cliff Edwards, Tom Northcott, Pat Hervey, Mark Max (The Courriers), Tony Tobias, Joey Gregorash, Don Breithaupt (Monkey House), Bob Wiseman, George Stevenson (Jarvis Street Revue), Bruce Morshead (Little Caesar & Consuls), Al Rain, Tom Lavin (Powder Blues Band), Barry Allen, Bruce Innis (Original Caste), Dave Harwood (Creemcheeze Good-Time Band), Bill Hill (J.B. & The Playboys), Chris Harvey and Wayne Scott (Streetnoise), Heather Leitner (Marty Butler), John Harris (Ocean),Bobby Curtola ,The Liverpool Set, and Bruce Wheaton (The Stitch In Tyme), Mike McKenna (McKenna Mendelson Mainline), Valdy, Don Grashey, Richard Green, Andy Forgie (Photograph), Carol Medina, Graham Dunnett (Dee & The Yeomen) Patti Jannetta, Peter Beacock (Major Hoople's Boarding House) and Gregory Donaghhey (The Carlton Showband).

Rick Jackson, 2016

Aarons and Ackley

Chuck Aarons (guitar, vocals)
Jim Ackley (keyboards, vocals)

Both Chuck Aarons and Jim Ackley were from the United States. The former was an ex New York session guitarist and writer, and the latter was an ex Los Angeles pianist and arranger/writer. Jim came up to Canada in 1969 and worked as a clerk in the promotion department of Capitol Records in Toronto. When Chuck came to Toronto in 1970, he ended up staying with Jim, and the two of them started writing songs together. Through producer Dennis Murphy at Sundog Productions, Aarons and Ackley signed a recording contract with Capitol Records, and in 1971 the label released their self-titled debut album. Their hits included Let It Shine and Devil Song. After the release of their second album, *You and I* in 1972, they spent the next two years producing albums for such artists as Bob McBride and the Irish Rovers. They also produced a series of jingles. In December, 1974 Aarons and Ackley signed a contract with GRT Records. Where Did The Music Go? was the first single in December 1974.

Singles:
Girl I've Been Waiting	Capitol 72665	1971
Let it Shine	Capitol 72648	1971
Devil Song	Capitol 72656	1971
Bonnie Blue	Capitol 72680	1972
Where Did the Music Go?	GRT 1230 83	1974
Detective of Love	GRT 1230 101	1975

Albums/CDs:
Aaron and Ackley	Capitol ST 6362	1971
You and I	Capitol ST 6379	1972

Abraham's Children

Ron Bartley (guitar)
Jim Bertucci (bass)
Brian Cotterill (percussion)
Bob McPherson keyboards)
Shawn O'Shea (guitar)

The beginnings of Abraham's Children go back to the late 1960s in Toronto when they were known as Just Us and Captain Midnight's Dirty Feet. The latter name was taken from an American comic strip. When the owners of the strip would not allow the use of the name in the United States, they changed their name to Abraham's Children. Signed to G.A.S. Records, their first hit single was Goodbye Farewell in 1972.

The group consisted of four members until April 1973 when Shawn O'Shea made it a quintet. Their first international hit was Gypsy. After the success of Goddess of Nature in 1973–74, the group went for a heavier sound, and changed their name to The Children. They broke up in 1976.

Shawn O'Shea formed a new group called Bang in 1976 with Ron Bartley, Joe Dinardo, formerly of Cycle, and Dave Babyn. Jim Bertucci record under the name of Jimi B (All American Boy/Strange Feeling A&M 573 1982), and signed to United Artists as an in house producer and artist. He also formed the bands Angel and Space Patrol. In 1982 he released a self-titled album on A&M. Three years later, he formed the electronic music group, Natopus, who recorded the album, *Transition* on Valley of the Sun Records. Today, he is working as a solo performer. Brian Cotterill died of cancer on September 11, 2007.

Singles:

Goodbye Farewell	Gas 1004	1972
Gypsy	Gas 1005	1972
Thank You	Gas 1011	1973
Goddess of Nature	UA/RAMPAGE 101	1973
Rockin' in the City	UAXW 421	1974
Deni	UAXW 580	1974

Album:

Time	Gas GLP 2001	1973

Ronney Abramson

Born in Paris, France, Ronney Abramson moved with her parents to Montreal where she learned to speak both English and French. Her early musical training was in classical music, and when she was fourteen she wrote her first song. While still in her teens she gave her first public performance, a solo guitar recital in Montreal.

She attended McGill University. While there, she became involved in Montreal's folk club scene. Her success as a folk singer led to dates in Eastern Canada and New York, and a recording contract with Capitol Records. She recorded only one with the label, the self-titled *Ronney Abramson*.

In 1972 she moved from Montreal to Toronto and became part of a rock trio with John Mills Cockell. She later formed her own band, and signed to True North Records. Her first single, Question For An Answer came out in 1976. An album of original songs was released at the end of the year.

Her next album on True North was *Stowaway* in 1977, which marked a departure in her music from folk to rock. Backing her up was the Stowaway Band which was comprised of Pat Ringley on bass, John Sheard on keyboards, and Bob DiSalle on drums.

Singles:

And the Child Will Smile	Capitol 72684	1972
Accident	Capitol 72697	1973
Question for an Answer	True North TN4 128	1976
S T O Please	True North TN4 135	1976
Never Seem to Get Along	True North TN4 138	1976
Your Love Gets Me Around	True North TN4 134	1977
Light Up Your Love	True North TN4 141	1978
Trouble	True North TN4 143	1978
I'm a Big Girl Now	True North TN4 154	1980
Get This Love Out of Here Alive	Duke Street DSR S9	1982
Won't Let You Get Away With That	Duke Street DSR S04	1983
Hold it, Surrender	Duke Street DSR 71004	1984

Albums/CDs:

Roney Abramson	Capitol SKA0 6378	1972
Stowaway	True North TN 27	1977
Jukebox of Paris	True North TN 3	1978

Bryan Adams

The eldest son of English parents, Jane and Conrad Adams, Bryan was born in Kingston, Ontario, on November 5, 1959. When his parents separated in 1975, he moved to Vancouver with his mother. After graduating from high school, he bought an Estey baby grand piano with the money his parents set aside for university. In 1976 Adams replaced Nick Gilder as lead singer of Sweeney Todd. Bryan left the group in 1977.

In 1978 Adams met Jim Vallance of the group Prism and together the pair began a long and fruitful songwriting partnership. They wrote songs for Prism, Loverboy, Tina Turner, Joe Cocker, and many others.

By 1980 Adams had recorded his self-titled album. During the next five years, he established himself as one of Canada's top male singers. In 1985 he received the Diamond Award for selling one million copies of his *Reckless* album in Canada, a first for a Canadian artist. Five Top Ten singles were released from it: Run To You, Heaven, Summer of '69, One Night Love Affair, and It's Only Love (a duet with Tina Turner). The album also sold four million in the U.S. Heaven became the first Canadian single to reach number one on Billboard's Hot 100 since Anne Murray's You Needed Me in 1978.

Adams also wrote with Vallance and David Foster, the Ethiopian famine relief anthem, Tears Are Not Enough, which brought many Canadian musicians together under one roof.

He also headlined the Prince's Trust Fund charity pop concerts in 1987 at Wembley Arena in London, England. Former Beatles Ringo Starr, George Harrison, and Paul McCartney, along with Eric Clapton, singer Boy George, and Mark King of the British pop group Level 42 joined the Canadian singer on three Beatles classics: While My Guitar Gently Weeps, With A Little Help From My Friends, and Here Comes The Sun. Other performers at the weekend concerts were Phil Collins, Paul Young, Midge Ure and Dave Edmunds, who also performed with Adams and his band.

In 1991 Bryan wrote, Everything I Do (I Do It For You) for the Warner Brothers film, Robin Hood: Prince of Thieves. The song was number one on Billboard's Hot 100 for seven weeks from July 27, 1991. It was certified a million seller on September 12, 1991.

Adams made headlines in 1992 when the Caadian Radio Television and Telecommunications Commission (CRTC) ruled that his album, *Waking Up the Neighbours,* could not be considered Canadian content, because many of the songs were co written with his producer, Robert "Mutt" Lange. At the time, the CRTC only recognized songs where 100% of the lyrics or music were written by Canadians. In the face of protests by Adams and his fans, the regulatory body changed the requirement to 50%, and Waking Up The Neighbours was declared Cancon on January 29, 1993.

Since his rise in popularity in 1985, Adams has recorded a successful string of hit singles and albums, and ranks as one of Canada's international superstars.

Singles:

Let Me Take You Dancing	A&M 468	1979
Hidin' From Love	A&M 220	1980
Give Me Your Love	A&M 497	1980
Lonely Nights	A&M 2359	1981
Fits Ya Good	A&M 551	1982

Cuts Like A Knife	A&M 602	1983
Straight From The Heart	A&M 2536	1983
This Time	A&M 619	1983
Best Was Yet To Come	A&M 629	1984
Run To You	A&M 2686	1984
Somebody	A&M 2701	1985
Heaven	A&M 2729	1985
Summer of '69	A&M 2739	1985
One Night Love Affair	A&M 2770	1985
Christmas Time	A&M 8651	1985
It's Only Love (w/Tina Turner)	A&M 2791	1986
Heat Of The Night	A&M 2921	1987
Hearts On Fire	A&M 2948	1987
Victim Of Love	A&M 2964	1987
Only The Strong Survive	A&M 745	1987
Everything I Do (I Do It For You)	A&M 1567	1991
Can't Stop This Thing We Started	A&M 1576	1991
There Will Never Be Another Tonight	A&M 1588	1991
Thought I'd Died And Gone To Heaven	A&M 15367	1992
Do I Have To Say The Words?	A&M 16111	1992
Please Forgive Me	A&M 0422	1993
All For Love	A&M 0476	1993
Have You Ever Really Loved A Woman	A&M 0551	1995
Rock Steady (with Bonnie Raitt)	Cap 58500	1995
The Only Thing That Looks Good On Me Is You	A&M 1579	1996
Let's Make A Night To Remember	A&M 1662	1996

Albums/CDs:

Bryan Adams	A&M Sp 4800/69902	1980
You Want It, You Got It	A&M Sp 4864/69555	1981
Cuts Like a Knife	A&M Sp 4919/69981	1983
Reckless	A&M Sp 5013	1984
Diana (Ep)	A&M Sp 23030	1985
Into The Fire	A&M Sp 3907	1987
Waking Up The Neighbours	A&M 15367	1991
So Far, So Good	A&M 0157	1993
Live Live Live	A&M 7094	1994
18 Til I Die	A&M 0551	1996
Bryan Adams: Unplugged	A&M 40831	1997
On A Day Like Today	A&M 541014	1998
The Best of Me	A&M 490513	1999
Anthology	A&M 555602	2005
Get Up	Universal 394302	2015

Susan Aglukark

Born in Churchill, Manitoba on January 27, 1967 Susan Aglukark made her public appearance at nine years of age as a choir member in her father's church. She grew up in the small, isolated community of Arviat on the west coast of Hudson Bay.

Through her music and personal appearances, she has become a role model for youth among Inuit. Rosemarie Kuptana, President of Inuit Tapirisat of Canada has called her an ambassador for Inuit, a woman of wisdom, and a leader.

In 1990 she made her first video, Searching which won the Top Cinematography award from MuchMusic. Her first recording was *Dreams for You*, an eight song cassette. Her second, *Arctic Rose*, was released in 1992 and featured songs in her native language of Inuktitut. She was backed by the Arctic Rose Band, led by singer/songwriter Terry Tufts.

Aglukark's music is a mix of contemporary pop, folk, rock and country. Her songs deal with such social issues as teenage suicide, child abuse, drugs and alcohol, and the spiritual and cultural estrangement of Inuit.

In 1993 she joined other Canadian celebrities in the Peter Gzowski Invitational Golf Tournament for Literacy in Inuvik, N.W.T., and performed at the Gzowski literacy fundraiser at Winter Gardens in Toronto. That summer she represented Canadian Inuit at the World Conference on Human Rights in Vienna, and at the Davvi Suuva Music Festival in Sweden.

The Northwest Territories magazine, *Up Here* named Susan Aglukark the 1993 Northerner of the Year. She was also chosen one of the 100 leaders to watch for by Maclean's magazine, and remains an integral voice for the Aboriginal community in Canada.

Singles:

Title	Catalog	Year
Searching	EMI 28605	1990
Old Toy Trains	EMI 227989	1993
Song Of The Land	EMI 28605	1994
Still Running	EMI 28605	1994
O Siem	EMI 32075	1995
Hina Na Ho (Celebration)	EMI 32075	1995
Breakin' Down	EMI 32075	1995/96
Shamaya	EMI 32075	1996
One Turn Deserves Another	EMI 53393	1999
Turn of the Century	EMI 53393	2000

Albums/CDs:

Arctic Rose	EMI 28605	1992
Christmas	EMI 227989	1993
This Child	EMI 32075	1995
Unsung Heroes	EMI 53393	1999
Big Feeling	EMI 714155	2004
Blood Red Earth	Arbor 229594	2006
White Sahara	Universal 592510	2011
Dreaming Of Home	E1 051063	2013

Chad Allan

Born Allan Peter Stanley Kowbel on March 29, 1943, he started playing the accordion at an early age. By 1956 he had picked up the guitar and organized his first group, The Rave Ons, named after the Buddy Holly song of the same name. When they disbanded, he started Allan's Silvertones, who eventually became known as The Guess Who, whom he left in 1966.

In 1967 he hosted the Winnipeg segment of CBC TV's Let's Go, and had formed Chad and The Good Time Music Appreciation Society with Micki Allen, Barry Stillwill and Karen Merklinger. Merklinger and Allan would later be joined by Bob McMullin and Corinne Cyca to form The Metro Gnomes. The Canadian Talent Library released a self-titled album of their songs in November 1969 (CTL S 5121).

During the 1970s and early 1980s, Allan wrote songs, played in clubs, and completed a master's degree in philosophy. He also recorded a few Singles:, including Spending My Time. In the early 1990s he was recording on his own Sea Breeze label as a Christian rock artist.

Singles:

Greeting Card	Quality 1907	1968
Through The Looking Glass	Quality 1925	1969
Looking Through Crystal Glass	Quality 1949	1969
West Coast Girl	Reprise 1003	1971
Spending My Time	GRT 1230 56	1973
Prairietown, Midwest City	GRT 1230 71	1974
Try (Diane Heatherington)	Daffodil DFS 1060	1975
Ballad Of A Middle Aged Rocker		1981
Don't Muscle In		1982

Allan Sisters

From Edmonton, Alberta, Jackie and Coralie Allan began singing as children. Jackie, the older sister, started performing at the age of seven. She began singing with her sister Coralie in and around Edmonton until they moved to Toronto to pursue a show business career.

There, Jackie met and married Art Snider, music director of CBC TV's Country Hoedown, in 1958. In 1963 Jackie and Coralie went to New York and cut their first single, Larry, which hit the Canadian charts in the summer of 1964. Although they were primarily a country act, they had two hits on the pop charts: Remember the Face and Dream Boy.

The Allan Sisters later joined The Tommy Hunter Show as regulars in 1966, where they stayed for the next eleven years. After leaving the show in 1977, they played together for five more years. Coralie retired in 1982, while Jackie continued to sing professionally in the group Tribute and as a solo act. She died of cancer on December 24, 1985.

Singles:
Larry	Shell 314	1964
Mr. Special	Red Leaf 102	1965
Remember the Face	Red Leaf 104	1965
Your Kind of Love	Red Leaf 107	1965
Dream Boy	Quality 1807	1966
I'm in with the Downtown Crowd	Quality 1841	1966
Lily the Pink	Sound Can Sr 701	1969
Somewhere There's A Mountain	Arpeggio Arps 1021	1973
Day After Tomorrow	Arpeggio Arps 1021	1973
Drummer Man	Op Art 303	1974
Mr. Songwriter	Snocan 120	1975
Rain	Snocan 127	1976

Albums/CDs:
Allan Sisters	Sound Canada Sc 7704	1969
Allan Sisters	Arpeggio Aprs 10006	1972
Drummer Man	Paragon Als 241	1974
Precious Moments	Ross Sound RS 1079	1983

Barry Allen

Born in Edmonton, Alberta on July 29, 1945, Barry Allen's music career goes back to 1963 when he joined Wes Dakus and The Rebels. A year later, his first hit single, Over My Shoulder/Flame Of Love, was released on Quality Records. He later signed a contract with Capitol, and in 1965 the label released his first album, *Goin' Places*, and the single, Easy Come Easy Go. His biggest success came in 1966 when Lovedrops, which was first recorded by Mickey and Sylvia in 1961, became a national hit.

Between 1965 and 1975, Barry became a freelance engineer and producer, hosted CTV's national music show, Come Together, worked with Norman Petty in Clovis, New Mexico, and was a member of the group Painter (West Coast Woman). Allen also received two Maple Leaf Awards, the forerunner to the Junos: Most Promising Male Vocalist in 1965, and Most Popular Male Vocalist in 1966.

From 1977 to 1987, he was involved in radio production at two Edmonton stations, CHED and CISN FM. He was also host and vocalist for ITV's CISN Country TV show. Since 1987, he has been owner and operator of Homestead Recorders in Edmonton, where he has produced a number of artists, such as Tony White, Laura Vinson and Free Spirit, Tommy Rogers, Danny Hooper, K.C. Jones, and Anne Beaumont.

Singles:

Over My Shoulder	Quality 1654	1964
Easy Come Easy Go	Capitol 72214	1965
It's Alright With Me Now	Capitol 72258	1965
Penny A Teardrop	Capitol 72306	1965
Hurry Santa Hurry/Pretty Paper	Capitol 72315	1965
Lovedrops	Capitol 72345	1966
Turn Her Down	Capitol 72391	1966
Armful Of Teddy Bears	Capitol 72430	1967
I Know (You Don't Want Me No More)	Capitol 72468	1967
I Don't Know What I'll Do	Apex 77094	1969
Well Allright	Barry 3512	1969
A Wednesday In Your Garden	Molten 2	1970
Take The Long Way Home	MCA 2005	1970

Albums/CDs:

Goin' Places	Capitol 6164	1965
Lovedrops	Capitol 6189	1966
Barry Allen	MCA 7005	1970

Tommy Ambrose

Born on October 19, 1939 in Toronto, Tommy Ambrose is a veteran of the Canadian pop music scene. At five, he sang at various Youth for Christ rallies at Massey Hall and Maple Leaf Gardens. When he was seventeen, he appeared regularly on CBC's Cross Canada Hit Parade. After three years of singing on the road, he had his own musical/variety series, The Tommy Ambrose Show, on CBC, sponsored by General Motors. In 1958 he had his first big hit, Remember Remember on Sparton Records.

When The Tommy Ambrose Show was canceled in 1963, Ambrose went on the road, but later gave it up to concentrate on studio work, which included cutting demos.

Ambrose went to New York in 1965 to work with producer Phil Ramone, who would later become Billy Joel's producer. A chance to sing with the Count Basie Orchestra brought him back to Canada.

In the late 1960s Tommy formed a partnership with Larry Trudell to create a radio and production company. A third partner, musician Doug Riley (of Dr. Music fame) was added in late 1979.

Ambrose tried his hand at television again in 1975 with the gospel music series called Celebration on CBC. With the formation of a jazz band in 1978, Ambrose recorded two albums for Phonodisc: *Sweet Times* and *Ambrose At Last* with The Doug Riley Band.

Today, Ambrose continues to be one of Canada's top jingle singers. He ran Jingles, his own restaurant and bar in Toronto from 1977 to 1989, where he played there occasionally with Doug Riley on keyboards, Rick Wilkins on sax and John McLeod on trumpet.

Singles:

Remember Remember	Sparton4 680R	1958
The Magic Of You	Sparton4 684R	1958/59
I Need Your Love	Sparton4 902R	1960
We're Not Too Young/Falling In Love	Sparton4 945R	1960
Unchained Melody/Jiminy Jum Jum	Chateau 122	1961
Casino Royale	Fontana F 1592	1967
Just Like A Man	Kanata 1001	1971
People City	RCA 75 1115	1972
Our Summer Song	RCA PB 50007	1974
Christmas Past	RCA PB 50038	1974
Long Street (Winding Through My Mind)	RCA PB 50117	1975
The Night Time And My Baby		1976

Albums/CDs:

YoungTommy Ambrose	Chateau CLP 1007	1962
Ann is Back	RCA PCS 1175	1970
Magic is the Night	RCA PCS 1215 LM 59	1970
Fuzzy Love	Kanata 4	1971
Sweet Times	New Ventures NV 5005	1978
Ambrose at Last	New Ventures NV 5009	1979
Songs Sinatra Taught Me	DMI Talent	1999

Bill Amesbury

Bill Amesbury was born in Kirkland Lake, Ontario in 1950. As a teenager in late 1960s, he was a member of the group Five Shy. When he grew tired of singing other people's songs he decided to become a songwriter, and later a producer and recording artist.

His first single was I Won't Let No One Get That Close To Me. It was followed by Virginia (Touch Me Like You Do) which became his first Top Ten hit in early 1974. That same year, he produced J.J. Barrie's No Charge which was a major hit in England. Casablanca Records also released his first album, *Jus' a Taste of the Kid*.

Amesbury's success as a singer/songwriter extended into Europe where he performed on every major TV variety show. In England he enjoyed further success with his self-penned songs, Every Girl In The World Tonight, Saturday Night I'll Be Waiting and I Remember in 1976 – 77.

His second album, *Can You Feel It*, on Capitol Records came out in June 1976. He retired from music altogether in the 1980s and became Barbara Amesbury, transsexual.

Singles:

I Won't Let No One Get That Close To Me	Yorkville YVM 45080	1973
Virginia (Touch Me Like You Do)	Yorkville YVM 45100	1974
Frogman Bradley	Yorkville YVM 45103	1974
Rock My Roll	Yorkville YVM 45102	1974
Every Girl In The World Tonight	RCA JB 50069	1975
(Say You Love Me) Sugar Pie	RCA PB 50094	1975
I Remember	Capitol 4287	1976
Can You Feel It	Capitol 72779	1976
You Belong To Me	Capitol 72785	1977

Albums/CDs:

Jus's Taste of the Kid	Casablanca 9005	1974
Can You Feel It	Capitol ST 11528	1976

Paul Anka

Born in Ottawa, Ontario on July 30, 1941, Paul Anka began performing at an early age in amateur talent contests, where he impersonated singers like Frankie Laine and Johnny Ray. During the summer of 1956 while working at the Los Angeles Civic Playhouse, he met Ernie Freeman of Modern Records, who was responsible for Anka's first record, Blau-Wile-Deveest-Fontaine. When it was unsuccessful, he decided to go to New York where The Rover Boys, a Canadian group, had a recording contract with ABC Paramount. After he met the label's A&R chief, Don Costa, Anka sang some of his own songs. One of them was Diana, inspired by his infatuation for a fifteen year old high school student named Diana Ayoub. ABC Paramount eventually signed him, and released Diana in the summer of 1957, which went on to sell nine million copies worldwide. Over the next five years Anka had other hits, including You Are My Destiny, Lonely Boy and It's Time To Cry.

In 1962 he began recording for RCA. That same year he played a cameo role in, and wrote the theme for, the film, The Longest Day. He also wrote the theme music for The Tonight Show starring Johnny Carson, which was played five nights a week for 30 years.

Anka was one of the hosts of the 1965 66 music series Hullabaloo and The Midnight Special in the early 1970s on NBC, and, in 1967, he was a guest on the 1967 comedy/variety series Spotlight. By the late 1960s he had changed to Buddah Records where he recorded Goodnight My Love, the old Jesse Belvin hit from 1956, Do I Love You and Jubilation. In 1969 Anka turned the French song, Comme d'Habitude into My Way, which was a Top 30 hit for Frank Sinatra. In 1971, Tom Jones recorded Anka's She's A Lady.

In 1974 he had a major hit with (You're) Having My Baby on the United Artists label, which became a number one hit and another million seller.

By the end of the 1970s Anka had opened his own restaurant in Las Vegas and taped a CBS TV special in Monte Carlo. On September 6, 1990 he became an American citizen, while retaining his Canadian citizenship. He has been back to Canada several times since, the last of which was in 2007 during his 50th anniversary as a Canadian artist. Diana, My Way, It Doesn't Matter Anymore. She's A Lady and Put Your Head On My Shoulder were inducted into the Canadian Songwriters Hall of Fame in 2008. In 2013, St. Martin's Press published his autobiography, My Way.

Singles:

I Confess/Blau Wile Deveest Fontaine	Regency539	1956
I Confess/Blau Wile Deveest Fontaine	RPM 472	1956
I Confess/Blau Wile Deveest Fontaine	RPM 499	1956
Diana	Sparton457	1957
Diana	ABC PAR 9831	1957
I Love You Baby	Sparton497	1957
I Love You Baby	ABC PAR 9855	1957
You Are My Destiny	Sparton529	1958
You Are My Destiny	ABC PAR 9880	1958

Encyclopedia of Rock, Pop & Folk Music in Canada

Crazy Love/Let The Bells Keep Ringing	Sparton 565	1958
Crazy Love/Let The Bells Keep Ringing	ABC PAR 9907	1958
Midnight	Sparton 598	1958
Midnight	ABC PAR	1958
Just Young	Sparton 650	1958
Just Young	ABC PAR 9956	1958
The Teen Commandments	ABC PAR 9974	1958
The Teen Commandments	Sparton 682	1958
(All Of A Sudden) My Heart Sings	Sparton 686	1958
(All Of A Sudden) My Heart Sings	ABC PAR 9987	1958
I Miss You So	Sparton 740	1959
I Miss You So	ABC PAR 10011	1959
Lonely Boy	Sparton 767	1959
Lonely Boy	ABC PAR 10022	1959
Put Your Head On My Shoulder	Sparton 800	1959
Put Your Head On My Shoulder	ABC PAR 10040	1959
It's Time To Cry	Sparton 829	1959
It's Time To Cry	ABC PAR 10064	1959
Puppy Love/Adam and Eve	Sparton 865	1960
Puppy Love/Adam and Eve	ABC PAR 10082	1960
My Home Town/Something Happened	Sparton 892	1960
My Home Town/Something Happened	ABC PAR 10106	1960
Hello Young Lovers/ I Love You In The Same Old Way	Sparton 922	1960
Hello Young Lovers/ I Love You In The Same Old Way	ABC PAR 10132	1960
Summer's Gone	Sparton 940	1960
Summer's Gone	ABC PAR 10147	1960
It's Christmas Everywhere	Sparton 949	1960
It's Christmas Everywhere	ABC PAR 10169	1960
Story Of My Love	Sparton 973	1960
Story of My Love	ABC PAR 10168	1960
Tonight My Love, Tonight	Sparton 988	1961
Tonight My Love, Tonight	ABC PAR 10194	1961
Dance On Little Girl	Sparton 1012	1961
Dance On Little Girl	ABC PAR 10220	1961
Kissin' On The Phone/Cinderella	Sparton 1038	1961
Kissin' On The Phone/Cinderella	ABC PAR 10239	1961
Loveland/The Bells At My Wedding	Sparton 1060	1961
Loveland/The Bells At My Wedding	ABC PAR 10279	1961
The Fools Hall Of Fame	Sparton 1067	1961
The Fools Hall of Fame	ABC PAR 10282	1961
I'd Never Find Another You/Uh Uh	Sparton 1081	1962
I'm Coming Home	Sparton 1110	1962
I'm Coming Home	ABC PAR 10338	1962
Love Me Warm and Tender	RCA 7977	1962
A Steel Guitar And A Glass Of Wine	RCA 8030	1962
Every Night (Without You)	RCA 8068	1962

Rick Jackson

I'm Coming Home	ABC PAR 10338	1962
Eso Beso (That Kiss!)	RCA 8097	1962
Ogni Giorno/Voglio Sapere	RCA 3299	1962
Ogni Volta/Statsera Resta Con Me	RCA 3316	1962
Love Me Warm And Tender	RCA 7977	1962
I'd Never Find Another You	SPAR 1081	1962
I'd Never Find Another You	ABC PAR 10311	1962
Love (Makes The World Go 'Round)	RCA 47-8115	1963
Remember Diana	RCA 47-8170	1963
Hello Jim	RCA 47-8195	1963
Did You Have A Happy Birthday?	RCA 47-8272	1963
Hurry Up And Tell Me	RCA 47-8237	1963
From Rocking Horse To Rocking Chair	RCA 47-8311	1963
In My Imagination	RCA 47-8396	1964
My Baby's Comin' Home	RCA 47-8349	1964
Sylvia	RCA 47-8493	1965
The Loneliest Boy In The World	RCA 47-8595	1965
Truly Yours	RCA 47-8764	1966
I Went To Your Wedding	RCA 47-8839	1966
I Can't Help Loving You	RCA 47-8893	1966
I'd Rather Be A Stranger	RCA 47-9228	1966
Poor Old World	RCA 47 9032	1966
Until It's Time For You To Go	RCA 47-9128	1967
That's How Love Goes	RCA 47-9268	1967
When We Get There	RCA 47-9457	1968
Goodnight My Love	RCA 47 9648	1969
In The Still Of The Night	RCA 74 0126	1969
Sincerely	RCA 74 0164	1969
Midnight Mistress	RCA 9746	1969
Happy	RCA 47 9767	1969
Do I Love You	Buddah 252	1971
Why Are You Leaning On Me Sir	Barnaby ZS7 2027	1971
Jubilation	Buddah 294	1972
Life Song	Buddah 314	1972
While We're Still Young	Buddah 337	1972
Hey Girl	Buddah 349	1973
Let Me Get To Know You	Fame 345	1973
(You're) Having My Baby	UA XW454	1974
One Man Woman, One Woman Man	UA XW569	1974
I Don't Like To Sleep Alone	UAXW 615	1975
(I Believe) There's Nothing Stronger	UAXW685	1975
Times of Your Life	UAXW 737	1975
Anytime (I'll Be There)	UAXW 789	1976
Make It Up To Me In Love	Epic 8 50298	1976
Happier	UAXW 896	1976
Wake Up/Papa	UAXW 8094	1976
My Best Friend's Wife	UAXW 972	1977
Everybody Ought To Be In Love	UAXW 1018	1977

If I Had My Life To Live Over	UAXW 1122	1977
I'll Help You		1977
This Is Love	RCA 11395	1978
Brought Up In New York	RCA PB 11351	1978
As Long As We Keep Believing	RCA PB 11662	1979
You And I (with Mireille Mathieu)	Polydor 2065 416	1979
Think I'm In Love Again	RCA PB 12184	1981
I've Been Waiting For You	RCA 12225	1981
Hold Me 'Til The Mornin' Comes	Columbia 38-03897	1983
Gimme The Word (with Karla DeVito)	Columbia 38 04187	1983
No Way Out (with J. Mignes)	Columbia 38-07358	1987
Mi Pueblo (with Juan Gabriel)		1996
Diana (with Ricky Martin)		1996

Albums/CDs:

Fabulous Paul Anka And Others	Riviera R0047	1956
Paul Anka	Sparton ABC 240	1958
My Heart Sings	Sparton ABC 296	1959
Swings For Young Lovers	Sparton ABC 347	1960
Anka At The Copa	Sparton ABC 353	1960
Paul Anka Sings His Big 15	Sparton ABC 323	1960
It's Christmas Everywhere	Sparton ABC 360	1960
Sings His Big 15 Volume 2	Sparton ABC 390	1961
Sings His Big 15 Volume 3	Sparton ABC 409	1962
Diana	Sparton ABC 420	1962
Paul Anka Live	PIA 2148	1962
Young, Alive And In Love	RCA LSP 2502	1962
Let's Sit This One Out	RCA LSP 2575	1962
Our Man Around The World	RCA LSP 2614	1963
Italiano	RCA 10130 (ITALY)	1963
Songs I'd Wish I'd Written	RCA LSP 2744	1963
21 Golden Hits	RCA LSP 2691	1963
Three Great Guys (w/Sedaka & Cooke)	RCA LPM 2720	1963
Excitement On Park Avenue	RCA LSP 2966	1964
Live In Germany	RCA PJL 1 8052	1964
Paul Anka	RCA SPC 3321	1964
On Tour	RCA LSP 9985	1964
Paul Anka Italiano	RCA LSP 10130	1964
A Casa Nostra	RCA LSP 10130	1964
In Paris	RCA LSP 430631	1964
Sonny Boy Undeine Sinorita	RCA LSP 10011 EIN	1965
Strictly Nashville	RCA LSP 3580	1966
Highlights From The O'keefe Centre Performance And Other Favorites	RCA LSP 3617	1966
Live At The Americana	RCA LSP 3875	1967
21 Golden Hits	RCA LSP 3808	1967
Goodnight My Love	RCA LSP 4142	1969

Sincerely	RCA LSP 4203	1969
Life Goes On	RCA LSP 4250	1969
Paul Anka in the 70s	RCA LSP 4309	1970
Paul Anka	Buddah BDS 5093	1972
Jubilation	Buddah BDS 5114	1972
My Way	RCA ACLI 0616	1974
Gold - 28 Original Recordings	Sire 3704	1974
Paul Anka Gold	Polydor 2669-020	1974
Anka	UA UALA 314	1974
Feelings	UA UALA 367	1975
This Is Paul Anka	Buddah 5622	1975
Paul Anka Live	Barnaby 6013	1975
Remember Diana	RCA ACLI 0896	1975
She's A Lady	RCA ACLI 1054	1975
Times Of Your Life	UA UALA 569	1975
The Painter	UA UALA 6530	1976
Sings His Favourites	RCA ACLI 1584	1976
My Way	RCA Camden 0616	1976
Essential Paul Anka	Buddah BDS 5667	1976
Puppy Love	Pickwick 3508	1976
Lonely Boy	Pickwick 3523	1976
Paul Anka	Pickwick 2087	1976
Music Man	UALA 746H	1977
Songs I'd Wish I'd Written	RCA ACLI 2482	1977
Paul Anka - His Best	LN 10000	1977
Vintage Years 1957-1961	Sire 6043	1977
Listen To Your Heart	RCA AFL 1-2892	1978
Live	GNP CRES. 2175	1978
Paul Anka - His Best	UALA 922	1978
Headlines	RCA AFL 1-3382	1979
Both Sides Of Love	RCA AFL 1-3926	1981
Very Best	Ranwood 8203	1981
Black Tie	Piccadilly 3403	1982
Walk A Fine Line	Columbia FC 38442	1983
Paul Anka Live	Columbia FC 39323	1984
Songs I Wrote And Sing	Pair 1129	1986
Best (14 Original Hits 1957 1961)	Rhino 70220	1986
Greatest Hits	Quality RSP 130	1986
Best Of Paul Anka	Pair 1204	1987
Italiano	RCA PC 1008	1987
His Best	EMI Manhattan 46739	1988
Freedom	A&M SP 9144	1988
30th Anniversary Anthology	RHINO 71489	1989
21 Golden Hits	RCA 38082	1989
Diana & Other Hits	RCA 2086 4 (CS)	1990
Five Decades Of Hits	Curb/WB 77467	1991
Sings His Big 10, Vol 1	Curb/WB 77557	1991
Sings His Big 10, Vol 2	Curb/WB 77558	1991

Classic Hits (w/Odia Coates)	Curb 77566	1992
Paul Anka In The 70s	RCA 66203 4	1993
Best Of The U.A. Years 1973 77	EMI 36993	1996
Amigos	Columbia CK 91110	1996
Duets	Paul Anka & Friends	1996
Body Of Work	Epic EK 69405	1998
Classic Songs My Way	Universal 726647	2007

Peter Appleyard

Born in Cleethorpes, Lincolnshire, England on August 26, 1928, Peter Appleyard's music career began as a drummer in the Central Royal Canadian Air Force Band and other British dance bands. He moved to Toronto in 1951 where he began playing the vibraphone.

From 1954 to 1956 he performed at the Park Plaza Hotel and CBC radio. He also played with Billy O'Connor and American pianist Cal Jackson on CBC TV's Jazz With Jackson.

In 1954, Peter formed his own combo that performed nightly at Jackie Rae's Stage Door in Toronto, appeared on Jackie Rae Show and Music Makers, both on CBC television. Three years later, he formed his own group in Toronto and toured with singer Gloria De Haven for a year.

He returned to CBC Radio in 1961 where he co-hosted with singer Patti Lewis, Patti & Peter, and on CBC TV in 1969 he co-hosted with Guido Basso, Mallets and Brass.

During the 1960s and 1970s Appleyard was popular in Toronto nightclubs. He played percussion in theatre, radio, TV and recording orchestras and toured the Middle East four times. In the early 1970s, he joined Benny Goodman's sextet, and later was in another orchestra that included Count Basie.

The late 1970s saw Appleyard perform annually at Ontario Place, and in 1977 he hosted his own TV variety show, Peter Appleyard Presents. He continued to tour into the year 2000 with his vibraphone stylings. He died on July 17, 2013.

Albums/CDs:

The Vibe Sound Of Peter Appleyard	Audio Fidelity AFLP 1901	1961
The Vibraphone Of Peter Appleyard	CTL S 5040	1963
The Many Moods Of Peter Appleyard	RCA CTLS 1112	1969
The Lincolnshire Poacher	CTL 477 5167	1973
Sophisticated Vibes	United Artists UALA 714G	1976
Peter Appleyard Presents	SALS D2D 001	1977

Peter Appleyard	New Ventnv 5007	1979
Peter Appleyard	Intercan IC 1020	1981
Prelude To A Kiss	RCA KKL1 0452	1982
Lost 1974 Sessions	Linus 270135	2012
Sophisticated Ladies	Linus 270151	2012

April Wine

David Henman (guitar) Replaced by Gary Moffet (1973)
Ritchie Henman (drums) Replaced by Jerry Mercer (1973)
Myles Goodwyn (guitar, lead vocals)
Jimmy Henman (guitar) Replaced by Jimmy Clench (1971);
Steve Lang (1975)
Brian Greenway (guitar)

Formed in Waverly, Nova Scotia in December 1969, the original four members moved to Montreal the following April with only $100 and their equipment. They recorded their first hit, Fast Train early in 1971 in Montreal at RCA with production by Billy Hill. In 1971 their self-titled debut album, also produced by Billy Hill, was released the same year. Soon after, bassist Jimmy Henman left and was replaced by Jimmy Clench.

The popularity of April Wine began to soar in 1972 following the release of You Could Have Been A Lady, the group's first number one hit in Canada. It was taken from the album, *On Record,* which also featured another single, Bad Side of the Moon, written by Elton John and Bernie Taupin.

Two more members of the band left during the recording of the album, *Electric Jewels* in 1973. David and Ritchie Henman were replaced by Jerry Mercer and Gary Moffet prior to a live debut at Toronto's Canadian National Exhibition on Labour Day, where they opened for T. Rex.

In the spring of 1974 April Wine went on their first national tour called "The Electric Adventure." Their big hit that same year was I'm On Fire For You Baby, the only single not included on any album.

After their summer tour in 1975 to promote their album *Stand Back*, Jimmy Clench left the group to join Bachman Turner Overdrive, and later Loverboy. He was replaced by bassist Steve Lang.

In 1976 their album, *The Whole World's Goin' Crazy*, shipped platinum (over 1,000,000 copies), the first by a Canadian group. The tour to promote the album became the first to gross $1 million. They were joined by Heart.

The band's other achievements included being the first to sell out the Regina Stadium on April 19, 1976 and the Kinsmen Field House in Edmonton, Alta. on April 23 and 24, 1976. Myles Goodwyn was the only original member of the group as of the mid 1970s. In 1977, the addition of guitarist Brian Greenway made the group a sextet.

April Wine toured for almost all of 1980 in Europe where they impressed audiences in Germany, United Kingdom and the Benelux countries. In January, 1981 their album, *Nature of the Beast*, produced the single Just Between You And Me, which became the biggest single ever for the group in the United States. Three years later, they recorded their last album, *Animal Grace*. Their farewell tour ended on July 31, 1984 at the Kokanee Bowl in Kelowna, British Columbia. Both Myles Goodwyn and Brian Greenway had solo Albums released in 1988. The former with Myles Goodwyn (AQR 548), the latter with Serious Business (Atlantic 78 18271).

April Wine reunited for a cross Canada tour in 1992. The lineup consisted of Myles Goodwyn, Brian Greenway, Steve Segal, Jim Clench, and Jerry Mercer. Early in 1993 they released their first single in eight years, If You Believe In Me on the independent fre label. It was followed by an album of all new material called Attitude.

In 2001 the group's lineup was comprised of Gerry Mercer, Myles Goodwyn, Brian Greenway and Jim Clench. They continue to tour today.

Singles:

Fast Train	Aquarius 5014	1971
Listen Mister	Aquarius 5019	1971
Strawberry Wine	Aquarius 5021	1972
You Could Have Been A Lady	Aquarius 5021	1972
Bad Side Of The Moon	Aquarius 5022	1972
Drop Your Guns	Aquarius 5024	1972
Lady Run, Lady Hide	Aquarius 5026	1973
Weeping Widow	Aquarius 5027	1973
Just Like That	Aquarius 5030	1974
Electric Jewels	Aquarius 5031	1974
I'm On Fire For You Baby	Aquarius 5032	1974
I Wouldn't Want To Lose Your Love	Aquarius 5035	1974/75
Cum Hear The Band	Aquarius 5037	1975
Oowatanite	Aquarius 5038	1975
Tonite Is A Wonderful Night	Aquarius 5043	1975
The Whole World's Goin' Crazy	Aquarius 5052	1976
Gimmie Love	Aquarius 5056	1976
Like A Lover, Like A Song	Aquarius 5060	1976
Forever, For Now	Aquarius 5061	1976
You Won't Dance With Me	Aquarius 5063	1977

Rick Jackson

She's No Angel	Aquarius 5067	1978
Rock And Roll Is A Vicious Game	Aquarius 5070	1978
Comin' Right Down On Top Of Me	Aquarius 5073	1978
Let Yourself Go	Aquarius 5076	1978
Roller	Aquarius 5079	1979
Get Ready For Love	Aquarius 5084	1979
Say Hello	Aquarius 5087	1979/80
I Like To Rock	Aquarius 5089	1980
Just Between You And Me	Aquarius 5097	1981
Sign Of The Gypsy Queen	Aquarius 5098	1981
All Over Town	Aquarius 5099	1981
Enough Is Enough	Aquarius 6001	1982
Tell Me Why	Aquarius 6004	1982
What If We Fall In Love Now	Aquarius 6005	1983
This Could Be The Right One	Aquarius 6009	1984
Sons of the Pioneers	Aquarius 6012	1984
Money Talks	Aquarius 6015	1984
Rock Myself To Sleep	Aquarius 6018	1985
Love Has Remembered Me	Aquarius 6020	1985
It's A Pleasure To See You Again	Aquarius 6046	1989
If You Believe In Me	FRE L0104	1993
Here's Looking At You Kid	FRE L0104	1993
That's Love	FRE L0104	1993
Voice In My Heart	FRE LO104	1993
I'm A Man	FRE L2109	1994
Driving With My Eyes Closed	FRE L2109	1994
If I Was A Stranger	FRE L2109	1994/95

Albums/CDs:

April Wine	Aquarius 502	1971
On Record	Aquarius 503	1972
Electric Jewels	Aquarius 504	1973
April Wine Live	Aquarius 505	1974
Stand Back	Aquarius 506	1975
The Whole World's Goin' Crazy	Aquarius 510	1976
Forever, For Now	Aquarius 511	1976
Live at the El Mocambo	Aquarius 515	1977
First Glance	Aquarius 517	1978
Greatest Hits	Aquarius 525	1978
Harder...Faster	Aquarius 527	1979
Nature of the Beast	Aquarius 530	1981
Power Now	Aquarius 533	1982
Animal Grace	Aquarius 535	1984
One for the Road	Aquarius 538	1985
Walking Through Fire	Aquarius 540	1985
The First Decade	Aquarius 563	1988
Over 60 Minutes...With the Hits	Aquarius 2549	1988

Over 60 Minutes...All the Rockers	Aquarius 2550	1989
Rock Ballads	Aquarius 256401	1990
The Wine Collection (box set)	Aquarius 2563	1990
Greatest Hits	Aquarius 2525	1991
Attitude	FRE L0104	1993
Frigate	FRE L2109	1994
Back to the Mansion	Civilian 610482	2001
Roughly Speaking	UNIV 222082	2008

Jann Arden

Born and raised in Springbank, Alberta on March 27, 1962, Jann Arden Richards received her first guitar at 15. When she graduated from high school, she decided to pursue a musical career instead of a university education. She played with various bands and sang everything from Billie Holiday to the Carpenters. In 1982 she began writing her own songs, such as I Just Don't Love You Anymore, which was included in her 1993 debut album on A&M Records, *Time for Mercu*.
In 1987 Arden was a member of the lounge duo, Heart and Soul when she met Neil MacGonigill, who had worked for a number of labels and had managed Ian Tyson.

Her debut album on A&M, *Time for Mercy* was released in February, 1993. The first single was Will You Remember Me. She released two more Albums with the label, *Living Under June*, in 1994 and, Happy? in 1997. Beginning in 2000, she had changed to Universal Music with the release of *Blood Red Cherry* and her *Greatest Hurts: Best Of* (2001). She was honoured with a star on Canada's Walk of Fame in 2006.

Singles:

Will You Remember Me	A&M 0071	1993
I Would Die For You	A&M 0071	1993
The Way Things Are Going	A&M 0071	1993
I'm Not Your Lover	A&M 0071	1993
Time For Mercy	A&M 0071	1993/94
Could I Be Your Girl	A&M 0248	1994
Insensitive	A&M 0248	1994/95
Wonder Drug	A&M 0248	1995
Unloved	A&M 0248	1995
Good Mother	A&M 0248	1995/96
Looking For It	A&M 0248	1996
The Sound Of	A&M 0789	1997
Wishing That	A&M 0789	1998

I Know You	A&M 0789	1998
Ode To A Friend	A&M 0789	1998/99
Sleepless	Universal 157527	2000
Into The Sun	Universal 157527	2000
If You Loved Me		2004

Albums/CDs:

Time for Mercy	A&M 0071	1993
Living Under June	A&M 0248	1994
Happy?	A&M 0789	1997
Blood Red Cherry	Universal 157527	2000
Greatest Hurts: Best Of	Universal 161652	2001
With the VSO	Universal 660392	2002
Love is the Only Soldier	Universal 383992	2003
Jann Arden	Universal 103953	2005
Uncover Me	Universal 712347	2006
Free	Universal 703235	2009
Spotlight	Universal 755207	2010
Uncover Me 2	Universal 956067	2011
Everything Almost	Universal 776253	2014
Christmas	Universal 576552	2015

John Arpin

Born in Port McNicoll, near Midland, Ontario, on December 3, 1936, John Arpin studied piano while growing up in his hometown. He began his music career in 1957 and later worked with Howard Cable, King Ganam, Leo Romanelli, and Stanley St. John.

From 1962 to 1987 John was a pianist in such Toronto bars and hotel lounges as The Port of Call, Mr. Tony's, and Pearcy House. He was also music director of two CTV shows, River Inn (1968–69) and Diamond Lil (1969–1970), and TV Ontario's Polka Dot Door from 1984.

He has also written a number of songs which have been recorded by Keath Barrie, Carlton Showband, Dick Damron, George Hamilton IV, Tommy Hunter and Roy Payne.

In the early 1960s, American pianist Bob Darch introduced ragtime music to Arpin, who later became Canada's foremost ragtime pianist.

He performed at the Mariposa Folk Festival and the St. Louis Ragtime Festival in the 1970s, and the Scott Joplin Festival in Sedalia, Mississippi in the 1980s. Arpin has served as chairman of the Toronto Ragtime Society and edited its publication, The Ragtimer from 1964 to 1968. Arpin has recorded albums of ragtime music as well as more contemporary music, including the CD, *John Arpin Plays George Gershwin* in 1991. He died on November 8, 2007.

Albums/CDs:

Title	Label/Number	Year
Concert In Ragtime	Scroll 101	1965
The Other Side Of Ragtime	Scroll 102	1966
Ragtime Piano	CTLS 5113	1969
Love And Maple Syrup: John Arpin Plays Lightfoot	CTL 477 548	1971
Barroom To Baroque	CTL 477 5165	1972
Direct To Disc	RCA Kpl1 0125	1975
I Write The Songs	RCA KKKl1 0258	1977
Music From The Movies	Nep Tunes Nep 101	1985
Plays His Anne Murray Favorites	Hom CHO HRCC 002	1986
Glad Rags And Sad Rags	Pro Arte CDD 373	1987
Scott Joplin's Greatest Hits	Pro Arte CDD 397	1987
You Keep Coming Back Like A Song: A Tribute To Irving Berlin	Pro Arte CDD 424	1988
Broadway Baroque	Pro Arte CDD 451	1988
Kings Of Ragtime	Pro Arte CDD 487	1989
Cakewalk: The Virtuoso Piano Music Of Louis Moreau Gottschalk	Pro Arte CDD 515	1989
Bach Meets Rodgers And Hammerstein	Pro Arte CDD 525	1990
Champagne Rags	Pro Arte CDD 497	1990
Broadway Baroque	Intersound 451	1990
Plays George Gershwin	Mastersound DFCD 1	1991
Best Of Honky Tonk Piano	Pro Arte CDD 3422	1992
Greatest Hits Volume 2	Pro Arte CDD 562	1993
Christmas With John Arpin	Intersound 3562	1994
My Romance	Intersound 3518	1995
Someone To Watch Over Me	Intersound 6119	1995
Ragtime Rarities: Scott Joplin	Intersound 3531	1995
Somebody Loves Me	Intersound 3530	1995
My Favorite Requests	Intersound 3593	1997
Greatest Hits Of Al Jolson	Intersound 3705	1998
Romance At The Movies	Intersound 3713	1998
Unchained Melody	Intersound 1436	1998
Blue Gardenia	Marquis Classics 81221	1998
Wishing Upon A Star & Other Childhood Favorites	Platinum 3731	1999

The Arrows

Peter Bleakney (bass)
Rob Gusev (keyboards)
Doug MacAskill (guitar)
Dean McTaggart (lead vocals, rhythm guitar)
Earl Seymour (sax)
Mike Sloski (drums)

This Toronto based band started out in 1981 as The Rejects, an R&B/pop band. They changed their name to The Arrows when everyone thought they were a punk band. The focal point of the group was Dean McTaggert's strong vocals, punctuated by Rob Gusev's textured keyboards, Doug MacAskill's driving guitar licks, and Earl Seymour's saxophone sounds. Bassist Peter Bleakney rounded out the group.

Their first single was Treat Her Right, a remake of Roy Head's 1965 hit, on El Mocambo Records. The following year, they released the EP, *Misunderstood*, on Spontaneous Records, which included a remake of the Animals' 1965 hit, Don't Let Me Be Misunderstood.

In 1984 they signed to A&M Records, whose first hit with the label was Meet Me In The Middle. That same year, their debut album, *Stand Back*, was released.

By the time their second album, *The Lines Are Open*, came out in November 1985, Bob Economou had replaced Sloski on drums, and Glenn Olive replaced Bleakney on bass.

The Arrows broke up in the late 1980s. McTaggart went on to write songs for other Canadian artists, notably Amanda Marshall.

Singles:

Treat Her Right	El Mocambo ESMO 515	1981
Lovelight	Spontaneous WRC3 2442	1982
Meet Me In The Middle	A&M 647	1984
Never Be Another One	A&M 671	1984
Say It Isn't True	A&M 2659	1984
Talk Talk	A&M 688	1985/86
Chains	A&M 699	1986
Heart of the City	A&M 695	1986

Albums/CDs:

Misunderstood (EP)	Sponataneous WRC2 2301	1982
Stand Back	A&M SP 79105	1984
The Lines Are Open	A&M SP 9119	1985

Bachman – Turner Overdrive

Chad Allan (vocals, rhythm guitar, mandolin, piano accordion) Replaced by Tim Bachman (1972); Blair Thornton (1974)
Randy Bachman (vocals, lead guitar, bass) Replaced by Jim Clench (1979)
Robin (Robbie) Bachman (drums)
C.F. (Fred) Turner (guitar)

Bachman Turner Overdrive began in 1970–71 when Randy Bachman, his brother Robbie, Chad Allan and Fred Turner joined together and called themselves Brave Belt. The genesis of Brave Belt began as a jam session when Randy, who had just left The Guess Who, went over to play some songs with longtime friend Chad Allan. In October 1970, they decided to form a group. Randy's younger brother, Robbie joined on drums. In 1971, Fred Turner was added to make Brave Belt a four-man band. That same year, they signed a contract with Reprise Records. In May 1971 their debut album, Brave Belt I was released. It was followed later that same year by Brave Belt II. Chad Allan left the group after it came out, and Brave Belt continued as a trio with Randy, Robbie and Fred. In April 1972, Randy Bachman's other brother Tim joined.

    The future of the band began to change when Terry David Mulligan, then host of ROQ in Toronto invited them to be on his show. Prior to their appearance, Randy sent a demo tape to Charley Fach at Mercury Records; he liked what he heard and immediately signed them. By now, the band had come up with a new name to fit the harder edge sound they played on stage Bachman Turner Overdrive. On May 1, 1973 their self-titled debut album on Mercury was released. It was the first of four successful albums.

    By 1976 the group had built up a loyal following in both Canada and the United States but the following year, Randy left the group due to musical differences. He formed the groups Ironhorse and Union, both of which failed to repeat the success of The Guess Who and Bachman Turner Overdrive.

    In 1978 the group adopted the acronym BTO. Robbie became group leader and a new album, *Rock and Roll Nights*, which included the single, Heartaches, were released on Mercury Records. Joining the group were Jim Clench, formerly with April Wine, and Blair Thornton who replaced Randy Bachman on bass and lead vocals. (see Randy Bachman)

    Chad Allan went on to have a solo career in the pop field in the 1970s and 1980s. Today, he records on his own Sea Breeze label as a Christian rock artist.

    BTO never really left the Canadian music scene even though in 1993 they were playing fairs and festivals in the United States. When Randy Bachman left after signing with Sony Music, he was replaced by Randy Murray. The rest of the group is comprised of Fred Turner, Robin Bachman, and Blair Thornton.

By Brave Belt
Singles:
Rock and Roll Band	Reprise 1023	1971
Crazy Arms, Crazy Eyes	Reprise 1039	1971
Never Comin' Home	Reprise 1051	1972
Dunrobin's Gone	Reprise 1083	1972
Another Way Out	Reprise 3659	1972

Albums/CDs:
Brave Belt	Reprise RS 6447	1971
Brave Belt II	Reprise MS 0257	1971
Bachman Turner Bachman As Brave Belt	Reprise MS 2210	1972
Brave Belt	Bullseye BLPCD 4054	2001

By Bachman Turner Overdrive
Singles:
Gimme Your Money Please	Mercury 73383	1973
Little Candy Dancer	Mercury 73383	1973
Hold Back The Water	Mercury 73417	1973
Blue Collar	Mercury 73417	1973
Let It Ride	Mercury 73457	1974
Takin' Care Of Business	Mercury 73487	1974
You Ain't Seen Nothin' Yet	Mercury 73622	1974
Roll On Down The Highway	Mercury 73656	1975
Hey You	Mercury 73683	1975
Quick Change Artist	Mercury 73710	1975
Down To The Line	Mercury 73724	1976
Take It Like A Man	Mercury 73766	1976
Lookin' Out For No. 1	Mercury 73784	1976
Gimme Your Money Please	Mercury 73843	1976
My Wheels Won't Turn	Mercury 73903	1977
Shotgun Rider	Mercury 73926	1977
Life Still Goes On	Mercury 73951	1977
Down The Road	Mercury 73987	1978
Heartaches	Mercury 74046	1979
Jamaica	Mercury 74062	1979
For The Weekend		1984
Mississippi Queen		1986
Wooly Bully	Penta Pro CD17 P	1989

Albums/CDs:
Bachman Turner Overdrive	Mercury SRM1 673	1973
Bachman Turner Overdrive II	Mercury SRM1 696	1973
Not Fragile	Mercury SRM1 1004	1974
Four Wheel Drive	Mercury SRM1 1027	1975
Head On	Mercury SRM1 1067	1975
Best of BTO (So Far)	Mercury SRM1 1101	1976

Freeways	MercurySRM1 3700	1977
Street Action	MercurySRM1 3713	1978
Rock and Roll Nights	MercurySRM1 3748	1979
BTO	Compleat CPL1 1010	1984
The Anthology	Mercury514902	1993
Gold	Mercury 547502	2005

Randy Bachman

Randall Charles Bachman was born September 27, 1943 in Winnipeg. His interest in music began as a child when his parents gave him a violin. At age three and one half, he sang Beautiful Brown Eyes on the show, King in the Saddle and won. From that moment he knew he wanted to be a singer. It was the guitar he discovered as a teenager that changed his life. He learned the instrument on his own by listening to the radio and records, and by studying it from Lenny Breau, one of the masters of the guitar. Randy learned the versatility of the guitar, and was soon able to pick up songs quickly by ear.

While still in his teens, he performed two original instrumentals, Randy's Rock and Playing It Cool on CKY Radio's Hi Fi Club. This led to his first vinyl recording with The Velvetones, who backed up Gary A. Cooper on the Quality single, Heartaches and Disappointments/Come On Pretty Baby.

Randy became a member of The Embers (later called The Jurymen) with

Garry Peterson. Together they later joined Allan's Silvertones who eventually became The Guess Who.

By 1970 Bachman had left The Guess Who to form Brave Belt, which later became Bachman Turner Overdrive or BTO. After writing such classic hits as You Ain't Seen Nothin' Yet, Takin' Care Of Business and Let It Ride, he left BTO in 1977 to concentrate on future solo projects, including producing Vancouver's Trooper, establishing the group Ironhorse, and recording more of his own songs.

Bachman released a solo album on Polydor Records in 1978 called *Survivor*. From it came the single, Is The Night Too Cold For Dancing? In 1989 he reunited with the original members of BTO for two years. He left again in 1991 and signed a solo contract with Sony Music in 1992. Early in 1993 the label released his first album, *Any Road* which contained both fast and slow versions of the single, Prairie Town, a tribute to the artist's Winnipeg days. The video for the fast version featured Neil Young, while the slow version, both Young and Margo Timmins of The Cowboy Junkies. A five song mini CD titled *Live In Seattle* came out in the fall of 1993. In 1996, True North Records released the full length CD, *Merge*.

Today, he remains active as a songwriter, singer and producer. In 2000 his autobiography, *Takin' Care of Business* (with John Einarson) was published by MacArthur & Company. Tal Bachman, Randy's son, released his self-titled debut album on Columbia (CK 67956) in 1999.

Singles:

Tally's Tune/La Jolla	RCA 1055	1970
Is The Night Too Cold For Dancing?	POL PD 14478	1978
Prairie Town	Col RBK1111	1993
Tailspin	Col RBK1111	1993
I Wanna Shelter You	Col RBK1111	1993
The Loner	Col RBK1111	1994
Made In Canada	TRNT TNSD 117	1996

Albums/CDs:

Axe	RCA LSP 4348	1970
Survivor	Polydor 6141	1978
Any Road	Columbia RBK1111	1993
Merge	True North TNSD 117	1996
BBachman and Turner	Linus ENT BOS-CD 002	2014
Heavy Blues (Bachman)	Linus ENT 270204	2015

The Band

Rick Danko (bass guitar)
Levon Helm (drums)
Garth Hudson (organ)
Richard Manuel (piano)
Jamie Robbie Robertson (guitar)

The origins of The Band go back to 1960–61 when Ronnie Hawkins recruited them as replacements for his backup band.

All five members had experience with high school bands: Robbie in Thumper and The Trombones; Garth in Paul and The Captors, Richard in The Rockin' Revols, Levon in The Jungle Bush Beaters and Rick in Rick and The Starliners and Rick and The Roxatones.

The Hawks played a blues/rock style of music that influenced other Canadian bands such as Luke and The Apostles, Mandela and Jack London and The Sparrows.

In 1965 The Hawks accompanied Bob Dylan on a world tour. When it ended, they returned with him to his home in the Catskill Mountains not far from

Woodstock. There, in a middle class ranch they nicknamed "Big Pink" they wrote with Dylan, who was recovering from a motorcycle accident, such landmark Albums as *The Basement Tapes, Music From Big Pink*, and *John Wesley Harding*.

During this time The Hawks changed their name to The Band and made their official debut in April 1969 at San Francisco's Winterland. That summer they played at the Woodstock Festival.

Recording for Capitol Records, The Band had a huge following, and between 1968 and 1973 they had a string of successful hit singles and albums.

In 1974 The Band reunited with Dylan on a sold out world tour which led to the release of the acclaimed concert album, *Before the Flood*.

On Thanksgiving Day 1976 The Band played Winterland for the last time. Filmed by director Martin Scorsese, The Last Waltz is considered by many the greatest concert film ever made.

The group reunited in 1983 without Robbie Robertson, and two years later they toured with Crosby, Stills and Nash. In the fall of 1985 they played in Richard Manuel's hometown of Stratford, Ontario. He died on March 4, 1986 at age forty-two.

The Band was honored with the Lifetime Achievement Award at the Juno ceremonies in 1989. In July 1990 they performed a live vesion of Pink Floyd's The Wall with Roger Waters, Van Morrison, Cyndi Lauper, Bryan Adams and Sinead O'Connor. The concert, which was taped and released on CD and home video, celebrated the tearing down of the Berlin Wall.

In the fall of 1992 The Band helped salute Bob Dylan on his thirtieth anniversary, and, the following year hosted the Absolutely Unofficial Blue Jean Bash at President Clinton's Inaugural Gala in Washington, D.C.

The individual members of The Band have all been successful as single acts. Levon Helm turned to writing music and acted in the Universal film, Coal Miner's Daughter (1980). Robertson acted in the film Carny (1980), worked as music director on Scorsese's The King of Comedy (1983), and released two solo albums. Garth Hudson wrote and performed an "Evening With Garth Hudson" at St. Ann's Cathedral in Brooklyn in 1989, and played on albums by such artists as Van Morrison and Marianne Faithful. Rick Danko toured extensively throughout Europe and America as a solo performer and member of ex Beatle Ringo Starr's All Starr Band in 1989 (along with Helm).

In 1993, The Band finished their first album of original material since *The Last Waltz*. Entitled *Jericho*, it was recorded at Levon Helm's studio in Woodstock, New York. The group's lineup was now comprised of original members Helm, Hudson, and Danko, along with Richard Bell, Jim Weider, and Randy Ciarlante.

The Band was the first Canadian act to be inducted into the Rock and Roll Hall of Fame in Cleveland, Ohio in January 1994.

Rick Danko died on December 10, 1999. He had recorded the following solo Albums: *Rick Danko,* (Arista AB 4141 1977), *Rick Danko In Concert* (Woodstock Records 1997), *Times Like These* (Breezehill 2000), and as *The Rick Danko Band, Live on Breeze Hill,* in 1999 on Breeze Hill Records. He had been one third of the trio, Danko/Fjeld/Andersen, with singer/songwriter Eric Andersen and Jonas Fjeld, a Norwegian roots artist, who recorded the CDs, *Danko/Fjeld/Andersen* (1993), and *Ridin' On The Blinds* (1997). Danko also had the single, Java Blues (Arista AS 0320) in 1977.

Singles:

By The Canadian Squires

Uh Uh Uh	Ware 6002	1965

By Levon and The Hawks:

The Stones I Throw	ATCO 6383	1965
Go Go Liza Jane	ATCO 6625	1968

By The Band:

Jabberwocky	Capitol 2041	1967
The Weight	Capitol 2269	1968
Up On Cripple Creek	Capitol 2635	1969
Rag Mama Rag	Capitol 2705	1970
Time To Kill	Capitol 2870	1970
The Shape I'm In	Capitol 2870	1971
Life Is A Carnival	Capitol 3199	1971
When I Paint My Masterpiece	Capitol 3249	1971
Don't Do It	Capitol 3433	1972
Caledonia Mission	Capitol 3500	1972
Third Man Theme	Capitol 3828	1973
The Great Pretender	Capitol 81572	1973
Ain't Got No Home	Capitol 3758	1973/74
Third Man Theme	Capitol 3828	1974
Ophelia	Capitol 4230	1976
Acadian Driftwood	Capitol 4316	1976
Georgia On My Mind	Capitol 4361	1976
Out Of The Blue	WB 8592	1978
Remedy	Pyramid 7048	1993
Stand Up	Pyramid 7172	1996
Free Your Mind	Pyramid 7187	1996

Albums/CDs:

Music From Big Pink	Capitol SKAO 2955/C46069	1968
The Band	Capitol SKAO 132/C46493	1969
Stage Fright	Capitol SW 425/C93593	1970
Cahoots	Capitol SMAS 651/C48420	1971
Rock of Ages	Capitol SABB 11045/C93595	1972
Moondog Matinee	Capitol SW 11214/C93592	1973
Northern Lights Southern Cross	Capitol ST 11440/C93594	1976
The Best of The Band	Capitol ST 11553/C46070	1976
Islands	Capitol 93591	1977
The Last Waltz	Warner Bros 3146	1978
Anthology Volume I	Capitol 11846/C48419	1978
Anthology Volume II	Capitol 48986	1978
To Kingdom Come: The Definitive Collection	Capitol CDP 792169	1989
Live At Watkins Glen	Capitol 231742	1989
The Night They Drove Old Dixie	Capitol 257260	1990
Jericho	EMI E 226599	1993
Across The Great Divide	Capitol 89565	1994
High On The Hog	EMI 23838	1996
The Collection	EMI 55078	1997
Jubilation	EMI 1420	1998
Greatest Hits	EMI 249412	2000

Barenaked Ladies

Andy Creeggan (congas, piano) Replaced by Kevin Hearn (1995)
Jim Creeggan (bass)
Steven Page (vocals, guitar)
Ed Robertson (vocals, guitar)
Tyler Stewart (drums)

This Toronto based quintet began as the duo of Steven Page and Ed Robertson in the fall of 1988. Robertson first played in a Max Webster cover band called Three Guys From Barrie, while Page in a Jazz Butcher inspired acoustic duo called Scary Movie Breakfast. In 1989 Andy and Jim Creeggan joined the group.

The band's music blends the Creeggan brothers' jazz background, Robertson's country roots, Page's pop culture diet, and Stewart's hard rock to create an original, quirky sound. Their music has fascinated fans and critics since the release of their five song cassette, Barenaked Lunch in 1991.

In the fall of 1990 Andy Creeggan left to take part in a student exchange program in Rwanda and Uruguay. In his absence, drummer Tyler Stewart filled in. When Andy rejoined the band in 1991, Stewart stayed on as the fifth member.

The Barenaked Ladies established themselves as one of Canada's most unusual groups. They sold out engagements in 7000 seat venues which was unprecedented for a band with no support from a major record company. They were the first in history to perform atop the BBC Broadcasting House.

In 1991 they won Toronto radio station CFNY's CASBY (Canadian Artists Selected By You) awards for Best Overall Group and Most Promising Songwriters. They later signed with Sire Records, distributed by Warner Music Canada, and in the summer of 1992 their first album, *Gordon* went on to sell more than 500,000 copies.

Andy Creeggan left in 1995, and was replaced by Kevin Hearn, a former member of Toronto's The Look People. Andy Creeggan's first solo effort was Andiwork (1997). With his brother Jim, they recorded the albums, *Brothers Creeggan* (Reprise CDW 46091 1995; reissued as BC 1322); *Brothers Creeggan II* (BC 111872 1997), and *Trunks* (Nettwerk 114672 2000). On March 25, 1997 the Barenaked Ladies appeared on the Fox network show, Beverly Hills 90210. Their CD, *Stunt* became their first million selling album in the United States. Steven Page left in 2009 and the group's resolve to continue together made it possible to keep on recording. In 2015, they went on tour to promote *Silverball*.

Singles:

Lovers In A Dangerous Time	Intrepid 0008	1992
Be My Yoko Ono	Reprise 26956	1992
Enid	Reprise 26956	1992
Grade Nine	Reprise 26956	1992
If I Had A Million Dollars	Reprise 26956	1992/93
Brian Wilson	Reprise 26956	1993
What A Good Boy	Reprise 26956	1993
Jane	Reprise 45709	1994
Alternative Girlfriend	Reprise 45709	1994
Life, In A Nutshell	Reprise 45709	1995
Shoebox	Reprise 46128	1996
The Old Apartment	Reprise 46128	1996
Break Your Heart	Reprise 46128	1996
One Week	Reprise 47011	1998
It's All Been Done	Reprise 47011	1998/99
Alcohol	Reprise 47011	1999
Call And Answer	Reprise 47011	1999
Get In Line	Elektra 62441	1999
Pinch Me	Reprise 47814	2000

Albums/CDs:

Barenaked Ladies	CBC/VAR 1013	1991
Gordon	Reprise 26956	1992
Maybe You Should Drive	Reprise 45709	1994
Shoebox (EP)	Reprise 46183	1996
Born on a Pirate Ship	Reprise 46128	1996
Rock Spectacle	Reprise 46393	1996
Stunt	Reprise 47011	1998
Maroon	Reprise 47814	2000
Disc One: 1991 2001	Reprise 48075	2001
Everything to Everyone	Reprise 482092	2003
Barenaked For the Holidays	Desperation 400152	2004
As You Like It	Desperation 213622	2005
Are Men	Desperation 432472	2006
Live in Michegan	Desperation GRP1940	2007
Snacktime!	Raisin 002076	2008
All In Good Time	Raisin891752	2010
Grinning Time	Raisin443895	2013
Silverball	Raisin784582	2015

The Barra Macneils

Kyle MacNeil (violin, guitar, mandolin, lead & harmony vocals)
Lucy MacNeil (violin, bodhran, Celtic harp, lead & harmony vocals, step dance)
Sheumas MacNeil (piano, synthesizers, bass vocals)
Stewart MacNeil (accordion, pennywhistle, bass, bodhran, lead & harmony vocals)

The Barra MacNeils, from Sydney Mines, Nova Scotia, have been performing from an early age. Their name comes from the Isle of Barra in Scotland, where their ancestors originally came from before they settled in Cape Breton about two hundred years ago.

Growing up, Kyle, Lucy, Sheumas and Stewart MacNeil were encouraged to join in the musical gatherings or "ceilidhs" held at their family home. Like The Rankin Family who followed them in 1989, they decided to make a living from the music they cherished so dearly.

Between 1986 and 1990 they released three independent albums: *The Barra Macneils, Rock In The Stream,* and *Timeframe.* The release of *Closer To Paradise* in 1993 marked their major label debut on Polygram. By 1999 they began recording for their own Barratone label.

Singles:

Row Row Row	Polydor 519029	1993
My Heart's in the Highlands	Polydor 519029	1993
Darling Be Home Soon	Polydor 521016	1993
Caledonia	Polydor 521016	1994
In The Wink of an Eye	Polydor 521016	1994
We Celebrate	Polydor 521016	1995
Myopic	Polydor 529077	1995/96
The Ballad of Lucy Jordan	Polydor 529077	1996
Mouth Music '97	Celtic Aire50731	1998
Queen of Argyle	Barratone99057	2000
By Northern Light	Barratone99057	2001

Albums/CDs:

The Barra Macneils	Polydor 519027	1986
Rock In The Stream	Polydor 519028	1989
Timeframe	Polydor 519029	1990
Closer to Paradise	Polydor 521016	1993
The Traditional Album	Polydor 521016	1994
The Question	Polydor 529077	1995
Until Now	Celtic Aire50731	1998
The Christmas Album	Barratone570003	1999
Racket in the Attic	Barratone990572	2000

Bearfoot

Jim Atkinson (vocals, guitar)
Hugh Brockie (lead and rhythm guitar, banjo)
Terry Danko (bass guitar)
Dwayne Ford (keyboards, flute, guitar, vocals)
Michael Tomlinson (drums, guitar, vocals)
Chris Vickery (bass guitar)

The origins of Bearfoot go back to 1970 when Ronnie Hawkins persuaded Hugh Brockie and Dwayne Ford to leave Edmonton and go to Toronto to become part of Ronnie's Rock'n'Roll Revival and Travelling Medicine Show.

When Dwayne left Hawkins he joined Terry Danko (brother of The Band's Rick Danko) and guitarist Atkinson at a farmhouse near Tillsonberg, Ont. It was not long before they became known as Atkinson, Danko and Ford. The addition of drummer Brian Hilton and Hugh Brockie made a name change to Atkinson, Danko and Ford with Brockie and Hilton.

After more personnel changes they finally settled on the name Bearfoot. In 1974 they had two major Canadian hits, Molly and Passing Time.

Bearfoot broke up in 1975. Dwayne Ford went on to pursue a solo career. In the fall of 1979 he recorded We'll Find A Way, a duet with Patsy Gallant. His first solo hit was Roll Me Away in 1980. In 1981 he recorded the album *Needless Freaking* which contained the singles Lovin' and Losin' You (1981) and Hurricane (1982). In 1997, he recorded the EP/CD, *Another Way To Fly*.

By Atkinson, Danko and Ford
Single:

Right On	Columbia 4 3076	1972

Albums/CDs:

Atkinson, Danko & Ford With Brockie & Hilton	Columbia ES 90134	1972
Friends	Columbia KE 32653	1973

By Bearfoot
Singles:

Only A Soldier	Columbia C4 3106	1973
Molly	Columbia C4 4027	1974
Sweet Virginia	Columbia C4 4056	1974
Passing Time	Columbia C4 4065	1974
Cable To Carol (Dwayne Ford & Bearfoot)	Columbia C4 4081	1975
Good Book (Dwayne Ford & Bearfoot)	CBS C4 4094	1975

Albums/CDs:

Passing Time (Dwayne Ford & Bearfoot)	CBS/Epic KE 33530	1975

Beau Dommage

Pierre Bertrand (vocals, bass)
Marie Michele Desrosiers (vocals, piano)
Real Desrosiers (drums)
Robert Leger (keyboards)
Replaced by Michael Hinton (1976)
Michel Rivard (vocals, guitar)

Beau Dommage began in 1970 as Quenouille bleue when founding member Michel Rivard (born: September 27, 1951) and author/composer Pierre Huet were attending the University of Quebec in Montreal. At first they performed only at art shows. With the addition of Robert Leger, their name changed to Theatre Sainfoin, and began playing at theatres. During this time, Marie Michele Desrosiers joined them on stage. By 1973 she had joined the group as a permanent member, and their name changed to Beau Dommage.

The group began practicing in Rivard's parents' basement at Boucherville. They played their first concert in October, 1973 at Luducie on the campus of the University of Montreal. Two years later, Capitol Records released their self-titled debut album. In 1976 Robert Leger left the group, and was replaced by Michael Hinton.

In 1977, Beau Dommage showed signs of breaking up. Rivard decided to make a solo album, because he wanted to express personally his own ideas without imposing on the other members.

The rest of the group had gone their separate ways by the end of the Seventies. Marie Michele went on to enjoy a solo career, and made her first public performance in 1981.

The group reunited during the summer of 1984 for the 450th anniversary celebrations of Jacques Cartier's landing. On December 9, 1984 they played at the Montreal Forum as part of the CBC TV's French series, Beaux Dimaches.

In 1985 two live albums were released from a reunion concert they gave at the Montreal Forum. The first was called, *Au Forum De Montreal*, and the second, *26 et 27 October 1984 Au Forum De Montreal*.

The solo careers of both Robert Leger and Michel Rivard sparked renewed interest in the group's recordings. Polygram reissued a greatest hits album by Beau Dommage in 1988 called, *Leurs Plus Grands Succes*.

Beau Dommage reunited in 1994 and released two albums on Audiogram Records: *Beau Dommage and Rideau*.

Singles:

Le picbois	Capitol 85.102	1975
Tous les palmiers	Capitol 85.105	1975
Harmonies du soir a Chateauguay	Capitol 85.109	1975
Le blues de l'a Metropole	Capitol 85.113	1975
Motel Mon repos	Capitol 85.118	1976
Heureusement qu'il y a la nuit	Capitol 85.122	1976
Montreal	Capitol 85.124	1976
Gisele en automne	Capitol 85.131	1977

Seize ans en 76	Capitol 85.134	1977
Tout va bien	Capitol 85.136	1977
Rouler la nuit	Capitol 85.140	1977
Une Amie d'enfrance	Capitol 85.141	1977
Le soeur endormi	Capitol 85.144	1978
Tellement on s'aimait	Polydor 73	1984
Le Rapide blanc	Polydor 85	1985
Echappe Belle	Audiogram 71089	1994
Rive Sud	Audiogram 71089	1995
Tout Simplement Jaloux	Audiogram 71089	1995/96

Albums/CDs:

Beau Dommage	Cap ST 70034/56353	1975
Ou Est Passe La Noce?	Cap ST 70037/56351	1975
Un Autre Jour Se Leve En Ville	Cap ST 70048/56352	1977
Passagers	Cap ST 70055/56355	1978
Les Grands Succes De Beau Dommage	Cap SK 70058	1978
Beau Dommage Au Forum, Vol. 1 26 ET 27 October 1984	POL 2424.050	1984
Au Forum De Montreal	POL 2424.253	1985
Plus De 60 Minutes Avec…	POL 7 48843	1987
Beau Dommage En Spectacle	POL 835.126	1988
Leurs Plus Grands Succes	Cap 56356	1988
Beau Dommage	Cap 56351	1991
L'integrale (Box Set)	Cap 56358	1991
Beau Dommage	Audiogram 71081	1994
Rideau	Audiogram 71089	1995

The Beau Marks

Joey Frechette (piano)
Ray Hutchinson (lead guitar, vocals)
Mike Robitaille (rhythm guitar)
Gilles Tailleur (drums)

Formed in 1958 this Montreal quartet began as The Del Tones. After the release of Moonlight Party on Quality Records in April, 1959, they were forced to change their name because a band in the United States had a legal right to it.

The new name originated from the Bomarc missile which was in the headlines at that time. Joey Frechette liked the sound of Bomarc, so he changed the spelling to Beau Marks.

Ray Hutchinson and Joey Frechette were the principal songwriters of the group, although credit went to all four. Frechette wrote Clap Your Hands. Moonlight Party and Billy Billy Went A Walking were written by Hutchinson.

Clap Your Hands was a number one hit in Canada and Australia. It was one of the first Canadian hits to be successful in the United States when it reached number forty-two in Cashbox, a trade weekly in the U.S.

They appeared on Dick Clark's American Bandstand and the Peppermint Lounge where they played for two weeks. As a result of their engagement at the latter, they were asked to play at a charity show at Carnegie Hall.

The Beau Marks broke up in 1963. Joey Frechette recorded his own version of Clap Your Hands in 1987 under the name, Joseph Conrad; Ray Hutchinson also recorded the Singles:, Rose Marie (1966), Mr. Rain (1966) and Every Bit As Wonderful (1972), while Mike Robitaille became a businessman. Gilles Tailleur died of a cerebral hemorrhage in 1977. Clap Your Hands was inducted into Canadian Songwriters Hall of Fame in 2005.

Singles:

Moonlight Party (as Del Tones)	Quality K 1881	1959
Moonlight Party	Quality 1881	1959
Rockin' Blues	Quality 1881	1959
Clap Your Hands	Quality 1966	1960
Billy Billy Went A Walking	Quality 1219	1960
Baby Face	Quality 1259	1961
Classmate	Quality 1315	1961
Oh Joan	TIME 1032	1961
Little Miss Twist	Quality 1307	1961/62
Yours	Quality 1337	1962
Clap Your Hands Once Again	Quality 1404	1962
The Tender Years	Quality 1423	1962
Dark Is The Night	Quality 1493	1962
Give Me One More Chance	Quality 1532	1963
Be Bop A Lula	Quality 1766	1965
Clap Your Hands	Quality 014	1968
Daddy Said	Quality 1966	1968
Clap Your Hands Once Again	Quality 040	1969

Albums/CDs:

High Flying Beau Marks	Quality V 1656	1960
The Beau Marks In Person Recorded On Location at le Coq D'or	Quality V 1683	1961
The Beau Marks	Quality V 1711	1962
High Flying Beau Marks	Birchmount 505	1969

The Bells

Cliff Edwards (vocals) Replaced by Charles Clark (1973)
Jacki Ralph (vocals)
Doug Gravelle (drums) Replaced by Skip Layton (1973)
Gord McLeod (percussion) Replaced by Mickey Ottier (1967)
Frank Mills (vocals, percussion) Replaced by Dennis Will (1970)
Mickey Ottier (keyboards, piano & organ)   Replaced by Frank Mills (1968)
Ann Ralph (Edwards) (vocals)
Mike Waye (bass)   Replaced by Wayne Cardinal (1973)

This group from Montreal started out as The Five Bells in 1965. Sisters Jackie and Ann Ralph were from the folk group, the Raymart Trio, while Cliff Edwards and Gord McLeod came from the Counts Four. Doug Gravelle rounded out the group. In 1967, McLeod left and was replaced by Mickey Ottier. Their first hit in 1969 was Moody Manitoba Morning, written by Winnipeg singer/songwriter Rick Neufeld, from their debut album, *Dimension*. That same year, Frank Mills replaced Ottier, and the group became known as The Bells. Their next hit, Fly Little White Dove, Fly, was written by Montrealers Marty Butler and Bob Bilyk. After its release in 1970, Frank Mills left to pursue a solo career, and was replaced by Dennis Will. The group's biggest hit was Stay Awhile in 1971, which was written by singer/songwriter Ken Tobias and was certified a million seller by R.I.A.A. on May 27, 1971. They first broke up in 1973 and, again, in the late 1970s, after the release of the album, *Edwards and Ralph* in 1977. Cliff's daughter, Jessica Edwards wrote and directed the documentary, Stay Awhile in 2014.

By The Five Bells
Single:
Moody Manitoba Morning	Polydor 540.007	1969

Album:
Dimensions	Polydor 542.004	1969

By The Bells

Singles:
Fly Little White Dove, Fly	Polydor 2065 040	1970
Stay Awhile	Polydor 2065 046	1971
Blanc Petit Oiseau Blanc	Polydor 2065 060	1971
Lady Dawn	Polydor 2065 064	1971

Sweet Sounds Of Music	Polydor 2065 077	1971
For Better For Worse	Polydor 2065 093	1971
Oh My Love	Polydor 2065 107	1972
Lord Don't You Think It's Time	Polydor 2065 124	1972
Sing A Song Of Freedom	Polydor 15063	1972
Maxwell's Silver Hammer	Polydor 2065 144	1972
He Was Me, He Was You	Polydor 2065 188	1973
The Singer	Polydor 2065 196	1973
Hey My Love	Polydor 2065 214	1973
All Over Again (At Every End There's A Beginning) (Edwards & Ralph)	Ariola AM. AA 7679	1978

Albums/CDs:

Fly Little White Dove, Fly (aka Stay Awhile)	Polydor 2424 022	1971
Love, Luck 'N Lollipops	Polydor 2424 035	1971
Studio "A"	Polydor 2424 038	1972
Pisces Rising	Polydor 2424 080	1973
Edwards And Ralph	Ariola AM. SW 50022	1977

Willie P. Bennett

William Patrick Bennett was born in Toronto on October 16, 1951. He started writing songs in 1966 and didn't start playing professionally until 1972. In 1973 he formed The Bone China Band who played in coffeehouses, small bars and universities throughout Ontario. In 1974 he began playing with the bluegrass band, The Dixie Flyers. A year later, his first solo album, *Tryin' to Start Out Clean* on Woodshed Records was released.

Since 1979 Willie has performed in every major folk festival in Canada, and his popularity extends to Europe where he has built up a loyal following. His songs have been recorded by Colleen Peterson, Sneezy Waters, Peter Pringle, J. J. Cale, Eric Anderson, k.d. lang, and Prairie Oyster.

In 1996, Colin Linden, Stephen Fearing and Tom Wilson of Junkhouse paid homage to Bennett by starting the trio, Blackie and The Rodeo Kings, named after one of his Albums.

He gave his last concert in Thunder Bay, Ontario on January 26, 2008. He died February 15, 2008.

Singles:

The Lucky Ones	Duke Street 71059	1989
You	Dark Light 12001	1992
Red Dress	Dark Light 12003	1994
Sometimes It Comes Easy	Dark Light 12003	1994

Albums/CDs:

Tryin' To Start Out Clean	Woodshed WS 004	1975
Hobo's Taunt	Woodshed WS 007	1977
Blackie & The Rodeo King	Posterity PWS 013	1979
The Lucky Ones	Duke Street DSR 31059	1989
Collectibles 1975 78	Dark Light DL 12001	1992
Take My Own Advice	Dark Light DL 12003	1993
Heartstrings	B Natural 0998	1998

Barney Bentall & The Legendary Hearts

Barney Bentall (vocals, guitar)
Will Froese (keyboards) Replaced by Cam Bowman (1985)
Jack Guppy (drums)
Doug Mc Fetridge (guitar) Replaced by Colin Nairn (1979)
Barry Muir (bass)

Formed in 1978, this Vancouver-based band began as Brandon Wolf, comprised of Barney Bentall, Will Froese, Jack Guppy, and Doug McFetridge. After the release of an independent EP in 1979, McFetridge left and was replaced by Colin Nairn. Following the release of the album, *Losing Control* there were more personnel changes. Froese left and was replaced by other keyboardists until Cam Bowman joined in 1985.

Barry Muir, formerly with The Payola$, had become a member in the early 1980s. They also changed their name to Barney Bentall and The Legendary Hearts.

For the next eight years they played clubs and bars until their big break came in the summer of 1987 when they made a live video performance of Something To Live For. Shortly after it aired on MuchMusic, Sony Music signed them up.

After the success of, Something to Live For, Barney Bentall and The Legendary Hearts continued to have more hits, such as Come Back To Me, Crime Against Love, Do Ya, and I'm Shattered. In 1996 a greatest hits package was released, followed by *Til Tomorrow* in 1997.

Singles:

Something To Live For	Epic 3050	1987
Come Back To Me	Epic 3064	1988
Black Clouds (12")	Epic CDN 443	1988
The House Of Love	Epic 3075	1988/89
Something To Live For	Epic 3050	1988
She's My Inspiration	Epic 3081	1989
Crime Against Love	Epic EK 80148	1990
Life Could Be Worse	Epic EK 80148	1991
I Gotta Go	Epic EK 80148	1991
Nothing Hurts (Like The Words)	Epic EK 80148	1991
Living In The '90s	Epic EK 80173	1992
Doin' Fine	Epic EK 80173	1992/93
If This Is Love	Epic EK 80173	1993
Belly Of The Sun	Epic EK 80173	1993
Family Man	Epic EK 80173	1993
Do Ya	Epic EK 80224	1995
I'm Shattered	Epic EK 80224	1995
Oh Shelley	Epic EK 80224	1996
Gin Palace	Epic EK 80224	1996
Fresh Jelly Roll	Epic CK 80259	1996/97
Be Inside You	Epic CK 80259	1997
You Should Be Having Fun	Col CK 80292	1997

Albums/CDs:

Barney Bentall & The Legendary Hearts	Epic BPEC 80131	1988
Lonely Avenue	Epic EK 80148	1990
Ain't Love Strange	Epic EK 80173	1992
Gin Palace	Epic EK 80224	1995
Greatest Hits 1986 1996	Epic CK 80259	1996
Til Tomorrow	Columbia 80292	1997
Gift Horse	True North TND 415	2006
The Inside Message	True North TND 530	2009
Flesh And Bone	True North TND572	2012

Bentwood Rocker

Eric Baragar (vocals, guitar, keyboards)
Mike Goettler (vocals, bass)
Tim Campbell (vocals, guitar)   Replaced by Barry Haggarty
Steve Smith (vocals, drums, keyboards)
Dan Thompson (vocals, guitar, percussion)

Based in Belleville, Ontario, this quintet evolved from The Sands of Time. Formed in 1977, *Bentwood Rocker* recorded some demos that caught the attention of Jack Richardson, who signed them to a production deal and produced eight of their songs. They were later part of the group's first album, *Not Taken* on their own independent label, Skyhawk Records. Shortly after the release of their Singles:, Forgive and Forget and It Won't Be Long, Tim Campbell left and was replaced by Barry Haggarty. In 1981 they signed with Quality Records, who released the album, Take Me To Heaven in 1982. In 1983 the group released the album, *Second Wind* under the name The Press, and in 1986 the single, Danger of Remembering as The Sands of Time. A self-titled CD came out in 1996.

Singles:

Forgive and Forget	Quality Q 2386X	1980
It Won't Be Long	Quality Q 2387X	1980
Take Me To Heaven	Quality Q 2408X	1982
Heart Says Go	Quality Q 2419X	1982
Second Wind (The Press)	Aquarius AQ 6013	1984
Danger Of Remembering (Sands of Time)	B&C Records BC025	1986
What Are We Doing Here?	Skyhawk CMDC 9563	1996

Albums/CDs:

Not Taken	Skyhawk BW1001	1979
Take Me To Heaven	Quality SV 2094	1982
Bentwood Rocker	Skyhawk CMDC 9563	1996

Art Bergman

Art Bergman's music career began in 1977 when he played in a band called The Schmorgs in the Vancouver suburbs. He later played with other bands such as The K Tels, subsequently called The Young Canadians, who released two EPs, *Hawaii* and *This Is My Life*.

From 1980 to 1983, Bergman was a member of Los Popularos. They released a single, Mystery To Me and an EP, *Born Free*.

In 1984 Bergman and a group of studio musicians called Poisoned released a six track EP, Yeah, I Guess. Another EP called, *Poisoned* came out in 1985.

He signed with Duke Street Records in 1988 and recorded his first solo album, *Crawl With Me*. His old backup group was rechristened, The Showdogs and included, Susann Richter, Taylor Nelson Little, and Ray Fulber. Bergman's second solo album was called, *Sexual Roulette*.

Turning to acting in 1991, Art played Otto in Bruce MacDonald's film, Highway 61. A deal with Polygram that same year resulted in his self-titled debut album for the label, and the single, Faithlessly Yours. A second hit from the album, If She Could Sing was released in November, 1991.

Singles:

Yeah, I Guess Who		1985
Poisoned		1985
Our Little Secret	Duke Street 71046	1988
Final Cliche	Duke Street 91046	1988
Bound For Vegas		1990
Faithlessly Yours	Polygram 511067	1991
If She Could Sing	Polygram 511067	1991/92
Contract	Sony EK80208	1995

Albums/CDs:

Poisoned (EP)		1985
Crawl With Me	Duke StreetDSR 31046	1988
Sexual Roulette	Duke StreetDSR 31062	1990
Art Bergmann	Polygram 511067	1991
What Fresh Hell Is This?	Sony EK80208	1995
Design Flaw	OPM 2121	1998
Vultura Freeway	Audio MonsterAM 0001	2000

Justin Bieber

Justin Bieber was born in Stratford, Ontario in March 1, 1994. He took second place in a local talent competition which later made him a phenomenon on You Tube. He later signed a recording contract with Usher. Signed to Def Jam he sold millions of records and was responsible for making Canadian music a dominant force on the Billboard Hot 100. What Do You Mean debuted at number one on September 19, 2015. In 2016 Love Yourself and Sorry chalked up number ones.

Singles:

One Time	Def Jam365691	2010
Love Me	Def Jam828003	2010
One Less Lonely Girl	Def Jam086150	2010
Favourite Girl	MIUCT 5791	2010
Baby	Def Jam297014	2010
U Smile	MIUCT 5800	2010
Never Let You Go	Def Jam820676	2010
Eenie Meenie	Epic 529292	2010
Somebody To Love	Def Jam266333	2010

Never Say Never	MercuryUSUM015391	2010
Next To You	Sony USJI 100078	2011
Mistletoe	Def JamUSUM 116290	2011
The Christmas Song	Def JamUSUM 116397	2011
Boyfriend	Def JamUSUM 202650	2012
Turn To You	Def JamUSUM 204878	2012
Die In Your Arms	MercuryUSUM 205353	2012
All Around The World	Def JamUSUM 205293	2012
As Long As You Love Me	Def JamUSUM 205320	2012
Beauty And A Beat	Def JamUSUM 205367	2012
Beautiful (w/Carly Rae Jrpsen)	Interscope 208954	2012
Nothing Like Us	Def JamUSUM 300154	2013
Heartbreaker	Def JamUSUM 314172	2013
All That Matters	Def JamUSUM 314567	2013
Hold Tight	Def JamUSUM 314690	2013
Wait For A Minute	Minute USCM 300919	2013
Recovery	DEF JSM USUM 314716	2013
All Bad	Def JamUSUM 317838	2013
Pyd (w/R. Kelly)	Def JamUSUM 318504	2013
Roller Coaster	Def JamUSUM 318563	2013
Change Me	Def JamUSUM 318861	2013
Confident	Def JamUSUM 319306	2013
Gas Pedal (w/Sage The Gemini)	USUYG 027384	2014
Where Are You Now (w/Skrillex&Diplo)	Atlantic USAT 500555	2015
What Do You Mean	Def JamUSUM 511919	2015
Sorry	Def JamUSUM 516760	2015
I'll Show You	Def JamUSUM 516758	2015
Love Yourself	Def JamUSUM 516761	2015
Company	Def JamUSUM 516762	2015
Mark My Words	Def JamUSUM 516757	2015
The Feeling	Def JamUSUM 516765	2015
No Pressure	Def JamUSUM 516763	2015
Purpose	Def JamUSUM 516767	2015
Children	Def JamUSUM 516766	2015
No Sense	Def JamUSUM 516764	2015
Been You	Def JamUSUM 516768	2015
Get Used To Me	Def JamUSUM 516769	2015
Trust	Def JamUSUM 516772	2015
All In It	DEF JSM USUM 516773	2015

Albums/CDs:

My World	Def Jam725523	2009
Never Say Never	Def Jam765149	2011
Under The Mistletoe	Def Jam 783390	2011
Believe	Def Jam706917	2012
Believe Acoustic	Def Jam728439	2013
Journals	Def Jam 689538	2014
Purpose	Def Jam 757641	2015

Big Sugar

Gordie Johnson (guitar, vocals)
Terry Wilkins (bass) Replaced by Garry Lowe (1995)
Al Cross (drums) Replaced by Walter "Crash" Morgan (1994);
Paul Brennan (1995); Gavin Brown (1998)
Kelly Hoppe (harmonica, melodica, steel guitar)

From Toronto, Ontario, this four-man band evolved in 1990 out of the Pine Trio when Gordie Johnson, who was invited on stage to sing with them, ended up replacing lead singer Rick "Hock" Walsh who left to rejoin the Downchild Blues Band. With the new name of Big Sugar, they ended up as backup group for such visiting blues acts as Lowell Fulson, Lazy Lester, Ray Charles, Etta James, and Aretha Franklin. In 1992 Big Sugar's self-titled debut CD was released on Hypnotic/A&M Records. The following year, their second CD, *500 Pounds,* was released. In 1993–94, Big Sugar expanded to four members with the addition of Kelly Hoppe. Al Cross also left the group and was replaced by Walter "Crash" Morgan, who died in October 1995. Big Sugar's third full length CD, *Hemi Vision* came out in 1996. In 1998 came the bilingual rock CD, *Heated* which included the first single, The Scene. Three years later, Universal Music released *Brothers And Sisters, Are You Ready* in both English and French (*Brothers And Sisters, Etes Vous Ready*).

In 2003 Big Sugar disbanded. Johnson recorded and toured with the Austin, Texas based metal band, Grady. Big Sugar reunited in 2010 and released albums with the same driving energy they have become famous in their live shows.

Singles:

Sleep In Late	Hypnotic 61005	1992
Dear Mr. Fantasy	A&M 1205	1995
Ride Like Hell	Silvertone 42287 7	1995
Diggin' A Hole	A&M 540600	1996
If I Had My Way	A&M 540600	1997
Gone For Good	A&M 540600	1997
Opem Up Baby	A&M 540600	1997/98
The Scene	A&M 40955	1998
Better Get Used To It	A&M 40955	1999
Turn The Lights On	A&M 40955	1999
Chauffe A Bloc	A&M 40955	1999
Nicotine	Universal 140292	2001
So Not Over	Universal 140292	2001
Red Rover	Universal 140292	2001
Natty Dread Rock		2015
Just Can't Leave You		2015

Albums/CDs:

Big Sugar	Hypnotic 61005	1992
500 Pounds	Hypnotic 61014	1993
Dear M.F.	A&M 1205	1995
Hemi Vision	A&M 54060	1996
Heated	A&M 40955	1998
Brothers & Sisters, Are You Ready	Universal 140292	2001
Hit And Run: Best Of	Universal 860643	2003
Big Sugar	True North 610052	2007
Five Hundred Pounds	True North 610142	2007
Revolutions Per Minute	Bread & Butter 400602	2011
Eliminate Ya Live	eOne BBP-DV-1012	2012
Yardstyle	Bread & Butter 208032	2014
Calling All The Youth	Bread & Butter 030947	2015

The Big Town Boys

Jimmy Arndt (sax)
Josh Collins (drums)
Tommy Graham (lead guitar, vocals)
John Henderson (organ, acoustic guitar) Replaced by Peter Sterback (1966)
Mike Lewis (trumpet, trombone, piano)
Brian Massey (bass) Replaced by Louis Yacknin (1966)

From Toronto, Ontario, The Big Town Boys formed in 1964, and were named after the hit of the same name by Shirley Matthews, who they also backed up. The original group consisted of Tommy Graham, Josh Collins, Jimmy Arndt, Mike Lewis and Brian Lewis. In 1965 John Henderson made the group a sextet. Signed to Capitol Records, their first single was Put You Down in 1965. That same year, they became the house band on CTV's After Four, Mike Lewis left the group to go back to school, and they were one of the acts who played at the opening night festivities for the new City Hall in Toronto. At Massey Hall they were among the first Canadian acts to play at the Teens Funarama shows, and they opened for The Beach Boys at Maple Leaf Gardens.

By the fall of 1966, they had changed their name to the B T B 4, and the group went through another personnel change: Louis Yacknin, from J.B. & The Playboys, replaced Brian Massey, and Peter Sterback replaced John Henderson. During their heyday, The Big Town Boys played with The Girlfriends, Jack London, Robbie Lane, and Bobby Curtola. They broke up in November 1967.

Singles:

Put You Down	RCA Victor 57 3339	1965
I Love Her So	Capitol 72252	1965
It Was I	Capitol 72284	1965
Hey Girl Go It Alone	Capitol 72327	1966
My Babe	Capitol 72398	1966
Do It To 'Em (B T B 4)	Yorkville 45007	1967
Jack Rabbit (B T B 4)	Yorkville 45010	1967

Album:

The Big Town Boys	Capitol T 6168	1966

Bim

Born Roy Forbes in Dawson Creek, British Columbia on February 12, 1953, he was nicknamed Bim by his late father who picked it up from the song, Bimbo, Where You Gonna Goyo. His interest in music came in 1968 when The Beatles released the "White Album." He played in a rock band called Crystal Ship and played nothing but Beatles songs from *The Beatles* and *Rubber Soul*.

Bim started playing professionally in 1971 in Vancouver, where he makes his home today. His first job was with a Rita Coolidge show in Edmonton. Early in 1973, he began playing coffeehouses on the west coast. Later he came east to Toronto and played at the Riverboat. Signed to A&M Records in 1975, he had a modest success on the charts in the mid-1970s.

Today, he still writes and records, and likes to try different musical styles. His seventh solo album, *The Human Kind* was a tribute to his country roots. In addition to recording and performing solo, he has been part of the trio, UHF (Ulrich, Henderson, and Forbes) since 1989.

Singles:

Me And My Baby	Casino C7 104	1975
Can't Catch Me	Casino C7 109	1975/76
Don't Try To Sleep	Casino C7 111	1976
Fly Back North	Casino C7 117	1976
So Close To Home	Casino C7 122	1976
Tender Lullaby	Casino C7 138	1978
Mincemeat Tart	ATR 110	1985
Away From Me (Roy Forbes)		1988
I'm So Lonesome I Could Cry (Roy Forbes)	AKA 1003	1995

Albums/CDs:

Kid Full Of Dreams	Casino CA 1007	1975
Raincheck On Misery	Casino CA 1009	1976
Thistles	Casino CA 1010	1978
Anything You Want	Stony SPL 1044	1982
A Christmas Album (Roy Forbes)	AUR TRAD ATR 109	1985
Love Turns To Ice (Roy Forbes)	AKA 1001	1987
The Human Kind (Roy Forbes)	AKA 1002	1992
Almost Overnight (Roy Forbes)	AKA 1003	1995
Crazy Old Moon (Roy Forbes)	AKA 1004	1998

Heather Bishop

Born on April 25, 1949 in Regina, Saskatchewan, Heather Bishop studied piano as a child and played guitar in her teens. In Winnipeg, under the tutelage of Alicja Seaborn she studied voice, and in the 1970s she was a member of a female dance band called Walpurgis Night. By 1976 she embarked on a solo career as both pianist and singer. In the 1980s she became one of Canada's leading performers in both feminist and children's music.

In 1986 she started to tour the United States and performed at such auspicious events as the Philadelphia International Theater Festival for Children, and the Michigan Womyn's Festival. In Canada she has played at various folk festivals from Vancouver to Winnipeg to Calgary. Her recordings can be found on the independent Mother of Pearl label. On May 11, 2001 she was invested into the Order of Manitoba, the province's highest honor.

Albums/CDs:

Grandmother's Song	Mother of Pearl001	1979
Celebration	Mother of Pearl002	1981
Bellybutton	Mother of Pearl003	1982
I Love Women Who Laugh	Mother of Pearl004	1983
Purple People Eater	Mother of Pearl005	1985
A Taste Of The Blues (CS)	Mother of Pearl006	1986
Walk That Edge	Mother of Pearl007	1989
A Duck In New York City (CS)	Mother of Pearl008	1990
Old New Borrowed Blue	Mother of Pearl009	1992
Daydream Me Home (CS)	Mother of Pearl010	1994
Chickee's On The Run	Mother of Pearl011	1997
Heather Bishop Live	Mother of Pearl012	2000
A Tribute To Peggy Lee	Mother of Pearl 320724	2004
My Face Is A Map Of My Time Here	CD Baby 579495	2009

Terry Black

Born in North Vancouver, B.C. on February 3, 1949, Terry Black began singing as a teenager, and at age fifteen his solo career started with the single Sinner Man on Arc Records in 1964. Other hits followed in the mid 1960s such as Little Liar and Baby's Gone, but his biggest hit was Unless You Care.

Dunhill Records in the U.S. promoted Black as "the Canadian Elvis" but he was bigger in Canada where his recordings were released on the Toronto independent label, Arc. Glen Campbell played as a session guitarist in Los Angeles where Black recorded. In 1964 he toured with The Beach Boys in Seattle.

In 1970 he met Laurel Ward while performing in the Toronto production of Hair. She had been in the group Prisms who recorded one album on Yorkville (PRISMS Yorkville YVS 33004) in 1968, produced by Rich Hubbard, aka Ritchie Knight.

As husband and wife, Terry Black and Laurel Ward became a popular Canadian duo. Their hits included Goin' Down (On The Road To L.A.) and Love Is The Feeling. They also recorded the EP, *All Night Long*.

Terry Black continued to record but less frequently. In 1982, he recorded, Waves Of Emotion on Duke Street Records. He died in Vancouver on June 28, 2009.

By Terry Black
Singles:

Sinner Man/Dry Bones	ARC 1063	1964
Unless You Care	ARC 1074	1964
Unless You Care	Tollie 026	1964
Say It Again	ARC 1080	1965
Little Liar	ARC 1090	1965
Only Sixteen	ARC 1103	1965
Only Sixteen	Dunhill 4005	1965
Poor Little Fool	ARC 1117	1965
Rainbow	ARC 1125	1966
Baby's Gone	ARC 1149	1966
Wishing Star	ARC 1173	1967
Ridin' A Daydream	GRT 1230 14	1971
Waves Of Emotion	DSR S09	1982

Albums/CDs:

Only Sixteen	ARC 5001	1965
The Black Plague	ARC 5002	1966

By Terry Black & Laurel Ward

Singles:

Goin' Down (On The Road To L.A.)	Yorkville YVM 45038	1972
Goin' Down (On The Road To L.A.)	Kama Sutra 540	1972
Warm Days and Warm Nights	Yorkville YVM 45065	1972
Love Is The Feeling	Yorkville YVM 45085	1974
Back Up (Against Your Persuasion)	RCA PB 50053	1975
Long Time	RCA PB 50137	1976

Album:

All Night Long (10" EP)	Duke StreetDSR 10/9 81	1982

Blue Rodeo

Cleave Andersen (drums) Replaced by Mark French (1989), and Glenn Milchem (1992)
Jim Cuddy (vocals, guitar)
Bazil Donovan (bass)
Greg Keelor (vocals, guitar)
Bobby Wiseman (piano) Replaced by Kim Deschamps (1992)

Jim Cuddy and Greg Keelor, who met at North Toronto High School in 1971, were the founding members of this Toronto-based band. They worked together in two other bands, The HiFis (1978 1981) and Fly To France (1981 84). When the latter broke up they formed Blue Rodeo in 1984, and were joined by bassist Bazil Donovan, pianist Bob Wiseman and drummer Cleave Andersen. In 1985, they began playing around Toronto and established themselves as a live act who could draw sellout crowds. They became regulars at The Horseshoe. Their debut album, Outskirts, was released in 1987 by Warner Music Canada.

After the release of their second album, Diamond Mine in December 1988, the group's reputation spread south of the border. By the end of 1989, Cleave Anderson had left the group, and was replaced by Mark French. In 1990 they played at the Montreux Jazz Festival, and appeared as Meryl Streep's backup band in the Columbia film, Postcards From The Edge.

Blue Rodeo's fourth album, *Lost Together* came out in June 1992. That same year, they had two major personnel changes: Bob Wiseman left to pursue a solo career, and was replaced by Kim Deschamps; and Mark French was replaced by Glenn Milchem, formerly with Change Of Heart. James Gray (Born December 8, 1960 and died August 5, 2013) joined on keyboards.

Their fifth album, *Five Days In July* came out in 1993. The first single was Five Days In May. Their sixth, Nowhere To Here was released in 1995, while their seventh, *Tremolo*, in 1997.

Greg Keelor released his first solo album, *Gone* (Wea 17513) in February 1997, and in September 1998, Jim Cuddy released his first solo album, All in Time (Wea 23107).

Singles:

Outskirts Of Love	Risque-Disque 751	1987
Try	Risque-Disque 82917	1987
Rebel	Risque-Disque 80107	1988
Day After Day	Risque-Disque 600	1987/88
How Long	Risque-Disque 56268	1989
Diamond Mine	Risque-Disque Pro 649	1989
House Of Dreams	Risque-Disque 56268	1989
Love And Understanding	Risque-Disque 56268	1990
Trust Yourself	Wea 72770	1991
Till I Am Myself Again	Wea 72770	1991
What Am I Doin' Here	Wea 72770	1991
After The Rain	Wea 72770	1991
Lost Together	Wea 82412	1992
Last To Know	Wea 82412	1992
Western Skies	Wea 82412	1992
Rain Down On Me	Wea 82412	1992/93
Angels	Wea 82412	1993
Flying	Wea 82412	1993
Already Gone	Wea 82412	1993
Five Days In May	Wea 77013	1993
Hasn't Hit Me Yet	Wea 77013	1994
Bad Timing	Wea 77013	1994
Dark Angel	Wea 77013	1994
Til I Gain Control Again	Wea 77013	1994
Head Over Heels	Wea 77013	1995
Side of the Road	Wea 10617	1995
Get Through To You	Wea 10617	1995/96
Girl in Green	Wea 10617	1996
Blew It Again	Wea 10617	1996
It Could Happen To You	Wea 19253	1997
Falling Down Blue	Wea 19253	1997
No Miracle No Dazzle	Wea 19253	1998
Somebody Waits	Wea 80936	1999
Always Getting Better	Wea 80936	2000
Home To You This Christmas	Wea 213504	2014

Albums/CDs:

Outskirts	Risque-Disque25 47181	1987
Diamond Mine	Risque-Disque25 62681	1989

Casino	Wea 72770	1990
Lost Together	Atlantic 82412	1992
Five Days in July	Wea 77013	1993
Nowwhere to Here	Wea 10617	1995
Tremolo	Wea 19253	1997
Just Like a Vacation	Wea 27394	1999
Days in Beteen	Wea 80936	1999
Greatest Hits, Volume 1	Wea 40932	2001
Blue Road	Wea 34072	2008
In Our Nature	Wea	2013
A Merrie Christmas To You	Wea 213504	2014
Live at Massey Hall	Wea 052349	2015

The Blue Shadows

Billy Cowsill (guitar, vocals)
Jeffrey Hatcher (guitar, vocals)
Jay Johnston (drums)
Elmar Spanier (bass)

Billy Cowsill who became famous as a member of The Cowsills (The Rain, The Park and Other Things, 1967) was instrumental in creating a band that played country music with the passion and energy of rock and roll. He later moved to Vancouver, B.C. where he joined Blue Northern, which split up in the early to mid 1980s.

The origins of The Blue Shadows goes back to The Billy Cowsill Band when it was a duo comprised of Cowsill and Spanier, they played spellbinding renditions of classic songs by Hank Williams Sr. and Roy Orbison.

The group expanded to a quartet with the addition of Jeffrey Hatcher and Jay Johnston. The former was singer, songwriter and guitarist with such bands as The Fuse, The Six and The Big Beat.

It was Billy and Jeff's smooth harmonies that resulted in a name change to The Blue Shadows. They described their sound as "Hank goes to the Cavern Club."

Signed to Sony Music, their debut album *On the Floor of Heaven* was released in 1993. The first single and video was Comin' On Strong. They broke up in 1995, shortly after the release of their second CD, *Lucky to Me*.

Singles:

Comin' on Strong	Col CK 80181	1993
The Fool is the Last One Tto Know	Col CK 80181	1994
Deliver Me	Col CK 80181	1994

(Born To Be) Riding Only Down	Col CK 80220	1995
Lucky To Me	Col CK 80220	1995
Field of Gold	Col CK 80220	1996
The Trouble With Trouble	Col CK 80220	1996

Albums/CDs:
| On the Floor of Heaven | Col CK 80181 | 1993 |
| Lucky To Me | Col CK 80220 | 1995 |

BLVD

Randy Burgess (bass)
David Forbes (lead vocals)
Randy Gould (guitar)
Mark Holden (saxophone, vocals)
Andrew Johns (keyboards)
Randal Stohl (drums)

Mark Holden and Randy Gould started Blvd in 1983 in Calgary, Alberta. Holden had returned from Frankfurt, Germany where he worked as a sound engineer at Hotline Studios. An offer to work at Thunderhead Studios in Calgary brought him back to Canada. While working there, he assembled the group that became Blvd. When the studio closed in 1985, he and the band relocated in Vancouver. In the spring of 1987, MCA released their self-titled debut album, *BLVD*. Their first charted single was In The Twilight in 1988. Blvd broke up in 1990 shortly after the release of their second album, *Inot the Street*.

Singles:
Never Give Up	MCA 53297	1988
Far From Over	MCA 53268	1988
Dream On	MCA 53395	1988
In The Twilight	MCA 8849	1988
Lead Me On	MCAD 42317	1990
Crazy Life	MCAD 42317	1990

Albums/CDs:
| BLVD | MCA 42111 | 1987 |
| Into the Street | MCAD 42317 | 1990 |

Bond

Bill Dunn (bass)
Jeff Hamilton (drums)
Alex Mac Dougall (lead guitar)
John Roles (rhythm guitar)
Ted Trenholm (keyboards)

The origins of this Toronto rock band go back to 1970 when John Roles placed an ad in the trades for interested musicians who wanted to form a band. In 1971 they recorded their first single, You Will Be The One/I Won't Be Here Tomorrow, on the Vintage label. Four years later, they signed with Columbia Records. Their first single, Dancin' On A Saturday Night was a major hit. The band's tight co ordination, vocals and Liverpudlian Sound made them one of Canada's most commercial bands in the mid 1970s. They broke up in 1979.

Singles:

You Will Be The One/		
I Won't Be Here Tomorrow	Vintage 1116	1971
Dancin' On A Saturday Night	Columbia C4 4061	1975
When You're Up, You're Up	Columbia C4 4083	1975
Hold On	Columbia C4 4103	1975/76
Back Seat Driver	Columbia C4 4117	1976
One Lives In My Life	CBS C4 4137	1976
I Can't Help It	Epic E4 4180	1978

Album:

Bond	Columbia ES 90301	1975

Mars Bonfire

Mars Bonfire was born Dennis Eugene McCrohan on April 21, 1943 in Oshawa, Ontario. He was one of the original members of Jack London and The Sparrows (later known as The Sparrows). When they split up in 1967, he decided to go solo and changed his name. His first solo effort was Ride With Me Baby in 1968. That same year, he wrote Born To Be Wild for Steppenwolf. Mars Bonfire's self-titled debut album also came out in 1968, followed by another album called, *Faster Than The Speed Of Life* in 1969.

Singles:

Ride With Me	UNI 55081	1968
Faster Than the Speed of Life	Columbia 4 44772	1969
Lady Moon Walker	Columbia 4 44888	1969

Albums/CDs:

Mars Bonfire	UNI 73027	1968
Faster than the Speed of Life	Columbia 9834	1969

Ray Bonneville

Ray Bonneville was born on October 11, 1948 in Hull, Quebec. A self-taught guitarist, he has played to wide acclaim from audiences in Canada, the United States and France. His music has been featured on several CBC programs, such as Swinging On A Star, Saturday Night Blues with Holger Peterson, and Home Run. In Quebec he has been a guest on Beau et Chaud and City Beat.

In his songs Bonneville combines a mix of musical influences from blues to country. They are often thoughtful and true to life. He has performed at many of the folk and jazz festivals across North America and France and has opened for B.B. King, John Hammond, Boz Scaggs, Muddy Waters, James Cotton, Charles Musselwhite, The Isley Brothers, Sonny Terry and Brownie McGhee, Little Anthony and The Imperials, and Dr. John.

In 1993 Ray's debut album, *On The Main*, was released on the independent label Blue Desert. It was followed two years later by *Solid Ground*. His third, *Gust Of Wind*, marked his debut on Stony Plain. Produced by Colin Linden, it featured Prairie Oyster's Keith Glass and Nashville's Tim O'Brien.

Singles:

The Good Times	Electric Desert EDR 9301	1995
Nothing to Lose	Audiogram ADCD 10097	1997
When The Night Time Comes		1998

Albums/CDs:

On the Main	Electric Desert EDR 9301	1993
Solid Ground	Audiogram ADCD 10097	1995
Gust of Wind	Stony Plain SPCD 1256	1999
Rough Luck	Prime PCD 68	2000

The Boomers

Peter Cardinal (bass, vocals)
Bill Dillon (guitars)
Rick Gratton (drums, percussion)
Ian Thomas (vocals, guitar, keyboards)

The Boomers came together in late 1990 while Ian Thomas was working on a solo album. He had invited some friends to help out: Peter Cardinal, a noted bassist and arranger whose worked with Anne Murray, Rick James, Oscar Peterson, and B.B. King; Bill Dillon, house guitarist for Daniel Lanois, and Rick Gratton, one of Canada's top session drummers with a series of instructional books, videos and clinics to his credit.

The chemistry among the four worked; what started out as a solo album became, The Boomers' debut album, *What We Do* in 1991. Despite its critical acclaim, it did not sell well in Canada. However, a buyer for a German record chain liked it enough to sell thousands of import copies before Wea Music of Canada (now Warner Music) started to sell it.

The Boomers were an immediate hit in Germany and when they played there live, it was to sold-out houses every night.

In 1993 the second album by The Boomers, *The Art of Living*, came out, and included their most popular song, You've Got To Know, which won a Socan award for the most performed song of the year.

Their third album, *25 Thousand Days*, on Alma/Polydor was released in 1996.

Singles:

Love You Too Much	Wea 74515	1991
One Little Word	Wea 74515	1991/92
Wishes	Wea 74515	1992
You've Got To Know	Wea 91854	1993
Art of Living	Wea 91854	1993
Good Again	Wea 91854	1993/94
I Feel A Change Coming	POL 42103	1996
Saving Grace	POL 42103	1997

Albums/CDs:

What We Do	Wea 74515	1991
The Art of Living	Wea 91854	1993
25 Thousand Days	POL 42103	1996

Bootsauce

Alan Baculis (bass)
Pere Fume (guitar)
Sonny Greenwich Jr. (guitar)
Rob Kazanel (drums)
Drew Ling (vocals)

Drew Ling was born in Liverpool, England, and came to Canada with his parents when he was a teenager. Settling in Calgary, Alberta, he met Pere Fume whose musical education began at age six with piano lessons. Sonny Greenwich Jr. was born in Montreal and he received his first guitar from his father, Sonny Greenwich Sr., who was a jazz guitarist. Sonny Jr. had started the band Dog Food (later called Dog Star).

Bootsauce formed in 1989 in Montreal at the club Le Biftech where Drew, Pere and Sonny met together. Allan Baculis and Rob Kazanel also joined the group.

That same year they signed a recording contract with PolyGram, who released the group's video and EP, *Scratching the Whole* in April 1990, and *The Brown Album* two months later.

In February 1991, Johnny Frappe joined on drums, and a month later, Bootsauce's Play With Me was voted the Alternative Song of the Year for 1991 by the Canadian Music Publishers Association.

Their second album, *Bull* cames out in February 1992, and was certified gold in Canada in seven weeks. *Sleeping Bootie*, their third, was released in November 1993.

During the summer of 1994, Pere Fume left Bootsauce, and was replaced by Fraser Rosetti from the group Exploited. The non-album track, Crack of Dawn, was released as a CD single in 120,000 cases of Labatt beer.

On March 22, 1995 the self-titled album, *Bootsauce* was released, and on May 5, 1996, Bootism The Bootsauce Collection.

Singles:

Masterstroke	POL 846247	1990
Scratching The Whole	Vertigo 510118	1990
Everyone's a Winner	Vertigo 510118	1991
Play With Me	Vertigo 510118	1991
Love Monkey #9	Vertigo 512027	1992
Whatcha Need	Vertigo 512027	1992
Big, Bad & Groovy	Vertigo 512027	1992
Rollercoaster's Child	Vertigo 512027	1992/93

Sorry Whole	Vertigo 518431	1993
Moanie	Vertigo 518431	1994
Caught Looking At You	Vertigo 518431	1994
Hey Baby	Vertigo 526778	1995
Each Morning After	Vertigo 526778	1995

Albums/CDs:

The Brown Album	POL 846247	1990
Reboot	Vertigo 510118	1991
Bull	Vertigo 572027	1992
Sleeping Bootie	Vertigo 518431	1993
Bootsauce	Vertigo 526778	1995
Bootism: The Bootsauce Collection	Vertigo 532290	1996

The Bourbon Tabernacle Choir

Gregor Beresford (drums)

Chris Brown (organ, clavinet, trombone, vocals)

Kate Fenner (vocals)

Gene Hardy (saxophone, vocals)

Jason Mercer (bass)

Chris Miller (guitar)

Chris Plock (keyboards) Replaced by Dave Wall (piano, vocals) (1988)

Andrew Whiteman (guitar, vocals)

The origins of The Bourbon Tabernacle Choir go back to 1985 when eight Toronto high school students joined together for a jam session later referred to as "The Sermon." Through subsequent performances they were able to smooth over the rough edges of their stage act. They eventually built up a local following in Toronto's nightclubs and bars. Chris Brown came up with the group's name in a dream.

In 1987 the group released the first of three independent cassettes, First Taste Of Bourbon. The other two were If Hell Had A Houseband in 1989 and Sister Anthony in 1990. Their first two Singles:, As Right As They Wanna Be and Put Your Head On were produced by ex-Blue Rodeo keyboardist Bob Wiseman. The accompanying video for Put Your Head On, debuted on MuchMusic in May of 1991. It was also included on the soundtrack of Bruce McDonald's feature film, Highway 61.

The year 1992 saw the Toronto octet record their first album, *Superior Cackling*

Hen for Yonder Records with distribution by Sony Music. Its title comes from a Jimi Hendrix song called Third Stone From The Sun (from the album Are You Experienced?) in which Hendrix mentions a majestic superior cackling hen.

Bourbon Tabernacle Choir broke up in 1995 after the release of their second album, *Shy Folk*. Dave Wall recorded a solo album, Lozenge, in 1993, which contained the first single, The Storm Is Passing Over. After the demise of the Bourbons, Chris Brown and Kate Fenner continued as a duo and recorded the albums *Other People's Heavens* (1998), *Geronimo* (DROG 00063 1999), *Great Lakes Bootleg* (2000), and *O Witness* (Ram Recordings RAMCD 75 2001).

Singles:
As Right As They Wanna Be	ATPC 0011 (cassette)	1990/91
Put Your Head On	ATPC 0011 (cassette)	1991
Make Amends	Yonder 0014	1992
Afterglow	Yonder 0014	1993
Original Grin	Yonder 0014	1993
All Peace	Yonder 0015	1995
Be My Witness	Yonder 0015	1995

Albums/CDs:
First Taste of Bourbon (EP)	Independent	1987
If Hell Had a House Band (EP)	Independent	1988
Sister Anthony (EP)	Independent	1990
Superior Cackling Hen	Yonder 0014	1992
Shyfolk	Yonder 0015	1995

The Box

Phillipe Bernard (drums)
Jean Pierre Brie (bass)
Guy Pisapia (keyboards)
Jean Marc Pisapia (lead vocals)
Claude Thibeault (guitar)

The Box formed in 1982 in Montreal when Jean Marc Pisapia was asked to be leader of a new Quebec group. He was an architecture major at the University of Montreal when he dropped out to play keyboards with former classmate and friend Ivan Doroschuk for a two month tour with his band, Men Without Hats. The music of The Box music was, according to Jean Marc Pisapia, "naive techno pop/rock. [Its focus] was on observations about the lighter side of life."

Although the group was a quintet, their sound engineer Luc Papineau played an integral part in creating the style of music they played on stage and recorded in the studio. At first they were called French Quebecers who sang in English.

Their 1986 hit, L'Affaire Dumoutier (Say To Me) broke the band in Quebec. It was not until the release of Closer Together in 1987 that the rest of Canada caught on to the band's music. The single of the same name was "an ordinary song that appealed to a lot more people."

Between 1985 and 1989, Sass Jordan played backup with The Box, although she was not a member of the group.

In 1992 the group changed from a sextet to a trio. The remaining members were Claude Thibeault, Jean Marc Pisapia and Jean Pierre Brie.

A Decade Of The Box, a single CD retrospective of the group's work, was released the following year.

Jean Marc Pisapia went on to pursue a solo career under the name John of Mark.

Singles:

Walk Away	Alert BDS 500	1984
Must I Always Remember	Alert BDS 501	1984
Dancing On The Grave (12")	Alert MBD 004	1985
Dancing On The Grave	Alert BDS 504	1985
With All This Cash (12")	Alert SBD 008	1985
L'Affaire Dumoutier	Alert BDS 510	1986
L'Affaire Dumoutier (12")	Alert MBD 006	1986
My Dreams Of You	Alert BDS 512	1986
Closer Together	Alert BDS 519	1987
Ordinary People	Alert BDS 522	1987
Crying Out Loud For Love	Alert BDS 524	1988
Temptation	Alert 81014	1990
Inside My Heart	Alert 81014	1990
Carry On	Alert 81014	1990

Albums/CDs:

The Box	Alert BD 1000	1984
The Box (EP)	Alert SBD 001	1984
All The Time, All The Time, All The Time	Alert BD 1003	1985
Closer Together	Alert BD 1005	1987
The Pleasure and the Pain	Alert 81014	1990
A Decade Of The Box	Kardiak KRKCD 2500	1993

Oscar Brand

Folksinger/songwriter Oscar Brand was born in Winnipeg, Manitoba on February 7, 1920. Before his family moved to Minneapolis, he lived on a wheat farm where he was exposed to the wonders of nature. He spent his childhood years in Chicago and New York. When he was in his late teens he left home to experience firsthand the hardships of the Depression.

While travelling across the U.S., he worked as a farmhand while playing folk songs on his banjo. He later returned to Brooklyn College where he majored in Abnormal Psychology. When World War II interrupted his studies, he worked up to the position of section chief of a psychology unit.

After his discharge from the army, he toured as a singer on the Herb Shriner Show. Eventually, he was hired as coordinator of folk music at radio station WNYC in New York, where he started his own program, Folksong Festival. During the 1950s and 1960s, the show was rebroadcast over the U.S. Information Service, and featured live performances of such folk music legends as Woody Guthrie, Richard Dyer Bennet and Bob Dylan among others.

In addition to his other shows on radio and television, Oscar built up a reputation as a singer/songwriter; he has appeared at many folk festivals and coffeehouses. He also recorded more than fifty albums on various labels, and wrote a number of books about folk music, notably Singing Holidays (Alfred A. Knopf, 1957) and The Ballad Mongers (Funk & Wagnalls, 1062). He continues to live in the United States.

Albums/CDs:

Noah's Ark	YPR 10013	1947
Sings Absolute Nonsense	RLP 12 825	1948
Old Time Bawdy Sea Shanties	AFLP 1884	1948
Riddle Me This (w/Jean Ritchie)	Riverside 12 646	1949
Give 'Im The Hook	Riverside 1118	1949
Bawdy Songs And Barroom Ballads I	Audio Fidelity 1906	1949
Bawdy Songs And Barroom Ballads II	Audio Fidelity 1803	1949
Songs And Poems Of The Sea	AUDMA LPA 1220	1949
Children's Concert	Wonderland 1438	1950
Courting Songs (w/Jean Ritchie)	Elektra 22	1950
G.I. (U.S. Army Songs)	Riverside 12 639	1950
Bawdy Songs And Backroom Ballads III	Audio Fidelity 1824	1950
Come To The PartY	YPR 15003	1950
Song Bag Of Folk Favorites	Riverside 12 7508	1951
Bawdy Songs Goes To College	Audio Fidelity 1952	1951
Bawdy Songs And Barroom Ballads IV	Audio Fidelity 1847	1951
Bring A Song Johnny	CRG	1951
Bawdy Sea Shanties	Audio Fidelity 1884	1952

Title	Label	Year
Rollicking Sea Shanties	Audio Fidelity 5966	1954
Bawdy Hootenanny	Audio Fidelity 2121	1955
Singalong Bawdy Songs & Backroom Ballads	Audio Fidelity 1970	1956
The Wild Blue Yonder: Songs Of A Fighting Air Force	Elektra 168	1956
Folksongs For Fun (w/Tarriers)	Decca 74275	1956
Bawdy Western Songs	Audio Fidelity 5920	1957
Sports Car Songs	Elektra 7188	1957
The Children's Almanac: The Singing Holidays	YPR 15019 15020	1958
Every Inch a Sailor	Elektra 169	1958
Up in the Air	Elektra 198	1959
Out of the Blue	Elektra 7178	1960
Tell it to The Marines	Elektra 174	1961
Sings for Adults	Sparton/ABC 388	1961
Snow Job for Skiers	Elektra 228	1961
Singalong Bawdy Songs	Audio Fidelity 1971	1961
Cough (Soldier Songs)	Elektra 242	1962
How to Steel an Election: A Dirty Politics Musical	RCA LSO 1153	1962
Election Songs of The United States	Folk FH 5280	1962
Folk Festival	Sparton/ABC 408	1963
Boating Songs	Elektra 183	1963
For Doctors Only	Elektra 204	1964
Morality	Impulse A 25	1964
On Campus Live	Kapp KS 3624	1965
JEAN Ritchie, Oscar Brand and Dave Sear at Town Hall	Folk FA 2428	1966
An Introduction To Folk Music & Folklore	Gold GW 223	1967
Laughing America	TraditionTLP 1014	1969
Pie in the Sky	TraditionTLP 1022	1969
Shivaree	Esoteric ES 538	1969
Live on Campus	Apex AL 7 1649	1969
Selections From The Bridge Of Hope	Celebration 1001	1970
Celebrate America (20 CS)	Westport Media	1971
Best Of	TraditionTLP 1053	1971
The Americans	Pickwick SPC 3322	1976
Paul Bunyan In Story And Song	Caedmon TC 1275	1977
Oscar Brand And His Young Friends Celebrate Singing Holidays	Caedmon	1978
Billy the Kid in Song and Story	Caedmon TC 1552	1979
Oscar Brand Celebrates The First Thanksgiving In Story And Song	Caedmon TC 1505	1980
My Christmas Is Best	Caedmon TC 1776	1983
Oscar Brand And Friends Celebrate Your Birthday In 14 Languages	Caedmon TC 1782	1985
American Dreamer	Biograph BLP 12067	1985
100 Proof Drinking Songs	Arabesque 6534	1987
Brand X	Roulette 42060	1987
I Sing, You Sing, And We All Sing I & II	Peter Pan 8082	1987

I Love Cats	Alcazar	1995
Get A Dog	Alcazar	1996
Presidential Campaign Songs Smithsonian Folkways	SFW CD 45051	1999

The British Modbeats

Joe Colonna (bass)
Greig Foster (guitar)
Mike Gorgichuk (guitar)
Robbie Jeffrey (drums)
Fraser Loveman (vocals)

Formed in 1963, this quintet from St. Catherines, Ontario played cover hits by such British rockers as The Rolling Stones, The Spencer Davis Group and The Pretty Things. On stage they presented themselves as true Brits. Robbie Jeffrey had a Union Jack on his bass drum, and the band name was written in old British script. Signed to Red Leaf Records, their first hit was, Whatcha Gonna Do About It, in the summer of 1966. They had three more hits in 1966-67. Their only album, *Mod is the British Modbeats* came out in 1967. The group disbanded in 1968.

Singles:

Whatcha Gonna Do About It	Red Leaf 620	1966
Love's Just A Broken Heart	Red Leaf 625	1966
Somebody Help Me	Red Leaf 632	1967
Try To Understand	Red Leaf 636	1967

Album:

Mod Is The British Modbeats	Red Leaf 002	1967

Charity Brown

Born in 1951 in Kitchener, Ontario, Phyllis Boltz started playing coffeehouses in Kitchener when she was fifteen. Influenced by Grace Slick of Jefferson Airplane, Brown sang psychedelic songs with the rock bands, Landslide Mushroom and Inner Light. She later changed her name to Charity Brown and joined Rain, a commercial rock band who had minor success with the hit single, Out of My Mind. When they broke up in 1973, she decided to go solo. In 1974 she signed with A&M Records. Her first of several hits was Jimmy Mack, a remake of the old Martha Reeves and The Vandellas hit. Her first album, *Rock Me*, came out in early 1976. Today, she lives in her hometown where she is married to a lawyer.

Singles:

Jimmy Mack	A&M 371	1974
You Beat Me to the Punch	A&M 375	1974/75
Take Me in Your Arms	A&M 391	1975
Our Day Will Come	A&M 391	1975
No Way to Treat a Lady	A&M 397	1975
Saving All My Love	A&M 1759	1976
Anyway You Want Me	A&M 410	1976
Stay With Me	A&M 421	1976
Ain't No Hurt Love Can Heal	A&M 425	1977
Forecast (Heartbreak, Rain and Tears)	A&M 439	1977
Hold on Baby	A&M 445	1977
All the Things You Told Me	A&M 453	1977

Albums/CDs:

Rock Me	A&M SP 9019	1976
Stay With Me	A&M SP 9022	1976
The Best of Charity Brown	A&M SP 9029	1977

Brunswick Playboys

Roger Cormier (lead guitar, bass, vocals)
Leo Doiron (drums)
George Hebert (guitar)
Gerry Holley (vocals)

This quartet from Moncton, New Brunswick started in 1957 as Roger and The Boys, Roger and The Playboys, and The Playboys before settling on the name the Brunswick Playboys. They became well known thanks to their eighteen appearances on CBC TV's Frank's Bandstand out of Halifax, Nova Scotia, and their tours of their home province, Nova Scotia, and Prince Edward Island. George Hebert, who joined the group in 1960, was able to improvise any guitar style and wrote many of their instrumentals, such as Too Blind To See, their 1965 hit on Arc Records.

The Brunswick Playboys broke up in 1967. Hebert is currently a member of Anne Murray's backup band.

Singles:

Too Blind To See	ARC 1084	1965
Trop Occupe	ARC 1104	1965
My Heart Is An Open Book	ARC 1106	1965
Heart	Excellent 5004	1966

Album:

Looking In On	Excellent 109	1966

Brussel Sprout

Jeff Benjamin (bass)
Ken Lush (flute)
Roger Manning (vocals, harp)
Danny Moses (vocals, bongos, violin)
Don Perrish (vocals, guitar)
Tom Treece (vocals)
John Vass (vocals, drum)

The history of Brussel Sprout goes back to 1972 when Don Perrish and Ken Lush, who had known each other from public school, started playing with some ex-members of a jug band called Custer's Last Stand. The occasion was to make a demo tape. After moving to Jordan, Ontario they spent the next year and a half working on their own material. They first called themselves The Amazing Vibrasonics.

After a series of personnel changes, the sextet was comprised of Don Perrish, Ken Lush, Roger Manning, Tom Treece, John Vass and Denny Moses. Jeff Benjamin made it a sextet in 1974. They signed a contract with MCA Records, and in the summer of 1975 their first single, Dance She Said was released. *One More Time* was the name of their debut album.

Their Singles:, High In The Rockies and Tryin' To Get Next To You, were written and arranged by Tom Treece. On the road Brussel Sprout has opened for Valdy, Gordon Lightfoot and The Good Brothers.

Singles:

Dance She Said	MCA 40360	1975
High In The Rockies	MCA 40503	1976
Tryin' To Get Next To You	MCA 40561	1976
Dance She Said	MCA 40638	1977

Album:

Brussel Sprout	MCA 2211	1976

Brutus

Bruce Gordon (trumpet, organ, guitar, bass)
Bill Robb (sax, trombone)
Len Sembaluk (drums)
Sandy White (bass)
Sonny Wingay (guitar)
Wally Zwolinski (organ, lead vocals)

Led by Walter Zwolinsky (aka Zwol), this Toronto band went through many personnel changes since its formation in 1969. Primarily a bar band, they dressed up in garish clothes co ordinated by artist Don Norman.

Their early hits, Funky Roller Skate on Quality Records, and Help Me, Free Me on Yorkville Records were not successful. In 1975, they scored their first hit with, Ooo Mama Mama, which was produced by Jack Richardson of The Guess Who fame. Their only album, *Brutus* was released in 1976.

When Brutus broke up 1977, Walter Zwol had a brief solo career with the hits New York City (1978), Call Out My Name (1979) and Shaka Shaka (1979). He also recorded two Albums, *Zwol* (1978) and *Effective Immediately* (1979). Zwol later formed a new band called Rage in 1981. Their only hit was Darlin' I'll Be True in 1981 from the album *Thrillz*.

Singles:

Funky Roller Skate	Quality 1953	1970
Duck Pond	Quality 1971	1970
Help Me, Free Me	Yorkville 45034	1971
Slow and Easy		1975
Ooo Mama Mama	GRT 1230 104	1975
Who Wants To Buy A Song	GRT 1230 114	1976
Sailing	GRT 1230 127	1976

Albums/CDs:

Brutus	GRT 9230 1057	1976
For The People	Bullseye BLPCD 4021	2001

Michael Bublé

Born in Burnaby, British Columbia on September 9, 1975, Michael Bublé has an international following. Unlike Paul Anka and Bobby Curtola his popularity did not come from the era of the chart. Produced by David Foster, he remains an ambassador for Canadian music wherever he performs. Home from his album, *It's Time* introduced him to a wide audience in 2005. Fouryears later, he gained acceptance with his album, *Crazy Love*. In 2012 his seasonal album, *Christmas*, was number one in Billboard and in December 2015, it became Bublé's biggest selling album. He was honoured with on Canada's Walk of Fame in 2015. His songs have been featured in several films: Down With Love (2003): Down With Love and For Once Kin My Life; Two Weeks Notice (2002) and Looney Tunes Back In Action (2003): Come Fly With Me; Memories of Matsuko (2006): Feeling Good; The Wedding Date (2007): Home, Sway and Save Thhe Last Dance For Me; 27 Dresses (2008): Call Me Irresponsible; Evening (2007): I've Got The World On A String; No Reservations (2007): Sway; Why Did I Get Married (2007) L-O-V-E; Stone of Destiny (2008) and The Proposal (2009): I've Got You Under ?My Skin, and Morning Glory (2010): Stuck in the Middle With You.

Singles:

Home	Reprise CDW 48946	2005
Everything	Reprise 2100373	2007
Lost	Reprise 2110373	2007
Haven't Met You Yet	Reprise 1174011	2009
Cry Me a River	Reprise 2520733	2009
Feeling Good	Reprise 844781	2009
Hollywood	Reprise 000764	2010
It Had to be Her Tonight	Reprise 700355	2011
It's Beginning to Look Like Christmas	Reprise 100700	2011
Have Yourself A Merry Little Christmas	Reprise 1100700	2011
Christmas Baby Please Come	Reprise 1100708	2011
Santa Claus is Comin' to Town	Reprise 100701	2011
It's a Beautiful Day	Reprise 30016	2013
Close Your Eyes	Reprise 300059	2013
Baby It's Cold Outside	Warner 402616	2014
Holly Jolly Christmas	Reprise 100705	2015

Albums/CDs:

Michael Bublé	Reprise 485352	2003
Come Fly With Me	Reprise 486832	2004
Michael Bublé	Reprise 489162	2004
It's Time	Reprise 489462	2005
Caught in the Act	Reprise 494442	2006
Call Me Irresponsible	Reprise 100313	2007
Meets Madison Garden	Reprise 497945	2009
Crazy Love	Reprise 520733	2009
Christmas	Reprise 528350	2011
To Be Loved	Reprise 534922	2013
Nobody But Me	Reprise 557530	2016

Bundock

Pierre Bundock (lead vocals, saxophone)
Marc Gendron (bass)
Dominique Lanois (guitar, vocals)
Martin Plante (keyboards)
Alain Roussel (drums)

The history of this quintet goes back to 1979 in Grand Mere, Quebec when music teacher Guy Pelletier and Pierre Bundock formed the first edition of the band. Four years later, they moved to Montreal. In 1985 they decided to write and record in English, the international language of music.

They were named after an Irish sailor named Bundock who got lost at sea. Irish legend has it that his young son transformed into an eagle and flew over the sea to find his missing father.

Pierre and Marc Bundock were first in a group called Windo, an electro pop band. They met while studying music at St. Laurent College.

Pierre had studied saxophone and piano at the conservatory in Trois Rivieres prior to attending St. Laurence.

Their Ep, Mauve (released in 1986) on Alert Records contained the song, American Singer, which was a tribute to the late Jim Morrison of The Doors. Released in 1987, it was their only national hit.

Singles:
American Singer	Alert SBD 012	1986/87
Hello I Love You	Alert BDS 526	1987/88

Albums/CDs:
Mauve (EP)	Alert BEP 001	1986
S.A. (Societe Anonyme)	Alert BD 1008	1988

Johnny Burt

Born in London, Ontario on March 31, 1914, Johnny Burt studied piano and composition in Toronto. In the 1930s he was a pianist with the dance bands of Luigi Romanelli, Jack Slatte, and George Wade among others, and he and his jazz trio were heard on CBC radio. Besides Burt, it was comprised of Murray McEachern and Danny Perri.

Johnny was also a member of the Trump Davidson Orchestra led by Ray Noble. They went to Great Britain in 1938 where they played with Bill Bissett's Orchestra.

The following year, he returned to Canada and played with various bands, notably Joe DeCourcy's dance band. Burt then spent three years as a bandsman with Royal Canadian Navy at HMCS York, Toronto.

After the Second World War, he worked as arranger and composer at the CBC where he became involved with the orchestras of Geoffrey Waddington, John Adaskin, Jean Deslauriers, Samuel Hershenhoren, Paul Scherman and others. From 1946 to 1948 Burt was heard on CBC radio, this time with Stan Wilson and Sam Levene.

With his own orchestra, Burt played on such CBC shows as Johnny Burt & Company in 1952, and others starring Elwood Glover, Wally Koster and Gisele MacKenzie.

From 1962 to 1972, Burt worked as music director for the Canadian Talent Library, where he chose the label's artists and supervised their recordings. His own recordings were on Canadian Talent Library and RCA.

Johnny also composed several music scores for the National Film Board, in addition to his orchestra's theme song, Theme For Susan. He died on September 21, 1980 in Toronto.

Singles:

Ik Ta Tuk/My Christmas Wish	CTL 477 811	1971
In The Arms of Home/Until You Came Along	CTL 477 819	1972

As Johnny Burt Society Albums/CDs:

The Strings of Johnny Burt	CTL M 1001	1962
Johnny Burt & His Orchestra	CTL M 1004	1962
Johnny Burt & His Orchestra	CTL S 5014	1962
Arrangements for Five Trombones	CTL S 5042	1964
Johnny Burt & His Orchestra	CTL S 5055	1964
Dance to the Trombones	Camden Cas 997	1966
Around The World	Camden Pcs 1199	1967
The Big Band of Johnny Burt	CTL S 5100	1968
A Christmas Wish	CTL 477 5154	1971
Come Summer	CTL 477 5160	1972
Double Exposure	CTL S 5213	1977

BUSH

Pentti "Whitey" Glan (drums)
Prakash John (vocals, bass)
Roy Kenner (vocals, percussion)
Domenic Troiano (vocals, guitar)

When Mandala broke up in the spring of 1969, Whitey Glan and Domenic Troiano formed Bush with Prakash John and Roy Kenner.

Signed to Dunhill Records, they had one self-titled album in 1970, which included the single, I Can Hear You Calling. The latter also became the B side to Three Dog Night's 1971 hit, Joy To The World.

Bush broke up after they finished playing their last show at The Bitter End in Los Angeles on July 6, 1971. Prakash John and Whitey Glann played with Alice Cooper and Lou Reed, and were part of Bette Midler's backup band in the film, The Rose (1979). Prakash John also later became involved in the groups, The Lincolns and The Hiptonics.

Roy Kenner and Domenic Troiano replaced Joe Walsh in the James Gang. (see Domenic Trolano) In 1995, Fusion reissued the group's only album on CD.

Single:
I Can Hear You Calling	Dunhill 4252	1970

Albums/Cds:
Bush	Dunhill DS 50086	1970
Bush	MAGADA 22	1995

Edith Butler

Born Marie Nicole Butler in Paquetville, N.B. on July 27, 1942, Edith Butler was first exposed to music while growing up in her hometown where she listened to country and western music on the radio. It was not until Edith left home to go to Notre Dame de l'Acadie, a girl's convent, that she received her first guitar from her brother. While there she learned all about Quebecois artists and the songs they sang. Later as an adult, she became interested in her Acadian past and researched the songs, ballads, stories, legends and tales of Acadian culture.

Although she liked to sing, her main vocation was teaching. She taught at a community school in Trudel, and later a secondary school in Bathurst, New Brunswick.

In 1964 she made her television debut on CBC's Singalong Jubilee. She was one of the first to perform in both English and French, when she sang Gordon Lightfoot's Song For A Winter Night.

After two years of teaching, she went to Laval University to study for her Master of Arts degree, where she realized that singing was going to be her career. In 1969 she recorded her first album, *Chansons d'Acadie.*

Her many accomplishments include a leading role in the National Film Board production of Les Acadiens de la dispersion (1964), a featured performer at the Canadian Pavilion at Expo '67 in Osaka, Japan and being made an Officer of the Order of Canada in 1975. She guest starred in the CBC series The Jubilee Years in the fall of 1992.

Singles:

Nos hommes ont mis la voile	Col C4 7221	1973
On parlera de nous someday	Col C5 4000	1973
Avant d'etre depaysee	Col C5 4045	1974
Mais je m'en vais demain	Col C5 4076	1974
Je vous aime, ma vie recommence	SPPS 9907	1976
Le fleve de lethe	SPPS 9909	1976
Anne, ma soeur Anne	SPPS 9916	1978
Y'a un temps pour dire	SPPS 9917	1978
Astheure qu'on est la	SPPS 9917	1979
Laissez moi derouler le soleil	SPPS 9923	1981
Escarmouche a Restigouche	SPPS 9924	1981
Un million de fois je t'aime	Kappa 1112	1985
Super Summertime I Love You	Kappa 1113	1985
Pas un jour, pas une heure	Party 1008	1986
On n'a pas tous les jours 20 ans	Party 1009	1986
Branchee sur le coeur	Star 3019	1987

Albums/CDs:

Chansons D'acadie	Radio Canada 390	1969
Avant D'etre Depaysee	Columbia FS 90156	1973
L'acadie S'marie	Columbia FS 90274	1975
Edith Butler	SPPS 19909	1977
L'espoir	SPPS 19904	1978
Asteur Qu'on Est La	SPPS 19905	1979
A Paquetville	SPPS 19911	1981
J'm'appelle Edith	SPPS 19916	1981
De Paquetville A Paris	Kappa Kpl 1111	1984
Un Million De Fois Je T'aime	Kappa Kpl 1112	1985
Le Party D'edith	Vamp VP 7007	1985
12 Grands Succes D'	Party 7008	1985
Et Le Party Continue	Party 7009	1986
Party Pour Danser	Star STR 8003	1987
Edith Butler	Kappa Ka 1990	1990
A L'annee Longue	Kappa KACD 2526	1995

Marty Butler

Born on July 10, 1943 in Montreal, Quebec, Butler first played in the Raymart Trio with Jacki and Ann Ralph, who left to join The Five Bells in 1964. A year later, Marty joined The Sceptres.

When they broke up in 1969, he decided to concentrate on a solo career and began writing songs with Bob Bilyk. Les Sceptres (no relation to The Scepters) was the first to record one of their songs. Their big break came in 1970 when their song, Fly Little White Dove Fly, was recorded by The Bells. They also wrote We Gotta Make It for Trini Lopez, Crowded By Emptiness for Ginette Reno, and, I Want To Be A Country Boy Again for Tommy Hunter.

Marty recorded such songs as, To A Place Near The River in 1971 and Saving It Up in 1980. On February 10, 1996 he died of cancer. (see The Sceptres)

Singles:
To A Place Near The River	Columbia C4 2988	1971
We Gotta Make It Together	Columbia C4 3025	1972
Time	Columbia C4 3054	1972
With All The Love In My Heart	Columbia C4 3054	1972
Can't You Hear The Music	Columbia C4 3081	1972/73
Once Loved Woman, Once Loved Man/ Love Vibrations	Columbia C4 3105	1973
If You Wanna Go To New York City	Columbia C4 4020	1973
Fly Little White Dove, Fly	Columbia C4 4047	1974
Lie To Myself	WAM.100	1978
Never Been In Love This Way	WAMX 110	1979
Saving It Up	WAMX 111	1980
Looks Like Love This Time	RCA PB 50701	1982
Christmas Prayer	Earwhacks 1 0001	1982
Take Another Look	RCA PB 50176	1984

Albums/CDs:
We Gotta Make It Together	Columbia ES 90092	1972
Love Vibrations	Columbia ES 90158	1973
Marty Butler	RCA NKL1 0478	1982

Meryn Cadell

This Toronto-based actress/singer songwriter played in the city's nightclubs for five years when she recorded her first independent cassette called *MARE-in Ka-DELL*. In 1989, she went into the recording studio to begin laying down tracks for her debut album which was released by Capitol Records in 1991. It was called *Angel Food For Thought*. The first single from the album was The Sweater, which did not become a national hit until the spring of 1992. That same year she had two other hits, Inventory and Barbie, neither of which equalled the success of her first.

Early in 1993 she recorded a single and video of the song Courage with The Infidels. That same year, Warner/Sire released her second solo album, *Bombazine*. The first single was Window of Opportunity. In 1997 her third, 6 Blocks was released. She underwent a gender transition in 2003 and became a man in 2004.

Singles:

The Sweater	Intrepid N21Y 0005	1991/92
Inventory	Intrepid N21Y 0005	1992
Barbie	Intrepid N21Y 0005	1992
Johnny and Betty	Sire/REP 45398	1993
Courage (with The Infidels)		1993
Window Of Opportunity	Sire/REP 45398	1993
Joe Roth	Handsome Boy0017	1997

Albums/CDs:

Angel Food For Thought	Intrepid N21Y 0005	1991
Bombazine	Sire/REP 45398	1993
6 Blocks	Handsome Boy0017	1997

John Allan Cameron

Born in Inverness, Cape Breton, Nova Scotia on December 16, 1938, John Allan Cameron grew up in a musical family. His mother and brother played fiddle, some of his cousins stepdanced or played piano, and his Uncle Dan Rory MacDonald composed more than 2,500 fiddle tunes. When he was a teenager, John started playing jigs and reels on guitar, an F hole type Kamico.

In 1957 he relocated from his native Inverness to Ottawa where he became a member of the The Order of the Oblate Fathers. Six months before becoming a priest, he left the order and priesthood. He ended up at St. Francis Xavier University in Antigonish, Nova Scotia, and began playing at coffeehouses and various college gatherings with a group called The Cavaliers. From 1965 to 1968 he performed regularly on Don Messer's Jubilee and Singalong Jubilee on CBC TV.

A contract with Apex Records in the late 1960s produced a couple of albums, *Here Comes John Allan Cameron* and *The Minstrel of Cranberry Lane*. In the early 1970s he signed with Balmur Ltd. and released two acclaimed albums, Get There By

Dawn And Lord Of The Dance. At one time he was frequently accompanied by four musicians who called themselves The Cape Breton Symphony: fiddlers John Donald Cameron, Winston "Scotty" Fitzgerald, and Wilfred Gillis, and piano/accordionist, Bobby Brown. With Cameron they recorded one album together in 1978 on the artist's own label, Glencoe.

In the mid 1970s he also headlined a weekly CTV variety series, and in 1988 he underwent a serious throat operation, and could not perform for two and a half years. In 1996 his CD, *Glencoe Station* was released.

He died November 22, 2006.

Singles:

Minstrel of Cranberry Lane	Apex 77105	1969
Streets of London	Col C4 3028	1972
Sit Down, Mr. Music Man	CYNDA 006	1972
Write Me A Picture	CYNDA 018	1973
I Can't Tell You	Columbia 4 4014	1973
Tie Me Down	Col C4 4135	1976
Please Don't Bury Me	Col C4 4162	1977
Overnight Success	Glencoe 150	1982
There Is A Comfort	Freedom FR 45 052	1987
Golden Ribbon	DWD 50549	1996
Getting Dark Again	DWD 50549	1996

Albums/CDs:

Here Comes John Allan Cameron	Coral CB 35000	1968
The Minstrel Of Cranberry Lane	Coral CB 35003	1969
The Minstrel Of Cranberry Lane	Apex AL7 1650	1969
Sit Down, Mr. Music Man	Cynda CNS 1005	1972
Get There By Dawn	Columbia ES 90089	1972
Lord Of The Dance	Columbia ES 90102	1973
Wedding, Wakes & Other Things	Columbia ES 90343	1976
Freeborn Man	Glencoe GM1 1002	1979
Song For The Mira	Glencoe GM1 1003	1981
Best Of John Allan Cameron	Great Atlantic Music CO	1982
Good Times	Freedom FR 019	1987
Wind Willow	Margaree Sound 9128	1991
Classic John Allan Cameron I & II	Margaree Sound 9231	1992
Glencoe Station	DWD 50549	1996

Canada Goose

Barbra Bullard (vocals)
Gary Comeau (lead guitar, steel guitar)
Paul Huot (guitar, vocals)
Wayne Leslie (bass, vocals)
John Matthews (vocals)
Richard Patterson (drums)

Early in 1970 three ex-members of The Esquires (Paul Huot, Gary Comeau and Richard Patterson) joined by Wayne Leslie, John Matthews and Barbra Bullard played as the house band at the Tabu Room of the Beacon Arms Hotel. They called themselves The New Esquires.

When they were approached about a recording a single, they decided to change their name because it was too dated. Guitarist Amos Garrett had told Patterson that The Maple Leafs or Canada Goose would be a good name. After clearing the use of the latter name with Garrett, the six-man band became known as Canada Goose with their first and only hit, Higher and Higher (1970) on Tonsil Records, a new record label in New York. In Canada it was distributed by Quality Records. It was originally recorded by Jackie Wilson in 1967.

Radio airplay of the song established the group among the teen set, and they graduated from the Tabu Room to bigger venues. As the demand for appearances grew, the individual members felt they could not give up their day jobs. They disbanded at the height of their success.

Other members of the group included Lock McFadden on guitar and vocals, Daryl ("D") Wadsworth on piano and vocals, Valerie ("Val") Tuck on vocals, Derek O'Neil on guitar and vocals, and Rick Lemieux on bass guitar and vocals.

Wadsworth decided to form another group under the name Canada Goose but they failed to impress fans of the old group and later disbanded.

Of the original six, Comeau went on to join James Leroy and Denim, Leslie toured with Neville Wells and Wells Fargo and American folksinger Tom Rush, Patterson became a member of several bands, including the David Wiffen Group, Sneezy Waters, Wells Fargo, Ian & Sylvia's The Great Speckled Bird and The Radio Kings.

Single:
Higher And Higher   Toncil 0002   1970

Cano

Marcel Aymar (guitar, vocals)
David Burt (guitar, harmonica)
Michel Dasti (drums, percussion)
John W. Doerr (bass, trombone, synthesizer, electric piano)
Michel Kendel (piano, bass)
Wasyl Kohut (violin, mandolin)
Andre Paiement (guitar, flute, vocals)
Rachel Paiement (vocals)

In 1971 a group of 65 individuals gathered together in Sudbury, Ontario to form a society where the artistic freedoms of both English and French Ontarians could express themselves musically under one national identity. By December, 1975 CANO had been established with a long term contract signed with A&M Records. The group's name is an abbreviation of Cooperative des Artistes de Nouvel Ontario.

Although the members of the group did not enjoy commercial success on the record charts, their vision of a united Canada in song remains an important contribution to Canadian music.

Andre Paiement committed suicide on January 21, 1978. He was 27.

From 1978 to 1980 Cano toured Canada, and, a year later, Rachel Paiement left the group to go solo. Cano changed their name in 1981 to Masque.

In November, 1981 Wasyl Kohut died. For the group's last album, *Visible* (1985), they returned to their old name.

Singles:

Le vieux Mederic	A&M 248	1976
Pluie estivale	A&M 441	1977
Frere Jacques	A&M 454	1977
Ryshnychok	A&M 470	1978
L'Autobus de la pluie	A&M 483	1979
Carrie	A&M 487	1979
Rebound	A&M 483	1979/80
Rendezvous	A&M 499	1980
Feel Your Fire	A&M 510	1980
Met tes gants	READY 541	1985

Albums/CDs:

Tous Dans L'meme Bateau	A&M Sp 9024	1976
Au Nord De Notre Vie	A&M Sp 9028	1977
Eclipse	A&M Sp 9033	1978
Rendezvous	A&M Sp 9037	1979

Spirit Of The North	A&M SP 9040	1980
Camouflage	A&M Sp 9060	1981
Visible	Ready LR 054	1985

The Carlton Showband

Gregory Donaghey (vocals, guitar)
Mike Feeney (vocals)
Seamus Grew (accordion, keyboards)
Bob Lewis (keyboards, bass, rhythm guitar, vocals)
Christy McLaughlin (harmonica, accordion, vocals)
Sean McManus (rhythm guitar, banjo, tin whistle, vocals)
Chris O'Toole (drums)
Johnny Patterson (trombone, bass, rhythm guitar)
Fred White (bass, rhythm guitar, banjo, mandolin, vocals)
Roddie Lee (drums, vocals)
R. Benoit (lead guitar, rhythm guitar, fiddle, mandolin)
Larris Benoit (bass, rhythm & lead guitars, vocals)
Aaron Lewis (keyboards, vocals)
Edwin Mitch McCoy (rhythm guitar, vocals)

The Carlton Showband started in 1963 as a trio comprised of Chris O'Toole, Seamus Grew, and Christy McLaughlin, three ex-patriate Irishmen who met in Toronto. That same year, Sean McManus joined to make the group a quartet. In 1964, Fred White, a rock 'n' roller from Cape Breton, Nova Scotia was invited to join as a replacement for McManus. But Sean stayed, and the Carlton Showband were now a quintet.

Originally, the group was called the Carltons Danceband. It was changed to the Carlton Showband when they were driving downtown Toronto and came to the corner of Carlton and Yonge Streets.

In 1965, they played every Saturday night at the Parkside Tavern on Yonge Street. While there they met Mike Feeney, who would later join the group and be instrumental in getting them into RCA studios in Toronto to record. On the 50th anniversary of the Easter Rebellion in April 1966, they made their first record: *The Merry Ploughboy*, aka *Off to Dublin in the Green*.

In 1967 they became the house band on the Pig 'n Whistle Show, and signed a recording contract with RCA Victor. That same year, they also added two new members, Edwin "Mitch" McCoy and Johnny Patterson. McCoy later left, and was replaced by Bob Lewis.

On May 15, 1968 the Carlton Showband toured Canada for the first time.

During this tour, on August 23 and 24, they played to the largest crowds in the band's history at the Central Canada Exhibition in Ottawa.

Throughout the 1970s, the group recorded several albums for RCA, toured the United States, and went through two personnel changes: Johnny Patterson left in 1975, and was replaced by Gregory Donaghey in July 1976; and Bob Lewis was replaced by Marty Wash in 1979.

During the next two decades, they continued to record and perform.

Chris O'Toole left and was replaced by Roddie Lee, who had been in The Caribou Showband, and Christy McLaughlin also left due to ill health.

The group continued as seven members until Marty Wash left in 1987, and was replaced by Robert Benoit. Two years later, Sean McManus died. Larris Benoit, Robert's brother, replaced him. In June 1991 Seamus Grew left, and was replaced by Aaron Lewis, and Mike Feeney left in 1992.

The Carlton Showband broke up in December 1996.

Singles:

The Merry Ploughboy	CASL 2106	1966
Up Went Nelson	CASL 2107	1966
Black Velvet Band		1967
March of the Maple Leaf	RCA 57 3455	1968
Westmeath Bachelor	RCA 75 1000	1968
Roll it Around in Your Mind		1972
The Leprechaun		1973
Biddy McGaw		1974
There's Nothing Like a Newfoundlander		1975
Any Dream Will Do	RCA PB 50044	1975
Harpers Ferry		1976
One Up on the World		1976
Sadie The Cleaning Lady		1976
More Than Yesterday		1977
Christmas in Killarney	RCA PB 50403	1977
Half an Hour Later in Newfoundland		1978
Hard Times		1979
He Believes in Me		1979/80
What's a Nice Guy		1982
Mother		1985

Albums/CDs:

The Carlton Showband	CASL BM 664	1966
We're Off to Dublin	MALA LP 4004	1966
The Carlton Showband	RCA PCS 1173	1967
A Night at the Pubb	RCA PCS 1177	1967
On Tour	RCA PCS 1203	1968
At the Pig Whistle	Arc ACS 5022	1969
Time Gentlemen Please	RCA LSP 4339	1970

Carlton Showband Special	RCA CASX 2597	1971
Carlton Country	RCA CASX 2620	1972
Best Of	RCA CASX 2483	1973
If You're Irish	RCA KCL1 5003	1973
Sing Irishmen Sing	RCA CASX 2539	1973
Best Of Vol Ii	RCA KCL1 7002	1974
Any Dream Will Do	RCA KPL1 0083	1975
First Choice	Tee Vee TA 1028	1975
One Up on the World	RCA KXL1 0142	1976
Best of Vol Iii	RCA Knl1 0218	1977
Here We Go Again	RCA KXL1 0259	1977
20 Gospel Favorites	RCA KSL2 7064	1977
Sixteen Most Requested	RCA KSL1 7067	1978
Hard Times	RCA KXL1 0333	1979
Back to The Sod	RCA Kxl1 0333	1980
Three Steps to Heaven	CSB WRC1 2634	1982
Reflections	CSB WRC1 4047	1985
We Wish You a Merry Christmas	CSB WRC1 4774	1986
25th Anniversary	CSBCD 02588	1988
Catch the Spirit	CSBCD 00190	1990
20 All Time Favorites	ROCD 001	1992
20 All Time Gospel Favorites	ROCD 002	1994
Family Christmas	ROCD 008	1995

Andrew Cash

Andrew Cash was born in Toronto, Ontario on January 22, 1962. His music is rooted in folk and acoustic rock and roll, while his songs reveal a realistic view of society.

His career began in 1980 when he formed the group L'Etranger with his friend Chuck Angus. They developed a local following on Queen Street in Toronto. Their first big break was coming in second in a band contest judged by Bob Segarini and Greg Godovitz. When L'Etranger broke up in 1986, Cash decided to pursue a solo career. He began playing once a week for nine months as a single acoustic act at The Spadina Hotel in downtown Toronto. In 1988 Cash became a solo artist and released his first album, *Time and Place* on Island Records. Another album, *Boomtown* followed in 1989.

Signed to MCA Records in 1993, his debut album for the label was called *Hi*. From it came the Singles:, A Lot Of Talk and Hey Maria.

He joined his brother Peter (The Skydiggers) in 1998 to form the Cash Brothers, who released the albums *Raceway* (2000), and *How Was Tomorrow* (ZOE 011431 2001).

Singles:

Trail of Tears	FringeFPE 3033	1986
Time And Place	Island97074	1988
Smile Me Down	Island97078	1988
What Am I Gonna Do With These Hands	Island97103	1989
100 Years	Island97113	1989
Boomtown	Island97098	1989
A Lot of Talk	MCA SD10930	1993
Hey Maria	MCA SD10930	1994

Albums/CDs:

Sticks And Stones (EP) (w/L'Etranger)	FringeFPE 3033	1986
Time and Place	IslandISL 1185	1988
Boomtown	IslandISL 1237	1989
Hi	MCA SD10930	1993

Cat

Jim Campbell (lead vocals)
Graham Fidler (bass, vocals)
Mike Mc Queen (guitar, vocals)
Phil Mulholland (drums)
Gary O'Connor (lead guitar, vocals)

This Toronto group began as The Spasstiks in 1964. They had two singles on the Apex label: Love's Got A Hold On Me/If That's What She Wants (1967) and I'm So Happy Now/Who's The Girl (1968). In 1968 they changed their name to Cat and recorded Doing The Best We Can, also on the Apex label. They also had hits on RCA (We're All In This Together) and Capitol (Riding Train). Cat split up in 1972. Gary O'Connor had a brief solo career as Gary O in the early 1980s, Jim Campbell became a record executive with Wea in 1974 and later with BMG Music Canada, and the rest of the group were members of Fast Eddie.

By The Spasstiks
Singles:

Love's Got A Hold On Me	Apex 77057	1967
I'm So Happy Now	Apex	1968

By Cat
Singles:

Doing The Best We Can	Apex 77080	1968
Light of Love	RCA 74 0279	1969

Solo Flight	RCA 74 0331	1970
We're All In This Together	RCA 74 0331	1970
Honey In The Sky	NNS 9013	1971
Save The Last Dance For Me	Cap 72788	1975/76

Album:

Cat	RCA LSP 4267	1970

Chalk Circle

Brad Hopkins (bass)
Derrick Murphy (drums)
Chris Tait (vocals, guitar)
Tad Winklarz (keyboards)

Chalk Circle, from Newcastle, Ontario, started out as a trio in 1983 with Chris Tait, Brad Hopkins, and Derrick Murphy. The group's name comes from the play, The Caucasion Chalk Circle by Bertolt Brecht. In the fall of 1984 Tad Winklarz, who had come to Canada from his native Poland, joined the group. In 1986 they signed a contract with Duke Street Records, and the group's first EP, The Great Lake was released, which included the hit Singles:, April Fool, and Me, Myself and I. Chalk Circle broke up in 1990. Brad Hopkins and Derrick Murphy went on to become members of the short lived Neurotic Ensemble, while Chris Tait formed Big Faith. The latter released the CD/EP, *Grounded*, in 1992, and the independent CD, *Undertow*, in 1994.

Singles:

April Fool	Duke DSR 71024	1986
Me, Myself and I	Duke DSR 81024	1986
This Mourning	Duke DSR 71035	1987
20th Century Boy	Duke DSR 81035	1987
Sons and Daughters	Duke DSR 71049	1989
Out of Control	PROCD 9002 J	1990

Albums/CDs:

The Great Lake	Duke DSR 41024	1986
Mending Wall	Duke DSR 31035	1987
As The Crow Flies	Duke DSR 31049	1990

The Chantones

Larry Desjarlais (tenor)
Jack Grenier (lead vocals)
Roy Lesperance (bass)
Jim Nantais (baritone)

The Chantones were a popular vocal quartet from Windsor, Ontario who played some of the top nightclub and supper clubs in Canada and the United States between 1954 and the late 1960s when they broke up.

Originally known as The Teen Tones, all four first sang together in the summer of 1953 when the Catholic Youth Organization (CYO) sponsored a Southwestern Ontario talent contest. The song they chose to sing was Have You Talked To The Man Upstairs by The Four Lads. When they won the contest it was their first big break. Their second was a chance meeting with Wally Spitzig, organist at Sacred Heart Church in Windsor, who knew The Four Lads. He arranged to have them sing his arrangement of You'll Never Walk Alone at the Michigan State Fair.

Their next big break came from the owner and manager of the Metropole supper club in Windsor when he asked them to fill in for an act that had cancelled. They were noticed by Lindsay Meehan, the 19 year old leader of the house band. He encouraged them to become a professional act. From their appearance at the Metropole they were able to play in other clubs in the Windsor area, such as the Elmwood Casino.

In 1958 singer Jack Scott, a native of Windsor, needed a backup group for the hit My True Love, and he chose The Chantones. Nothing happened to the song until Joe Carlton, owner of Carlton Records, bought the song and and promoted it. It became a Top 5 hit in the summer of 1958. After the success of My True Love, the group made their own record. The A side was Five Little Numbers, the B side If I Loved You. Although it was not a major hit, it was a big seller. They had two other hits, Tangerock/Don't Open That Door in 1960 on Top Rank Records, and Stormy Weather/Sweet Georgia Brown on Capitol Records in 1961.

During the summer of 1962 Roy Lesperance left the group to get married and raise a family. His last show was at the Michigan State Fair with Roy Orbison and The Platters. Lesperance was born with congenital cataracts and has never had more than five per cent of normal sight. Today, he is totally blind and currently works with the CNIB. Jack Grenier runs his own theatrical production company in Stirling Heights, Michigan, and Larry Desjarlais and Jim Nantais live in Detroit.

Singles:
Anne Marie	Sparton 491	1957
Five Little Numbers	Carlton 485	1959
Tangerock	Top Rank 2066	1960
Stormy Weather	Capitol 4661	1961

Robert Charlebois

A pioneer in the art of combining French Canada's joual (slang) language with rock 'n' roll, Robert Charlebois was a respected singer, songwriter, guitarist and actor. Born in Montreal, Quebec on June 25, 1945, he studied piano for six years, and in his teens he took acting lessons at the National Theater School in Montreal for three years (1962-65).

In 1965 he recorded his first album, *Ma Boule.* Three years later he wrote a song called Lindberg which earned him the grand prize at the Fifth International Festival of French Song at Spa, Belgium, and in 1969, the Prix Leclerc at Festival du disque.

Charlebois often sang in concert and on record with Louise Forestier and Mouffe (real name Claudine Monfette).

By the late 1960s he projected the image of a "Superfrog." He wore a Montreal Canadiens hockey sweater and sang in joual with a jazz/rock group. His act became a novelty in French pop music and established his career as a performer. His first hit was Lindberg which was written by poet Claude Peloquin who had never written for music before.

Throughout his career Charlebois has turned to poets and novelists for inspiration. He has also shared the stage with The Band, Janis Joplin, The Grateful Dead, and Tom Rush.

He made his first appearance outside Quebec at the Toronto Pop Festival in Toronto in 1969. A year later, he joined other Canadian rock stars as a member of the Festival Express which travelled across Canada by train.

Charlebois's second major hit was Ordinaire in 1970. He also started writing scores for Quebec's burgeoning film industry. They included Jusqu'an coeur (1969), A Soir, on fait peur au monde (1969), Deux femmes en or (1970) and Bulldozer (1971). In the early 1970s he added Cajun music to his act after he heard one of his uncles play a record called French chansons de la Lousianne. His other French singles include Entre Deux Joints, Que Can Blues and Cauchemar. The first single he recorded in English was The Greatest Idea/Halloween in 1972.

In 1974, Robert took a two-year sabbatical from his music to act in the films,

Sombre Vacances (1975) and in Italian director Sergio Leone's *Un genie, deux associes, un cloche* (1976).

He returned to the concert stage in 1976 and entertained audiences with his special brand of music. As a singer songwriter he was arguably the first to use an electric guitar in the chansonnier tradition, a style of music derived from poetic expression.

Charlebois was absent from the Quebec music scene from 1984-89. Some of the songs he became known for during this period were Moi Tarzan, Toi Jane, Les Talons Hauts, C'est Pas Physique, C'est Electrique, Graziella, and J't'Aime Comme Un Fou.

In 1992 he released *Immensement*, an album that earned him France's Victoire, the equivalent of the Grammy Award. He also recorded his first rock opera, *Cartier* which was performed throughout the francophone world as a radio broadcast.

His current style is called musique du monde (world beat) in France. It is an amalgam of rock, ballad, Latin rhythm, rap and mock metal.

Singles:

Title	Label	Year
Divertimento	Carnaval CT 33873/4	1965
Demain L'hiver	GammaAA 1020	1968
Dolores	GammaAA 1030	1968
Lindberg	GammaAA 1026	1968
La fin du monde	GammaAA 1034	1968
Coeur en Chomage	GammaAA 1036	1969
Tout Ecartille	GammaAA 1044	1969
Demain L'hiver	GammaAA 1058	1969
Te V'la	GammaAA 1063	1970
Deux femmes en or	GammaAA 1076	1970
Mon Pays/Ordinaire	GammaAA 1081	1970
Sensation 1	GammaAA 5003	1970
Le violent seul	GammaAA 1108	1971
La valse Reno	GammaAA 1139	1971
Yasa Pichou	GammaAA 1130	1971
The Greatest Idea	Barclay 30014	1972
Conception	Barclay 60207	1972
Cauchemar	Barclay 60257	1973
Entre Deux Joints	Barclay 60273	1973
Je reve a Rio	Barclay 60300	1975
Que Can Blues	Barclay 60318	1975
The Frog Song	Solution 9002	1976
Je reviendrai a Montreal	Solution 9008	1976
Sombres vacances	Solution 9009	1977
Coup d'soleil	Solution 9024	1977
Je l'savais	Solution 9034	1977
Saint Jerome	Solution 9043	1979
J't'hais	Solution 9053	1979

Moi Tarzon, Toi Jane	Solution9101	1981
Heureux en amour	Solution9120	1982
Faut qu'ca change	Solution9141	1982
Super Baby	Solution8353	1982
Les Talons hauts	Solution9157	1982
Je t'aime comme un fou	Solution8301	1983
Consomme, consomme	Solution8302	1983
Je Suis monte	Girafe4008	1984
C'est pas physique, c'est electrique	Solution8303	1985
Juke Box	Solution8304	1985
Zoodiac	Solution8305	1985
Champion	Solution8306	1987
Tarari	Solution8307	1987
Yuppie	Solution8308	1987
J'veux p'us qu'tu m'aimes	Solution8309	1988
Silence on danse	Solution8310	1989
Graziella	Solution8311	1989
J'savais pas	Solution8312	1989
Madonna Tremblay	Solution8313	1989
Cette chanson la	Solution8314	1990

Albums/CDs:

Robert Charlebois Vol I	SelectSP 12131	1965
Robert Charlebois Vol II	SelectSP 12147	1966
Terres Des Bums	Phonadisc PHL 5006	1967
Robert Charlebois	GammaGS 115	1967
Robert Charlebois/Louise Forestier	GammaGS 120	1968
Quebec Love	GammaGS 136	1969
Un Gars Ben Ordinaire	GammaGS 144	1971
Robert Charlebois	GammaGS 146	1971
Les Grand Succes De..	GammaG2 1003	1972
Charlebois	Barclay 80123	1972
Solidaritude	Barclay 80173	1973
Charlebois	Barclay 80200	1974
Longue Distance	SolutionSN 905	1976
Live a Paris	SolutionSN 925/926	1976
Swing Charlebois Swing	SolutionSN 939	1977
Solide	SolutionSN 964	1979
Heureux En Amour	SolutionSN 531	1981
Robert Charlebois	SolutionSN 801	1983
Ma Premiere Chanson	Girafe1006	1984
Super Position	SolutionSN 802	1985
Charlebois Vol Un	SolutionSN 803	1987
Charlebois Volume 1	SNC 975 1	1991
Charlebois Volume 2	SNC 975 2	1991
Charlebois Volume 3	SNC 975 3	1991
Le Meilleur De Robert Charlebois	WM 120 661014	1991
Immensement	Solution805CD	1992
La Maudite Tournee		1995

The Checkerlads

Robert Buchholtz (organ, background vocals)
Harvey Frasz (drums)
Robert Frei (lead and rhythm guitar, background vocals)
Larry Reich (lead and rhythm guitar, harmonica, background vocals)
Arnold Ripplinger (lead vocals, bass, rhythm guitar)

This group from Regina was popular from mid to late 1960s. They were managed by Joe Vargo and produced by Don Grashey and Chuck Williams. Their first national hit on RPM's Top Singles Chart was Baby Send For Me in the fall of 1966. In 1969 their song, *So Much in Love* was included on a compilation album released by Birchmount/Quality.

Singles:
Baby Send For Me	Gaiety116	1966
The Dreamer	Gaiety123	1966
Behind Ev'ry Man	RCA 57 3443	1967

The Checkers

Jerry Arnold (guitar)
Gary Fabbi (drums)
Dennis Goshinmon (guitar)
Wes Kucheran (guitar)

The Checkers started in Lethbridge, Alberta in 1957. At first they were a trio comprised of Dennis Goshinmon, Wes Kucheran, and Gary Fabbi.

Jerry Arnold, who had been in the city's first rock band, The Rockers, joined in 1958. Managed by Ed Ryan, a local disc jockey, the group played throughout Southern Alberta, Minot, South Dakota, and Cranbrook, British Columbia.

On stage they wore black pants, red shirts, and white sport coats. In their hometown they played regularly at the Henderson Lake Pavilion on Saturday nights, and also toured with Buddy Knox and Roy Orbison.

In 1959, Ryan was instrumental in getting the group signed to Barry Records. Their first single was Chinook/Stormin' later that same year.

A second single, Twilight Twist/Twistin' Inn followed in 1960.

During this time, Robbie Jeacock replaced Fabbi and the group toured

Alberta, Saskatchewan, Manitoba, and the Lakehead. Jeacock then quit the group and returned to Lethbridge. His replacement was Rick

Belanger, who changed his name to Rick Bell, was later in the Five Man Electrical Band.

The Checkers broke up in 1963 when Arnold left. He continued to play in various rock groups until 1978. Today, he runs his own art gallery in Lethbridge.

Singles:
Chinook/Stormin'	Barry 3054X	1959
Twilight Twist/Twistin' Inn	Barry 3107X	1960

The Chessmen

Bill Lockie   (guitar)
Terry Jacks   (vocals, rhythm guitar)
Bruce Peterson (electric accordion)
Guy Sobell   (lead guitar)
Al Wiertz   (drums)

This Vancouver group had a sound similar to other instrumental groups like The Ventures and Cliff Richards' The Shadows. Formed in 1963, The Chessmen had many different musicians come and go but Guy Sobell and Terry Jacks were the two mainstays of the group until they broke up in 1966. In addition to the Bill Lockie, Bruce Peterson, and Al Wiertz, other members of the group included Miles Kingan and Larry Borisoff.

Originally, Jacks played rhythm guitar but he was so terrible that he was almost forced out of the group. He ended up staying when he started writing songs and became their lead singer.

The Chessmen's first recording was the double-sided instrumental Mustang/Meadowlands in 1963. Their second, The Way You Fell featured Jacks on vocals.

After their breakup, Sobell went on to become producer/manager and husband for Denise McCann, while Jacks became famous as a member of The Poppy Family and as a solo artist. One of his songs, There's No Blood In Bone, originally recorded after The Chessmen disbanded, turned up on the first Poppy Family album.

Singles:

Meadowlands/Mustang	London 17334	1963
The Way You Feel/She Comes By Night	London 17340	1964
Love Didn't Die/You Lost Your Love	Mercury 72498	1965
What's Causing This Sensation/ Running Wild	Mercury 72559	1965

Chester

Mike Argue (lead guitar, vocals)
Jim Mancell (lead vocals)
Wedge Monroe (drums, piano, guitar)
Glen Morrow (keyboards, guitar, vocals)

This Toronto-based group was together seven months when Make My Life A Little Better began to climb the Canadian charts in the summer of 1973. Billed as a "Happiness Group" they recorded their only major hit, Make My Life A Little Bit Brighter at Eastern Sound in Toronto.

In 1974 Mike Argue left to concentrate on a solo career. Two years later, in 1976, the group broke up.

Glen Morrow, who formed the original group, later recruited Fran Cheslo as lead singer of the reformed Chester, who recorded You Give Me Strength in 1977.

Singles:

Make My Life a Little Better	Celebration 2078	1973
Start a Dream	Celebration 2092	1974
Let the Telephone Ring		1975
You Give Me Strength	Quality 2209	1977

Rita Chiarelli

This Hamilton born singer/songwriter began her music career in high school. After graduation she and her backup band Battleaxe toured North America. When they played the Nickelodeon in London, Ont., its owner, Ronnie Hawkins was impressed by their sound. A year later, Rita left Battleaxe to be a vocalist with Hawkins.

In 1982 Rita was unhappy with the progress of her musical career and moved to Italy for five years. Upon her return to Canada in 1987, she wrote Have You

Seen My Shoes? which became her first single release. It also attracted attention of movie producer Brian McDonald who used the song for the soundtrack of his movie, Roadkill.

Rita went on to win the Q107 Homegrown contest for the song, Love Overload and received first prize in the Molson Canadian Rocks Showdown in 1991.

Her other achievements include Most Deserving Artist of a Recording Contract (1987), Toronto's Rising Star (1988) and a nomination for Female Vocalist in 1991 at the Toronto Music Awards.

Chiarelli's debut album, *Road Rockets* which is also the name of her backup band, came out in 1992 on Edmonton's Stony Plain label, distributed by Warner Music. In 1994 came her second album, *Just Getting Started*, and in 1997 her third, *What A Night Live!*, which was recorded in Germany in 1996. She then switched to the Northern Blues label out of Toronto. Her debut release was *Breakfast at Midnight* (2001).

Singles:
Have You Seen My Shoes?	R&R Records 00101	1987
Give Me A Reason To Change	Roto Noto 1037	1987
Love Overload	Stony PlainSPCD 1173	1992
Satisfied	Stony PlainSPCD 1197	1994
Heartbreak of the Week	Stony PlainSPCD 1197	1994
Just Getting Started	Stony PlainSPCD 1197	1995

Albums/CDs:
Road Rockets	Stony Plainspcd 1173	1992
Just Getting Started	Stony Plainspcd 1197	1994
What A Night Live!	Stony Plainspcd 1236	1997
Breakfast At Midnight	Northern Blues Nbm 0003	2001
No One To Blame	Mad Iris 026211	2007
Italian Sessions	Mad Iris 13232	2008
Sweet Paradise	Mad Iris 198337	2010
Music From The Big House	Mad Iris 593883	2011

Chilliwack

Ab Bryant (bass)
Howard Froese (guitar)
Bill Henderson (guitar, vocals)
Claire Lawrence (keyboards, sax)
Brian MacLeod (guitar, keyboards, drums, sax)
Glenn Miller (bass guitar)
Ross Turney (drums)
Howie Vickers (vocals)

This Vancouver band was first known as The Classics when they started playing together in 1961. They were comprised of Glenn Miller (bass), Claire Lawrence (sax), Gary Taylor (drums), Howie Vickers (lead vocals), Brian Russell (guitar), and Tom Baird (keyboards) who wrote their first hit single, Aces High (1964). The Classics developed a local following and were the house band on Let's Go, a weekly show on CFUN TV.

In 1967 they changed their name to The Collectors, and had a string of hit records between 1967 and 1970, notably Fisherwoman and Lydia Purple. By 1971 they had changed their name to Chilliwack. The latter group was comprised of Howie Vickers on vocals, Bill Henderson on guitar and vocals, Claire Lawrence on saxophone and vocals, Glenn Miller on bass and Ross Turney on drums.

The nucleus of the group was Henderson, Lawrence, and Turney. When Vickers and Miller left the group, the three original members found it difficult to replace them and they became a trio.

Howard Froese joined in 1973, while Brian MacLeod in 1977. The latter was responsible for writing some of their big hits, such as My Girl (Gone, Gone, Gone) in 1981.

Henderson reunited with Lawrence in 1984 and together they brought Chilliwack back for a reunion concert. Two years later, in 1986, Henderson and Lawrence with drummer Jerry Adolph, bassist Brian Newcombe, guitarist John Roles and keyboardist Robbie Gray played as Chilliwack at the Ontario Place Forum.

MacLeod died on April 25, 1992 in Vancouver after a year long fight with cancer. He had produced such acts as the Good Brothers, Billy Newton Davis, Chrissy Steele, and The Headpins, and wrote songs for Loverboy and Chicago among others. Froese, who left Chilliwack in 1978, died in 1993.

Bill Henderson went on to become one third of the trio UHF (Ulrich, Henderson & Forbes).

By The Classics/Canadian Classics*
Singles:
Aces High	Jaguar 2001	1964
Til I Met You*	Jaguar 2002	1964
I Don't Know*	Jaguar 2003	1965
Why Don't You Love Me	GNP Crescendo 342	1966

By The Collectors
Singles:
Looking At A Baby	New Syndrome16	1967
Fisherwoman	New Syndrome19	1967
We Can Make It	Warner Bros WB 7159	1968

Lydia Purple	Warner Bros WB 7211	1968
Early Morning	Warner Bros WB 7297	1969
I Must Have Been Blind	London17379	1970
Sometimes We're Up	London17383	1970

Albums/CDs:

The Collectors	Warner Bros WB 1746	1967
Grass and Wild Strawberries	Warner Bros WB 1774	1968

By Chilliwack
Singles:

Chain Train	Parrot 350	1970
Rain O	Parrot 2535	1970
Sundown	Parrot 2536	1971
Lonesome Mary	A&M 321	1971
Groundhog	A&M 1395	1973
There's Something I Like About That	Goldfish GF 105	1974
Crazy Talk	Goldfish GS 110	1974
Come On Over	Goldfish GS 114	1975
Last Day In December	Casino C7 107	1975
California Girl	Mushroom M 7022	1976
Something Better	Mushroom M 7025	1977
Baby Blue	Mushroom M 7024	1977
Fly At Night	Mushroom M 7024	1977
Arms Of Mary	Mushroom M 7033	1978
Never Be The Same	Mushroom M 7038	1978
Road To Paradise	Mushroom M	1979
Communication Breakdown	Mushroom M 7046	1980
My Girl (Gone, Gone, Gone)	Solid Gold SGS 712	1981
(Don't Wanna)Live For A Living	Solid Gold SGS 716	1981
I Believe	Solid Gold SGS 716	1982
What You Gonna Do (When I'm Gone)	Solid Gold SGS 725	1982
Lean On Me	Solid Gold SGS 736	1982
Gettin' Better	Solid Gold SGS 757	1983
Don't Stop	Solid Gold SGS 747	1983
Don't Go	Solid Gold SGS	1983
Got You On My Mind	Solid Gold SGS 752	1984

Albums/CDs:

Chilliwack	Parrot PAS 71040	1970
Chilliwack	A&M SP 3509	1971
All Over You	A&M SP 4375	1973
Riding High	Goldfish CA 1003	1975
Rockerbox	Casino CA 1006	1976
Dreams, Dreams, Dreams	Mushroom MRS 5006	1976
Lights From The Valley	Mushroom MRS 5011	1978
Breakdown In Paradise	Mushroom MRS 5015	1979

Wanna Be A Star	Solid Gold SGR 1006	1981
Opus X	Solid Gold SGR 1014	1982
Segue	Solid Gold SGR 1020	1983
(Reissued on CD as "Greatest Hits")	Cbs VCK 80129	1988
Look In, Look Out	Solid Gold SGR 1023	1984
Lights From The Valley	Linus MRS 5011	2013
Dreams Dreams Dreams	MRS 5006	2013

Choya

Paul Clinch (guitar)
Joe Dinardo (bass)
Gary Gries (drums)
Bruce Ley (keyboards)
Debbie Schall (viola)
Rickie Yorke (congas)

This sextet from Toronto was led by Paul Clinch, who was a former member of Cycle and Magic Cycle. They achieved minor success in the spring of 1976 with Linda Write Me A Letter.

Clinch also had minor success as a solo artist with the hits, Don't Take The Sun (1972), Lovin' You Tonight (1974), and Band Bandit (1979).   He died on November 8, 1988.

Singles:

Let The Children Boogie Part 1	CUE 502	1973
We Can Make It Together	Realistic RE.102	1976
(shown as Paul Clinch with Choya)		
Linda Write Me A Letter	Realistic 68 8200	1976

Album:

Living Like A Rich Man	Realistic RL 1000	1977

Christmas

Bob Bryden (vocals)
Tyler Reizanne (bass)
Rich Richter (drums)
Lynda Squires (vocals)   Replaced by Robert Bulger

This four-member band from Oshawa, Ontario began as Reign Ghost in 1968. It was comprised of Bob Bryden, Lynda Squires, Dave Hare, Jerry Dulek, and Jim and Bob Stright. Over the next two years, they released one single and two albums.

In 1970 Lynda Squires left to join the Toronto production of Hair, and was replaced by Robert Bulger. That same year, the group's name changed to Christmas, later The Spirit of Christmas. They broke up in 1975.

Bryden later had a solo career, and in 1982 he released the independent album, *See This Brick*. He later formed the groups Benzene Jag (1981 – 85) and Age of Mirrors (1985 – 86), and was half of the duo of Bellma (Diana) and Bob, who recorded the cassette, *One Spirit*. As a solo act, he recorded the cassettes, *Songs From St. James*, and *Ditties For Kiddies*. He is also youth pastor for the Word Faith Christian Centre in Burlington, Ontario.

By Reign Ghost
Single:
Long Day Journey	Paragon 1020	1970

Albums/CDs:
Reign Ghost	Allied 12	1969
Reign Ghost	Paragon 19	1970
Reign Ghost	Laser's Edge	1991

By Christmas
Singles:
Don't Give It Away	Daffodil 1002	1970
Point Blank	Daffodil 1008	1971
I'm A Song, Sing Me	Daffodil 1010	1971

By Spirit of Christmas
Single:
Graveyard Face	Daffodil 1058	1975

Albums/CDs:
Christmas	Paragon 18	1970
Heritage	Daffodil 16002	1970
Lives To Live By	Daffodil 10047	1974
Christmas Live At Massey Hall	Indie	1989
Lies To Live By	Laser's Edge	1990
Heritage	Laser's Edge	1993

Les Classels

Michel Caron (guitar, vocals)
Jean Clement Drouin (guitar)
Serge Drouin (drums)
Gilles Gerard (vocals)
Pierre Therrien (bass)

This quintet from Montreal, Quebec dyed their hair white, wore white suits and played white instruments. They became as famous as The Beatles but the popularity of Les Classels continued into the late 1970s, long after the Fab Four broke up.

The origins of the group go back to 1960 when five school friends decided to form a rock band. They called themselves The Special Tones, and played small clubs, road houses and The Windsor Hotel in St. Jean, Quebec where they established a local following. Their material ranged from Duke Ellington and Frankie Laine to Little Richard.

In 1964 they recorded their first hit, Avant de me dire adieu. It went to the top of the charts in Quebec and the group was suddenly inundated by autograph seekers. The Montreal tabloids ran articles on each of the members and soon became known as the Quebec Beatles.

They later changed their appearance by getting rid of the white hair. Outside of French Canada, their success was limited to good reviews of their hit records, but they failed to impress record buyers.

In 1970 they recorded a French version of The Guess Who's 1969 international hit, These Eyes as Le Temps de L'Amour.

They broke up in 1971. Twenty years later they reunited to record the song, Je pense a toi for the CD compilation, Les Classels Vol 1.

Singles:

En marchand sur la plage	Jeunesse-Franco 4007	1964
Avant De Me Dire Adieu	Jeunesse-Franco 4013	1964
Ton Amour A Change Ma Vie	Trans-Canada TC 3105	1964
Le sentier de neige	Trans-Canada OR 738	1964
Qu'est devenu notre passe	Trans-Canada TC 3119	1965
Please Wait For Me	Trans-Canada TC 3127	1965
Tomorrow May Be Too Late	Trans-Canada	1965
N'attendons Pas Qu'il Soit Trop Tard	Trans-Canada TC 3129	1965
les revoltes	Trans-Canada TC 3143	1965
Tu le regretteras	Vogue INT 18005	1965
Le vent de la nuit	Trans-Canada TC 3161	1966
Et maintenant	Trans-Canada TC 3170	1966
Exodus	Trans-Canada TC 3187	1966
Les soirs d'hiver	Trans-Canada OR 779	1966

Lorsque j'entends	Trans-Canada 0R 813	1967
Everybody's Coming To Montreal	Trans-Canada TC 3202	1967
Lo per te darei la mia vita	Trans-Canada OR 805	1967
Je l'ai fait pour toi	Trans-Canada TC 3207	1967
Un peu d'espoir, un peu de toi	Trans-Canada TC 3228	1967
Les trois cloches	Trans-Canada TC 3237	1968
Mes jeunes annees	Trans-Canada TC 3254	1968
Dalila	Trans-Canada OR 838	1968
C'est toi	Trans-Canada TC 3273	1969
En marchant sur la plage	Trans-Canada TC 4007	1969
Si j'etais millionaire	Trans-Canada TC 4016	1970
Le Temps de L'Amour	Trans-Canada TC 4027	1970
L'herbe de la paix	Trans-Canada TC 4038	1970

Albums/CDs:

Les Classels	Trans-Canada TF 330	1964
Les Classels En Spectacle	Trans-Canada TF 336	1965
Et Maintenant Les Classels	Trans-Canada TSF 1353	1966
Blanc Sur Neige	Trans-Canada TSF 1371	1966
Les Classels (En Couleurs)	Trans-Canada TSF 1398	1968
Au Theatre Des Varietes	Trans-Canada TSF 1429	1968
Les Classels	Trans-Canada TCR 1074	1968
Les Classels Vol 1	Merite 22 917	1991
Les Classels Vol 2	Merite 22 923	1992

David Clayton-Thomas

Best known as the lead singer of Blood, Sweat & Tears, David Clayton Thomas, whose real name is David Thomsett, was born on September 12, 1941 in Walton on Thames, England. His first hit was Boom Boom on the Acta label in 1964. That same year, he recorded Barby Lee with his first group, The Fabulous Shays (later The Shays). They were comprised of Tony Collacott on piano, Jamie Todd on bass, Billy Ross on lead guitar, Al O'Brien on drums, and Jack Craig on rhythm guitar. In 1965 they had a major hit with Walk That Walk. A year later, The Shays became known as The Bossmen. Their single Brainwashed on the Roman label was a national hit in the summer of 1966, and featured a rock guitar section with a jazz piano.

Clayton Thomas' experiment into what became known later as jazz rock paved the way for groups like Blood, Sweat & Tears and Chicago.

During his initial period with Blood, Sweat & Tears, David wrote the hits Spinning Wheel and Lucretia MacEvil. He left the group in 1972. Although he moved to the United States, he remained a Canadian citizen.

After a three year solo career, he returned to Blood, Sweat & Tears. They became the first rock group to play the prestigious Metropolitan Opera and to headline at the Waldorf Astoria in New York City.

In 1980, Bobby Economou, who played with Blood, Sweat & Tears until 1977 when he left to tour with Maynard Ferguson, rejoined the group.

That same year, they signed to MCA Records, who released the album, *Nuclear Blues*. It featured cover versions of Jimi Hendrix's Manic Depression and Henry Glover's blues classic, Drown In My Own Tears.

David Clayton Thomas was inducted into the Juno Hall of Fame in 1996. In 2010 Penguin Books published his autobiography, Blood, Sweat And Tears.

By David Clayton Thomas
Singles:

Title	Label	Year
Boom Boom	ACTA 6901	1964
Barby Lee	ACTA 6904	1964
Walk That Walk (& His Quintet)	Red Leaf 65001	1965
Take Me Back/Send Her Home	Roman 1101	1965
Out Of The Sunshine	Roman 1102	1965
Brainwashed (& The Bossmen)	Roman 1105	1966
Brainwashed (& The Bossmen)	Tower 263	1966
This Hour Has Seven Days (& The Shays)	Roman 1104	1966
No, No, No	Roulette 7048	1969
Say Boss Man	Decca 732556	1969
Father, Dear Father	York 45020	1970
Sing A Song	Columbia 4 45569	1972
Magnificent Sanctuary Band	Columbia 4 45603	1972
Yesterday's Music	Columbia 4 45675	1972
Harmony Junction	RCA 74 0966	1973
Yolanda	RCA APBO 0216	1973
Anytime...Babe	RCA APBO 0296	1974

Albums/CDs:

Title	Label	Year
David Clayton Thomas & The Shays A Go Go	Roman 101	1965
Sings Like It Is	Roman 102	1966
David Clayton Thomas	Decca 75146	1969
David Clayton Thomas	Pickwick 3245	1969
David Clayton Thomas	Columbia KC31000	1972
Tequila Sunrise	Columbia KC31700	1972
David Clayton Thomas	RCA APL1 0173	1973
Clayton	ABC 1104	1978
Blue Plate Special	Stony Plain SPCD 1246	1997

Tom Cochrane

Born in Lynn Lake, Manitoba on May 13, 1953, Tom Cochrane began playing the guitar in a blues band in 1969 when he was fifteen years old. In 1971 he formed the country rock band Harvest in Toronto, but left a year later to concentrate on a solo career. He also signed a recording contract with Daffodil Records, who released You're Driving Me Crazy (Faith Healers), the first of several singles that were included on the album, *Hang on to Your Resistance*.

In 1976 he wrote the music score for Al Waxman's film, My Pleasure Is My Business. He also formed Red Rider, a trio comprised of Rob Baker, Peter Boynton, and Ken Greer. In 1978 bassist Jeff Jones, formerly in the group Ocean, made Red Rider a quartet.

Capitol Records released the group's debut album, *Don't Fight It* in 1980. Between 1981 and 1984 three more albums were released: *As Far as Siam*, *Neruda*, and, *Breaking Curfew*. They became officially known as, Tom Cochrane, and Red Rider, with the release of the album of the same name in 1986. Other albums followed, including *The Symphony Sessions*, which was a collaborative effort with the Edmonton Symphony Orchestra.

In the fall of 1990, Red Rider disbanded and Tom continued to record on his own. His first solo effort was, Mad Mad World in 1991, which included the seminal pop hit, *Life is a Highway*. Two years later, the box set, *Ashes To Diamonds: A Collection* was released. It was followed by, *Ragged Ass Road* (1995), *Songs of a Circling Spirit* (1997), and *Xray Sierra* (1998).

By Cochrane
Singles:

You're Driving Me Crazy	Daffodil DFS 1045	1973
Hang On To Your Resistance	Daffodil DFS 1048	1974
I Wish I Could See You Now	Daffodil DIL 1053	1974
Gabriella	Daffodil DIL 1061	1975
Hang On To Your Resistance	Daffodil DIL 1063	1975

By Tom Cochrane
Singles:

Softly Walk Away	Daffodil 1216 1070	1976
Sail On	Daffodil 1216 1072	1976
Life is a Highway	Capitol 97723	1991
No Regrets	Capitol 97723	1991/92
Sinking Like a Sunset	Capitol 97723	1992
Mad Mad World	Capitol 97723	1992
Washed Away	Capitol 97723	1992
Bigger Man	Capitol 97723	1992/93
I Wish You Well	EMI 32951	1995

Wildest Dreams	EMI 32951	1995/96
Dreamer's Dream	EMI 32951	1996
Just Scream	EMI 32951	1996
Crawl	EMI 32951	1996
Lunatic Fringe	EMI 37239	1997
Good Man, Feeling Bad	EMI 37239	1997
I Wonder	EMI 93924	1999
Willie Dixon Said	EMI 93924	1999
Stonecutter's Arms	EMI 93924	1999

Albums/CDs:

Hang On To Your Resistance	Daffodil 10043	1974
Mad Mad World	Capitol 97723	1991
Ashes To Diamonds: A Collection	EMI 80743	1993
Ragged Ass Road	EMI 32951	1995
Songs of a Circling Spirit	EMI 37239	1997
Xray Sierra	EMI 93924	1998
No Stranger	Universal 706042	2006
Take It Home	Universal 718016	2015

By Tom Cochrane and Red Rider
Singles:

White Hot	Capitol 72821	1980
Don't Fight It	Capitol 4868	1980
What Have You Got To Do	Capitol 72861	1981
Human Race	Capitol 5211	1983
Can't Turn Back	Capitol 5229	1983
Young Thing, Wild Dreams (Rock Me)	Capitol 5335	1984
Breaking Curfew	Capitol 5383	1984
Boy Inside the Man	Capitol 72301	1986
The Untouchable One	Capitol 5641	1986
One More Time (Some Old Habits)	Capitol 73017	1987
Ocean Blue (Emotion Blue)	Capitol 73023	1987
Big League	Capitol 73068	1988
Different Drummer	Capitol 73094	1989
Victory Day	Capitol 73085	1989
Good Times	Capitol 73076	1989
White Hot (Live)	Capitol 73102	1990
Bird On A Wire	Capitol 73110	1990

Albums/CDs:

Don't Fight It	Capitol ST 12028	1980
As Far As Siam	Capitol ST 12145	1981
Neruda	Capitol ST 12226	1983
Breaking Curfew	Capitol ST 12317	1984
Tom Cochrane And Red Rider	Capitol ST 12484	1986
Victory DAY	Capitol C1 26570	1987
The Symphony Sessions	Capitol C1 26574	1989

Bruce Cockburn

Bruce Cockburn was born on May 27, 1945 in Ottawa. He worked as a street musician in Paris and studied theory, composition and arranging at the Berklee College of Music in Boston (1964-66). In the mid 1960s he switched to rock and was a member of The Esquires and The Children. By 1967 he went solo and sang in coffeehouses, and made his first solo appearance at the Mariposa Folk Festival. He then joined the folk group, Three's A Crowd in 1969. That same year at Toronto's famous folk club, The Riverboat, he replaced Neil Young who joined Crosby, Stills and Nash. In 1969 Cockburn signed a recording contract with True North Records and began work on his self-titled debut album for the label. It also marked a long association with Bernie Finkelstein, the founder and producer of the label. Cockburn's first album on True North was released in early 1970. That same year, he wrote the music score for film director Don Shebib's classic film, Goin' Down The Road.

In the fall of 1993, he released his first Christmas album, where he sang in four different languages: French (Les anges dans nos campagnes), Spanish (Riu Riu Chiu), Huron (The Huron Carol) and English (traditional Christmas songs).

Cockburn has built an international loyal following and continues to speak out in his songs which deal with subjects he feels compelled to address, such as the environment (If A Tree Falls), land mines (Mines of Mozambique), and a world observer of current events (Get Up Jonah and The Whole Night Sky). Musically, he has gone from acoustic guitars (Bruce Cockburn) to acoustic jazz (In The Falling Dark), electric guitars (Humans), and roots music (Nothing but a Burning Light). He received the Order of Canada in 1983.

Singles:

Title	Label	Year
Going To The Country	True North TN4 100	1970
Musical Friends	True North TN4 103	1970
One Day I Walk	True North TN4 105	1971
Up On The Hillside	True North TN4 112	1971
It's Goin' Down Slow	True North TN4 109	1972
Burn	True North TN4 127	1975
I'm Gonna Fly Someday	True North TN4 132	1976
Vagabondage	True North TN4 133	1976
Free To Be	True North TN4 140	1977
Laughter	True North TN4 142	1978
Wondering Where The Lions Are	True North TN4 147	1979
I'm Okay (Fascist Architecture)	True North TN4 158	1980

Tokyo	True North TN4 149	1980
Rumours of Glory	True North TN4 156	1980
Coldest Night Of The Year	True North TN4 160	1981
I Wanna Go Walking	True North TN4 166	1981
You Pay Your Money	True North TN4 168	1981
The Trouble With Normal	True North TN4 178	1983
Tropic Moon	True North TN4 182	1983
Lovers In A Dangerous Time	True North TN4 189	1984
Making Contact	True North TN4 190	1984
If I Had A Rocket Launcher	True North TN4 193	1984/85
Peggy's Kitchen Wall	True North TN4 197	1985
People See Through You	True North TN4 206	1986
Call It Democracy	True North TN4 208	1986
See How I Miss You	True North TN4 209	1986
Waiting For A Miracle	True North TN4 210	1987
If A Tree Falls	True North TN4 212	1989
Don't Feel Your Touch	True North TN4 213	1989
Shipwrecked At The Stable Door	True North TN4 214	1989
A Dream Like Mine	True North TN 77	1991
Great Big Love	True North TN 77	1992
Mighty Trucks of Midnight	True North TN 77	1992
Somebody Touched Me	True North TN 77	1992
Mary Had A Baby	True North TN 77	1993
Listen For The Laugh	True North TN 82	1994
Scanning These Crowds	True North TN 82	1994
Someone I Used To Love	True North TN 82	1995
Night Train	True North TND150	1997
Pacing The Cage	True North TND150	1997
The Whole Night Sky	True North TND150	1997
Last Night of the World	True North TND 0183	1999

Albums/CDs:

Bruce Cockburn	True North TN1	1970
High Winds White Sky	True North TN3	1971
Sunwheel Dance	True North TN7	1972
Night Vision	True North TN11	1973
Salt, Sun And Time	True North TN16	1974
Joy Will Find A Way	True North TN23	1975
In The Falling Dark	True North TN26	1977
Circles In The Stream	True North TN30	1977
Further Adventures Of Bruce Cockburn	True North TN33	1978
Dancing In The Dragon's Jaws	True North TN37	1979
Humans	True North TN42	1980
Mummy Dust	True North TN45	1981
Inner City Front	True North TN47	1982
Trouble With Normal	True North TN53	1983

Stealing Fire	True North TN57	1984
World Of Wonders	MCA 5772	1986
Waiting For A Miracle	True North TN68&69	1987
Big Circumstancee	True North TN70	1988
Bruce Cockburn Live	True North TN73	1990
Nothing But A Burning Light	True North TN77	1991
Christmas	True North TN83	1993
Dart To The Heart	True North TN82	1994
Mummy Dust	True North TND 045	1995
The Charity of Night	True North TND 150	1997
You Pay Your Money and You Take Your Chance (Ep)	True North TND 0161	1998
Breakfast in New Orleans, Dinner in Timbuktu	True North TND 0183	1999
You've Never Seen Everything	True North TND 301	2003
Life Short Call Now	True North TND 425	2006
Slice Of Life –Solo Live	True North TND 520	2009
Small Source Of Comfort	True North TND 536	2011

Leonard Cohen

Singer, songwriter, author and poet, Leonard Cohen was born into a prosperous Jewish family in the suburb of Westmount in Montreal, Quebec on September 21, 1934. While attending a socialist camp in 1950, he learned to play the guitar. At 15, he was influenced by country and western music and played in a band called The Buckskin Cowboys. After earning a Bachelor of Arts degree in 1955 from McGill University, he wrote his first volume of poetry, *Let Us Compare Mythologies*, and gave poetry readings in a Montreal nightclub accompanied by jazz.

In 1963 his first novel, *The Favorite Game* was published, and a year later, he received the Quebec prize for literature. In 1966, his second novel, *Beautiful Losers*, was published simultaneously in Canada and the United States. Its theme focused on what reviwer John Wain in The New York Times referred to it as "a frightening vacuum of modern Canada and the Canadian's uncertainty as to who he is and where his allegiances lie, both historically and in the present."

By 1967 he sang at the Newport Folk Festival, and his appearance on CBC TV's Camera Three led to a recording contract with Columbia Records.

Cohen's most popular song was Suzanne in 1968, which was inspired by a woman Cohen had seen on the dance floor of a club called Le Vieux Moulin in the early 1960s. Her name was Suzanne Verdal, a dancer and artist's model, who, in the 1980s, was still active as a dancer who was known for her fiery, barefooted rhythms and outlandish costumes.

In the mid 1960s, The Stormy Clovers, a folk singing group from Toronto, began singing Cohen's songs.

With the release of The Future in 1992, Cohen was back in the limelight. The first single and video, Closing Time, was a big hit.

Cohen remains an international figure and has been the subject of several books and tribute Albums. His son, Adam released his self-titled debut album on Columbia (CK 67957) in 1998. In 2006, Ain't No Cure For Love, Everybody Knows, Halleluah, and Suzanne were inducted into Canadian Songwriters Hall of Fame. In 2008 he was inducted into The Rock and Roll Hall of Fame.

His final album was released in the fall of 2016 three weeks before his passing. He died in LA on November 7, 2016.

Singles:

Suzanne	Columbia 4 44439	1968
So Long Marianne	Columbia 4 2785	1968
Bird on a Wire	Columbia 4 44827	1969
Dress Rehearsal Rag	Columbia 4 2991	1970
Passing Thru	Columbia 4 45852	1973
Dance Me to the End of Love	CBS C5 7081	1984
First We'll Take Manhattan	Columbia	1988
Closing Time	Columbia CK 53226	1992/93
The Future	Columbia CK 53226	1993
Never Any Good	Columbia CK 68636	1997
In My Secret Life	Columbia CDNK 1587	2001
Show Me the Place		2012
Almost Like the Blues		2014

Albums/CDs:

The Songs of Leonard Cohen	Columbia CS 9533	1967
Songs From a Room	Columbia CS 9767	1969
Songs of Love and Hate	Columbia C 30103	1971
Live Songs	Columbia KC 31724	1973
New Skin for the Old Ceremony	Columbia KC 33167	1974
The Best of Leonard Cohen	Columbia ES 90334	1975
Death of a Ladies Man	Columbia PES 90436	1977
Recent Songs	Columbia JC 36264	1979
Various Positions	Columbia PCC 90728	1984
I'm Your Man	Columbia FC 44191	1988
The Future	Columbia CK 53226	1992
Cohen Live	Columbia CSK 80188	1994
More Best of	Columbia CK 68636	1997
Field Commander Cohen: Tour of 1979	Columbia CK 66210	2001
Ten New Songs	Columbia CK 85953	2001
The Essential Leonard Cohen	Columbia 2CK 86884	2002
Dear Heather	Columbia CK 92891	2004
Live at the Isle of Wight 1970	Columbia 570701	2009

Live in London	Columbia 405022	2009
Songs From the Road	Columbia 777112	2010
Old Ideas	Columbia 986712	2012
Popular Problems	Columbia 014292	2014
Live in Dublin	Columbia 035592	2014
I Can't Forget: A Souvenir of the Grand Tour	Columbia 074162	2015
You Want it Darker	Columbia 365D72	2016

Holly Cole Trio

Born and raised in Halifax, Nova Scotia, Holly Cole and her bandmates, bassist David Piltch and pianist Aaron Davis started playing together as a trio in the mid 1980s on Queen Street in Toronto. Their music was an amalgam of jazz, pop, rhythm & blues, and country. In 1989 their EP, *Christmas Blues* was released. *Girl Talk*, their first full length CD came out in June 1990, followed by *Blame It On My Youth* in October 1991. Both albums showcased a diverse selection of songwriters ranging from Hank Williams and George and Ira Gershwin, to Tom Waits and Smokey Robinson. In 1993 the trio's third, *Don't Smoke in Bed* added strings to compliment their sound, while *Temptation* in 1995 was a reinterpretation of sixteen songs by Waits. The following year came *It Happened One Night*, a live and enchanced CD which included eight audio tracks, four full-length live videos, two promotional videos, a discography and a question and answer with Holly. Piltch and Davis, a CD by the other two members of the trio also came out in 1996. *Dark, Dear Heart* in 1997 featured more original songs with more keyboards, horns, percussion, and guitars. A greatest hits collection called *Treasure 1989-93* came out in 1998. Holly Cole has toured throughout Canada and the United States, Europe, Japan, several Asian countries, and Mexico.

Singles:

Talk to Me Baby	Alert 81016	1990
Calling You	Alert 81018	1991/92
Downtown	Alert DPRO 225	1992
I Can See Clearly Now	Alert 81020	1993
Cry (If You Want To)	Alert DPRO 238	1994
Jersey Girl	Alert 81026	1995
I Want You	Alert 81026	1996
Don't Let the Teardrops Rust Your Shining Heart	Alert 81030	1996/97
I've Just Seen a Face	Alert 81034	1997/98
Onion Girl	Alert 81034	1998
Make it go Away	Alert 81037	2000

Albums/CDs:

Christmas Blues (EP)	Alert BDS 543	1989
Girl Talk	Alert 81016	1990
Blame it on My Youth	Alert 81018	1991
Don't Smoke in Bed	Alert 81020	1993
Temptation	Alert 81026	1995
It Happened One Night	Alert 81030	1996
Dark, Dear Heart	Alert 81034	1997
Treasure 1989 1993	Alert 81035	1998
Romantically Hopeless	Alert 81037	2000

Dorothy Collins

She was born Marjorie Chandler on November 18, 1926 in Windsor, Ontario. Using Dorothy Collins as her stage name, she went on to have a successful career as both a singer and recording artist. She was discovered in Chicago by her future husband, bandleader Raymond Scott, who hired her to sing with his band in the early 1940s. He worked with her until she became a star on Your Hit Parade in the 1950s. In addition to singing on the show, she sang commercials for such sponsors as Lucky Strike.

In 1953 Scott married Collins, and she continued to remain popular with audiences until the late 1950s, then she appeared in clubs and made guest appearances on TV. In the late 1960s she started playing summer stock and road shows. She made a brief comeback in 1971 as the girl next door in the Broadway hit, Follies, with Yvonne De Carlo and Alexis Smith.

Collins recorded for MGM in the 1940s and other labels in the 1950s. Her two major hits were My Boy Flat Top in 1955, and Seven Days in 1956, both on Coral Records. She died on July 21, 1994.

Singles:

We Knew It All The Time	MGM 10006	1947
I Love You, Yes I Do	MGM 10132	1948
You'd Be Surprised	MGM 10282	1948
I'm Playing With Fire	MGM 10753	1950
How Many Times?	MGM 11020	1950
Mountain High, Valley Low	MGM 11036	1951
From The Time You Say Goodbye	Decca 28251	1952
If'n	Decca 28421	1952
I Will Still Love You	Decca 28461	1952
Small World	Decca 28574	1952
My Heart Stood Still	Audiovox 100	1954
Mother Talk	Audiovox 102	1954
Singin' In The Rain	Audiovox 104	1954

Crazy Rhythm	Audiovox 107	1954
Break My Heart Gently	Audiovox 108	1954
My Boy Flat Top	Coral 61510	1955
Seven Days	Coral 61562	1956
Baciare Baciare (Kissing Kissing)	Top Rank 2024	1959/60
Banjo Boy	Top Rank 2052	1960

Albums/CDs:

Songs By Dorothy Collins	Coral CRL 57106	1955
Dorothy Collins	Vocalation 3724	1965

The Collins/Pickell Project

James Collins (vocals)
Dave Pickell (keyboards)

The Collins Pickell Project is made up of the songwriting team of James Collins and Dave Pickell. The two of them started their long distance songwriting partnership in 1994 through Anne Marie Smith of Warner/Chappell Music.

They have collaborated on over thirty nationally charted singles by Gavin Hope, V.I.P., Amy Sky, Switzerland's Code 5, West End Girls, Carol Medina, Anne Murray, Aaron Neville, Temperance, D Cru, Dan Hill, and Robbie Robertson.

In 1998 the Collins/Pickell Project released their first single, Since Tomorrow featuring singer Amy Soloway. Their second, I Wish You Were Here, came out in late 1998.

Singles:

Since Tomorrow	Warner Comp 98369	1998
I Wish You Were Here	Popular 32822	1998/99
I Wanna Write A Song For Celine Dion	PopularDPOP 006	1999

The Cooper Brothers

Darryl Alguire (guitar)
Glenn Bell (drums)
Brian Cooper (vocals, bass)
Richard Cooper (vocals, guitar)
Terry King (vocals, steel guitar)
Charles Robertson (vocals, reeds)
Al Serwa (keyboards)

The history of The Cooper Brothers goes back to 1964 when Richard Cooper saw The Beatles on The Ed Sullivan Show. From that moment he wanted to carve out a career as a musician. He and his brother, Brian, played in several cover bands in Eastern Canada, such as The Cat Dragged In. They sang Paul Mc Cartney medleys.

The sons of an Ottawa songwriter, Richard and Brian grew up listening to the music of the Big Band era and Cole Porter. The decision to form their own rock band came in 1972, when Richard was halfway through his studies for a master's degree in English Literature at the University of Ottawa.

In 1974 the Cooper Brothers had their own band, and put out three singles (Finally (With You), Miss Lonely Heart and From Day To Day) but none was a hit. They were produced by Les Emmerson of the Five Man Electrical Band.

During this time the group had expanded to seven members. Their manager, Allan Katz helped the group sign a deal with Capricorn in the United States. In the summer of 1978 they had a national hit with Rock and Roll Cowboys, followed by The Dream Never Dies, which won an ASCAP award for its performance by American country singer Bill Anderson. Some of the group's other hits included I'll Know Her When I See Her and Show Some Emotion.

The Cooper Brothers broke up in 1983. Terry King died on July 27, 1998.

Singles:

Finally (With You)	Polydor 2065 220	1974
Miss Lonely Heart	Polydor 2065 237	1974
From Day To Day	Diana DO 1008	1975
Rock And Roll Cowboys	Capricorn CPS 0303	1978
The Dream Never Dies	Capricorn CPS 0308	1978
Away From You	Capricorn CPS 0315	1979
I'll Know Her When I See Her	Capricorn CPS 0325	1979
Show Some Emotion	Capricorn CPS 0330	1979

Albums/Cds:

Cooper Brothers	Capricorn CPN 0206	1978
Pitfalls of The Ballroom	Capricorn CPN 0226	1979
Learnin' To Live With It	Salt Records SR 104	1980

Copper Penny

Blake Barrett (drums)
Ron Hiller (bass)
Kenny Hollis (lead vocals)
Bill Monomen (guitar)
Rich Wamil (keyboards, clavinets, vocals)

This quintet from Kitchener, Ontario began in 1965 when original members Kenny Hollis and Rich Wamil formed their own group. They had seven singles released but none was a hit. While other groups of that period, like J.B. and The Playboys and The Big Town Boys had broken up, Copper Penny survived by staying together. They were first known as The Penny Farthings. In 1966 they changed their name to Copper Penny, which came from the B side of If I Call You By Some Name, a hit by The Paupers.

In the late 1960s they finally had a hit with Nice Girl on Columbia Records, but it didn't give them the national exposure they needed to become a hit group. They switched to RCA for another hit, Stop (Wait A Minute). It, too, was not a major hit.

Their big break came in the early 1970s when they signed to London Records subsidiary label, Sweet Plum. The success of their first single on the new label, You're Still The One (1973) attracted national attention and it became their biggest hit.

When it came time to record Sittin' On A Poor Man's Throne, they turned to Richard Becker of Pac III studios in Detroit. He helped create the R&B sound that made it their second biggest song.

Backing up Copper Penny in Detroit were Joyce Vincent Wilson and Thelma Hopkins of Tony Orlando & Dawn fame.

Two of their four albums were recorded in Detroit, and two at RCA studios with Jack Richardson, who also produced The Guess Who.

Hollis and Wamil had seen a number of personnel changes since they started playing together. Shortly after signing to Sweet Plum, Ron Hiller, a former member of Rain, another Kitchener group, joined Copper Penny.

They played 150 dates a year in the United States, mostly in arenas, universities and high schools. They toured with such big names as Led Zeppelin, Uriah Heep, and Bob Seger. In Canada, they shared the same stage with The Guess Who and The Five Man Electrical Band.

In 1975 the group began recording for Capitol Records. Their hits included Disco Queen and Goodtime Sally. Their last single, Suspicious Love was issued under the name Rich Wamil and Copper Penny. When Copper Penny broke up in the late 1970s, Kenny Hollis had a brief solo career. One of his hits was "Goin' Hollywood" in 1979.

Singles:

Nice Girl	Columbia 4 2817	1968
Just A Sweet Little Thing	Nimbus Nine 74 0263	1969
Stop (Wait A Minute)	Nimbus Nine 75 1031	1970
You're Still The One	Sweet Plum 9912	1973
Sittin' On A Poor Man's Throne	Sweet Plum 9914	1973
Rock And Roll, Boogie Woogie And Wine	Sweet Plum 9919	1973/74

Where Is The Answer	Sweet Plum 9921	1974
Summertime	Sweet Plum 9925	1974
Help Your Brother	Capitol 72741	1975
Disco Queen	Capitol 72751	1975
Goodtime Sally	Capitol 72757	1975
Going Down To Miami*	Capitol 72764	1975
Run Rudolph Run*	Capitol 72765	1975
Needing You	Capitol 72774	1976
Suspicious Love*	Capitol 72776	1976

*as Rich Wamil & Copperpenny

Albums/CDs:

Copper Penny	RCA 4291	1970
Sittin' On A Poor Man's Throne	Sweet Plum PLP 951	1973
Fuse (Rich Wamil & Copperpenny)	Capitol ST 6410	1976

Corbeau

Roger Belval (drums)
Pierre Harel (vocals) Replaced by Marjolene Morin (1979)
Donald Hince (guitar)
Michel Lamothe (bass)
Jean Millaire (guitar)

From Montreal, Quebec, Corbeau formed in 1977 from former members of Offenbach, with the exception of Donald Hince and Marjolene Morin, who replaced Pierre Harel in 1979 when he left after the release of the group's self-titled debut album. With their second album, *Fou* in 1980, Corbeau became one of the exponents of hard rock in Quebec. In 1981 and 1982 they won the Felix Award for Group of the Year, and Music Express honored them as Best Group of 1982. Unable to break into the French market in continental Europe, Corbeau broke up in 1985. Marjolene Morin went on to have a successful solo career as Marjo.

Singles:

Cash moe	London LFX 1101	1979
Agriculture	London LFX 1104	1979
J'lache pas	Kebec Disc KD 9094	1980
Suite 16	Kebec Disc KD 9112	1981
Illegal	Kebec Disc KD 9135	1982
Maladie d'amour	Kebec Disc KD 9155	1982

Slow Motion	Kebec Disc KD	1983
Ti verret	Kebec Disc KD 9216	1983
Amoureuse	Kebec Disc KD 9262	1984

Albums/CDs:

Corbeau	London LFS 9031	1979
Fou	Kebec Disc KD 515	1980
Illegal	Kebec Disc KD 540	1982
Corbeau	Kebec Disc KD/EPKD 592	1983
Corbeau: Dernier ICI	Kebec Disc KD 619/620	1984
Corbeau: L'integrale	Musi Art MAC 678	1992

The Courriers

Russell Kronick (vocals, banjo, guitar)
Mark Max (vocals, guitar)
Cayla Mirsky (vocals) **Replaced by Jean Price 1962; Pamela Fernie 1964**

This Ottawa folk group began in late 1958 as The Folklores, when Russell Kronick, Mark Max, and Cayla Mirsky were invited to sing at a local charity ball. It led to exposure on local and national television, with other appearances at the Venus de Milo Lounge (Montreal), Le Hibou (Ottawa), The Purple Onion (Toronto), Gate of Horn (Chicago), and Padded Cell (Minneapolis). They sang songs of French, Scottish, English, Anglo Canadian and American Negro origins.

In 1961 they recorded the single, Joe Bean which was released on the Barry record label. The following year, Cayla left and was replaced by Jean Price. By this time they had changed their name to The Courriers.

They then recorded the album, *The Courriers Carry On* for Mercury in 1962. By the release of their first album for RCA Victor in 1965, *Sing Hallelujah*, Pamela Fernie had joined as their new female singer. Their last album, *From Sea to Sea* came out in 1966.

The Courriers broke up in 1966. Thirty years later, Russell and Mark invited Ann Steinberg to join the revamped Courriers who performed at the Ottawa Folk Festival in 1998.

Singles:

Joe Bean	Barry 3066	1961
Run To Your Mama	RCA 57 3319	1964
Cherry Bough Tree	RCA 57 3328	1964

| The Long River | RCA 57 3351 | 1965 |
| Sing Hallelujah | RCA 57 3390 | 1965 |

Albums/CDs:

The Courriers Carry On	MercuryMG/SR 20772	1963
Sing Hallelujah	RCA PCS 1048	1965
From Sea to Sea	RCA LCP 1079	1966

Cowboy Junkies

Alan Anton (bass)
Margo Timmins (vocals)
Michael Timmins (guitar)
Peter Timmins (drums)

The origins of the Cowboy Junkies go back to 1980 when Michael Timmins and Alan Anton started a band called Hunger Project. When it broke up in England a year later, Michael and Alan formed Germinal, a strictly instrumental noise band. In 1985, they returned to Toronto where the Cowboy Junkies was born. Margo Timmins, Michael's sister, became their lead singer, while her brother Peter was added on drums.

One of the group's key influences was the Velvet Underground whose simple but effective sounds created a groove that fit similarly with the rhythmic artistry of the Cowboy Junkies. Margo's distinctive voice added to their overall appeal.

In October 1986, they released their debut album, *Whites Off Earth Now!!* on an independent label. The following year, the band arranged to record live at the Church of the Holy Trinity in Toronto, Ontario. The one 14 hour session resulted in the album, *The Trinity Session* (1988).

By the release of their third album, *The Caution Horses* in 1990, they had signed to RCA/BMG. After two more Albums with the label, *Black Eyed Man* (1992) and *Pale Sun, Crescent Moon* (1993), they switched to MCA (now Universal Music) until 1998. Their next two releases were *Rarities, B Sides And Slow, Sad Waltzes* (1999) on Latent, and *OPEN* (2001) on Zoe.

Singles:

Misguided Angel (12")	RCA JD 10027	1989
Sweet Jane (12")	RCA JD 10027	1989
Cause Cheap is How I Feel (12")	RCA 2612 1 RDAB	1990
Rock And Bird	RCA 2058	1990
Sun Comes Up, It's Tuesday Morning	BMG 91802	1990
Southern Rain	RCA 61049	1992
Horse in the Country	RCA 61049	1992

If You Were the Woman, I Was the Man	RCA 61049	1992
The Post	BMG 16808	1993
Hard to Explain	BMG 16808	1993/94
First Recollection	BMG 16808	1994
A Common Disaster	GEF GEFSD 24952	1996
Angel Mine	GEF GEFSD 24952	1996
Speaking Confidentially	GEF GEFSD 24952	1996
Come Calling	GEF GEFSD 24952	1997
Miles From Our Home	GEFSD25201	1998

Albums/CDs:

Whites Off Earth Now!!	Latent Latex 4	1986
Whites Off Earth Now!!	Latent/Rca 23	1990
The Trinity Session	Latent Latex 5	1988
Blue Moon Revisited (EP)	RCA 64427 2	1990
The Caution Horses	RCA 2058	1990
Sun Comes Up (10" EP)	RCA PT 49288	1990
Black Eyed Man	RCA 61049	1992
Cowboy Junkies Live!	BMG 62329	1992
Pale Sun Crescent Moon	BMG 16808	1993
200 More Miles	BMG 29643	1994
Essential Junk	BMG KCDP 51199	1994
Lay it Down	Geffen GEFSD 24952	1996
Studio	BMG 42657	1997
Miles From Our Home	Geffen GEFSD 25201	1998
Rarities, B Sides And Slow, Sad Waltzes	Latent 11	1999
Waltz Across America	Latent 12	2000
Best Of	RCA/BMG 68052	2001
Open	Zoe 1020	2001

Johnny Cowell

Johnny Cowell was born John Marwood on January 11, 1926 in Tillsonburg, near London, Ontario. His father and three uncles were members of the Tillsonburg Town Band where Johnny played his first trumpet solo at six years of age. Although he taught himself how to play the instrument, he did study with Edward Smeale in Toronto after joining The Toronto Symphony Orchestra in 1941.

During World War II he served with the Royal Canadian Navy in Victoria, British Columbia. From 1943 to 1945 he played first trumpet with the Victoria Symphony Orchestra.

Back in Toronto he studied composition at the Toronto Conservatory of Music with two of the city's top teachers and composers, Oskar Morawetz and John Weinzweig. From 1952 he played with the Toronto Symphony Orchestra.

In 1956 he began to compose his own songs, one of which was Walk Hand In Hand, which several artists recorded, including Tony Martin,

Andy Williams, and Denny Vaughan among others. Another, Our Winter Love was recorded by Bill Pursell in 1963 and The Lettermen in 1967. Cowell's other songs include Just My Luck To Be 15, Stroll Along With The Blues, and These Are The Young Years.

He has also composed a number of pieces for symphony orchestras, such as Girl On A Roller Coaster (1969), Anniversary Overture (1972), Sangre de Toro Bravo (1974), and Trumpet Concerto (1978).

Singles:

Quiet Girl	Ampersand 477 623	1971
Goodbye Sunshine	Broadland BR 2149	1975
These Are The Days	TRC 451	1982

Albums/CDs:

His Girl	Stone SXS 3731	1968
Bridge Over Troubled Waters	CTL 477 5127	1970
The Tender Loving Care	Ampersand 477 1601	1971
Hot Brass	Audat 477 4007	1973
These Are The Days	Broadland BR 1921	1975
It's Gotta Be Love	Scope 477 5700	1978
The Virtuoso Trumpet Of	Fanfare DFL 8013X	1985
Carnival Of Venice	Fanfare DFCD1 010	1990
The Art Of Johnny Cowell: Virtuoso Trumpet Gems	Do-Re-Mi DHR 71127	1998

Deborah Cox

From Toronto, Ontario on July 13, 1974, Deborah Cox began singing when she three years old when she sang along to commercials on television. By age twelve she was singing them professionally, after she won a Tiny Tot Talent contest sponsored by a local TV station. In her teens she played around Toronto and attended the Claude Watson School For The Arts.

She was raised in a strict Roman Catholic household by Guyanese immigrants, Jeanette and Ernie, Deborah's stepfather, where there were regular family meals, daily prayers and church weekly. While growing up she was influenced by her mother's love for calypso, jazz and blues.

In 1989 she met Lascalles Stephens, who was producing Maestro and developing such acts as Simone Denny who later became a member of Love, Inc. Stephens and Cox later married in 1998.

Cox won the lead role in the off Broadway musical, Mama I Want To Sing in 1990 and, two years later, she moved to Los Angeles and where she signed a recording contract with Arista Records. Her self-titled debut CD was released in September 1995. In 1997 she recorded Things Just Ain't The Same for the soundtrack of Money Talks, and in 2001, Absolutely Not for the soundtrack of Dr. Doolittle 2.

In 1999 Cox's single, Nobody's Supposed To Be Here became the longest running number one song on Billboard's Rhythm & Blues singles & Tracks. It was number one for fourteen weeks from November 7, 1998 to February 6, 1999.

She made her acting debut in the film Love Come Down, which premiered at The Toronto Film Festival in September 2000.

Singles:

Sentimental	Arista 8781	1995
Who Do U Love	Arista 8781	1996
Where Do We Go From Here	Arista 8781	1996
Things Just Ain't The Same	Arista 19022	1997
Nobody's Supposed To Be Here	Arista 13550	1998/99
It's Over Now (CS/s)	Arista 3614/13656	1999
We Can't Be Friends (CD/s)	Arista 3691	1999
Absolutely Not	J Records 21080	2001

Albums/CDs:

Deborah Cox	Arista 8781	1995
One Wish	Arista 19022	1998

Crack of Dawn

Trevor Daley (trombone)
Gabriel Dwight (trumpet)
Carl Harvey (lead guitar)
Rupert Harvey (rhythm guitar)
Alvin Jones (saxophone, flute)
Glen Ricketts (vocals)
Jacek Sobotta (keyboards)
Andree Smith (bass)

From Toronto, Ontario, Crack of Dawn organized in the fall of 1973 and were best known for their brand of energetic and boisterous stage shows, and infectious dance songs that made them one of Canada's top dance bands. Signed to Columbia Records they had a minor success on the charts with It's Alright (This Feeling) and Keep The Faith.

Most of the group's material was written by Glen Ricketts and brothers Carl and Rupert Harvey. All three had moved from Kingston, Jamaica to Kitchener, Ontario. Ricketts was a member of various Toronto bands before he helped found Crack of Dawn.

Despite their lack of success record wise, they continued to perform in clubs with their blend of disco and soul music into the late 1970s.

Singles:
The Key	Columbia C4 4089	1975
It's Alright (This Feeling)	Columbia C4 4129	1976
Keep The Faith	Columbia C4 4111	1976

Album:
Crack Of Dawn	CBS ES 90336	1976

Crash Test Dummies

Ben Darvell (harmonica, mandolin)
Mitch Dorge (drums, accordion)
Ellen Reid (keyboards)
Brad Roberts (lead vocals)
Dan Roberts (bass)

From Winnipeg, Manitoba, the Crash Test Dummies started out in 1986 as a band organized to play at the Blue Note, a local club, where they eventually became the house band. They went through several name changes, such as the Rhythm Pigs, the Chemotherapists, and Skin Graft before a friend suggested the name Crash Test Dummies. On stage, they played a mixture of Celtic music with songs by Kiss and Aerosmith.

Originally, the group was comprised of Brad Roberts on vocals and guitar, Ellen Reid on keyboards, accordion and vocals, Megan Saunders on vocals, Benjamin Darvill on mandolin, George West on bass, and Vince Lambert on drums. Saunders and West left in 1989; the latter was replaced by Dan Roberts, Brad's brother. Lambert left in 1991, and was replaced by Michael Dorge. Two other members of the group were Paul Hogan, who was the group's bass player under the name of the Rhythm Pigs, and Daniel Koulack.

On April 14, 1989 the group called themselves Crash and Test when they opened up for Valdy at the West End Cultural Centre in Winnipeg.

Signed to Polygram Records, they achieved success with their debut album, *The Ghosts That Haunt Me* in 1991. It became the top selling Canadian album of the year, and its success was due in large part to the video of the single Superman's Song.

They continued to have success in 1993 with their second album, *God Shuffled His Feet* and with the video for the song, Ballad Of Peter Pumpinkhead, from the soundtrack of the film, Dumb and Dumber. Their next two albums were *A Worm's Life* (1996) and *Give Yourself a Hand* (1999).

Singles:

Superman's Song	Arista AL 8677	1991
The Ghosts That Haunt Me	Arista AL 8677	1991
Androgynous	Arista AL 8677	1992
Mmm Mmm Mmm Mmm	Arista 16531	1993
Swimming In Your Ocean	Arista 16531	1994
Afternoons and Coffeespoons	Arista 16531	1994
God Shuffled His Feet	Arista 16531	1994/95
Ballad of Peter Pumpinhead	BMG 66523	1995
He Liked To Feel It	Arista 39777	1996
My Own Sunrise	Arista 39777	1997
My Enemies	Arista 39777	1997
Keep A Lid On Things	VIK 74321	1999
Get You In The Morning	VIK 74321	1999

Albums/CDs:

The Ghosts That Haunt Me	Arista AL 8677	1991
God Shuffled His Feet	Arista 16531	1993
A Worm's Life	Arista 39777	1996
Give Yourself A Hand	VIK 74321	1999
I Don't Care That You Don't Mind	Cha-Ching 168012	2001
Jingle On The Way	KocH 8439	2002
Songs Of The Unforgiven	Deep Fried 00052	2004
Very Best Of	Arista/Legacy 870512	2008
Ooh-La-La	Deep Fried	2010
Demo-Litions	Deep Fried	2011

Crash Vegas

Colin Cripps (guitar)
Jocelyne Lanois (bass) Replaced by Darren Watson (1991)
Ambrose Pottie (drums)
Michelle Mc Adorey (vocals)

Crash Vegas was a Toronto-based quartet comprised of musicians who had played in other bands: Colin Cripps worked with The Spoons and The Heavenly Brothers, Ambrose Pottie with The Thin Men and White Noise, and Jocelyne Lanois with Martha and the Muffins. The group's principal songwriters were Cripps and Michelle Mc Adorey, whose musical career started in England where she tried to break into the British music scene. After five years she became disillusioned about a music career and returned to Toronto where she gave up music altogether. It was Blue Rodeo's Greg Keelor who encouraged her to pursue a career as a songwriter and to form her own group. He was an early member of Crash Vegas in the late 1980s, and co-wrote five songs on their first album and four on their second.

Their debut album, *Red Earth* (1990) on Blue Rodeo's Risque Disque label was more a studio effort. In December 1990, Jocelyn Lanois left the group, and was replaced by Darren Watson, who joined in February 1991.

Crash Vegas's second album called *Stone* was released on Polygram Records in the spring of 1993. Marked by Mc Adorey's insightful lyrics, it was closer to their stage act. Four of the tracks were recorded with renowned English producer John Porter who has worked with The Smiths, Bryan Ferry, and Miracle Legion. One of them, Nothing Ever Happened featured an inventive mix by American garage rock godhead Butch Vig. The only non original song, One Way Conversation was composed by Soul Asylum's Dave Pirner.

Other contributors on Stone were legendary Faces keyboardist Ian Mc Lagan and Robbie Robertson/Daniel Lanois collaborator Bill Dillon on guitar and pedal steel.

The group broke up in 1995 shortly after the release of the album, *Aurora* on Epic Records, distributed by Sony Music.

Colin Cripps went on to become a member of Junkhouse, while Michelle McAdorey released her debut solo album, *Whirl* (Quilt 74783) in 2001.

Singles:

Inside Out	Risque-Disque27 0770	1990
Sky	Risque-Disque27 0770	1990
Smoke	Risque-Disque27 0770	1990
You and Me	London422 828409	1993
1800 Days	London422 828409	1993
My City Has A Place	London422 828409	1993
Keep It To Myself	London422 828409	1993
Pocahontas	Sony EK 80217	1994
On and On	Sony EK 80217	1995
Old Enough	Sony EK 80217	1995

Albums/CDs:

Red Earth	Risque-Disque27 0770	1990
Stone	London422 828409	1993
Aurora	Sony EK 80217	1995

Creamcheeze Good Time Band

Dave Harwood (bass)
Billy Kell (guitar, lead vocals)
Pat Kell (washboard, tambourine, vocals)
Jimi Kell (drums)
Barb Payne (fiddle, recorder) Replaced by Doug McNaughton (1972)

The members of the Creamcheeze Good Time Band from Stratford, Ontario were first known as The Badgerz from 1965 to 1969. They played at local dances and the Canadian National Exhibition in Toronto. On New Year's Day, 1971 the Creamcheeze Good Time Band was born, when the Kells, Dave Harwood and Barb Payne joined together for a practice session at the Kell family farm. Well known in the Stratford Kitchener area, the group appeared on The Tommy Hunter Show, and played at Ontario Place and The Royal Winter Fair. The Creamcheeze Good Time Band's first album, *Perth County Green*, on Dominion Records, was released in June 1971, while their second, Home Cookin', on MCA Records, came out in June 1973. Louisiana Man and Redwood Hill were charted on RPM's country chart. The group broke up in 1976. Billy Kell died of lung cancer in July 1991.

Singles:
Uncle Jed	Dominion 146	1971
Dynamite But Annie Wouldn't	Dominion 155	1972
Living Without You	MCA 40089	1973
Fleetwood Plain	MCA 40163	1973

Albums/CDs:
Perth County Green	Dominion 21022	1971
Home Cookin'	MCA 398	1973

The Crew Cuts

Pat Barrett (tenor)
Rudi Maugeri (baritone)
John Perkins (lead)
Ray Perkins (bass)

The origins of The Crew Cuts go back to St. Michael's Cathedral School in Toronto, Ontario where they first met and studied as students of voice, harmony and arranging together. Johnnie Perkins and Rudi Maugeri began singing and performing locally with Bernard Toorish and Connie Codarini in the group the Otnorots, which is Toronto spelled backwards. After their graduation, Toorish and Codarini left to become members of another Toronto group, The Four Lads.

Johnnie's younger brother Ray and tenor Pat Barrett replaced them, and all four became known as The Canadaires. They spent the early 1950s performing at fashion shows, church functions, the Canadian National Exhibition in Toronto, and local clubs.

They eventually decided to turn professional and hired an agent, who booked them for a month at McVans, a club in Buffalo, New York.

They also auditioned for Arthur Godfrey's Talent Scouts TV show which didn't work out.

In 1953, the Canadaires recorded the single, Chirp Chirp Sing A Song Little Sparrow for Thrillwood Records in New Jersey. When it failed to become a hit, they returned to Toronto.

Their agent secured them a spot on the Gene Carroll Show in Cleveland, Ohio, where they were well received. During their second visit to the show, they met Cleveland disc jockey Bill Randle who took them around to various clubs and record labels. It was he who suggested they change their name, so they chose the Crew Cuts. The only record label interested in signing them up was Mercury Records in Chicago.

In March 1954, Crazy Bout Ya Baby was released and it became their first big hit. It was followed by Sh Boom which spent seven weeks at number one on Billboard's singles chart during the summer of 1954. Other hits followed such as Earth Angel, Gum Drop, Angels In The Sky and Mostly Martha.

From 1958 1960 the group was signed to RCA but they had no hits. In the early 1960s, they recorded on several independent labels.

The Crew Cuts broke up in June, 1964. Their farewell appearance was at a club in Pittsburgh, Pennsylvania.

Singles:

Crazy 'Bout You Baby	Mercury70341	1954
Sh Boom	Mercury70404	1954
Oop Shoop	Mercury70443	1954
All I Wanna Do	Mercury70490	1954
Dance Mr. Snowwman Dance	Mercury70491	1954
The Whippenpoof Song	Mercury70494	1955
Ko Ko Mo	Mercury70529	1955
Earth Angel	Mercury70529	1955
Don't Be Angry/Chop Chop Boom	Mercury70597	1955
Unchained Melody	Mercury70598	1955

A Story Untold	Mercury 70634	1955
Gum Drop	Mercury 70668	1955
Slam Bam	Mercury 70710	1955
Angels In The Sky	Mercury 70741	1955
Mostly Martha	Mercury 70741	1955
Seven Days	Mercury 70782	1956
Out Of The Picture	Mercury 70840	1956
Tell Me Why	Mercury 70890	1956
Thirteen Going On Fourteen	Mercury 70922	1956
Love In A Home	Mercury 70977	1956
Halls Of Ivy	Mercury 70988	1956
Young Love	Mercury 71022	1957
Angelus	Mercury 71076	1957
Susie Q	Mercury 71125	1957
I Sit In My Window	Mercury 71168	1957
Be My Only Love	Mercury 71223	1957
Forever My Darling	RCA 47 7320	1958
Baby Be Mine	RCA 47 7359	1958
Fraternity Pin	RCA 47 7446	1959
Gone, Gone, Gone	RCA 47 7509	1959
No, No, Evermore	RCA 47 7667	1959
Kin Ni Ki Nic	RCA	1959
An American Beauty Rose	RCA 47 7734	1960
Aura Lee	RCA	1960
Over The Mountain	Warwick 558	1961
Number One With Me	Warwick 623	1961

Albums/CDs:

Crazy 'Bout You Baby (EP)	Mercury 13261	1954
The Crew Cuts on the Campus	Mercury MGW 12145	1954
Three Cheers For the Crew Cuts (EP)	Mercury 13274	1955
Three Cheers For the Crew Cuts (EP)	Mercury 13275	1955
The Crew Cuts Go Long Hair	Mercury MGW 12195	1955
Rock And Roll Bash	Mercury MGW	1955
Tops in Pops (EP)	Mercury MGW 13290	1956
The Crew Cuts a La Carte	Mercury MGW 12177	1956
Crew Cuts Surprise Package	RCA LPM/LSP 1933	1959
You Must Have Been a Beautiful Baby	RCA LPM/LSP 2067	1960
Best Of: The Mercury Years	Mercury 532731	1996

Crosstown Bus

Brian Anderson (bass, vocals)
Jeff Boyne (guitar, congas, lead vocals)
Mike Killeen (drums, vocals)
Frank Ludwig (piano, guitar, organ, vocals)
Rob Sommerville (organ, congas, vocals)

This quintet from Vancouver, B.C. was first known as Self Portrait and was comprised of Frank Ludwig, Jim Taylor, Ron Sullivan, and Graham Crowell. After recording one single, He's A Man, on the Rumble record label, the group evolved into Crosstown Bus, with Ludwig being the only one left from the first group. As Crosstown Bus, they had two hits in the early 1970s, Rochester River and I'm Lost Without You, which were included on their only album, *High Grass*, released in the fall of 1971.

Singles:
Rochester River	MCA 2003	1970
I'm Lost Without You	MCA 2013	1971
High Grass	MCA 2018	1971

Album:
High Grass	MCA 7015	1971

Crowbar

Sonnie Bernardi
Jozef Chirowski
John Gibbard
Roly Greenway
Kelly Jay (Real name: Blake Fordham)
Rheal Lanthier

The history of Crowbar goes back to 1962 when Roly Greenway and Rheal Lanthier were in a group called The Ascots. Six years later, with the addition of John "The Ghetto" Gibbard and Kelly Jay, whose real name was Blake Fordham, they changed their name to The Ascot Revue. From 1968 1970, they played as The Hawks, Ronnie Hawkins' backup group. In 1970, Sonnie Bernardi and Josef Chirowski (Mandela) joined the group. In the spring of that year, they renamed themselves Crowbar, and recorded the album *Official Music* with King Biscuit Boy. They later played together at the 1970 Strawberry Fields Rock Festival.

Corrina, Corrina was the first single release by King Biscuit Boy and Crowbar in September, 1970. Crowbar had also released their own album, *Bad Manors* in January, 1971, named after an old farmhouse outside Hamilton, Ontario.

Crowbar first split up in 1974. Jozef Chirowski went to work with the Alice Cooper Band. In November, 1977 the original members (Lanthier, Jay, Gibbard and Bernardi) reunited with new members Ray Harrison, who played the organ on Del Shannon's 1961 number one hit, Runaway, on keyboards and Rick Birkett on bass. Roly Greenway left to join Next, whose only hit was Only A Friend in 1976.

A new version of Crowbar toured Canada in the winter of 1977 78. The lineup consisted of Kelly Jay, Sonny Bernardi, Rheal Lanthier, John "Ghetto" Gibbard, Roly Greenaway and Ray Harrison.

Kelly Jay had brief success in the 1970s as a solo artist with such hits as Play Your Cards Right (1975) and Cherry Pie (1977). He previously had recorded the song Curlers And Cream in 1966 (Quality 1816X and Now Records RS 602). In 1993 he returned to the recording studio to make his first solo record in ten years. Entitled, *There's More Lovin'* (Where That Came From), it was written by Denis Keldie, a longtime keyboardist and friend of Jay's. Jay currently resides in Calgary, and in 1999 he reunited with other original members of Crowbar to play at a benefit rock revival in Toronto. The rest of the band continues to play occasionally in and around Metro Toronto. O What A Feeling was inducted into Canadian Songwriters Hall of Fame in 2011.

Singles:

Corrina Corrina (King Biscuit Boy & Crowbar)	Daffodil DFS 1001	1970
Oh What A Feeling	Daffodil DFS 1004	1971
Happy People	Daffodil DFS 1009	1971
Too True Mama	Daffodil DFS 1012	1971/1972
Ask Me No Questions	Daffodil DFS 1019	1972
Dreams	Daffodil DFS 1029	1972
Fly Away	Daffodil DFS 1014	1972
Hey Baby	Daffodil DFS 1021	1972
House Of Blue Lights	Daffodil DFS 1038	1972
Higher And Higher	Epic 5 11008	1973
Million Dollar Weekend	Epic 5 11050	1973/4
All The Living Things	Epic 5 11104	1974
Run Rudolph Run	Puck SL 7609	1977
Blue Light Boogie	Promo	1986/87

Albums/CDs:

Official Music (King Biscuit Boy & Crowbar)	Daffodil SBA 16000	1970
Bad Manors	Daffodil SBA 16004	1971
Larger Than Life	Daffodil SBA 16007	1972
Heavy Duty	Daffodil SBA 16013	1972
CROWBAR CLASSICS	Daffodil SBA 16030	1973
KE32746	Epic KE 32746	1973

Susan Crowe

Susan Crowe grew up in a musical family in Cow Bay, Nova Scotia. She later made for herself as a folksinger on the Maritime coffeehouse and festival circuit. In 1982 she left performing to work in the service industry and Canada Post. She returned to singing in 1993 when she wanted to record some of her own songs. A year later came her debut CD, *This far from Home*, which was nominated for a Juno Award in the category of Best Roots/Traditional Recording.

In 1998 her second CD, *The Door to the River* was released, and three years later, her third, A Pilgrim's Mirror.

She has performed at almost every major folk festival in Western Canada, and her passionate voice has been widely praised from Montreal to Vancouver.

Albums/CDs:

This Far From Home	Corvus	CR001	1994
The Door To The River	Corvus	CR003	1995
A Pilgrim's Mirror	Corvus	CR005	1998
Book Of Days	Corvus	CR011	2005
Greytown	Corvus	CR017	2009

Cub

Robynn Iwata (guitar, vocals)
Valeria (drums, vocals) Replaced by Lisa G. (1993)
Lisa Marr (bass, vocals)

Cub formed in May 1992 in Vancouver, British Columbia. Later that same year, they signed a recording contract with Mint Records. In 1993 they toured across Canada and the eastern United States with The Smugglers, Seaweed, and The Hanson Brothers. The following year, they went on a west coast U.S. tour with The Ne'er do Wells and DOA, and a Canadian tour with Huevos Rancheros, The Leather Uppers, NFA. Valeria, the original drummer, left in 1993 and was replaced by Lisa G. Cub's first full length CD, *Betti Cola* was released in October 1993. Although they were less known in eastern Canada, the group developed a following in their hometown and on the U.S. west coast. Their sound has been described jokingly as "cuddlecore" and on stage they played mostly original material with some cover versions of songs like The Beach Boys' Surfer Girl. Cub broke up in 1997.

Singles:

Go Fish	Mint MRD 002	1993
Your Bed	Mint MRS 009	1994
My Chinchilla	Mint MRD 002	1994
Nicolas Bragg	Mint MRD 002	1994
My Flaming Red Bobsled	Mint MRD 005	1995
Cub & The Potatomen	Mint MRD 008	1995
Cub & The Potatomen	Mint MRS 013	1995
Freaky	Mint MRD 021	1996
T.J./She's a Rainbow	SPIN ART MRM 107	1996

Albums/CDs:

Pep (EP)	Mint MRS 003	1992
Hot Dog Day (EP)	Mint MRS 004	1993
Betti Cola	Mint MRD 002	1993
Betti Cola (EP)	Mint MRS 005	1993
Come Out Come Out	Mint MRD 005	1995
The Day I Said Goodbye (EP)	Mint MRD	1995
Box of Hair	Mint MRS 021	1996
Mauler! a Collection of Oddities	ANDA 214	1997

Burton Cummings

Born on December 31, 1947 in Winnipeg, Manitoba, Burton Lorne Cummings took piano lessons at an early age. In the early 1960s, he was a member of The Deverons, and with them he recorded the Singles:, Blue Is The Night and Lost Love on Reo Records.

In December 1965 he replaced Bob Ashley as lead singer in The Guess Who. During the next ten years he helped write some of their biggest hits, including These Eyes, Laughing and No Time.

Cummings left The Guess Who in 1975 to concentrate on a solo career. In the fall of 1976, CBS Records released his self-titled debut album. Stand Tall, the first single, was a Top Ten hit in both the United States and Canada. Some of his other hits included My Own Way To Rock, Break It To Them Gently and You Saved My Soul.

From 1976 to 1984 he had several including his self-titled effort in 1976, followed by My Own Way To Rock, Dream Of A Child, and Woman Love. Six years after the release of Plus Signs in 1990, he re recorded some of his best songs for the album, *Up Close and Alone*.

Singles:

Stand Tall	Portrait6 7001	1976
I'm Scared	Portrait6 7002	1977
Timeless Love	Portrait6 7003	1977
My Own Way To Rock	Portrait6 7007	1977
Your Back Yard	Portrait6 70011	1977/78
Break It To Them Gently	Portrait6 70016	1978
I Will Play A Rhapsody	Portrait6 70024	1979
Meanin' So Much	PortraitL4 4107	1979
Draggin' Them Down The Line	Portrait48338	1979
Fine State Of Affairs	Epic E4 4248	1980
Mile A Second	Epic E4 4257	1980
One And Only	Epic E4 4262	1980
You Saved My Soul	Epic E4 4284	1981
Mother Keep Your Daughters In	Epic E4 4294	1981/82
Whatever Happened To Your Eyes	Epic E4 7067	1984
One Day Soon	Capitol 93938	1990
The Rock's Steady	Capitol 93938	1990
Free	Capitol 93938	1990
Take One Away	Capitol 93938	1990
Permissible To Cry	Capitol 93938	1991

Albums/CDs:

Burton Cummings	PortraitPR 34261	1976
MY OWN WAY TO ROCK	PortraitPR 34698	1977
Dream Of A Child	PortraitJR 35481	1978
The Best Of Burton Cummings	Columbia CK 81015	1980
Woman Love	Epic XPEC 80040	1980
Sweet Sweet	Epic XPEC80054	1981
Heart	Epic XPEC80100	1984
Plus Signs	Capitol 93938	1990
The Burton Cummings Collection	Rhino 71717	1994
Up Close And Alone	MCA 81010	1996

Bobby Curtola

He was born Robert Curtola in Port Arthur (now Thunder Bay), Ontario, on April 17, 1944. His musical career started in high school when he used to sing at high school dances with his group, The Bobcats.

At one of the dances, he met Basil and Dyer Hurdon of Tartan Records. They were so impressed with Bobby's stage performance, they ended up signing him to their label. His first single, Hand In Hand With You came out in 1960. Two of his single releases, Fortune Teller and Aladdin, were the first two gold records ever to be awarded a Canadian recording artist. Other hits on Tartan were Don't You Sweetheart Me in 1961 and Three Rows Over in 1963.

Bobby's popularity among the teens led to Curtolamania across Canada in the early 1960s. For more than twenty years he has appeared in Las Vegas where he became the first performer to sign a multi-million contract as a lounge act. He also hosted the CTV variety show, Shake, Rock, Roll in 1973.

His major achievements and awards include being a headliner for twenty years as a lounge performer in Las Vegas, recording the first jingle that sounded like a Top 40 record that started a trend in advertising ("Things go better with Coke") and receiving the Order of Canada in 1998. He has also been inducted as a member of the Ochapowace Tribe of Saskatchewan, and honored in recognition for his charitable work in Ecuador with the Bobby Curtola Centre of the World Children's Foundation. In addition to North America, he has performed in Southeast Asia, South America, and Europe. He died on June 5, 2016.

Singles:

Title	Label/Number	Year
Hand In Hand With You	Tartan1001	1960
Ever Near You	Tartan1002	1960
You Must Belong To Me	Tartan1003	1960
Call Me Baby	Tartan1004	1961
Don't You Sweetheart Me	Tartan1005	1961
Don't You Sweetheart Me	Del FI 4163	1961
Never Be Alone Again	Tartan1006	1961
Hitchhiker	Tartan1007	1961/62
Hitchhiker	DEL FI 4195	1961/62
Fortune Teller/Johnny Take Your Time	Tartan1008	1962
Fortune Teller/Johnny Take Your Time	Del FI 4177	1962
You Must Belong to Me (re released)	Tartan1009	1962
I Cry and Cry	Tartan1010	1962
Aladdin	Tartan1011	1962
Aladdin	Del FI 4185	1962
My Christmas Tree	Tartan1012	1962
Destination Love	Tartan1013	1962/63
Gypsy Heart	Tartan1014	1963
Indian Giver	Tartan1015	1963
Three Rows Over	Tartan1016	1963
Three Rows Over	Del FI 4223	1963
Move Over	Tartan1018	1963/64
Little Girl Blue	Tartan1019	1964
You're Not a Goody Goody	Tartan1021	1964
As Long as I'm Sure of You	Tartan1022	1964
Come Home Little Girl	Tartan1024	1964
Alone and Lonely	Tartan1025	1964/65
It's About Time	Tartan60 1026	1965
Mean Woman Blues	Tartan60 1027	1965

Walkin' With My Angel	Tartan60 1028	1965
Makin' Love	Tartan60 1029	1965
Forget Her	Tartan60 1030	1965
While I'm Away	Tartan60 1031	1966
The Real Thing	Tartan60 1032	1966
Wildwood Days	Tartan60 1033	1966
It's Not Funny Honey	Tartan60 1034	1966/67
Give Me A Reason To Stay	Tartan60 1035	1967
Quando, Quando, Quando	Tartan60 1036	1967
Footsteps	Tartan60 1040	1967
Sandy	Tartan60 1041	1968
Pretty Blue Eyes	Tartan60 1043	1968
Step By Step	Tartan60 1044	1968
Unless You Care	Tartan60 1045	1969
Mammy Blue	Tartan60 1045	1969
Gotta Give Love/My Christmas Tree	Tartan60 1046	1969
Jean	Capitol 72615	1970
Way Down Deep	Capitol 72639	1971
Songman		1973
Oh My Marie	RCA PB 50234	1976
Stickin' With Beautiful Things	RCA PB 50272	1976
May The Force Be With You	Bamb A-2001	1977
Have You Ever Really Been There	Tartan TA-009	1984
Answer Me Carrie	Tartan 60-1033	1984
Freda Lee (as Boby Curtola)	BCI 451	1987
Playin' In The Shadows of Glory	RBI 8904	1990
Drivin' Down A Phantom Road	RBI 8906	1990

Albums/CDs:

Hitch Hiker	Tartan101	1961
Mr. Personality	Tartan102	1962
Truly Yours	Tartan103	1963
12 Tickets To Cloud 9	Tartan104	1964
Love Story In Stereo	Tartan105	1965
Magic Moments	Tartan106	1965
Twelve Golden Hits	Tartan107	1966
Bobby Curtola's Greatest Hits Vol 1	Tartan108	1967
Bobby Curtola's Greatest Hits Vol 2	Tartan109	1968
Bobby Curtola's Greatest Hits Vol 3	Tartan110	1969
Bobby Curtola's Greatest Hits Vol 4	Tartan111	1969
Changes	Capitol ST 6354	1970
Curtola	Capitol ST 6361	1971
Songman	CTL 477 5166	1973
Shake, Rock, And Roll	Tuff 113	1974
Stickin' With Beautiful Things	RCA KPL1 0165	1976
Curtola: His Greatest Hits	Tee Vee Ta 1071	1977
Curtola 2 Decades of Hits		1984
15 Greatest Hits	Bmg 17248	1991

Christmas Flashback	Tartantar 0014	1992
Gotta Get Used To Being Country	Tartantar 0016	1993
Turn The Radio Up	RRN 10301	1996

Wes Dakus & The Rebels

Bob Clarke (lead guitar)
Wes Dakus (bass)
Maurice Marshall (guitar)
Gary McDonald (trumpet)
Doug Michetti (piano)
Don Paches (drums)
Wallace Petruk (alto sax, tenor sax)
Lennie Richards (vocals)
Orest Urchak (tenor sax)

This group from Edmonton, Alberta began as Club 93 Rebels in 1957, and were comprised of Wes (Jack) Dakus, Don Paches, and Bob Clarke. In 1959, they recorded the single, Pink Canary on Quality Records, and, a year later, Dakus left the band.

Between 1958 and 1963, Bob Clarke had started an instrumental group called The Nomads. The rest of the group consisted of Max L'Hirondelle (guitar), Jack Paul (vocals), Hugh Bolton (piano), Lyn Wallace (drums), Gary Peterson (trumpet), Bill Eccleston (sax), and Dave McLachlan (bass). During that period, Clarke was known to have played in both The Nomads and The Rebels. The Nomads recorded the single, Teem Twist in 1960.

When Wes Dakus returned to The Rebels in 1963, Clarke chose to stay in Dakus's group. There were two new additions: Stu Mitchell on drums, and Barry Allen on rhythm guitar and vocals. In 1965, Clarke quit. When Wes Dakus and The Rebels disbanded in 1967, the lineup of the group included Dakus, Allen, Mitchell, Dennis Paul and Maurice Marshall. Barry Allen went solo and had several hits, such as Lovedrops. Dennis Paul formed The Skeptics, who later became the Gainsborough Gallery.

By Club 93 Rebels
Singles:

Taboo	Quality K 1023	1958
El Ringo	Quality K 1250	1958
Pink Canary	Quality K 1982	1959

By Wes Dakus & The Rebels
Singles:

Side Winder	Quality 1631	1964
Las Vegas Scene	Quality 1660	1963
Hobo	Capitol 72213	1965
Come on Down	Capitol 72259	1965
Hoochi Coochi Coo	Capitol 72305	1965/66
She Ain't No Angel	Capitol 72350	1966
We've Got a Groovy Thing Going	Capitol 72396	1966
Mama's Boy	Capitol 72442	1967
Shotgun	Capitol 72457	1967
Manipulator	Capitol 72484	1967
The Chaser	Capitol 72532	1968

Albums/CDs:

Wes Dakus With the Rebels	Capitol 6120	1965
Wes Dakus' Rebels	Kapp 3636	1967

Lisa Dal Bello

Born in Woodbridge, Ontario on May 22, 1959, Lisa Dal Bello learned to play the guitar from a neighbour. At eleven years of age, she wrote her first song, Oh Why?, which was an attempt at a protest song. At thirteen, she began singing professionally, and at fifteen she sang her first advertising jingle, a beer commercial. By her late teens she had become a regular performer on CBC TV's Music Machine. The exposure led to a record contract with MCA. In the spring of 1977 her self-titled debut album was released. It was to be her only one with the label.

Her next two albums were released by Capitol Records, *Pretty Girls* (1978) and *Drastic Measures* (1981). The single, Pretty Girls was a major hit in 1979. That same year in the U.S., Melissa Manchester covered the song which became a Top 40 hit.

In 1981 she stopped her musical career to concentrate on her reading and poetry. She also took courses in Women and Law at Toronto's York University.

Three years later former guitarist/producer Mick Ronson (Mott The Hoople) saw Lisa in a CBC documentary and convinced her to return to the recording studio. She later signed a contract with Capitol Records. In 1984 her debut album, *Whomanfoursays* (the title was a play on "human forces") was released. It marked a change in her stage name, which was shortened to Dal Bello, and in her image and attitude since her sound had matured from mainstream dance music to more diverse stylings. Her fifth album, *She* was first released in Europe in late 1987, and in North America on January 23, 1989. Tango was the first single.

In between albums she wrote the lyrics for 99 Red Balloons for Nena, and composed songs for the soundtrack of director Adrian Lyne's film 9 1/2 Weeks (1986).

Singles:
(Don't Want To) Stand In Your Way	MCA 40806	1977
Pretty Girls	Talisman TAL 100	1979
Never Get To Heaven	Capitol 72853	1981
She Wants To Know	Capitol 5006	1981
Gonna Get Close To You	Capitol 72952	1984
Animal (12")	EMI 75074	1984
Tango	Capitol 73074	1989
Talk To Me	Capitol 73083	1989
Eleven	EMI 37985	1996/97

Albums/CDs:
Lisa Dal Bello	MCA 2249	1977
Pretty Girls	Talisman 1000	1978
Drastic Measures	Capitol ST 12140	1981
Whomanfoursays	Capitol ST 12318	1984
She	Cap C1 48286	1989
Whore	EMI 37985	1996

Daybreak

Harry Busby (trumpet)
Lamar Dodsworth (sax)
Graham Dunnett (guitar, vocals)
Len Lytwyn (drums)
John Lovatt (guitar, vocals)
Ian Mutch (organ)

From Toronto, Ontario, Daybreak was a six man band organized by Graham Dunnett in 1969. They evolved from Dee and The Quotum, formerly Dee and The Yeomen. Their only single was Greatest Story Ever Told on London Records in 1970. Daybreak broke up in 1971.

Single:
Greatest Story Ever Told	London17391	1970

Dee & The Yeomen

Graham Dunnett (Dee) (lead guitar, vocals) Replaced by Laurie Keller and Bob Smith (1967)
Len Lytwyn (drums)
Terry Watkinson (organ)

Dee and The Yeomen formed in Toronto in 1964. Dee, whose real name was Graham Dunnett, was born in Middlesex, England, where he was a member of several bands such as The Starliners. He moved to Canada in March 1963 and settled in Toronto, Ontario. A year later, he started his own group called Dee & The Yeomen. Dee had been Dunnett's nickname since he was a teenager. The group played regularly at a coffeehouse called The Night Owl in Yorkville Village, and toured throughout Ontario.

Wolff Records released their first single, Say Baby (Who Am I) in January 1965. Take The First Train Home followed on Can Cut Records later that same year. In 1967, Dee left and was replaced by Laurie Keller and Rob Smith. The group then added Terry Watkinson and Len Lytwyn and they called themselves The Rock Show of the Yeomen. Dee went on to organize Dee & The Quorum, later Dee & The Quotum and Daybreak.

By Dee & The Yeomen
Singles:

Say Baby (Who Am I)	Wolff 101	1965
Take The First Train Home	Can Cut 8880	1965
Take The First Train Home	Bell 633	1965
A Love Like Mine	Reo 8909	1966
Baby It's All Worthwhile	Reo 8940	1966
In A Minute Or Two	Reo 8966	1966

By Dee & The Quotum
Single:

Someday You'll Need Someone	Sound Canada 705	1969

Deja Vu

Bob Bonnell (vocals)
Wally Cameron (drums)
Cal Dodd (vocals)
Paul Gordon (vocals)
John Pimm (guitar)
John Sheard (keyboards)
Terry Wilkins (bass)

This seven member band hailed from Toronto, Ontario. Its beginnings go back to November, 1974 when Skip Prokop of Lighthouse encouraged them to go in the studio and produce an album of their own songs. Signed to Capitol Records International, their first album was called, *A Song For Everyone*. Hot on the heels of its release, they opened for Joe Cocker as part of his Canadian tour. Dance was their first hit single in the summer of 1976. A second album, *Get It Up For Love*, also on Capitol, came out in 1977.

Singles:
Dance	Capitol 4277	1976
Be Happy	Capitol 4321	1976
Love I'd Like To Thank You	Capitol 4396	1977

Albums/CDs:
A Song For Everyone	Capitol ST 11527	1976
Get It Up For Love	Capitol ST 11604	1977

Dewline

Al Gibson
Francis Munoz
Pat Murphy
Allan Watta
Dwayne Wells

The Dewline was a five man band from Calgary, Alberta. Their first single, on Capitol Records, was Recipe For Love in 1969. The following year, they recorded If You Can Dig It and Ode To A Cucumber, Blueberry And A Flower, the two sides of their second single on Reo Records, produced in Hollywood by Don Grashey and Chuck Williams. They broke up in 1970.

Singles:
Recipe For Love	Capitol 72557	1969
If You Can Dig It	REO 9033X	1970

The Diamonds

Stan Fisher (lead singer) Replaced by Dave Somerville (1954)
Ted Kowalski (tenor) Replaced by John Felton (1959)
Phil Levitt (baritone) Replaced by Mike Douglas (1957)
Bill Reed (bass) Replaced by Evan Fisher (1959)

The Diamonds were a vocal quartet from Toronto, Ontario, originally comprised of Stan Fisher, Ted Kowalski, Phil Levitt and Bill Reed. Formed in 1953, they were first known as The Four Diamonds, a name suggested by Kowalski. A year later, Fisher left to finish college. He was replaced by Dave Somerville, an audio engineer at the CBC, who wanted to make a career as a singer. By 1955, they had shortened their name to The Diamonds, and had started playing in the United States. Signed to Coral Records, their first two Singles:, Black Denim Trousers And Motorcycle Boots and Smooch Me, went unnoticed.

When they heard that Bill Randle had discovered The Crew Cuts, The Diamonds arranged to play at the Alpine Valley Club in Cleveland, Ohio where they hoped to meet him. When they did, he was instrumental in signing them to a contract with Mercury Records. Their first hit was a cover version of Frankie Lymon and The Teenagers' Why Do Fools Fall In Love, which reached #12 in 1956 on Billboard's Hot 100. Its success convinced the group to do more cover versions, including The Willows' Church Bells May Ring, The Clovers' Love, Love, Love, The Gladiolas' Little Darlin', and The Rays' Silhouettes.

In 1987 Levitt left and was replaced by Mike Douglas. Two years later, Reed and Kowalski also left, and were replaced by Evan Fisher and John Felton respectively. With Somerville's departure in 1961, the original Diamonds had broken up.

Somerville continued to perform under the name David Troy and later joined the Four Preps. The original Diamonds reformed in the 1970s. Felton died in a plane crash in May 1982 near Mount Shasta, California. The Diamonds were inducted into the Juno Hall of Fame in 1984.

Bill Reed died on Oct. 22, 2004, Ted Kowalski on August 8, 2010, and Diamond Dave" Somerville on July 14, 2015.

Singles:

Black Denim Trousers & Motorcycle Boots	Coral 61502	1955
Smooch Me	Coral 61577	1955
Why Do Fools Fall In Love	Mercury70790	1956
Church Bells May Ring	Mercury70835	1956
Love, Love, Love	Mercury70889	1956
Ka Ding Dong	Mercury70983	1956
Soft Summer Breeze	Mercury70983	1956
My Judge And Jury	Mercury70934	1956
A Thousand Miles Away	Mercury71021	1956
Little Darlin'	Mercury71060	1957
Words Of Love	Mercury71128	1957
Zip Zip	Mercury71165	1957
Silhouettes	Mercury71197	1957
The Stroll	Mercury71242	1958
High Sign	Mercury71291	1958

Kathy O	Mercury 71330	1958
Happy Years	Mercury 71330	1958
Walking Along	Mercury 71366	1958
She Say (Oom Dooby Doom)	Mercury 71404	1959
Gretchen	Mercury 71449	1959
Sneaky Alligator	Mercury 71468	1959
Young In Years	Mercury 71505	1959
Walkin' The Stroll	Mercury 71534	1959
Tell The Truth	Mercury 71586	1960
Slave Girl	Mercury 71632	1960
You'd Be Mine	Mercury 71735	1960
I Sho' Lawd Will	Mercury 71782	1960
Woomai Ling	Mercury 71818	1960
One Summer Night	Mercury 71831	1961
Horizontal Lieutenant	Mercury 71956	1961
The Slide	Nathaniel 101	1961

Albums/CDs:

The Diamonds	Mercury MG 20309	1957
America's Famous Song Stylists	Mercury W MGW 121	1958
Pop Hits	Mercury W MGW 121	1958
Songs From The Old West	Mercury 60159	1959
The Diamonds Meet Pete Rugolo	Mercury MG20368	1959
The Diamonds Collection	Stardust CD 1010	1993
The Best Of: The Mercury years	Mercury 532734	1996

Celine Dion

Born in Charlemagne, Quebec on March 30, 1968, Celine Dion came from a showbusiness family. Her parents were traditional folk musicians who toured with Celine's older brothers and sisters as The Dion Family.

Her mother, Therese, played the violin; her father the accordion.

In January, 1981, Celine met Rene Angelil who became her manager after hearing her sing, Ce n'etait qu'un reve on cassette.

Angelil signed her to his independent TBS label and two Dion Albums were released together, *La Voix Du Bon Dieu* and *Celine Dion Chante Noel*.

The following year Celine represented France at the 1982 Yamaha World Popular Song Festival in Tokyo. She won a gold medal for performing Tellement j'ai d'amour pour toi.

In 1985 she stopped performing to plan the next step in her career. She signed with CBS Records Canada in 1987. Her debut album, *Incognito* produced six Top

Ten Singles:. Later that year, she sang Just Have A Heart in English at the Juno Awards in Toronto and received a standing ovation. A year later, she won the Eurovision Song contest in Dublin.

Before she released her first English album, *Unison* in 1990, she was Quebec's princess of pop. She had recorded eight French language Albums that sold more than 900,000 copies and won 15 Felix Awards, the equivalent to the English Juno Award and awarded annually in Quebec since 1979. In Quebec she is known as "la petite Quebecoise."

For *Unison*, Sony Music set aside a million dollars, the largest budget ever for a Canadian artist. Several singles were culled from the album, including the Top 5 hit, If You Asked Me To. Written by Diane Warren, it was first recorded in 1989 by Patti Labelle for the James Bond film, Licence to Kill, and was on Billboard's Rhythm and Blues and Adult Contemporary charts. Polly Anthony, head of promotion at Epic Records in the U.S. suggested Celine record If You Asked Me To, which became a hit in 1992.

Her other English hits have included Beauty and The Beast, a duet with American singer Peabo Bryson, Because You Loved Me, and My Heart Will Go On, which is on both her, *Let's Talk About Love*, album and the soundtrack to the motion picture Titanic. My Heart Will Go On was the eighth single to enter Billboard's Hot 100 at No. 1 on February 28, 1998.

Celine has also contributed the songs, (You Make Me Feel Like) A Natural Woman to Tapestry Revisited: A Tribute To Carole King (Atlantic 92604 1995), Brahms Lullaby to For Our Children, Too (Rhino 72494 1996), and God Bless America to A Tribute To Heroes (Sony CK 86300).

She received both the Order of Quebec and the Order of Canada on April 30 and May 1, 1998 respectively. In 1999 she was honored with her own star on Canada's Walk of Fame in Toronto.

Singles:

Ce n'etait qu'un reve	Showbuzz 334	1981
La voix du bon	Super Etoiles 353	1981
L'amour viendra	Super Etoiles 381	1982
Tellement j'ai d'amour pour toi	Saisons SNS 6518	1982
D'amour ou d'amitie	Saisons SNS 6524	1983
Mon ami m'a quitte	Saisons SNS 6527	1983
Un enfant	Saisons SNS 6536	1983
Ne me plaignez pas	Saisons SNS 6543	1984
Un Colombe	Triangle 201	1984
Mon reve de toujours	TBS 5555	1984
Un amour pour moi	TBS 5557	1985
C'est pour toi	TBS 5560	1985

C'est pour vivre	TBS 5561	1985
Dans la main d'un magicien	TBS 5562	1985
La ballade de michel	TBS 5563	1985
Fais ce que tu voudras	TBS 5564	1986
L'univers a besoin d'amour	TBS 5565	1986
On travers un miroir	CBS C5 3000	1987
Incognito	CBS C5 3009	1987
Lolita	CBS C5 3018	1987
Comme un coeur froid	CBS C5 3028	1988
Delivre Moi	CBS C5 3037	1988
D'abord, c'est quoi l'amour	CBS C5 3059	1988
Can't Live With You(w/N. Davies)	CBS C5 3088	1989
(If There Was) Any Other Way	CBS C5 3132/CK 80150	1990
Unison	CBS CXP3138/CK 80150	1990
Where Does My Heart Beat Now	CBS C5 3151/CK 80150	1990/91
The Last To Know	CBS C5 3161/CK 80150	1991
Ziggy	CBS CK 80168	1991
Have A Heart	Columbia CK 80150	1991
Beauty And The Beast (w/Peabo Bryson)	Columbia 74090	1991/92
If You Asked Me To	Columbia CK 54273	1992
Des mots qui sonnent	Columbia CK 80168	1992
Je danse dans ma tete	Columbia CK 80168	1992
Nothing's Broken But My Heart	Columbia CK 54273	1992
Love Can Move Mountains	Columbia CK 54273	1992/93
Water From The Moon	Columbia CK 54273	1993
When I Fall In Love (w/Clive Griffin)	Columbia EK 53764	1993
Did You Give Enough Love	Columbia CK 54273	1993
The Power of Love	Columbia CK 57555	1993/94
Misled	Columbia CK 57555	1994
Think Twice	Columbia CK 57555	1994
L'Amour Existe Encore	Columbia CK 80212	1994
Only One Road (CD)	Sony XEUK11661450	1995
Pour Que Tu M'Aimes Encore (CD)	Columbia 66129	1995
Je sais pas (CD)	Columbia Sony 662102	1995
A Natural Woman	Atlantic 92604	1995/96
Because You Loved Me	Columbia CK 33068	1996
Because You Loved Me (CD)	Sony XUSK1178224	1996
It's All Coming Back To Me Now(CD)	Columbia 38 K78345	1996
Les Derniers Seront Les Premiers	Columbia CK 80238	1996/97
To Love You More	Columbia CK 80238	1996/97
All By Myself	Columbia CK 33068	1997
Tell Me (with Barbra Streisand)	Columbia CK 68861	1997
My Heart Will Go On	Columbia CK 68861	1997/98
Immortality	Columbia CK 68861	1998
I'm Your Angel (CD)(w/R.Kelly)	Jive 42557	1998/99
On ne change pas	Columbia CK 80438	1999
That's The Way It Is	Columbia CK 63760	1999/00
I Want You To Need Me	Columbia CK 63760	2000

Albums/CDs:

Title	Label/Number	Year
La Voix Du Bon Dieu	Super Etoiles 4101	1981
Tellement J'ai D'amour Pour Toi	Saisons SNS 80007	1982
Chantes Et Contes De Noel	Saisons SNS 90002	1983
Les Chemins De Ma Maison	Saisons SNS 90001	1983
Les Grands Succes De Celine Dion	TBX XX001	1984
Melanie	TBS 501	1985
C'est Pour TOI	TBS 503	1985
Celine Dion En Concert	TBS 504	1985
Les Chansons En Or	TBS 507	1986
Incognito	CBS PFC 80119	1987
Dion Chante Plamondon	CBS CK 80168	1991
Unison	CBS CK 80150	1990
Celine Dion	Columbia CK 52473	1992
The Colour Of My Love	Columbia CK 57555	1993
Les Premieres Annees	Columbia CK 74653	1993
Celine Dion A L'olmypia	Columbia CK 80212	1994
Love Can Move Mountains (EP)	Sony 174817	1995
D'eux	Columbia CK 80219	1995
Gold VOL 1	Sony/VER 480287	1995
Gold VOL 2	Sony/VER 481431	1995
Falling Into You	Columbia CK 33068	1996
Live A Paris	Columbia CK 80238	1996
Let's Talk About Love	Columbia CK 68861	1997
S'il Suffisait D'aimer	Columbia CK 80339	1998
These Are Special Times	Columbia CK 69523	1998
Au Coeur Du Stade	Columbia CK 80438	1999
All The Way A Decade Of Song	Columbia CK 63760	1999
Collector's Series Volume 1	Columbia CK 85148	2000
Taking Chances	Columbia 081142	2007
Taking Chances The Concert	Columbia 673649	2010
Sans Attendre	Columbia 457462	2012
Loved Me Back To Life	Columbia 137159	2013
Une Seule Fois Live	Columbia 065122	2014

Dionysos

Phil Bech (flute, keyboards)
Eric Clement (guitar)
Fern Durand (bass)
Bob Lepage (drums)
Paul Andre Thibert (flute, guitar, lead vocals)

Dionysos was the first Quebec band to compose and sing in both English and French. Based in Montreal they developed a local following in the Montreal Sept

Iles Chibogamu circuit. They also played in Toronto and New York.

In 1971 they made their first album, *Le Grand Tour* on Jupiter Records. Their second, *Le Prince Croule* on Zodiaque Records followed in 1971. They composed the score for Sam Sheppard's play The Tooth Of Crime which opened in January February of 1974 at the Centaur Theatre in Montreal. Dionysos also performed six songs on stage based on the lyrics from the script.

They went on hiatus in 1974, and reunited in the fall of 1975 when they returned to the studio to record a self-titled album on Deram Records.

Although the band sang in both languages, they still considered themselves a Quebec group. Other members of the group included Jean Pierre Forget, Andre Mathieu, and Jean Pierre Legault.

Dionysos broke up in 1978. Paul Andre Thibert pursued a solo career and released an album on Solo Records, *Musique de Mes Amis Dionysos* (1983), which included the first single, Du fond de la nuit.

Singles:

L'age d'or	Jupiter 1216	1970
The Golden Age Pt. 1	Jupiter 2002	1970
J'ai jamais	Zodiaque 319	1973
L'age d'or 2	Solo 11413	1978
Du Fond de la Nuit (Paul Andre Thibeault)	Saisons SNS 6522	1983

Albums/CDs:

Le Grand Jeu	Jupiter YDS 8032	1971
Le Prince Croule	Zodiaque ZOX 6001	1971
Collection Dionysos	Trans World TWK 6028/6029	1974
Dionysos	Deram XDEF 125	1976
Musique De Mes Amis (Paul Andre Thibeault)	Solo SO 25507	1983

Melanie Doane

Melanie Doane was born in Truro, Nova Scotia on December 19, 1967. While growing up in nearby Halifax, she was exposed to music at an early age from her mother who taught piano, and her older sister and younger brother who took music lessons. Melanie learned to play the violin at age three, and grew up listening to a wide range of music, from the Big Bands and Dixieland to The Beatles and Queen.

After graduating from high school, she went to Dalhousie University where she studied to be a teacher. However, after two years she dropped out and worked in local theatre productions. In 1988 she moved to Toronto where she appeared in TV commercials and various stage productions. While she continued to act, she took up songwriting. In 1993 she recorded the independent EP, *Harvest Train*. Three years later, Sony Music released her first CD, *Shakespearean Fish*, and in 1998, came her second for the label, *Adam's Rib*.

Singles:
I Pray	Page Pub. MRD 026	1995
Tell You Stories	Sony CK 80233	1996
Emmanuel	Sony CNDNK 1207	1996
My Sister Sings	Sony CK 80233	1997
Adam's Rib	Sony CK 80325	1998
Waiting For The Tide	Sony CK 80325	1998/99
Goliath	Sony CK 80325	1999
Happy Homemaker	Sony CK 80325	1999

Albums/CDs:
Harvest Train (EP)	Page Pub. MRD 026	1993
Shakespearan Fish	Sony CK 80233	1996
Adam's Rib	Sony CK 80325	1998
Melvin Live	Maple Recordings 295002	2002
You Are What You Love	Wea 468627	2003
Emerald City	CD Baby 289269	2006
A Thousand N Ights	Prairie Ocean 403014	2009
Up To The Light	Prairie Ocean 634566	2015

Bonnie Dobson

Bonnie Dobson was born in Toronto, Ontario on November 13, 1940.

She began singing folk songs in her early teens. Between 1960 and 1964 she toured all over the United States, and lived in Chicago and New York. In 1965 she returned to Toronto where she sang in local coffeehouses. On CBC radio she sang regularly on the show, 1967 And All That, and was co host of La Ronde (1968 70) with Chantal Beauregard. In 1970, she moved to England where she performed on both the BBC and ITV.

As a songwriter she has written many popular songs, one of which was Morning Dew, a song she composed in 1961 and first recorded by American folksingers Fred Neil and Tim Rose in the mid to late 1960s.

Lulu, Duane and Greg Allman, Long John Baldry, Grateful Dead, Lee Hazlewood, and Nazareth are among those who have also recorded it.

Dobson recorded for various labels, including two for RCA: *Bonnie Dobson* and *Good Morning Rain*.

Single:

I Got Stung	RCA 74 0208	1969

Albums/CDs:

For The Love Of Him	MercuryMG 20987	1964
Dear Companion	Prestige 7801	1969
Bonnie Dobson	RCA LSP 4219	1969
Good Morning Rain	RCA LSP 4277	1970
She's Like A Swallow	Prestige 13021	1972
Bonnie Dobson At Folk City	Prestige 13057	1973
Merry Go Round Of Children's Songs	Prestige 13064	1973
Children's Songs	Prestige 13064	1973
Bonnie Dobson	Argo ZFB 79	1974
Morning Dew	Polydor 2383 400	1975

Rich Dodson

Born in Sudbury, Ontario, Rich Dodson moved to Calgary where he became a member of The Rebounds who later changed their name to The Stampeders. He wrote many of their songs including their biggest hit, Sweet City Woman (1971). A year later he had success as a solo artist with the song, Julia Get Up. When he left the group in December 1976, he continued to write and record his own songs on his own label, Marigold Productions in Mississauga, Ontario, and has co-written and produced for several oMarigold Records. He also produced other Canadian artists, such as Debbie Johnson, Aashna, Alanis Morissette, Eddie M, Rikki Rumball, and Monkey House. Today he remains a member of The Stampeders who are actively touring.

Singles:

Julia Get Up	Music World Creations 1010	1972
Give You That Love	Marigold MPL 728	1979
Natalie	Marigold MPL 703	1980
Lookin' Back	Marigold Mpl 705/MPL 709	1981
Hollywood	Marigold MPL 712	1982
If You Got A Heart	Marigold MPL 722	1983
Givin' It Up For Love	Marigold MPL 724	1984
No Time To Say Goodbye	Marigold MPL 726	1984
She's Comin' Back	Marigold MPL 727	1985
Your Own Kinda Music	Marigold MPL 728	1985

Album/CD:

Secret Hits	Aquarius 00575	1994

Denny Doherty

He was born Dennis Gerard Stephen Doherty in Halifax, Nova Scotia on November 29, 1940. At fifteen, he started in the dance band, Peter Power and from there was in such pop/folk groups as The Hepsters.

In 1961 he was in a group called The Colonials which later became The Halifax Three. When they broke up in late 1963, Doherty went to New York where he was first in The Mugwumps, with Cass Elliott, Zal Yanovsky and James Hendricks, then The New Journeymen with John and Michelle Phillips and Marshall Brickman.

From the summer of 1965 to 1968 Doherty was a member of The Mamas and The Papas who had several hits including; Monday Monday, California Dreamin', and Twelve Thirty. After the demise of the group, he recorded two solo Albums, *Whatcha Gonna Do?* and *Waiting For A Song*.

He returned to Nova Scotia in 1977 where he acted at The Neptune Theatre and hosted "Denny's Sho" on CBC during the summer of 1978.

During the 1980s he toured with John Phillips, Spanky McFarlane, Scott MacKenzie and Mackenzie Phillips in a new version of The Mamas and The Papas. Doherty also sang in the gospel rock musical, Fire, which was composed by fellow Canadians Paul Ledoux and David Young.

In 1996 Denny was inducted into the Juno Hall of Fame. He was host of the CBC children's series, Theodore Tugboat and in 1998-99 was filming another series for the network called, Pet Pony. He has also starred in the stage production, The Nearly True Story of The Mamas and The Papas: Dream A Little Dream. He died on January 19, 2007.

Albums/CDs:

Whatcha Gonna Do?	Dunhill DS 50096B	1972
Waiting For A Song	Ember Records EMS 1036	1975

The Doughboys

Jonh Bond Head (bass, vocals) Replaced by Peter Arsenault
Jonathon Cummins (guitar, vocals)
John Kastner (lead vocals, guitar)
Brock Pytel (drums, vocals) Replaced by Paul Newman

Formed in Montreal in late 1986, this Montreal quartet was first signed to the independent Pipeline Records. Although they were primarily a rock band, they played heavy metal, too. The original members of the group were John Kastner, Brock Pytel, Jonah Bond Head and Scott McCullough.

Their first album, *Whatever* came out in late 1987. In February of 1988 they made a video of the song, You're Related, which was included in the soundtrack of the film, Hit and Run.

Between 1988 and 1991 they toured extensively. They also went through some personnel changes. By the release of *Happy Accidents* in 1990, the lineup was comprised of Kastner, Peter Arsenault, Jon Widdabee Cummins and Paul Newman.

In 1992 the group signed with A&M Records. They also took the year off to write new material and to reevaluate the group's future. In 1993 came Crush, their debut album. Three years later, their second, *Turn Me On* was released.

The Doughboys broke up in 1997. John Kastner went on to form the group All Systems Go! with Frank Daley and Mark Arnold (from the American group, Big Drill Car) and Toronto drummer Matt Taylor.

Singles:

You're Related	Restless	1988
Fix Me	A&M 540124	1993
Shine	A&M 540124	1993
Neighbourhood Villain	A&M 540124	1994
I Never Liked You	A&M 540576	1996
Everything And After	A&M 540576	1996

Albums/CDs:

Whatever	Pipeline (No #)	1987
Home Again	Restless 7 72345 1	1988
Home Again (Ep)	Restless	1988
Happy Accidents	Restless 72510	1990
When My Up Turns To Down	Restless 72585	1992
Crush	A&M 540124	1993
Blanche (EP)	A&M 540148	1993
Turn Me On	A&M 540576	1996

Doug and The Slugs

Rick Baker (guitar)
Doug Bennett (vocals, guitar)
John Burton (guitar)
Steve Bosley (bass)
Simon Kendall (keyboards)
Wally Watson (drums)

Formed in 1977 by Doug Bennett, this Vancouver-basement band developed a loyal club following in Toronto's El Mocambo and Kingston's Prince George

Hotel. The band's name referred to the slimy, black creatures found on Vancouver's lawns and sidewalks.

Bennett was principal songwriter for the group. At first they played cover tunes until Bennett started writing original songs. In Vancouver they became well known at their "slug dances" that had various themes, such as beach blanket bingos, Ricky Ricardo Romps, and psychedelic 60s soirees. The popularity of Slugmania, as it was called, led to the group's signing on Ritdong Records, their own label, which was distributed by RCA.

Their first hit single, Too Bad came out in 1980. Other hits followed throughout the 1980s, including Chinatown Calculation and Tomcat Prowl. Leader Doug Bennett decided to leave music temporarily to star in John Gray's hit play, Rock and Roll. In 1992, the band released the CD, *Tales From Terminal City*. The following year came the retrospective collection, *Slucology 101: A Decade Of Doug And The Slugs*. Doug Bennett died on October 16, 2004.

Singles:

Too Bad	Ritdong 0001	1980
Chinatown Calculation	Ritdong PB 50595	1980
Drifting Away	Ritdong PB 50611	1981
Partly From Pressure	Ritdong PB 50663	1981
Real Enough	Ritdong PB 50648	1981
Who Knows How To Make Love Stay	Ritdong PB 50711	1983
Making It Work	Ritdong PB 50731	1983
Love Shines	A&M AMS 105	1984
Day By Day	A&M AMS 102	1984/85
I'll Be Waiting For You	A&M AMS 106	1985
White Christmas	A&M AMS 107	1985
It's Got To Be Monday	A&M AMS 108	1986
Tomcat Prowl	A&M AMS 115	1988
(I Don't Want To) Walk Away	A&M AMS 116	1988
It's A Powerful Thing	A&M AMS 117	1989
Terminal City	TCT 92102	1992
Rusty Bus	TCT 93202	1993

Albums/CDs:

Cognac and Bologna	Ritdong KKL1 0375	1980
Wrap It	Ritdong KKL1 0430	1981
Music For The Hard Of Thinking	Ritdong KKL1 0480	1983
Ten Big Ones	Ritdong KKL1 0551	1983
Popaganda	A&M AMD 1003	1984
Animato! (Doug Bennett)	A&M AMD 1005	1986
Tomcat Prowl	A&M AMD 1007	1988
Tales From Terminal City	TCT 92102	1992
Slucology 101: A Decade of Doug and The Slugs	TCT 93202	1993

Downchild Blues Band

Donnie (Mr. Downchild) Walsh (guitar)
Chuck Jackson (vocals)
Michael Fonfara (keyboards)
Pat Carey (sax)
Tyler Burgess (drums)
Gary Kendall (bass)

The origins of Downchild go back to July 1969 in Toronto when they became the first blues band to play at Grossman's Tavern. Their name came from a song by blues legend Sonny Boy Williamson. The group lists Willie Dixon, B.B. King, Muddy Waters, and Elmore James among their musical influences. Other founding members of the band included Jim Milne, Richard "Hock" Walsh, who originally played with the band from 1969 to 1976, Cash Wall, and Dave Woodward (Powder Blues).

Brothers Donny and Richard Walsh were the inspiration for Dan Aykroyd's 1980 film, The Blues Brothers.

Downchild is best known for their remake of Joe Turner's Flip, Flop & Fly, from their 1973 album, *Straight Up*. In 1978 they reformed as a three piece band called Mister Downchild, with Jane Vasey (who died on July 6, 1982), Don and Rick Walsh, who had returned to Downchild after a brief stint with his own band. Rick Walsh appeared on the group's album, *Gone Fishing* in 1989. He spent the 1990s performing with a number of different musicians, and died on January 2, 2000. Tony Flaim, who played with the group in the 1970s and 1980s, died on March 10, 2000.

Over the years, other members of Downchild have included John Witmer, Bill Bryans (M.G. & The Escorts, Mama Quilla, The Parachute Club), Wayne Jackson, Paul Nixon, James Warburton, and Vic Wilson.

Singles:

Flip, Flop and Fly	Special 1230 60	1973
Almost	Special 1230 67	1974
One More Chance	GRT 1230 111	1975
Caldonia	GRT 1230 125	1975
Tell Your Mother	Special 1230 82	1975
Goin' Dancin'	Special 1230 94	1975
Old Ma Belle	GRT 1230 106	1975/76
Stagger Lee	Posterity PT 103	1977
Tryin' To Keep Her 88's Straight	Attic AT 227	1980
Road Fever	Attic AT 232	1980
Stages of Love	Attic AT 242	1980
Hey Hey Little Girl	Attic AT 253	1981

Albums/CDs:

Bootleg	Special SS001	1972
Straight Up	GRT 9230 1029	1973
Dancing	GRT 9230 1049/LAT 1141	1974
Ready to Go	GRT 9230 1060	1975
So Far: A Collection Of our Best	Posterity PTR 13004	1977
We Deliver	Attic LAT 1085	1980
Road Fever	Attic LAT 1099	1980
Blood Run Hot	Attic LAT 1117	1981
But I'm on the Guest List	Attic 1 DJ	1982
It's Been So Long	Stony Plain SPL 1113	1987
Straight Up/We Deliver	Attic ACD 4102	1988
Gone Fishing	Stony PL SPL 1139	1989
Dancing/Road Fever	Attic ACD 24114	1992
Good Times Guaranteed	Downchild DMCD 025	1994
Lucky 13	Downchild DMCD 0013	1997
It's Been So Long/Ready To Go	Stony Plain SPCD 1242	1997
A Case of the Blues	Attic ACD 1516	1998
Come on In	DMCD 014	2004
Live at the Palais	Royale Borealis 270069	2007
I Need a Hat	True North TNR 70112	2009
Can You Hear the Music	Linus 270187	2013

Drake

Drake was born Aubrey Drake Graham in Toronto on October 24, 1986 to an African-American fathner and a Jewish Canadian Jew. He started out acting under his real name. Best known for playing Jimmy Brooks in Degrassi: The Next Generation for seven seasons, he also starred in such shows as Out-of-Towners, Blue Murder, Being Erica before being a voice for Ethan in Ice Age: Continental Drift (2012) and a supporting role in Anchorman 2: The Legend Continues In 2013.

The transition to recording artist came in 2006 with the hip hop collection, Room For Improvement. The following year, Comeback Session included his first single, Replacement Girl.

In 2008 Lil Wayne invited him to join his tour which led to 2009's *So Far Gone*, featuring the single, Best I've Ever Had. Signed to Lil Wayne's Young Money Entertainment, his debut album, *Thank You Later*, came out in 2010. After the release of, Take Care in 2011,

Drake received acclaim and earned the Grammy for Best Rap Album in 2013. His first number one on Billboard's Hot 100 was One Dance on May 21, 2016.

Singles:

Forever	Interscope 014785	2009
Over	Island820630	2010
Find Your Love	Universal 957128	2010
Right Above It	Island078003	2010
What's My Name	Def JamUSUM 025031	2010
Moment 4 Life	IslandUSCM 00003	2011
All Of The Lights	ROC-A-FELLA USUV 100318	2011
I'm On One	IslandUSCM 100126	2011
Headlines	IslandUSCM 100290	2011
She Will	IslandUSCM 100309	2011
Make Me Proud	IslandUSCM 100505	2011
Take Care	IslandUSCM 100547	2011
The Motto	IslandUSCM 100731	2012
Crew Love	IslandUSCM 100546	2012
F***Problem	Polo RCA 201 220	2012
Started From The Problem	IslandUSCM 300065	2013
Love Me	IslandUSCM 300002	2013
Hold On We're Going Home	Cash Money USCM 300690	2013
From Time	Cash Money USCM 300744	2013
Too Much	Cash Money USCM 300752	2013
The Emotion	Cash Money USCM 300760	2013
Furthest Night	Cash Money USCM 300736	2013
Mine	Def Jam400720	2014
Believe Me	Cash Money USCM 400174	2014
0 To 100-Catch Up	Cash Money USCM 400222	2014
Only	Cash Money USCM 500010	2015
Energy	Cash Money USCM 500014	2015
Know Yourself	Cash Money USUM 502037	2015
Back To Back	Cash Money USCM 500241	2015
Hotline Bling	Cash Money USCM 500328	2015
Right Hand	Cash Money USCM 500244	2015
Jumpman	Cash Money USCM 500300	2015
Work	Roc Nation QMFT 600116	2016
Summer Sixteen	Cas Money USCM 600001	2016
One Dance	Cash Money USCM 600028	2016

Albums/CDs:

Thank Me Later	Cash Money 743307	2010
Take Care	Cash Money 783262	2011
Nothing Was The Same	Cash Money 752186	2013
If You're Reasing This It's Too Late	Island728879	2015
What A Time To Be Alive	Cash Money 516661	2015

Dr. Music

This 16-member band was the brainchild of Douglas Brian Riley, born in Toronto on April 24, 1945. He had been playing music since his teens when he was with the R&B group, The Silhouettes, who built up a local following at the Toronto nightclub, The Blue Note.

By the late 1960s, he had worked with Ray Charles as his arranger and keyboard player, and then worked on shows at Canada's two major TV networks. For the CTV network there was The Ray Stevens Show (1969 70), and Rolling On The River (1970 72), and at the CBC, Music Machine (1973 74), Tommy Ambrose's Celebration (1975 76) and The Wolfman Jack Show (1976 77).

The "DR." was taken from his first and last names. Backing him up were Laurel Ward, Rhonda Silver, Brenda Gordon, Terry Black, Michael Kennedy, Brian Russell and Steve Kennedy (Motherlode). Dr. Music was together from 1971 to 1976, and they were signed to the now defunct GRT record label. Sun Goes By was one of their major hits in the summer of 1972. Some of their other songs included Try A Little Harder, written by Steve Kennedy, and One More Mountain To Climb by Neil Sedaka. Doug Riley died on August 27, 2007.

Singles:

Try A Little Harder	GRT 1233 06	1971
One More Mountain To Climb	GRT 1233 07	1971
Gospel Rock	GRT 1233 10	1972
Sun Goes By	GRT 1233 13	1972
Long Time Comin' Home	GRT 1233 15	1972
Tryin' Times	GRT 1233 17	1973

Albums/CDs:

Dr. Music	GRT 9233 1003	1972
Dr. Music Ii	GRT 9233 1004	1973
Retrospective	GRT 9230 1070	1975
Dreams (Doug Riley)	PM Records PMR 007	1976
Dr. Music Circa 1984 (EP)	CTL S5261	1984
Freedom (Doug Riley)	Duke DSRC 31066	1990

Annette Ducharme

Born and raised in the Francophone community of La Salle in Windsor, Ontario, Annette Ducharme's musical career started in the 1970s when she was in various bands. She moved to Vancouver in 1979 where she began to hone her craft as a songwriter, and became a member of the Bowers Ducharme Trio, who recorded the EP, *Slavery In Real Life* (Harvest 3001).

In 1985 at the West Coast Music Awards, she not only won for Most Promising Artist, but also caught the attention of Capitol Records, who signed her in 1988. The following year, the label released her debut album, *Blue Girl*.

Ducharme began releasing on her own label, Beggar's Bliss Records, beginning with, Sanctuary, in 1994.

Tom Cochrane recorded one of Ducharme's songs, Sinking Like a Sunset on his 1990 album, *Mad Mad World*. He also included three of her songs on his Ragged Ass Road album, one of which, *Best Waste of Time*, also appeared on *Ducharme's Bloom*.

Singles:
No Such Thing	Capitol 73082	1989
Sanctuary	Bliss CD 1000	1994
Change Your Mind	Bliss BK 9595	1995/96
Moral	Bliss BK 9595	1996
Tortured	Attack 1298	1997

Albums/CDs:
Blue Girl	Capitol 91980	1989
Sanctuary	Bliss 1000	1994
Bloom	Bliss BK 959 5	1995
Tortured	Attack 1298	1997

Earthboy

Mike Fonfara (keyboards)
Michael Hanson (vocals, guitar)
Marty Jones (bass)
Mladen (guitar)

Toronto based Earthboy started in 1996 when Michael Hanson, formerly the drummer for Glass Tiger, wanted to start his own group. Their sound has an orchestral pop style complemented by the contributions of Mladen, Marty Jones, and Mike Fonfara. In 1998 Rah Rah Records released their self-titled debut album, featuring Showers Over Everyone, the first single.

Singles:
Showers Over Everyone	Rah Rah 98 5001	1998
Shot	Rah Rah 98 5001	1998

Albums/CDs:
Earthboy	Rah Rah 98 5001	1998

Econoline Crush

Don Binns (bass)
Hack (guitars) Replaced by Ziggy Sigmond
Trevor Thornton Hurst (vocals)
Gregg Leask (drums) Replaced by Robert Wagner (1997);
Nico Quintal (1998)
Robbie Morfitt (guitars)
Daniel Douglas Yaremko (bass) Replaced by Ken Fleming (1997);
Tom Christianson (1998)

This Vancouver rock band was formed in 1992 by Trevor Thornton Hurst and Tom Ferris, formerly with Moev. In 1993 EMI released their EP, PURGE. Before the release of their first full length CD, *Affliction* in 1995, Hack had left the band. There were more personnel changes before the release of their second full length CD, *The Devil You Know* in 1997: Gregg Leask was replaced by Robert Wagner, Daniel Douglas Yaremko by Ken Fleming, and Ziggy Sigmond joined on guitars. Early in 1998, Fleming was replaced by Tom Christianson, and Wagner by Nico Quintal.

Singles:

T.D.M.	EMI 28989	1993
Wicked	EMI 32072	1995
Wicked (12")	EMI SPRO 1053	1995
Nowhere Now (12")	EMI SPRO 1113	1995
Nowhere Now	EMI 32072	1995
All That You Are	EMI 38244	1997/98
Sparkle And Shine	EMI 38244	1998
Surefire	EMI 38244	1999

Albums/CDs:

Purge (EP)	EMI 28989	1993
Affliction	EMI 32072	1995
Affliction (Blue Vinyl)	EMI 32072	1995
The Devil You Know	EMI 38244	1997
Brand New History	EMI 24574	2001

Edward Bear

Larry Evoy (drums, vocals)
Danny Marks (guitar) Replaced by Roger Ellis (1971)
Paul Weldon (organ) Replaced by Bob Kendall (1972)

Edward Bear started out as a five-piece band in 1967. They have the distinction of being the first Canadian act to have an album released without a prior hit single. Released on Capitol Records the album was called, *Bearings*. You, Me & Mexico, the first single, peaked at #3 on RPM's singles chart in 1970.

Originally classed as a rock and blues band, the success of Mexico made them a commercial hit and it led to the release of their second album, *Eclipse*. Evoy's vocalizing was recognized by critics as the main reason for Edward Bear's instant success. In September, 1972 came another hit single, Last Song. Written and sung by Evoy it went on to become a Number One smash in both Canada and the United States and sell sold over a million copies.

The group went through some personnel changes beginning with Danny Marks (who was replaced by Roger Ellis) after the completion of, *Eclipse*. Weldon left in 1972 to concentrate on his graphic arts business and was replaced by Bob Kendall. When Ellis left in 1973 to start his own band in Los Angeles, Edward Bear became a duo. But Kendall was unhappy and he left after the release of the Capitol single, Walking On Back, written by Kendall. He was replaced by Barry Best in 1974.

The backup group for Edward Bear was Potatoes who played with the band until 1975 when they went out on their own. They were comprised of Randy Gulliver, Tim Wynveen, Denny Deporter, Carl Pamminger and Bill Loop.

Evoy continued to perform until the mid 1970s as Edward Bear with the backup group Horizon. In 1978 he recorded under his own name and had minor success as a solo artist.

In 1984 Capitol released, *The Best of Bear*. From it came the single, God Bless Us Now, which was only serviced to radio stations Last Song was certified a million seller on March 15, 11973 and was inducted into Canadian Songwriters Hall of Fame in 2015.

Singles:

You, Me & Mexico	Capitol 72603	1970
You Can't Deny It	Capitol 72622	1970/71
Spirit Song	Capitol 72638	1971
Fly Across the Sea	Capitol 72653	1972
Masquerade	Capitol 72662	1972
Last Song	Capitol 72677	1972/73
Close Your Eyes	Capitol 72692	1973
Walking On Back	Capitol 72709	1973
Coming Home Christmas	Capitol 72715	1973
Same Old Feeling	Capitol 72722	1974
Freedom For The Stallion	Capitol 72734	1974
On And On	Capitol 72756	1975
Perfect Strangers (Larry Evoy)	Attic AT 135	1976

Here I Go Again (Larry Evoy)	Attic AT 171	1978
Dreams (Larry Evoy)	Attic AT 199	1978
God Bless Now	Capitol 72943	1984
Feels Right	URS 101	1985

Albums/CDs:

Bearings	Capitol SKAO 6238	1969
Eclipse	Capitol SKAO 6349	1970
Eclipse (EP)	EB1	1970
Edward Bear	Capitol ST 6387	1972
Close Your Eyes	Capitol SKAO 6395	1973
Larry Evoy	Attic LAT 1049	1978
The Best of The Bear	Capitol SN 66154	1984
The Edward Bear Collection	Cap C2 26585	1991

Cliff Edwards

Montreal born Cliff Edwards became a professional entertainer in 1963, when he was lead singer of The Counts Four, a rock 'n roll group that played clubs, dances, and some concerts. In 1965 they became known as The Five Bells who they played in New York's Copacabana, Miami's Americana Hotel, and Bermuda's Princess Resort. Shortened to The Bells in 1970, they had a major hit with Stay Awhile, written by Ken Tobias.

Cliff left The Bells in 1973 and recorded as a solo artist for Polydor, Columbia, A&M, Boot Records, and Cliff's own label, Timeframe. He also attended Loyalist College in Belleville, Ontario where he studied television. He then worked as a camera operator and set designer at CKWS TV in Kingston, Ontario, associate producer and actor in the sitcom, Bright Side on CJOH TV in Ottawa, an account executive at Pontiac Buick for MacLaren Advertising, and artistic director for the Town Hall Heritage Theatre in Wingham.

Singles:

Uncle Dad and Auntie Mom	Polydor 2065 150	1972/73
Carry On (as Cliff & Ann Edwards)	Polydor 2065 194	1973
Carpenter of Wood	Polydor 2065 203	1973
Say Goodbye To Anne	Polydor 2065 218	1974
Love May Be The Answer	Columbia 4 4026	1974
Singer of Songs	A&M 400	1975
Song For Wendy	A&M 406	1976
(There's A) Fire Burning Still	A&M 417	1976

What's Forever For	Boot 280	1980
Grab The Money And Run	Boot 299	1981
Easier Said Than Done	Polydor 2065 124	1981
Keep Your Hands Off	Boot 317	1982
Storm	LMS 002	1984
She's My Woman	TFP 001	1989
Highway #1		1989/90
Sailing (EP)	Concept Audio	2013

Albums/CDs:

Transitions	Polydor 2424 071	1974
Singer Of Songs	A&M SP 9021	1976
What's Forever For	Boot BOS 7222	1981
From A Quiet Room	TimeFrame	1989
Through The Years	Summit Sound	2013
Undercurrent	Artisan 703679	2016

Shirley Eikhard

Born on November 7, 1955 in Sackville, N.B., Shirley Eikhard grew up in a showbusiness family. At 13 she was a hit at the Mariposa Folk Festival, had her first recording contract at 14, and at 17 played in Las Vegas. Growing up in Oshawa, Ontario, her father drove her to auditions and concerts, where she played all kinds of music from folk to blues to rock. Early in her musical career she demonstrated an ability to write songs, such as, It Takes Time, which Anne Murray recorded in 1971. She also wrote Something in Your Face, recorded in 1971 by Donna Ramsey, and Don't Try to Please, also recorded in 1971 by The Sanderlings, a teenaged singing group from Newfoundland.

Eikhard's first single as a recording artist was Smiling Wine in the spring of 1972. Her biggest hit was Say You Love Me in the summer of 1976. The following year she stopped recording and concentrated on writing more of her own music, and for the next ten years she experimented on her own record label, which was called Eika Records. Two Singles:, It's Understood (her first bilingual record) and Someone Else came out in 1986, and the album, *Taking Charge* in 1987.

She won a 1991 Grammy award for her song, Something To Talk About which Bonnie Raitt recorded on her Grammy winning album, *Luck Of The Draw*. Eikhard also wrote Kick Start My Heart for Alannah Myles on her self-titled debut album. She changed musical styles with two jazz collections, *Going Home* (1998) and, *The Last Hurrah* (2000).

Singles:

It Takes Time	Capitol 3197	1971
Smiling Wine	Capitol 3281	1972
Right On Believin'	Capitol 3578	1973
Rescue Me	Capitol 3798	1974
Play A Little Bit Longer	Attic AT 109	1975
Sure Thing	Attic AT 120	1975
I Just Wanted You To Know	Attic AT 125	1976
Say You Love Me	Attic AT 129	1976
Let Me Down Easy	Attic AT 141	1976
Someday Soon	Attic AT 162	1977
Don't Let Me Down	Attic AT 166	1977
I Don't Want To Lose Your Love	Attic AT 176	1977
Never Givin' Up On You	Eika 45 01	1982
Clever Girl	Eika 45 02	1983
Rumours	Eika 45 03	1983
Always Someone Else	Eika 45 04	1985
It's Understood	Eika 45 05	1986
Someone Else	Eika 45 07	1986
Take The Fall	Denon CAN9023	1995/96

Albums/CDs:

Shirley Eikhard	Capitol ST 6371	1972
Child Of The Present	Attic LAT 1007	1975
Let Me Down Easy	Attic LAT 1021	1976
Horizons	Attic LAT 1032	1977
Taking Charge	Eika 25 48531	1987
If I Had My Way	Denon CAN9023	1995
Going Home	Artisan 57890	1998
The Last Hurrah	SEM 1199	2000
Stuck In The Groove	SEM 079312	2007
Riding On The 65	SEM 084992	2008
Just Call Me Alice	SEM 2009	2009
Dream Of A Perfect Day	SEM 005422	2012
My Day In The Sun	SEM 2014	2014

The Emeralds

John Hayman (electric guitar, background vocals)
Ron Musselwhite (drums, lead vocals) Replaced by Wayne Connors (1964)
Earl Newhall (bass, background vocals)
Ross Sully (alto and baritone sax, background vocals)
Paul Wright (piano, background vocals)

The Emeralds started in 1960 in their hometown of Richmond Hill, Ontario. Dressed in green uniforms, they played all over Ontario and opened for Bobby Curtola, Sandy Selsie, The Charmaines, and many others.

Ooh Poo Pah Do, the group's first single in 1962, was a remake of R&B singer Jesse Hill's 1960 hit. The Emeralds second single, Please Believe Me, came out in 1963. That same year, Ron Musselwhite left and was replaced by Wayne Connors from Little Caesar and The Consuls. The Emeralds also changed their name to The Shades of Blue and The Suedes before calling it quits in 1967.

Singles:
Ooh Poo Pah Do	Hallmark 7370	1962
Please Believe Me	Tamarack TTM 605	1963

Rik Emmett

Born on July 10, 1953 in Toronto, Ontario, Rik Emmett was a member of the Toronto rock band Triumph. In 1987, he was offered to play guitar in such groups as Asia and Damn Yankees. However, he turned them all down because he liked the freedoms associated with being a solo performer.

In 1990 Duke Street Records released his debut solo album, *Absolutely*. His second effort, *Ipso Facto*, was released in 1992. The song, Out of the Blue was written with Stevie Ray Vaughn in mind, while Rainbow Man was Emmett's tribute to blues legend Robert Johnson and the impact his music had on Muddy Waters, Howlin' Wolf, T. Bone Walker, B.B. King and Chuck Berry.

Recently, Emmett has recorded a series of instrumental recordings that bridge all guitar styles from flamenco and folk to soft jazz, and blues oriented swing and rock. His first, *Ten Invitations From the Mistress of Mr. E*, originally came out in 1997 and was re released in 1998.

Singles:
Big Lie	Duke StreetDSR 31068	1990
When A Heart Breaks	Duke StreetDSR 31068	1990/91
Saved By Love	Duke StreetDSR 31068	1991
World Of Wonder	Duke StreetDSR 31068	1991
The Way That You Love Me	Duke StreetDSR 31068	1991
Bang On	Duke StreetDSR 31079	1992
Dig A Little Deeper	Duke StreetDSR 31079	1992/93
Heaven In Your Heart	Duke StreetDSR 31079	1993
Let Me Be The One	Duke StreetDSR 31096	1995
Anything You Say	Duke StreetDSR 31096	1995

Albums/CDs:
Absolutely	Duke Street31068	1990
Ipso Facto	Duke Street31079	1992

The Spiral Notebook	Duke Street 31096	1995
Ten Invitations From The Mistress Of Mr. E	Open House 174	1997
Swing Shift	Open House 305	1998
Raw Quartet	Open House 93022	1999
Live At Berklee	Open House 11712	2000

Eric's Trip

Julie Doiron   (bass, vocals)
Chris Thompson (guitar)
Ed   Vaughan   (drums) Replaced by Mark Gaudet (1992)
Rick White   (guitar, vocals)

Named after a song recorded by Sonic Youth on their 1988 album *Daydream Nation*, Eric's Trip hailed from Moncton, New Brunswick where they formed in June 1990. In 1991, Ed Vaughan left the group and was replaced by Mark Gaudet, who joined in January 1992. Signed to the Seattle based Sub Pop label in 1992, they became well known on the alternative music scene in Halifax, Nova Scotia. Eric's Trip broke up in 1996. Rick White formed Elevator To Hell with Mark Gaudet, who renamed themselves Elevator Through in 1999 with the release of their third album on Sub Pop, *Vague Premonition* (SPCD 461). As Elevator To Hell, their two previous releases were Parts 1 – 3 (SPCD 365) and *Eerieconsiliation* (SPCD 399).

Julie Doiron recorded under the moniker of Broken Girl on Sappy Records including *Dog Love Part II* (1993), a seven inch single called Nora (1995), and a self-titled CD, *Broken Girl* (SAPPY 009   1996). In 1997 Julie Doiron's debut solo album, *Loneliest in the Morning*, was released on the Sub Pop label (SPCD 398). Two years later came an EP, *Will You Still Love Me* (Tree 13) and the full length CD, *Julie Doiron and The Wooden Stars* (Sappy 0202) and the all French recording, *Desormis* (Endearing   NDR 030) in 2001.

Singles:
Belong		1992
My Room	Subpop 234B	1993
View Master	Subpop 268B	1994
Stove	Subpop 234B	1994
The Gordon Street Haunting	Subpop 266B	1994
Sun Coming Up	Subpop 333	1996

Albums/CDs:

Songs About Chris (Ep)	Subpop 205B	1993
Love Tara	Subpop 234B	1993
Peter (EP)	Murder 002	1993
The Gordon Street Haunting(Ep)	Subpop 266B	1994
Forever Again	Subpop 268B	1994
Eric's Trip	Sonic Unyon Ss02B	1995
Julie and The Porthole To Dimentia (Ep)	Sappy 001	1995
Purple Blue	Subpop 333	1995
Long Days Ride Til Tomorrow	Sappy SAP 017	1997
The Eric's Trip Show	Teen 3025	2001

Eritage

Marc Benoit (bass, guitar)
Benoit Bourque (jig dancer extraordinaire)
Yvan Brault (piano)
Raynald Ouellet (accordion)
Vincent Ouellet (fiddle)
Raymond Philippe (percussion, flute)

This six-member bilingual folk group from Quebec was formed in the spring of 1977 by Raynald Ouellet, Jean Pierre Joyal and Marc Benoit. They began their musical career at the Tele Capitale television network in Quebec City, where they taped shows for two folk based music shows, Gentil' Alouette and Folklore en Tete. On stage, Eritage specialized in a program of songs, dances, jigs, reels, rags and cakewalks.

Eritage played at many folk festivals throughout Canada and the United States. They recorded five Albums, three of which were produced for the Catholic School of Quebec: *LA Poulette Grise, L'alouette Chante Encore,* and *Chansons De Toutes Les Couleurs.*

Their first non-children's album was their 1979 self-titled debut on Son D'Or Records, *Eritage*. In 1982 they recorded *La Ronde Des Voyageurs,* which was produced by the late Stan Rogers. Eritage broke up on April 12, 1985.

Albums/CDs:

Eritage	Son D'or SD 2000	1979
La Poulette Grise	SelectSSC 13077	1980
L'alouette Chante Encore	SelectSSC 13080	1981
Chansons De Toutes Les Couleurs	SelectSSC 13081	1981
La Ronde Des Voyageurs	Fogarty's Cove Music 006	1982

The Esquires

Gary Comeau (lead guitar) (1962 66)
Bob Harrington (lead vocals) Replaced by Don Norman (1964); Brian Lewis (1966)
Clint Herlihy (bass guitar) (1962 66)
Paul Huot (rhythm guitar)(1962 65)
Richard Patterson (drums)

Formed in 1962, the Ottawa-based Esquires played their first public performance at the Rockcliffe Air Base Teen Club. After joing the Musician's Union in 1963 they signed a two-year contract to play every Friday and Saturday night at the Pineland Dance Pavilion.

The major influence of the original members (Harrington, Comeau, Herlihy, Huot and Patterson) was Cliff Richard and The Shadows whose sound they wanted to duplicate. On stage they were a carbon copy of the English group.

Managed by Sandy Gardner who was a columnist for The Ottawa Journal, the Esquires played with many rock 'n roll stars of the early and mid 1960s. On July 18, 1963 they were among the Canadian acts featured on Dick Clark's Caravan of Stars at Faucher Stadium with Gene Pitney, The Dovells, Paul and Paula and The Tymes. The Esquires also toured with The Dave Clark Five, The Beach Boys, Roy Orbison and The Rolling Stones.

Signed to Capitol Records, their first single was Atlantis in 1963, followed by the instrumental smash, Man From Adano in 1964. Their album, *Introducing The Esquires*, was released the same year. They switched to Columbia Records in 1966. At Bell Studios in New York City they recorded two singles for the label, It's A Dirty Shame and Love Hides A Multitude of Sins.

In 1967 the Esquires disbanded. They reunited in 1987 for the 25th anniversary of the group. The lineup was comprised of Don Norman, Gary Comeau, Clint Hierlihy, Paul Huot, Brian Lewicki, and Richard Patterson.

Through the years 1962 – 66 the members of the group included Gail Thompson, Bert Hurd, Ted Gerow, John Cassidy, Bernie Jessome, Doug Orr, Bruce Cockburn, Robert Coulthart and Mike Argue.

Two music videos made by The Esquires in 1964 aired on MuchMusic in the mid-1990s: Man From Adano and Gee Whiz It's You. Bob Harrington died on February 7, 2005 in Victoria, B.C. and Richard Patterson on April 3, 2011.

Singles:

Atlantis/I've Lost My Girl	Capitol 72126	1963
Man From Adano/Gee Whiz It's You	Capitol 72137	1964
So Many Other Boys/The Oldest Story	Capitol 72193	1964/65
Cry Is All I Do/We've Got A Future	Capitol 72219	1965

Love's Made A Fool Of You/Summertime	Capitol 72277	1965
It's A Dirty Shame/Devoted To You	Columbia C4 2698	1966
Love Hides A Multitude Of Sins/ Why Should I Care?	Columbia C4 2705	1966/67

Albums/CDs:

Introducing The Esquires	Capitol T 6075	1964

David Essig

Born on December 2, 1945 in Frederick, Maryland, David Essig became a naturalized Canadian in 1978. Educated at George Washington University and the University of Wisconsin, he moved to Elmsdale, Ontario (near Huntsville) in 1971 to start a career as a folksinger.

He began appearing at film festivals across Canada and in 1974 he founded his own record label, Woodshed (later New Woodshed). From 1983 to 1985 he was writer and host for the CBC country music radio show, Six Days On The Road, and has been a commentator on other CBC variety and music programs.

His popularity extended to Italy and Switzerland. In the latter, he made his European debut at Mahogany Hall in Berne in 1980. He was also the first Canadian to perform at the National Folk Festival of Australia in 1989.

Essig's first recording was, *Redbird Country* on his Woodshed label. His other Albums include *Stewart Crossing, In The Tradition*, and *Rebel Flag: David Essig Live In Italy*. He has also recorded for the Appaloosa label.

Albums/CDs:

Redbird Country	Woodshed WS 001	1974
High Ground	Woodshed WS 002	1975
Stewart Crossing	Woodshed WS 006	1976
Sequence	POS/Wood PWS 012	1978
In the Tradition	Phonadisc PHE 6014	1981
While Living in the Good Years	Appaloosa AP 041/NWS 016	1984
Whose Muddy Shoes	Appaloosa AP 051	1986
Two Kayagum Solos (CS)	New Woodshed NWS 018	1986
Running Light (CS)	New Woodshed NWS 019	1987
Morning Calm (CS)	New Woodshed NWS CD1	1988
Rebel Flag: David Essig Live In Italy	Appaloosa AP 072	1990
Tremble and Weep	Appaloosa AP 126	1996
Declaration Day	Appaloosa AP-154	2002
Stone in My Pocket	Pacific Music 12032	2004

Double Vision	Watershed 021245	2008
Moon on Rough Bay	Watershed	2012

The Eternals

John Hildebrand (guitar)
Harry Hildebrand (bass)
Ron Paley (keyboards)
Ted Paley (drums)

This five-man band made a name for themselves in their native Winnipeg by recording covers of old and established hits, such as the Del Vikings' Come Go With Me and Buddy Holly's Raining In My Heart. Group members Ron Paley and Harry Hildebrand wrote some of the band's original material, such as Girl In The Window, which the group recorded on Quality Records.

Their 1968 hit, Falling Tears was written by Ottawan Dave Britten, and featured string and horn arrangements by CBC musical director Bob Mcmullin. Randy Bachman, then a member of The Guess Who, wrote their last hit, The Real World of Marianne.

Singles:

Girl In The Window	Quality 1856	1967
Come Go With Me	Quality 1884	1967
Raining In My Heart	Quality 1889	1967
Santa Claus Is Comin' To Town	Quality 1896	1967
Falling Tears	Quality 1902	1968
The Real World of Marianne	Quality 1915	1968
My Woman	Quality 1922	1969

Everyday People

David Hare (keyboards)
Pamela Marsh (vocals, vocals)
Alan Muggeridge (drums)
Christ Paputts (rhythm guitar, vocals)
Carson Richards (bass)
Bruce Wheaton (vocals, lead guitar)

Formed in Toronto in the fall of 1969 by Bruce Wheaton, Everyday People was signed to GRT Records. Of their many single releases, I Like What I Like was called "the hottest dance song to come along in years" by Cream Magazine. The group broke up in 1974 when Wheaton moved to Halifax, Nova Scotia to start the group Molly Oliver with Carson Richards.

Singles:
You Make Me Wonder	GRT 1233 01	1970/71
I Get That Feeling	GRT 1233 05	1971
Don't Wait For Tomorrow	GRT 1233 08	1972
I Like What I Like	GRT 1233 12	1972
Feelin' Better Already	GRT 1233 14	1972
Today I Feel Like Being Happy	GRT 1233 16	1972
Memories		1972

Album:
Everyday People	GRT 9233 1002	1971

Eria Fachin

Born in Hamilton, Ontario, Eria Fachin had accomplished a lot in her short career. Her work included performing on jingles, movie soundtracks and syndicated television shows. Her biggest success came in 1988 with the release of her album, *My Name is Eria Fachin*. The first single, Savin' Myself became an international dance hit and was charted in both the United Kingdom and United States, where it reached #50 in 1988 on Billboard's Hot 100.

She entertained across Canada and the United States, and often helped out the less fortunate by attending fundraising charity events.

On May 9, 1996 she died of cancer in Oakville, Ontario.

Singles:
Savin' Myself	Power PX7 200	1988
Your Love Just Came Too Late	Power PX7 201	1988
I Hear A Symphony	Power PX7 211	1989

Albums/CDs:
My Name Is Eria Fachin Power	PXH 2000	1988

Percy Faith

Born in Toronto on April 17, 1908, Percy Faith was one of Canada's foremost composer/conductors. When he was an eighteen-year-old student at the Toronto Conservatory of Music he burned his hands putting out a fire on the clothing of his three year old sister. The accident forced him to change his promising career as a pianist, so he turned to conducting and arranging.

In 1933 he was hired by the CBC as composer/conductor, and in 1940 he moved to United States where he became musical director of such radio shows as The Contented Hour. He also became an American citizen.

Faith joined Columbia Records in 1950 and it was not long before he had a string of hits beginning with I Cross My Fingers, On Top Of Old Smoky and Song From Moulin Rouge. His biggest success was The Theme From A Summer Place, which was number one for nine weeks on Billboard's Hot 100 in 1960.

At Columbia he arranged music for many of the label's stable of artists, including Guy Mitchell, Tony Bennett, Doris Day, The Four Lads, and Frankie Laine, and he recorded more than fifty Albums. Faith died on February 9, 1976.

Singles:

I Cross My Fingers	Columbia 38786	1950
All My Love	Columbia 38918	1950
Christmas In Killarney	Columbia 38918	1950
On Top Of Old Smoky	Columbia 39328	1951
When The Saints Go Marching In	Columbia 39528	1951
I Want To Be Near You	Columbia 39528	1951
Delicado	Columbia 39708	1952
Swedish Rhapsody	Columbia 39944	1953
Song From Moulin Rouge	Columbia 39944	1953
Return To Paradise	Columbia 39998	1953
Many Times	Columbia 40076	1953
Genevieve	Columbia 2332	1953
Dream Dream Dream	Columbia 40185	1954
The Bandit	Columbia 40323	1954
Petite	Columbia 40390	1954
Song For Sweethearts	Columbia 40277	1954
Land of the Pharoahs	Columbia 40482	1955
Valley Valaparaiso	Columbia 40633	1956
We All Need Love	Columbia 40644	1956
With A Little Bit Of Luck	Columbia 40696	1956
The Last Dance	Columbia 40826	1957
Theme From A Summer Place	Columbia 41490	1960
Theme For Young Lovers	Columbia 41655	1960
Zorba	Columbia 44734	1968

Hello Tomorrow	Columbia 44932	1969
Spinning Wheel	Columbia 44987	1969
I Don't Know How To Love Him	Columbia 45297	1971
Anytime of the Year	Columbia 45374	1971
Airport Love Theme	Columbia 45114	1971
Diamonds Are Forever	Columbia 45525	1971
Love Theme From The Godfather	Columbia 45563	1972
Theme From Chinatown	CBS 10010	1974
Summer Place '76	CBS 10233	1975

Albums/CDs:

Continental Music	Columbia CL 525	1952
Romantic Music	Columbia CL 526	1952
Music Until Midnight	Columbia CL 551	1952
Music From Kismet	Columbia CL 550	1952
Music From Hollywood	Columbia CL 577	1953
Music Of Christmas	Columbia CL 588	1953
Music From House Of Flowers	Columbia CL 640	1954
Amour, Amor, Amore	Columbia CL 643	1955
Viva The Music Of Mexico	Columbia CS 8038	1957
Football Songs	Columbia CL 6148	1957
AMERICAN Waltzes	Columbia CL 6178	1957
Fascinating Rhythms	Columbia CL 6203	1958
Carnival Rhythms	Columbia CL 6242	1958
Music For Her	Columbia CL 702	1958
Bouquet	Columbia CS 8124	1959
Malaguena	Columbia CS 8081	1959
My Fair Lady	Columbia CL 895	1959
Touchdown!	Columbia CL 1182	1959
Hallelujah!	Columbia CL 1187	1959
Music Of Christmas	Columbia CL 1381	1960
Bon Voyage!	Columbia CS 8214	1960
The Sound Of Music	Columbia CS 8215	1960
Jealousy	Columbia CS 8292	1960
Greatest Hits	Columbia CL 1493	1960
Camelot	Columbia CS 8370	1960
Tara's Theme & Other Themes	Columbia CS 8427	1960
Carefree	Columbia CS 8360	1961
Mucho Gusto!	Columbia CS 8439	1961
Bouquet Of Love	Columbia CS 8481	1961
Subways Are For Sleeping	Columbia CS 8533	1962
Hollywood's Great Love Themes	Columbia CS 8583	1962
The Music Of Brazil	Columbia CL 1822	1962
Great Folk Themes	Columbia CL 2108	1963
THEMES FOR Younglovers	Columbia CS 8823	1963
Broadway Bouquet	Columbia CL 2356	1964
Themes For The In Crowd	Columbia CS 9241	1965
Christmas Is	Columbia CS 9377	1965

Plays The Academy Award Winner	Columbia CS 9450	1966
For Those In Love	Columbia CS 9610	1968
Angel Of The Morning	Columbia CS 9706	1968
Those Were The Days	Columbia CS 9762	1969
Windmills Of Your Mind	Columbia CS 9835	1969
Love Theme From Romeo & Juliet	Columbia CS 9906	1969
Leaving On A Jet Plane	Columbia CS 9983	1970
Today's Great Movie Themes	Columbia CS 1019	1970
Percy Faith Play The Beatles	Columbia KC 30097	1970
Time For Love	Columbia KC 30230	1971
I Think I Love You	Columbia KC 30502	1971
Black Magic Woman	Columbia KC 30800	1971
JESUS CHRIST Superstar	Columbia CA 31042	1971
Joy	Columbia CA 31301	1972
Day By Day	Columbia KC 31627	1972
New Thing	Columbia KC 32803	1974
Disco Party	Columbia KC 33549	1975
Summer Place '76	Columbia KC 33915	1975

Robert Farnon

Born in Toronto, Ontario on July 24, 1917, Robert Farnon studied piano at age seven with his mother. In 1930 he began playing drums in his brother Brian's dance band and also studied percussion under Duncan Snider. Four years later, he switched to the trumpet and played in several dance bands of Gus Browne, Stanley St. John, Bob Shuttleworth, Geoffrey Waddington, and Percy Faith's CRBC (CBC) orchestra. From 1937 to 1943 Farnon was a member of The Happy Gang.

In addition to arranging music for Faith in the 1930s, Farnon also started writing his own symphonies. His first, Symphonic Suite, was completed in 1940 and made its premiere on January 7, 1941 when it was performed by The Toronto Symphony Orchestra. His second symphony was first heard on the CBC radio program, Concert Hour in 1943.

During World War II he was music director for The Army Show, where he conducted the Canadian band of the Allied Expeditionary Forces in Canada and later in England, where they were heard on the BBC.

While in England he started writing film scores for such British and Hollywood films as Elizabeth of Ladymead (1947), His Majesty O'Keefe (1953), The Little Hut (1957), and The Road To Hong Kong (1962).

Farnon's recordings date back to the late 1940s and early 1950s when he recorded for Decca. His compositions range from classical pieces to contemporary tunes. Among those who have recorded his music include Oscar Peterson (The Pleasure of Your Company) and The Winnipeg Symphony Orchestra (Scherzo for Trumpet and Orchestra). In 1959 Pye Records in England released the two volume set, *The Music of Robert Farmpm Volume I* (NPL 18025) and *Volume II* (NPL 18033), which honored Farnon's contribution to popular music. In 1958 he makes his home in Guernsey in the Channel Islands where he lived until his death on April 23, 2005.

Albums/CDs:

Robert Farnon Concert	Decca LM 4509	1950
Flirtation Walk	LondonLL 1053	1954
Something To Remember You By	LondonLL 1231	1955
Canadian Impressions	LondonLL 1267	1956
Melody Fair: The Music Of..	LondonLL 1280	1956
Sensuous Strings Of...	Phillips PHM 200 058	1958
Pictures In The Fire	LondonLL. 1667	1959
Music Of Robert Farnon	Dominion 1230	1959
Robert Farnon Concert	LondonLPB. 126	1960
Cocktails For Two	RHP B 20005	1963
By A Waterfall	RHP B 20006	1963
Stephen Foster Melodies	LondonLPB. 258	1964
Robert Farnon And Orchestra Play The Hits Of Sinatra	Phillips BL 7672	1965
Conducts My Fair Lady And Other Musical Bouquets	Phillips 652 064	1968
Portraitof THE WEST	Long SYM LW 156	1969
Rhapsody For Violin & Orchestra	Chappell 44900	1969
Pop Makes Progress	CPS.39001	1970
The Music Of Robert Farnon	Poly NCB 2382.008	1971
Showcase For Soloists	Invicta CINV 105	1973
At The Royal Festival Hall	Pey NSPH 400	1975
Golden Hour Presents the Best..	GH 601	1975
Conducts His Music For Captain Horatio Hornblower And Rhapsody For Violin & Orchestra	Citadel CT 7009	1979
Captain Horatio Hornblower: Concert Works	RR 47 CD	1992
Journey Into Melody	Conifer Classics	1996
British Light Music	Marco Polo/Nexus 93401	1997
The Lost Recordings	Cowtown CD 01	1997
More Lost Recordings	Cowtown CD 02	1998
Sketches Of Sinatra And Bennett	Castle/SEL/CD 533	1999

Stephen Fearing

Stephen Fearing was born in Vancouver, British Columbia on January 12, 1963. At the age of seven, Stephen Fearing moved with his family to Dublin, Ireland where he spent his formative years. By the mid 1980s, he had returned to his hometown of Vancouver. In 1988 he released his first independent album, *Out To Sea*, followed two years later by his second, *Blue Line*.

Stephen's abilities as a songwriter, along with his smokey voice and unique guitar stylings, has contributed much to his success. He impressed Bernie Finkelstein enough to get him signed to his True North label in 1991. Fearing's debut album, *The Assasin's Apprentice* came out in 1993. The first single was Expectations.

During the winter of 1995 96, Fearing joined Colin Linden and Tom Wilson of Junkhouse to form Blackie and *The Rodeo Kings*. Their first CD, released in 1996, was *High Or Hurtin': The Songs Of Willie P. Bennett*.

Singles:
Race Of Fractions	True North CDNK 650	1991
Expectations	True North TNK 84	1993
The Bells of Morning	True North TNK 76	1994

Albums/CDs:
Out To Sea	Aural Tradition ATR 301 1	1988
Blue Line	True North TNK 76	1990
The Assassin's Apprentice	True North TNK 84	1993
Industrial Lullaby	True North TSND 0151	1997
So Many Miles Live	True North TND0215	2000
That's How I Walk	True North TND0266	2002
Yellow Jacket	True North TND 110	2006
Fearing And White	Lowden 20111	2011
Between Hurricanes	Lowden 20131	2013

Ferron

Born Debbie Foisy on June 2, 1952 in Vancouver, Ferron (a name which means iron and rust) learned to play the guitar at eleven. She made her professional debut in 1974 at a benefit for The Women's Press Gang, with the song Who Loses. A former waitress, cab driver and jack of all trades, her music has attracted a strong following. Her self-titled debut album came out in 1977 on her own label, Lucy

Records. Her album, *Testimony* became a feminine anthem in the 1980s, and helped establish her as one of today's most respected poet/songwriters. She made her major label debut on Warner Brothers 1996 with the release of *Still Riot*.

In addition to recording her own material, her songs have been included in three compilations: *Ain't Life a Brook* in the acoustic collection, *The Acoustic Edge*; Sunshine in the lullaby collection, *Hand in Hand*, and *It Won't Take Long*, written by Ferron and recorded by the Indigo Girls, on *Spirit of '73: Rock for Choice*.

Among those who have recorded Ferron's songs are James Keelaghan, Holly Near, Cathy Fink and Lucie Blue Tremblay.

Single:

Who Loses	Stony PlainSPL 1036	1981

Albums/CDs:

Ferron	Lucy Records LR 001	1977
Backed Up	Lucy Records LR 002	1978
Testimony	Lucy Records LR 003	1980
Shadows on a Dime	Lucy Records LR 004	1984
Phantom Center	Chameleon 74830	1990
Resting with the Question	Cherrywood Station CW 006	1992
Not a Still Life	Cherrywood Station CW 007	1992
Driver	Earthbeat 942564	1994
Phantom Center	Earthbeat 942576	1995
Still Riot	Warner CDW 46292	1996

The Fifth

Jimmy Grabowsky (organ)
Richard Gwizdak (bass)
Melvyn Ksionzek (guitar)
Ron Rene (vocals) Replaced by George Belanger
Barry Zdbiak (drums) Replaced by Vance Masters

This Winnipeg based group's origins began in the northern Manitoban town of Gimli. Their first hit single was Yesterday's Today written by bassist Melvyn C. Ksionzek on London Records. It received the Lloyd C. Moffat Award in 1968 as the year's best Canadian produced rock recording. The Fifth had one more national hit in December 1967 and early 1968 with Tears, also on London Records. They changed their name to Next in 1970, and released the album, Dusty Shoes in 1971. The lead singer of Next was George Belanger, who later fronted Harlequin. Ron Rene later joined the punk band, The Litter in Minneapolis.

By The Fifth
Singles:
Yesterday's Today	London17355	1967
Tears	London17358	1967
All I Want Is Love	London17362	1968
Sunshine People	London17368	1969
You Don't Seem To Care	Franklin 635	1970
Gotta Get Up	Franklin 637	1970

By Next
Single:
Which Way	Warner Bros WB 4011	1971

Album:
Dusty Shoes	Warner Bros WB 9009	1971

54-40

Phil Comparelli (guitar, trumpet, vocals)
Brad Merritt (bass)
Darryl Neudorf (drums)   Replaced by Matt Johnson (1985)
Neil Osborne (vocals)

Formed in 1980 in Vancouver, British Columbia, 54-40 was the brainchild of Neil Osborne and Brad Merritt. They first opened for DOA at the Smilin' Buddha, which they later immortalized in their 1994 CD, *Smilin' Buddha Cabaret*. After establishing themselves throughout the Pacific Northwest, they recorded two EPs on the independent Mo Da Mu label: Things Are Still Coming Ashore and Selection. During those early days they toured with such bands as PiL, Wall of Voodoo, and Romeo Void.

Originally a trio comprised of Osborne, Merritt, and Darryl Neudorf, the addition of Phil Comparelli in 1984 complemented the band's sound. In 1985 Neudorf left and was replaced by Matt Johnson, formerly with the group French Letters.

The name 54-40 came from a U.S. presidential slogan, "54 40 or fight", used by James Polk, to expand the U.S. border north past the 49th parallel. The numbers "54 40" indicate the precise geographical reference where the stars and stripes were supposed to fly.

In June 1986 Warner/Reprise released the self-titled debut album, which included the Singles:, I Go Blind and Baby Ran. A year later came the album, *Show Me*, and in July 1989 came their next album, *Fight for Love*.

By 1991 they had signed with Sony Music, who released their critically acclaimed, *Dear Dear*. Their popularity continued with subsequent releases in the 1990s, and they are now one of Canada's most successful bands.

Singles:

What To Do Now	Wea 25 54361	1984
Sound Of Truth	Wea 25 54361	1984
Christmas Time	Wea	1984
Baby Ran (12")	PRO 5440	1986
One Day In Your Life	Warner 92 79237	1988
Walk In Line	Wea 92 57721	1988
One Gun	Wea 92 57721	1988
2000 Years Of Love	Wea	1988
Miss You	Reprise 92 59611	1989
Baby Ran	Reprise 92 54401	1989
I Go Blind	Reprise 92 54401	1990
Baby Have Some Faith	Reprise 92 59611	1990
Nice To Luv You	Columbia CK 05440	1992
She La	Columbia CDNK 714	1992
Music Man	Columbia CK 05540	1992
You Don't Get Away (That Easy)	Columbia CDNK 786	1993
We Are, We Pretend	Columbia CK 05440	1993
Blame Your Parents	Columbia CK 80190	1994
Assoholic	Columbia CDNK 971	1994
Ocean Pearl	Columbia CK 80190	1994
Radio Luv Song	Columbia CK 80190	1995
Lucy	Columbia CK 80190	1995
Love You All	Columbia CK 80231	1996
Lies To Me	Columbia CK 80231	1996
Crossing A Canyon	Columbia CK 80231	1996/97
I Love Candy	Columbia CK 80231	1997
Since When	Columbia CK 80336	1998
Lost And Lazy	Columbia CK 80336	1999
Ocean Pearl	Columbia CK 80461	1999
Casual Viewin'	Columbia CK 80540	2000

Albums/CDs:

Selection (Ep)	Mo Da Mu	1982
Set The Fire	Wea 25 54361	1984
54-40	Reprise 92 54401	1986
Show Me	Wea 92 55721	1987
Fight For Love	Reprise 92 59611	1989
Sweeter Things	Warner 30857	1991
Dear Dear	Columbia CK 05440	1992
Smilin' Buddha Cabaret	Columbia CK 80190	1994

Trusted By Millions	Columbia CK 80231	1996
The Sound Of Truth	Columbia CK 80279	1997
Since When	Columbia CK 80336	1998
Heavy Mellow (Live)	Columbia C2K 80461	1999
Casual Viewin'	Columbia CK 80540	2000
Goodbye Flatland	Divine Industries SBCK 3012	2003
Yes To Everything	True North TND 365	2005
Essentials	Warner 262516	2005
Northern Soul	True North TND 517	2008
A History Unplugged	Ounded Bird	2010
Lost In The City	Smilin' Buddah SBEC 1082	2011
La Difference		2016

Figgy Duff

Geoff Butler (button accordion, flute)
Bruce Crummell (electric guitar)
Noel Dinn (vocals, drums, bodhran, keyboards)
Philip Dinn (bodhran, backing vocals)
Rob Laidlaw (bass)
Frank Maher (accordion)
Pamela Morgan (lead vocals, acoustic guitar, keyboards, tin whistle)
Dave Panting (bass, acoustic guitar, mandolin)
Derek Pelley (bass, background vocals)
Kelly Russell (violin)
Jamie Snider (vocals, fiddle, electric guitar)
Art Stoyles (accordion)

Noel Dinn founded Figgy Duff in 1974 in Newfoundland. The genesis of the group goes back to the 1960s when he was a member of the 1960s rock band, Lukey's Boat. Travelling across Newfoundland to Montreal and London, England, he wanted to form a group that played the music of his ancestors with his powerful drumming.

Pamela Morgan's classical background and Dinn's rock influence combined to help make the group's music take shape. Although their music is rooted primarily in folk, they tried to incorporate a few elements of rock, especially in their jigs and reels.

Their self-titled debut album was first released on Dingle's Records in 1980. In 1990 they began writing their own songs on the album, *Weather Out The Storm*. Their last album, *Downstream*, contained all original material.

The group dissolved following the death of Noel Dinn on July 26, 1993.

Pamela Morgan recorded the album, *The Colour of Amber* with Anita Best (Amber Music ACD 9008 1991) and the solo album, *On a Wing and a Prayer* in 1996 (A&M/Sleeping Giant Music 7001).

Albums/CDs:

Figgy Duff	Dingle's Records DIN 326	1980
Weather Out The Storm	Hypnotic 1000	1990
After The Tempest	Boot BOS 7243	1991
DOWNSTREAM	Hypnotic 1009	1993
A Retrospective 1974 1993	Duckworth 50325/EMI 23627	1995

The Five D

Jack Arsenault (rhythm guitar, vocals)
Brian Bradfield (drums)
Brad Campbell (bass, vocals)
Marc Corbin (guitar, vocals)
Jim Pagliaro (drums)
Dave Poulin (lead vocals)
Keith Richardson (vocals, guitar)

From Ottawa, Ontario, The Five D, were a pop/rock group who recorded for the Sir John A label.

They started out in 1965 as The Fifth Dimension but had to change their name to avoid conflict with an American group of the same name. Their first hit was Baby Boy in 1967.

That same year, Marc Corbin and Jim Pagliaro joined the group when two members left. The band appeared on a live broadcast of the Centennial Celebrations on Parliament Hill with Queen Elizabeth II and Prince Philip. The group's farewell concert was also in July 1967 when they opened for The Who, The Troggs, and Ohio Express.

Singles:

Baby Boy	RG 1017	1967
Runnin' Around In Circles	Sir John A 1	1967
She Can't Be My Girl	Sir John A 5	1968

Fludd

Jorn (John) Anderson (drums, vocals)
Greg Godovitz (bass, vocals)
Brian Pilling (lead vocals, guitars)
Ed Pilling (lead vocals, harp, percussion)
Mick Walsh (guitar)

Fludd was formed in 1969 by brothers Brian and Ed Pilling, who had previously played in the band The Wages of Sin and had backed up Cat Stevens.

Originally a quartet, Peter Czankey made it a five-man band in 1972. In 1974 Gord Waszek was added as a replacement for Brian Pilling who left because of ill health. When he returned, Gord remained with the group. Godovitz, who left in 1974, formed the group Goddo.

Fludd's first two Singles:, Turned 21 and Get Up, Get Out and Move On were on the Warner Brothers label and were big hits. They continued to have hits on both Daffodil Records (1972 74) and Attic Records (1974 1976). The latter released a retrospective collection of the group's hits in 1977 called From The Attic '71 '77. They broke up when Brian Pilling died of cancer in 1978.

Singles:

Turned 21	Warner Bros 753	1971/72
Get Up, Get Out and Move On	Warner Bros 7576	1972
Always Be Thinking Of You	Daffodil DFS 1025	1972/73
Yes	Daffodil DFS 1032	1973
C'Mon C'Mon	Daffodil DFS 1037	1973
Cousin Mary	Daffodil DFS 1042	1973
I Held Out	Daffodil DFS 1047	1974
Brother And Me	Attic AT 100	1974
Dance Gypsy Dance	Attic AT 103	1974
What An Animal	Attic AT 107	1975
I'm On My Way	Attic AT 114	1975/76
Help Me Back	Attic AT 134	1976

Albums/CDs:

Fludd	Warner Bros 2578	1972
On!	Daffodil SBA 16020	1972
Great Expectations	Attic LAT 1001	1975
From The Attic '71 TO '77	Attic LAT 1027	1977
Greatest Expectations Best Of	Pace 003	1995

Flying Circus

Greg Grace (vocals, electric guitar, tambourine, kazoo)
Replaced by Sam See (1973)
Doug Rowe (lead vocals, electric & acoustic guitars, banjo, kazoo)
Colin Walker (drums)
Terry Wilkins (vocals, bass, mandolin, harmonica, kazoo)

Originally from Australia where they started in 1968, Flying Circus had a hit in 1969 with Hay Ride in their home country. From 1971 to 1974 they moved to Canada where they had major success with the Capitol single, Old Enough To Break My Heart.

After the release of their first album, Gypsy Road, Greg Grace was replaced by Sam See.

Doug Rowe died on July 23, 2015.

Singles:
Run Run Run	Columbia DO 8989	1972
Maple Lady	Capitol 72676	1972
Old Enough To Break My Heart	Capitol 72688	1973
Gypsy Road	Capitol 72711	1973
Morning Sets You Free	Capitol 72724	1973

Albums/CDs:
Flying Circus	Capitol ST 6391	1972
Gypsy Road	Capitol SKAO 6383	1972
Last Laugh	Capitol ST 6400	1973

FM

Martin Deller (drums, percussion)
Cameron Hawkins (synthesizers, vocals
Nash The Slash (violin, mandolin, vocals)

FM started out in Toronto in 1976 as a two-man electronic band comprised of Cameron Hawkins and Nash The Slash.

Hawkins was born in Toronto and first studied the cello at the Royal Conservatory of Music. When his friends in high school were all in rock bands he was organizing recitals for his twelve piece chamber orchestra. He eventually dropped classical music and picked up the bass guitar and later formed his own rock band. Cameron's love for the synthesizer helped bridge the gap between his classical training and yen for rock. At a CBC recording session he met Nash The Slash and the two of them started experimenting with the synthesizer, electric violin and mandolin.

They became a trio in 1977 when Martin Deller joined on drums. Born in Winnipeg, he was classically trained on piano and was first introduced to drums and percussion while attending high school in Nairobi. After graduation, he returned to Canada where he studied composition and electronic music at York University in Toronto. When he he wasn't playing with FM, he studied and taught music.

FM became an established act on the Toronto music scene, and recorded their debut album, Black Noise, which included the first single, Phasors On Stun. Shortly after its release, Nash The Slash left to start a solo career. Ben Mink, who would later produce k.d. lang and others, joined the group. He left in 1981. The group disbanded in 1987. Their album Black Noise was reissued on October 14, 2014 on vinyl and a collector's edition CD.   (see Nash The Slash)

Singles:

Phasors On Stun	Passport 1167 7916	1978
Rocket Roll	Passport PS 703	1979
Power	Passport PS 705	1980
It's Up To You	Passport PS 707	1980
Surface To Air	Passport PS 708	1980
Just Like You	Quality 2463	1985
All of The Dreams		1986
Why Don't You Take It	MCA 52840	1986
Dream Girl		1987
Good Vibrations	Duke 71042	1987
Magic (In Your Eyes)		1988
Retroactive	NSHSD 1194	

Albums/CDs:

Black Noise	Passport PL 4001	1977
Direct To Disk	Labyrinth LBR 1001	1978
Surveillance	Passport PB 2001	1979
City Of Fear	Passport PB 2028	1980
Con Test	Quality SV 2138	1985
Tonight	Duke DSR 31042	1987
Hideaway (Interactive CD ROM)	Now See Hear NSH 1095	1995

Peter Foldy

This Hungarian born singer/songwriter moved to Sydney, Australia with his parents in 1956, and arrived in Toronto, Ontario, nine years later. In 1976, Peter Foldy became a Canadian citizen.
He scored a major hit in Canada with the self-penned hit Bondi Junction in 1973, which was about a place in Australia.
   Shortly after its release he went to Hollywood where he played bit parts in such movies as The Last Detail (1973) and The Paper Chase (1973). In the late 1970s he moved to Los Angeles where he later appeared in the film, Roadie (1980) with Alice Cooper, Meat Loaf and Blondie.
In the early 1980s Foldy returned to music. He co-wrote with fellow Canadian David Daniels the hit, Let's Start Again for Australian singer Samantha Sang. Foldy then performed in the Los Angeles production of Hair.
Today, he is a writer/director of films.

Singles:
Bondi Junction	Kanata 1015	1973
I'll Never Know	Kanata 1019	1973
When I Am So In Love	Kanata 1020	1974
Christmas Eve With You	Kanata 1022	1974
Roxanne	Capitol 72775	1976
Julie Ann	Capitol 72783	1977
Love City	Free Flight PB 11692	1979
School of Love		1981

Album:
Peter Foldy	Kanata KAN 12	1974

49th Parallel

Dennis Abbott (vocals) Replaced by Doran Beattie (1969)
Terry Bare (drums)
Dan Lowe (guitar)
Rob Carlson (guitar)
Dave Petch (organ) Replaced by Jack Velker (1968)
Mick Woodhouse (bass) Replaced by Dan Severins & Gary Stasiuk (1966), Dave Downey (1968)

This Calgary group started out in 1966 as The Shades and The Shades of Blonde when they dyed their hair. Under the latter name, they recorded the song, All Your Love, which was only available on an EP with other groups of their vintage until a CD retrospective of their work came out in 1997.

The lineup of the group consisted of Dennis Abbott, Dan Lowe, Rob Carlson, Dave Petch, Mick Woodhouse, and Terry Bare. In 1966 they had two other bass players, Dan Severins and Gary Stasiuk. Other members of the group included Alf Cook (on bass) and Dennis Mundy (on organ).

In 1967 The Shades of Blonde changed their name to the 49th Parallel. Their first two singles were Labourer and She Says on RCA.

Their only album, *49th Parallel*, came out in 1969.

By the following year, many of the original members of the group had left and they changed their name to Painter, and then Hammersmith.

(see Painter and Hammersmith)

Singles:

Labourer	RCA 57 3428	1967
She Says	RCA 57 3447	1968
Blue Bonnie Blue	Venture 612	1968
Twilight Woman	Venture 1004	1969
Now That I'm A Man	Venture 1011	1969
I Need You	Barry 3518	1970

Albums/CDs:

49th Parallel	Maverick MAS 7001	1969
49th Parallel (CD R)	Pace 019	1997

David Foster

Born on November 1, 1949 in Victoria, British Columbia, David Foster started playing the piano at age five. In his teens he worked in England with a Victoria band called The Strangers. He later went to Toronto where he played with Ronnie Hawkins.

While a member of the Vancouver group, Skylark, he went to Los Angeles where he worked as a studio musician for the likes of Michael Jackson, George Harrison, Rod Stewart, Barbra Streisand and others.

Under the tutelage of Quincy Jones, Foster became a producer began in 1976. Some of the acts he has produced over the years include Celine Dion, Peter Allen, Chicago, Alice Cooper, Hall and Oates, and Boz Scaggs.

In 1982 he released his first album as a solo artist, *The Best of Me*. Three years later, he returned to Vancouver where he co wrote and produced Tears Are Not Enough, a benefit recording for Ethiopian famine relief.

David Foster was inducted into the Juno Hall of Fame in 1997.

Singles:

Love Theme From St. Elmo's Fire (Man In Motion)	ATL 78 98257	1985
The Best of Me (with Olivia Newton John)	ATL 78 94207	1986
Who's Gonna Love You Tonight	ATL 78 93767	1986
Winter Games	ATL 78 91407	1988
And When She Danced (w/Marilyn Martin)	ATL 78 90297	1988

Albums/CDs:

David Foster	Atlantic 78 16421	1986
The Symphony Sessions	Atlantic 78 17994	1988
River of Love	Atlantic 82162	1991
Play it Again	Atlantic 82296	1991
The David Foster Christmas Album	Interscope INTSD 92295	1993

Fosterchild

Barry Boothman (bass)
Jim Foster (guitar, vocals)
Gerry Wand (drums)
Vern Wills (guitar, vocals)
Peter Sweetzir (keyboards)

Jim Foster, a native of Victoria, British Columbia, was a radio addict and began playing guitar at thirteen. Vern Wills was an army brat born in Calgary, who joined his first band at the age of twelve. Foster and Wills first met when their respective bands performed at a local teen hangout, The Haunted House, in Calgary. Not content to remain with a bar band, Wills left Canada for New York where he became a member of the group, The Walkers. When he had problems renewing his work visa, he returned to Calgary and rejoined Foster.

After a number of personnel changes, the group Fosterchild was born in 1976. The following year, they signed a record deal with CBS Records. Until We Meet Again was their first hit in 1977. They continued to record for CBS and broke up in the early 1980s. Foster recorded the solo album, *Power Lines* (RCA NFL1 8056) in 1986.

Singles:

Magic Is In The Air	Columbia C4 4163	1977
Until We Meet Again	Columbia C4 4171	1977
I Need Somebody Tonight	Columbia C4 4174	1978
It's Too Late Now	Columbia C4 4195	1978
Behind The Eight Ball	Columbia C4 4202	1978

Albums/CDs:

Fosterchild	CBS PES 90382	1977
Troubled Child	CBS PCC 80003	1978
On The Prowl	Vera Cruz VCR 1008	1980

The Four Lads

James Arnold (first tenor)
Frank Busseri (baritone)
Connie Codarini (bass)
Bernard Toorish (second tenor)

Growing up in Toronto, Ontario, this vocal quartet started out as choirboys in St. Michael's Cathedral Choir School. James Arnold, Frank Busseri, Connie Codarini and Bernard Toorish became known as The Four Dukes in 1947. They also went under the name The Jordanaires when they sang religious music. In 1949, they made their CBC radio debut on Elwood Glover's Canadian Cavalcade.

In 1950 they went to a concert by their favorite group, The Golden Gate Quartet, a major gospel act at that time. When the four from Toronto went backstage to mimic them, Olandus Wilson of the Golden Gate Quartet encouraged them to send a demo to their manager Mike Stewart, who arranged for them to sing at Le Ruban Bleu, a nightclub in New York owned by impressario Julius Monk. He suggested they change their name to the Four Lads, since another group in Detroit called themselves The Four Dukes.

When Mitch Miller at Columbia Records heard the Four Lads, he arranged for them to sing backup for Johnny Ray. On October 16, 1951 they recorded Cry. They also continued to sing backup on other artists associated with the label, including Doris Day and Frankie Laine.

After signing a contract with Columbia Records in 1952, The Four Lads recorded their first hit, The Mockingbird. Throughout the 1950s they had a number of hits, including Istanbul (Not Constantinople), Moments To Remember, Standing On The Corner, and Put A Light In The Window.

On television, they made their debut on The Ransom Sherman Show on NBC in 1950. Other TV appearances included The Pat Boone Chevy Showroom on ABC, and The Steve Allen Show on NBC. The Four Lads also hosted Upbeat on CBS during the summer of 1955, and were regulars on Perry Presents on NBC in July 1959.

Today, The Four Lads are still together, with Frank Busseri being the only original member left. They were inducted into the Juno Hall of Fame in 1984.

Singles:

Tired of Loving You	OKEH 6860	1952
The Mockingbird	OKEH 6885	1952
Somebody Loves Me	Columbia 39865	1952
He Who Has Love	Columbia 39958	1953
Down by the River Side	Columbia 2218/40005	1953
I Should Have Told You Long Ago	Columbia 40082	1953
Istanbul (Not Constantinople)	Columbia 40082	1953
Oh, That'll be Joyful	Columbia 2435	1954
Gilly Gilly Ossenfeffer Katenellen Bogen by the Sea	Columbia 40236	1954
Skokiaan	Columbia 40306	1954
Rain, Rain, Rain	Columbia 40295	1954
Moments to Remember	Columbia 40539	1955
I Heard The Angels Singing	Columbia 40600	1955
No, Not Much	Columbia 40629	1956
I'll Never Know	Columbia 40629	1956
Standing on the Corner	Columbia 40674	1956
My Little Angel	Columbia 40674	1956
The Mocking Bird	Epic 9150	1956
The Bus Stop Song (A Paper of Pins)	Columbia 40736	1956
A House With Love in It	Columbia 40736	1956
Who Needs You	Columbia 40811	1957
It's So Easy to Forget	Columbia 40811	1957
I Just Don't Know	Columbia 40914	1957
Put A Light in the Window	Columbia 41058	1957/58
There's Only One of You	Columbia 41136	1958
Enchanted Island	Columbia 41194	1958
The Mocking Bird	Columbia 41266	1958
The Girl on Page 44	Columbia 41310	1959
The Fountain of Youth	Columbia 41365	1959
Happy Anniversary	Columbia 41497	1959

Albums/CDs:

Stage Show	Columbia CL 2576	1954
On The Sunny Side	Columbia CL 912	1956
The Four Lads Sing Frank Loesser	Columbia CL 1045	1957
Four on the Aisle	Columbia CL 1111	1958
Breezin' Along	Columbia CL 1223	1958
Greatest Hits	Columbia CL 1235	1958
Four Lads Swing Along	Columbia CL 1299	1959
High Spirits	Columbia CL 1407	1959
Love Affair	Columbia CL 1502	1960
Hits of the 60s	Dot DLP 3438	1960
Twelve Hits	Kapp KL 1224	1961
Dixieland Doin's	Kapp KL 1254	1961
This Year's Top Motion Picture Songs	UA UAL 3356	1962

Songs Of World War II	UA UAL 3399	1962
Moments To Remember	CSP 14391	1986
16 Most Requested Songs The 50S I	Columbia CK 45110	1989
16 Most Requested Songs The 50S II	Columbia CK 45111	1989
16 Most Requested Songs	Legacy CK 46158	1991

Freedom

Rene Boileau (bass)
Del Desrosiers (bass) Repld Les Larue (1970)
Franki Hart (lead vocals, piano, recorder)
Bill Hill (lead guitar)
Eddie Kaye (drums)
Rick St. Jean (rhythm guitar, vocals)

Montreal's Freedom started in 1969. Their first single and album, both titled *Doctor Tom*, came out in 1970 on the Aquarius label. When they learned that an American group had the same name as theirs, Freedom became Freedom North. After two more singles in 1971, they broke up.

Singles:
Doctor Tom	Aquarius 5005	1970
Losing You	Aquarius 5006	1970
Ordinary Man	Aquarius 5008	1971
Gone Forever	Aquarius 5015	1971

Album:
Doctor Tom	Aquarius 501	1970

Frozen Ghost

Sammy D. Bartel (keyboards)
John Bouvette (drums)
Wolf Hassel (bass)
Arnold Lanni (vocals, guitar)

Formed in 1985 by Arnold Lanni and Wolf Hassel, both former members of Sheriff, Frozen Ghost released their self-titled debut album in 1987 with Warner Music Canada.

Lanni is the singer, songwriter, producer, and leader. As a member of Sheriff, he wrote When I'm With You, which was a hit in 1983 and 1989. The second time around it went to number one on Billboard's Hot 100.

Their second album, *Nice Place To Visit*, came out in 1988, and their third, *Shake Your Spirit*, in 1992. In the four years between albums, Lanni worked on new material and produced other artists such as Wild T & The Spirit.

Singles:

Should I See	Wea 25 84097	1987
Round And Round	Wea PRO 621	1988
Yum Bai Ya	Wea 25 80927	1988
Pauper In Paradise	Wea 25 77657	1989
Dream Come True	Wea PRO 642	1989
Head Over Heels	Wea 75149	1992
Shake Your Spirit	Wea 75149	1992
Cry (If You Want You)	Wea 75149	1992
Shine On Me	Wea 75149	1992

Albums/CDs:

Frozen Ghost	Wea 25 45651	1987
Nice Place To Visit	Wea 25 57051	1988
Shake Your Spirit	Wea 75149	1992

Georgette Fry

Born in St. Jerome, Quebec, Georgette Fry first became interested in music through her father, who played the guitar. She received her first guitar at age ten from her parents, and not long after fell in love with the blues after hearing Etta James.

She started playing professionally in 1975, and has been in several bands. Her first, Comfort, played country/rock, and were together from 1976 to 1978. Other members included Bill Joslin, Fred Hannah, Bruce Hamilton, and Jeff Green. She was then in The Bill Joslin Band, which was comprised of Joslin, Fry, Robin Roberts, Jim Gore, and Grant Heckman. When Joslin grew tired of playing in the band that bore his name, he changed it to the Running Shoe Review. By 1981 the group was down to the duo of Joslin and Fry, and together they played for six years. Georgette then moved to London, Ontario where she became involved in two bands, an acoustic blues trio called One Flight Up and the R&B flavored Georgette Fry Band. She has been a member of Electricity and played with the duo of Haines and Leighton.

In 1992 she recorded the four song cassette, *Ankle Deep*, which included Slow Water and Don't Leave Me Guessin', the two songs that helped her win a songwriting competition in London a year earlier. Fry has performed with the Kingston Symphony Orchestra, the Prince George Symphony and at the Standard Bank Jazz Festival in Grahamstown, South Africa. She is backed up by The B Sides Blues Band: Jim Preston on guitar, Zak Colbert on bass, Dirt Clancy on drums, and Pete Pereira on sax.

Albums/CDs:

Rites Of Passage	SRR 002	1995
Georgette Live	SRR 003	1997
Let Me Drive	SRR 004	2001
Back In A Moment	EMI 491758	2007

Nelly Furtado

Nelly Furtado was born on December 2, 1978 in Victoria, B.C. Her love of music started in childhood when she sang duets with her mother in church. At age nine she learned to play the ukulele and trombone and by the time she was twelve she had started writing songs. In her teens she was in a marching band. After she graduated from Mount Douglas Secondary School in 1996, she joined the hip hop group, the Plains of Fascination and sang vocals on their album, Join The Ranks. After this experience she invited Newkirk to become half of a hip hop duo, Nelstar, but it didn't last.

At a Honey Jam Talent Show she met singer Gerald Eaton from The Philosopher Kings who helped her release her debut album, *Whoa, Nelly* in 2000. Her next, Folklore(2003), featured the song, Foria, which became the official anthem of the 2004 European Football Championship.

She was criticized for the theme of female sexuality over her album, Loose (2005). She became the first North American artist to reach number one on the Billboard Latin Albums Chart with, *Mi Plan*, on October 3, 2009.

Singles:

I'm Like A Bird	Dreamworks DRMD 509192	2000
Turn Off The Light	Dreamworks DRMD 450891	2001
On The Radio (Remember The Days) Powerless	Dreamworks DRMD 450856	2002

(Say What You Want)	Dreamworks DEMD 504645	2003
Try	Dreamworks DRMD 505113	2004
Forca	Dreamworks DRMD 862823	2004
Maneater	Geffen 859585	2006
Promiscuous	Geffen 706030	2006
All Good Things Come To An End	Geffen 714378	2006
Say It Right	Geffen 729728	2007
Give It To Me	Interscope 732199	2007
Do It	Polydor MIUC 77028	2007
Jump	Atlantic 346898	2009
Morning After Dark	Interscope 728036	2009
Who Wants To Be Alone	Musical Freedom MIUCT 8388	2010
Hot'n'Fun	Interscope 492731	2010
Big Hoops (Bigger The Better)	Interscope 203454	2012

Albums/CDs:

Whoa Nelly!	Dreamworks 503292	2000
Folklore	Dreamworks 505089	2003
Loose	Geffen 853919	2006
Loose – The Concert	Geffen 032102	2007
Mi Plan	Universal 331802	2009
Best Of	Geffen 755381	2010
Spirit Indestructible	Intersccope 14406	2012

B.B. Gabor

B.B. Gabor (Gabor Hegedus), a refugee from Hungary and a talented singer/songwriter/producer, built up a loyal following in Toronto in the early 1970s. By 1980 he had formed his own backup group, The Instabands.

He signed a contract with Anthem Records, and his first single was the two sided hit, Nyet, Nyet Soviet (Soviet Jewellery) and Moscow Drug Club, a Russian folk song that describes an underground location where people used to escape from the KGB. As producer, he worked with the female new wave group, The Curse, Jimi Bertucci and Dean Taggert. B.B. Gabor died in Toronto on January 17, 1990.

Singles:

Nyet Nyet Soviet (Soviet Jewellery)	Anthem ANS 019	1980
Jealous Girl	Anthem ANS 038	1981
Little Thing	Anthem ANS 040	1981

Albums/CDs:

B.B. Gabor	Anthem ANR 1 1021	1980
Girls Of The Future	Anthem ANR 1 1034	1981

André Gagnon

The youngest of nineteen children, André Gagnon was born in Saint Pacome de Kamouraska, Quebec in 1942. He became fascinated by the piano at age three while watching his older sister, who was an organist at the local church. At age four, he took piano lessons and at six he began composing short pieces. In 1961 he went to study in Paris on a grant from the Quebec government. A year later, he returned to Canada and worked with fellow Quebec singer/songwriter Claude Leveillee. In 1967 he received his diploma from the Conservatoire de musique de Montreal and arranged to put on an all Mozart program, which launched his career.

A year later he signed a contract with Columbia Records.

Although his achievements have been mostly in the classical field, his 1976 album *Neiges* became a best seller and earned him a Juno Award.

His subsequent recordings, such as Surprise, Donna and Mouvements, quickly established him in the pop and disco fields. He has also composed music for such movies such as Running and The Pianist. In 1979 he received the Order of Canada, and the William Harold Moon Award in 1993 from the Society of Composers, Authors and Music Publishers (SOCAN). Today he ranks as one of Canada's internationally known pianists, and is the most popular instrumental recording artist in Japan. Star Records released Gagnon's soundtrack to the movie Juliette Pomerleau in 1999.

Singles:

Pour les amants	Columbia C4 7016	1968
Don't Ask Why	Columbia C4 2831	1968
Notre Amour	Columbia C4 7055	1969
Song For Petula	Columbia C4 2892	1969
Et Ariane	Columbia C4 7077	1969
Format 30	Columbia C4 7112	1970
Les chemins d'ete	Columbia C4 7119	1970
Summer Roads	Columbia C4 2927	1970
Rainbow	Columbia C4 2981	1970
Butterfly	Columbia C4 2990	1970
Wow	LondonL.2582	1976
Surprise	LondonL.2607	1976
Night Flight	Tekson 513	1977

Piano In The Sun	London L.2632	1977
Weekend	London L.2633	1977
Donna	London L.2646	1977
Comme en vacances	London L.2647	1977
Rendez Vous	London L.2672	1978
Ride To Ville Emard	London L.2695	1980
Rio Non Stop	CBS C5 4276	1981
Virage a gauche	CBS C5 4283	1981
Septieme ciel	CBS C5 4295	1982
Beau et chaud	CBS C5 4324	1982
Violetta	CBS 7CDN 32	1986
Comme dans un film	CBS 7CDN 43	1987
Cher Jean Paul	Star3045	1988
Des Dames de coeur	Star3049	1989

Albums/CDs:

Andre Gagnon, Piano Et Orchestre	Columbia FL 325	1964
Leveillee Gagnon	Columbia FL 331	1965
Une Voix, Deux Pianos	Columbia FL 662	1967
Pour Les Amants	Columbia FS 680	1968
Notre Amour	Columbia FS 694	1969
Mes Quatres Saisons	Columbia ES 90293	1969
Let It Be Me	Columbia ES 90034	1971
Les Grand Succes D'andre Gagnon	Columbia PCC 80070	1971
Projection	Columbia 90159	1973
Saga	LondonSP 44219	1974
Neiges	LondonSP 44252	1976
Le Saint Laurent	LondonSP 44301	1978
Mouvements	LondonSP 44311	1980
Virage A Gauche	Columbia PFC 80052	1981
Greatest Hits	CBS PCC 80070	1982
Impressions	CBS PCC 80085	1983
Comme Dans Un Film	Columbia PFC 80116	1986
Des Dames De Coeur	Star STR 4 8010	1988
Noel	Star STR 78038	1992
Presque Blue	Star STR 78039	1993
Les Jours Tranquilles	Star STR 78040	1993
Romantique	Star STR 78057	1994
Twilight Time	Star STR 8073	1995
Eden	Star STR 78096	1997
Juliette Pomerleau	Star STR 78108	1999

Gainsborough Gallery

Mel Degan (vocals)
Ray McAndrew (drums)
Tim McHugh (keyboards)
Peter Marley (guitar, vocals)
Denny Paul (bass)
Henry Small (violin, vocals)

From Calgary, Alberta, this sixman band started out in 1966 67 as The Skeptics. By the time they recorded their first single, My Little Red Book/Little By Little on Apex Records, they had changed their name to the Gainsborough Gallery.

In 1969 they went down to Clovis, New Mexico to record their only album, *Life is a Song*, which was produced by Norman Petty (Buddy Holly, Roy Orbison, Buddy Knox and another Alberta group, Wes Dakus and The Rebels).

By the end of 1972 the Gainsborough Gallery had broken up.

Singles:
Little Red Book/Little By Little	Apex 77075	1968
If You Knew	Apex 77081	1968
Life Is A Song	Reo 9026	1969/70
Ev'ry Man Hears Different Music	Reo 9030	1970
House On Soul Hill	Reo 9034	1970

Albums/CDs:
Life Is A Song	Reo 703	1970
Life Is A Song (U.S.)	Evolution 2012	1970

Lennie Gallant

Born in South Rustico, Prince Edward Island, Lennie Gallant has travelled extensively across Canada, Europe, the Middle East, and Mexico. His songwriting reflects his experiences, both at home and abroad, and often take the shape of story songs, while his music combines the Celtic and Acadian roots of his upbringing.

Gallant's debut album was the critically acclaimed Breakwater in 1988, which Canadian Composer called "a near perfect contemporary folk album." His subsequent albums ranged from Believing In Better, which showed the artist's versatility with a fusion of musical styles, to The Open Window, a more serious effort because it focused on songs about love and the hard life of the fishermen in the Maritimes. Both, Lifeline, and, Live, continued the artist's love for the folksong.

Singles:

Believing In Better	Revenant LGCD 102	1991
The Cry Of Love	Revenant LGCD 102	1992
Man Of Steel	Revenant LGCD 102	1992
Is It Love I Feel (Or The Courage I Lack)?	Revenant LGCD 102	1992/93
How Many Bridges	Revenant LGCD 102	1993
Embers	CBS CK 80196	1994
Which Way Does The River Run	CBS CK 80196	1994
Looking At The Moon	CBS CK 80196	1994
Peter's Dream	CBS CK 80196	1995
The Open Window	CBS CK 80196	1995
The Band's Still Playing	Force Ten	1997/98
Meet Me At The Oasis	Force Ten	1998

Albums/CDs:

Breakwater	Revenant LGC 101	1988
Believing In Better	Revenant LGCD 102	1991
The Open Window	CBS CK 80196	1994
Lifeline	Force Ten	1997
Live	Revenant 08622	2000

Patsy Gallant

From Campbellton, New Brunswick, Patsy Gallant was born in 1948. At a very young age her mother insisted she perform with her three older sisters. Billed as The Gallant Sisters, they performed in Quebec and recorded several singles in Montreal.

In 1967, Patsy decided to go solo, and recorded the single, Mon vin d'ete with Joel Denis. It led to TV appearances on Music Hop, Discotheque, Jeunesse Oblige, and Smash. She could sing in both English and French.

She met songwriter Yves Lapierre in 1969 and they become involved in a commecial jingle business. Her most famous jingle was for the Ford Motor Co, and her group was dubbed the Ford A Maniacs. She also met her future manager, Ian MacDonald. In Quebec she began singing movie themes, notably Theme From L'Initiation and Theme From Ya Pas De Trou A Perce.

Her English debut came in 1972 with the album, Upon My Own, and the single Get That Ball. Although she made other recordings in the 1970s and 1980s, her best known hit was From New York To L.A., an English disco version of Gilles Vigneault's Mon Pays.

Throughout the 1990s she has been performing in France and Quebec. In 1993, she played the leading role in a musical about French singer Edith Piaf that toured only in Quebec.

By The Gallant Sisters
Singles:

Viens chez moi	Fontaine 1514	1964
Mon coeur	ABC 4508	1965
Les hommes de 40 ans	Fantastic 3623	1965
Noel dans le vent	Fantastic 3637	1965

By Patsy Gallant
Singles:

Mon vin d'ete (w/Joel Denis)	Fantastic 3690	1967
La musique et la danse	Chance 607	1967
Mister Lewis	Barclay 60002	1968
Maman ne m'a pas dit	Initiation 501	1970
Nous irons ensemble	Gap 204	1971
Get That Ball	Columbia C4 3056	1972
I Don't Know Why	Columbia C4 3092	1971
Toi l'enfant	Columbia C4 4028	1972
Power	Columbia C4 4032	1972
Tout va trop vite	Columbia C4 7230	1972
Thank You Come Again	Columbia C4 7252	1973
Save The Last Dance For Me	Columbia C4 4041	1974
Raconte	Columbia C4 4050	1974
Karate	Columbia C4 4064	1974
Le lit qui craque	Columbia C4 4078	1974
Doctor's Orders	Columbia C4 4059	1974/75
Make My Living At Night	Columbia C4 4063	1975
Making Love In My Mind	Columbia C4 4084	1975
Les femmes	Columbia C4 4096	1975
Can't Make It	Columbia C4 4102	1975
J'ai le droit	Attic	1975
Mon Pays	Kebec DISC 10105	1976
From New York To L.A.	Attic AT 134	1976
Libre pour l'amour	Attic AT 146	1976
Are You Ready For Love	Attic AT 147	1977
Sugar Daddy	Attic AT 161	1977
Besoin d'amour	Attic AT 500	1977
Sugar Daddy	Attic AT 501	1977
Back To The City	Attic AT 172	1977/78
Will You Give Me Your Love		1978
Stay Awhile With Me	Attic AT 185	1978
Every Step Of The Way	Attic AT 187	1978
C'est l'amour	Attic AT 502	1978
Oh Michel	Attic AT 197	1978

Love Affair	Attic AT 202	1978
Michel	Attic AT 503	1978
C'est l'amour	Attic AT 504	1979
It's Got To Be You	DSP 132	1979
We'll Find A Way (with Dwayne Ford) 1979		
Everlasting Love	Hot Vinyl 1001	1980
How Many Lonely Nights	Hot Vinyl 1004	1980
Ce matin la	Trans-Canada TC 4	1980
Don't Forget About Me	Hot Vinyl 1007	1981
On peut croire au soleil	Trans-Canada TC 8	1981
Sasha	Trans-Canada TC 12	1981
Hit The Streets Tonight	Vamp 7504	1984
High Tech Girl	Vamp 7509	1984
Si je chante	Star 3003	1985

Albums/CDs:

Y'a Plus De Trou A Perce	Gap APS 2052	1971
Toi L'enfant	CBS FS 90096	1971
Upon My Own	CBS FS 90114	1972
Patsy Gallant	Columbia FS 90115	1972
Power	Columbia FS 90246	1974
Are You Ready For Love	Attic LAT 1017	1976
Besoin D'amour	Attic LATC 50000	1976
Will You Give Me Your Love	Attic LAT 1037	1977
Patsy	Attic LAT 1051	1978
Patsy Gallant Et Star	Attic LATF 5001	1978
Ses Plus Grands Succes	Attic LATF 5002	1978
Greatest Hits	Attic LAT 1078	1979
Stranger In The Mirror	Hot Vinyl 2001	1980
Amoureuse	Trans Can TCM 1004	1981
Take Another Lover	Vamp VR 102	1984

Garfield Band

Dennis French (drums, percussion)
Jacques Fillion (keyboards)
Garfield French (lead vocals)
Walter Lawrence (guitar, electric cello)
Paul O'Donnell (guitar, harmonica, banjo)
Chip Yarwood (flute, synthesizer)

The genesis of Garfield goes back to 1971 when its lead vocalist Garfield French graduated from high school in Scarborough, Ontario. After travelling to Europe where he honed his skills as a composer, he and Paul O'Donnell worked as a duo back in Toronto. They later merged with Dennis French's band and became known as Garfield in 1973. For the next three years they worked hard to perfect their sound, and in 1976 Mercury Records released their debut album, Strange Streets. From it came their first hit, Old Time Movies. A second album, *Out There Tonight* followed in 1977. After taking two years off to reassess the band's future, they returned to the studio to record their third album, *Reason To Be*, which was released in December 1979. Two years later came their fourth, and last album, *Flights of Fantasy*. Other members of the group included Maris Tora, Neil Nickator and Dan Donovan on bass, Barry Hutt and Terry Watkinson on keyboards, Mike Phillips on congas, and Steve Kennedy on sax.

Singles:
Old Time Movies	MercuryM 73800	1976
Give My Love to Anne	MercuryM 73845	1976
All Alone Again	Polydor 2065 377	1978
Buffalo to Boston	Polydor 2065 420	1980
Like I Love You		1981
High Class		1981

Albums/CDs:
Strange Streets	MercurySRM 1 1082	1976
Out There Tonight	Polydor 2424 167	1977
Reason to Be	Polydor 2424 183	1979
Flights of Fantasy	Polydor 2424 225	1981

Gary and Dave

Gary Weeks (vocals)
Dave Beckett (vocals)

This duo from London, Ontario, began performing together in 1966 when they auditioned at a United Appeal concert and came in fourth. Both were psychology majors at the University of Western Ontario.

On stage, Gary was the straight man, while Dave played the clown. They sang original compositions, comedy numbers, and hits by such artists as Creedence Clearwater Revival and Three Dog Night. Dave would add his own funny imitations of Stay Awhile (The Bells hit) as a fourteen-year-old Viennese choirboy, and an a capella song called Linoleum in which Dave used his own absurd lyrics. Together they would perform Lighthouse's One Fine Morning with a kazoo. Their act was widely acclaimed throughout Europe, especially in Holland.

In 1970, Quality Records released Tender Woman, the duo's first single. They were one of the first acts signed to Greg Hambleton's Axe Records in April 1972. Their first single was You Can't Do It Now, and their biggest hit was Could You Ever Love Me Again in 1973. Twelve-year-old Michel Lesage from Montreal recorded a French version in 1974.

After a few more hits, the duo decided to stop recording and began working as pilots for Air Canada in 1975. A year later, they realized that music meant more to them than flying, and returned to music on a full-time basis with the backup group, the Stewart Brothers Band. In 1977 Axe released the album *14 Greatest Hits*. Two years later, they left the music business.

Singles:

Tender Woman	Quality 1977	1970
Can't You do it Now	Axe 2	1972
Here it Comes Again	Axe 7	1973
Could You Ever Love Me Again	Axe 10	1973
I Fell in Love With You Sometime	Axe 11	1974
It Might as Well Rain Until September	Axe 17	1974
I May Never See You Again	Axe 19	1974
What Can You Do About It?	Axe 22	1975
All in the Past Now	Axe 22	1975
I Can't Find the Words	Axe 25	1975
You Send Me	POL 2065 324	1976
It's Alright, My Darling	Axe 45	1977
I'll Always Love You	Axe 53	1978

Albums/CDs:

Together	AXS 503	1973
14 Greatest Hits of Gary & Dave	AXS 519	1977

Gary O

Gary O is the son of Billy O'Connor, who had one of the first Canadian music series on Canadian television.

Going back to the 1960s, Gary O's musical career started with the groups the Synics, Cat, Liverpool, and Aerial. In Liverpool, he and the rest of the group played covers of Beatles songs and released the Singles:, Dolly (Taurus TR 004) and Down To Liverpool (Taurus TR 007) in 1976. When they grew tired of playing covers, they played under the name of, Aerial and released two singles; Easy Love in 1978 and Tears That You Cry in 1980, and two albums, *In The Middle of The Night* (Anthem ANR 1 1011 1978) and *Maneuvers* (Anthem ANR 1 1026 1980).

After Aerial split up, Gary spent four years on the executive board of the Toronto Musician's Association, and formed the band, Kid Rainbow.

In January 1981 Gary decided on a solo career and shortened his last name. From his self-titled debut album came a cover of the old Hollies hit, Pay You Back With Interest.

Singles:
Pay You Back With Interest	Capitol	1981
I Believe in You	Capitol 72859	1981
Get It While You Can	RCA PB 13870	1984
Shades of 45	RCA PB 13985	1985

Albums/CDs:
Gary O	Capitol ST 12157	1981
Pretty Boy	RCA	1984

The Gemtones

Johnny Belser (drums)
Daryl Cail (bass, vocals)
Paul Marleau (lead vocals, guitar)
George Randall (rhythm guitar)
Brice Sinclair (vocals, piano)

This instrumental group from Moncton, New Brunswick formed in 1961 when Johnny Belser was invited to try out for a neighbourhand band. Johnny's mother was so impressed by them that she became their manager and booking agent. In their hometown they made a guest appearance at the local YMCA.

They were soon in popular demand and ended up playing throughout the Maritime provinces. Their first big break came when they were invited to appear on CFCF TV's Like Young teen show in Montreal.

Signed to the Banff/Rodeo label, their first album, The Fabulous Gemtones Play And Sing Hit Selections, came out in 1962. Before their next album was released, The Fabulous Gemtones Play Reno & Other Hits, Melbourne Records released the hit Singles:, Reno and Peace Pipe.

In addition to playing cover versions of hits from such bands as The Ventures and The Shadows, The Gemtones wrote their own instrumentals, one of which was Reno.

Singles:
Reno	Melbourne WG 3176	1963
Peace Pipe	Melbourne WG 3183	1963

Albums/CDs:

The Fabulous Gemtones Play & Sing Hit Selections	Banff RBS 1156	1962
The Fabulous Gemtones Play Reno & Other Hits	Banff RBS 1201	1963

Gettysbyrg Address

Orest Andrews (vocals)
Mike Hanford (keyboards, vocals)
Ron Savoie (drums) Replaced by Craig Hamblin
Bill Wallace (bass)
Kurt Winter (guitar)

This Winnipeg group began as The Shondels in 1964. Led by Mike Hanford, the rest of the group was comprised of Jack Wong, Gary Shaw, and Kenny Hordichuk. Their debut single on Eagle Records was Don't Put Me Down (1964). Wong later left to be replaced by Bill Wallace, who would later join The Guess Who in 1972. Danny Thompson replaced Shaw, while Hordichuk by Bob Hunter.

In 1967 they changed their name to Gettysbyrg Address, and began recording on the Winnipeg-based Franklin label which was distributed by Caravan. They also changed their singing style, from Hanford's British-influenced lyrics to the Motown sound. After Come Back To Me Baby in 1968, they broke up. Their final recording session produced two songs, Nothing Better To Do and Someday Sunday, which were released in 1969 under the name The Mind Explosion. A year later, a new version of Gettysbyrg Address was formed. They recorded the song Baby True for Franklin's compilation album, *Winnipeg Vol. 1*. Winter, who was in the first incarnation of Gettysbyrg Address, was a member of The Guess Who from 1972-74. He died on December 14, 1997.

By The Shondels
Singles:

Don't Put Me Down	Eagle 106	1964
Another Man	Col C4 2673	1966
In the World of Today	Col C4 2711	1966
I Take it Back	Col C4 2717	1967

By Gettysbyrg Address
Singles:

Love is a Beautiful Thing	Franklin 0100	1967
My Girl	Franklin 546	1967

Come Back Baby	Franklin 601	1968
Nothing Better to Do (as The Mind Explosion)	Franklin 621	1969

Nick Gilder

Born on December 21, 1951, in London, England, Nick Gilder moved to Vancouver, British Columbia when he was ten years old. In 1971 he formed the group Sweeney Todd with guitarist Jimmy McCulloch. Their biggest hit was Roxy Roller in 1976. That same year, he and McCulloch left the group and moved to Los Angeles. Gilder signed a recording contract with Chrysalis Records, who released his debut album, You Know Who You Are in 1977. In 1978, Gilder's Hot Child In The City went to number one on Billboard's Hot 100 on October 28, 1978. Although he had other hits into the 1980s, he was unable to duplicate the success of his only number one hit. He later relocated to Los Angeles. In 1994 he returned to Vancouver where he recorded with The Drive in 1997 and The Time Machine (since 1999). Today, he remains active as a singer/songwriter and performer.

Singles:

She's A Star (In Her Own Right)	Chrysalis CHS 2108	1976
Runaways In The Night	Chrysalis CHS 2161	1977
Rated X	Chrysalis CHS 2174	1977
Hot Child In The City	Chrysalis CHS 2226	1978
Here Comes The Night	Chrysalis CHS 2264	1978/79
(She's) One of The Boys	Chrysalis CHS 2304	1979
(You Really) Rock Me	Chrysalis CHS 2332	1979
Electric Love	Chrysalis CHS 2357	1979
Metro Jets	Chrysalis CHS 2382	1980
Wild Ones (Feeling Better)	Casablanca NBS 2289	1980
She Talks (Body Talk)	Casablanca NBS 2336	1981
Catch 22	Casablanca NBS 2302	1981
Prove It	Casablanca NBS 2333	1981
Let Me In	RCA PS 14177	1985
Let Me In (12" on red vinyl)	RCA JR 14182	1985
Footsteps	RCA PS 14268	1985/86
Cafe Heaven (with The Drive)	Gilder Records	1997
You're Everything	Spinner	1997
You're Everything	Page Music NG2000	1999
Roxy Roller/Hot Child In The City	Page Music NG2000	2000

Albums/CDs:

You Know Who You Are	Chrysalis CHR 1147	1977
City Nights	Chrysalis CHR 1202	1978
Frequency	Chrysalis CHR 1219	1979
Rock America	Casablanca NBLP 7243	1980
Body Talk Muzik	Casablanca NBLP 7259	1981
Nick Gilder	RCA NFL1 8051	1985
Stairways (The Drive)	Gilder Records SP 649	1997
Longtime Coming (The Time Machine)	Page/Oasis NG 2000	1999
The Best Of Nick Gilder: Hot Child In The City	Razor&Tie/BMG	2001

Bobby Gimby

Bobby Gimby was born on October 25, 1918 in Cabri, Saskatchewan.

His parents, two sisters and a brother were all musical. Together they formed a small band, and he bought his first trumpet through the mail.

From 1941 to 1943 he was lead trumpeter for Mart Kenney and His Western Gentlemen, one of Canada's most famous dance bands. He later served as storyteller and performer on CBC Radio's The Happy Gang from 1945 to 1955. On CBC TV he was musical director for the Juliette show.

His visit to Malaysia in the early 1960s inspired him to write the tune, Malaysia Forever, which topped the country's charts and became an unofficial national anthem.

Gimby's greatest contribution is the Centennial song, Canada, which he wrote in 1966. Two years earlier, in 1964, he was playing a band date in La Malbaie, Quebec on St. Jean Baptiste Day, and he was moved by the sight of fifty children parading through the streets in colorful costumes and singing a folk song in French. From that experience, he came up with Canada, which he wrote in both English and French.

During Canada's centennial year, he became known as "The Pied Piper of Canada." The cape he wore was designed by his daughter Lynn, who also decorated the heraldic trumpet he used to march with the children in each place he visited. His centennial song united young Canadians from coast to coast and there have been more than thirty recorded versions. All the royalties were donated to the Boy Scouts of Canada.

Up until his death on June 20, 1998, Gimby lead the band at the Leisure World Retirement Home in North Bay, Ontario.

Singles:

Santa Claus Rides Again	RCA 57 3269	1964
The Cricket Song	RCA 57 3274	1964
Canada (w/The Young Canada Singers)	Quality 1967	1967
Let's Get Together Canada Forever	Quality 1919	1968
What A Wonderful World	Quality 1929	1969
Manitoba Hundred		1970
The Cricket Song	Quality 2003	1971
Go British Columbia		1971

Albums/CDs:

The Golden Trumpet of Bobby Gimby	CTL S 5028	1963
Let's Get Together (The Pied Piper & The Kids)	Quality SV 1820	1970
Canada The Pied Piper & The Kids	ER 1377X	1973
Bobby Gimby And The Kids Present The Bunny Hop	Bobby Gimby 22	1977
Bobby Gimby Now	Bobby Gimby 23	1978

Ginger

Chris Hooper (drums)
Tom Hooper (bass)
Vincent Jones (keyboards)

With the departure of Kevin Kane in The Grapes of Wrath in 1992, the remaining three members reformed under the new name of Ginger. In 1993, they released a self-titled six song EP and toured Canada, opening for Sarah McLachlan. The following year came their first full length CD, Far Out, which included the hits Solid Ground, The Earth Revolves Around You, and the title track. By 1996 their second album, *Suddenly I Came To My Senses*, was released. The first single was Everything You're Missing. In 1997 Ginger dissolved when Kane reconciled with his former bandmates. (see Grapes Of Wrath)

Singles:

Earth Revolves Around You	Nettwerk 206320	1993
Try To Believe Me	Nettwerk 206320	1994
Solid Ground	Nettwerk 203084	1994
Far Out	Nettwerk 233086	1995
Everything's Funny	EMI 253959	1996
Here With Me	EMI 253959	1997

Albums/CDs:

Ginger (EP)	Nettwerk 206320	1993
Far Out	Nettwerk 230096	1994
Suddenly I Came To My Senses	EMI 253959	1996

The Girlfriends

Diane Miller (vocals)
Rhonda Silver (vocals)
Stephanie Taylor (vocals) Replaced by Patrician Anne (1966)

The Girlfriends from Toronto, Ontario were created by Les Pouilot and Stan Jacobson for the CBC TV show, Music Hop in 1963. In 1964 they recorded the single, I Will on the Hallmark label. Because there was an American group by the same name, The Girlfriends changed their name to The Willows in 1965.

Diane Miller was an experienced singer and dancer who had worked on The Tommy Ambrose Show and the C.N.E. Grandstand show. She also recorded two singles on Columbia Records in 1965: Mr. Teperman/Baby That's The Way It Goes and Hello Young Lovers/How Do You Feel. Rhonda Silver had been a professional singer since she was six, and had recorded three singles on Barry Records: Rockin' Reindeer (1960), Am I Old Enough To Know (1961), and Blue Party Dress (1963). Stephanie Taylor was the tall and serious one of the group, who played bit parts on some TV dramas and sang on CBC TV's Country Hoedown. In 1966, she left the trio and was replaced by Patrician Anne. Taylor became one of the female vocalists in Hagood Hardy's backup group The Montage, and later recorded on her own in the 1970s. The Girlfriends broke up in 1967.

By The Girlfriends
Single:

I Will	Hallmark	1964/65

By The Willows
Singles:

My Kinda Guy	MGM 13484	1966
Outside The City	MGM 13714	1967

Glass Tiger

Al Connelly (guitar)
Alan Frew (vocals)
Michael Hanson (drums)
Wayne Parker (bass)
Sam Reid (keyboards)

From Newmarket, Ontario, Glass Tiger was first known as Tokyo when they formed in 1982. In 1984, after they opened for the British group, Culture Club at Maple Leaf Gardens in Toronto, Tokyo were approached by Capitol Records who later signed the group under the new name of Glass Tiger.

Jim Vallance, who had written with Bryan Adams among others, produced Glass Tiger's debut album, *The Thin Red Line*, which was released in February 1986 and included the Singles:, Don't Forget Me (When I'm Gone), Someday, and the title track.

After the release of their second album, *Diamond Sun*, in April 1988, Michael Hanson left and was replaced by Tony Thompson, who had worked with David Bowie, Rod Stewart, Power Station, and Randall Coryell of Red Rider.

Glass Tiger broke up in 1992. Sam Reid opened his own studio in Toronto, Alan Frew released his first solo album, Hold On, in 1994, and Hanson started the group Earthboy.

Singles:

Don't Forget Me (When I'm Gone)	Capitol B 72992	1986
Someday	Capitol B 73004	1986
The Thin Red Line	Capitol B 72996	1986
You're What I Look For	Capitol B 73014	1987
I Will Be There	Capitol B 73021	1987
I'm Still Searching	Capitol B 73052	1988
Diamond Sun	Capitol B 73059	1988
Send Your Love	Capitol B 73071	1988/89
My Song	Capitol B SPRO 364	1988
Watching Worlds Crumble	Capitol B 73081	1989
Animal Heart	Capitol 92922	1991
The Rhythm Of Your Love	Capitol 92922	1991
My Town	Capitol 92922	1991
Rescued (By The Arms Of Love)	Capitol 92922	1991/92
Touch Of Your Hand	Capitol 27022	1993

Albums/CDs:

The Thin Red Line	Capitol ST 6527	1986
Diamond Sun	Capitol C1 48684	1988
Simple Mission	Capitol 92922	1991
Best Of The Best: Air Time	Capitol 27022	1993
Live In Concert	Linus 279006	2006

Goddo

Greg Godovitz (vocals, bass)
Marty Morin (drums) Replaced by Doug Inglis (1976)
Gino Scarpelli (guitar)

The genesis of Goddo goes back to 1964 when Greg Godovitz was in other rock bands such as The Pretty Ones, The Pyggs, Mushroom Castle (with Eddie Schwartz) and Sherman and Peabody. Goddo started in late 1974 after Godovitz left Fludd. Their first hit single, Louie Louie, in the summer of 1975 was a remake of The Kingsmen's 1963 hit.

Goddo's self-titled debut album on Polydor Records came out in 1977. In 1981, Attic Records released Pretty Bad Boys.

By 1983 the band shortened its name by one "d" and the members were all new: J.F. Leary (guitar), Matt Meehan O'Leary (drums), and Tommy Mack (bass).

In 1990 Attic released the retrospective CD, 12 Guauge Goddo: Blasts From The Past.

Godovitz's memoir, Travels With My Amp was published by Abbeyfield Publishers in 2001.

Singles:

Louie Louie	A&M 398	1975
There Goes My Baby	Polydor 2065 383	1977
Fortune In Men's Eyes	El Mocambo Esmo 511	1980/81
Pretty Bad Boy	Attic AT 250	1981/82
If Tomorrow Never Comes	Attic AT 263	1982
Was It Something I Said		1992

Albums/CDs:

Goddo	Polydor 2424 901	1977
Who Cares	Polydor 2424 902	1977
An Act of Goddo	Polydor 2424 189	1979
Best Seat In The House	Attic LAT 1107	1981
Pretty Bad Boys	Attic LAT 1120	1981
12 Gauge Goddo: Blasts From The Past	Bullseye BEBBD 6	1990
King Of The Broken Hearts	Justin Entertainment JED 21	1992
2ND Best Seat In The House	Bullseye BLPCD 2504	2001
Live	Linus 279011	2008

Gogh Van Go

Sandra Luciantonio (vocals)
Dan Tierney (vocals, guitar)

Daniel Tierney and Sandra Luciantonio first met in 1980 when they were students at the University of Guelph. Tierney, from Montreal, studied biology, while Luciantonio, from Sarnia, the fine arts. It was not until 1985 when they both moved to Montreal that they decided to form a group called The Hodads. For the next four years, they played the club circuits in Montreal and Toronto. They also opened for such diverse acts as Los Lobos, Chris Isaak, John Hiatt, and The Tragically Hip.

In 1989, The Hodads recorded a two-song, twelve-inch disc featuring Routine and Quand le soleil dit bonjour aux montagnes. The independent release was charted at many college radio stations across Canada.

Sandra and Don changed their moniker to Gogh Van Go in 1991. Signed to Audiogram Records in Montreal, their self-titled debut album was released in February 1993 and was produced by Pierre Marchand, whose credits included Sarah McLachlan's SOLACE, and The McGarrigle Sisters' Heartbeats Accelerating. Instant Karma, a remake of John Lennon's 1970 hit, was the first single from Gogh Van Go; the accompanying video was directed by James Di Salvio.

Singles:
Instant Karma	Audiogram ADCD 10058	1992
Bed Where We Hide	Audiogram ADCD 10058	1993
Say You Will	Audiogram ADCD 10058	1993
Call It Romance	Audiogram ADCD 10058	1994
Tunnel Of Trees	Audiogram ADCD 10058	1994
Meet Me In Heaven	Audiogram ADCD 10099	1997
Big Cook	Audiogram ADCD 10099	1997

Albums/CDs:
Gogh Van Go	Audiogram ADCD 10058	1993
Bliss Station	Audiogram ADCD 10099	1997

Matthew Good Band

Ian Browne (drums)
Dave Genn (guitar, keyboards)
Matthew Good (vocals, guitar)
Geoff Lloyd (bass) Repld by Rich Priske (1998)

Matthew Good started out as a folk singer in his native Vancouver. In the early 1990s he had an acoustic folk group, who released two independent cassettes, *Broken* in 1993 and *Euphony* in 1994, both on Good's Black Spinning Disks label. Shortly after the release of their independent debut album, *Last of the Ghetto Astronauts* in November 1995, Good decided to start a rock band.

In May 1997 they released the EP, Raygun on its own MGB label. They later signed to A&M Records, who released the group's major label debut, Underdogs later that same year. By November 1998 bassist Geoff Lloyd had been replaced by Rich Priske. In 2001 Universal released the limited edition numbered EP, Loser Anthems of which there were only 35,000 made, followed by the full length CD, The Audio Of Being.

Singles:

Alabama Hotel Room	MGB 290671	1995
Symbolistic White Walls	MGB 290671	1996
Raygun	Darktown 90500	1997
Everything is Automatic	Darktown 94001	1997
Rico	Darktown 94001	1998/99

Albums/CDs:

Last of the Ghetto Astronauts	MGB 290671	1995
Raygun (EP)	Darktown 90500	1997
Underdogs	Darktown 94001	1997
Beautiful Midnight	Darktown 37862	1999
Loser Anthems (EP)	Universal 142342	2001
The Audio of Being (Limited Edition)	Universal 162282	2001
The Audio of Being (Regular Release)	Universal 161842	2001

Lawrence Gowan

Born in Glasgow, Scotland on November 22, 1957, Lawrence Gowan first studied classical music in the mid 1970s when he left high school after Grade 12. From 1977 to 1980 he was a member of Rheingold, a theatrical rock band that made music similar to Queen and Genesis. His self-titled debut album on CBS Records came out in 1982. His next album, Strange Animal (1985), was produced by David Tickle (Peter Gabriel) at Ringo Starr's recording studio at Tittenhurst Park in Ascot, a suburb of London, England.

With the release of his third album, Great Dirty World (1987), he had become popular both as a touring and recording artist. Songs from Lost Brotherhood, his fourth, were first performed to appreciative audiences during his 1988 tour. His last album for Sony Music was *But You Can Call Me Larry!* in 1993, which was a critical success. He has since started his own label, Gowan Productions. With the release of the 1997 CD, *No Kilt Tonight*, he started appearing at various folk festivals. In 1997 he wrote Healing Waters, a tribute to Princess Diana. More recently, he has been the lead singer of Styx.

Singles:

A Criminal Mind	Columbia C4 7061	1985
(You're A) Strange Animal	Columbia C4 7082	1985
Guerilla Soldier	Columbia C4 7108	1985
Cosmetics	Columbia C4 7125	1986
Moonlight Desires	Columbia C4 7206	1987
Awake The Giant	Columbia C4 3011	1987
Living In The Golden Age	Columbia C4 3020	1987
All The Lovers In The World	Columbia	1987
Lost Brotherhood	Columbia FC 80160	1990
Out Of A Deeper Hunger	Columbia FC 80160	1990/91
When There's Time For Love	Columbia CK 80183	1993
Dancing On My Own Ground	Columbia CK 80183	1994
Soul's Road	Columbia CK 80183	1994
Your Stone Walls	Columbia CK 80183	1994
Heart Of Gold	SelectGPCD 1100	1995
Guns And God	SelectGPCD 1100	1995
I'll Be There In A Minute	SelectGPCD 1100	1995/96
Laura	SelectGPCD 1100	1996
The Good Catches Up	SelectGPCD 1100	1996
Get It While You Can	SelectGPCD 1100	1996/97
Healing Waters	Sony CK 80306	1997

Albums/CDs:

Gowan	Columbia PCC 80069	1982
Strange Animal	Columbia PCC 80099	1985
Great Dirty World	Columbia FC 40754	1987
Lost Brotherhood	Columbia FC 80160	1990
But You Can Call Me Larry!	Columbia CK 80183	1993
The Good Catches Up	SelectGPCD 1100	1995
No Kilt Tonight	Algae LG 10001	1997
Best Of	Sony CK 80306	1997
Home Field	Panoramic Music 1001	1998
Live In Concert	Linus 279005	2007

Tommy Graham

Tommy Graham first became involved in the Toronto music scene in 1958 with his high school band. After playing at the Blue Note Club when it opened in 1960, he moved to Los Angeles. In 1963 he returned to his home town and later joined The Big Town Boys who backed up Shirley Matthews on her hits, Big Town Boy and Private Property. When The Big Town Boys broke up in 1967, Graham decided to travel around the world, stopping in India where he became interested in the country's music and took lessons from Ravi Shankar's sarode player, Ali Akbar Kahn.

In 1970 he returned to Canada where he worked with his friend and record producer, Brian Aherne. Graham backed up Anne Murray on her international hit, Snowbird. Paul White, then an executive producer at Capitol Records, invited Graham to make a solo record; the result was Planet Earth, released in December 1970. Backing him up were studio musicians Skip Beckwith (bass), Ron Rully (drums), Bill Speer (piano), and Buddy Gage (steel guitar). Graham's solo career was short lived.

Singles:
Things Ya Say	Capitol 72632	1971
Sahajiya	Capitol 72651	1971
After The Goldrush	Capitol 72663	1972
My Happy Song	Capitol 72706	1973
Sea Cruise	Capitol 72726	1974

Album:
Planet Earth	Capitol SKAO 6356	1970

The Grapes of Wrath

Chris Hooper (drums)
Tom Hooper (bass)
Vincent Jones (keyboards)
Kevin Kane (vocals, guitar)

This quartet began in 1979 as a punk band called Kill Pigs in Kelowna, British Columbia, with Tom and Chris Hooper, Kevin Kane, and Chuck Unpleasant. When they split up, the Hooper Brothers and Friendly Giant joined another punk band, Gentlemen of Horror, while Kevin Kane played in the group Empty Set.

The former split up in 1982, and Tom, Chris and Kevin form a group called Honda Civic. After playing for a one night engagement, they decided to stay together. They also changed their name to The Grapes of Wrath, after the John Ford film of the same name, because Chris was a film buff.

The band moved to Vancouver, where they were signed to the independent Nettwerk label. In 1984 a four song EP was released. A year later came their debut album, *September Bowl of Green.*

Their next album, *Tree House,* was produced by Tom Cochrane and released in October 1987. Two years later, their third, *Now and Again,* came out, and featured guest performances by Chuck Leavell of the Allman Brothers and "Sneaky" Pete Kleinor of the Flying Burrito Brothers and Byrds fame. In August of 1991 their fourth album, *These Days,* was recorded at Vancouver's Mushroom Studios and mixed at Abbey Road Studios in London, England.

Their first of several hit Singles:, Backward Town, was released in 1985. They continued to have hits until 1992 when Kevin Kane left the group. Due to legal problems over their name, the remaining members of The Grapes of Wrath became known as Ginger. When Kevin Kane rejoined the rest of the group in 1998, The Grapes of Wrath were back. They recorded the single, Like a Fool (1998), followed by the CD, *Field Trip* (2000), which included a six song EP with the first 10,000 copies.

Singles:

Backward Town	Capitol B 73051	1985
Backward Town	Capitol SPRO 79286	1985
Misunderstanding	Nettwerk NT7 302	1986
Misunderstanding (12")	Nettwerk 12 NTWK 13	1986
When Love Comes Around	Nettwerk NT7 303	1986/87
Peace of Mind	Capitol B 73035	1987
O Lucky Man	Capitol B 73047	1987
All The Things I Wasn't	Capitol B 73089	1989
Do You Want To Tell Me	Capitol B 73101	1990
Do You Want To Tell Me	Capitol 12CL 570	1990
What Was Going Through My Head	Capitol 92581	1990
I Am Here (12")	Capitol SPRO 566	1991
You May Be Right	Capitol 96431	1991/92
A Fishing Tale	Capitol 96431	1992

Albums/CDs:

The Gentlemen Of Horror (EP)		1980
September Bowl Of Green	Nettwerk 16/Cap 93337	1985
Treehouse	Capitol CLT 48018	1987
Now And Again	Capitol C 92581	1989
These Days (Colored vinyl)	Capitol SPRO 79897	1991

These Days	Capitol 96431	1991
The Grapes Of Wrath	Capitol SPRO 79046	1992
Seems Like Fate 1984 1992	EMI 31185	1994
Field Trip (W/6 Song EP)	Song 2002	2000

Greaseball Boogie Band

John Bride (lead guitar)
Tommy Frew (drums)
Duncan White (lead vocals)
Ray Harrison (keyboards)
Wayne Mills (saxophone)

The Greaseball Boogie Band was started in Toronto in 1971 by Duncan White (a.k.a. King Grease). Their act consisted mainly of 1950s rock and roll standards, and they first became famous in their hometown in such nightspots as the El Mocambo. On stage, King Grease wore a sleeveless T shirt, spattered jeans, biker boots, and a chain link belt.

When the band started to sing Gene Vincents's 1956 rocker, Be Bop A Lula, King Grease would squeeze a tube of Brylcreem over his head and belch out loud.

GRT Records released their self-titled debut two album set in 1973, which included the single, Be Bop A Lula, a cover version of Gene Vincent's 1956 hit.

Besides White, the other main members were Ray (Rabbit) Harrison,
John (Animal) White, Wayne (Pig Boy) Mills, and Tommy (Short Ass) Frew.

Their last show as The Greaseball Boogie Band was a Liberal campaign rally for Pierre Trudeau in the spring of 1974. That same year they became known as The Shooter Review. The Murphy Sisters, formerly with Winnipeg's Sugar 'n Spice, sang backup.

They shortened their name to Shooter, and GRT released their first hit, I Can Dance (Long Tall Glasses) in 1975, which was also a hit that same year by Leo Sayer, who wrote the song. The group broke up in 1978. Harrison, Mills, and Bride became members of Toronto's Cameo Blues Band.

By Greaseball Boogie Band
Single:
| Be Bop A Lula | GRT 1230 70 | 1975 |

Album:
| Greaseball Boogie Band | GRT 9230 1042 | 1973 |

By Shooter
Singles:

I Can Dance (Long Tall Glasses)	GRT 1230 93	1975
Train	GRT 1230 97	1975
Hard Times	GRT 1230 115	1976
Standing On The Inside	GRT 1230 109	1976
Cherokee Queen	Casino C7 125	1978

Great Big Sea

Alan Doyle (vocals, guitar)
Bob Hallett (button accordion, fiddle, mandolin)
Sean McCann (tin whistle, bodhran, guitar)
Darrell Power (bass)

Great Big Sea started in 1991 when Alan Doyle first met Sean McCann in the tiny fishing village of Petty Harbour, Newfoundland. With the addition of Bob Hallett and Darrell Power, they became known as Great Big Sea.

Their music is a combination of traditional Newfoundland roots mixed with a rock and roll influence and upbeat lyrics, and each member of the group contributes to their overall sound. Doyle carries each song with his expressive vocal style; McCann adds a Celtic touch with the tin whistle, bodhran, and guitar; Power gives the group its rock edge on bass, and Hallett demonstrates his prowess on a half dozen instruments, including the button accordion, fiddle, and mandolin.

In 1993 the group released their self-titled independent album, which Warner Music Canada re released in 1995. It was followed by UP (1995) and PLAY (1997). Sire Records in the United States released the album, Rant And Roar in 1998, which included songs from Play.

Sean McCann left at the end of 2013, while Alan Doyle pursued his interest in acting and composing music for television and the movies.

Singles:

Fast As I Can	Wea 12277	1996
Going Up	Wea 12277	1996
When I'm Up (I Can't Get Down)	Wea 18592	1997
Ordinary Day	Wea 18592	1997/98
It's The End Of The World As We Know It (And I Feel Fine)	Wea 18592	1998
How We Did From Saying...	Wea 18592	1998
Consequence Free	Wea 27734	1999
Feel It Turn	Wea 27734	1999

Albums/CDs:

Great Big Sea	NRA 10088	1993
Up	Wea 12277	1995
Play	Wea 18592	1997
Turn	Wea 27734	1999
Road Rage	Wea 284666	2000
Sea Of No Cares	Wea 243310	2002
Something Beautiful	Wea 261387	2004
The Hard And The Easy	Wea 262606	2005
Courage & Patience & Grit	ZOE 01143-11062	2006
Fortune's Favour	Wea 2951727	2008
Safe Upon The Shore	Wea 283179	2010

The Great Scots

Gerry Archer (drums)
Dave Isner (bass)
Wayne Forrest (rhythm guitar)
Rick McNeil (lead vocals)
Bill Schnare (lead guitar)

From Halifax, Nova Scotia, The Great Scots started in 1962 as The Beavers, who played rock'n roll and rhythm and blues. With the arrival of Beatlemania in 1964, they became one of the first groups to feature two-part harmonies.

They went to New York in December 1964 where they signed a recording contract with Epic Records. Their first single was Don't Want Your Love. They also did a remake of Bobby Day's 1958 hit, Rockin' Robin which was never released. A third single, That's My Girl (Rotten To The Core) was recorded in Los Angeles, but it didn't go anywhere except in the group's hometown.

By late 1965 they had made several TV appearances on Shindig, Where The Action Is, Shivaree, 9 Streetwest, and Shebang, a local Los Angeles show. They also played at the Rose Bowl with Herman's Hermits and The Lovin' Spoonful.

Signed to Triumph Records in 1966, they recorded two Singles:, Ball and Chain, and, The Light Hurts My Eyes. On the Challenge label, they recorded the single, Blue Monday/Show Me The Way under the name The Free For All. The Great Scots disbanded in the fall of 1966.

Singles:

Give Me Lovin'	Epic 9805	1965
Lost In Conversation	Epic 9866	1966

Ball And Chain	Triumph 66	1966
The Light Hurts My Eyes	Triumph 67	1966
Blue Monday	Challenge 59339	1966

Albums/CDs:

The Great Lost Great Scots Album	Sundazed SC 11048	1997

Great Urban Band

Robert Arlidge (vocals, bass) Replaced by Duffy King (1979)
Douglas Atkinson (vocals, keyboards, synthesizers)
Frode Nilson (vocals, guitars, piano)
Jim Sherwood (vocals, drums, percussion)

This Kingston band formed in 1976. They played a mix of blues, rock and classical music, in addition to some original songs that were more elaborate than the average three-chord rock. Their self-titled album on Rage Records was recorded live on May 18, and 19, 1979 in Dollar Bills, a local nightspot at the Prince George Hotel. When Duffy King joined that fall, they were a five-piece band until Robert Arlidge left.

The Great Urban Band broke up in 1980.

Album:

Great Urban Band	Rage WRC 1 910	1979

Lorne Greene

Born in Ottawa on February 12, 1915, Lorne Greene was best known as Ben Cartwright in the long running western TV series, Bonanza (1959–73).

Greene started his radio career in the 1930s at radio station CBO in Ottawa. Between 1940–43 he was the "Voice of Doom" on the Canadian Broadcasting Corporation (CBC). Greene made his first Broadway appearance in 1953 in The Prescott Proposals, opposite Katherine Cornell.

After starring in a few movies: The Silver Chalice (1954), Peyton Place (1957), and, The Buccaneer (1958), he was offered the part of Ben Cartwright.

In the 1960s he turned to recording, with his best-known hit, Ringo, reaching number one on Billboard's Hot 100 on December 5, 1964.

When Bonanza went off the air, he hosted Lorne Greene's New Wilderness for five years. He later starred in two short lived TV series, Battlestar Galactica and Code Red.

Greene died on September 11, 1987 of complications from an operation for a perforated ulcer. In 2015 he was honoured on Canada's Walk of Fame.

Singles:
Ringo	RCA 8444	1964/65
The Man	RCA 8490	1965
An Old Tin Cup	RCA 8554	1965

Albums/CDs:
Cartwrights	RCA LSP 2503	1963
Christmas With the Cartwrights	RCA LSP 2757	1963
Welcome to the Ponderosa	RCA LSP 2843	1965
The Man	RCA LSP 3302	1966
Portrait of the West	RCA LSP 3678	1967
Five Card Stud	Camden CAS 2391	1969
Lorne Greene	BMG 17225	1991

Joey Gregorash

Born on June 23, 1950 in Winnipeg, Manitoba, Joey Gregorash's showbusiness career started in 1964 in an instrumental group called The Wellingtons with Jim Brennan, John Nykon, and Peter Rutherford. They later changed their name to The Mongrels, a name suggested by Joey because it was his favorite dog. In 1968, he left the group and was replaced by Alan Schick.

Signed to Polydor Records in 1970, Joey had a number of hits, including Jodie, Don't Let Pride Get You Girl, and Take The Blindness.

He also recorded two albums, *North Country Funk*, and, *Tell The People*.

By 1975 he had stopped touring and joined Moffatt Broadcasting. On CKY radio in Winnipeg, he became host of the morning show. Seven years later, he moved to mornings at CHMM FM.

In the mid 1970s at a friend's wedding, Joey first sang Together (The Wedding Song), which became the B side to the independent single, Love Is Gonna Bring Us Together in 1983. In 1987, it was released by Attic Records and became one of four gold records by a Canadian artist for that year. The other three were Corey Hart, Glass Tiger, and Bryan Adams.

Over the years, Joey has become a TV personality on such shows as Young As You Are, followed by Joey & The Hits, Dance Party,

S'kiddle Bits, and Hi Noon. In the late 1970s, he recorded under the name of Jay Anthony on RCA Records.

In addition to having studied Bel Canto voice under Alicjia Seaborn of the Warsaw Opera Company, he has recorded new versions of his old hits, such as Together (The New Wedding Song) and Jodie. He is currently host at McPhillips Street Station, one of the Manitoba Lotteries Corporations' two gaming/entertainment centres in Winnipeg.

Singles:

Stay	Polydor 2065 023	1970
Tomorrow Tomorrow	Polydor 2065 034	1970/71
Jodie	Polydor 2065 055	1971
Don't Let Pride Get You Girl	Polydor 2065 073	1971
Down By The River	Polydor 2065 073	1971
My Love Sings	Polydor 2065 100	1972
Bye Bye Love	Polydor 2065 118	1972
Take The Blindess	Polydor 2065 148	1972
Tell The People	Polydor 2065 168	1973
Liza	Polydor 2065 205	1973
You've Been Wrong	Polydor 2065 219	1974
I Know We'll Make It Together	Sonogram SG 9033	1975
Love Is Gonna Bring Us Together	Lite Rock 97 03	1983
Together (The New Wedding Song)	Attic AT 357	1987
Together (The New Wedding Song) (with Lorraine Lawson)	Popular CD 3166	1997

Albums/CDs:

North Country Funk	Polydor 2424 025	1971
Tell The People	Polydor 2424 066	1972

Bobby G. Griffith

Bobby G. Griffith was a Winnipeg artist whose success came from the United States when he signed with Lawrence Welk's publishing company, Teleklew Productions Inc. Signed to his Ranwood label, he had a major hit with The Badger's Song in Canada in 1973. Backing Griffith up was George Dearling on drums, Lou Fortin on bass, Valentine Bent on lead guitar, and Jimmy Carver on electric piano.

During Griffith's early years, he fronted The New Movement and recorded on various labels, Canadian American, Stone, M.T.C.C. and Polydor.

Singles:

Cheater Cheater	CAN AM 123	1960
Tough Guy/Yes It's True	Stone 720	1967
Living on a Wishbone	MTCC 1001	1970
709	POL 2065 052	1971
In Her Loving Way	POL 2065 090	1971
Sound of Peace	Ranwood 933	1972/73
The Badger's Song	Ranwood 951	1973
You Can't Get It All		1974
Give My Love to Lady Canada	Badger BA 005	1975
Keep An Eye on Your Friends	Badger BA 007	1975/76

Album:

Bobby G. Griffith	Celebration 1892	1978

The Guess Who

The story of The Guess Who began in Winnipeg, Manitoba with Allan Kowbel in the late 1950s, when he formed the group Allen's Silvertones, a name derived from a guider model manufactured by Sears. In addition to Allan, the rest of the group included Johnny Glowa, Brian "Ducky"

Donald, Jim Kale, and Bob Ashley. In 1961, Randy Bachman and Garry Peterson replaced Glowa and Donald. That same year, the group changed their name to Chad Allan and The Reflections, and, in 1962, made their first recording, Tribute To Buddy Holly, which was followed by Shy Guy in 1963.

By the time their next record came out, Stop Teasing Me, in 1964, Bob Burns, a local radio/TV personality, had become their manager. When an American group called The Reflections had a big hit with Just Like Romeo and Juliet in 1964, the Winnipeg group became known as Chad Allan and The Expressions. Their first recording under the new name was Shakin' All Over, a cover version of the 1960 British hit by Johnny Kid and The Pirates.

Quality Records executive George Struth renamed Chad Allan and The Expressions, The Guess Who, in early 1965. While Shakin' All Over was becoming a national hit in Canada, New York based Scepter Records wanted to release it in the U.S. In June 1965 it peaked at #22 on the Billboard Hot 100.

In December 1965 Bob Ashley left the group, and was replaced by Burton Cummings, who had come from another Winnipeg group, The Deverons.

Chad Allan left in the spring of 1966. For the next four years, The Guess Who was comprised of Bachman, Kale, Peterson, and Cummings.

Jack Richardson became their new producer and manager in 1968. He signed them to his label, Nimbus 9 Productions. In the fall of 1968, their first three singles for the label were When Friends Fall Out, Of A Dropping Pin, and These Eyes, which became their first million seller.

The Guess Who continued to have more hits, notably Laughing/Undun, No Time, and American Woman, which went to number one on Billboard's Hot 100 in the spring of 1970.

Shortly after the release of the album, *American Woman*, there were a number of changes in the group. Bachman quit and was replaced by two new members, Kurt Winter and Greg Leskiw. In 1972 Leskiw was replaced by Don McDougall, and Kale by Bill Wallace. Two years later, Winter and MacDougall were replaced by Domenic Troiano (Robbie Lane & The Disciples, Mandala, Bush). Burton Cummings left in 1975 to pursue a solo career.

Kale, McDougall, Winter, drummer Vance Masters, and guitarist Dave Inglis began touring as The Guess Who in 1978. Since then there have been several versions of the group. Winter died on December 14, 1997. Three of their singles were certified million sellers by RIAA.

These Eyes on June 25, 1969, Laughing on October 28, 1969 and American Woman on May 22, 1970. In 2005, No Time, These Eyes and American Woman were inducted into the Canadian Songwriters Hall of Fame. Today they are one of Canada's top touring acts. The current line-up consists of Garry Petersen, Jim Kale, Leonard Shaw, Derek Sharp and Laurie Mac Kenzie.

By Chad Allan and The Reflections
Singles:
Tribute To Buddy Holly	Canada/American 802	1962
Shy Guy	Quality 1559	1963
Stop Teasing Me	Quality 1644	1964

By Bob Ashley and The Reflections
Single:
Made in England	Reo 8735	1963

By Chad Allan and The Expressions
Single:
Shakin' All Over	Quality 1691	1965

By The Guess Who
Singles:
Tossin' & Turnin'	Quality 1724	1965
Hey Ho (What You Do To Me)	Quality 1752	1965
Hurting Each Other	Quality 1778	1965

Believe Me	Quality 1797	1966
And She's Mine	Quality 1832	1966
Clock On The Wall	Quality 1815	1966
His Girl	Quality 1863	1967
Pretty Blue Eyes	Quality 1874	1967
This Time Long Ago	Quality 1876	1967
Flying On The Ground	Quality 1890	1967
Miss Felicity Grey/ Flying On The Ground (Brit.)	Fontana TF 861	1967
This Time Long Ago/ Flying On The Ground	Quality 1933	1967
Hurting Each Other	Quality 1974	1968
When Friends Fall Out	Nimbus Nine9002	1968
Of A Dropping Pin	Nimbus Nine9004	1968
These Eyes	Nimbus Nine9005	1968/69
Maple Fudge	Nimbus Nine9007	1969
Laughing/Undun	Nimbus Nine74 0195	1969
No Time	Nimbus Nine74 0300	1969
American Woman/No Sugar Tonight	Nimbus Nine74 0325	1970
Hand Me Down World	Nimbus Nine74 0367	1970
Share The Land	Nimbus Nine74 0388	1970
Hang On To Your Life	Nimbus Nine74 0414	1971
Albert Flasher/Broken	Nimbus Nine74 0458	1971
Rain Dance	Nimbus Nine74 0522	1971
Life In The Bloodstream	Nimbus Nine74 0578	1972
Heartbroken Bopper	Nimbus Nine74 0659	1972
Guns, Guns, Guns	Nimbus Nine74 0708	1972
Runnin' Back To Saskatoon	Nimbus Nine74 0803	1972
Follow Your Daughter Home	Nimbus Nine74 0880	1973
Orly	Nimbus Nine74 0926	1973
Glamour Boy	Nimbus Nine74 0977	1973
Star Baby	Nimbus NineAPBO 0217	1974
Clap For The Wolfman	Nimbus NineAPBO 0324	1974
Loves Me Like A Brother	Nimbus NinePB 10216	1975
Dancin' Fool	Nimbus NinePB 10075	1975
Rosanne	Nimbus NinePB 10306	1975
When The Band Was Singin' Shakin' All Over	Nimbus NinePB 10410	1975
Silver Bird	Nimbus NinePB 10716	1976
C'Mon Little Mama	Aquarius 5072	1978
Sweet Young Thing	Aquarius 5075	1978
Sharin' Love	Aquarius 5081	1979
Lovelite	Esmos 516	1981
Let's Watch The Sun Go Down	Ready SR 491	1984

Albums/CDs:

Shakin' All Over	Quality V1756	1965
Hey Ho (What You Do To Me)	Quality V1764	1965
It's Time	Quality V1788	1966
A Wild Pair	Nimbus Nine100	1968

Wheatfield Soul	Nimbus Nine102	1968
The Guess Who	Birchmount BM 525	1968
SUPER Golden Goodies	Quality SV 1827	1969
The Guess Who (U.S.)	MGM SE 4645	1969
Canned Wheat	RCA LSP 4157	1969
American Woman	RCA LSP 4266	1970
Share The Land	RCA LSP 4359	1970
Best Of The Guess Who Vol I	RCA LSP 1004	1971
The Guess Who Play The Guess Who (U.S.)	Pickwick PIP 6806	1971
So Long Bannatyne	RCA LSP 4574	1971
Rockin'	RCA LSP 4602	1972
Live At The Paramount	RCA LSP 4779	1972
Shakin' All Over (U.S.)	Springbd SPB 4022	1972
History Of (U.S.)	Pride 0012	1972
Wild One (U.S.)	Pickwick SPC 3246	1972
Artificial Paradise	RCA LSP 4830	1973
Number Ten	RCA APL1 0130	1973
Best Of The Guess Who Vol II	RCA APL1 0269	1973
Road Food	RCA APL1 0405	1974
Flavours	RCA APL1 0636	1975
Power In The Music	RCA APL1 0995	1975
The Way They Were	RCA APL1 1778	1976
20 Original Hits	K TEL NC 458	1976
The Greatest Of The Guess Who	RCA AFL1 2253	1977
Guess Who's Back	Aquarius AQR 518	1978
All This For A Song	Aquarius AQR 522	1979
Together Again	Ready LR 049	1984
The Best Of The Guess Who Live (U.S.)	Compleat 6672012	1986
Track Record: The Guess Who Collection	BMG KXL7115	1988
The Guess Who: The Ultimate Collection	RCA 67300	1997
Running Back Thru Canada	VIK 81182	2000
This Time Long Ago	Bullseye 2CD 2509	2001

Bruce Guthro

Bruce Guthro, from Sydney Mines, Nova Scotia, had a minor country hit in 1993 with Livin' in the 90s. His first independent CD, Sails to the Wind (1994) was produced by Bill MacNeil and Gilles Godard. He has written songs with Susan Aglukark, Amy Sky, Scott Dibble, and toured with Anne Murray, Jann Arden and Natalie MacMaster. In 1997 Guthro won SOCAN's Songwriter of the Year award at the East Coast Music Awards (ECMA). EMI Music Canada released his second album, *Of Your Son*, in 1998. The first single was Walk This Road.

Singles:

Livin' in the 90s	AGL CD01	1993
I'll Surrender	AGL CD01	1995
Him & God & Me	AGL CD01	1995
Stan's Tune		1996
Walk this Road	EMI 57175	1998
Falling	EMI 57175	1998
Ivey's Wall	EMI 57175	1998/99
Good Love	EMI 57175	1999

Albums/CDs:

Sails to the Wind	AGL CD01	1994
Of Your Son	EMI 57175	1998

The Halifax Three

Richard Byrne (vocals, acoustic guitar)
Denny Doherty (vocals, acoustic guitar)
Pat La Croix (vocals, washtub bass)

On December 31, 1960 they first sang together as The Colonials at a jazz club in Halifax, Nova Scotia. Pat La Croix and Denny Doherty met at a pawn shop on Barrington, Street, and Richard Byrne was singing songs by The Kingston Trio. They all thought they sounded good together and decided to become a trio. Pat already had his own TV show on CBC Halifax. By the summer of 1961, they were on both the CBC and CTV networks and had their own CBC-TV program, Headin' On Home. By the end of 1961, they changed their name to The Halifax Three. When their sixteen week contract ended, they went to Montreal where they sang in such clubs as the Venus DiMilo and Lou Black's Living Room. They later went to Toronto where they played in various clubs and coffeehouses, such as The Bohemian Embassy, The Village Corner, The Purple Onion, and The Fifth Peg where they opened for Bill Cosby.

In 1962 while they were playing at the Folksway Motor Inn in Niagara Falls they went to Buffalo, New York to audition for Harry Altman, who ran a supper club called The Town Casino. Through him the trio met Burt Block, head of I.T.A. (International Talent Associates), who signed them to a two-year contract. Block then took The Halifax Three to Dave Caplan, the head of A&R at Columbia who signed them to a two-year, two-album contract.

Being signed to an exclusive American agency led to appearances on CBC

TV's major shows and work on the Ivy League circuit in the United States where they played on college campuses. In Greenwich Village, they met the late Cass Elliott who was then in The Big Three. Between engagements, The Halifax Three went into the recording studio and made their first self-titled album for Epic Records.

They also made appearances on American TV, notably The Merv Griffin Show, The Mike Douglas Show, and The Mitch Miller Show.

The Halifax Three finished their second album for Epic, San Francisco Bay Blues in late 1963, and then went on The Hootenanny Tour where they travelled across fifteen southern states and ended up at Carnegie Hall in New York City. On the tour they were joined by Glenn Yarbrough, Jo Mapes, and John and Michelle Phillips who were in The Journeymen. By then, Zal Yanovsky had joined The Halifax Three as a full-time accompanist.

By the end of 1963, The Halifax Three split up. Denny and Zal were in The Mugwumps together; then Denny joined John, Michelle and Cass in The Mamas and The Papas, while Zal became a member of The Lovin' Spoonful.

Denny also released two solo albums (see Denny Doherty), while Pat La Croix released the CD/EP, *This Is All I Ask* (TBGCD D195) in 1994. Luscious Records released, Pat's daughter Dana's debut CD, *Pride* (DL 002) in 1998. Two songs by The Halifax Three appeared on the CD, Before They Were The Mamas and Papas *The Magic Circle* (Varese Sarabande VSD 5996 1999): *Oh Mary Don't You Weep* and *The Man Who Wouldn't Sing Along With Mitch*. Richard Byrne died on January 7, 2007 and Denny Doherty on January 19, 2007.

By The Colonials
Single:

All My Trials	Rodeo 280	1961

By Halifax Three
Singles:

Bull Train	Epic 5-9560	1963
The Man Who Wouldn't Sing Along With Mitch	Epic 5-9572	1963

Albums/CDs:

The Halifax Three	Epic BN 26038	1963
San Francisco Bay Blues	Epic BN 26060	1963

Albums:

The Complete Halifax Three	Sony 202982	2002

Hammersmith

Doran Beattie (lead vocals)
Jeff Boyne (rhythm guitar, vocals) Replaced by Craig Blair (1975 76)
Dan Lowe (lead guitar)
Royden Morice (bass, keyboards, synthesizer, vocals)
James Llewellyn (drums) Replaced by Dale Buchner (1975 76)

The last name change for this Calgary group that began as The Shades in 1966 was Hammersmith. They recorded two albums for the Mercury label; their self-titled debut in 1975, and, It's For You, in 1976. Hammersmith were together from 1974 to 1978. Comprised of Dan Lowe, Doran Beattie, Jeff Boyne, Royden Morice, and James Llewellyn, the lineup changed between albums. Boyne was replaced by Craig Blair, while Llewellyn by Dale Buchner.

Singles:
Feelin' Better	MercuryM 73717	1976
Late Night Lovin' Man	MercuryM 73749	1976
Good Bye Good Bye	MercuryM 73874	1976

Albums/CDs:
Hammersmith	MercurySRM 1 1040	1975
It's For You	MercurySRM 1 1102	1976

Keith Hampshire

Born on November 23, 1945 in London, England, Keith Hampshire took ballet and tap dancing lessons as a child. His parents who were stage actors moved to New York where they triumphed as stage actors they decided to move to New York. They triumphed on stage and then took a train north to Toronto where they bought a car and headed west to Calgary. While growing up there, Keith sang in the local Anglican church choir and took weekly vocal lessons. At 16 he made a good enough soprano.

When rock'n'roll became more popular, Hampshire decided to form his own group called The Intruders. When it folded he started another one, Keith and The Bristols. It, too, quickly disbanded. A third group, however, Keith and The Variations lasted three years on the club circuit.

After graduating from high school, he was hired at CFCN Radio and Television as a cameraman. Unhappy with CFCN's radio format he started playing

British rock on his after-midnight show. He was one of the first to introduce Canadians to Brian Poole and The Tremeloes, The Swinging Blue Jeans, The Animals and The Searchers.

In 1966 he applied for a job on Radio Caroline, Amsterdam's 50 kilowatt pirate radio station in the North Sea. For thirteen months he became an English idol with "Keefer's Uprising" morning show and later "Keefer's Commotion" in the afternoon. Back in Canada for Expo 67, radio station CKFH in Toronto hired him as a disc jockey where he remained for three years.

Through a friend he met producer Bill Misener (ex Paupers) at RCA and recorded I Wish I Could Wish Away which was retitled Ebenezer. Daytime Night time, written by Mike Hugg of Manfred Mann, was an immediate smash, along with the follow up hit, First Cut Is The Deepest, written by Cat Stevens. In 1974 Hampshire remade Hallelujah Freedom, a hit for Junior Campbell in England.

Since the late 1970s, Keith has made a living singing commercials for a variety of products such as Aquafresh, Miss Mew, Imperial Margarine, Seven Up, Elk's Clothing and McCain's "Tastey Taters.". He returned to the recording studio in 1982 to record the album, Variations, on Freedom Records. The first single, I Can't Wait Too Long, was not a national hit.

Singles:

Millions of Hearts	King KG 1068	1967
Ebenezer	RCA 74 0472	1971
Daytime, Night time	A&M 330	1972
First Cut is The Deepest	A&M 337	1973
Big Time Operator	A&M 356	1973
Forever and Ever		
(Baby I'm Gonna Be Yours)	A&M 370	1974
Hallelujah Freedom, Waking Up Alone	A&M 381	1974
Something Good, Just Another Fool	Axe 34	1976
I Can't Wait Too Long, Nobody's Child	FR 45 004	1982
OK Blue Jays, OK Blue Jays	BJ-01 KOSINEC	1983

Albums/CDs:

The First Cut	A&M SP 9006	1973
Variations	Freedom FR 005	1981

The Happy Feeling

Jim Aiello (vocals, keyboard)
Danny Ferguson (vocals, lead guitar)
Gordon Moffatt (vocals, guitar, keyboards)
Robert Moffatt (vocals, guitar)
Gerry Mudry (drums)
Bob Wagner (vocals, bass)

This Calgary group started out as Plus Four in 1966 with Gerry Mudry, Danny Ferguson, and Gordon Moffatt. In 1967, Gordon's brother Robert, whose distinctive harmony bass helped create the group's trademark vocal sound, joined the group. That same year, Jim Aiello also joined, with Bob Wagner, from Eatonia, Saskatchewan, in 1968.

During 1968 the group changed its name to The Happy Feeling and recorded at Norman Petty's studio in Clovis, New Mexico. Their first single, Happy Feeling, on Barry Records came out in the fall of that year and went to #1 on CKXL's....

Between 1968 and 1970 they opened for a number of American groups who came to Calgary, such as Tommy James and The Shondells, Paul Revere and The Raiders, The Fireballs and Three Dog Night.

They also performed on the Festival Express Show in Calgary, and appeared on Young As You Are, a local TV show hosted by Joey Gregorash, and CTV's Come Together.

The Happy Feeling also had their own TV show which combined original and cover tunes with comedy bits choreographed with fast and slow motion film footage a la Buster Keaton and The Three Stooges. The group broke up in 1971.

Singles:
Happy Feeling	Barry 3499	1968
Hey Little Man	Barry 3507	1969
Good Neighbour Day	Barry 3513	1969
Still Hill	Barry 3517	1970
Sacroiliac Boop	Barry 3523	1970
Children	Barry 3525	1971

Albums/CDs:
Happy Feeling	Barry BSR 357	1970
Happy Feeling (U.S.)	AVE 33011	1970

Hagood Hardy

Born in Angola, Indiana on February 26, 1937, Hagood Hardy came to Canada as an infant and was raised in Oakville, where he studied piano with Edna Lawrence and Ellen Scott. He became a professional musician at eighteen years of age, and played the vibraphone at Toronto's House of Hambourg jazz club while studying political science and economics at the University of Toronto.

In 1961 he moved to New York where he played and recorded with such jazz greats as the George Shearing Quintet, Herbie Mann Sextet, and Martin Denny Group. Returning to Toronto in 1966, he formed the Hagood Hardy Trio with bassist Ian Henstridge and drummer Richard Marcus. A year later, Hardy's first album, STOP 33, was released. It was followed by Here's Hagood Hardy in 1968.

In 1969, he fronted Hagood Hardy and The Montage which stayed together until 1972. The Montage was comprised of Dave Lewis on drums, Rick Homme on bass, Bill Bridges on lead guitar, and Stephanie Taylor and Lynne McNeil on vocals and percussion.

Hardy is best known for The Homecoming, which was originally used in a Salada Tea commercial before it was a major hit in 1975.

He also composed the music for more than fifty films and TV shows, notably his Gemini Award winning score for CBC's Anne of Green Gables, and other CBC shows, notably Bethune, The Wild Pony, and Rituals.

Among the other honors he has received during his career are the Order of Canada in 1992, and the Toronto Arts Foundation's Lifetime Achievement Award in 1996.

Hagood Hardy died of cancer on January 1, 1997.

Singles:

Title	Catalog	Year
Just A Little Lovin' (w/The Montage)	POL 2001 204	1971
The Garden Path (w/The Montage)	GRT 1230 31	1972
The Homecoming	Attic AT 112	1975
Wintertime/Jennifer's Song		1975
Love Theme From Missouri Breaks	Attic AT 132	1976
Maybe Tomorrow	Attic AT 142	1976
Nightwalker	Attic AT 182	1977
Reunion	Attic AT 170	1977
The Harlequin Theme (A Time For Love)		1978
Love Song	Attic AT 201	1978
The Birdwalk	Attic AT 212	1979
Working in L.A.		1981
Love Makes the Water Taste Like Wine	Attic AT 261	1982
Chasing A Dream	DSR 71000	1983

Albums/CDs:

Title	Catalog	Year
Stop 33	CTLS 1096/GRT 9211	1967
Here's Hagood Hardy	CTL S 5096	1968
Hagood Hardy And The Montage	CBC LM 81	1970
Hagood Hardy And Montage	CTLS 0155/GRT 9230 1012	1972
The Homecoming	CTLS 5191/Attic LAT 1003	1975
Maybe Tomorrow	Attic LAT 1011	1976
Tell Me My Name	Attic LAT 1034	1977
Reflections	Attic LAT 1052	1978
A Very Special Christmas	K TEL NC 496	1978
The Hagood Hardy Collection	Attic LAT 1073	1979
As Time Goes By	Attic LAT 1097	1980
The Christmas Album	Attic LAT 1098	1979
Love Me Closer	Attic LAT 1116	1982
Chasing A Dream	Duke ST DSR 310000	1983
Night Magic	Duke ST DSR 31014	1985
Hagood Hardy	Duke ST DSR 3130	1986
All My Best	Duke ST DSMD 31052	1988
All My Best II	Duke ST DSMD 31063	1989
Morocco	SACK CD 2 2018	1989
A Christmas Homecoming	ISIS 1002	1989
Walk With Me	Channel CD 2292	1992
Anne	ISIS 1003	1992
In My Heart	Duke 31083	1992
After Hours	Solitudes CD02	1995
Alone	Solitudes CD01	1995
My Song	Solitudes CD19	1996
Between Friends	Solitudes CD20	1996

Harem Scarem

Mike Gionet (bass) Replaced by Barry Donaghy (1995)
Harold Hess (vocals)
Pete Lesperance (guitars)
Darren Smith (drums)

Harem Scarem is a Toronto quartet who has been together since 1987. Each member of the band comes from a different musical background. Harold Hess began his career at the age of 12. He played and sang in various bands before he joined a heavy metal group when he was 15. Pete Lesperance started playing the guitar at 8 and seven years later also joined a heavy metal band that opened for Anvil. He joined Harem Scarem in 1988 after trying to make a living as a guitarist on the road. Mike Gionet has had conservatory training in piano and guitar. He spent his teens playing bass in polka bands and showbands. Darren Smith is an accomplished musician and can play several instruments. He first met Hess when the two of them were in the band Blind Vengeance. Before Smith joined Harem Scarem, he sang lead vocals and played guitar in various group. Together the foursome learned all aspects of the music business including writing, performing, producing, engineering and touring. In 1989 they put together an eleven-song demo CD and spent the following year writing and recording new material, and, a year later, the group negotiated a recording contract with Warner Music Canada, after finishing second in Toronto radio station Q 107's Homegrown competition. Their self-titled debut album for Warner and first hit single, Slowly Slippin' Away were released in 1991. After the group finished their 1995 album, *Voice of Reason*, bassist Mike Gionet left, and was replaced by Barry Donaghey. Harem Scarem changed their name to Rubber in 1999 and in 2000 came their self-titled debut CD (Wea 29884), featuring the first single, Sunshine.

Singles:
Slowly Slippin' Away	Wea 75150	1991
Love Reaction	Wea 75150	1991/92
Honestly	Wea 75150	1992
With A Little Love	Wea 75150	1992
Something To Say	Wea 75150	1992
No Justice	Wea 93139	1993
Change Comes Around	Wea 93139	1993
Had Enough	Wea 93139	1993/94
If There Was A Time	Wea 93139	1994
Blue	Wea 10613	1995
Hail, Hail	Wea 19146	1997

Albums/CDs:
Harem Scarem	Wea 75150	1991
Mood Swings	Wea 93139	1993
Live and Acoustic	Wea 96585	1994
Voice of Reason	Wea 10613	1995
Live in Japan	Wea 14250	1996
Karma Cleansing	Wea 19146	1997
Big Bang Theory	Wea 24208	1998

Harlequin

George Belanger (lead vocals)
John Hannah (guitar) Replaced by Glen Willows
Ralph James (bass)
John White (keyboards) Replaced by Gary Golden
Denton Young (drums) Replaced by David Budzak

From Winnipeg, Manitoba, Harlequin formed in 1970 when Ralph James, John Hannah, Denton Young, and John White decided to form a band. After playing at fairs, teen dances, and the club circuit in North and South Dakota, Northern Ontario, and Manitoba, they headed east to Toronto. In 1972 Denton Young left the group to form Zon, while Hannah left to form another Winnipeg group, Streetheart.

For a short time, Harlequin was renamed Holy Hannah with David Budzak on drums, Gary Golden on keyboards, Glen Willows on guitar (as Hannah's replacment), and George Belanger on vocals.

Signed to Epic Records in 1979, their debut album was Victim Of A Song, which was originally released on the Inter Global Music label. After a string of hits, beginning with Survive, they broke up in the late 1980s.

Singles:

Survive	Epic E4 8357	1979
You are the Light	Epic E4 8375	1980
Innocence	Epic E4 4261	1981
Thinking of You	Epic E4 4271	1981
Superstitious Feeling	Epic E4 4310	1982
I Did it For Love	Epic E4 4322	1982
Take This Heart	Epic E4 7027	1984
(It's) No Mystery	Epic E4 7185	1986
(It's) No Mystery (12")	Epic 12CDN 296	1986

Albums/CDs:

Victim of a Song	Epic PEC 90566	1979
Love Crimes	Epic PEC 80048	1980
Radio Romances	Epic PEC 80115	1986
Harlequin's Greatest Hits	CBS WEK 80134	1986

Harmonium

Pierre Daigneault (flute, piccolo, soprano sax, clarinet)
Serge Fiori (guitar, flute, zither harp, bass drum, vocals)
Serge Locat (piano, mellotron, synthesizer)
Michel Normandeau (guitar, accordion, vocals)
Louis Valois (bass guitar, electric piano, vocals)

The origins of Montreal's Harmonium go back to 1973 when Serge, Michel and Louis formed a trio. Like most groups in Quebec in the early 1970s, their popularity began on the coffeehouse circuit of Old Montreal and university campuses.

During the summer of 1974 they played to packed houses at the Place des Arts and the Sports Centre of the University of Montreal.

Signed to Quality Records, their first two albums, *Harmonium* and *Les Cinq Saisons*, sold well.

There were also personnel changes in the group: in 1976, Pierre Digneault was replaced by Libert Subirana, while Michel Normandeau by Robert Stanley; and, in 1977, Serge Locat was replaced by Jeff Fisher. Between 1976 and 1978, two new members were added:

Denis Farmer on drums, and Monique Fouteaux on vocals and keyboards.

The band broke up in 1980. Six years later, Serge Fiori went solo. In 1986 Polygram Records released his self-titled debut album.

Michel Normandeau was only a member between 1972 and 1976. He had a brief solo career in 1979 with the release of his first album, *Jouer* on Polydor Records. Since 1988 he has been a civil servant in Montreal.

Singles:
100,000 raisons	Celebration CEL 2093	1974
Dixie	Celebration CEL 2132	1975

Albums/CDs:
Harmonium	Celebration CEL 1893	1974
Les Cinq Saisons	Celebration CEL 1900	1975
L'heptade	CBS PGF 90348	1976
Harmonium En Tournee	CBS PFC 2 80045	1977

Corey Hart

Corey Hart was born in Montreal, Quebec on May 31, 1961. He grew up in Spain, Mexico, Florida and Quebec. When he was a teenager, he approached Montreal record companies with cassettes of his songs without success. At seventeen, he ran away from home to live in New York where he became friends with Billy Joel's backup band. He later returned to Montreal, and in 1983 signed a contract with Aquarius Records. Sunglasses At Night was his debut hit single in the spring of 1984. Some of his other hits included Boy In The Box, Eurasian Eyes, and a cover version of Elvis Presley's Can't Help Falling In Love. Never Surrender was his biggest hit during the summer of 1985. In 1992, Sire released 92 Days Of Rain and in 1996, Columbia released a self-titled effort, followed by Jade (1998). He is married to French chanteuse Julie Masse.

Singles:

Sunglasses at Night	Aquarius AQ 6007	1984
It Ain't Enough	Aquarius AQ 6011	1984
She Got the Radio	Aquarius AQ 6014	1984
Lamp at Midnight	Aquarius AQ 6016	1985
Never Surrender	Aquarius AQ 6017	1985
Boy in The Box	Aquarius AQ 6019	1985
Everything in My Heart	Aquarius AQ 6021	1985
Rudolph the Red Nosed Reindeer	Aquarius AQ 6021	1985
Eurasian Eyes	Aquarius AQ 6022	1986
Eurasian Eyes (12")	Aquarius SPRO AQ 6022	1986
I Am by Your Side	Aquarius AQ 6023	1986
Can't Help Falling in Love	Aquarius AQ 6024	1986
Take My Heart	Aquarius AQ 6028	1987
Too Good to be Enough	Aquarius AQ 6027	1987
Dancing With My Mirror	Aquarius AQ 6025	1987
In Your Soul	AQ 6037/EMI PB50134	1988
In Your Soul (12")	EMI SPRO 04059	1988
Spot You in a Coalmine		1988
Still in Love	Aquarius AQ 6042	1989
Don't Take Me to the Racetrack	Aquarius AQ 6045	1989
A Little Love	Aquarius 92513	1990
Bang! (Starting Over)	Aquarius 92513	1990
Rain on Me	Aquarius 92513	1990
Diamond Cow	Aquarius 92513	1990
92 Days of Rain	Sire 26815	1992
Baby When I Call Your Name	Sire 26815	1992
Always	Sire 26815	1992
I Want (Cool Cool Love)	Sire 26815	1993
Hymn to Love (CD/S)		1994

Black Cloud Rain	Columbia 80240	1996
Tell Me	Columbia 80240	1997
Third of June	Columbia 80240	1997
Someone	Columbia 80240	1997
Break The Chain	Columbia 80240	1999

Albums/CDs:

First Offense	Aquarius AQR 537	1983
Boy in the Box	Aquarius AQR 539	1985
Fields of Fire	Aquarius AQR 542	1986
Young Man Running	Aquarius AQR 551	1988
Bang!	Aquarius 92513	1990
The singles Collection (1983 1990)	Aquarius 2561	1991
Attitude & Virtue	Sire 26815	1992
Corey Hart	Columbia 80240	1996
Jade	Columbia 80387	1998

The Lisa Hartt Band

Long before Lisa Hartt started her own band in 1974, she was a music veteran. Born Lisa Eisenhardt on January 3, 1949, her fledgling music career started in 1960 when she sang a jingle with Dorval's United Church Choir for La Belle Fermiere hotdogs. Two years later, she played regularly at various folk clubs in Montreal, Toronto and Le Hibou in Ottawa. In 1963, she became a member of The Lonesome Valley Three with Bob Gauthier and Mike Wheatfield. The following year, she recorded two singles for RCA Victor: Simon Simon and Know One 'Cept Me.

From 1965 to 1967 she was in the folk groups, The New Mode Grass with John and Lucky Cripton and Derek Smith, and The Chrystal Staircase with Ken Tobias, Don Stevens and Charlie Clark from 1967 to 1969. They recorded the single, Lady Laughter, written by Tobias. Lisa then played in The First Amendment with Brian Edwards, Skip Layton, Ian Hully and Clark.

During the early 1970s, she travelled to Bermuda, England, Egypt, and Germany and joined the all-female Big Band, The Christine Lee Set. She also was a vocalist with Gino Vannelli. In 1972, Lisa recorded her first single, Touch Me, on Polydor. That same year, she joined the trio, Touchstone, with Barry McMullen and Dave Graziatto, and in 1973 she was in a group called Oz, with Rayburn Blake, Richard Yuen, Marty Deller, and Wayne Cardinal. They later changed their name to The Lisa Hartt Band with Blake, Yuen, ex Pauper Denny Gerrard and Marty Cordrey.

Their first single, The Last Blues I'll Ever Sing was released in 1975. In 1976 they had a national hit with Old Time Movie, written by Blake. The Lisa Hartt Band broke up in 1978.

In 1979 Hartt moved to Los Angeles where she worked with Natalie Cole and later as a singer/songwriter with David Foster, Brenda and Brian Russell, Alan Thicke, Jay Gruska and Bobby David.

The early 1980s saw her back in Canada where she hosted two CBC specials, Listen To The Music and A Little Special. She also was involved in the bands, The Muscles of Expression, The Times, and Suma. In 1985 she formed the duo Flame with her husband Michael Spillane, and graduated from Concordia University with a degree in communications. She also recorded the jingle, The Best Is Yet To Come for the Special Olympics. Today, she lives in Mississauga where she remains active as a singer/songwriter.

Singles:
Old Time Movie	Rising Sun RI.003X	1976
Easy Come, Easy Go	Rising Sun RR.006	1976
All Over The World	Rising Sun RR.008	1976
Sweet Serenade	Rising Sun RR.010	1976

Album:
Starwatcher	Rising Sun RRLP 104	1976

Hart Rouge

Annette Campagne (vocals)
Michelle Campagne (vocals, acoustic guitar, synthesizer, piano)
Paul Campagne (vocals, bass, acoustic guitar)
Suzanne Campagne (vocals)

Born and raised in the Metis community of Willow Bunch, Saskatchewan, Annette, Michelle, Paul and Suzanne Campagne grew up singing harmony to a diverse range of songs from The Monkees to McDonald's commercials. In the 1970s they formed the group Folle Avoine. In 1986 they began writing and performing under the name of Hart Rouge, the original name of their hometown.

Signed to Trafic Records, their self-titled debut album came out in 1988, and the following year the group moved to Montreal.

Their second album, *Inconditionnel* (1991) was produced by Daniel Lavoie. The title track earned a Socan award as one of the most played songs on Quebec radio, while C'est elle was co-written with singer/songwriter Connie Kaldor.

Hart Rouge began to headline festivals across Quebec, and later performed abroad at Francovision in Paris, and The Rock Summer Festival in Eastonia.

Global CanWest network's French documentary of the band, So Many Miles and Words Between Us, won a silver medal at the Houston International Film Festival.

The group released a jazz gospel/blues album of French Christmas classics entitled, LE Dernier Mois De L'annee, which earned rave reviews and a fifteen date Christmas tour of Quebec.

In 1993 MCA released their folk/rock album, Blue Blue Windows, which featured a cappella version of Neil Young's Helpless. After the release of Bonsoir Quebec in 1995, the eldest sister Anne left to pursue a solo career.

By the release of their 1997 album, *Beaupre's Home*, the group had changed from pop to a more roots style of music, with the addition of Michel Dupire on percussion and multi-instrumentalist Davy Gallant.

Singles:

Double Take	Trafic F4 87201	1987
The Heart of the Matter	Trafic F4 88216	1988
Et apres tout ca	Trafic	1989
Rosa	Trafic	1989
Raconte moi une histoire	Trafic 89248	1989
Inconditionnel	Trafic 8953	1991
C'est elle	Trafic 8953	1991

Albums/CDs:

Hart Rouge	Trafic 8732	1988
Inconditionnel	Trafic 8953	1991
Le Dernier Mois De L'annee	Independent	1992
Blue Blue Windows	MCA 10807	1993
La Fabrique	FACD 0594	1994
Bonsoir Quebec	Independent	1995
Beaupre's Home	H13 0297	1997

The Haunted

Bob Burgess (bass, vocals) Replaced by Glen Holmes (1964), Mason Shea (1966), Michael St. Germain (1966)
Pierre Faubert (guitar) (Replaced by Allan Birmingham (1965)
Tim Forsythe (organ) (1963 64)
Jurgen Peter (guitar)
Jim Robertson (vocals) (1963 64)
Peter Symes (drums) Replaced by Brian Roberts (1965), Dave Wynne (1965)

From Montreal, Quebec, the history of The Haunted goes back to late 1959 when Jurgen Peter was playing guitar at his parents' house in Chateaugay, Quebec. He and some of his friends often gathered together to play tunes by Lonnie Mack and The Ventures. Peter later joined The Blue Jays with Bob Burgess in late 1963. When they broke up, Peter and Burgess formed The Haunted. Joining them were Tim Forsythe, Jim Robertson, and Pierre Faubert.

By the fall of 1964 they were playing in and around Montreal.

When Forsythe and Robertson left, the band added Glen Holmes on bass while Burgess sang lead vocals.

Between 1964 65 the group played cover songs by The Beatles, Chuck Berry and The Rolling Stones. It was during this time that Dave Boxer, a radio host at CFCF Montreal, became interested in promoting them. He booked them at the Bonaventure Curling Club, one of the local top spots.

Between 1964 and 1966, there were a number of personnel changes: Allan Birmingham replaced Faubert on lead guitar;

Peter Symes was replaced first by Brian Roberts who defected to join The Raving Madd, and then by Dave Wynne. Holmes was replaced by Mason Shea, while Michael St. Germain, formerly from The Beat Boys, joined on bass. Burgess and St. Germain initially left to join The Esquires in Ottawa. When that didn't happen, St. Germain formed another band called The Cavemen. Brothers Pierre and Gilbert Faubert also went on to form their own band, Sir Bradley and The Screams, with Holmes and Greg Tomlinson.

On January 3, 1966, The Haunted took part in a battle of the bands contest at the Montreal Forum. First prize was a contract with Quality Records. Their first hit single for the label was 1 2 5 in the summer of 1966. Their second, I Can Only Give You Everything, followed in the fall of the same year.

They broke up in 1970.

Singles:

1 2 5	Quality 1814	1966
I Can Only Give You Everything	Quality 1840	1966
Vapeur Mauve/Pourquoi	Mark XII	1966
Searching For My Baby	Transworld 1674	1967
Out Of Time	Transworld 1682	1967
Land Of Make Believe/An Act Of Leisure	Transworld 1702	1968

Album:

The Haunted	Transworld 6701	1967

The Hawks (See "The Band")

Ronnie Hawkins

Ronald (Ronnie) Hawkins was born on January 10, 1935 in Huntsville, Arkansas. He first became interested in music when he was going to university to study for an arts degree. At the same time he was enlisted in the United States National Guard as part of his service obligation. The first time he showed any interest in singing on stage was at a campus pub where Moses and The Teacups played around 1954. However, he had more of an interest in hot rods and movie stars when he arrived in Hollywood and ended up working for Esther Williams at MGM as a clown diver. Returning to Fayetteville, Arkansas in 1956, he served two years in the military where he became involved in the group, The Black Hawks. This led to Ronnie starting his own group, The Hawks with Willard Jones, Jimmy Ray Paulman (Jimmy Luke) and Mark Lavon (Levon) Helm.

In 1958 Hawkins and The Hawks played in Hamilton and London, Ontario before making a name for themselves at Le Coq D'Or in Toronto. Hawkins also became known as Rompin' Ronnie. During the summer of that same year, he recorded Hey Bo Diddley on Quality Records. He then signed a recording contract with Roulette Records in the United States in 1959. Forty Days, his first single with the label, was released in Canada on Apex.

Ronnie became a Canadian citizen when he married Wanda Nagurski on March 10, 1962.

The most famous lineup of The Hawks came in the early 1960s when it included three future members of The Band: Robbie Robertson, Rick Danko, and Garth Hudson. By 1964 they had left to form Levon and The Hawks.

In 1964, Hawkins started his own Hawk label, with Robbie Lane and The Disciples and Doug Lycett among those on the artist roster.

Other members of The Hawks include a Who's Who of Canadian Rock: Bob Boucher, Gordon Fleming, Dave Lewis, John Till, Eugene "Jay" Smith (The Majestics), Hal Greer, Rick Bell (Ritchie Knight & The Mid Knights), David Clayton Thomas, Bob McBride, Richard Newell (King Biscuit Boy), Larry Atamniuk, Wayne Cardinal, Bobby Starr, Scott Cushnie, and Roly Greenway, Rheal Lanthier, John Gibbard and Kelly Jay Fordham, all of whom became Crowbar.

Singles:

Hey Bo Diddley	Quality 1827	1958
Forty Days	Apex 76499	1959
Mary Lou	Apex 76561	1959
Southern Love	Apex 76623	1960
Clara	Roulette R4228	1960
The Ballad of Cheryl Chessman	Roulette R4231	1960
Ruby Baby	Roulette R4249	1961
Summertime	Roulette R4267	1961
Cold Cold Heart	Roulette R4311	1961
I Feel Good	Roulette R4400	1961
Bo Diddley/Who Do You Love	Roulette R4483	1963
High Blood Pressure	Roulette R4502	1963
Get My Mojo Working	Hawk HR 002	1964
Bluebirds Over The Mountain	Hawk HR 106	1965
Goin' To The River	Hawk HR 107	1965
Home From The Forest	Yorkville 45016	1967/68
Reason To Believe	Yorkville 45019	1968
Go Go Liza Jane		1968
Matchbox	Hawk IT 301	1969
Down In The Alley	Hawk IT 302	1970
Bitter Green	Hawk IT 305	1970
Patricia	Hawk 1205 01	1971
Cora Mae	Monument 8548	1972
Lonesome Town	Monument 8561	1972
Diddley Daddley	Monument 8571	1973
Lonely Hours	Monument 8573	1973
Lady Came From Baltimore	Polydor 2065 303	1976
(Stuck In) Lodi	Quality 2392	1981
Only The Lucky	Quality 2399	1981
Wild Little Willie	Quality 2426	1983
Ode To A Truck Drivin' Man	Trilogy TR 50	1984
Hello Again, Mary Lou	Epic E4 3022	1987
Days Gone By	Epic E4 3026	1987

Albums/CDs:

Ronnie Hawkins	Roulette SR 25078	1959
Mr. Dynamo	Roulette SR 25102	1960
Folk Ballads	Roulette SR 25120	1960
Songs Of Hank Williams	Roulette SR 25137	1960
Best Of Ronnie Hawkins	Roulette SR 25255	1965
Mojo Man	Roulette SR 25390	1967
Home From The Forest	Yorkville YVS 33002	1968
Ronnie Hawkins	Hawk SD 9019	1970
The Hawk	Hawk 9205 9039	1971
Rock And Roll Resurrection	Monument KZ 31330	1972
The Giant Of Rock And Roll	Monument KZ 32940	1974
The Hawk In Winter	Polydor 2424 121	1976
Sold Out	Roulette SR 42045	1978

The Hawk	United Artists LA968H	1979
Greatest Hits	Quality SV 2074	1981
Legend In His Spare Time	Quality SV 2092	1981
The Hawk And Rock	Trilogy TR 50000	1983
Making It Again	Epic PEC 80104	1985
Hello Again...Mary Lou	Epic PEC 80127	1987
Greatest Hits (3 Lps)	Silver Eagle SE 10873	1989
Treasure Chest	Polydor 871739	1989
Rock 'N Roll Favorites	Silver Eagle SED10873	1989
Then And Now	Elite 845648	1991
Let It Rock	Quality QCD 2104	1995
Can't Stop Rockin'	Sony RK 24110	2001

Haywire

Marvin Birt (guitar)
Sean Kilbride (drums)
Paul Mac Ausland (vocals)
David Rashed (keyboards)
Ron Switzer (bass)

This band from Charlottetown, P.E.I. was originally a quartet when they formed in 1982. They later added Sean Kilbride on drums to make a five-man band. Constant touring tightened up their sound and they quickly became one of the most popular acts in the Atlantic Provinces.

In 1984 they won Q104 Halifax's homegrown contest. It resulted in the release of a five-song EP in June, 1985. Signed to Attic Records in January, 1986, their debut album, *Bad Boys* went on to sell more than 100,000 copies.

The group's popularity was acknowledged by the readers of Music Express magazine who voted them Best New Group of 1986.

In 1987 they represented the nation at the Yamaha World Popular Song Festival in Tokyo. They won the Golden Award for Best Song.

By the end of 1987 their second album, Just Don't Stand There had been released. Haywire's success continued into the early 1990s. Attic Records released a greatest hits album by the group in the fall of 1993.

Singles:

Bad Bad Boy	Attic AT 335	1986
Standing in Line	Attic AT 343	1986
Shot in the Dark	Attic AT 347	1986
Dance Desire	Attic AT 360	1987
Black And Blue	Attic AT 365	1987/88

Thinkin' About The Years	Attic AT 371	1988
Fire	Attic AT 378	1988
Short End Of A Wishbone	Attic ACD 1283	1990
Operator Central	Attic ACD 1283	1990/91
Taken The Pain	Attic ACD 1283	1991
Buzz	Attic ACD 1334	1992
Get Back	Attic ACD 1334	1992
Wanna Be The One	Attic ACD 1334	1992

Albums/CDs:

Bad Boys	Attic LAT 1220	1986
Don't Just Stand There	Attic LAT 1239	1987
Nuthouse	Attic ACBD 1283	1991
Get Off	Attic ACD 1334	1992
Wired: The Best of Haywire	Attic ACDM 1383	1993

The Headpins

Bernie Aubin (drums)
Ab Bryant (bass)
Brian Mac Leod (guitar, keyboards)
Darby Mills (lead vocals)

Founded in 1980 by Chilliwack's Brian MacLeod and Ab Bryant, The Headpins was a Vancouver quartet who first played part time for fun and money. The band's original lead singer was Denise McCann, but she was quickly replaced by Darby Mills, who was from Vernon, B.C. During the six years The Headpins were together, Brian MacLeod and Ab Bryant were also members of Chilliwack, and did double duty until the group's last album, *Opux X* came out in 1983. The Headpins' debut album, *Turn it Loud* on Solid Gold Records, sold well when it was released in 1982, as did their other two, Line Of Fire (1983), and Head Over Heels (1985). They broke up in 1986.

Singles:

Don't It Make Ya Feel	Solid Gold SGS 720	1982
Breakin' Down	Solid Gold SGS 731	1982
Celebration	Solid Gold SGS 741	1983
Just One More Time	Solid Gold SGS 746	1984
Feel It (Feel My Body)	Solid Gold SGS 749	1984
Staying All Night	MCA 5630	1985

Albums/CDs:

Turn it Loud	Solid Gold SGR 1010	1982
Line of Fire	Solid Gold SGR 1017	1983
Head Over Heels	MCA 6530	1985
Greatest Hits	CBS CK 80130	1988

Jeff Healey Band

Jeff Healey (lap top guitar, vocals)
Mischke Matthews (background vocals) (1993)
Tuku Matthews (background vocals) (1993)
Joe Rockman (bass, keyboards)
Washington Savage (keyboards) (1993)
Tom Stephen (drums)

Blind at the age of one, Jeff Healey, who was born on March 25, 1966, has been playing the lap top guitar since he was three years old. His guitar technique has been praised by blues legend B.B. King and the late Stevie Ray Vaughn.

In 1982 Healey recorded an independent video called Adriana, which was released as a vinyl single by an independent label in 1986. Three years later at Grossman's, a small Toronto nightclub, the Jeff Healey Band came together when bassist Joe Rockman and drummer Tom Stephen decided to join forces.

After signing a record deal with BMG Music Canada Inc. who released their debut album, See The Light in 1988, they soon established themselves as a hot new Canadian group.

MGM/UA in Hollywood wanted Healey to star in the film, Road House opposite Patrick Swayze. Its box office success helped draw attention internationally to Healey and his band.

In 1990 came their second album, *Hell to Pay*. It featured a guest appearance by ex-Beatle George Harrison on a cover version of While My Guitar Gently Weeps. The first single, I Think I Love You Too Much featured Mark Knopfler of the British band Dire Straits.

On November 6, 1992 came their third album, *Feel This* which showed how much the band had grown since their debut four years earlier. They also added keyboardist Washington Savage, and vocalists Mischke and Tuku Matthews.

In addition to writing music, Jeff Healey has hosted his own radio on the CBC network called My Kinda Jazz. In 1995 Arista released Cover To Cover, a collection of cover songs.

He died March 2, 2008.

Singles:

Adrianna	Procan CCR 9259	1986
See The Light	Arista 87062	1988
Confidence Man	Arista 87062	1988
My Little Girl	Arista 87062	1988
Angel Eyes	Arista AS1 9808	1989
While My Guitar Gently Weeps	Arista 8632	1989
I Think I Love You Too Much	Arista 8632	1990
How Long Can A Man Be Strong	Arista 8632	1991
How Much	Arista 8632	1991
Cruel Little Number	Arista 87062	1992/93
Heart Of An Angel	Arista 87062	1993
Lost In Your Eyes	Arista 87062	1993
It Could All Get Blown Away	Arista 87062	1993
Leave The Light On	Arista 87062	1993
You're Coming Home	Arista 87062	1993
I Got A Line On You	Arista 23888	1995
Angel	Arista 23888	1995
Stuck In The Middle With You	Arista 23888	1995
I Tried	Forte 641001	2000
Daze of the Night	Provogue 74892	2016

Albums/CDs:

See The Light	Arista 8553	1988
Hell To Pay	Arista 8632	1990
Feel This	Arista 87062	1992
Cover To Cover	Arista 23888	1995
Get Me Some	Forte 641001	2000
Songs From The Road	Ruf 1154	2009
Last Call	Stony Plain 32135	2010
Heal My Soul	Provogue 74892	2016

Heart

Mike DesRosier (drums)
Howard Leese (guitar)
Ann Wilson (lead vocals)
Nancy Wilson (vocals, guitar, keyboards)
Mike Fisher (guitar)
Roger Fisher (guitar)
Steve Fossen (bass)

The origins of Heart go back to 1963 in Seattle, Washington when the group was comprised of Steve Fossen and brothers Roger and Mike Fisher and were known as The Army. Ann Wilson joined in 1970. When Mike Fisher became their manager, he was replaced by Ann's sister Nancy. In 1972 the group changed its name to White Heart and then Heart two years later.

They moved to Vancouver in 1975 where they were given immigrant status for seven years, and added drummer Mike DeRosier to their lineup. Their debut album, *Dreamboat Annie* on Mushroom Records was released in 1976. The group became known for their hard-edged pop vocals on such songs as Crazy On You and Magic Man.

In 1976 they returned to Seattle and signed with Portrait Records. Other personnel changes included the Fisher brothers who both left in 1979, and the addition of Howard Leese in 1980.

By the end of 1982 the group's status as Canadian immigrants terminated. In 1993 the Wilson Sisters recorded Battle of Evermore as The Lovemongers. They continued to release material as Heart, including a greatest hits CD in 1998. They were inducted into the Rock And Roll Hall Of Fame in 2013.

Singles:

How Deep It Goes	Mushroom M 7008	1975
Magic Man	Mushroom M 7011	1975
(Love Me Like Music) I'll Be Your Song	Mushroom M 7014	1975
Crazy On You	Mushroom M 7021	1976
Dreamboat Annie	Mushroom M 7023	1977
Barracuda	Portrait6 70004	1977
Little Queen	Portrait6 70008	1977
Kick It Out	Portrait6 70010	1977
Heartless	Mushroom M 7031	1978
Without You	Mushroom M 7035	1978
Straight On	Portrait6 70020	1978/79
Dog And Butterfly	Portrait6 70025	1979
Even It Up	Epic 50847	1980
Tell It Like It Is	Epic 50950	1981
Unchained Melody	Epic 51051	1981
This Man Is Mine	Epic 02925	1982
How Can I Refuse	Epic 04047	1983
Allies	Epic 04184	1983
What About Love	Capitol 5481	1985
Never	Capitol 5512	1985
These Dreams	Capitol 5541	1986
Nothin' At All	Capitol 5572	1986
If Looks Could Kill	Capitol 5605	1986
Alone	Capitol 44002	1987
Who Will You Run To	Capitol 44040	1987
There's The Girl	Capitol 44089	1987
I Want You So Bad	Capitol 44116	1988

All I Wanna Do Is Make Love	Capitol 44507	1990
I Didn't Want To Need You	Capitol 44553	1990
Stranded	Capitol 44621	1990/91
Will You Be There (In The Morning)	Capitol 58041	1994

Albums/CDs:

Dreamboat Annie	Mushroom MRS 5005	1976
Little Queen	PortraitPR 34799	1977
Magazine	Mushroom MRS 5008	1978
Dog & Butterfly	PortraitFR 35555	1978
Bebe Le Strange	Epic FE 36371	1980
Greatest Hits/Live	Epic FE 36888	1980
Private Audition	SMI 138049	1982
Passionworks	Epic IDK 38800	1983
Heart	Capitol ST 12410	1985
Bad Animals	Capitol C1 12546	1987
Brigade	Capitol C1 91820	1990
Rock The House Live!	Capitol 95797	1991
DESire Walks On	Capitol 99627	1993
The Road Home	Capitol 30489	1995
Greatest Hits	Epic/Legacy 69015	1998
Dreamboat Annie	Capitol CD 21184	1999
The Essential Heart	Epic TV2K 615557	2002

Helix

Bruce Arnold (drums) Replaced by Brian Doerner
Paul Hackman (lead guitar)
Leo Niebudek (guitar) Replaced by Greg "Fritz" Hinz (1982 99)
Don Simmons (keyboards) Replaced by Paul Hackman
Rick Tremblay (guitar)
Brian Vollmer (lead vocals)
Ron Watson (guitar) Replaced by Brent Doerner, Denny Balicki (1990)
Keith Zurbrigg (bass)

This Kitchener-based heavy metal group started out in 1974 as The Helix Field Band. The original lineup was comprised of Ron Watson, Bruce Arnold, Don Simmons, Brian Vollmer, Keith Zurbrigg, and Rick Tremblay. In 1975, Watson and Tremblay left and in 1976, Simmons and Arnold. Over the years, other members included Mike Uzelac, Brent and Brian Doerner, Gary Borden, Greg Fraser, Danny Balicki, Leo Niebudek, and Gary "Fritz" Hinz.

In 1979 they recorded their first single for H&S Records, Billy Oxygen. By the early 1980s, they had switched to Capitol Records and built up a loyal following with their heavy rock sounds. Their single, The Storm (1990) was Zepplinesque, while Give It To You, another song, was reminiscent of AC/DC.

On Sunday, July 5, 1992 lead guitarist Paul Hackman died of injuries suffered in an accident when the group's van flipped on the Coquihalla Highway in British Columbia.

In 1993, Helix released a new album on Aquarius Records called, *It's a Business Doing Pleasure*. It featured Kim Mitchell on, Sleeping In The Doghouse Again, and a duet with Lee Aaron called Look Me Straight In The Heart. The first single from the album, *That Day is Gonna Come* was a tribute to Hackman. The accompanying video was comprised of Super 8 home movies that were shot on the road between 1976 and 1982.

Their 1984 album, Live At The Marquee, which was released only to radio, was reissued on CD in 1998. Vollmer recorded the solo albums, *Cherry St.* (Perris Records, 1999) and *When Pigs Fly* (Vollmer Records, 1999).

Today, the band is still touring and recording with Mike Hall and Gerry Finn (both from The Killer Dwarfs), Glenn "Archie" Gamble, Daryl Gray and Brian Vollmer.

Singles:

Billy Oxygen	H&S 1002	1979
Don't Hide Your Love		1980
It's Too Late	H&S 2002	1981
Don't Get Mad Get Even	Capitol 72925	1983
Does A Fool Ever Learn (12")	Capitol SPRO 236	1983
Rock You	Capitol 72949	1984/85
(Make Me Do) Anything You Want	Capitol SPRO 264	1985
Deep Cuts The Knife	Capitol 5490	1985
The Kids Are All Shakin'	Capitol 72981	1985
Live At The Marquee (12")	Capitol SPRO 263	1985
Wild In The Streets	Capitol	1987
The Storm	Capitol 26573	1990
The Storm (12")	Capitol CD PRO 471	1990
Runnin' Wild In The 21st Century	Capitol 26573	1990
Good To The Last Drop	Capitol 26573	1991
That Day Is Gonna Come	Aquarius Q2570	1993
Tug Of War	Aquarius Q2570	1993

Albums/CDs:

Breaking Loose	H&S 101	1980
White Lace and Black Leather	H&S 202	1981
No Rest For the Wicked	Capitol ST 12281	1983
Walkin' on the Razor's Edge	Capitol ST 12362	1984
Long Way to Heaven	Capitol ST 12411	1985
Wild in the Streets	Capitol ST 46920	1987
OVER 60 Minutes with Helix	Capitol 93571	1989

Back For Another Taste	Capitol C1 26573	1990
The Early Years	Maximum 11001	1992
It's a Business Doing Pleasure	Aquarius Q2570	1993
Half Alive	Derock DER 9012	1998
Live at the Marquee		1998
Deep Cuts: The Best of Helix	Razor & Tie	1999
B Sides	Beak Records	1999

Hemingway Corner

Johnny Douglas (bass, lead guitar, percussion, background vocals) (1992 94)
David Martin (rhythm guitar, lead vocals)
Scott Dibble (guitar, vocals)
Mark Stirling (electric guitar, harmonica, vocals)

These two multi-talented singer/songwriters forged a musical collaboration that led to the birth of Hemingway Corner. The sound of their acoustic guitars led to comparisons to Crosby, Stills, Nash and Young, America, the Indigo Girls and R.E.M.

David Martin hails from Atlanta, Georgia. He lived in Nashville for several years where he honed his craft as a songwriter before moving to Los Angeles. Johnny Douglas is from Toronto. He left Los Angeles to set up roots in Nashville to concentrate on his songwriting. The two met while writing songs for Sony Music, and began working together in December, 1992.

Their self-titled debut album on Epic/Sony came out in 1993. The first single was Man on a Mission.

In 1994 Douglas, a family man, left the group, because he grew tired of touring and wanted to be closer to home. Scott Dibble, one of the founders of the Toronto-based band Watertown, and Mark Stirling joined Hemingway Corner to make it a trio. Sony Music released their CD, Under A Big Sky, in 1995.

Singles:

Man on a Mission	Epic 80180	1993
So Long JFK	Epic 80180	1993
Love Love Love	Epic 80180	1994
Ride it Out	Epic 80180	1994
King of New York	Epic 80180	1994
Tell Me Why	Epic 80180	1994/95
Big Sky	Epic 80218	1995
Watch Over You	Epic 80218	1995/96
Make it Up as You Go	Epic 80218	1996
Wild Honey	Epic 80218	1996

Albums/CDs:
Hemingway Corner	Epic 80180	1993
Under The Big Sky	Epic 80218	1995

Wade Hemsworth

One of Canada's traditional folksingers was Wade Hemsworth, whose natural delivery endeared him to folk music enthusiasts.

Some of his songs have recently been re-discovered thanks to the reissue of two three CD sets, Canada: A Folksong Portrait, and, Singers and Songs of Canada.

Born in Brantford, Ontario on October 23, 1916, Hemsworth's interest in folk music goes back to Newfoundland where he was stationed during World War II. Once he started hearing the province's many folksongs his interest in folk music grew to the point where he was sitting down and writing his own songs while he was a draftsman for the Canadian National Railway and Ontario Hydro.

Some of his more famous songs include, The Black Fly Song, The Wild Goose, Foolish You, and, The Story of the I'm Alone.

He made only one album, *Folk Songs of the Canadian North Woods* on the Folkways label in 1955. In 1963 Hemsworth sang at the Mariposa Folk Festival.

In 1979 his song, The Log Driver's Waltz was made into a three minute animated film short, while The Black Fly Song inspired the National Film Board cartoon of the same name which was nominated for an Academy Award in 1995.

Hemsworth died on January 19, 2002.

Album:
Folk Songs of the Canadian North Woods	Folkways FW 6821	1955

Pat Hervey

Born and raised in Toronto, Ontario, Pat Hervey was one of Canada's first successful female singing stars. She first sang in public at age eight, and as a teenager began her professional singing career with the single, Stormy Weather (1961).

She began her television career on such CBC shows as Holiday Ranch, Wayne and Shuster, Parade, The Jack Kane Show, and Don Messer's Jubilee. During the

1960s she became a national celebrity when she appeared regularly on two CBC TV shows, Country Hoedown and The Tommy Hunter Show, where she sang pop, country and gospel songs.

Producer Art Snider was instrumental in getting her to record on his own label, Chateau Records. The result was her first hit, Stormy Weather, in 1961. The following year she went to Nashville where she recorded her first number one smash, Mr. Heartache. She later recorded two Albums for RCA Victor, *Pat Hervey* and *Peaceful*.

In 1969 she moved to Vancouver, British Columbia where she appeared on her own CBC show, Miss Patricia's Songs and Things, and started a new career in jazz. She later married Oliver Gannon, who as one of Canada's top jazz guitarists, introduced her to Brazilian Jazz and such Vancouver jazz notables as Al Wold, Ron Johnston, Ian McDougall, John Nolan, Torben Oxbol, Blaine Wikjord, Jack Stafford, the late Fraser MacPherson. Today, she continues as a singer/bassist in the jazz field in Vancouver. She died on July 31, 2016.

Singles:

Stormy Weather	Chateau 135	1961
Mr. Heartache	Chateau 143	1962
A Mother's Love/Heaven For Awhile	Chateau 149	1962
Tears of Misery	RCA 47 8135	1963
I Wouldn't Blame You		1963
Walking in Bonnie's Footsteps	RCA 47 8281	1963/64
Think About Me	Red Leaf 103	1965
He Belongs to Yesterday	Red Leaf 105	1965
Ain't A Girl Allowed to Cry	Red Leaf 106	1965
The Land I Dream Of	AME 108	1971

Albums/CDs:

Pat Hervey	RCA Victor International PC 1021	1965
Peaceful	RCA Camden CAS 2393	1970

The Hi-Fis

Jim Cuddy (vocals, guitar)
Greg Keelor (vocals, guitar)
Malcolm Schell (vocals, bass)
Jimmy Sublett (vocals, drums)

In the fall of 1979 while Jim Cuddy and Greg Keelor were in high school they began writing songs together, and formed a band called The Hi Fis. Originally a trio, they added Jimmy Sublett, from the Montreal band The Scavengers, in 1980. Along with covers of songs by The Beatles, The Rolling Stones, and The Yardbirds, they also used some of their own original material.

They recorded one single, Look What You've Done/I Don't Know Why (You Love Me), on Showtime Records in 1980. The following year, the group broke up when Cuddy and Keelor went to moved to New York City. They returned to Toronto in 1984 and started Blue Rodeo.

Single:
Look What You've Done   Showtime 001   1980

Dan Hill

Born on June 3, 1954 in Don Mills, Ontario, Dan Hill started in the music business when he finished grade 12. He had been writing songs since he was fourteen and sent a tape of six of them to RCA.

Two of them, Peter Pan and Nobody's Right, became two sides of a single when it was released in 1973. Unfortunately, it was not a hit. He later signed a recording contract with GRT Records. You Make Me Want To Be, released in 1975, was the first single.

His biggest hit to date was Sometimes When We Touch, which he recorded in 1977. Written by Hill and American songwriter Barry Mann, it was number one in Canada, Australia, and ten other countries. Hill's next big success came in 1987 when he recorded a duet called Can't We Try with Vonda Sheppard.

After its success he took a break from recording to concentrate on his songwriting. He wrote songs for such artists as Jeffrey Osborne, George Benson, Tina Turner, and Celine Dion.

In the fall of 1991 Hill reunited with his old friend Russ Regan, co-founder of Quality Records. The result of their new collaboration was the album, *Dance of Love*, which included the first single, I Fall All Over Again. Two years later came Let Me Show You: Greatest Hits And More, followed by an album of original material called, *I'm Doing Fine*.

Today, he lives in Toronto where he focuses on his songwriting.

He co-wrote two Top Ten country hits in 1998 with Keith Stegall: Sammy Kershaw's Love of My Life and Mark Wills' I Do (Cherish You).

Singles:

Peter Pan/Nobody's Right	RCA KPBO 0002	1973
You Make Me Want To Be	GRT 1230 100	1975
Growing Up	GRT 1230 107	1975
You Say You're Free	GRT 1230 110	1976
Hold On	GRT 1230 122	1976
Phonecall	GRT 1230 126	1976
Sometimes When We Touch	GRT 1230 137	1977/78
Let The Song Last Forever	GRT 1230 155	1978
All I See Is Your Face	GRT 1230 158	1978
Dark Side of Atlanta		1978
(Why Did You Have To Go And) Pick On Me	GRT 1230 168	1978
Hold On To The Night	Magnum 8805	1979
When You Smile		1979/80
I Still Reach For You	Columbia C4 4243	1980
Don't Give Up On Love		1981
I'm Just A Man		1982
Helpless	MS 76208	1983
You Pulled Me Through	MS 76215	1983
Love In The Shadows	Mercury 76204	1983
Can't We Try (with Vonda Sheppard)	Columbia C4 7050	1987
Never Thought (That I Could Love)	Columbia C4 7681	1988
Carmelia	Columbia C4 7772	1988
Unborn Heart	Columbia C4 8754	1989
I Fall All Over Again	Quality QLP 2001	1991/92
Is It Really Love	Quality QLP 2001	1992
Through It All (CD/S)	Quality QSP 736	1992
Hold Me Now	Quality QLP 2001	1992
Flirting With A Heartache	Quality QCD 2016	1993
Healing Power of Love	Quality QCD 2016	1993
Let Me Show You	Quality QCD 2016	1993/94
In Your Eyes*	Quality QCD 2016	1994
Love Theme From Napoleon* (CD/S)	EMI PROMO	1994
Sometimes When We Touch*	Quality QCD 2016	1994
Wrapped Around Your Finger	SPON 81012	1996
I'm Doing Fine	SPON 81012	1996/97
Everytime We Say Goodbye (with Vann Johnson)	SPON 81012	1997
Love of My Life	TVK 24055	1999
Once Upon a Time	TVK 24055	2000

(* w/Rique Franks)

Albums/CDs:

Dan Hill	GRT 9230 1061	1975
Hold On	GRT 9230 1065	1976
Longer Fuse	GRT 9230 1073	1977

Frozen In The Night	GRT 9230 1079	1978
If Dreams Had Wings	Columbia FC 3644	1980
Partial Surrender	Epic FE 37418	1981
Love In The Shadows	MercurySRM 1 4081	1983
Dan Hill	Columbia FC 40456	1987
Real Love	CBS FC 45162	1989
The Dan Hill Collection	CBS WCK 80141	1989
Dance Of Love	Quality QLP/CD 2001	1991
Let Me Show You: Greatest Hits And More	Quality QCD 2016	1993
I'm Doing Fine	SPON 81012	1996
Love Of My Life: Best Of	Columbia TVK 24055	1999

Honeymoon Suite

Dave Betts (drums)
Ray Coburn (keyboards)
Johnny Dee (guitar, vocals)
Derry Grehan (guitar, vocals)
Gary Lalonde   (bass, vocals)

The genesis of Honeymoon Suite goes back to September 1982 when Derry Grehan and Johnny Dee first met in the group's hometown of Niagara Falls, Ontario. Grehan had been in the bands Stytch and Steve Blimkie and The Reason, when he asked Dee to form a new group to compete in a homegrown talent search in Toronto, with the Grehan-penned song, New Girl Now, which became their first hit single when they signed to Wea.

In 1986 they achieved success simultaneously in U.S. and Canada when their hit single, Feel It Again started climbing up the charts. Their next hit single, What Does it Take was featured in an episode of NBC's Miami Vice, and the soundtrack of the Warner Brothers' movie, One Crazy Summer (1986).In 1987 they also contributed the title song to Warner Brothers'Lethal Weapon.

After fifteen hit Singles:, the group changed management and became a trio when Dave Betts and Gary LaLonde left. Other members of the group have included Rob Preuss, Troy Feener, Tim Harrington, Steve Skingley, Steve Webster, Tom Lewis, Stan Miczek, Jorn Andersen, and Creighton Doane. Their lineup in 2001 featured Dee, Grehan, Peter Nunn, Brett Carrigan and Rob Laidlaw.

Singles:

New Girl Now	Wea 25 94867	1984
Stay In The Light	Wea 25 91527	1985
Burning In Love	Wea 25 92627	1985
Wave Babies	Wea 25 90277	1985
Feel It Again	Wea 25 87717	1986
What Does It Take	Wea 25 8638	1986
All Along You Knew	Wea 25 85357	1987
All Along You Knew (12")	Wea PRO	1987
Lethal Weapon	Wea	1987
It's Over Now	Wea 25 78197	1988
Love Changes Everything	Wea 25 80327	1988
Lookin' Out For Number One	Wea 25 79137	1988
Still Lovin' You	Wea 69791	1989/90
Long Way	Wea 69791	1990
Say You Don't Love Me	Wea 75532	1991
The Road	Wea 75532	1991/92

Albums/CDs:

Honeymoon Suite	Wea 25 07301	1984
Stay In The Light (EP)	Wea 25 91260	1985
The Big Prize	Wea 25 28241	1986
What Does It Take (EP)	Wea PRO 49	1986
Lethal Weapon	MKCD 01	1987
Racing After Midnight	Wea 54451	1988
Honeymoon Suite: The singles	Wea 69791	1989
Monsters Under The Bed	Wea 75532	1991
13 Live	Magada CD 49	2001
Lemon Tongue		2001

Gavin Hope

Born in Scarborough, Ontario on August 2, 1973, Gavin Hope moved to Calgary when he was seven years old. He became the youngest member of the Calgary Opera Chorus in the early 1990s and performed in various stage productions, notably Romeo and Juliet.

He has also won several talent competitions and sang backup for Michael Bolton during his Time, Love and Tenderness Tour in Western Canada.

Gavin also performed and recorded with the Calgary pop group, The EarthTones, and was invited to perform with The Nylons, a group he joined in 1994.

While still with The Nylons, he recorded his first single, Can I Get Close, which was followed by The Tears I Cry (the same song Carol Medina first recorded in 1989), and It's OK, It's Alright.

In October 1997 Gavin left The Nylons to join the Toronto production of the musical Rent. Two years later, his first full length CD, *Anything Like Mine*, was released. The first single was the title track.

Singles:
Can I Get Close	Quality QCDS 7282	1996
The Tears I Cry	Quality QCDS 7282	1996/97
It' OK, It's Alright	PopularPR2S 3198	1997
Anything Like Mine	PopularDPOP 001	1999

Album:
Anything Like Mine	Popular 83293	1999

Lorence Hud

Born in Saskatoon, Saskatchewan in 1947, Lorence Hud is an accomplished musician who can play fourteen instruments, including the organ, piano, vibes, harpsichord, bass guitar, drums, saxophone, and glockenspiel. Before he was a music major at the University of Saskatchewan between 1968 and 1970, he played in a Calgary group called For Keeps, which was managed by Doug Hutton. Hud also recorded some of his own songs on RCA and Apex in Los Angeles.

After moving to Toronto in the early 1970s, he signed a contract with A&M Records. Sign of the Gypsy Queen was his first single with the label.

In 1976 he moved to Los Angeles where he worked for Carmen Productions at Sound City Studios, where he was a part of a songwriting team with Rick Springfield and Les Emmerson. Hud returned to Toronto in 1981 and resumed his solo career. Quality Records released the single, Here's To You/Feel The Pulse in 1982 but it was not a hit.

Singles:
Natural Loved Boy	Apex 77083	1968
Sign Of The Gypsy Queen	A&M AM 332	1972/73
Master of Pantomime	A&M AM 335	1973
Guilty of Rock'n'Roll	A&M AM 358	1974
The Song That Annie Sings	A&M AM 365	1974
(Out On The Road) Rollin' Home	A&M AM 376	1974/75
Love You All Night Long (Belly Up To The Bar)	A&M AM 382	1975

| Flashing Signs & Neon Lights | A&M AM 396 | 1975 |
| Here's To You/Feel The Pulse | QUA 2421X | 1982 |

Albums/CDs:
Lorence Hud	A&M SP 9004	1972
Dancin' in my Head	A&M SP 9009	1973
Here's To You (EP)	Quality EPQ2	1982

Huevos Rancheros

Brent J. Cooper (guitar)
Graham Evans (electric bass)
Richie Lazarowich (drums)

From Calgary, Alberta, Huevos Rancheros started in the summer of 1990. Brent Cooper had previously played in other Calgary bands such as The Presence, Cryin' Helicopters, and the Ted Clarke Five.

In 1991 they recorded the self-titled independent cassette, Huevosaurus. Their three CDs, Endsville (1993), Dig In (1995) and Get Outta Dodge (96) celebrated a musical style that brought back surf music from the early 1960s with a 1990s twist that was inventive and nondescript in its delivery. Their album, *Muerte Del Toro* (Death Of The Bull) in 2000 was recorded at Sundae Sound in Calgary with Dave Alcock from the group Chixdiggit and included a new version of Wild Turkey Surprise.

Singles:
Cindy With An "S"		1992
Rockin' In The Henhouse	Loud 3	1994
Gump Worsley's Lament	Loud 3	1995
64 Slices Of American Cheese/Telstar	RF 703	1995
Come In Tokyo/Mrs. Fothergill	SLOO14	1997
Wild Turkey Surprise	Mint MRS 034	1999

Albums/CDs:
Rocket To Nowhere (EP)		1992
Endsville	C/Z Records CZO63	1993
Dig In!	Mint MRD 007	1995
Get Outta Dodge	Mint MRD 024	1996
Muerto Del Toro	Mint MRD 040	2000

Ian and Sylvia

Ian Tyson (born in Victoria, B.C. on September 25, 1933) and Sylvia Fricker (born in Chatham, Ont. on September 19, 1940) played an integral role as one of Canada's first successful folk duos.   They met in 1959 and first sang together at Massey Hall in 1961 when Pete Seeger invited them to come on stage and sing a couple of songs. Later that summer, Ian and Sylvia played at the first Mariposa Folk Festival and the Newport Folk Festival.

Signed to Vanguard Records, their self-titled debut album was released in 1961.

A year later he began writing his songs, including Four Strong Winds, the title track on the duo's second album. They later hired bassist Felix Pappalardi, who would later produce New York's first folk/rock group, The Mugwumps with Canadians Denny Doherty from The Halifax Three and Zal Yanovsky.

On June 26, 1964 Ian and Sylvia were married at St. Thomas' Anglican Church in Toronto.

They continued to record for Vanguard, then MGM and Columbia.

During Canada's centennial year they toured Canadian Army bases, and in 1968 Ian and Sylvia formed The Great Speckled Bird.

The fall of 1969 they hosted their own CTV show, Nashville North, which was later changed to The Ian Tyson Show. Its success kept the group together although there were many personnel changes.

In 1975 Ian Tyson left the show to concentrate on a solo career. He and Sylvia divorced a year later. They reunited in 1986 for a concert at the Kingswood Music Theatre in Toronto. Since their breakup, they have both carved out successful careers in the country field.Four Strong Winds was inducted into the Canadian Songwriters Hall of Fame in 2003.

Singles:

Four Strong Winds	Vanguard 35021	1963
You Were On My Mind	Vanguard 35025	1964
Lovin' Sound	MGM 13686	1967
House of Cards	Vanguard 35062	1968
Trucker's Cafe	Ampes 11006	1970
Creators Of Rain	Columbia 4 45430	1971
More Often Than Not	Columbia 4 45475	1971
You Were On My Mind	Columbia C4 3047	1972
Salmon In The Sea	Columbia C4 45680	1972

Albums/CDs:

Ian & Sylvia	Vanguard VRS 9109	1962

Four Strong Winds	Vanguard VRS 9133	1963
Northern Journey	Vanguard VRS 9154	1964
Early Mornin' Rain	Vanguard VRS 9175	1965
Play One More	Vanguard VRS 9215	1966
So Much For Dreaming	Vanguard VRS 9241	1967
Lovin' Sound	MGM E 4388	1967
Best of Ian & Sylvia	Vanguard VSD 79269	1968
Nashville	Vanguard VRS 9284	1968
Full Circle	MGM SE 4550	1968
Great Speckled Bird	Ampes A 10103	1969
Ian & Sylvia's Greatest Hits Volume I	Vanguard VSD 5/6	1969
Ian & Sylvia's Greatest Hits Volyme II	Vanguard VSD 23/24	1970
Ian & Sylvia	Columbia C 30736	1971
You Were On My Mind	Columbia KC 31337	1972
The Best of Ian & Sylvia	Columbia G 32516	1973

I Mother Earth

Edwin (vocals)
Bruce Gordon (bass)
Christian Tanna (drums)
Jagori Tanna (guitar)

I Mother Earth was a four-man band from Toronto. Formed in September, 1990, the group's artistic vision came from the music of Pink Floyd, Santana and Led Zeppelin.

Brothers Christian and Jagori Tanna first played in their parents' basement as teenagers, and later played in a number of garage bands until mid 1989 when they met Edwin, who became vocalist for the group in June, 1990. The addition of Bruce Gordon made it a four-man band, when his previous band, Roctopus broke up.

Signed to EMI, their first album, *Dig,* was released on July 27, 1993. The first single and video was Rain Will Fall.

Edwin left in 1997 to pursue a solo career. He was replaced by Brian Byrne. In 1999 Edwin's debut CD, Another Spin Around the Sun (EK 80392) Was Released By Columbia/Sony.

Singles:

Rain Will Fall	EMI 98912	1993
Not Quite Sonic	EMI 98912	1993/94
So Gently We Go	EMI 98912	1994
Levitate	EMI 98912	1994/95

One More Astronaut	EMI 32919	1996
Used To Be Alright	EMI 32919	1996/97
Raspberry	EMI 32919	1997
Summertime In The Void	MER 46246	1999

Albums/CDs:

Dig	EMI 98912	1993
Scenery and Fish	EMI 32919	1996
Blue Green Orange	MER 46246	1999
Earth, Sky and Everything In Between	EMI 32326	2001

The Inbreds

Mike O'Neill (vocals, bass)
Dave Ullrich (drums)

The Inbreds started in Kingston, Ontario in January 1992 when Mike O'Neill and Dave Ullrich first played together in a late night jam session. The chemistry between them worked, and during the next two years they released three independent cassettes, *Darn Foul Dog* (February 1992), The *Let's Get Together* Ep (June 1992), and *Egrog* (April 1993), and the CD, *Hilario* (December 1993).

They played in clubs across Southern Ontario and toured with The Rheostatics prior to the release of their second CD, *Kombinator* in November 1994.

During the second half of 1995, they were part of, The Tragically Hip's Another Roadside Attraction, and later toured with, Jale and The Super Friendz.

By the spring of 1996, The Inbreds, relocated to Halifax, Nova Scotia where they recorded their third CD, It's Sydney or The Bush.

They split up in 1998. Mike O'Neill recorded the solo album, *What Happens Now* (Perimeter 300062) in 2000.

Singles:

Shermans	PF 009	1992
You Will Know	PF 92639	1993
Any Sense of Time	PRCD 6399	1994
Yelverton Hill	Shine US20	1997
Moustache	Murder 029	1997

Albums/CDs:

Darn Foul Dog (EP/CS)	PF 001	1992
Let's Get Together (EP)	PF 004	1992
Egrog (CS)	PF 005	1993
Hilario	PF 012	1993
Kombinator	PF 017	1994
It's Sydney Or The Bush	PF/TAG 16325	1996
Winning Hearts	MURD 034	1998

The Infidels

Molly Johnson (vocals)
Norman Orenstein (guitar)

The Infidels, a Toronto band featuring Molly Johnson, have been together since 1980 when they were first known as Alta Moda (Julian). They were named after the title of a 1991 article in The Toronto Star written by Murray McLauchlan. The name "Infidels" refers to the various musical influences that comprise their sound, and because Molly has always felt like an infidel or an unbeliever.

Molly and Norman Orenstein have known each other since high school. The former lived above the infamous Cameron House Pub and sang jazz and rhythm and blues to help pay the bills, while the latter played guitar in various local bands.

Their self-titled debut album on I.R.S. Canada was released in 1991. From it came their first single, 100 Watt Bulb. In January, 1993 the duo joined Meryn Cadell in a video of the funk/dance/rock song Courage. Written by the Infidels, it was part of a campaign to promote sustainable development and the responsible use of our resources.

Singles:
100 Watt Bulb	I.R.S. 13110	1991
Celebrate	I.R.S. 13110	1991/92
Without Love	I.R.S. 13110	1992
Shaking	I.R.S. 13110	1992

Albums/CDs:
The Infidels	I.R.S. 13110	1991

Influence

Jack Geisinger (bass)
Bobo Island (organ, piano)
Louis Campbell Mc Kelvey (guitar)
Andrew Keiler (lead vocals)
Walter Rossi (guitar)
Dave Wynne (drums)

This Montreal-based group was known more for their stage act which included a mini opera. It featured the guitar stylings of Walter Rossi, who began his career as as one of the Soul Mates in 1965 and then toured as a sideman with Wilson Pickett. In 1967–68 Rossi joined Influence, a band that played in Toronto and New York.

The short time that Influence was together, they made one album which contained the mini opera, Man Birds Of Prey. It was released in 1968, the same year the band broke up.

Rossi, who was born on May 29, 1947 in Naples, Italy, went on to play in the Buddy Miles Express and his own short-lived band, Charlee in 1972. From 1976 to 1980 he recorded several singles and four albums for Aquarius Records (*Walter Rossi* – AQ 514; *Six Strings Nine Lives* – AQ 519; *Diamonds For The Kid* – AQ 526; and *Picks* – AQ 531).

Album:
Influence   Sparton630   1968

The Irish Descendants

D'Arcy Broderick (fiddle, banjo, guitar, bouzouki) Repld by Eamonn O'Rourke (1998)
Gerard Broderick (vocals, bodhran, piccolo)
Larry Martin (vocals, bass)
Con O'Brien (vocals, guitar)
Kathy Phippard (keyboards) Replaced by Bill McCauley (1996)
Ronnie Power (vocals, guitar, tin whistle, bouzouki)

Formed in 1990 in St. John's, Newfoundland, The Irish Descendants have been one of the most popular Celtic groups in Atlantic Canada. Con O'Brien and Ronnie Power are natives of Bay Bulls on Newfoundland's South Shore, while D'Arcy Broderick hails from Bay de Verde, on the north tip of Conception Bay and was formerly in the Irish group, Sons of Erin. Larry Martin was born near Grates Cove, near Bay de Verde.

The success of the group depends largely on the group's overall appeal to both older audiences and a younger generation of fans who have discovered the energy and fun of traditional music.

Their first independent album, Misty Morning Shore, was released in 1991. Over the next two years they were nominated for two awards at the 1991 East Coast Music Awards for best roots traditional group and best live act. They also played their first international show in Boston, Massachusetts on St. Patrick's Day 1992. Their many other appearances included performing live with the Newfoundland Symphony Orchestra in 1992, and at Canada's Greatest Party on Canada Day, 1992. In 1993 Warner Music Canada released their second, Look To The Sea.

D'Arcy Broderick left the group in 1996, and founded the group The Fables in August 1997. That same year, the Irish Descendants were honored as the official band for Newfoundland's 500th Anniversary Celebrations.

Singles:

Useta Love Her	WAR 40174	1993
Last of the Great Whales	WAR 40174	1993/94
Catch The Wind	WAR 98237	1994
Rock And A Hard Place	WAR 14827	1996
Shamrock City	WAR 14827	1996/97
Rollin' Home	WAR 22717	1998
Catch The Wind	Wea 29128	1999

Albums/CDs:

Misty Morning Shore	Independent	1991
Look To The Sea	War 40174	1993
Gypsies & Lovers	War 98237	1994
Livin' On The Edge	War 14857	1996
Rollin' Home	War 22717	1998
So Far So Good: The Best Of	War 29128	1999
Blooming Bright Star	Sextant 0001	2001

The Irish Rovers

Jimmy Ferguson (vocals)
Wilcil McDowell (accordion)
George Millar (guitar)
Joe Millar (accordion, bass)
Will Millar (vocals, guitar, banjo)

The history of the Irish Rovers goes back to 1963 in Calgary, Alberta, when Will Millar became a featured performer on a daily kids TV show. His appearance caused such a sensation that he was invited to host the show five days a week for the next two years.

At the end of each show, he'd say, "Hey kids, if you're not doing anything, get your parents to take you down to Phil's Pancake House cause that's where I'll be after the show."

After he arrived he sang at each table and one of the songs he ended up recording was a rare acoustic performance of The Unicorn.

When his younger brother George and Jimmy Ferguson heard about Will's success in Toronto, they moved to Calgary. It wasn't long before The Irish Rovers was born, with the addition of Joe Millar, and later Wilcil McDowell in 1967.

A twenty-week run at the Purple Onion Club in San Francisco led to the group being signed to a contract with Decca Records. Their first single was The Unicorn in 1968. Written by Shel Silverstein, it became an international hit and sold over eight million copies.

Other hits by the band ranged from the cute novelty number, The Biplane Evermore to the whimsical Lily The Pink, which was also recorded by the English group, The Scaffold.

From 1971–74 they were hosts of their own weekly variety show on CBC. They did not have another major hit until 1980 with Wasn't That A Party, from album, *Party with the Rovers*, released by Attic Records in 1985. In 1989 they celebrated their 25th anniversary.

In 1994, Will Millar left the group to concentrate on a solo career. On October 7, 1997 Jimmy Ferguson died while the group was playing in Massachusetts.

By The Irish Rovers
Singles:

The Unicorn	Decca 32254	1968
Whiskey On A Sunday	Decca 32333	1968
The Biplane Evermore	Decca 32371	1968
Lily The Pink	Decca 32444	1969
Peter Knight	Decca 32529	1969
Rhymes and Reasons	Decca 32616	1970
Years May Come, Years May Go	Decca 32723	1970
Morning Town Ride	Potato 3001	1973

By The Rovers
Singles:

Wasn't That a Party	Attic AT 231	1980/81
Mexican Girl	Attic AT 237	1981
Chattanoogie Shoe Shine Boy	Attic AT 254	1981

No More Bread and Butter	Attic AT 260	1982
Pain in My Past	Attic AT 260	1982
Grandma Got Run Over By Reindeer	Attic AT 275	1982
Merry Bloody Xmas	Attic AT 275	1982
Everybody's Making it Big But Me	Attic AT 325	1985
All Sing Together	Attic AT 385	1989
Other Side of the Morning	Attic AT 391	1989

Albums/CDs:

First of The Irish Rovers	Decca DL 74855	1967
The Unicorn	Decca DL 4951	1968
All Hung Up	Decca DL 75037	1968
Tales to Warm Your Mind	Decca DL 75081	1969
The Life of a Rover	Decca DL 75157	1969
On the Shores of Americay	Decca DL 75302	1971
Irish Rovers Live	Attic LAT 1028	1972
Emigrate! Emigrate!	Attic Lat 1029	1972
Irish Rovers Special	K Tel NC 420	1972
Greatest Hits	Mca 4066	1973
Children of The Unicorn	K Tel NC 445	1976
Irish Rovers in Australia	Attic LAT 1038	1976
Tall Ships and Salty Dogs	Attic LAT 1086	1979
15th Anniversary	Video Memories 100	1980
The Rovers	Attic LAT 1095	1980
No More Bread and Butter	Attic LAT 1118	1982
It Was a Night Like This	Attic LAT 1149	1982
Party With The Rovers	Attic LAT 1205	1985
Party Pack	Potato 1300	1986
Hardstuff	Attic ACD 1253	1989
Silver Anniversary	Attic ACD 1303	1989
When The Boys Come Rollin' Home	Attic ACD 1381	1993
Years May Come, Years May Go	MCA Mcbbd 20307	1993
Celebrate: The First 30 Years	Rover ROV 30 2	1994
Celtic Collection: Next 30 Yrs.	Rover IRD 001	1995
Children of The Unicorn	Attic KCB3000	1995
Irish Rovers' Gems	Rover IRD 002	1996
Come Fill Up Your Glasses	Rover Ird 003	1998
Best of The Irish Rovers	MCA 11958	1999
Ramblers and Gamblers	Carlton Sounds 01142	1999
Upon a Shamrock Shore	MCA 112162	2000
Down by The Lagan Side	Rover Ird 006	2000
Songs of Christmas	Phantom 499343	2000
Another Round	Rajon 307827	2002
Boys of Belfast	Varese Sarabande 066422	2003
40 Years a Rovin	Rover 9334338	2005
The Irish Rovers Live	851785	2009
Gracehill Fair	Rover 96922	2010
Still Rovin'	Varsse Fontana067017	2010

Home in Ireland	Optv Media 007527	2011
Drunken Sailor	OPTV Media	2012
Celtic Celebration	Universal 61037	2013
Merry Merry Time of Year	Optv Media CD-87	2013

Jackson Hawke

Chris Castle (keyboards)
Bob Clarke (drums) Replaced by Bucky Berger (1977)
Gene Falbo (bass, vocals)
Tim Ryan (acoustic guitar, vocals)
Bob Yeomans (electric and acoustic guitar, vocals)

Tim Ryan and Bob Yeomans first started working together in 1963 when they were in a band called Amen. Their manager was Bernie Finkelstein, who also looked after Kensington Market at the time. When Amen split up in mid 1965, Ryan went to work at the steel mills in Sault Ste. Marie, his hometown.

In 1973 he moved to Montreal after Andre Perry who had worked with John Lennon and Yoko Ono heard some demos that Ryan and Yeomans had put together. Perry suggested that they get together to put out an album which would be produced by Frazer Mohawk. When Bob left the project, the result was a solo album by Tim Ryan.

Back in Toronto in 1973, Tim and Bob met again. This time they decided to form their own band called Hero. They later represented Canada at the World Popular Song Festival in Tokyo with the song, Sweet December. Ryan left to concentrate on his writing and became a solo performer. On August 1, 1975, Ryan returned to the group.

When they signed a recording contract with CBS Records on April 1, 1976, they changed their name to Jackson Hawke, and added Bob "Crow" Clarke on drums, and Chris Castle on keyboards.

Their first hit single, You Can't Dance was an immediate success, and was recorded by England Dan and John Ford Coley in 1978 on Big Tree Records (BTS 16117). Radio programmers turned it into a double-sided hit when they played the flip side, Into The Mystic, which was written by Van Morrison.

In late 1977, the group added two more new members, Gary Holt on guitar and Bucky Berger on drums. The latter replaced Bob Clarke. By the end of 1979 Jackson Hawke had disbanded.

Singles:
You Can't Dance/Into The Mystic	Columbia C4 4131	1976
She's The One	Columbia C4 4150	1976
Set Me Free	Columbia C4 4165	1977

Albums/CDs:
Forever	Columbia PES 90375	1976
Jackson Hawke	Columbia PES 90417	1977

J.B. and The Playboys

Bill Hill (lead guitar, vocals)
Andy Kaye (rhythm guitar) Repld by J.P. Lauzon 1966
Allan Nicholls (lead vocals)
Doug West (drums) Repld by Gaetan Dany 1967
Louis Yachnin (bass) Repld by Peter Carson 1966

J.B. and The Playboys formed in September 1963 in Montreal, Quebec. Originally, they were a quartet comprised of Bill Hill, Allan Nicholls, Doug West, and Andy Kaye. Louis Yachnin joined during the winter of '63. J.B. was the group's mascot. Their first single on RCA Victor was Chances in 1965. Other hits followed, including I'm Not Satisfied and Don't Ask Me To Be True. With the release of Poor Anne in late 1965, they had changed their name to The Jaybees.

In November 1966 Andy and Louis left the group, and were replaced by J.P. Lauzon and Peter Carson respectively. Doug left the group in 1967 and was replaced by Gaetan Dany.

By 1968 the Jaybees had become known as the Carnival Connection. Poster Man was their only hit on Capitol Records.

In May 1969 they changed their name again to Feathers, and was comprised of Nicholls, Hill, Les Lanie, and Nick Katsos.

The group broke up in September 1969 when Nicholls joined the cast of the Broadway musical Hair in New York. Hill became a member of the group Freedom, a.k.a. Freedom North, while Lauzon joined the group Life.

By J.B. & The Playboys
Singles:
Chances	RCA 57 3342	1965
I'm Not Satisfied	RCA 57 3344	1965
Love, Happiness & Sweet You	RCA 57 3355	1965
Don't Ask Me To Be True	RCA 57 3345	1965

Album:
J.B. & The Playboys	RCA 1086	1965

By The Jaybees
Singles:
Poor Anne	RCA 57 3376	1965
I'm A Loner	RCA 57 3398	1966
Footsteps In The Snow	RCA 57 3404	1966
I Think Of Her	RCA 47 9001	1966/67

By Carnival Connection
Single:
Poster Man	Capitol 2244	1968

Shawne Jackson

From Toronto, Ontario, Shawne Jackson began singing when she was a teenager in a church choir in Toronto. She then was in the a cappella rhythm and blues group Sneakers and The Tierras that played at the Club Bluenote.

In 1967 she and her brother Jay Jackson joined The Majestics.

Two years later, Shawne left for New York where she worked as a secretary and went to modelling school. Later in Los Angeles, she worked with fashion designer Lucy Johnson. By the end of 1971 she had met Domenic Troiano who encouraged her to resume her music career in Toronto.

Shawne worked with Keith Hampshire on his CBC variety show, and in 1974 she had a major hit with Just As Bad As You, written and produced by Troiano, on Playboy Records.

Her next hit was Get Out of the Kitchen on RCA, followed by, Come Back Boy, on, El Mocambo Records.

She continued to sing backup for other Canadian acts such as Luba, and had a small role on CTV's Night Heat.

Singles:
Just As Bad As You	Playboy P 50053	1974
Along For The Ride	RCA PB 50232	1975
Get Out Of The Kitchen	RCA PB 10428	1976
T'Eloigner de Mon Coeur	RCA PB 50171	1976
Come Back Boy	ESMO 504	1980

Album:
Shawne Jackson	RCA APL1 1320	1975

Susan Jacks

Born Susan Pesklevits on August 19, 1948 in Saskatoon, Saskatchewan. She later married Terry Jacks and together they started The Poppy Family in 1967.

Like Terry, she also began recording solo and had success with such hits as You Don't Know What Love Is, I Thought of You Again, and You're A Part of Me.

After both the breakup of her marriage and the group, she continued to record solo on various labels. In 1996 she recorded Christmas Angel, which was included on the CD, Uniting The Spirit (1996 Gilles Godard Productions 01382) a special collection of Christmas music to benefit Special Olympics in Canada. She is currently working in Nashville.

Singles:

You Don't Know What Love Is	LondonL.182	1973
I Thought Of You Again	Goldfish G.102	1973/74
I Want You To Love Me	Goldfish G.104	1974
Build A Tower	Goldfish GS.109	1974
You're A Part Of Me	Goldfish GS.113	1975
Love Has No Pride	Casino C7 102	1975
Anna Marie	Casino C7 105	1975
Dream	Casino C7 108	1975/76
Memories Are Made Of You	POL 2065 312	1976
Daytime Hustler	POL 2065 369	1977

Albums/CDs:

I Thought Of You Again	GoldFH GFLP 1002	1973
Dream	Casino CA 1005	1975

Terry Jacks

Terry Jacks was born on March 29, 1944 in Winnipeg, Manitoba and raised in Vancouver, where he became involved in the music scene there. From 1963 to 1966 he was a member of The Chessmen. When they disbanded, Jacks married Susan Pesklevits, and together they started The Poppy Family in 1967.

In 1970 Jacks recorded his first solo hit, I'm Gonna Capture You on London Records. He later started his own label, Goldfish Records, and in 1973 recorded Seasons In The Sun, an English adaptation of Jacquel Brel's Le Moribund which was first recorded in 1964 by The Kingston Trio. It went on to sell more than nine million copies.

By 1973 The Poppy Family had broken up. Terry's other solo hits included If You Go Away, another English adaptation of a Jacquel Brel song, and Rock and Roll (I Gave You The Best Years of My Life), which was also recorded by Mac Davis.

Singles:

I'm Gonna Capture You	LondonM.17381	1970
Someone Must Have Jumped	LondonM. 17427	1971
Concrete Sea	LondonL.181	1972
I'm Gonna Love You Too	LondonL.188	1972/73
Seasons In The Sun	Goldfish 101	1973
If You Go Away	Goldfish 108	1974
Rock And Roll (I Gave You The Best Years Of My Life)	Goldfish 111	1974
Christina	Quality 2135	1975
Holly	Goldfish 1	1975
Y'Don't Fight The Sea	Goldfish GO.3	1976
In My Father's Footsteps	Goldfish GO.6	1976
Ghost In Your Mind	Goldfish GO.7	1976
You Keep Me Up	Goldfish GO.9	1977
Hey Country Girl	Goldfish GO.12	1977
You Fooled Me	A&M 611	1983
Voice of America	A&M 626	1983
Where Evil Grows	A&M 637	1984
Tough Guys Don't Dance	A&M 681	1985
I Can't Forget It	Attic AT 351	1987
Just Like That	Attic AT 354	1987

Albums/CDs:

Seasons In The Sun	Goldfish GLFP 1001	1974
Y'don't Fight The Sea	Goldfish GLFP 1	1975
Pulse	A&M SP 9096	1983
Just Like That	Attic LAT 1229	1987
Into The Past.Terry Jacks Greatest Hits	A&M SP 69881	1989

Les Jaguars

Jean Guy Cossette (guitar)
Gilles Morissette (vocals, guitar)
Reynald Morissette (drums)
Doris Thibault (bass)

This instrumental vocal group from Quebec evolved from another band called Les Harmos from Arvida, who were comprised of brothers Reynald and Gilles Morissette, Doris Thibeault, and Jean Guy Cossette, whom they joined in 1962 form Les Jaguars, and played in ballrooms and hotels in Lac Saint Jean, Saquenay and La Cote Nord. Tournesol Records released their self-titled debut album in late 1963, which included the two sided hit, Mer Morte/Supersonic Twist.

The Jaguars were similar to The Ventures, except they added more electric guitars with reverb and echo. After The Jaguars's second album, *Les Jaguars Pour La Danse*, came out in 1964, they played in Montreal and the rest of Quebec.

Before they broke up in the spring of 1966, they had added Yvon Vaillancourt from Les Vampires on sax, and Tommy Manderson on vocals.

Jean Guy Cossette went on to work with Les Bohemes, a group from Sherbrooke, Quebec. He also toured under the name of Jean Guy (Arthur) Cossette, was in other Quebec groups, such as Les Sinners and La Revolution Francaise, and starred with Robert Charlebois in the film, A Soir on fait peu in 1969. By the early 1980s he had started le son des Jaguars with guitarist Michael Murphy, bassist Andre Parenteau, and drummer Pierre Rinquet. They toured Quebec and put out a Jaguars album that combined old and new material. Two other drummers in the group were Andre Leclerc and Pierre Martin. With Guylaine Maroist and Peter Sandmark, Cossette has toured as The Travelling Blueberries.

Singles:

Mer Morte/Supersonic Twist	Tournesol TL 17	1963
Dead Sea	Reo 8842	1963
Solitude	Tournesol TL 29	1964
Mlle. Ye Ye	Tournesol TL 39	1964
Dors Mon Amour	Tournesol TL 46	1966
Devant la croix	Tournesol TL 65	1966
L'Horloge/Hanky Panky	Tournesol TL 83	1966
Maitre de la guerre	Teledisc TD 34	1967

Albums/CDs:

Les Jaguars	Tournesol TL 6002	1963
Les Jaguars Pour La Danse	Tournesol TL 6006	1964
Les Jaguars, Volume 2	Tournesol TL 402	1964
Long Jeu Ouest Turn (Jean Guy Cossette)	RCA CGPS 383	1973
Les Nouveaux JaguarS: Pour La Danse	Passe Temps 50	1973
Jaguars	Pro Culture PPC 4004	1982

By Jean Guy "Arthur" Cossette
Singles:

Le fermier de la guerre	Youpi 7052	1970
Je change	RCA 75 5064	1973
Saint Jerome Jamboree	RCA 75 5105	1973
Tourne en rond (Arthur & Les Jaguars)	Pacha 4414	1974
Mer morte/Solitude (re release)	Millionaires MG 100136	1974

Jale

Eve Hartling (guitar, vocals)
Alyson MacLeod (drums, vocals) Replaced by Mike Belitsky (1995)
Jennifer Pierce (guitar, vocals)
Laura Stein (bass, vocals)

From Halifax, Nova Scotia, Jale was an all-girl group that started in April of 1992. The name of the group was taken from the initials of all four members. Jennifer Pearce came from another group called No Damn Fears. An EP, Aunt Betty, on the Cinnamon Toast independent label was released in 1992. By the spring of 1993, they had signed with the Seattle based label Sub Pop, and was included on the label's east coast compilation, Never Mind The Molluses.

In 1994, Sub Pop released Jale's first full-length CD, *Dream Cake*. A year later, Alyson MacLeod left the group, and was replaced by Mike Belitsky. Jale's second CD, So Wound came out in 1996. In 1997 they disbanded.

Singles:
Three Days	Subpop 235	1994
Not Happy	Subpop 256	1994
Long Way Home		1995
Jesus Loves Me		1995
All Ready		1996
Ali		1996
True What You Say	Sealed Fate (NO #)	1997

Albums/CDs:
Aunt Betty (EP)		1992
Promise (EP)	Subpop PROCD #31	1994
Dream Cake	Subpop SPCD 256	1994
Closed (EP)	Murder MURBD018	1995
So Wound	Subpop SPCD 350	1996

Colin James

Born on August 17, 1964 in Regina, Saskatchewan, Colin Munn grew up listening to a wide variety of music, from folk music to soul to the blues. In his early teens he learned the penny whistle and mandolin, and in his mid teens he quit school to form his own trio, The Hoo Doo Men. They played the Winnipeg Folk Festival and opened for such artists as Mississippi bluesman John Lee Hooker and Delaware rocker George Thorogood.

The year 1983 was a turning point in his career. He moved to Vancouver and joined David Burgin in the group, The Night Shades, who were the opening act for Texas singer Stevie Ray Vaughan's show in Saskatoon. James ended up opening for Vaughn during the rest of his Canadian tour.

Tired of being introduced as Colin Munn because it was often the butt of many jokes, Vaughn suggested he change his last name to James, and encouraged him to start his own band.

Back in Vancouver, James and his manager Stephen Macklam put a band together. In 1988 James's self-titled debut album on Virgin/EMI was released, and it became the fastest selling debut in Canadian music industry. Two years later, the label released his second album,

After a string of commercial hit Singles:, beginning with Voodoo Thing in 1988, James recorded the blues album, Colin James And The Little Big Band, which was released in 1993. His songs have been recorded by Maria Muldaur, Johnny Halliday, Maia Sharp, Paul Thorn, Bernard Allison, Colin Linden and Blackie And The Rodeo Kings.

Singles:

Voodoo Thing	Virgin 1444	1988
Five Long Years	Virgin 1455	1988/89
Why'd You Lie	Virgin 1468	1989
Chicks 'n Cars	Virgin 1492	1989
Dream of Satin	Virgin 86062	1989
Back In My Arms Again	Virgin 86168	1990
Keep On Loving Me Baby	Virgin 86168	1990
Just Came Back	Virgin 86168	1990
Give It Up	Virgin 86168	1990/91
If You Lean On Me	Virgin 86168	1991
Love Thang	Virgin 86168	1992
Cadillac Baby	Virgin 39190	1993
Surely (I Love You)	Virgin 39190	1994
Saviour	Wea 10614	1995
Freedom	Wea 10614	1995/96
Real Stuff	Wea 10614	1996
C'mon With The C'mon	Wea 23010	1999

Albums/CDs:

Colin James	Virgin 86062	1988
Sudden Stop	Virgin 86168	1990
Colin James and The Little Big Band	Virgin 39190	1993
Then Again	Virgin 40179	1995
Bad Habits	Wea 10614	1995
National Steel	Wea 19634	1997
Colin James And The Little Big Band II	Wea 23010	1998
Fuse	Wea 84633	2000

Traveler	Wea 47389	2003
Rooftops & Satellites	MRCD 6521	2009
Fifteen	EMI 946915	2012
Hearts on Fire	Universal 715466	2015

Patti Jannetta

Born and raised in Toronto, Patti Jannetta started singing in high school. She was discovered by a local disc jockey who saw her perform in a production of, What's Wrong World, which she also co-wrote. At sixteen, she started singing professionally.

She appeared in the documentary feature, Superstar, which starred Thai singing sensation, Manee, whom Patti opened for throughout Europe and Thailand.

As a songwriter, Patti has written many songs for inclusion on other people's albums, notably *Make Up Your Mind* which she co-wrote and recorded with the legendary Bo Diddley, as his first-ever female singing partner.

Over the years she has worked with many charities, such as Variety The Children's Charity and The Hospital For Sick Children. She has also hosted her very own TV special, Family Christmas with Patti Jannetta.

Today she continues to write her own songs and record them, including Tell Me You Love Me with James Collins and Carol Medina.

Singles:

You've Got No One	Janta JM 8298	1981
Don't Change	Janta JM 83141	1981
Ready For Your Love	Janta JM 8349	1983
Don't You Want My Love	Trilogt TR 060	1984
I Am Your Child	Attic AT 341	1984
Party Girl	Trilogy TR 550	1988
Name of the Game	Trilogy TR 550	1988
I Know You'll Wait	Trilogy 9102	1991
Mark On My Heart	Trilogy 9102	1992
Even Though You're Gone	Trilogy 9102	1993

Albums/CDs:

Patti Jannetta	Janta JMC 8293	1983
Breathless	Trilogy TR 550	1988
Mark On My Heart	Trilogy TR 9102	1991

Paul Janz

Born in Three Hills, Alberta, 50 miles northeast of Calgary, Paul Janz's formal music training was at the Conservatory of Music in Basil, Switzerland, where he studied opera under the tutelage of bass baritone Sandoz. He also took up the piano and after a year's study he arranged and conducted studio sessions with the Basil Symphony.

His musical interests eventually turned to pop music and he formed the group Deliverance in 1978 with his brother Ken. In the U.S. they enjoyed brief success with the hit song, Leaving L.A. in 1980 on CBS Records. When the producers of the movie Deliverance threatened to sue over the use of the name, the group disbanded in 1980. Before Paul returned to Canada in 1981, he had a top-five hit in Germany with Steine.

Settling in Vancouver, he began singing jingles and enrolled as a philosophy major at Simon Fraser University. He also worked on his first solo album, *High Strung* which A&M released in 1985.

The artist's other accomplishments included writing, producing and performing Something Special, the theme of the CTV show Neon Rider; and writing Enemies Like You And Me, the love theme for the film Iron Eagle II. In 1992 he was media spokesman World Vision, a non-profit organization that appeals for funds to help the Third World.

A string of hit singles in the 1980s continued to keep Janz in the spotlight, and in 1992 A&M released a "best of" compilation called Presence. That same year he switched to Attic Records who released the album, Trust.

Singles:

Go To Pieces	A&M AM 676	1984
Don't Cry Tonight	A&M AM 668	1985
High Strung	A&M AM 687	1985
Close My Eyes	A&M AM 693	1985
One Night (Is All It Takes)	A&M AM 2946	1987
Believe In Me	A&M AM 738	1987/88
I Won't Cry	A&M AM 750	1988
Send Me A Miracle	A&M AM 755	1988
Every Little Tear	A&M 5288	1990
Rocket To My Heart	A&M 5288	1990
Stand	A&M 5288	1990
Hold Me Tender	A&M 5288	1990/91
This Love Is Forever	A&M 19179	1992
Wind Me Up	Attic ACDM 1365	1992
Amazon Rain	Attic ACDM 1365	1993
Calling My Personal Angel	Attic ACDM 1365	1993

Albums/CDs:

High Strung	A&M SP 9108	1985
Electricity	A&M SP 5156	1987
Renegade Romantic	A&M 5288	1990
Presence: A Collection of Hit Singles	A&M 19179	1992
Trust	Attic ACDM 1365	1992

Jarvis Street Revue

Tom Cruikshank (drums)
Wayne Faulconer (vocals, lead guitar)
Tom Horricks (vocals, sax)
George Stevenson (bass)

From Thunder Bay, Ontario, the Jarvis Street Revue started in 1970. Tom Horricks had been in other bands from the area, such as Donny B and The Bonnvils, The Plague, and Lexington Avenue; George Stevenson in Donny B and The Bonnvils, and Wayne Faulconer in Satan and The D Men. The Jarvis Street Revue had three singles and one album, all released on Columbia Records in the early 1970s. They broke up in 1974.

Singles:

Uncle Benny	Gaiety 343	1970
20 Years	Columbia C4 2969	1971
Tambourine	Columbia C4 3008	1972
I Believe In Freedom	Columbia C4 3064	1972

Album:

Mr. Oil Man	Columbia ES 90020	1971

Carly Rae Jepsen

Carly Rae Jepsen was born in Mission, British Columbia on November 21, 1985. She aspired to be a singer at an early age. In 2007 she came in third on Canadian Idol. In 2008 her debut album, *Tug of War* included the single Call Me Maybe. Originally a folk song, it's upbeat rhythm caught on in 2012 after the album *Kiss* was released. Call Me Maybe was issued as a single and went to number one on Billboard's Hot 100 on June 23, 2012 where it remained for nine weeks. It also tied the same number of weeks in 1954 when Sh Boom by The Crew Cuts was number one. In 2014 she played the title role in a new version of Rodger and Hammerstein's Cinderella on Broadway. Emotion, her third CD, *Emotion* came out in 2015.

Singles:
Call Me Maybe	604 Records 100615	2012
Good Time (w/Owl City)	Interscope USUM 206288	2012
Beautiful	Interscope USUM 208954	2012
Tonight I'm Getting Over You	Interscope USUM 208958	2013
I Really Like You	Interscope USUM 500234	2015
Run Away With Me	Interscope USUM 507009	2015

Albums/CDs:
Tug of War	Fontana CJM 0002	2008
Kiss	Interscope 715354	2012
Emotion	Interscope 738531	2015

Jericho

Frank de Felice (drums)
Gord Fleming (organ, piano, vocals)
Denny Gerard (bass, vocals)
Fred Keeler (lead guitar, vocals)

From Toronto, Ontario, Jericho was one group that had only one major hit and one album, both on Ampex Records and produced by Todd Rundgren.

Fred Keeler was once lead guitarist for The Shays, and had played with The Majestics. Denny Gerard had been a member of The Paupers for seven years, and had recorded with Richie Havens, and Peter, Paul and Mary. He had also been nominated for Playboy's Jazz Award for two consecutive years. Frank de Felice hailed from Brantford, Ontario, and had played in various bands in and around the Toronto area. Gord Fleming had studied at the University of Toronto's music school, and had done some studio work with David Clayton Thomas, Ronnie Hawkins, Jesse Winchester, and John Hammond Jr.

Single:
Make It Better	Bearsville 31003	1971

Album:
Jericho	Ampes 10112A	1971

France Joli

Born in Montreal, Quebec in 1963, France Joli was a teenaged pop sensation who started singing at a very early age. At eleven, she began singing on amateur talent shows and commercials, and by the time she was fifteen she was headed for stardom.

On July 7, 1979 she performed Come To Me at New York's Fire Island in front of five thousand screaming fans. She left the stage a star, while the song went on to become her first hit, reaching number thirteen on Billboard's Hot 100.

Joli's popularity continued on television where she made appearances on Solid Gold, The Merv Griffin Show, Dinah Shore, The Midnight Special, The Bob Hope Special, and many others.

She toured Europe, Japan, Mexico and South America, and also performed at the Riviera Hotel in Las Vegas and New York City's Radio City Music Hall.

In 1984 she received The Grand Prize award and The Most Outstanding Performance Award at the Yamaha World Popular Song Festival in Tokyo.

Tony Green, who produced her until 1981, reunited with Joli in 1996 to produce the six song EP, Touch.

Singles:

Come To Me	TGO TGS 500	1979
This Time	Prelude 8013	1980
Feel Like Dancin'	Prelude 8016	1980
Gonna Get Over You	Manhattan M U7777	1982
Still Thinking Of You	Manhattan 002	1982
Dumb Blonde	Epic 15 7003	1983
Girl In The 80s	Epic 34 04048	1983
Blue Eyed Technology	Epic 34 04254	1983
Party Lights	Epic 7055	1984
Does He Dance	Epic 34 04863	1985
Save Me	Monogram MNG 0001	1998

Albums/CDs:

France Joli (EP)	TGO TG 7000	1979
Tonight	TGO 7002	1980
France Joli Now	Manhattan 001	1982
Attitude	Epic FE 38829	1983
Witch Of Love	Epic FE 39934	1985
Touch (EP)	Popular 3074 SLP	1996
If You Love Me	Monogram MNG 0001	1998

Jon and Lee and The Checkmates

Hilmar Ajak (sax)
Al Dorsey (guitar) Replaced by Larry Leishman
John Finley (vocals)
Michael Fonfara (keyboards)
Dave McDevitt (bass) Replaced by Peter Hodgson
Lee Jackson (lead vocals)
Paul Rothchild (drums) Replaced by Wes Morris, Jeff Cutler

The history of this Toronto group goes back to 1963 when they were first known as Lee Jackson And The Checkmates, and were comprised of Lee Jackson (Mike Ferry), Michael Fonfara, Al Dorsey, Dave McDevitt, Paul Rothchild, and Hilmar Ajak. They were one of the first rhythm & blues bands with a strong gospel/soul influence.

In March 1964 they became known as Jon and Lee and The Checkmates when John Finley joined up. There were other personnel changes: Dorsey was replaced Larry Leishman, Rothchild by Wes Morris and Jeff Cutler, and McDevitt by Peter Hodgson. By late 1966 they changed their name to the Jon Lee Group, and they broke up in 1967. During the four years they were together, they only recorded the single, Bring It Down Front as the Jon Lee Group.

Finley, Hodgson, Leishman and Fonfara went on to become members of the group Rhinoceros, who had a commercial hit with the instrumental, Apricot Brandy in 1969. Fonfara later worked with Lou Reed, Black Stone, Mercy and Eleventh Hour among others. He is currently a member of the Downchild Blues Band.

Leishman died in Mattawa, Ontario on March 4, 2013.

Single:
Bring It Down Front Sparton1617 1967

Debbie Johnson

Born in Port of Spain, Trinidad on September 8, 1961, Debbie Johnson moved to Canada in 1971. Coming from a musical family, she joined her sister, two brothers, mother and father in The Johnson Family, who had two singles on Atlantic Records produced by Bob Ezrin. In 1981, Debbie became a member of the group Sweet Ecstasy who were known for their flashy theatrical stage show. They also won four Black Music Awards in 1983 on the strength of their independent single, Pull Our Love Together (1983), produced by Rich Dodson at Marigold Studios. When Sweet Ecstasy broke up in 1985, Rich encouraged Debbie to go solo. Her first single was a duet with Dodson called Lonely Lovers in 1986. Two years later, her debut album, *Just Like Magic*, was released.

Debbie later met Don Breithaupt of Monkey House fame, who with Rich Dodson wrote some of Debbie's hits, two of which were I'll Respect You and Power To The People.

Singles:

Lonely Lovers		1986
Just Like Magic		1987
Secret Love		1987
Mama Said Why		1988
Just My Imagination		1988
Love Of My Life	Marigold MPL 753	1990
Touch The Sky	Marifold MPL 1204	1990
I'll Respect You	Aquarius 562	1991/92
I Know You Very Well	Aquarius 562	1992
Power To The People	Aquarius 562	1992
Behind Closed Doors	Aquarius 562	1992
Everlasting Love	Aquarius 562	1992
So Excited	Aquarius 562	1992
Let Me Go	Aquarius 562	1992/93

Albums/CDs:

Just Like Magic	Marigold MPL 1203	1988
Just My Imagination (EP)		1988
Touch The Sky	Marigold MPL 1204	1989
So Excited	Aquarius 562	1991
The Remixes		1992

Marc Jordan

Marc Jordan was born on March 6, 1948 in Buffalo, New York. In 1970 he left Brock University where he was studying film to become a professional musician. His musical influences included Joni Mitchell, Van Morrison, James Taylor and Steely Dan.

He first tried out for a part in the Toronto musical production of Hair but ended up getting an understudy's role. During that time he was a backup singer for Bobby Vee. Jordan later returned to university, but left again and formed a duo that sang Burt Bacharach songs in cocktail lounges. He then travelled to Europe where he concentrated on his abilities as a singer and songwriter.

Back in Toronto, he met Edmonton publisher Doug Hutton who signed him to a publishing, recording and management contract. Jordan then became involved in two disastrous music projects: a song saga double album called *Cantata Canada* (Capitol), and an album that paid tribute to the RCMP on its golden anniversary.

Jordan recorded his first single, It's A Fine Line, in 1973. His next single was New York Kids in 1975. Neither of them were a hit. In 1978, Jordan signed a recording contract with Warner Brothers, who released his debut album, Mannequin. The single, Marina Del Ray, was the first of several hits.

In 1990, after a ten year absence, he returned to the charts with Burning Down The Amazon and Edge of the World, and in 1993 he recorded 'Til The Last Teardrop Falls with Exchange and Amy Sky. That same year, Warner Music released Jordan's album, *Reckless Valentine*, which included the first single, Waiting For a Miracle.

Jordan is married to singer/songwriter Amy Sky.

Singles:
It's A Fine Line		1973
New York Kids	CBS C4 4080	1975
Marina Del Ray	WAR WBS 8659	1978
Survival	WAR WBS 6904	1978
I'm A Camera	WAR WB 0141	1979
Release Yourself		1979/80
Twilight		1979/80
Generalities	WAR FWB 0174	1980
New York New York	Rio 708	1980
Secrets	Rio 714	1980
You Found Out	Arista ASO 622	1981
Burning Down The Amazon	RCA 9640	1990
Edge Of The World	RCA 9640	1990
Waiting For A Miracle	Sin Drome 8899	1993
Back Street Boy	Sin Drome 8899	1994
The Same Mistake	Sin Drome 8899	1994
Beautiful Disguise	Cafe PMK76	1996
Flowers For Jane	Cafe PMK76	1997
Charlie Parker Loves Me	Blue Note 20419	1999

Albums/CDs:
Mannequin	Warner KBS 3143	1978
Blue Desert	Warner QBS 3362	1979
Talking Through Pictures	RCA 5907 1 R	1987
Cow	RCA 9640 1 R	1990
Reckless Valentine	Sin Drome 8899	1993
Cool Jam Black Earth	Cafe PMK76	1996
This Is How Men Cry	Blue Note 20419	1999

Sass Jordan

Born in 1962 in Montreal, Quebec, Sass Jordan captured the country by storm with her first hit single, Tell Somebody in 1988. Her raunchy vocal style made her unique among the new breed of Canadian pop/rock singers.

When she was seventeen years old, she learned the bass guitar and later joined a group called The News, later called The Pin Ups, who she left at twenty-one to work as a television interviewer, a house painter and a backup singer for The Box, a Montreal band.

In 1985 she decided to try a solo career and was eventually signed by Aquarius Records in Montreal. She began working with guitarist, arranger, and composer Bill Beaudoin. Her first two songs were Steel On Steel and No More, which would be included on her debut album, *Tell Somebody* in 1988.

Her second album, *Racine* (1992) was a tribute to the artists she listened to when she a teenager: The Rolling Stones, David Bowie, Bad Company, Free, and Faces.

Singles:

Tell Somebody	Aquarius AQ 6040	1988/89
So Hard	Aquarius AQCD 522	1989
Double Trouble	Aquarius AQ 6044	1989
Stranger Than Paradise	Aquarius AQCD 522	1989
Rescue Me	Aquarius AQCD 522	1990
Make You A Believer	Impact 10524	1992
I Want To Believe	Impact 10524	1992
You Don't Have To Remind Me	Impact 10524	1992
Goin' Back Again	Impact 10524	1992/93
Who Do You Think You Are	Impact 10524	1993
High Road Easy	MCAD 10980	1994
Pissin' Down	MCAD 10980	1994
Give	MCAD 10980	1994
Sun's Gonna Rise	MCAD 10980	1994
I'm Not	MCAD 10980	1994/95
Ugly	MCAD 10980	1995
Do What I Can	Aquarius Q2 00583	1997/98
Desire	Aquarius Q2 00583	1998

Albums/CDs:

Tell Somebody	Aquarius AQR 522	1988
Racine	Impact IPTD 10524	1992
Rats	MCAD 10980	1994
Present	Aquarius Q2 00583	1997
Hot Gossip (Sass Jordon)	Aquarius 00594	2000

Juliette

Of Polish Ukrainian descent, she was born Juliette Augustina Sysak in Winnipeg, Manitoba on August 26, 1927. At six years of age she started singing at local amateur night shows in her hometown and in Vancouver where she moved at ten. At the Orpheum Theatre there, she sang There'll Always be an England, which Pierre Berton, then writing for the University of British Columbia's student newspaper, predicted stardom for Juliette. Dal Richards heard about her and invited her to sing with his orchestra at the Hotel Vancouver.

She later joined them for a live radio broadcast from the Panorama Roof. From 1942 on, she was heard regularly on CBC radio, including George Calangis' Sophisticated Strings, Alan Young's show where she became a regular, and on local Vancouver radio shows like Burns Chuckwagon with The Rhythm Pals in which she was nicknamed The Belle of the Chuckwagon, and her own show, Here's Juliette.

In 1954 she flew to Toronto to make a guest appearance on CBC TV's Holiday Ranch with host Billy O'Connor, and ended up becoming a regular on the show. Two years later, she was given her own weekly half hour show which was broadcast live every Saturday night after Hockey Night In Canada. Until 1966 she was affectionately known as Our Pet Juliette and she ended each show with "Goodnight, Mom."

Other CBC TV shows followed, including After Noon, Juliette & Friends, and It's Your Choice. She also hosted two CBC Super Specials: Juliette's Favorite Things (1977) and Juliette's Return Engagement (1981). For eight years she was a judge who travelled across the country looking for new talent for du Maurier's Search For The Stars.

Juliette recorded with the Rhythm Pals on Aragon Records back in the 1950s and she made three albums for RCA Camden in the late 1960s.

In 1999 she was honored with her own star on Canada's Walk of Fame in Toronto.

Singles:
(Recorded with The Rhythm Pals)

I Keep Telling Myself/Bought For A Song	Aragon 253	1956
I Caught The Bride's Bouquet/What's The Use	Aragon 254	1956
Christmas Is A Day For Miracles	RCA SPC 45 81	1970

Albums/CDs:
(Recorded with Jimmy Dale Singers)

Juliette	RCA Camden CAS 2223	1968
Christmas World	RCA Camden CAS 2279	1968
Country World	RCA Camden CAS 2341	1969

Junkhouse

Dan Achen (electric guitar, vocals)
Ray Farrugia (drums, vocals, percussion)
Grant Marshall (bass)
Russ Wilson (vocals)   Replaced by Colin Cripps (1997)
Tom Wilson (acoustic guitar, vocals)

Tom Wilson and Ray Farrugia started Junkhouse in Hamilton, Ontario in 1990. Wilson had been a folk singer in various bands, and was a member of the Florida Razors in 1981 who recorded the independent EP, Half A Rock 'N Roll Record and the album, *Beet Music* before breaking up in 1987. Farrugia was in the group, The Trouble Boys. After releasing independent records, they signed a recording contract with Sony Music, and in 1993 their debut CD, *Strays* was released. In 1995 came their second CD, Birthday Boy, and in 1997 their third CD, *Fuzz*.

Principal songwriter for the group is Tom Wilson. In 1996 he joined Colin Linden and Stephen Fearing to form the trio, Blackie and The Rodeo Kings, whose debut effort, High or Hurtin', was a tribute to Willie P. Bennett.

In 1997, Russ Wilson left the group, and was replaced by Colin Cripps, formerly with Crash Vegas. Bassist Grant Marshall also joined the group. Tom Wilson released his first solo album, Planet Love on Columbia in 2001.

Singles:

Out Of My Head	Epic EK 80184	1993
The Sky Is Falling	Epic EK 80184	1994
Praying For The Rain	Epic EK 80184	1994
Gimme The Love	Epic EK 80184	1994
Big Brown Turtle	Epic EK 80184	1994/95
Be Someone	Epic EK 80228	1995
Brown Shoe	Epic EK 80228	1996
Burn For You	Epic EK 80228	1996
Pearly White	Epic CK 80285	1997
Shine	Epic CK 80285	1997/98

Albums/CDs:

Strays	Epic EK 80184	1993
Strays (EP)	Epic CDNK 863	1993
Birthday Boy	Epic EK 80228	1995
Fuzz	Epic CK 80285	1997

Diane Juster

Born on March 15, 1946 in Montreal, Quebec, Diane Juster began her musical training at age five. She studied piano under Marie Therese Paquin and Mme. Legoff, and in her teens showed an interest in singing while attending College Andre Grasset. While there she sang under the name of Marie Octobre, and played keyboards at all the school shows. She started writing her own songs at seventeen. In the mid 1970s newcomer Julie Arel made her famous when she recorded seven of Juster's original compositions.

When Diane was twenty-five years old a record company executive convinced her to record; the result was the single, Ce Matin, which became a hit after she introduced it on Jeunesse, a popular TV show in Quebec.

In May, 1974 she began performing her own songs, which included Ma Maison, C'est une ile and Quands tu partiras. That same year, her debut album, *Melancolie* was released. In 1975 she performed for the first time at Montreal's Places des Arts. After the release of her second album, *M'aimeras Tu Demain*, Juster announced that she was quitting the stage to concentrate on her songwriting. She wrote songs for such artists as Robert Charlebois, Celine Dion and Ginette Reno. Juster's 1980 composition, Je ne suis qu'une chanson, which was recorded by Reno, won the Felix Award as best song of 1980. By 1991 it had become the best selling song in Quebec. In 1981 Diane became a founding member of the Societe Professionelle des Auteurs Compositeurs du Quebec (SPACQ).

In addition to writing songs, she has composed film scores for Jean Claude's Eclair au chocolat, Danielle Suissa's The Morning Man, and the music of Monsieur Amilcar for the Eddy Tousaint Ballet.

More recently, she has become a crusader for the songwriter's rights, and is a vice president of Quebec's songwriter's association. In 1993 she released a self-titled album of sixteen songs.

Singles:

Title	Label	Year
Parle moi	LondonFC 825	1972
Vive les roses/Ce Matin	Fleur 471	1974
Ma Maison, c'est une ile	Fleur 746	1974/75
Je me retourne	Fleur 482	1975
Hey le monde	Fleur 489	1975
Tout est fini	Fleur 498	1976
Va t en	Kebec DISC 9018	1977
Eclair au chocolat	CAM 1002	1978
Se faire l'amour	Kebec Disc KD 9019	1981
Tristes jeudis	Kebec DISC KD 9093	1981
Soiree a l'opera	Marguerite 471	1984

Crazy Love	Kebec DISC KD 9358	1987
J'ai besoin de parler	Kebec DISC KD 9368	1988

Albums/CDs:

Melancolie	Fleur FLP 202	1974
M'aimeras Tu Demain	Fleur FLP 205	1975
Mes Plus Belles Chansons	Fleur FLP 217	1976
Regarde En Moi	Kebec Disc KD 917	1977
Tu As Laisee Passer L'amour	Kebec Disc KD 518	1981
Rien Qu'amoureuse	Marguerite MAR 8088	1984
J'ai Besoin De Parler	Kebec Disc KD 660	1987
Diane Juster	BMG 12665	1993

Justin Tyme

Don Gunter (guitar, vocals)
Jim Maxwell (drums)
Garnet Schneider (bass)
John Wittman (guitar) Replaced by Bob White

This Winnipeg group was first called, Donny and The Footprints, in 1964. They later changed their name to Justin Tyme and signed a three-year recording contract with Warner Brothers Seven Arts in 1969. Their first single was Nonsense Child, which had as its flipside, Miss Felicity Grey, written by Jerome Langely and Jimmy Stewart and originally recorded by The Guess Who as the B side to the British release of their hit, Flying On The Ground Is Wrong. Shortly after the release of Justin Tymes's second single, Child of Dawn in 1970, the group disbanded.

Singles:

Nonsense Child/Miss Felicity Grey	WB 5020	1969
Child Of Dawn	WB 5022	1970

Connie Kaldor

Connie Kaldor was born in Regina, Saskatchewan on May 9, 1953.

Her career as a singer/songwriter did not begin until 1979 when she left the theatre. Although she sang at the Regina Folk Festival as a teenager, she decided on a dramatic career. She studied dramatic arts at the University of Alberta. This led to performances at the Theatre Pass Muraille in Toronto and 25th Street House in Saskatoon.

She also appeared on radio and television.

In her mid twenties she switched to a singing career, and toured the Prairies with Heather Bishop. She also sang at the Vancouver Music Festival in 1980. The following year she recorded her first album, *One of These Days*, on Coyote Records, and toured Canada to promote it.

Her subsequent recordings on various labels included one on Oak Street, Lullaby Berceuse (1988), in which she was joined by French singer Carmen Champagne.

Kaldor's best known songs include Bird On A Wing, Maria's Place, Wood River, Wanderlust, and I Go Walking. Among those who have recorded her songs are Roy Forbes, Ronnie Gibson, Priscilla Herdman, Hart Rouge, and Garnet Rogers.

Albums/CDs:

One Of These Days	Coyote WRC1 1317	1981
Moonlight Grocery	Coyote CR 1002	1984
Lullaby Berceuse	Oak OSL 1011	1988
Gentle Of Heart	BOSCD 019	1989
Wood River	CEGCD 1010	1992
Small Cafe	Outside CEGCD 10205	1996
Love Is A Truck	Outside CEGCD-1025	2000
Vinyl Songbook	Outside CEGCD 1020	2003
Sky With Nothing To Get In The Way	Outside CEGCD 1035	2005
Postcards From The Road Outside	CBGCD 1040	2009
Love Sask	Outside	2014

Kashtin

Claude McKenzie
Florent Vollant

This popular Montagnais duo started singing together in 1984. The name "Kashtin" means tornado in the Montagnais Innu Aionum language. Their first performances were at the Innu Nikamu festival at Maliotenam and other native communities along the Lower North Shore of the St. Lawrence River.

Montreal composer/producer Guy Trepanier saw potential in this duo, and he encouraged them to record their self-titled debut album in 1989, which featured the Quebec hits, E Uassiuian (Mon enfance in French and My Childhood in

English), Tipatshimun (Chanson du diable in French and Song of the Devil in English), and Tshinanu (Nous Autres in French and Ourselves in English).

1989 marked the duo's debut in Paris, France at the Theatre de la Ville and La Cigalle. A year later, they played at the New Music Seminar in New York.

After the release of their second album, *Innu* in 1991, Florence Vallant went on hiatus, while Claude McKenzie recorded the solo album, *Innu Town*.

Albums/CDs:

Kashtin	Groupe Concert Musique PPFL 2009	1989
Innu	Musicor PPFLC 2011	1991
Akua Tuta	Columbia CK 80209	1994

Christopher Kearney

Born in Toronto on December 6, 1947, Christopher Kearney was four years old when he moved with his parents to Lindsay, Ontario. He grew up on Buddy Holly and the Everly Brothers, and learned to play the guitar left handed. His musical career started in the mid to late 1960s when he lived and worked on the American West Coast. He later met Gordon Lightfoot who encouraged him to be a singer/songwriter. In 1970 Kearney recorded Theme for Jody on Apex Records. He returned to Toronto in mid 1971. He wrote a number of songs, some of which were published by Lightfoot's Early Morning Music.

Capitol Records released his self-titled debut album in 1972. The first single was Loosen Up. Kearney played at various folk clubs throughout the United States, such as the Bitter End in New York. He also toured with Anne Murray.

He represented Canada, along with The Stampeders, at the Seventh Rio International Pop Song Festival in Rio de Janeiro, Brazil in 1972. The following year Capitol released Kearney's second album, *Pemmican Stash*.

Although he never achieved the same success as Lightfoot, he remains as one of Canada's most popular singer/songwriters of the early 1970s.

In 1993 he wrote A Letter From Sarajevo, a public awareness video which featured Tom Cochrane, Rik Emmett, Molly Johnson, Murray McLauchlan and Ian Thomas. Directed by John Grierson, the namesake and grandson of the National Film Board founder, it showed footage of the Niagara Children's Chorus singing with children on the streets of Toronto set against war footage from Bosnia. Kearney wrote the song with Scott Lane and Neil Dobson.

Singles:

Theme For Jody	Apex 77113	1970
Rocking Chair Ride	MCA 2008	1971
Loosen Up	Capitol 72664	1972
Country Lady	Capitol 72675	1972
One Helluva Rock'n Roll Band	Capitol 72691	1973
Runnin' Child	Capitol 72742	1975

Albums/CDs:

Christopher Kearney	Capitol ST 6372	1972
Pemmican Stash	Capitol ST 6392	1973
Sweetwater	Capitol ST 6424	1975

James Keelaghan

Caglary singer/songwriter James Keelaghan's musical career began in 1983 when he played guitar with Scottish folksinger Margaret Crystal. He later played in several groups, notably Ernie The Band, an acoustic punk/folk group who played everything from the late Stan Rogers to The Talking Heads.

In 1985 folksinger/songwriter Garnet Rogers heard him sing Jenny Bryce and encouraged James to make music a full-time career. In 1987 he released his first independent cassette, *Timelines*; a second, *Small Rebellions*, came out in 1989.

Keelaghan has played at many folk festivals around the world, such as the Australia National Festival, Ann Arbor Folk Festival, Lunenberg Folk Festival, Santa Monica Festival, and the Vancouver, Edmonton, and Winnipeg Folk Festivals. Until 1992 he toured with Bill Eaglesham on bass and background vocals, and Gary Bird on six string and steel guitars.

His songs recall the history of Western Canada, from the Red River Rebellion to stories about immigrants, settlers, and the Great Depression. There are also some songs that are personal, such as Kiri's Song which came to him through his sister and a friend whose grandparents were interned during the Second World War because they were Japanese. Others include Gladys Ridge, about the joys of returning home after being on the road; Hillcrest Mine that tells the story about Canada's largest mining disaster; Rebecca's Lament chronicles the tale of the great Indian chief Tecumseh, and Small Rebellion about the Beinfait mining massacre.

Often compared to the late Stan Rogers, Keelaghan continues to build on his reputation as a chronicler of Canadiana. Since 1993 he has toured and recorded with Spanish born Calgarian Oscar Lopez.

Albums/CDs:

Timelines	Tranquilla TMCD 001	1987
Small Rebellions	Tranquilla TMCD 002	1989
My Skies	Redbird/Green Linnet GLCD 2112	1993
A Recent Future	Justin Time JTR8453	1995
Sweet Sweet Love	True North TND 353	2005
House Of Cards	Borealis BCD 198	2009

Mart Kenney

He was born Herbert Martin Kenney in Tweed, Ontario on March 7, 1910. When he was still a baby, he moved to Vancouver. Growing up he was exposed to music from her Aunt Sara, a concert pianist and teacher, and the radio where he heard the saxophone, the most compelling instrument ever.

In 1925 he procured a Conn alto saxophone at Roland's Music Store and took lessons from Charlie Williams, a famous Vancouver musician in the 1920s. Kenney quit school in 1927 and ended up working for the Underwood Typewriter Company. A year later, Len Chamberlain, another local musician, offered him his first professional job.

Kenney went on to play other orchestras in Western Canada until he formed his own band in 1931 when he was hired for an engagement at Vancouver's Alexandra Ballroom. They became known as Mart Kenney and The Seven Western Gentlemen, and were comprised of Glen Griffith on piano and trumpet, Jack Hemmings on trumpet, Bert Lister on banjo and alto sax, Hec McCallum on bass, violin and Sousaphone, Ed Emel on drums, and Art Hallman on vocals and saxophone (1932 1944).

In 1934 they made their radio debut on station CJOK from the Alexandra Ballroom, and introduced Lister's arrangement of The West, The Nest, And You Dear at Henderson Lake in Lethbridge, Alberta, which later became the band's theme song.

During the 1930s, Kenney and his band were popular on the CRBC program, Sweet and Low, toured Eastern Canada, and began recording for RCA.

In 1940 they moved to Toronto where their radio broadcasts were picked up by NBC network in the U.S. and the BBC in Great Britain. They established Mart Kenney's Ranch, a dance hall in Woodbridge, Ontario, in 1949. Kenney continued to tour into the late 1960s, and in 1969 the Ranch closed and his band broke up.

Besides Hallman, other featured singers in Kenney's group over the years included Eleanor Bartelle (1936), Georgia Dey (1937), Beryl Bolen (1940), Judy Richards (1940 43), Veronica Foster (1943 44), Roy Roberts (1946 49), and Wally Koster (1949 1952). Norma Beth Locke, who married Kenney in 1952, was also a singer in her husband's band. She was born in Montreal on October 15, 1923 and died in Mission, B.C. on September 17, 1990.

Other members of Kenney's band included Bobby Gimby, pianist Jack Fowler, and saxophonist Stan Patton.

In 1980 Kenney was made a member of the Order of Canada. He died February 8, 2006.

Singles: (78s)

Title	Label	Year
There's Rain In My Eyes	RCA Victor 216592	1938
The West, The Nest And You, Dear	RCA Victor 216593	1938
Sailing At Midnight	RCA Victor 216594	1938
Jingle Bells	RCA Victor 216595	1938
Blue Tahitian Moonlight	RCA Victor 216596	1939
Steamboat Bill	RCA Victor 216597	1939
Beloved	RCA Victor 216598	1939
We're In The King's Navy	RCA Victor 216601	1939
Heart of Mine	RCA Victor 216602	1939
I'd Love To Live In Loveland	Bluebird 4679	1940
French Minuet	Bluebird 4681	1940
We're Proud of Canada	Bluebird 4683	1940
There'll Come Another Day	Bluebird 4689	1941
Captains of the Clouds	Bluebird 4730	1941
I'm Sorry I Made You Cry	Bluebird 4731	1941
A Little On The Lonely Side	RCA Victor 56 0000	1945
You Belong To My Heart	RCA Victor 56 0001	1945
Cuddles	RCA Victor 56 0008	1945
Let Him Go, Let Him Tarry	RCA Victor 56 0009	1945
The First Time I Kissed You	RCA Victor 56 0027	1948
When I Get Back To Calgary	Dominion 12	1951
I Love The Way You Say Goodnight	Dominion 13	1951
The West, A Nest And You, Dear	RCA Victor 56 0048	1951
Canadian College Medley	RCA Victor 56 0049	1951
The West, A Nest And You, Dear	RCA 57 5038	

Albums/CDs:

Title	Label	Year
Mart Kenney And His Orchestra	CTL M1053/S5053	1964
The West, A Nest And You	RCA Camden 776	1965
50th Anniversary Musical Tribute	World WF1 101	1981
Live! The Swinging Orchestra Of Mart Kenney	Nomadic NR7502	
Swinging Musical Showcase	WAP CD CD100	2000

Kensington Market

Alex Darou (bass)
Luke Gibson (vocals, guitar)
Eugene Martynec (vocals, guitar, piano)
Keith Mc Kie (vocals, guitar)
John Mills Cockell (Moog synthesizer)
Jimmy Watson (drums)

Named after a downtown neighbourhood in Toronto, the group was founded in 1967 by Bernie Finkelstein who later guided the careers of Bruce Cockburn and Murray Mc Lauchlan in the 1970s.

Comprised of Alex Darou, Luke Gibson (Luke & The Apostles), Eugene Martynec (Bobby Kris & The Imperials), Keith McKie, and Jimmy Watson, they first recorded for Stone Records. Their first single, Mr. John came out in 1967, and was charted nationally in RPM.

Warner Brothers Records released their debut album, *Avenue Road* in June 1968. By the release of their second album, Aardvark, in April 1969, John Mills Cockell joined the group. With his Moog synthesizer the group was able to record an album that represented the psychedelic sound of Yorkville. It was produced by Felix Pappalardi (The Lovin' Spoonful, The Youngbloods and Cream).

Shortly after its release, Alex Darou died, and the group had broken up by the end of 1969.

Singles:
Mr. John	Stone 714	1967
Bobby's Birthday	Stone 721	1967
Help Me	Warner Bros 6061	1968
I Would Be The One	Warner Bros 7221	1968
Witch's Stone	Warner Bros 7265	1969

Albums/CDs:
Avenue Road	WB 1754	1968
Aardvark	WB 1780	1969

The Killjoys

Gene Champagne (drums)
Mike Trebilcock (guitar, vocals)
Shelley Woods (bass)

Gene Champagne and Mike Trebilcock were in a band called The Monday Nuns, when they recruited Shelley Woods and changed their name To The Killjoys in 1993. From Hamilton, Ontario, they released their debut album, *Starry*, independently in 1994. Later that same year, Warner Music Canada signed the group and re-released it. In 1996, their second, Gimme Five came out, and in 1998 their third,

Melos Modos, which is pronounced Mee los Moe dos and is Latin for "the root of melody." Trebilcock left in the late 1990s and released his first solo album, *Shield Millions* (Jolleycut Records CD 7181) in 2000.

Singles:
Today I Hate Everyone	Wea 98970	1994/95
Dana	Wea 98970	1995
Any Day Now	Wea 98970	1995
Rave + Drool	Wea 13450	1996
Soaked	Wea 13450	1996
Look Like Me	Wea 13450	1996/97
Sick Of You	Wea 13450	1997
Perfect Pizza	Wea 22190	1998
I've Been Good	Wea 22190	1998

Albums/CDs:
Starry	Wea 98970	1994
Gimme Five	Wea 13450	1996
Melos Modos	Wea 22190	1998

Kilowatt

Bob Brett (drums)
Steve Hegyi (lead guitar, vocals)
Greg Leskiw (guitar, vocals)
Bill Wallace (bass, vocals)

This Winnipeg-based band was formed by ex-Guess Who members Greg Leskiw and Steve Hegyi, when their previous band, Les Q broke up in 1979. The addition of bassist Bill Wallace, another Guess Who alumnus, and drummer Bob Brett rounded out the quartet.

They were the first act sign with RCA's independent Dallcorte label. Their self-titled debut album in 1982 contained their first two Singles:, Lovers On The Run and Kids Are Krazy.

By the time their second album, *Currents* was released, Brett had left, and the group remained a trio. Both of their albums were produced by Domenic Troiano (*Robbie Lane* & The Disciples, Mandala, Bush, James Gang, Guess Who).

Singles:
Lovers On The Run	Dallcorte	1982
Kids Are Krazy	Dallcorte DCS 0102	1983
Not A Kid Anymore	Dallcorte DCS 0111	1983

Albums/CDs:
The Two Sides Of Kilowatt (EP)	Dallcorte DLS 1002	1982
Kilowatt	Dallcorte DLP 0701	1982
Currents	Dallcorte DLP 0706	1983

Andy Kim

Born and raised in Montreal, Quebec, he was born Andre Joachim on December 5, 1952. Kim wanted to be a singer when he first heard Elvis Presley and Buddy Holly. While attending Pius X High School in Montreal, he listened to The Beatles and The Rolling Stones. Convinced that he could make it as a singer, he went to New York where he recorded two songs: I Loved You Once for United Artists in 1963, and I Hear You Say I Love You for Red Bird in 1965. It was not until he signed with Dot Records in 1967 that he found success with such hits as How'd We Ever Get This Way, Shoot'em Up Baby, Baby, I Love You, So Good Together, Be My Baby, and It's Your Life.

In the late 1960s Kim collaborated with Jeff Barry on some of the songs for The Archies cartoon series. They included Bang Shang A Lang, Sugar, Sugar, and Jingle Jangle.

In 1973, Andy moved to Los Angeles where he ended up being cast as singer Rick Michaels in the episode, Sing A Song Of Murder for the CBS TV show, Barnaby Jones.

The following year, Andy had started his own record label, Ice Records and had number one hit with the single, Rock Me Gently. Others followed such as The Essence of Joan and Fire, Baby I'm On Fire.

During the 1980s and 1990s, Kim began recording under the name of Baron Longfellow, a name given to him by Gordon Mills, who had managed Engelbert Humperdinck and Tom Jones. As Baron Longfellow, he recorded Amour, one of the top five selling singles in Canada in 1980. Four years later, PolyGram released the album, *I'm Gonna Need a Miracle Tonight*. In the early 1990s, he had a minor hit with the single, Powerdrive. SugarSugar which he wrote with Jeff Barry was inducted into Canadian Songwriters Hall of Fame in 2006.

Two of Kim's songs were million sellers: Baby I Love You on October 14, 1969, and Rock Me Gently on October 3, 1974.

By Andy Kim
Singles:

I Loved You Once	UA 591	1963
Give Me Your Love	20th 6709	1964
I Hear You Say (I Love You Baby)	Barry 3381	1965
I Hear You Say (I Love You Baby)	Red Bird 10040	1965
How'd We Ever Get This Way	Steed 707	1968
Shoot'em Up Baby	Steed 710	1968
Rainbow Ride	Steed 711	1968/69
Tricia Tell Your Daddy	Steed 715	1969
Baby I Love You	Steed 716	1969
So Good Together	Steed 720	1969
A Friend in The City	Steed 723	1970
It's Your Life	Steed 727	1970
Be My Baby	Steed 729	1970
I Wish I Were	Steed 731	1971
I Been Moved	Steed 734	1971
Who Has the Answer	UNI 55332	1972
Love the Poor Boy	UNI 55353	1972/73
Oh What A Day	UNI 55356	1973
Rock Me Gently	Ice IC 1	1974
Fire, Baby I'm On Fire	Ice IC 2	1974
The Essence Of Joan (Ain't It Funny How Love Can Own You)	Ice IC 3	1975
Mary Ann	Ice IC 4	1975
Baby You're All I Got	Ice IC 5	1975
Harlem (as Andy Kimm)	Ice IC 7	1976
I See The Light (as Andy Kimm)	Ice IC 8	1976
Lonely Again (as Andy Kimm)	Ice IC 9	1976

Albums/CDs:

How'd We Ever Get This Way	Dot ST 37001	1968
Rainbow Ride	Dot ST 37002	1969
Baby I Love You	Dot ST 37004	1969
Andy Kim	Uni 73137	1973
Greatest Hits	Dot PIN 1021	1974
Rock Me Gently (Andy Kim U.S.)	Ice IC 100	1974

By Baron Longfellow
Singles:

Go It Slow	Ice ICR 001	1980
Amour	Ice ICR 002	1980

I'm Gonna Need A Miracle Tonight	Ice ICR 004	1984
Hold Me	Ice ICR 005	1984
In The Night Machine	Ice ICR 006	1985
Powerdrive (Longfellow)	Ice 001	1991

Albums/CDs:
Baron Longfellow	Ice ICLP 1001	1980
Prisoner By Design	Ice ICLP 1002	1984
Sacrifice To Satisfy (Unissued)	Ice 002	1991

Tom Kines

Tom Kines was born in Roblin, Manitoba on August 3, 1922. He first sang in public at age five. As a teenager he played drums in local brass, pipe and dance bands. While attending the University of Manitoba, his studies were interrupted by World War II and he was drafted into the Royal Canadian Navy. He became interested in performing and researching folk music when he was posted to Northern Ireland. After the war he moved to Ottawa and became a founding member of The Tudor Singers of Ottawa, whose repertoire included songs from the Elizabethan era.

Kines was also a member of the Ottawa Choral Society and and Toronto Bach Society. Best known as a folksinger, he performed in Montreal and Stratford and played on CBC Radio and at the Mariposa Folk Festival. In 1958 he appeared on two children's shows on CBC TV, The Song Shop and Magic In Music. He later hosted his own show, The Song Pedlar.

In 1966, he was appointed national director of Care Canada, a job he held until his retirement in 1987. He died on February 1, 1994.

Albums/CDs:
Of Maids and Mistresses	Elektra EKL 137	1957
Songs From Shakespeare's Plays and Popularsongs of Shakespeare's Time	Folkways FW 8767	1961
An Irishman In Americay	Folkways FW 3522	1962
Folk Songs of Canada	RCA PCS 1014	1965

Bill King

Born in Jeffersonville, Indiana on June 19, 1946, Bill King first came to Canada in the summer of 1963 when he was enrolled in Oscar Peterson's Advanced School of Contemporary Music. He joined the U.S. Army in 1968 but quit a year later to come to Canada to pursue a career in music. He played with Janis Joplin, Chuck Berry, and Linda Ronstadt before he joined his first Canadian band, Homestead, who recorded the single, We The People (1970) and album, Every Living Thing (1970), both on Nimbus Nine.

Signed to Capitol Records as a solo act, he had such hits as Superdad, Canada, and Wheel of Fortune. After recording for Raunch and Change Records, King formed the group China, with Christopher Kearney and Danny McBride.

King then switched from pop to jazz and recorded three albums in the 1980s, *Avenue B* and *Ice* (both 1984) and *City Of Dreams* (1985). In 1987, he started The Jazz Report which was also the name of a nationally syndicated radio program until September 1991.

In 1998, Radioland released East Side Symphony, an album that showcased the artist's ability to combine jazz and the classics. Today, King lives in Toronto where he continues to publish The Jazz Report and write and perform.

Singles:
Superdad	Capitol 72694	1973
Canada	Capitol 72712	1973
Give Me Love	Capitol 72712	1973
Wheel Of Good Fortune	Capitol 72720	1974
Blue Skies, Blue Skies	Capitol 72732	1974
Top Dollar Man	Capitol 72745	1975
Street Walker	Raunch R 76001	1976
Love And Affection	Change CH 45027	1980

Albums/CDs:
Goodbye Superdad	Capitol ST 6398	1973
Dixie Peach	Capitol ST 6422	1974
East Side Symphony	Radioland 10012	1998

King Biscuit Boy

Born on March 9, 1944 in Hamilton, Ontario, Richard Newell grew up listening to the blues on American radio shows. In his teens he began playing harmonica and between 1961 and 1965 worked with the blues/rock band, The Barons. They made one record in 1961 called Bottleneck.

In the early 1960s, The Barons changed their name to Son Richard and The Chessmen, and played Chuck Berry, Little Richard, Hank Ballard and Huey Smith.

By 1966 Richard had left the Chessmen, and had replaced Richie Hubbard as the lead singer of the Mid Knights. Two years later he joined Ronnie Hawkins, who nicknamed him King Biscuit Boy after a radio show at KFFA in Helena, Arkansas.

He left Hawkins to play with Crowbar in 1970, and later that same year he recorded the album, Official Music.

After recording a few solo projects in the 1970s, he went on hiatus from the music business. He has since been performing some new songs along with his older material, which has been reissued on CD on Stony Plain. He died in Hamilton, Ontario on January 5, 2003.

Singles:

Corrina Corrina (w/Crowbar)	Daffodil DFS 1001	1970
Biscuit's Boogie	Daffodil DFS 1005	1971
Lord Pity Us All	Daffodil DFS 1013	1971
29 Ways/Boom Boom	Daffodil DFS 1015	1972
Boogie Walk Part 1	Daffodil DFS 1020	1972
Barefoot Rock	Daffodil DFS 1030	1972
Deaf, Dumb, Crippled and Blind	Epic 11150	1974
New Orleans	Epic 50129	1975

Albums/CDs:

Official Music (with Crowbar)	Daffodil SBA 16000	1970
Gooduns	Daffodil SBA 16006	1972
King Biscuit Boy	Epic E 32891	1974
Mouth Of Steel	Stony Plain SPL 1076	1982
Badly Bent: Best Of	Daffodil DFN 667	1983
Richard Newell Aka King Biscuit Boy	Stony Plain SPL 1120	1988
The Best Of King Biscuit	Bullseye BEIBD 24	1992
Official Music	Stony Plain SPCD 1220	1995
Gooduns	Stony Plain SPCD 1222	1995

The Kings

David Diamond (lead vocals, bass)
Sonny Keyes (keyboards)
Max Styles (drums)
Aryan Zero (guitar)

Formed in 1979 in Hamilton, Ontario, this quartet captured Canadian and American audiences with their first hit, Switchin' To Glide in 1980. On   stage they projected the image of a new wave group, but were a rock and roll band.

David Diamond wrote the music, while Aryan Zero the lyrics. Their debut album, *The Kings Are Here* was produced by Bob Ezrin (Pink Floyd, Alice Cooper, Kiss). After a long hiatus the original members reunited to record the CD, *Unstoppable*, which was released in 1993. In the spring of 1999 Warner Music released *The Kings are Here,* a compilation of songs that were popular in the group's heyday.

Singles:

Partyitis	Extreme EF 90337	1980
This Beat Goes On/ Switchin' to Glide	Extreme/Kings I	1980
Switchin' to Glide	Extreme E 47006	1980
Don't Let Me Know	Extreme E 47110	1981
All the Way	Extreme E 47213	1981
Fools Are in Love	Extreme EF 90388	1981
As if I Cared	Dizzy DZ 72903	1982
Shoulda Been Me	Dizzy DZ 7751	1988
Unstoppable	Dizzy DZ 4953	1993
Lesson to Learn	Dizzy DZ 4953	1993
Tonight I Got You	Dizzy DZ 4953	1994

Albums/CDs:

The Kings are Here	Extreme X6E 274	1980
Amazon Beach	Elektra X5E 543	1981
The Kings (EP)	Dizzy DZLP 3004	1982
Unstoppable	Dizzy DZ 4953	1993
The Kings Are Here And More	Dizzy/Wea 37375	1999
Party Live In '85	Bullseye BLPCD 4043	2000

Klaatu

Terry Draper (drums)
Dee Long (guitar)
John Woloschuk (keyboards)

Named after a character in the science fiction classic, The Day The Earth Stood Still (RKO, 1951), this trio from Toronto wrote and sang all their own material. Formed in 1973 they prided themselves on their anonymity until 1982 when they publicly identified themselves through radio and print interviews. At first Klaatu was a duo made up of John Woloschuk and Dee Long. In 1974 the addition of Rusty Draper made it a three-man band. They recorded six albums between 1973 and 1982. The Carpenters recorded a remake of their song, Calling Occupants Interplanetary Craft in 1977.

For the title of their first album, Klaatu chose 3:47 E.S.T., the time in which Michael Rennie arrived in Washington in The Day The Earth Stood Still. When the album was released in 1976, it was the subject of much talk in both the United States and Canada, because they sounded a lot like The Beatles. A rock music writer for the Providence Journal in Rhode Island started the controversy with an article he wrote, "Is Klaatu Band The Beatles?"

Late in 1981 the group released their fifth album, *Magentalane*, and added three new members: Gary McCracken on drums, Michael Gingrich on bass, and Gerald O'Brien on keyboards.

Klaatu broke up in the mid 1980s. They reunited in 1988 to record Tatort, a song for West German television. Terry Draper released two solo albums, *Light Years Later* (Bullseye BLPCD 4010   1997) and *Civil War and Other Love Songs* (Bullseye CD 4030   2001).

Singles:

Hanus of Uranus	GRT 1233 18	1973
(Reissued on Daffodil DIL 1066 in 1975)		
California Jam	Daffodil 1057	1975
Sub Rosa Subway	GRT 1216 1075	1977
Calling Occupants	GRT 1216 1075	1977
We're Off You Know	Daffodil 1216 1077	1977
Dear Christine	Daffodil 1079	1978/79
A Routine Day	Daffodil 1081	1979
Knee Deep in Love	Daffodil 1083	1980
I Can't Help It	Daffodil 1085	1980
Love of a Woman	Capitol 72865	1981
December Dream	Capitol 72871	1981

Albums/CDs:

3:47 E.S.T.	Daffodil 9216 10054	1976
Hope	Daffodil 9216 10057	1977
Sir Army Suit	Daffodil SBA 16059	1978
Endangered Species	Daffodil SBA 16060	1980
Magentalane	Capitol ST 6487	1981
Klaatu Klassics	Capitol/DAF DFN 664	1982
Peaks: Best of	Attic ACDM1374	1993

Ritchie Knight & The Mid Knights

Rick Bell (keyboards)
Mike Brough (sax)
Doug Chappell (bass)
Ritchie Knight (vocals) RPLD by Richard Newell
Barry Lloyd (organ) RPLD by Ray Reeves
George Semkiw (guitar)
Barry Stein (drums)

The history of Ritchie Knight and the Mid Knights goes back to 1961 when George Semkiw and a friend from school, Leo Donahue decided to start their own group. They went through several personnel changes until 1962 when the lineup was comprised of Semkiw (who was going under the name of George Kash), Richard Hubbard (who was Ritchie Knight), Doug Chappell, Barry Stein, Barry Lloyd and Mike Brough.

The group was first known as The Mid Knights, who played regularly at the Balmy Beach Canoe Club in the east end of Toronto, and around Ontario. Their stage act consisted mainly of rhythm and blues cover tunes, one of which was Charlena. Their version became so popular that Arc Records approached the group to record it. The record company insisted they change their name to Ritchie Knight and The Mid Knights. On June 24, 1963 it went to number one on 1050 CHUM in Toronto.

Following the success of Charlena, the group went through more personnel changes. Lloyd left and was replaced by Ray Reeves, and Brough left to finish college.

After the release of That's Alright on RCA Victor in 1966, Ritchie Knight left. Richard Newell, who later became famous as King Biscuit Boy, was his replacement. With the addition of Rick Bell as a second keyboard player, the group called themselves The Mid Knight Blues Band. They recorded one single for Warner Brothers, Somebody Somewhere Needs You in 1968. After several more personnel changes, the band broke up in 1969.

Singles:

Charlena	ARC 1028	1963
The Joke	ARC 1037	1963
Homework	ARC 1047	1964
Think It Over	ARC 1076	1965
One Good Reason	ARC 1110	1965
That's Alright	RCA 57 3392	1966
Somebody Somewhere Needs You (as Mid Knights)	WAR 7180	1968

Moe Koffman

Born on December 28, 1928 in Toronto, Ontario, Morris (Moe) Koffman's interest in music began at the age of nine when he studied the violin, and the alto saxophone as a teenager. In his mid teens he played in dance bands, and eventually became one of the best Canadian jazzmen around. He was among the first to adopt the new be bop style of New York in the 1940s. In 1948 he won a CBC Jazz Unlimited poll as best alto saxophonist of the year.

His first recordings were 78s made in Buffalo, N.Y. In 1950 he moved to the United States where he played in such big bands as Jimmy Dorsey and Sonny Dunham. While in New York, he studied flute with Harold Bennett of the Metropolitan Opera Orchestra, and clarinet with Leon Russianoff, principal of The New York Philharmonic Orchestra.

In 1955 he returned to Toronto where he became a booking agent for George's Spaghetti House. His band, The Moe Koffman Quartet (and sometimes Quintet) made weekly appearances there until 1990.

Jubilee Records released his best known composition, Swinging Shepherd Blues in 1958. It was re-released on the GRT label in in 1973.

Koffman also joined Doug Riley (of Dr. Music fame) and together they made several popular recordings. Moe also made many recordings of his own music, and also played in several jazz-oriented TV orchestras led by Guido Basso, Jimmy Dale, and Rob McConnell and The Boss Brass.

Two years after joining the Boss Brass in 1972, he led his own band for Global TV's Everything Goes. In 1982 he began working with Dizzy Gillespie at concerts throughout Canada and the United States.

He also toured with Peter Appleyard in Western Canada and the Maritimes in 1991. Koffman also appeared with several orchestras, notably The Toronto Symphony, Hamilton Philharmonic, Sudbury Symphony Orchestra, Orchestra London Canada, Kitchener Waterloo Symphony Orchestra, and the Calgary and Edmonton Symphony Orchestras.

He was appointed to the Order of Canada on July 6, 1993 in recognition of his outstanding achievement and service to the arts and music community. In 1997 he was inducted into the Canadian Jazz Hall Of Fame. On March 28, 2001 he died in Orangeville, Ontario. In 2016, Swinging Shepherd Blues was inducted into The Canadian Songwriters Hall of Fame.

Singles:

Swinging Shepherd Blues	Jubilee J 5311X	1957/58
Little Pixie	Jubilee J 5324X	1958
Shepherd's Hoedown	Jubilee J 5367X	1958
Soul Brothers	Jubilee J 5485X	1958

Two Bourrees (Suite III)	GRT 1230 21	1972
The Gig (ue)	GRT 1230 30	1972
Swinging Shepherd Blues	GRT 1230 51	1973
Cavern Of The Mountain Trolls	GRT 1230 66	1973
It's All Right	GRT 1230 121	1976
Irish Tea Party	Anthem ANS 015	1980
Lonely Girl	Elektra 96 99087	1982
Koff Drops (Allegro Sonata II)	Anthem ANS 051	1983
(originally the flipside to GRT 1230 30)		

Albums/CDs:

Hot And Cool Sax	Jubilee JLP 1037	1957
The Shepherd Swings Again	Jubilee JLP 1074	1958
Moe Koffman The Swinging Shepherd Plays For Teens	ASCOT 16001	1962
Tales Of Koffman	UA JAZZ UAJ 14209	1962
The Moe Koffman Quartet	CTL 5029	1962
The Moe Koffman Quartet	CBC EXPO 31/RCI 268	1967
Moe Koffman Goes Electric	Jubilee JGS 8009	1967
Turned On Moe Koffman	Jubilee JGS 8016	1968
Moe's Curried Soul	Revolver RLPS 502	1970
Moe Koffman Plays Bach	GRT 9230 1008	1971
The Four Seasons	GRT 9230 1022	1972
Sorcerer's Dance	HOPI VHS.902	1972
Master Session	GRT 9230 1041	1973
Solar Explorations	GRT 9230 1050	1974
Best Of Moe Koffman	GRT 9230 1053	1975
Live At George's	GRT 9230 1005	1975
Jungle Man	GRT 9230 1066	1976
Museum Pieces	GRT 9230 1072	1977
Things Are Looking Up	GRT 9230 1078	1978
Back To Bach	GRT 9242 2004	1979
If You Don't Know Me By Now	Elektra XE1 60046	1982
Best Of Moe Koffman Vol I	Anthem ANR 1 639	1983
Best Of Moe Koffman Vol Ii	Anthem ANR 1 643	1983
The Magic Flute	Polytel PTL 17002	1985
One Moe Time	Duke DSR 31023	1986
Moe Mentum	Duke DSR 31036	1987
Oop Pop A Da	Duke DSR 31048	1988
Moe Koffman Quintet Plays	Duke DSR 31060	1990
Music For The Night: A Tribute To Andrew Lloyd Webber	Duke DSR 31073	1991
Moe Koffman With The Moe Koffman Quintet		1996
The Best Of Moe Koffman I&Ii	Anthem ANBD 1057	1996
Devil's Brew	Duke DSR 31100	1997
Project	Universal 59271	2000

Tony Kosinec

From Toronto, Ontario, Tony Kosinec was a performer/songwriter who had gained an international reputation as an actor, and as an opening act for such diverse acts as Seals and Crofts, Poco, Laura Nyro, Procol Harum and Blood, Sweat and Tears.

In 1971 Tony had a major success with the song, 48 DeSoto on Columbia Records. He switched to Smile Records, an independent label distributed by London Records of Canada Ltd., in 1973. His only album with the label, *Consider the Heart*, was released that same year, which also contained the hit single, All Things Come From God.

He changed labels again in 1974, this time to GRT Records. His first single, Love Hurts, failed to become a hit. Two other singles followed, A Little Road And A Stone To Roll and So Long.

In 1984 he recorded the song, My City Toronto (in honor of the Ontario city's sesquicentennial), as part of the duo Kosinec and Lenz.

Today, he resides in the United States where he has been writing music for television.

Singles:

You Got Me Crazy	Columbia 4 44932	1969
48 DeSoto	Columbia 4 45313	1971
All Things Come From God	Smile SLE 102	1973
Love Hurts	GRT 1230 79	1974
A Little Road and a Stone To Roll	Smile SLE 105	1974
So Long	Smile SLE 107	1974
My City Toronto (The Sesqui Song) (as Kosinec & Lenz)	A&M MC 02	1984
Whose Love	True North 4 199	1985
Listen to the Hukilau	True North 4 203	1985

Albums/CDs:

Processes	Columbia	1969
Bad Girl Songs	Columbia	1971
Consider the Heart	Smile SMS 1	1973
Passerby	True North TN62	1985

Wally Koster

He was born Walter Serge on February 14, 1923 in Winnipeg, Manitoba. In 1939 he began singing with Joe DeCourcy's dance band in his hometown. He later performed on radio station CJRC in Winnipeg, and made his CBC radio debut when he replaced George Murray on the Woodhouse and Hawkins Comedy Show.

During World War II Wally served as a bandsman and sang with Ellis McLintock's dance band in Toronto. From 1949–52 he was trombonist and featured vocalist with Mart Kenney.

Koster appeared on his first CBC TV show in 1952 and two years later he hosted CBC radio's Trans Canada Hit Parade, and co-hosted Cross Canada Hit Parade with Joyce Hahn. In 1960 he was host of CBC TV's The World of Music.

During the early 1960s he was in the musical comedies, Guys and Dolls (as Sky Masterson) and Carousel (as Billy Bigelow). He also played at the O'Keefe Centre in the Toronto production of The Most Happy Fella. He began singing and playing trombone in nightclubs with his band, The Music Men in the mid 60s.

He also acted in various CBC TV dramas.

He died on December 11, 1975 in Toronto.

Singles:

That's Amore/Changing Partners	Sapphire 101	1954
From The Vine Came The Grape/ Young At Heart	Sapphire 102	1954
Radisson/The Man With The Bright Silver Badge	Spiral S 16	1957
Alberta Trail/Sunset March	RCA T 35776	
Christmas Is Here/Christmas My Time of Year	CBC LM 147	1974

Albums/CDs:

Broadway Hit Parade	Capitol SN 6301	
The Songs Of Wally Koster	CTL S 5066	1965
Wally Koster	RCI 173	

Chantal Kreviazuk

Chantal Kreviazuk was born in Winnipeg, Manitoba on May 18, 1974. At age three she started playing the piano, which she later studied at the University of Manitoba. In her teens she was a member of a band. The inspiration to write songs came to her after she injured her jaw and femire while riding on a moped in Italy. She concentrated on writing jingles and handling background vocals. Signed to Sony Music, her debut CD, *Under These Rocks and Stones* was released in October 1996. It was produced by Matt Wallace and Peter Asher, one half of the British duo Peter and Gordon, and producer of albums by such artists as Linda Ronstadt and James Taylor. On the Armageddon soundtrack, she contributed a cover version of Leaving on a Jet Plane, and on 1999's soundtrack to the TV show Dawson Creek, Feels Like Home. Her cover version of The Beatles' In My Life was used as the theme of the NBC TV series, Providence. In 2001 she made her film debut in Century Hotel (TVA International Pictures). In 2012 she recorded a live album with the Niagara Symphony.

Singles:

God Made Me	Col CK 80246	1996/97
Believer	Col CK 80246	1997
Wayne	Col CK 80246	1997
Surrounded	Col CK 80246	1997/98
Leaving on a Jet Plane	Epic 69440	1998/99
Feels Like Home	Col CK 69853	1999
Before You	Col CK 80391	1999
Dear Life	Col CK 80391	2000
Souls	Col CK 80391	2000
Far Away	Col CK 80391	2001

Albums/CDs:

Under These Rocks And Stones	Col CK 80246	1996
Color Moving And Still	Col CK 80391	1999
What If It All Means Something	Col CK 86482	2002
Ghost Stories	Sony BMG 673797	2006
Since We Met: Best Of 1996-2006	Commercial Canada 834214	2008
Plain Jane	Universal 7446520	2009
In This Life	Col CSK 58293	2012

Robbie Lane & The Disciples

Terry Bush (guitar)
Doug Copeland (drums)
William Cudmore (harmonica, sax)
Paul Denyes (keyboards) Replaced by Bill Davis (1988)
Robbie Lane (vocals)
Paul Mifsud (tenor sax)
Gene Track (bass)

Robbie Lane, born Robin Curry, had previously been in a band called B.J. and The Rebels in Toronto in 1959. A year later he started Robbie Lane and The Lincolnaires. Comprised of Lane, Domenic Troiano (guitar), Gene Track (bass), Marty Fisher (keyboards), Sonny Milne (drums), and Bert Hermiston (tenor sax), the original group changed their name to Robbie Lane and The Disciples in December 1962 at Troiano's suggestion.

Their first single was Fannie Mae on Hawk Records in 1964, a cover version of Buster Brown's 1960 hit of the same name. They later signed with Capitol where they had such hits as What Am I Gonna Do and You Gotta Have Love.

In 1965 they recorded two singles as Butterfingers: Too Early In The Morning and Baby Ruth, the latter written by Doug Riley and Terry Bush went on to make sales history for a Canadian instrumental, and was first recorded by Dave Allan and The Arrows on Tower Records in the U.S.

By Robbie Lane and The Disciples
Singles:

Fannie Mae	Hawk 001	1964
Ain't Love A Funny Thing	Hawk 005	1964/65
Sandy/Where Love Has Gone	Capitol 72253	1965
Tiger In The Tank	Capitol 72271	1965
What Am I Gonna Do	Capitol 72357	1966
You Gotta Have Love	Capitol 72394	1966
It's Happening	Capitol 72503	1967

Albums/CDs:

It's Happening	Capitol ST 6182	1966
Ain't Dead Yet	Chicken CRCD-1	1996
The Best Of	Pace 023	1997

By Butterfingers
Singles:

Too Early In The Morning	Hallmark 1514	1965
Baby Ruth	Red Leaf 610	1965

By Robbie Lane
Singles:

M'Lady	Celebration 2094	1974
Missing You	Celebration 2114	1975
Stay With Me	Celebration 2151	1975

k.d. lang

She was born Katherine Dawn Lang on November 2, 1961 in Consort, Alberta. Her first single release was Friday Dance Promenade in 1983, which was pressed on white vinyl and is now considered a collector's item. At the beginning of her career, she was largely unknown since her music was rarely played on Canadian radio stations, and her performances on stage were compared to the late Patsy Cline. Owen Bradley, who produced Patsy Cline among others, came out of retirement to produce Lang's 1988 album, *Shadowland*.

In concert she wowed audiences with her frenetic performance and vocal stylings. At the closing ceremonies of Calgary's Winter Olympics in 1988, she led a rousing square dance. That same year, Chatelaine magazine chose her as their woman of the year. In 1989 she made her sixth appearance on The Tonight Show Starring Johnny Carson, and performed at New York City's Radio City Music Hall at the invitation of Barbara Orbison, Roy Orbison's widow. Lang and Orbison recorded the duet, Crying, a remake of his 1961 pop hit, in 1987, from the film, Hiding Out.

Lang admitted publicly in the early 1990s that she was a lesbian, and offended her critics when she became a spokesperson in a "Meat Stinks" campaign. In 1992, lang had a hit in Canada and the United States with Constant Craving, from her album *Ingenue*, and in 1997 she was awarded the Order of Canada.

Her album, *Drag* (1997) focused on the theme of addiction, and featured songs recorded by other singers, such as Peggy Lee (Don't Smoke In Bed), Les Paul and Mary Ford (Smoke Rings), Jane Siberry (H'Aint It Funny), and The Hollies (The Air That I Breathe).

Singles:

Hanky Panky	Bum 842	1984
Crying (with Roy Orbison)	Virgin 99388	1987/88
Diet of Strange Places	Sire 92-1987	1987
I'm Down To My Last Cigarette	Sire 92-79197	1988
Lock, Stock And Teardrops	Sire 92-78137	1988
Full Moon Full Of Love	Sire 29327	1989
Three Days	Sire 7-22734	1989
Pulling Back The Reins	Sire 92 58771	1989
Big Boned Gal	Sire 92 58771	1990
Constant Craving	Sire/War 26840	1992
Miss Chatelaine	Sire/War 26840	1992
The Mind of Love (Where Is Your Head Kathryn?)	Sire/War 26840	1992
Just Keep Me Moving	Sire/War 45433	1993

Hush Sweet Lover	Sire/War 45433	1994
If I Were You	Sire/WAR 46034	1995/96
You're OK	Sire/WAR 46034	1996
Sexuality	Sire/WAR 46034	1996
Anywhere But Here	Warner 83234	1999/00
Summer Fling	Warner CDW 47605	2000
Extraordinary Thing	Warner CDW 47605	2001
What A Wonderful World	Draw 2850	2002
Leavin' On Your Mind	MCA 02465	2003
Helpless	Nonesuch 15040	2004
Confess (with Siss Boom Bang)	Nonesuch	2005
Simple	Nonesuch 15449	2006
I Dream Of Spring	Nonszuch	2007
Coming Home	Nonesuch	2008

Albums/CDs:

A Truly Western Experience	Bum 842	1984
Angel With A Lariat	Sire 92 54411	1986
Shadowland	Sire 92 57241	1988
Absolute Torch And Twang	Sire 92 58771	1989
Ingenue	Sire/War 26840	1992
Even Cowgirls Get The Blues	Sire/War 45433	1993
All You Can Eat	Sire/War 46034	1995
Drag	Sire/War 46623	1997
Invincible Summer	Warner cdw 47605	2000
Live By Request	Warner Cdw 48108	2001
A Wonderful World	RPM	2002
Hymns Of The 49th Parallel	Nonesuch 279847	2004
Sing 17 Loud	Nonesuch	2011

Penny Lang

Born in Montreal in 1942, Penny Lang's musical career began in her late teens when she played at the student cafe at Sir George Williams University. She then went to New York's Greenwich Village where she played at The Bitter End. In the audience that night were her folk heroes, Ramblin' Jack Elliott, Mary Travers, and Phil Ochs.

Between 1962 and 1968 she toured constantly and she also began to write her own songs, which were often compared to Leonard Cohen and Joni Mitchell. During this time, Lang carved her own niche in the folk music world by interpreting the music of Leonard Cohen, Bob Dylan and Tim Hardin among others. She played at various clubs, such as The Back Door Cafe and Cafe Andre in Montreal, The Riverboat in Toronto, and Gerdes Folk City in Greenwich Village, and at many folk festivals throughout Canada and the United States. Audiences at her performances would often sing in a campfire manner, which helped build Lang's reputation as the First Lady of The Montreal Folk Music Scene. She left the club circuit in 1970 following the birth of her son, Jason, but returned to performing in 1988 when her fans kept asking the manager at Montreal's Golan coffeehouse if she was ever coming back. Her music is a mix of blues, gospel, folk and country.

Albums/CDs:

Yes	She-Wolf SWPL 9701-2	1991
Live (Cs)	PL 92	1992
Ain't Life Sweet	Silver Wolf SWPL-9302	1993
Carry On Children	Silver Wolf SWPL-9601	1996
Live At The Yellow Door	Silver Wolf SWPL-9702	1997
Penny Lang And Friends Live	She-Wolf SWPL-9801	1998
Somebody Else	She-Wolf SWPL-9901	1999
Gather Honey	Borealis BCD 1137	2001
Stone +Sand+ Sea+Sky	Borealis BCD 176	2006

Daniel Lanois

Daniel Lanois was born in Hull, Quebec on September 19, 1951. When he was ten years old, his family moved to Hamilton, Ontario where he later operated his first studio in the basement of his mother's house. His first effort as a singer/songwriter was *Acadie*, which was praised by music critics in both Canada and the United States. It featured the song, Jolie Louise which was featured on the hit CBS-TV series Northern Exposure and on the 1992 soundtrack compilation from the show.

Early in 1993 Lanois released his second solo album, *For the Beauty of Wynona*. Like his first album, the songs reflected the singer's roots from his French-Canadian ancestors to his own personal experiences.

He is best known more for his work as a producer than as a singer/songwriter. Since the 1980s he has produced such acts as Martha and The Muffins, The Parachute Club, Luba, Ian Tyson, Willie P. Bennett, Sylvia Tyson, Bob Dylan, Peter Gabriel, Robbie Robertson, The Neville Brothers, Brian Eno, and U2.

Lanois has also written and produced the music for such films as the Oscar-winning Sling Blade and All The Pretty Horses, both directed by Billy Bob Thornton.

Singles:
The Maker	Opal 92-59694	1989
Still Water	Opal 92-59694	1990
Jolie Louise	Opal 92-59694	1990
Lotta Love To Give	Warner Bros 45030	1993

Albums/CDs:
Acadie	Opal 92-59694	1989
For The Beauty Of Wynona	Warner Bros 45030	1993

The Last Words

Ron Guenther (vocals, drums)
Brad Campbell (bass)
Bill Dureen (lead vocals)
Graeme Box (guitar)

This group from Toronto started in April 1965. Their repertoire consisted of forty original tunes, and on stage it was Ron Guenther's driving big beat on drums combined with his harmony vocals, and Graeme Box's guitar and vocal stylings that contributed much to the band's sound. Brad Campbell was a part-time horticulturalist as well as bassist for the group. Lead vocalist Bill Dureen, whose hometown is St. John, New Brunswick, has written with Box many of the group's hits, including I Symbolize You.

They broke up in 1967.

Singles:
The Laugh's On Me	RCA Victor 57-3361	1965
I Symbolize You	Columbia 4-2707	1966
Give Me Time	Columbia 4-2726	1967

The Lavender Hill Mob

Chuck Chandler (vocals, keyboards)
Victor Fiory (drums, percussion)
Gerald Hardy (vocals, flute, soprano sax)
Hector Jacob (vocals, rhythm guitar)
Ronny Jones (vocals, guitars)
Nicky Pregeno (lead vocals, bass)

The Lavender Hill Mob started in a basement rehearsal hall in Montreal, Quebec in 1976. Commonly known as "The Mob," this six-piece band was discovered by former Mahogany Rush manager Robert Nickford. They made their first national appearance on the Juno Award Show on March 16, 1977. Their only two national hits on RPM's 100 singles Chart were The Party Song in 1977 and Dream Away in 1978. The group's self-titled debut album came out in 1976 on United Artists. By the release of their second album, *Street of Dreams* in 1977, Hector Jacob had left the group.

Singles:
The Party Song	United ArtistsUAXW 9254	1977
Chibougamou	United ArtistsUAXW 1001	1977
Dream Away	United ArtistsUAXW 1109	1978
The Ballad of Molly Maguire	United ArtistsUAXW 1202	1978

Albums/CDs:
The Lavender Hill Mob	United Artistsuala 719G	1976
Street Of Dreams	United ArtistsUALA 818G	1977

Leahy

Agnes Leahy (vocals, fiddle, piano, stepdancer)
Angus Leahy (fiddle, piano, stepdancer)
Donnell Leahy (fiddle, stepdancer)
Erin Leahy (vocals, paino, fiddle, stepdancer)
Doug Leahy (fiddle, sax, stepdancer)
Frank Leahy (drums, fiddle, stepdancer)
Julie Leahy (vocals, piano, mandolin, stepdancer)
Maria Leahy (vocals, guitar, piano, fiddle, mandolin, stepdancer)
Siobheann Leahy (vocals, bass, piano, fiddle, stepdancer)

From Lakefield, Ontario, the Leahy family's eleven children each started learning musical instruments at an early age, in addition to stepdancing. During the 1970s and early 1980s they played at various county fairs and rural weddings, and recorded on their label, Donlea, Panther, and RCA.

Tired of competing, they soon began performing to local crowds in and around their hometown, and by the mid-1990s they had played at many of the prestigious shows around the world, notably, the Austrian Musikantenstall Television Show, which was broadcast to 100 million people throughout Europe, the Folk Dream Gala at Toronto's Massey Hall, Global TV's Variety Village Telethon, the Chicago Irish Festival, and New York's A Day In The Bog Irish Festival. They also performed at the Opening Ceremonies Finale of The Special Olympics and The Breeder's Cup. Signed to Virgin Records, their self-titled CD came out in March 1997.

Singles:
You've Got The Fiddle (And I've Got The Bow)	Panther	1986/87
Rudolph The Red-Nosed Reindeer	RCA	1987
The Call To Dance	Virgin 42955	1997
B Minor	Virgin 42955	1997

Albums/CDs:
The Leahy Family	Donlea A 100	1983
The Leahy Family	RCA KKKL1-0576	1986
On The Move	Panther	1987
Leahy	Virgin 42955	1997
Lakefield	Virgin 45716	2001

Avril Lavigne

Born in Belleville, Ontario on September 27, 1984, she grew up in Napanee, Ontario. When she was sixteen, she moved to Manhattan, New York where she began writing songs for her first album. Signed to Arista Records by producer Antonio L.A. Reid, Let Go marked her debut in 2002. Complicated, the first single, was number one at MuchMusic in Toronto the weeks of June 15 and 22, 2002.

In 2006 she played a waitress in the documentary, Fast Food Nation and performed during the closing ceremony of 2006 Olympics in Turin, Italy.

On her third CD, *The Best Damn Thing*, it featured the song, Girlfriend, which had a chorus which was recorded in eight languages: Spanish, German, Italian, Portuguese, Hindi, Mandarin, Japanese, and English.

In 2011, her CD, *Goodbye Lullaby* was delayed because of creative differences. Its contrasting styles from bubble gum, What The Hell to the more acoustic closing, Goodbye.

Singles:
Complicated	Arista 965782	2002
Complicated	RCA 955782	2002

Sk8er Boi	Arista 977852	2002
I'm With You	Arista 506702	2003
Losing Grip	Arista 534542	2003
Don't Tell Me	Arista 608422	2004
My Happy Ending	Arista 636492	2004
Nobody's Home	Arista 663652	2004
He Wasn't	Arista 683052	2005
Girlfriend	RCA 073522	2007
When You're Gone	RCA 119262	2007
Hot	RCA MICT 3267	2007
Alice	Walt Disney 758577	2010
What The Hell	RCA 000915	2011
Here's To Never Growing Up	Epic USSM 301439	2013
Rock'N'Roll	Epic USSM 304458	2013
Let Me Go (with Chad Kroeger)	Epic USSM 304489	2013

Albums/CDs:

Let Go	Arista 949312	2002
Under My Skin	Arista 517872	2004
The Best Damn Thing	RCA 037742	2007
Goodbye Lullaby	Sony 558702	2011
Avril Lavigne	Epic 496332	2013

Brent Lee & The Outsiders

Ron Desjarlais (guitar)
Brent Lee (vocals, guitar)
Mike Lynch (bass)
Naoise Sheridan (guitar)

This quartet from Vancouver started playing together in 1990. As one of Canada's hardest working country/rock bands from the west coast, they relocated to Toronto in the summer of 1991. After cutting a demo tape of original material they decided to release their debut album, *Rose Tattoo*. Signed to Justin Entertainment, a small label distributed by MCA, in 1992, the group's first single was Would You Love Me. By the fall of 1992, the group had broken up.

Singles:

Would You Love Me	Justin JED-19	1992
Where I'm Going	Justin JED-19	1992
Mexican Bandits	Justin JED-19	1992
Take It To The Mountain	Justin JED-19	1992

Albums:

| Rose Tattoo | Justin JED-19 | 1992 |

Lee Aaron

Lee Aaron (vocals) Real Name: Karen Sue Greening
John Albani (guitar)
Greg Doyle (guitar)
Kimio Oki (drums)
Chas Rotunda (bass)

This hard rock band from Toronto took its name from their female lead singer whose powerful vocals have made them one of the most respected groups on the international rock scene. Born Karen Sue Greening in Belleville, Ontario, Lee Aaron grew up listening to her mother's Anne Murray and Supremes records. Her first exposure to heavy metal music occurred in high school when she was introduced to Deep Purple, Led Zeppelin and other heavy rockers.

In 1983 her band made their debut at The Marquee Club in England, and they later played at various European rock festivals, notably The Reading Festival in England.

Lead singer Aaron has graced the covers of many English and European magazines, and has ranked in the Top 10 of two British publications, Kerrang! and Sounds Female. Aaron has also been voted as the second-best instrumental vocalist by the German magazine, Metal Hammer.

Attic Records released Powerline: The Best Of Lee Aaron in 1992. Eight years later, Barking Dog released the CD, Slick Chick with her latest backup group, The Swingin' Barflies, which was characteristic of her change in musical direction to pop/jazz standards.

Singles:

Shake it Up	Attic LAT 1188	1984
We Will Be Rockin'	Attic LAT 1188	1984
Only Human	Attic AT 350	1987
Dream With Me	Attic LAT 1231	1987
Goin' Off The Deep End	Attic AT 358	1987
Whatcha Do To My Body	Attic AT 394	1989
Sweet Talk	Attic LAT 1257	1990
Hands On	Attic LAT 1257	1990
Sex with Love	Attic ACD 1322	1991
Some Girls Do	Attic ACD 1322	1991
Peace On Earth	Attic ACD 1369	1992

Albums/CDs:

Lee Aaron Project	Freedom FR-014	1983
Metal Queen	Attic LAT 1188	1984
Call Of The Wild	Attic LAT 1212	1985

Lee Aaron	Attic LAT 1231	1986
Bodyrock	Attic LAT 1257	1989
Some Girls Do	Attic ACD 1322	1991
Powerline: The Best Of	Attic ACD 1369	1992
Slick Chick	Barking Dog 007	2000

Leigh Ashford

Joe Agnello (bass)
Dave Cairns (drums, vocals)
Newton Garwood (keyboards)
Buzz Sherman (vocals)
Gord Waszek (guitar)

Named after a sixteenth-century prostitute, the original lineup of Leigh Ashford was comprised of Joe Agnello, Gord Waszek, Newton Garwood and Dave Cairns. They evolved from various Toronto bands such as The Demons, G.W. and The Demons, and Tom and Ian and The Soul Set. By the time they went into the recording studio in 1970, they had gone through some personnel changes. Cairns had left and was replaced by Lance Wright of Terry And The Pyrates, who also left and was replaced by Craig Kaleal from the Saskatchewan group, The Witness. Douglas "Buzz" Sherman from the Hamilton group, Flapping joined as vocalist. He had previously been in Mushroom Castle with Eddie Schwartz and Greg Godovitz (Fludd). In 1970 Bruno Weckerle replaced Garwood.

Signed to Revolver Records, their first single, Dickens came out in late 1970. The following year, their only album, *Kinfolk* was released. In 1972, they recorded the single, Workin' All Day on the Hopi label. By then Don Elliot, formerly with Mandala, had joined Wally Cameron and early member Newton Garwood to form another version of Leigh Ashford with Waszek and Sherman. When Waszek left in 1973-74, the band recruited Earl Johnson, Bill Wade, and Terry Juric and they changed their name to Moxy. (see Moxy)

Singles:
Dickens	Rrevolver 0010	1970/71
Everything Is Easy	RCA 75-1026	1971
Never Give Myself	RCA 75-1054	1971
Workin' All Day	Hopi P1.1001	1972

Album:
Kinfolk	RCA LSP 4520	1971

James Leroy

Born in Martintown, Ontario on April 3, 1947 James Leroy started out in Ottawa, as a folksinger in the mid-1960s.

In 1970 he turned his attention to the contemporary field and eventually put together a backup group comprised of Chuck Bergeron on bass, Gibb Lacasse on drums, David Oslund on lead guitar, Gary Comeau (of The Esquires) on pedal steel guitar, and Valerie Tuck on vocals. They called themselves Denim, after the song You Look Good In Denim, which was written by Leroy during a lunch break while rehearsing for a new album. Signed to GRT Records, his other hits included Touch of Magic and Make It All Worthwhile. An album called *James Leroy with Denim* came out in 1973. In 1976 he led the reformed Kitchener group, The Boarding House, formerly Major Hoople's Boarding House. On May 10, 1979 he died in Ottawa at the age of 32.

Singles:
Touch of Magic	GRT 1230-47	1973
Touch of Magic (U.S.)	JANUS J219	1973
Touch of Magic (Britain)	MAM R98	1973
You Look Good In Denim	GRT 1230-53	1973
Make It All Worthwhile	GRT 1230-65	1973
Some Kind Of Fool	GRT 1230-80	1974
Lady Ellen	GRT 1230-86	1974

Album:
James Leroy With Denim	GRT 9230-1034	1973

Leslie Spit Treeo

Laura Hubert (vocals)
Pat Langner (vocals)
Jack Nicholsen (vocals)

The origins of this folk/rock group began on the streets of Toronto where founders Laura Hubert, Jack Nicholsen and Pat Langner were buskers at the Leslie Street Spit, the lakefront near Toronto that bears the group's name.

After winning the 1991 Juno Award for Most Promising Group, the original three members quickly became one of the nation's hottest new bands.

In 1992, the trio added keyboardist Jason Sniderman and bassist Frank

Randazzo to their lineup. They helped create the group's new rock 'n' roll sound which can be heard on their second album, *Book of Rejection*. It's first single, In Your Eyes featured Randy Bachman on guitar.

The group changed its name in 1993 to Leslie Spit, when Jack Nicholsen left to become an actor. He performed with the band until May of '93 when he was cast to play a role in The Civilization of A Shoe Shine Boy at the Buddies In Bad Times Theatre in Toronto. The group later returned to using their old name.

Singles:

Angel From Montgomery	Capitol 94856	1991
Like Yesterday	Capitol 94856	1991
Heat	Capitol 94856	1991
In Your Eyes	Capitol 99646	1992
Sometimes I Wish	Capitol 99646	1992/93
Happy	Cap 99646	1993

Albums/CDs:

Don't Cry Too Hard	Capitol 94856	1990
Book of Rejection	Capitol 99646	1992
Hell's Kitchen	DL 12005	1995

Monique Leyrac

Born on February 26, 1928 in Montreal, Quebec, Monique Leyrac has carved out a successful career as both a singer and actress. She has recorded and sung the songs of such composers as Pierre Petel (in the film, Les Lumieres de ma ville), Charles Aznavour, Jean Rafa, Charles Trent, Gilles Vigneault, Claude Leveillee, and Felix Leclerc. She studied with Jeanne Mauberg, and in 1943 took the role of Bernadette in Frank Werfel's Le Chant de Bernadette. RCA Victor released her first single, La fille a Domingo in 1949.

In 1963, Columbia Records released her debut, Monique Leyrac Chante Vigneault Et Leveillee. Two years later, she was chosen by the CBC to sing at the International Song Festival in Sopot, Poland, and won the Grand Prix of International Day for her rendition of Vigneault's Mon Pays. In 1967 she played Toronto's Massey Hall, New York's Carnegie Hall, and Expo '67. She was made an Officer of the Order of Canada in 1968, and in 1970 she starred with Genevieve Bujold in the film, Act of the Heart. At the Stratford Festival in 1972 she appeared in The Three Penny Opera, and in 1976 she performed at the

Kennedy Centre in Washington. In 1978 she received the prestigious Prix de musique Calixa-Lavallee.

Since 1980 she has taken part in tributes to Vigneault and Leclerc, written the romance novel, Mon enfance a Rosemont, and appeared in the English and French versions of Sarah Bernhardt et la bete.

Singles:

La fille a Domingo	RCA 56-5171	1949
Au Chili	RCA 56-5172	1949
Bal des faubourgs	RCA 56-5184/57-0022	1949
Le bel Ecossais	RCA 56-5185/57-0037	1950
Pedro de Mexico	RCA 56-5194/57-0059	1950
Argentine	RCA 56-5195/57-0060	1950
Les lumieres de ma ville	RCA 56-5207/57-0101	1950
Jardin d'automne	RCA 56-5208/57-0102	1950
Le p'tit bonheur	RCA 57-0184	1952
Les filles de Trois-Rivieres	RCA 57-0185	1952
Mon Pays	Columbia C4-6898	1964
Les beaux dimanches	Comedie-Canadienne	1965
Flowers, Perfume, Candy	Columbia C4-2771	1967
Tous les enfants du monde	Columbia C4-6956	1967
Love Is Blue	Columbia C4-2783	1967
Ashes of the Flame	Columbia C4-2805	1968
Beautiful Morning	Columbia C4-2825	1968
La joie de vivre	Columbia C4-7051	1969
Le bonheur	Columbia C4-7052	1969
Pour cet amour	Columbia C4-7053	1969
Qui a tue Leon-Boule-de-gomme	Columbia C4-7107	1970
C'est tout une musique	Columbia C4-7117	1970
Petit garcon, ne grandit pas	Columbia	1970
Sainte-Adele, P.Q.	LondonFC-823	1970
Soirs d'hiver	LondonFC-827	1971
Tous les amants	Zodiaque 323	1973
Le ragtime a musique	Kebec-Disc KD 9048	1978

Albums/CDs:

Monique Leyrac Chante Vigneault Et Leveillee	Columbia FL-301	1963
Chansons Sur Mesure	Adagio 198.001	1963
Pleins Feux Sur Monique Leyrac (Re-Released As Mes Premieres Chansons - Harmony KHF-90232 - In 1973)	Columbia FS-622	1964
Monique Leyrac En Concert	Columbia FS-644	1966
Monique Leyrac	Columbia Els-316	1967
Monique Leyrac A Paris	Columbia FS-657	1967
Beautiful Morning	Columbia	1968
Monique Leyrac Chante La Joie De Vivre	Columbia FS-695	1968

Beautiful Morning	Columbia Els-324	1968
Monique Leyrac	Columbia FS-720	1969
L'hiver	Columbia FS-741	1970
Les Grands Succes	De Monique Leyrac GFS-90008	1971
Parlez-Moi De Vous	GFS-90117	1971
Monique Leyrac: 1678-1972	Zodiaque 6003	1972
Chansonniers Du Quebec	Radcan 360	1972
Qui Etes-Vous Monique Leyrac?	Radcan F-679	1975
Monique Leyrac Chante Nelligan	Barclay 9001	1975
Monique Leyrac Chante Felix Leclerc	POL 2424.157	1977
Les Grands Succes De Monique Leyrac	Sony BUK-50215	1991

Life

J.P. Lauzon (guitar)
Marty Simon (drums, vocals)
Dan Zimmerman (bass, vocals)
Lorraine Zimmerman (vocals)

This Montreal group was first known as The Scene with Michael Ship, Marty Simon, Dan Zimmerman, and guitarist Barry Albert. In 1969 they changed their name to Life, and recorded a self-titled album on Polydor Records, which included the hit single, Hands of the Clock. Their follow-up single, Strawberry Fields was a remake of the old Beatles hit from 1967. Life broke up in 1970. As a solo act, Lorraine Zimmerman later recorded three singles Don't Twist My Mind (Grand Slam 2014 – 1971), Why Did They Take It Away (Grand Slam 2033 – 1972), and I'd Like To Know (Sweet Plum 9910 – 1973).

Singles:

Hands of the Clock	Polydor 540-009	1969
Strawberry Fields	Polydor 2065-005	1970
Sweet Lovin'	Polydor 540-013	1970
Needing You	Polydor 540-017	1970

Album:

Life	Polydor 2424-001	1970

Gordon Lightfoot

Born on November 17, 1938 in Orillia, Ontario, Lightfoot was one of Canada's top folksingers. In the 1960s he wrote many songs that have become pop standards, three of which became hits for other artists in 1965: Ribbon of Darkness was a number one country hit for Marty Robbins, and Peter, Paul & Mary recorded For Lovin' Me and Early Mornin' Rain.

At eight years of age he took piano lessons and later sang in the local United Church junior choir. He played at civic centers and local radio shows in his teens. Jazz was another kind of music that influenced him, and he played in various jazz groups. In junior high he gave up the piano for the guitar and drums.

In 1955 he placed second in a province-wide competition of barbershop quartets. Two years later when he left high school, he still wanted to be a performer and wrote The Hula Hoop Song. On CBC-TV's Country Hoedown, he was one of the Swinging Singing Eight. In those early years he was influenced by country music. When he heard the Weavers's Carnegie Hall album he turned to traditional folk music.

In the early 1960s Lightfoot recorded for Chateau Records, owned by the late Norman Snider, who was instrumental in launching the young singer's recording career. Lightfoot and Terry Whelan (ex-barbershopper) formed a duo called The Two Tones. They recorded a live album in January, 1962 on Chateau Records.

By 1965 he was becoming well known since he frequently played at Toronto's Riverboat. He signed a contract with United Artists in 1966 and his self-titled debut album was released. In the mid-to-late 1960s his hits included Spin Spin, Go Go Round and The Way I Feel. In 1969 he signed with a $1,000,000 deal with Reprise/Warner which was unheard of for an artist at that time. In 1970 he received the Order of Canada.

Lightfoot became an international star in the 1970s. The song, If You Could Read My Mind was a smash hit in both Canada and the United States. In 1974 Sundown became his first US gold single, and first number one hit on Billboard's Hot 100 on June 29, 1974. Since the early 1980s, Lightfoot has recorded infrequently. If You Could Read My Mind was inducted into Canadian Songwriters Hall of Fame in 2003.

Singles:

(Remember Me) I'm The One	Chateau 142	1962
It's Too Late, He Wins/Negotiations	Chateau 148	1962/63
I'll Meet You In Minoochan	Chateau 152	1963
I'm Not Sayin'	WB 5621	1965

Just Like Tom Thumb's Blues	UA 929	1965
Spin Spin	UA 50055	1966
Go Go Round	UA 50114	1967
The Way I Feel	UA 50152	1967
Black Day In July	UA 50281	1968
Bitter Green	UA 50447	1968
Me And Bobby Mc Gee	REP 0926	1970
If You Could Read My Mind	REP 0974	1970/71
This Is My Song	AME 102	1971
Talking In Your Sleep	Rep 1020	1971
Summer Side Of Life	Rep 1038	1971
Beautiful	Rep 1088	1972
Same Old Obsession	Rep 1128	1972
You Are What I Am	Rep 1128	1972
Can't Depend On Love	Rep 1145	1973
It's Worth Believin'	Rep 1145	1973
Sundown	Rep 1194	1974
Carefree Highway	Rep 1309	1974
Rainy Day People	Rep 1328	1975
The Wreck Of The Edmund Fitzgerald	Rep 1369	1976
Race Among The Ruins	Rep 1380	1977
The Circle Is Small	WBS 8518	1978
Daylight Katy	WBS 8579	1978
Dreamland	WBS 8644	1978
Dream Street Rose	WBS 49230	1980
If You Need Me	WBS 288	1980
Baby Step Back	WBS 50012	1982
Blackberry Wine	WBS 92-99637	1982
Anything For Love	WBS 92-86557	1986
Stay Loose	WBS 92-85537	1986
I'll Prove My Love	REP 45208	1993
Inspiration Lady	CNR 998892	2004

Albums/CDs:

Two Tones Live At The Village Corner	Chateau Clp-1012	1962
Lightfoot	Uas 6487	1965
The Way I Feel	Uas 6587	1967
Did She Mention My Name	Uas 6649	1968
Back Here On Earth	Uas 6672	1968
Sunday Concert	Uas 6714	1969
Sit Down Youngstranger (Aka If You Could Read My Mind - U.S.)	Rep RS 6392	1970
Early Lightfoot	Ame 7000	1971
Classic Lightfoot (Best Of, Vol 2)	UAS 5510	1971
Summer Side Of Life	Rep Ms 2037	1971
Don Quixote	Rep MS 2056	1972
Old Dan's Records	Rep MS 2116	1972
Sundown	Rep MS 2177	1973

Very Best Of Gordon Lightfoot	UALA 243	1974
Cold On The Shoulder	Rep MS 2206	1975
Gord's Gold	Rep 2RS 2237	1975
Summertime Dream	Rep MS 2246	1976
Endless Wire	War KBS 3149	1978
Dream Street Rose	War XHS 3426	1980
The Best Of Gordon Lightfoot	UAS 6754/E2-48396	1980
Shadows	War Xbs 3633	1982
Salute	War 92-39011	1983
East Side Of Midnight	War 92-54821	1986
Over 60 Minutes With...	Cap 48844	1987
Gord's Gold Vol Ii	War 92-57841	1988
The Original Lightfoot (3 Cds)	EMI S2 80747	1992
Waiting For You	Rep 45208	1993
A Painter Passing Throught	Rep 46949	1998
Songbook (4 Cds)	War 75802	1999
Complete Greatest Hits	Rhino 78287	2002
Harmony	War 70027	2004

Lighthouse

Dick Armin (cello)
Ralph Cole (guitar)
Pinky Dauvin (voxals)
Don DiNovo (violin)
Paul Hoffert (keyboards, vibes)
Keith Jollimore (sax, flute)
Bob Mc Bride (vocals)
Peter Pantaluk (trumpet)
Skip Prokop (drums)
Howard Shore (sax, flute)
Larry Smith (trombone)
Louis Yackniw (bass)

Founded by drummer Skip Prokop in 1968, Lighthouse remains one of the best groups to emerge on the Canadian rock music scene.

Prokop started on drums in 1963 when he played with small bands in legion halls in Toronto. His first group was the Riverside Three. Six months later they broke up and he ended up playing in other city bands. In the mid-1960s he met Bill Misener, Chuck Beale and Danny Gerard and together they became The Paupers. (see The Paupers) In 1968 Prokop left the latter to organize a 13-piece group called Lighthouse.

The first musician asked to join the group was Ralph Cole, whom Prokop had met while still a member of The Paupers. Signed to MGM Records in the United States, they were managed by Vinnie Fusco, a music publisher in New York, who was impressed by their demo tape. Prokop began recruiting other members for the group. They were Grant Fullerton and Pinky Dauvin (Lighthouse's first lead singer) from Toronto's Stitch In Tyme. They were joined by saxophonist Howard Shore, a composer friend of Hoffert's. They were the first rock act to play at the Newport, Monterey and Boston Globe jazz festivals, the Atlantic City Pop Festival, and the Isle of Wight Festival in England.

In 1969 they signed a contract with RCA Records. After two singles and three albums with the label, they switched to GRT Records, where they had success with such songs as One Fine Morning, Sunny Days and Pretty Lady.

The 1970s also saw more changes within the group. In 1973, Paul Hoffert and Bob Mc Bride left in 1973, and Skip Prokop in 1974. The rest of the group disbanded in 1976.

On September 10 and 11, 1982 the original members of Lighthouse reunited for four shows at the Ontario Place Forum, and during the summer of '93 they reunited for a concert at Toronto's City Hall Square. Original members Hoffert, Prokop, and Cole were joined by new lead singer Danny Clancy and keyboardist Donald Quan.

Jollimore died in January 1986, Bob Mc Bride on February 20, 1998 and Pinky Dauvin on April 21, 2013. Howard Shore went on to become a successful film composer, notably for directors David Cronenberg and Peter Jackson. Shore won three Oscars: Original Music Score for Lord Of The Rings: Fellowship Of The Ring (2001), Original Music Score and Original Song (Into The West)for Lord Of The Rings: Return Of The King (2003).

Singles:

Title	Catalog	Year
Feels So Good	RCA 74-0285	1969
The Chant	RCA 47-9808	1970
Hats Off (To The Stranger)	GRT 1230-04	1971
One Fine Morning	GRT 1230-10	1971
Take It Slow	GRT 1230-19	1971
I Just Wanna Be Your Friend	GRT 1230-25	1972
Sunny Days	GRT 1230-39	1972
You Girl	GRT 1230-46	1973
Broken Guitar Blues	GRT 1230-52	1973
Pretty Lady	GRT 1230-63	1973
Can You Feel It	GRT 1230-61	1974
Good Day	GRT 1230-77	1974

Albums/CDs:

Lighthouse	RCA LSP 4173	1969
Suite Feeling	RCA LSP 4241	1970
Peacing It All Together	RCA LSP 4325	1970
Thoughts Of Movin' On	GRT 9230-1010	1971
One Fine Morning	GRT 9230-1002	1972
Lighthouse Live!	GRT 9230-1018	1972
Sunny Days	GRT 9230-1021	1972
Can You Feel It	GRT 9230-1039	1973
Good Day	GRT 9230-1046	1974
The Best Of Lighthouse	GRT 9230-1052	1975
Best of - Sunny Days Again	Denon CAN 9002	1989
Song of The Ages	Denon CAN 9026	1996

Little Caesar and The Consuls

Wayne Connors (drums) Replaced by Gary Wright (1963)
Bruce Morshead (vocals, keyboards)
Ken Pernokis (guitar)
Norm Sherrat (sax)
Tom Wilson (bass)

Little Caesar and The Consuls first formed in 1957 in Toronto, Ontario. They were named after a British sedan called the Consul. The original lineup consisted of Bruce Morshead, Norm Sherrat, Peter Deremiccious, Ken Pernokis, and Gene Mac Lellan, who would later write Snowbird for Anne Murray. Morshead was nicknamed "Little Caesar", after Edward G. Robinson's title character in the 1931 gangster film of the same name.

During their early years, Robbie Robertson and Gene MacLellan had been members. By 1960 their lineup was comprised of Bruce Morshead, Norm Sherratt, Ken Pernokis, Wayne Connors, and Tom Wilson Gary Wright replaced Connors in 1963.

In 1963 they had their first hit, If I Found A New Girl on Columbia Records. Two years later, they recorded My Girl Sloopy on the Red Leaf label. On December 13, 1965, Little Caesar and The Consuls' version of The Miracles' You Really Got A Hold On Me was #1 on RPM's singles chart. They returned to Columbia for their last two hits, Mercy Mr. Percy (1966) and My Love For You (1967).

There have since been more personnel changes in the group. Morshead left the band to return to Kodak where he worked while attending night school in the 1950s. He was replaced by Steve Macko. Tom Wilson left in 1969 to become an agent, where he handled April Wine, Ronnie Hawkins and Bachman-Turner Overdrive.

The group broke up in 1971, but reunited in 1973 for a six week tour. Their lineup was comprised of originals Norm Sherrat (vocals), Gary Wright (drums) and Tom Wilson (bass), with new members Paul Denyes (keyboards) and Tommy Graham (guitar).

In 1976 they reunited again. This time with new members John Bradley on guitar, and Bob Oliffe on bass. Under the leadership of Steve Macko, they opened for the Bay City Rollers on their Canadian tour. They also recorded a new version of Sloopy on Raunch Records, which was more uptempo, and retitled Hang On Sloopy.

With a different lineup, Little Caesar and The Consuls were back in 1993. This time the members were Sherrat, Wright and Wilson, along with Vic Wilson (baritone, tenor sax, vocals), Steve Macko (piano, tenor sax, vocals) and Tony Crivaro (guitar and vocals). Vic Wilson had co-managed Rush with Ray Danniels.

Their reunion also marked a return to the recording studio where they made the CD, *Since 1956* in 1993. They broke up in September 2001.

Singles:

If I Found a New Girl	Columbia C4-2637	1963
Troubles and Trials/Something Funny, Something Wrong	Columbia C4-2641	1963
Sea Cruise	ARC 1066	1964
My Girl Sloopy	Red Leaf 612	1965
You Really Got A Hold on Me	Red Leaf 613	1965
You Laugh Too Much	Red Leaf 616	1966
One Thousand Miles Away	Red Leaf 619	1966
Don't Make a Fool of Me/ Little Heartbreaker	Red Leaf	1966
Mercy Mr. Percy	Columbia C4-2793	1966
My Love for You	Columbia C4-2747	1967
Hang on Sloopy	Raunch R 76003	1976

Albums/CDs:

Little Caesar And The Consuls	Red Leaf 1001	1965
Since 1956	RRC RRCD 101	1993

Colin Linden

Colin Linden was born in Toronto on April 16, 1960 in Toronto.

Since meeting Howlin' Wolf at the age of eleven, Colin has become one of our top blues guitarists. In his teens he began playing coffeehouses and folk festivals, and travelled throughout the southern states where he met and played with many of the surviving blues legends of the 1920s and 1930s.

In 1976 he left school to join David Wilcox's Teddy Bears and a year later, Colin started his own band. By the end of the 1970s he had toured with Leon Redbone and recorded with Mississippi bluesman Sam Chatmon on his album, *Sam Chatmon & His BBQ Boys* on Flying Fish Records.

The 1980s saw Linden record his first solo album, *Colin Linden Live* on Ready Records. He also played with Amos Garrett, Willie P. Bennett, Gwen Swick, Mendelson Joe, Morgan Davis, African singer Tony Bird, and Rick Danko and Garth Hudson of The Band.

During the next decade he worked as a session guitarist, writer and/or producer on Albums by Rita Coolidge, The Band, Bruce Cockburn, Lori Yates, Gowan, Lennie Gallant, Colin James, Prairie Oyster, and American artist Brookes Williams. Linden also co-wrote such hits as The Band's Remedy and Michelle Wright's Guitar Talk.

After recording one album each for Stony Plain and A&M Records, he switched over to Columbia. His 1995 album, *Through The Storm, Through The Night* was heavily influenced by gospel and the blues.

During the second half of the 1990s, he joined Tom Wilson of Junkhouse and Stephen Fearing to form the trio, Blackie and The Rodeo Kings.

Albums/CDs:

Colin Linden Live	Ready LR 011	1981
The Immortals	Stony PlainSPL 1097	1986
When the Spirit Comes	A&M SP 9143	1988
North At Eight, South At Nine	Columbia CK 80178	1993
Through the Storm, Through the Night	Columbia CK 80225	1995
What's the Matter With...(EP)	Columbia CDNK 1343	1998
Raised ty Wolves	Columbia CK 80329	1998
Sad & Beautiful World 1975-1999	Columbia CK 80522	2000
Big Mouth	Columbia CK 80615	2001

Little Daddy and The Bachelors

Tommy Chong (guitar)
Wes Henderson (guitar)
Little Daddy (vocals)
Floyd Sneed (drums)
Bernie Sneed (keyboards)

This quartet was one of the most popular club bands in Vancouver. They were voted Best Group at the Pacific National Exhibition Teenage Fair in 1964, and the prize was a recording session set up by RCA Victor. They recorded a cover version of Too Much Monkey Business, which was originally recorded by Chuck Berry.

Little Daddy's real name was Tommy Melton. The group went through three name changes, such as Four Niggers and A Chink and Four Colored Fellows And An Oriental and Four N's And A C, before they broke up in the mid-1960s.

Tommy Chong and Wes Henderson were later members of Bobby Taylor and The Vancouvers, while Floyd Sneed, from Calgary, Alberta, was the drummer for Three Dog Night from 1968-1975. Chong also was half of the comedy/acting team of Cheech and Chong in the 1970s and 1980s.

Single:
Too Much Monkey Business   RCA 57-3363   1964

The Liverpool Set

Kent Daubney (drums)
Dave Donnell (lead guitar)
Evan Hunt (vocals) Replaced in 1966 by Jack Douglas
Eve Lancing (vocals)
Gary Nelson (rhythm guitar) Replaced in 1966 by Jack Douglas
Shane Sennet (bass)

This group started in Toronto in 1962 as Strangers Incorporated. They later moved to Hawksbury, Ontario where they played with many Quebec groups, such as Les Classels. Strangers Incorporated were managed by Bill Anthony, a.k.a. Liam Ryan, who had the idea to promote them as an English act, which is why their name was changed to the Liverpool Set. With the exception of Kent Daubney and Evan Hunt, the other members of the group had fictitious names: Shane Sennet was Leo Cannon, Eve Lancing was Ivars Lidums, Gary Nelson was Gary Jolicoeur, and Dave Donnell was Lachlan Mac Fadyen.

In 1964-65 they made their first appearance in Niagara Falls, Ontario, and later became the first Canadian band to sign an American recording contract. Signed to Columbia Records, they went to Nashville where they recorded some songs, one of which became their first single, Must I Tell You (I Love You), which was launched on July 15, 1965 in Miami, Florida at a Columbia Records convention.

By 1966 Gary Nelson and Evan Hunt were replaced by Jack Douglas, formerly a member of Wild Child and The Violations. Later that same year, the Liverpool Set became known as The Night Shift, and recorded the single, After The Lights Go Out. They broke up in 1967.

Singles:
Must I Tell (I Love You)	Columbia 4-43351	1965
Oh Gee Girl	Columbia 4-43512	1966
Change Your Mind	Columbia 4-43813	1966

The Lords of London

Greg Fitzpatrick (vocals)
Sebastian Agnello (keyboards)
Danny Taylor (drums)
John Richardson (guitar)
Hughie Leggatt (bass)

The origins of the group go back to 1966 when five teenagers joined together to form their own group. All with the exception of Leggat, who was from Scotland, were from the east end of Toronto.

They called themselves The Lords of London and were a mainstream pop band who recorded for Apex Records. Their first hit was Cornflakes and Ice Cream in 1967. Their other singles were 21,000 Dreams and Candy Rainbow.

By 1969, the group had changed to a heavier sound and they also changed their name to Nucleus. Sebastian Agnello had left the group and was replaced by Bob Horne. In 1970 they became known as Leather.

In 1971 the group went through another change in personnel. Greg Fitzpatrick, Danny Taylor and John Richardson all left. Bob Horne and Hughie Leggatt were joined by Alex Machin and Paul Naumann. The group also became known as A Foot In Coldwater. Signed to Daffodil Records, A Foot In Coldwater had several hits, notably (Make Me Do) Anything You Want, and (Isn't Love Unkind) In My Life.

When the band split up in 1977, Leggat went on to form the bands Thunder Road and Private Eyes. He also joined his brother Gordon as a duo. In 1982, they recorded the album, Illuminations on Capitol Records. A Foot In Coldwater reunited for a series of concerts in 1988.

As The Lords Of London
Singles:

Cornflakes and Ice Cream	Apex 77054	1967
21,000 Dreams	Apex 77068	1967
Candy Rainbow	Apex 77074	1968

As Nucleus
Albums:

Nucleus	Mainstream S 6120	1969

As A Foot In Coldwater
Singles:

(Make Me Do) Anything You Want	Daffodil DFS 1017	1972
(Isn't Life Unkind) In My Life	Daffodil DFS 1028	1973
Lady True	Daffodil DFS 1033	1973
Love Is Coming	Daffodil DFS 1040	1973
So Long/Who Can Stop Us Now	Daffodil DFS 1046	1974
(Make Me Do) Anything You Want	Daffodil DFS 1058	1975
Para-Dice	Daffodil DFS 1058	1975
I Know What You Need	Daffodil DFS 1065	1975
Midnight Lady	Daffodil DFS 1068	1976
It's Only Love	Daffodil DFS 1087	1977

Albums/CDs:

A Foot In Coldwater	Daffodil SBA 16012	1972
Second Foot In Coldwater	Daffodil SBA 16028	1973
All Around Us	Daffodil SBA 10048	1974
Breaking Through	Anthem ANR1-1008	1977
Footprints - Best Of Vol 1	Daffodil DFN 665	1983
Footprints - Best Of Vol 2	Daffodil DFN 666	1983

Lost and Profound

Lisa Boudreau (vocals)
Terry Tompkins (vocals)

The history of this Toronto based duo began in Calgary where Lisa and Terry met as members of different bands: Lisa in The Now Feeling, and Terry in The Left Book Club. They eventually teamed up as The Psychedelic Folk Virgins, and moved from Calgary to Toronto. Lisa began her musical career while still in high school in Moncton, N.B. She occasionally played back up for The Nerves. When they split up in search of separate careers, they coincidentally all ended up in Calgary and formed The Left Book Club.

Born in Hamilton, Terry became interested in music when he received The Beatles 1964-66 album. He spent much of his youth writing songs in both Hamilton and Calgary. When he talked to groups like The Sex Pistols and The Ramones about music, they convinced him to join a band. Before joining The Now Feeling he was a member of The Snots, The Deceitful Concubines and Hamilton's The False Idols.

Lost and Profound was first comprised of Allan Baekeland, Bartok Guitarsplat, Boudreau and Tompkins, and they released an independent cassette, The Bottled Romance Of Nowhere. When Guitarsplat left, he was replaced by Curtis Driedger of The Ceedees.

Later, he and Baekeland left, and Terry and Lee continued as Lost and Profound. Their self-titled debut album on Polygram was released in the spring of 1992.

Singles:
Brand New Set of Lies	Polydor 513251	1992
Curb The Angels	Polydor 513251	1992
Winter Raging	Polydor 513251	1992
All Consuming Mistress	Polydor 513251	1993
Miracles Happen	Polydor 519518	1994

Albums/CDs:
Lost and Profound (EP)	Polydor PCD 195	1992
Lost and Profound	Polydor 513251	1992
Memory Thief	Polydor 519518	1994
Love's Sweet Messenger	LWR 1017	1996

Loverboy

Paul Dean (guitar)
Matt Frenette (drums)
Doug Johnson (keyboards)
Mike Reno (lead vocals)
Scott Smith (bass)

The origins of Loverboy go back to Calgary, Alberta in 1978 when Paul Dean met Mike Reno. They were joined later by Doug Johnson, Matt Frenette (Tom Cochrane), and Scott Smith.

Early in 1979 their first demo attracted the attention of Lou Blair and Bruce Allen who were instrumental in getting the band signed to Columbia Records. Their self-titled debut album was released in July 1980.

In 1981 their sophomore set, Get Lucky, came out. While on tour to promote it they broke attendance records across Canada. After their third album, Keep It Up, in 1983 they took a break from touring.

They wrote Nothing's Gonna Stop Us Now for the Olympics in 1984, and, later that same year, Mike Reno and Ann Wilson collaborated on the song Almost Paradise for the soundtrack of Footloose. In 1984 they contributed the song, Destruction to the soundtrack of Giorgio Moroder's reissue of the silent classic, Metropolis, and Heaven In Your Eyes, to Top Gun (1986).

During the next three years they toured extensively where they broke more box office records across Canada. In 1989 came the album, Big Ones, a greatest hits compilation that also included the new songs, Too Hot and Ain't Looking For Love. They also decided to go on hiatus.

In 1992-93 Mike Reno was in the band called Just If I with Neil Shilkin, Neal Schon, Matt Frenette, Russel Kline and Ken Sinaeve.

Spinner released their only CD, *All One People* (SP 0614) in 1993.

During the spring of 1994, Loverboy reunited. They toured the United States for the first time in seven years. Two years later came their first album of all-new material, *Temperature's Rising*. It was followed by another called, *Six* in 1997.

In November 2000, they lost bassist Scott Smith who was swept away from his sailboat by an eight-metre wave off the California coast near San Francisco.

Singles:

The Kid Is Hot Tonite	Columbia C4-4255	1980
Turn Me Loose	Columbia C4-4266	1980
Lady of the '80s	Columbia C4-4272	1981
Working For The Weekend	Columbia C4-4291	1981/82
When It's Over	Columbia C4-4300	1982
It's Your Life	Columbia C4-4300	1982
Hot Girls In Love	Columbia 38-03941	1983
Queen of The Broken Hearts	Columbia C4-4347	1983
Gangs In The Street	Columbia C4-4314	1984
Lovin' Every Minute Of It	Columbia 38-05569	1985
Dangerous	Columbia 38-05711	1985
This Could Be The Night	Columbia 38-05765	1986
Lead A Double Life	Columbia 38-05867	1986
Heaven In Your Eyes	Columbia 38-06178	1986
Notorius	Columbia 38-07324	1987
Too Hot	Columbia 73066	1989
Ain't Looking For Love	Columbia CK-45411	1990

Albums/CDs:

Loverboy	Columbia JC-36762	1980
Get Lucky	Columbia FC-37638	1981
Keep It Up	Columbia QC-38703	1983
Lovin' Every Minute Of It	Columbia FC-39953	1985
Wildside	Columbia OC-40893	1987
Big Ones	Columbia CK-45411	1989
Classics	Columbia CK-80198	1994
Temperature's Rising	SMS IDK 85238	1996
Six	BMG 62202	1997
Just Getting Started	Rockstar066920	2009
Unfinished Business	LVBY 74214	2014

The Lowest of The Low

Dave Alexander (drums)
John Arnott (vocals, bass)
Ron Hawkins (lead vocals, guitar)
Steve Stanley (vocals, lead guitar)

The genesis of this Toronto band goes back to the late 1980s when Ron Hawkins and Dave Alexander were in a band called Social Insecurity. When it broke up, the two of them joined Steve Stanley in the group, Popular Front. With the addition of John Arnott, they became The Lowest of the Low in March 1991. Their independent debut album, *Shakespeare My Butt*, was released later that same year. Their second, Hallucigenia, came out in March 1994. The group broke later that same year.

Hawkins went on to form his own group, The Rusty Nails, who have released three albums, *The Secret Of My Excess* (Shake The Record/Warner SALC 225 - 1996), *Greasing The Starmachine* (Outside Music - 102223), and *Crack Static* (2000).

The group reunited to do an album in 2002.

Albums/CDs:

Shakespeare My Butt	L.S.D. LDD 79303	1991
Hallucigenia	A&M 40228	1994

Luba

Michael Bell (bass)
Doug Corrivo (keyboards)
Alain Couture (guitars, vocals)
Luba Kowalchyk (vocals)
Mark Lyman (rhythm & lead guitar)
Pierre Marchand (keyboards & vocals)
Peter Marunzak (drums)
John Nestorowich (rhythm guitar, vocals)
Doug Short (keyboards)
Jeff Smallwood (guitar & banjo)
Mike Zwonok (bass)

Luba Kowalchyk was born in Montreal in 1958. Of Ukrainian extraction she began singing as a teenager when she travelled across Canada to sing traditional folk tunes in Canadian Ukrainian communities.

Growing up in Montreal's working class neighborhood of St. Leonard, Luba learned to speak Ukrainian and English, and later picked up Polish and Russian. She began taking vocal lessons as a child and learned to play the guitar, flute and piano by the time she was a teenager. All of this training led to her first recordings in Ukrainian.

At Montreal's Concordia University in 1979, Luba, Peter Marunzak, and guitarist Mark Lyman formed a rock group and released a min-album featuring, Every Time I See Your Picture, a song dedicated to Luba's late father.

In 1984 she recorded her first album. Two years later came her second, *Between the Earth and Sky*, which included the single, How Many (Rivers To Cross).

After having such hits as Storm Before The Calm, Secrets and Sins, and Little Salvation, Luba broke up in 1990.

Luba, the singer, made a comeback in 2000 with the release of the CD, *From the Bitter to the Sweet*, on her own Azure music label, which included the first single, Is She a Lot Like Me.

Singles:

Everytime I See Your Picture	Capitol 72899	1983
Let It Go (12")	Capitol 75077	1984
Let It Go	Capitol 72947	1984
Storm Before the Calm (12")	Capitol SPRO 266	1984
Storm Before the Calm	Capitol 72959	1984/85
Secrets and Sins (12")	Capitol SPRO 266	1985
Secrets and Sins	Capitol 72966	1985
How Many (Rivers To Cross)	Capitol 72997	1986

How Many (Rivers To Cross) (12")	Capitol S-75157	1986
Innocent (With An Explanation)	Capitol 73003	1986
Strength in Numbers	Capitol 73012	1986
Act of Mercy	Capitol 73018	1987
When a Man Loves a Woman	Capitol 73043	1987/88
Giving Away a Miracle	Capitol C1-93176	1989
No More Words	Capitol C1-93176	1990
Little Salvation	Capitol C1-93176	1990
Is She a Lot Like Me?	Azure CD 712002	2000

Albums/CDs:

Chain Reaction	Parlophone TGO 7003	1980
Luba (EP)	DLP 3003	1982
Secrets and Sins	Capitol ST 12351	1984
Between the Earth and Sky	Capitol ST 12472	1986
Over 60 Minutes With	EMI 48553	1987
All or Nothing	Capitol C1-93176	1989
From the Bitter to the Sweet	Azure CD 712002	2000

Luke and The Apostles

Luke Gibson (lead vocals, guitar)
Peter Jermyn (keyboards)
Jim Jones (bass)
Pat Little (drums)
Mike McKenna (lead & rhythm guitars)

This group from Toronto started out as Mike's Trio in 1964 with Mike McKenna on vocals and guitar, Rick MacMurray on drums, and Graham Dunsmore on bass. They played in Yorkville Village at the Cafe La Patio. Later that same year, Luke Gibson joined them and they became known as Luke and The Apostles. They played at the Cellar Club, which specialized in rhythm & blues. In 1967 they recorded their only single, Been Burnt on Bounty Records, and shortly thereafter, they broke up.

Luke joined Kensington Market, Mike became one of the Ugly Ducklings and later Mc Kenna Mendelson Mainline, Little started with Tranfusion which later became known as Crazy Horse.

The original members of Luke and The Apostles reunited in 1970 and had a minor success with the hit, You Make Me High. By the end of the year they had disbanded again.

Gibson recorded the album, Another Perfect Day (TN6) on True North and acted opposite Genevieve Bujold in the film, Journey in 1972. After Mainline broke up in 1972, McKenna was in the band Diamondback from 1974 to 1976, and has been in a group called Sidewinder since 1995.

Singles:
Been Burnt	Bounty 45105	1967
You Make Me High	True North T4-102	1970

Doug Lycett

Doug Lycett was born in Oshawa, Ontario in 1937. He moved to Toronto in his twenties where he figure skated, danced, and became a recording star. His first single, You Don't Want To Go was released by Quality Records in 1961. After recording for Arc, Columbia and Hawk Records, he settled in Bowmanville where he worked in a testing lab at Goodyear Canada. In the mid-1980s he bought a farm in Orono, Ontario, where he pursued another interest - breeding and racing thoroughbred horses. Up until his untimely death from a heart attack on September 15, 1998, Doug had been raising daylilies on his farm, the only place in Canada where new strains of the plant have been developed. He grew interesting and beautiful formations and colors.

By Doug Lycett
Singles:
You Don't Want To Go	Quality 1245	1961
One of the Lonely	ARC 1024	1963
Build a Scaffold Way Up High	Columbia 2751	1967

By Doug Lycett & The Kingston Monarchs
Single:
What Does a Boy Do	Hawk 004	1964

Ray Lyell and The Storm

James Anthony (drums)
Luc Grenier (bass, background vocals)
Ray Lyell (lead vocals, acoustic guitars)
David Kristan (lead & rhythm guitars)
Vince Renaldo (keyboards)   RPL by George Manz
Paula Tessaro (lead & background vocals) RPL by Tim Tyler

This Hamilton based singer/songwriter released his first single, Take This Heart on H&S Records in 1987. Two years later he and his backup band The Storm released their self-titled debut album in 1989 on Spy Records. His heartland rock 'n' roll sound was evident in his music which had a lot to do one theme: the Wild West. Many of the ideas for his songs came from personal experience. To help prepare him for his second album, Desert Winds, he lived in a tent in the desert 30 miles from Phoenix in 1991. The band recorded the album in the Bearsville studio in New York, Winfield Studios in Hamilton and The Metal Works in Mississauga. Between recording albums he learned about another band who called themselves The Storm. To avoid a legal suit, they dropped the name and became known simply as Ray Lyell.

Singles:
Take This Heart	H&S 7CDN-48	1987
Another Man's Gun	Spy 1002	1989
Cruel Life	Spy 1002	1990
Carry Me	Spy 1002	1990
Gypsy Wind	Spy 1011	1993
Desert Nights	Spy 1011	1993
Don't Let Go	Spy 1011	1993
Bitter Creek	Spy 1011	1993
One For The Old Guard	Spy 1011	1993/94

Albums/CDs:
Ray Lyell and The Storm	Spy 1002	1989
Desert Winds	Spy 1011	1993

Ashley MacIsaac

Born and raised in Creignish, Inverness, Cape Breton, Nova Scotia, Ashley MacIsaac experimented with old traditional fiddling and different styles of music to come up with Celtic punk. His success made him one of Canada's top contemporary fiddlers.

In his teens, he toured the small Celtic communities in Massachusetts and California. He recorded two independent releases, Close To The Floor and A Cape Breton Christmas in 1991 (reissued on CD in 2001).

Inspired by Zamfir, the master of the pan flute, Ashley's first full-length album of original material, Hi, How Are You Today (1995), named after a common Cape Breton greeting, combined the musical origins of the seventeenth century Scottish highlands with hypnotic urban dance anthems in Sleepy Magee (with smooth Gaelic incantations by Mary Jane Lamond), and molten jig-rock salvos in Rusty D Con-Struck-Tion, to the uptempo fiddle breakdown of The Devil In The Kitchen.

With the Toronto dance act BKS, he recorded The Square Dance Song (I Wanna Go Higher), and he has performed with Paul Simon, Edie Brickell, David Bryne and The Chieftains.

In 1999 he switched from A&M to the independent Loggerhead label. His first CD for the label was *Helter's Celtic*.

Singles:
Devil In The Kitchen	A&M 220012	1995/96
Sleepy Magee (CD/S)	A&M 205002	1996

Albums/CDs:
Close To The Floor	Reel Time RT18	1991
Close To The Floor	A&M 022002	1994
Hi How Are You Today	A&M 220012	1995
Fine Thank You Very Much	A&M 220022	1996
Helter's Celtic	Loggerhead 2192	1999
A Cape Breton Christmas With	Fiddle Music 101	2001
Live At The Rehearsal Hall	Linus ENT 279003	2003
Pride	Linus 270065	2005
Live At The Savoy	Linus 270054	2005

Gisele MacKenzie

Born Marie Marguerite Louise Gisele Lefleche on January 10, 1927, this native of Winnipeg, Manitoba first studied the violin with Flora Matheson Goulden and Kathleen Parlow in her hometown. She mastered the instrument so well that she had a promising career as a concert violinist, but she gave it all up for a career as a pop singer. Her first professional job was in the band of Bob Shuttelworth who later became her husband and manager.

From 1946 to 1950 she had her own radio show on CBC called Meet Gisele. When the show finished, she moved to the United States and adopted her father's second given name of MacKenzie as her professional name. She also sang with Percy Faith on his CBS radio show in New York, and Bob Crosby's CBS-TV show, Club 15.

In 1952 she started recording for Capitol Records. One of four songs she recorded that year was Don't Let The Stars Get In Your Eyes, which was also a hit for Perry Como.

From 1953 on she began a long association with Jack Benny and frequently appeared on his long running TV show until it was cancelled in 1965.

She became an American citizen in 1955. Two years later, she was a regular on NBC's Your Hit Parade (1953-1957), and hosted her own show on the same network (1957-58).

MacKenzie continued to record on various labels and appeared in the musical productions of South Pacific, Annie Get Your Gun and The King And I among others. She died September 5, 2003.

Singles:

Fairyland/Jolie Jacqueline	Capitol 1722	1951
Please/Love Makes The World Go 'Round	Capitol 1878	1952
La Fiacre	Capitol 1907	1952
What'll I Do/I'm So Easy to Satisfy	Capitol 2059	1952
Adios	Capitol 2156	1952
Water Can Quench The Fire Of Love	Capitol 2266	1952
Don't Let The Stars Get In Your Eyes	Capitol 2256	1952
Gone/The New Wears Off Too Fast	Capitol 2307	1953
Lipstick-a-Powder-'n Paint	Capitol 2404	1953
I Didn't Want To Love You/ I'd Rather Die Young	Capitol 2501	1953
Half-Hearted/Till They've All Gone Home	Capitol 2556	1953
Doggone It, Baby, I'm In Love/ Ridin' To Tennessee	Capitol 2743	1954
Hard To Get	X 0137	1955
Pepper Hot Baby	X 0172	1955
The Star You Wished Upon Last Night	VIK 0233	1956
Oh, Pain! Oh, Agony! (Know What I Mean Jelly Bean)	VIK 0274	1957

Albums/CDs:

Orchids From Gisele	Capitol CC 1001	1953
Gisele	Vik LX-1055	1956
Mam'selle Gisele	Vik LX 1075	1956
Gisele	Camden CAL-532	1958
At The Empire Room Of The Waldorf	Sun 5155	1960
Christmas With Gisele	Vik LX 1099	1956
Gisele	Rca LSP-1790	1961
Sings Lullaby and Goodnight	Cricket CR-29	1963
Loser's Lullabies	Mercurymg-20790	1963
Chansons Folklorique Pour Enfants	Nou-Gen NG-1727	1964
Sings Dominique In French And English	Meteor SDLP-168	1964
Sings And Tells Cinderella & Alice In Wonderland	Pickwick SPC-3184	1965

Tara MacLean

Tara MacLean was born on October 25, 1973 in Charlottetown, Prince Edward Island. Her father was a singer and dancer, her stepfather a country gospel singer, and her mother an actress. Tara started singing at an early age, and one of her earliest public appearances was on television with her father when she was eleven. Signed to Nettwerk Records in Vancouver in April 1995, her debut CD, Silence was released in 1997. She also recorded Let Her Feel The Pain for the CD compilation, Slow Brew, the proceeds of which went to rape crisis centers.

Singles:
Evidence (Can You Hear Me Now)	Nettwerk 30106	1997
If I Fall	Nettwerk 30144	1999

Albums/CDs:
Silence	Nettwerk 30106	1997
If You See Me (EP)	Nettwerk 36323	1998
Passenger	Nettwerk 30144	1999

Gene MacLellan

One of the most sought after songwriters in Canada in the late 1960s and early 1970s was Gene MacLellan. Born in Val d'or, Quebec in 1938, he later moved to Toronto with his parents. As a teenager he was a member of Little Caesar and The Consuls. When he was eighteen, he left to work as a bus boy on Rhode Island, and he sang in churches and outdoor rallies across Canada with travelling evangelist Bud Kena.

Gene loved Prince Edward Island and often worked picking apples and digging potatoes to earn a living while living with his aunt. He returned to songwriting when he was invited to appear on The Don Messer Show. It led to a four month tour with American country singer Hal Lone Pine.

Returning to Canada, MacLellan moved to Halifax where he was offered a job on CBC-TV's Singalong Jubilee. He later went on to write such pop standards as Snowbird for Anne Murray and Put Your Hand In The Hand for Ocean.

In 1972 he stopped performing and went to live on Prince Edward Island. Four years later he recorded his third album for Capitol,

If It's Alright With You. He also performed sporadically during the late 1970s and 1980s. Up until his death on January 19, 1995 he had lived the life of a recluse on Prince Edward Island.

Atlantica Music in Nova Scotia released the CD, A Gene Maclellan Tribute by John Gracie in 1995. Two years later, EMI released Lonesome River in 1997, a compilation of songs from MacLellan's three albums for Capitol.

Singles:

The Call	Capitol 72607	1970
Thorn In My Shoe	Capitol 72628	1970
Pages of Time	Capitol 72644	1971
Lonesome River	Capitol 72660	1972

Albums/CDs:

Gene Maclellan	Capitol ST 6348	1970
Street Corner Preacher	Capitol ST 660	1970
If It's Alright With You	Capitol ST 6444	1976
Gene & Marty	Pilgrim PMC 7015	1979
Lonesome River	EMI CD 57587	1997

Natalie MacMaster

Natalie MacMaster was born on June 13, 1972 in Troy, Cape Breton, Nova Scotia. Her uncle, Buddy MacMaster was one of the province's fiddling legends. Both sides of her family share a common bond in either fiddling, singing or dancing. When she was five years old, her mother taught her step-dancing. At nine she was introduced to the fiddle.

In 1989 she recorded her first independent album, *Four on the Floor (1989)*. They were followed by *Road To The Isle* (1991) and *Fit As A Fiddle* (1993).

On stage, Natalie incorporated her modern and traditional dance steps with her fiddle playing, and she has captivated audiences in the United States, Europe, New Zealand, Japan, Denmark, and Canada.

After signing to Warner Music, the label released a compilation of her earlier work in 1996.

Albums/CDs:

Four On The Floor	Independent	1989
Road To The Isle	Independent	1991
Fit As A Fiddle	Rounder/Wea 16260	1993
A Compilation	Mcmaster/Wea 16561	1996
No Boundaries	Wea 15697	1996
My Roots Are Showing	Wea 22715	1998
In My Hands	Wea 28398	1999

Rita MacNeil

Rita MacNeil was a descendant of the Barra MacNeils who came to Canada in the early 1800s and settled in Big Pond, Nova Scotia around 1809. Born on May 28, 1944, she was the fifth of eight children born to Neil and Catherine MacNeil. Rita's music ranges from Celtic-tinged country folk to R&B, gospel, blues and rock.

At seventeen years of age, she left home for Toronto where she hoped to develop her first love, a singing career. At thirty-one, she saw her first album, *Born a Woman* released by Boot Records. But it was a huge success. Other recordings followed, including two independent albums, *Part of the Mystery* and *I Am Not What I Seem*.

Not until 1987 when Virgin Records released her debut album, *Flying on Her Own*, did Rita's career finally take off.

In the twelve years since its release, she has built up a loyal following with her homespun songs that are drawn from her own personal hardship, pride, and humility. Her song, Reason To Believe was written in remembrance to her mother who was always there for her.

She performed at the Royal Albert Hall in London, England in 1991, and the following year was awarded the Order of Canada from then Governor General Ray Hnatyshyn.

On the CBC-TV network, she had her own show, Rita and Friends, which ran from 1994-1997. In 1998 she appeared on her first CTV special entitled Rita MacNeil Celtic Celebration, and her autobiography, On A Personal Note was published by Key Porter Books.

She died on April 16, 2013.

Singles:

Flying On Your Own	Lupins RMS-101	1986/87
Used To You	Virgin RMS-102	1987
Fast Train To Tokyo	Virgin RMS-103	1987
Leave Her To Memory	Lupins RMS-105	1988
Working Man	Lupins RMS-106	1988
Walk On Through	Lupins RMS-107	1988
I'll Accept The Rose	Lupins RMS-111	1989/90
We'll Reach For The Sky Tonight	Virgin 4001	1990
When Love Surrounded You And I	Virgin 4001	1990
Why Do I Think Of You Today	Virgin 4001	1990
You Taught Me Well	Virgin 5001	1990
Watch Love Go Strong	Virgin 5001	1990/91
Call Me And I'll Be There	Virgin 5001	1991
The Hurtin' Kind	Virgin 5001	1991
Bring It On Home To Me	Virgin 6001	1992

Broken Heart Strings	Virgin 6001	1992/93
Moment In Time	Virgin 6001	1993
Shining Strong	Virgin 6001	1993

Albums/CDs:

Born A Woman	Boot BOS 7154	1975
Part Of The Mystery	Big Pond (NO #)	1981
I Am Not What I Seem	UCCBP 1006	1983
Flying On Your Own	Lupins RM-1001	1987
Reason To Believe	Virgin RM-2001	1988
Now The Bells Ring	Virgin RM-3001	1988
Rita	Virgin RM-4001	1989
Home I'll Be	Virgin RM-5001	1990
Thinking Of You	Virgin RM-6001	1992
Once Upon A Christmas	Virgin 35754	1993
Volume One: Songs From The Collection	Virgin 35747	1994
Porch Songs	EMI 35469	1995
Joyful Sounds: A Seasonal Collection	EMI 53394	1996
Joyful Sounds (Box Set)	EMI 54175	1996
Music Of A Thousand Nights	EMI 56328	1997
Live At The Orpheum With The Vancouver Symphony 1999	EMI 98974	2001

Alan MacRae

Alan MacRae was born in Edinburgh, Scotland in 1935. The song of an eminent bagpiper from The Royal Scots Regiment, Alan worked at a variety of jobs before he became a folksinger/songwriter. He left Scotland and came to Canada in the 1950s after serving a tour of duty in the Royal Air Force.

One of his first jobs in Canada was in a gold mine in Timmins, Ontario. He then became interested in a singing career and moved to Vancouver, where he was part owner and performer of the city's first coffeehouse, The Question Mark. Exposure on local television helped him gain more notoriety and he was later invited to write his first musical score for a CBC TV documentary.

In 1961 he played at the first Mariposa Folk Festival in Orillia, Ontario. It was there he met Klaus Van Graft, a folk singer from Holland who emigrated to America in 1955. They sang sea shanties together and eventually teamed up with Beverlie Sammons to form the singing group, The Chanteclairs. In 1962 they recorded the album, *Just For a Lark* on Continental Maple Leaf Records (CML 1000).

During this time Alan became interested in writing his own songs and contemporary music. Some of them included Mr. Troubadour, Down To Mexico, Shake The Dust, It's All Over, What I Feel, and Everything's Going For Me, all of which were included on the Canadian Talent Library album, The Songs Of Alan Macrae, released in January, 1970.

He died on January 4, 1985 at the age of fifty.

Album:
The Songs Of Alan Macrae   CTL S-5123   1970

Bob McBride

Born in Toronto in 1946, Bob McBride was best known as the lead singer of Lighthouse from 1970-73. He had replaced Pinky Dauvin of The Stitch In Tyme who left to pursue a solo career. McBride's melodic and distinctive vocals contributed much to Lighthouse's success as one of Canada's best groups. His voice was heard on such hits as One Fine Morning, You Girl, and Sunny Days among others. He left due to a drug addiction problem and to help make ends meet he sang commercial jingles for beer and jello.

He also recorded for Capitol, London, MCA and Aurora Meadows. His solo hits included Pretty City Lady and Do It Right.

On September 10 and 11, 1982 he returned as Lighthouse's lead singer when the group reunited for four shows at the Ontario Place Forum.

During his last years he was plagued by drug problems. The tragic death of his teenaged step daughter in 1992, from an allergic reaction to peanuts, plunged him further into the abyss he was unable to cope. He died in Toronto on February 20, 1998.

Singles:
Pretty City Lady   Capitol 72681   1972
Butterfly Days   Capitol 72695   1973
Treasure Song   Capitol 72696   1973
Do It Right   Capitol 72718   1974
Mighty Eagle   Capitol 72730   1974
Seasons   MCA 40664   1977
Sail On   MCA 40697   1977
My World Is Empty Wihout You   MCA 30853   1978
Wild Eyes   Aurora Meadows 78-474   1978
Roaring Twenties Queen   Aurora Meadows 78-475   1978

Albums/CDs:

Butterfly Days	Capitol ST 6348	1972
Sea of Dreams	Capitol ST 6397	1974
Bob Mc Bride	LondonCM 501	1978
Here to Sing	MCA 2318	1978

Bob McCord and The Vibrations

Tom Bennett (drums)
Pat Brynes (organ)
Roger Cooke (lead guitar, vocals)
Al Duff (rhythm guitar)
Bob Mc Cord (lead vocals)
Keith Mc Donnell (bass)

Bob McCord and The Vibrations were one of Kingston, Ontario's top bands. Formed in late 1961 and early 1962, they performed mostly in high schools in the Kingston-Brockville area, and Alexandria Bay, New York. Pat Byrnes, Al Duff and Roger Cooke were all from Kingston. Tom Bennett and Keith Mc Donnell lived on Wolfe Island. Both Pat and Al were still in school. The former attended Regiopolis College, while the latter QECVI. Bill Tyler was one of the band's early members, but he didn't stay.

Each of the members were self-taught. One of the highlights of their musical career was sharing the same stage on one of their Wednesday night shows with Roy Orbison.

They played show tunes and covers of the Top 40 hits of the day. The latter included such instrumentals as Walk Don't Run by The Ventures, Sleepwalk by Santo and Johnny, and Green Onions by Booker T. & M.G.'s.

Lead vocals were shared by McCord and Cooke. The latter sang lead on some songs because he had a higher vocal range. Cooke sang on the Del Shannon hits (Runaway & Hats Off To Larry).

In 1964 John Bermingham, who was then program director of CKLC Radio in Kingston, wrote two original songs that the band recorded in Toronto on the Star label, a subsidiary of Arc Records. It was the first disc pressed by the new record company.

The "A" side was I Missed My Year, while Grain of Sand was the "B" side. During the summer of 1964, it was a Top 5 hit in Kingston and some cities out west.

Mc Cord left the band in 1965 to pursue other interests. The Vibrations continued to play the bar circuit and broke up later that same year.

Single:

I Missed My Year/Grain of Sand	StarST 14	1964

John McDermott

John McDermott was born in Priesthill, Scotland on March 25, 1955. He grew up in a household where music was part of his upbringing. When he was nine years old, he moved to Canada where the McDermott family settled in Toronto. Because of his interest in singing, John spent two years at St. Michael's Choir School.

After he graduated from high school he worked as a shipper and salesman at Specialty Chemical. In 1980 he began working in the circulation department of The Toronto Sun. During this time he occasionally played at weddings, family gatherings, and friends' parties. He never considered a career in music until newspaper magnate Conrad Black asked him to sing at a dinner that John was hosting. Black and several Toronto businessmen were impressed enough to finance his first album and jumpstart his music career.

McDermott's debut album, *Danny Boy* was originally a collection of songs to honor his parents' 50th wedding anniversary. It was released by EMI/Angel in late 1992.

His subsequent recordings continued to impress audiences and fans alike, with his appreciation of both the music and songs of his Scottish ancestry.

Albums/CDs:

Title	Catalog	Year
Danny Boy	EMI 54772	1992
Old Friends	EMI 27467	1994
Christmas Memories	EMI 27468	1994
Love is a Voyage	EMI 34632	1995
When I Grow Too Old to Dream	EMI 54637	1997
Buy Victory Bonds	EMI 84684	1998
If Ye Break Faith	EMI 94632	1998
Daughter of Mine (EP)	EMI 86602	1999
A Day to Myself	EMI 29332	2001
Great Is My Faithfulness	EMI 58235	2003
Timeless Memories	Angel 031607	2006
Journeys	Universal 060031	2010
Holly & The Ivy	Reflections 55579	2013
Raised on Songs and Stories		2015

Kate and Anna McGarrigle

Born of French-Canadian and Irish parents in St.-Saveurs-des-Monts, Quebec, Kate, born on February 6, 1946, and Anna McGarrigle, born on December 4, 1944, started singing together in 1959. Fluent in both English and French, they studied music at a local convent where they learned the piano, banjo, guitar and button accordion. While in their teens they played in public, but did not take music seriously until the McGarrigle family moved to Montreal in the early 1960s.

In 1963 Kate and Anna began playing in Montreal's coffeehouses and colleges as the female half of the Mountain City Four, a folk group that also included Jack Nissenson and Peter Weldon, both of whom recorded for the Folkways label.

During this time both Kate began studying engineering at McGill, while Anna took an art course at the Ecole des Beaux Arts.

Kate moved to New York in 1970 where she immersed herself in music.

Anna occasionally joined her on stage. Both of them began to write songs, some of which helped gain them international recognition as songwriters. One of their best known songs was Heart Like A Wheel which was recorded in 1972 by McKendree Spring and, in 1975, by Linda Ronstadt.

As a result of their growing fame, Warner Brothers signed the duo in 1975. Their self-titled debut album was released in 1976. It was followed by *Dancer With Bruised Knees* (1977) and *Pronto Monto* (1978).

The sisters made their debut at Victoria Palace in London, England on July 25, 1976, and that same year also appeared at the 1976 Charley Wakes Folk Festival in Lancashire.

The McGarrigles's repertoire included songs inspired by the various styles of popular music and French-Canadian folk music. They have performed in Ireland, England, Belgium, Holland, United States and Canada.

Their subsequent releases in the 1990s continued to show their marked determination to keep alive the folk traditions of English and French Canada.

Kate's son Rufus Wainwright carried on the family tradition with the self-titled CD, Rufus Wainwright (Dreamworks DRMSD 50030) in 1998 and *Poses* (Dreamworks DRMSD 450237) in 2001. On their 1998 album, *The Mcgarrigle Hour*, Rufus sang background vocals, along with Anna's two children, Sylvian and Lily. Kate McGarrigle died on January 18, 2010.

Singles:

Complainte Pour Ste.-Catherine	WB 8193	1975
Pronto Monto	WB FWB.0051	1978
Mais quand tu danses	KD-9085	1980

Move Over Moon	POL 2065.479	1982
Sun, Son (Shining on the Water)	POL 2065.478	1982
Love Over and Over	POL 2065.469	1982
A Place In Your Heart	POL PDS-2280	1985

Albums/CDs:

Kate & Anna Mcgarrigle	Warner BS 2862	1976
Dancer with Bruised Knees	Warner BS 3014	1977
Pronto Monto	Warner BSK 3248	1978
French Record	Hannibal HNBL 1302	1980
Love Over and Over	Polydor 2424-240	1982
Heartbeats Accelerating	BMG 2070-P	1990
Matapedia	Hannibal HNCD 1394	1996
The Mcgarrigle Hour	Hannibal HNCD 1417	1998

McKenna Mendelson Mainline

Michael Mc Kenna (vocals, guitar)
Joe Mendelson (vocals, guitar, bass, harmonica)
Tony Nolasco (vocals, drums)
Franklin "Zeke" Sheppard (vocals, bass, mandolin, harmonica)

McKenna Mendelson Mainline started in Toronto in 1968. They recorded a self-titled album on Paragon that same year. This was followed by *Stink* in 1969. The original bass player for the group was Danny Gerrard, formerly with The Paupers. In 1971 the name of the group was shortened to Mainline, and the band broke up in 1972.

Franklin "Zeke" Sheppard, born in Kentville, Nova Scotia on May 23, 1941, played with The Dutch Mason Band in 1956, and later The Dovermen before joining Mainline. When they broke up he formed his the group, Blackstone Rangers with Jon Finlay. Sheppard then performed as a harmonica player on The Tommy Hunter Show (CBC) and The Ronnie Prophet Show (CTV), and played on albums by prominent country acts. Sheppard moved to Nashville in 1975 and prior to his death from cancer on October 10, 1997, he was entertainment director of The Cheyenne Saloon in Orlando, Florida.

Joe Mendelson went on to record several albums as Mendelson Joe, while Tony Nolasco and Mike McKenna went on to form the group Diamondback. They recorded two Singles:, Just My Way (Of Loving You) - Atlantic 40002 and Wait My Time - Atlantic 40004 (both released in 1974). Today, McKenna is in the Toronto-based group Sidewinder.

By Mc Kenna Mendelson Mainline
Singles:
Better Watch Out	Liberty 56120	1969
One Way Ticket		1970

Albums/CDs:
Stink	Liberty LBS 83251	1969
Stink (U.S.)	United ArtistsUAS 6729	1969
Blues (CD/R)	Pacemaker 012	1996

By Mainline
Singles:
Get Down To	GRT 1230-22	1972
Games Of Love	GRT 1230-32	1972

Albums/CDs:
Canada, Our Home and Native Land	GRT 9230-1011	1971
Live at the Victory Theatre	GRT 9230-1015	1972

Loreena McKennitt

Born in Morden, Manitoba on February 17, 1957, Loreena McKennitt first wanted to be a veterinarian. She loved music, too, and studied piano with Olga Friesen and voice with Elma Gislason.

In her teens, Loreena switched from classical to folk music, where she played in a folk club in Winnipeg, down the street from the girls' school she attended.

By the late 1970s when she had started university, she had been introduced to Celtic music. After hearing Alan Stivell's recording of The Celtic Harp Renaissance, she fell in the love with the instrument. In 1984 she bought a second-hand harp that she still uses to this day. She also uses such Celtic-style folk instruments as the fiddle, tin whistle, the Russian balalaika, the Indian sitar and tamboura, as well as the more modern synthesizers and electric guitars.

In 1981 she moved to Stratford, Ontario where she worked as a composer, actor and singer in the Shakespearan Festival. Using Diane Rapaport's book, How To Make Your Own Recordings, she recorded Elemental (1985), her first of three independent recordings.

McKennitt also has written film scores for Bayo (1985), the TV movie Heaven On Earth (1986), and several National Film Board Productions: The Burning Times, Goddess Revisited, To A Safer Place, and Full Circle.

The Visit in 1991 marked her debut with Warner Music Canada.

By the release of her EP, A Winter Garden (Five Songs For The Season), she had sold more than two million records worldwide.

Her last release with the label was The Book Of Secrets in 1997, featuring The Mummers' Dance, which was released as a limited edition CD single in February 1998 to meet consumer demand.

Singles:

Greensleeves	Quinlan Road 75151	1991
All Souls Night	Quinlan Road 75151	1991
The Old Ways	Quinlan Road 75151	1992
The Bonny Swans	Quinlan Road PRO 6794	1994
God Rest Ye Merry Gentleman	Quinlan Road CDN 65	1995
The Mummer's Dance	Quinlan Road 22507	1998
Marco Polo	Quinlan Road 21082	1999

Albums/CDs:

Elemental	Quinlan Road 101	1985
To Drive the Cold Winter Away	Quinlan Road 102	1987
Parallel Dreams	Quinlan Road 103	1989
The Visit	Quinlan Road 75151	1991
The Mask and Mirror	Quinlan Road 95296	1994
A Winter Garden (Ep)	Quinlan Road 12290	1995
The Book of Secrets	Quinlan Road 19404	1997
Live In Paris and Toronto	Quinlan Road 21082	1999

Catherine McKinnon

Catherine McKinnon was born on May 14, 1944 in Saint John, New Brunswick. At age 8 she made her radio debut in Saint John and at 12 her TV debut in London, Ont. After graduating from Mount Saint Vincent College in Halifax in the early 1960s, she was a regular on CBC-TV show, Singalong Jubilee. She also appeared on other CBC shows such as Don Messer's Jubilee, Music Hop, and had her own show called on the network, That McKinnon Girl.

Between 1964 and 1969 she recorded on Arc Records. Her debut album in 1964 was Voice of An Angel. Until It's Time For You To Go, a song written by Buffy Ste. Marie, charted nationally in RPM Weekly in 1966. She continued to record until 1976 when she took a four-year absence.

Another of McKinnon's talents is acting. She has starred in several musical stage productions such as Spring Thaw (1967), Rainbow Stage, The Wizard of Oz and My Fair Lady. Her first straight acting role was in Same Time Next Year in the summer of 1976.

On television McKinnon also became well known in the "Come Back To Ireland" commercial and as the Florida "Sunshine Girl" in the orange juice commercials.

She returned to the studio in 1980 to make her self-titled debut album on Pickwick's Intercan label. The album was comprised of such songs as Baby In The Morning, Singing The Blues, and Mother, a John Lennon song she once sang regularly in her stage show.

In December, 1992 she recorded her second Christmas album, *Images of Chrismtas*, and the following year performed at benefit concerts for the Multiple Sclerosis Society of Canada, of which she was its national spokesperson. One of the concerts was in Kingston, Ontario where she sang two songs with The Vimy Band, which were later released on an independent CD. Her younger sister, Patrician Anne, was also a singer.

Singles:

Until It's Time For You To Go	ARC 1130	1966
Share The Good Times With Me	ARC 1146	1966
Everybody's Got The Right To Love	Capitol 2781	1970
Peaceful Mountain	Capitol 2867	1970
This World of Mine		1976/77
That's When You Know	Intercan 10005	1980
Give Yourself Up	Intercan 10010	1980
Sail On		1984
We Are All Canadians		1992

Albums/CDs:

Voice of An Angel	ARC 628	1964
Voice of Angel Ii	ARC 666	1965
Catherine Mckinnon Christmas Album	ARC Ac17	1966
Both Sides Now	ARC 777	1968
Everybody's Talkin'	ARC 814	1969
Catherine Mckinnon	Intercan IC-1002	1980
Images of Christmas	Attic 1370	1992
Voice of An Angel (CD-R)	EMI 21703	1997

Patrician Anne McKinnon

Patrician Anne McKinnon was born on March 17, 1948 at Camp Shilo, Manitoba. At age six, the family moved to London, Ontario where she won several talent contests without any musical training.

When the McKinnons moved to Halifax, their youngest daughter enrolled at Mount St. Vincent Academy where she won honors for herself and her school. At fourteen she made her first TV appearance on High Society, and at eighteen she recorded her first single for Arc Records, Blue Lipstick. She also appeared on several TV shows, such as Singalong Jubilee, Music Hop, Show of the Week, The Ian Tyson Show, A Go-Go 66 and After Four. She died on October 10, 2001 of lymphatic cancer.

Singles:

Blue Lipstick	ARC 1113	1966
Doesn't Anybody Here Know It's Christmas	Harrae HR-175	1976
Suddenly	Tembo 8407	1984

Album:

Suddenly	Tembo TMT 4326	1984

Sarah McLachlan

Sarah McLachlan was born in Halifax, Nova Scotia on January 28, 1968. She studied classical guitar, piano and voice at the Maritime Conservatory of Music in her hometown. At seventeen, she performed in a band called October Game.

In September 1987 she moved to Vancouver and began work on her debut album, *Touch*, on Nettwerk Records, which was released two years later and featured guest musicians Kevin Kane of The Grapes of Wrath, and David Kershaw of Water Walk.

Her sophomore album, *Solace*, came out in 1991, which was a success both critically and commercially. *Fumbling Towards Ecstasy* in 1993 was a more personal album and was produced by Pierre Marchand in Montreal. *Possession*, her next album, included the song Hold On, inspired by the documentary, A Promise Kept, about a woman whose fiance discovers he has Aids.

McLachlan's success continued with a compilation album called, *Rarities, B Sides and Other Stuff*, which included three movie songs: I Will Remember You from The Brothers McMullen; a cover version of Lightfoot's Song For A Winter Night from Miracle on 34th Street (1994), and Full of Grace from Moll Flanders.

With the release of Surfacing, McLachlan became an international star. It entered Billboard's Top 200 Album Chart at number two on August 2, 1997. Her next album, *Mirror Ball* entered the same chart at number three on July 3, 1999.

She is also responsible for the all-woman show, Lilith Fair, one of the most popular road shows in North America which helped raise money for women's groups.

Singles:

Vox	Nettwerk 387	1989
Touch	Nettwerk NTL 30024	1989
Steaming	Nettwerk NTL 30024	1990
The Path of Thorns	Nettwerk W2-30055	1991
Into The Fire	Nettwerk W2-30055	1991
Drawn To the Rhythm	Nettwerk W2-30055	1992
Possession (CD/S)	Nettwerk 06319	1993
Hold On	Nettwerk W2-30081	1994
Fumbling Towards Ecstasy	Nettwerk W2-30081	1994
Good Enough (CD/S)	Nettwerk 33081	1994
I Will Remember You	Nettwerk 230105	1995
Dear God	Nettwerk 230105	1995
Full of Grace	Nettwerk 230105	1996
Building A Mystery	Nettwerk 30116	1997
Sweet Surrender	Nettwerk 30116	1997
Angel	Nettwerk 30116	1998
Angel (CD/S)	Warner Sunset13621	1998
I Will You Remember You (Live)	Nettwerk 30140	1999
Possession	Nettwerk 30140	1999
Ice Cream	Nettwerk 30140	1999

Albujms/CDs

Touch	Nettwerk NTL 30024	1989
Solace	Nettwerk 30055	1991
Live (Ep)	Nettwerk W-6313	1992
Fumbling Towards Ecstasy	Nettwerk 30081	1993
The Freedom Sessions	Nettwerk 36321	1994
Rarities, B-Sides and Other Stuff	Nettwerk 30105	1996
Surfacing	Nettwerk 30116	1997
Mirror Ball	Nettwerk 30140	1999
Remixed	Nettwerk 30200	2001
Afterglow	Nettwerk20332	2003
Afterglow Live	Nettwerk30404	2004
Bloom the Remix Album	Nettwerk30402	2005
Mirrorball-Complete Concert	Arista 87284	2006
Wintersong	Nettwerk30621	2006
Laws Of Illusion	Arista 55367-2re1	2010

Murray McLauchlan

Born in Paisley, Scotland on June 30, 1948, Murray McLauchlan came to Canada in 1953 where his family settled in Toronto. At the age of 12 he began playing the guitar. In school he had shown an aptitude for art and won a $250 scholarship from Hallmark Cards. When he graduated from art school, he decided to pursue another interest which was music. His earliest musical influences were Tony Joe White, Woody Guthrie, Bob Dylan, and Ramblin' Jack Elliott.

It was not long before he started performing at the Village Corner Club in Yorkville. In the mid-1960s he left Toronto for New York's Greenwich Village.

In 1968 Murray returned to Toronto where he made his first appearance at a nightclub called the Riverboat, and he was beginning to be noticed as a songwriter. Two of his songs, Child's Song and Old Man were recorded by American folksinger Tom Rush.

Finkelstein, who managed such Canadian groups as The Paupers and Kensington Market in the 1960s, became Murray's manager in 1970. In 1971 Murray's debut album, *Songs From the Street* was released on Finklestein's label, True North Records.

Throughout the 1970s, McLauchlan had such hits as The Farmer's Song, Little Dreamer, The Shoeshine Working Song, Down By The Henry Moore, On The Boulevard and Whispering Rain.

The 1980s saw Murray become a CBC radio host with the series, Swingin' On A Star.

The Canadian Rehabilitation Council for the Disabled chose If The Wind Could Blow My Troubles Away as its theme song for the 1981 International Year of Disabled Persons. That same year, Murray wrote Alligator Shoes, the theme for the film of the same name which was written, co-produced and directed by Clay Borris.

Murray's other humanitarian efforts were Christmas Seals Chairman for the Canadian Lung Association in 1984, and a participant in several benefits for the Barrie tornado victims and to the Northern Lights for African Relief Aid record, Tears Are Not Enough (1985).

In 1988, he switched from True North to Capitol Records. His first release was *Swingin' On a Star*.

Three years later came his second album, *The Modern Age*. The first single was the title track. The accompanying video featured native dancers from the Six Nations Reserve in Brantford, Ontario who were recruited with the assistance of prominent Mohawk photographer Greg Staatz. In 1998 Viking Press published his autobiography, Getting Out Of Here Alive.

Singles:

Jesus Please Don't Save Me	True North TN4-110	1972
Farmer's Song	True North TN4-113	1973
Hurricane of Change	True North TN4-116	1973
Linda Won't You Take Me In	True North TN4-118	1974
Shoeshine Working Song	True North TN4-119	1974

Do You Dream of Being Somebody	True North TN4-124	1975
Maybe Tonight	True North TN4-124	1975
Down By the Henry Moore	True North TN4-125	1975
Little Dreamer	True North TN4-126	1975
On the Boulevard	True North TN4-129	1976
Love Comes and Grows	True North TN4-137	1977
Straight Outta Midnight	True North TN4-139	1978
Whispering Rain	True North TN4-144	1979
You Can't Win	True North TN4-146	1979
Try Walkin' Away	True North TN4-150	1980
Don't Put Your Faith in Men	True North TN4-150	1980
Into a Mystery	True North TN4-151	1980
If the Wind Could Blow		
My Troubles Away	True North TN4-161	1981
Never Did Like That Train	True North TN4-194	1983
Red River Flood	True North TN4-186	1984
Everything Reminds Me of Loving You	True North TN4-188	1984
Railroad Man	True North TN4-191	1984
Song For Captain Keast	True North TN4-195	1985
I'm Best at Lovin' You	True North TN4-204	1985
Me & Joey/Golden Fields	True North TN4-207	1986
My Imaginary Tree	Capitol B-73070	1988
Love With a Capital L	Capitol B-73080	1989
Please Don't Call It Running Away	Capitol B-73090	1989
The Modern Age	Capitol 95523	1991
Back With You	Capitol 95523	1991
So I Lost Your Love	Capitol 95523	1991

Albums/CDs:

Songs From the Street	True North TN-4	1971
Murray Mclauchlan	True North TN-9	1972
Day to Day Dust	True North TN-14	1973
Sweeping the Spotlight Away	True North TN-18	1974
Only the Silence Remains	True North TN-19	1975
Boulevard	True North TN-25	1976
Hard Rock Town	True North TN-29	1977
Greatest Hits	True North TN-35	1978
Whispering Rain	True North TN-36	1979
Into a Mystery	True North TN-41	1980
Storm Warning	True North TN-44	1981
Windows	True North TN-49	1982
Timberline	True North TN-54	1983
Heroes	True North TN-59	1984
Midnight Break	True North TN-68	1985
Swingin' on a Star	Capitol B-73070	1988
The Modern Age	Capitol 95523	1991
Gulliver's Taxi	True North TND131	1996
Hard Rock Town	True North TND 549	2015
Windows	True North RND 552	2015
Timberline	True North TND 555	2015

Ellis Mclintock

Born in Toronto on November 18, 1921, Ellis McLintock came from his musical family. His father played the euphonium, while his mother, the piano. They decided Ellis should have piano lessons, but they were cut short when he broke his leg playing hockey. His father decided he should try to play the coronet. By watching his parents he was able to learn the scales and it was not long before Ellis mastered the instrument.

In 1936 he was invited to audition for the Canadian contingent of the British Empire Boys Band. At 17, Sir Ernest MacMillan offered him a job as principal trumpeter with The Toronto Symphony, which included supervising the brass department at the Royal Conservatory. Ernest Williams, who was on the staff at Julliard, helped Ellis get a job playing with Leopold Stokowksi.

During the Second World War, Ellis played in the Royal Canadian Air Force Central Band in Ottawa. However, the starchy food and woollen uniforms of the army gave him psoriasis, so he was given a medical discharge.

On June 2, 1944 Ellis opened at Casa Loma where he became an instant hit.

After the war when Big Band music began to wane, he found a new career in television, and he was playing on seventeen shows a week at the CBC. They included Cliff McKay's Musical Kitchen, CBC Symphony, CBC Wednesday Night, and The Wayne and Shuster Show.

His appearances continued throughout the 1950s and 1960s. He also became a favorite at the Old Mill in Toronto where couples would dance the night away to McLintock's dance band.

During the 1970s he taught music at Thornlea Secondary School and Orillia High School until he retired in 1986.

He died on September 25, 1997.

Albums/CDs:

At The Old Mill	RCA LCP 1052	1963
Ellis Mclintock & Trumpets-A-Plenty	CTL S 5054	1964
His Trumpet And Orchestra	CTL S 5070	1965
At Expo 67	RCA PCS 1179	1967

Ben McPeek

Ben McPeek was born Benjamin Dewey in Trail, British Columbia on August 28, 1934. Although he received his musical training out west, his music career did not begin until he moved to Toronto in 1953. As a teenager he started playing the piano in various dance bands and eventually sang with The Five Playboys on CBC radio.

In 1960 he became involved in musical theatre where he became director of Up Tempo '60. He later wrote the music for other stage productions in Toronto, such as That Hamilton Woman, Suddenly Last Summer and Actually This Autumn. By 1963 Ben had written the opera bouffe, The Bargain.

The following year he started Ben McPeek Ltd, a company that produced jingles. In 1966 he co-founded Nimbus Nine Productions that fostered Canadian talent. Among the artists signed were Bonnie Dobson, Tyme and a Half (later Noah), Alastair & Linda, Copper Penny, Fast Eddy, Tobi Lark, Bill Marion, and Robbie MacDougall.

Ben started recording in 1966, and his first album, *Ben Mcpeek: His Voices and Orchestra* was released by the Canadian Talent Library. He also recorded for other labels, including RCA and Attic.

In 1972 he wrote the score for the film, The Rowdyman, starring Gordon Pinsent. Among the others he scored was the documentary Catch The Sun in 1973. With Harry Freedman he formed The Canadian Film Company Guild in 1979.

During the 1970s his recordings included more of his own music, and he continued to write for theatre and film. He also wrote piano sonatas, rags, orchestral works and pop novelty songs under the name of the Pucker and Valve Society Band. In 1977, Monica Gaylord recorded the album, Plays Mcpeek (Boot BMC 3007).

On January 14, 1981 he died in Toronto.

Singles:

Thinking of You	Attic AT 126	1976
Baked Apple Rag	Attic AT 155	1976
Little White Lies	RCA PB-50437	1977

Albums/CDs:

Ben Mcpeek, His Voices and Orchestra	CTL S-5060	1966
Mcpeek Pyrotechnics	CTL M 1080	1966
Ben Mcpeek's Latest Fling At The Record Scene		
Peace Train	RCA CASX-2553	1972
Play Me	RCA KXL-1-0032	1973
Thinking of You	Attic LAT 1008	1976
The Pucker and Valve Society Band	Attic LAT 1030	1977
Music To Do Anything By	CTL S-5214	1977

Maestro

Born Wesley Williams on March 31, 1968 to Guyanese immigrants in Toronto, he grew up in the suburb of North York. At age seven he began writing poetry and at eleven he was writing his own music. Under the tutelage of New York hip-hop pioneers, Grandmaster Flash and The Furious Five, Sponnie G., Jimmy Spicer and Kurtis Blow, the then eleven-year-old Wesley began writing and performing rap.

In 1983 under the stage name of Melody MC, he took part in a rap fest on college station CKLN. He later joined a fellow rapper, Ebony MC, whose real name is Marion Bruce, to form The Vision Crew which lasted until 1987.

By mid-1988 Williams decided to go solo and chose the moniker, Maestro Fresh Wes. He recorded his first demo, You Can't Stop Us Now, and another, I'm Showin' You with DJ LTD (aka Alvin Swaby).

However, no record company was interested in producing.

A visit to New York with the song, Let Your Backbone Slide in 1989 resulted in a contract with LMR Records. Al Mair of Attic Records agreed to distribute the U.S. label in Canada.

Maestro Fresh Wes became the first successful rap artist in Canada with such hits as Drop The Needle and Private Symphony. After the release of his album, *Black Tie Affair* he went to the United States but he was not very well received. The release of Naah! This Kid Can't Be From Canada! in 1994 was not a huge success.

He returned to Canada and decided to go under the name of Maestro.

Attic Records released his fourth CD, *Built To Last* on October 20, 1998.

Singles:

Drop the Needle	Attic ACD 1272	1990
Private Symphony	Attic ACD 1272	1990
Let Your Backbone Slide	Attic ACD 1272	1990
Don't Play SHARE-AIDS (w/D-SHAN)		1990
Louie Louie (12")	Cypress CTI-1200	1990
Conductin' Thangs	Attic ACD 1312	1991
Nothing at All	Attic ACD 1312	1991
It's On the Mike Mechanism		1993
Fine Tune Da Mic		1993
Search Without the Retsin	Attic ACD 1397	1994
Stick to Your Vision	Attic ACD 1518	1998/99
416/905	Attic ACD 1518	1999

Albums/CDs:

Symphony In Effect	Attic ACD 1272	1990
Black Tie Affair	Attic ACD 1312	1991
Naah! Dis Kid Can't Be From Canada	Attic ACD 1397	1994
Built to Last	Attic ACD 1518	1998

The Magic Cycle

Kevin Barry (drums, vocals)
Paul Craig (rhythm guitar, vocals)
Peter Goodale (organ)
Joey Rome (bass, vocals)
Stan Theriault (lead guitar, vocals)
Pete Young (guitar)

Formed in Toronto in 1966, The Magic Cycle recorded their first hit, Let's Run Away on Red Leaf Records in early 1967. The original lineup was comprised of Paul Clinch, aka Paul Craig, Stan Theriault, Pete Young, Joey Rome, and Kevin Barry. In the spring of 1970 they became a sextet with the addition of Peter Goodale.

The principle songwriters of the group were Joey Rome and Paul Craig. The Magic Cycle later became known as The Cycle in 1970 when they recorded on Tamarac Records. The release of their 1973 single, Magic Music marked the 10th anniversary of the label. In 1976 The Cycle had changed personnel and became known as Choya. Paul Clinch died on November 8, 1988.

Singles:
Let's Run Away	Red Leaf 633	1967
Give Me the Right	Red Leaf 637	1967
Doctor Lollipop	Giant 904	1968
Groovy Things	Fingerprint 101	1970
Wait for the Miracle (TheCycle)	Tamarac TTM 642	1971
Gimme Some Time	Tamarac TTM 643	1971
Come Back Again	Tamarac TTM 645	1972
All I Really Need is You (TheCycle)	Tamarac TTM 646	1972
If You Call Out My Name	Tamarac TTM 647	1973
Magic Music	Tamarac TTM 648	1973

Albums/CDs:
Saturday Afternoon Rummage Sale	Tamarac 1003	1970
Magic Music	Tamarac 1004	1973

Mahogany Rush

Jim Ayoub (drums)
Paul Harwood (bass)
Frank Marino (guitar)

This group from Montreal formed in 1970, and was more popular in the United States than they were in Canada. Their popularity suddenly took off after the death of Jimi Hendrix, whom Marino idolized. In the U.S. they headlined shows with The Chambers Brothers, Graham Central Station, Ted Nugent, and The Amboy Dukes.

Their first single Buddy was recorded at the little Coyotte Studio in Quebec City, and their debut album was called Maxoom.

In 1975 Marino added an "e" to his first name because of his interest in numerology.

Three years later, the group went on a mini-tour of Japan.

After appearing at the Quebec Coliseum in 1982, Marino left the group to go solo. He subsequently had two albums released; *Juggernaut on Columbia* in 1980, and *Full Circle* on Maze in 1986.

In 1988 Marino and a group of musicians returned to their old name and released *Double Live* on Maze.

Since the early 1990s, Marino has been playing solo in various nightclubs in and around Montreal.

Singles:

Buddy	Kot'ai 151	1972
Child of the Novelty	Kot'ai 4502	1973
A New Rock and Roll	Kot'ai 4502	1974
Satisfy Your Soul	Kot'ai 4508	1975
Dragonfly	CBS C4-4143	1976
All Along the Watchtower	Columbia 34109	1979
Strange Dreams	Columbia 8508	1982

Albums/CDs:

Maxoom	Kot'ai KOT 3001	1972
Child Of the Novelty	Kot'ai KOT 3302	1974
Strange Universe	Kot'ai KOT 3308	1975
Mahogany Rush IV	Columbia 34190	1976
World Anthem	Columbia 34677	1977
Frank Marino and Mahogany Rush	Columbia 35257	1977
Tales of the Unexpected	CBS 35753	1979
What's Next	CBS 36204	1980
Power of Rock and Roll	CBS 37099	1981
Juggernaut (Frank Marino)	CBS 38023	1982
Full Circle (Frank Marino)	Maze ML-8011	1986
Double Live	Maze MMAL-6004	1988

The Majestics

Bearded John Crone (baritone sax)
Orlando Guierri (trombone)
Jay Jackson (vocals)
Shawne Jackson (vocals)
Dave Kon (lead guitar)
Brian Lucrow (trumpet)
Wes Morris (drums)
Russ Strathdee (tenor sax)
Chris Vickery (bass)

Formed in late 1962, The Majestics were one of the most popular rhythm & blues bands in Toronto. They also were known to play some Big Band tunes, whose sound was described by bookers and fans alike as unbelievable and powerful. They were led by Jay Smith until 1965 when he left to join Ronnie Hawkins.

On stage they had a brass section made up of Brian Lucrow; Bearded John Crone on baritone sax, whose height dwarfed the other musicians; Orlando Guierri on trombone, and Russ Strathdee on tenor sax. There was also a string section comprised of Chris Vickery on bass, and Dave Kon on lead guitar, complemented by Wes Morris' infectious drum beat.

Shawne and Jay Jackson joined the group in 1965. Shawne had been in The Tiarras who performed regularly at the Club Bluenote, while Jay had previously been in The Pharoahs from 1961-64.

The group recorded for Arc Records in the late 1960s, and never had a commercial hit. Billed as Shawne and Jay Jackson and The Majestics, Shawne left in 1969 to pursue a solo career. The Majestics broke up in 1971.

Singles:
Respect	ARC 1178	1967
No Good To Cry	Arc 1179	1967
Hey Joe	Goodgroove 5002	1968

Albums/CDs:
Instrumental R&B	Arc A732	1966
Funky Broadway	Arc A752	1967
Tribute To Otis Redding	Arc A770	1968
Here Come Da Judge	Arc AS780	1968

Major Hoople's Boarding House

Peter Beacock (vocals, keyboards)
Rena Gaile (vocals, flute, piano)
Grant Heywood (vocals, drums)
James Leroy (vocals, keyboards)
Dave Lodge (vocals, bass, sax)
Peter Padalino (vocals, guitar)
Rick Riddell (vocals, drums)
Gail Selkirk (vocals)

The history of this Kitchener, Ontario-based group goes back to 1965 when they were first known as The Swinging Shan-de-Leers. The core of the group consisted of Rick Riddell, Peter Padalino and Rocky Howell. By the time they recorded Can't Mend A Broken Heart in 1967, the name of the group had been shortened to The Shan-De-Leers.

Dave Lodge then joined, followed by Gail Selkirk. Later that same year, they became Major Hoople's Boarding House, with permission from the owners of the comic strip of the same name, because there had been so many personnel changes.

Their first single, on Polydor Records, was Beautiful Morning in 1969. They played throughout Ontario, Eastern Canada and New York State. During the 1970s and 1980s the group went through more personnel changes, Selkirk and Riddell left in 1973 and were replaced by Peter Beacock and Ed Miller. Two years later, Padalino and Lodge left, which left Howell as the only original member.

The band continued to record more Singles:, such as Everything's The Same, Face On The Wind, She's Got All Of My Body, Lady, and I'm Running After You, which was their biggest hit.

In 1976 singer/songwriter James Leroy joined as leader of the group, but it was short-lived. The band then took a short hiatus and regrouped in June 1979 for a week long reunion at a local club in Kitchener. Axe Records released their single, Someone, in time for the group's second reunion in June 1980.

Rena Gaile became the group's latest female singer in 1981. Originally from London, Ontario, she would later be successful as a country singer with such hits as Make Time For Love, Better Off Blue, and The Hand That Rocks The Cradle.

In September 1981, the group performed with Kitchener-Waterloo Symphony, which was hailed as an electrifying show in The Kitchener-Waterloo Record. On November 5, 1986 Dave Lodge died of cancer.

Howell gathered together a new group called Boardinghouse in 1988, which also included Grant Heywood on vocals and drums, Gary Hintz on bass, and Ralph Hetke on keyboards. The group finally broke up in 1990.

Singles:

Beautiful Morning	Polydor 540.014	1969
Lady	Much 1004	1970
Everything's The Same	Poly 2065-155	1972
Face On The Wind	Chelsea BCBO-0147	1973
She's Got All Of My Body	Poly 2065-075	1974
I'm Running After You	Axe 24	1975
Above Record As It Was	Priv STK PS 45,041	1975
You Girl	Axe 32	1976
I've Got You On My Mind	Axe 36	1976
Someone	Axe 59	1980
This Song Reminds Me Of You	Axe 62	1981
What Took So Long	Axe 64	1981
We Can't Give Up	Axe 66	1983
You're Hurting Everyone	Axe 68	1983
Trudy	Axe 70	1983
Never Gonna Let You Go	Major Records MJ-002	1984
Late Night Invitation	Major Records MJ-002	1985
You're Right	Major Records MJ-003	1986

Albums/CDs:

Reunion (EP)	Board/House MHBH001	1979
The Hooples Album	Axe AXM 1002	1981
The New Adventures Of Hooples	Major Records MJA 1001	1986

Malka and Joso

Malka Himel (Maroom)
Joso Spralja

Malka and Joso were one of our more unique duos in that they sang in more than one language and their appeal transcended the coffeehouse circuit. They played in concert halls, college campuses, and made radio and TV appearances.

Malka Himel was born in Kfar-Saba, Israel on January 21, 1936. She was the daughter of a cantor. When she was very young she starred in Israel's famous children's theatre, and performed as a dancer at the renowned Dalia Theatre. As an actress she starred in The Village Tale, one of the first Israeli movies.

Joso Spralja was born in Zadar, Yugoslavia on May 23, 1929.

Encouraged by a parish priest on the Dalmation Coast, he sang in cathedrals and theatres of Dalmatia where he became well known. He also earned a scholarship at the Zagreb Conservatory.

Malka moved to Toronto in 1954, while Joso in 1961. They met at Yorkville 71, a local coffeehouse, and made their debut at the Lord Simcoe Hotel on April 1, 1963. That same year, they sang at the Mariposa Folk Festival.

Signed to Capitol Records in 1964, their first album, *Introducing Malka and Joso* came out in early 1965. Later that same year the label released their second, *Mostly Love Songs*.

On November 26, 1966 they played at Carnegie Hall in New York and the following year in England. During Canada's Centennial Year they participated at a Royal Command Performance at the Canadian Centennial Ball. By the end of 1967, Malka and Joso split up.

Malka went to work at CBC Radio, and received an ACTRA award in 1977 for her four part documentary, A Bite of the Big Apple. She is also the author of the novel, Sulha, which received praise from Leonard Cohen, Joni Mitchell, and Nobel Laureate Elie Wiesel. Joso is famous for his restaurant, Joso's, which ranks among the most popular in Toronto.

Albums/CDs:

Introducing Malka and Joso	Capitol ST 6108	1964
Mostly Love Songs	Capitol ST 6129	1965
Jewish Songs	Capitol ST 6169	1966
Malka Et Joso - Autour Du Monde	Capitol ST 70.007	1968
Forever	EMI 24675	2000

Mandala

Josef Chirowski (organ)
Donny Elliot (bass)
Whitey Glann (drums)
George Olliver (guitar, vocals)
Domenic Troiano (guitar, vocals)

The history of this Toronto group goes back to 1964 when they were the house band at the Club Bluenote and were known as The Five Rogues. After they left in June 1965, they changed their name to the Mandala.

Their first two singles, Opportunity and Give and Take, both on KR Records, were released in 1967. That same year, Olliver and Chirowski left the group, and were replaced by Roy Kenner and Henry

Babraj. Hugh Sullivan later replaced Babraj.

They had two more hits, Love-Itis and You Got Me, on Atlantic Records, before breaking up in the spring of 1969.

Troiano, Glann and Kenner formed Bush with Prakash John later that summer. George Olliver went on to form the groups George Olliver and The Children, and Natural Gas before going on to several solo projects. (see Domenic Troiano, Bush)

Singles:
Opportunity	KR 0119	1967
Give And Take	KR 0121	1967
Love-Itis	Atlantic 2512	1968
You Got Me	Atlantic 2567	1968

Albums/CDs:
Soul Crusade	Atlantic SD8184	1968
Mandala - Classics	Wea 25-23291	1986

Maneige

Alain Bergeron (flute, saxophone)
Jerome Langlois (piano, clarinet, keyboards)
Vincent Langlois (keyboards, percussion)
Denis Lapierre (guitar)
Yves Leonard (bass)
Paul Picard (percussion)
Gilles Schetagne (drums, percussion) Replaced by Pierre Gauthier (1981)

This jazz/rock fusion band from Montreal, Quebec formed in 1972. Denis Lapierre, Yves Leonard, Alain Bergeron, Vincent and Jerome Langlois were first members of the rock band Lasting Weep, who changed their name to Maneige in 1973.

Although they were from Quebec, they sang in both English and French. After building up a local following in their native province, Maneige decided to break into the English market where they were well received in Western Canada and Northern Ontario.

Their self-titled debut album on Harvest/Capitol Records was released in 1974. It was followed by Les Porches De Notre Dame a year later.

In 1976 Vincent Langlois left the group. The group continued to perform in Quebec and English Canada. By 1982 they had stopped performing. Bergeron, Schetagne, Leonard with guitarist Michel Lefrancois later revived the group and in 1983 they made their last album, *Images*. In 1984 Paul Picard rejoined the group.

They wrote the music for the films, Quebec On The Sunny Side and Quebec Plus.

Singles:

Troixix	Polydor DJ-20	1978
Quebec Saint-Malo (12")	Saisons SNS-500/SNS-6541	1984

Albums/CDs:

Maneige	Harvest ST-70035	1974
Les Porches De Notre-Dame	Harvest ST-6438	1975
Ni Vent...Ni Nouvelle	POL 2424.143	1977
Libre Service	POL 2424.176	1978
Composite	POL 2424.206	1980
Montreal, 6a.M.	INT-33007	1980
Images	Saisons SNS-80008	1983

Amanda Marshall

From Toronto, Ontario, Amanda Marshall has been involved in music since she was three years old, when her parents enrolled her in a toddler's music program at The Royal Conservatory of Music.

While growing up she was exposed to her father's standard pop fare to her mother's Caribbean music that she brought with her from her native Trinidad.

In her teens, Amanda sang at various clubs and was hailed by music critics as the next Janis Joplin because of her strong emotive voice. She played on stage with Jeff Healey who became a close friend, and opened for Healey and Tom Cochrane.

In the fall of 1991 when she was nineteen she signed a recording contract with Sony, but dropped out because she wanted to rethink her career. She later contributed her version of Don't Let It Bring You Down, on the Neil Young tribute album, Borrowed Tunes.   She signed with Columbia in 1993 and two years later her long awaited debut album was released. It featured a mix of musical styles from pop to blues, and featured the pop hit, Dark Horse, which was covered by American country artist Mila Mason in 1997.

In 1999 Marshall's sophomore effort, Tuesday's Child featured the lead off single and video, Love Lift Me. Her third CD, Everybody's Got A Story came out in 2001.

Singles:

Don't Let It Bring You Down	CBS Z2K80199	1994
Let It Rain	Epic EK 80229	1995
Birmingham	Epic EK 80229	1996
Fall from Grace	Epic EK 80229	1996

Sitting On Top of the World	Epic EK 80229	1996
Beautiful Goodbye	Epic EK 80229	1996
Dark Horse	Epic EK 80229	1996/97
Trust Me (This Is Love)	Epic EK 80229	1997/98
Believe In You	Epic 68971	1999
Love Lift Me	Epic EK 80380	1999
If I Didn't Have You	Epic EK 80380	1999
Shades of Grey	Epic EK 80380	2000
Why Don't You Love Me	Epic EK 80380	2000
Everybody's Got A Story	Epic EK 80702	2001

Albums/CDs:

Amanda Marshall	Epic EK 80229	1995
Tuesday's Child	Epic EK 80380	1999
Everybody's Got a Story	Epic EK 80702	2001

The Marshmallow Soup Group

Tim Cottini (drums)
Timothy Eaton (vocals) (real name: Timothy Harrower)
John Lemmon (keyboards)
Ron Smith (bass)
Wayne Sweet (guitar)

This group, originally from Kingston, Ontario, started out in 1968 as The Ethic Souls. When they moved to Ottawa, they changed their name to The Marshmallow Soup Group. In late 1969 RCA released their debut single, I Love Candy. It was followed by Sing To My Lover in 1970. A year later, the group broke up.

Until 1974, Ron Smith, David John Lemmon, Wayne Smith, and Tim Cottini were part of the touring band called Buffalo.

Timothy Eaton, whose real name was Timothy Harrower, recorded with his own group named Timothy. Their hits were Timothy (RCA 75-1088 - 1972), Brotherhood (RCA - 1972), and Rock and Roll Music (RCA 75-1108 - 1972/73). In 1974 Eaton recorded Falling Out of Love (RCA PB-10023) under the name of Buster Brown.

Singles:

I Love Candy	RCA 75-1014	1969/70
Sing To My Lover	RCA 75-1028	1970

Martha and The Muffins

Carl Finkle (bass)
Mark Gane (guitar)
Tim Gane (drums)
Andy Haas (sax)
Martha Johnson (vocals, keyboards)
Martha Ladly (vocals, keyboards, trombone)

The history of Martha and The Muffins goes back to 1975 when all of lived in the same neighbourhood in Thornhill, in the north end of Toronto. By 1975 they all had moved to downtown Toronto. Martha Johnson was in a band called The Doncasters. In 1977 Mark Gane, David Millar and Carl Finkle asked her to play keyboards in their new band, which also included Mark's brother Tim and Martha Ladley. They called themselves Martha and The Muffins.

After they made their first independent single, Insect Love/Suburban Dream in 1979, they were offered an eight album deal with Virgin Records in the United Kingdom.

Their debut single on Virgin was Echo Beach, which was initially released in the U.K. and later became a top ten hit in Canada.

In 1981 Joceyln Lanois replaced Ladley, and their album, *This is the Ice Age*, co-produced by Daniel Lanois, was released on Virgin. Lanois also co-produced Danseparc.

By 1984 the group had become a duo comprised of Mark and Martha, and their name was shortened to M+M. They also began work on their next album, *The World is a Ball*, with co-producer David Lord (XTC, Peter Gabriel, Echo & The Bunnymen) at Le Studio in Quebec, and Lord's Crescent Studios in Bath, England.

Mark and Martha won Best Music Video Production at the Yorkton Short Film and Video Festival in 1987 for their self-produced video of Only You from The World Is A Ball. They also moved to England.

Three years later, they composed, recorded and produced the soundtrack for Michael Gibson's critically acclaimed feature-length, Defy Gravity.

Their next album, *Modern Lullaby*, was released in 1992 on Intrepid Records, and Martha began to work as a children's entertainer. She and Mark performed together in schools and other venues.

In 1995 Martha's album, Songs From The Tree House was released.

It was later adapted for the stage by the duo for Youththeatre, a children's theatre group in Montreal. In 1996-97 it was performed throughout Ontario, Quebec, and Winnipeg, Manitoba.

EMI released the CD, Then Again: A Retrospective in 1998 which included the new song, Resurrection.

Singles:

Insect Love/Suburban Dream		1979
Echo Beach	Virgin VS 1111	1980
Paint by Number Heart	Virgin VS 1115	1980
Was Ezo	Virgin VS 1125	1980
About Insomnia	Dindisc DIN 19	1980/81
Women Around the World at Work	Virgin VS 1131	1981
Swimming	Virgin VS 1136	1981/82
Danseparc	Current Wake 1	1983
Black Stations/White Stations	Current/Wake 7	1984
Mystery Walk (as M+M)		1984
Cooling the Medium (as M+M)	Current/Wake 8	1984
Cooling the Medium (12")	Current Wash 5	1984
Song in My Head (as M+M)	Current/Wake 14	1986
Rainbow Sign	INT N215-0014	1992

Albums/CDs:

Metro Music	Virgin VL 2142	1980
Trance and Dance	Virgin VL 2207	1980
This is the Ice Age	Virgin VL 2228	1981
Danseparc	Current Wave-1	1983
Mystery Walk	Current Wave-3	1984
The World is a Ball	Current Wave-006	1986
Far Away in Time	Virgin 86710	1987
Modern Lullaby	INT N215-0014	1992
Then Again: A Retrospective	EMI 96001	1998

Mashmakhan

Rayburn Blake (guitar)
Brian Edwards (bass, lead vocals)
Pierre Senecal (flute, organ)
Jerry Merce (drums)

Rayburn Blake, Jerry Mercer, Pierre Senecal and Brian Edwards all grew up in the same neighbourhood in Montreal, and were first in a band called The Dominoes, then Trevor Payne and The Soul Brothers.

In 1965 Edwards left and was a member of three other bands before he rejoined his former bandmates four years later.

Between 1965 and 1969, Blake, Mercer and Senecal were members of The Triangle, who recorded the single, Les montagnes russes/Deux mirrors (GammaAA-1042 - 1969). When Edwards returned in the spring of 1969, they changed their name to Mashmakhan, which was an exotic plant that grew in

Jamaica. They made their debut at a club called Laugh-In, where they presented the ultimate in visual and audio communication. They signed with Columbia Records that same year, and, a year later, they had a national hit with As Years Go By from their self-titled debut album. It was also a hit in the United States where it reached #31 on Billboard's Hot 100, and in Japan it made the Top Ten.

Their second album, *The Family*, came out in 1971, and the following year the group broke up. Senecal revived the group in 1973 with Brian Greenway and Steve Lang (ex-April Wine), and Lorne Nehring. As The Years Go By was inducted into Canadian Songwriters Hall of Fame in 2015.

Singles:

As The Years Go By	Col C4-2924	1970
Children of the Sun	Col C4-2960	1971
Start All Over	Col C4-2979	1971
Love Is	Col C4-3011	1972
Light Blue	Col C4-3012	1972
Ride Johnny Ride	Col C4-3055	1972
Dance A Little Step	AQ 5025	1973

Albums/CDs:

Mashmakhan	Col ELS-365	1970
The Family	Col ES 90000	1971

Ray Materick

Born in Brantford, Ontario in 1949, Ray Materick was introduced to rock and roll music by his brothers. As a teenager he was inspired to write songs after listening to Bob Dylan, John Fogerty, Gordon Lightfoot and Van Morrison. In 1972 Materick signed with Kanata Records. His debut album with the label was Side Streets. After a self-titled effort on One Heart Records in 1974, he signed with Asylum. His only song to receive national attention was Linda Put the Coffee On in 1975. He continued to release albums independently until 1980 when he left music to work in a Toronto wooodworking shop. Before the end of the decade he had started to write songs again, and in 2000 started King Kong Records with his partner, Dan Quinlan.

Singles:

A Hard Life Alone	Kanata KAN 1010	1972
Season Of Plenty	Kanata KAN 1010	1972
Linda Put The Coffee On	Asylum ASC 5001	1975
Northbound Plane	Asylum ASC 5002	1975
Feelin' Kinda Lucky Tonight	Asylum ASC 5003	1976

Ride Away	Asylum ASC 5005	1976
Bring On The Light	One Heart-C/N One-3333	1981

Albums/CDs:

Sidestreets	Kanata 10	1972
Ray Materick	One Heart C/N One 1111	1974
Neon Rain	Asylum 7ESC 10001	1975
Best Friend Overnight	Elektra ESC 10002	1975
Midnight Matinee	Asylum 7ESC-10003	1976
Fever in Rio	Casino CA 1012	1979
Rough Serenade	King Kong KKRC 100	2000
Melting Pot	King Kong KKRC 200	2000
Man in the Thunderbird	King Kong KKRC 300	2000
Wild World	King Kong KKRC 500	2000
Ashes and Dust	King Kong KKRC 600	2000
Sunflowers	King Kong KKRC 700	2000
Violent Flood	King Kong KKRC 1200	2000
Here at Home	King Kong KKRC 1400	2000
The Songwriter	King Kong	2001

Shirley Matthews

From Harrow, Ontario, Shirley Matthews started singing in church and school. At 19 she sang part-time as a hobby and performed at high school dances. She also played at the Club Bluenote in Toronto. Her first single was Big Town Boy on Tamarac Records in late 1963 and early 1964. When she performed it live she was backed up the Big Town Boys, who had their own hits on Capitol Records. Today, Shirley works at a fitness club in Toronto.

Singles:

Big Town Boy	Tamarac 602	1963/64
He Makes Me Feel So Pretty	Red Leaf 608	1964
Private Property	Tamarac 603	1964
Stop the Clock	Red Leaf 611	1965

Max Webster

Paul Kersey (drums) Replaced by Gary McCracken (1977)
Kim Mitchell (guitar, vocals)
Mike Tilka (bass)
Terry Watkinson (keyboards) Replaced by Dave Stone (1980)

Formed in Sarnia in 1973 by Mitchell, the group moved to Toronto three years later. They were best known for their unpredictable musical progressions and abstract lyrics written by longtime friend Pye Dubois. The band's self-titled debut album on Taurus Records came out in May, 1976, and in January, 1977 they signed an international record deal with Anthem Records.

In the spring of 1981 the group broke up and Mitchell went on to pursue a successful solo career. (See Kim Mitchell)

Singles:

Blowing The Blues	Taurus TR-006	1976
Words To Words	Anthem ANS-003	1977
Let Go The Line	Anthem ANS-012	1979
A Million Vacations	Anthem ANS-013	1979
Paradise Skies	Anthem ANS-014	1980
Check	Anthem ANS-	1980
Blue River Liquor Store	Anthem ANS-027	1981
Hot Spots	Anthem ANS-037	1981

Albums/CDs:

Max Webster	Taurus TR 101a	1976
High Class Borrowed Shoes	Anthem ANR-1-1007	1977
Mutiny Up My Sleeve	Anthem ANR-1-1012	1978
A Million Vacations	Anthem ANR-1-1018	1979
Live Magnetic Air	Anthem ANR-1-1019	1980
Universal Juveniles	Anthem ANR-1-1027	1980
Diamonds Diamonds	Anthem ANR-1-1033	1981
Best Of Max Webster	Anthem ANR-1-1058	1989

Carol Medina

Carol Medina was born in Melbourne, Australia on October 25, 1966. Of Croation, Portuguese and English descent, she moved to Toronto when she was a year old. While growing up she was influenced by Tina Turner, Heart, Pat Benatar, and Taylor Dayne.

At 12 Carol became a professional singer and actress, and travelled to the Orient on a USO tour. In 1994 she won Best Vocalist at the So Danse Awards in Montreal, which are handed out by a Montreal DJ record pool.

Among the songwriters who have collaborated on her songs are James Collins, Patti Jannetta, Don Breithaupt and producers Brad Daymond and Greg Kavanaugh (Secret Fantasy).

Carol's debut single release was The Tears I Cry on Rich Dodson's Marigold label, which was later covered by Gavin Hope. Her other songs include I'll Just Say Goodbye, a heartwrenching ballad about a close friend's passing, and pop/dance tracks, Tell Me You Love Me, I Had A Dream, and You Don't Know (Where My Lips Have Been).

Most of her songs have been issued on compilations, although some of her early songs appeared on her first full-length CD, *Secret Fantasy*.

Singles:

The Tears I Cry	Marigold CD/EP	1989
So Good For You	Marigold CD/S	1990
Wait 'Til My Heart Finds Out	Marigold CD/S	1991
Sooner or Later Medley (Duet w/Mark Cassius Ferguson)	Marigold CD/S	1993
Love Me Just Enough	Marigold CD/S	1993
And The Song Goes..(Doo Dit)	Quality QCD2032	1993
I Had A Dream	Quality QCD2074	1994
Tell Me You Love Me	Quality QCD2090	1995
You Don't Know (Where My Lips Have Been)	Quality QCD/S7126	1995
Wait 'Til My Heart Finds Out (w/Billy Newton-Davis)	Quality QCD 2058	1995
Secret Fantasy	Quality QCD 2058	1995
Let The Music Play	Quality CD/S	1995
You Never Done It Like That	Quality QCD 2058	1996
I'll Just Say Goodnight	Quality QCD 2139	1996
One Day of Kisses	PopularPR2S 3192	1997
Wonder Woman (Theme Song)	PopularPR2S 3230	1998
Are You Tempting Me?	Popular28220	1998

Album/CDs

Sooner or Later (Promo EP)	Marigold	1993
Secret Fantasy	Quality QCD 2058	1995

Sue Medley

Born in 1962 in Courtenay, B.C., Sue Medley first became interested in music when she was given a drum set at the age of nine. Four years later, she acquired a guitar and soon began writing songs. At 15 she turned professional and became half of a folk/country duo. In June 1987 she recorded the independent single, Cryin' Over You, which was well received in Western Canada. A second independent release, Angel Tonight, came out in 1989.

Signed to Polygram in 1989, her self-titled debut album came out a year later, which was produced by Medley and John Cougar Mellencamp's guitarist Michael Wanchic. Supplying background vocals on that album was John Hiatt's backup group, The Goners.

Throughout 1990 she toured Canada and the United States, where she opened for Bob Dylan on some dates.

Medley's first hit was called *Dangerous Times*, which was inspired by the events in Tienanmen Square.

In 1992 came her second album, *Inside Out*. Her next, Velvet Morning came out on Egg Records in 2000.

Singles:

Dangerous Times	Mercury842982	1990
That's Life	Mercury842982	1990
Love Thing	Mercury842982	1990
Maybe the Next Time	Mercury842982	1991
Queen of the Underground	Mercury842982	1991
When the Stars Fall	Mercury512527	1992
Inside Out	Mercury512527	1992
Jane's House	Mercury512527	1992/93
Forget You	Mercury512527	1993
Gone	Egg 9700	2000

Album/CDs:

Sue Medley	Mercury842982	1990
Inside Out	Mercury512527	1992
Velvet Morning	Egg 9700	2000

Shawn Mendes

Shawn Mendes was born in Pickering, Ontario on August 8, 1998 to an English mother and Portuguese father. In 2012 Shawn's acoustic version of Justin Bieber's As Long As You Love Me was launched on Vine, a video sharing service. Its success made him a teenage sensation. In 2014 he entered Ryan Seacrest's Best Cover Song Contest with Great Big World's Say Something and won. It attracted the attention of Andrew Gertler who became his manager. He also was instrumental in getting Mendes signed to Island Records. A self-titled EP was released in 2014 featuring the song, Life of The Party.

His debut album, *Handwritten* came out in 2015. That same year, Believe was featured on the soundtrack of the TV movie, The Descendants and he opened for Taylor Swift on her North American tour.

Singles:

Life of the Party	EMI USUM 407508	2014
Stitches	EMI USUM 500658	2015
I Know What You Did Last Summer	EMI USUM 516597	2016

Album:

Handwritten	EMI 713555	2015

Men Without Hats

Jeremie Arrobas (bass) RPL by Stefan Doroschuk
Colin Doroschuk (keyboards)
Ivan Doroschuk (vocals, keyboards)
Allan McCarthy (drums)

The core of this group from Montreal were the Doroschuk brothers, who began as a trio comprised of Jeremie Arrobas, Ivan Doroschuk and Allan McCarthy in 1980. Two years later, Arrobas left and was replaced by Stefan Doroschuk. His brother Colin also joined to make the group a quartet.

They were jokingly called Men Without Surnames because they didn't want anyone to know three of its members were brothers.

Their first single release in 1983 was The Safety Dance, which peaked at #3 on Billboard's Hot 100. Their other hits included Where Do The Boys Go, Pop Goes The World, and In The 21st Century.

By the early 1990s the group took a hiatus from the music business. In 1997 Ivan Doroschuk recorded the CD, *The Spell* under the name of Ivan, which produced the hits Open Your Eyes, Super Bad Girls and 1972 (Slippin' Away).

Singles:

The Safety Dance	Sire 25-99567	1983
Living In China	Sire ST-12	1983
I Got The Message	Sire ST-14	1983
Where Do The Boys Go	Sire TAK-15/MCA 52460	1984
The Great Ones Remember	Sire ST-20	1984
I Like	Sire ST-21/MCA 52293	1984
Nationale 7	Sire 25-90477	1985
The Safety Dance	Statik 2412	1985
Fotonuvela (Ivan Doroschuk)	CBS IS-7091	1985
Pop Goes The World	MercuryMS 76260	1988
Moonbeam	MercuryMS 76264	1988
O Sole Mio	MercuryMS 76268	1988

Hey Men	Mercury876-162	1989/90
In The 21st Century	Mercury876-696	1990
Here Come The 90s	Mercury888-712	1990
You And Me	Mercury872-291	1990
Sideways	Mercury848569	1991

Albums/CDs:

Rhythm of Youth	Sire Statik 10	1983
Folk of The 80s	Sire Statik 18	1984
Freeways	Sire Statik 25-22261	1985
Pop Goes The World (The Adventures of Women and Men Without Hate)	Mercury832730	1987
In The 21st Century	Mercury842000	1989
Sideways	Mercury848569	1991
Greatest Hats	AQR 2579	1996

Messenjah

Errol Blackwood (vocals, bass)
Hal Duggan (keyboards, bass, background vocals)
Rupert "Ojiji" Harvey (vocals, guitar)
Tony King (percussion)
Crash Morgan (drums)
Raymond Ruddock (drums, keyboards, percussion, background vocals)
Charles Sinclair (bass guitar)
Eric Walsh (rhythm guitar, background vocals)
Haile Yates (percussion)

The origins of Canada's first reggae band go back to 1980 in Kitchener, Ont. where Errol Blackwood and Rupert Harvey enjoyed playing together and decided to form a band.

Brought up by Jamaican parents, Blackwood was tired of playing in rock bands and wanted to get back to his roots. Harvey was a Toronto musician and producer of such groups as Crack of Dawn. Together, Blackwood and Harvey developed a strong following in the United States, particularly California, Texas and New Mexico.

After a year of touring they recorded an independent album called Rock You High in California. In 1982 they had signed with Wea Records of Canada (now Warner Music) who decided to reissue Rock You High as their first release. They became the first Canadian reggae band to sign with a major label.

With their second album, Jam Session in 1984, the group added a Tony King on percussion. Between their second and third albums there was a period of three years when the group went through a major personnel change. Errol Blackwood left in 1986 to pursue a solo career. He was replaced by Harvey.

Messenjah's next album was *Cool Operator* in 1987. It was followed by another three-year hiatus when Donovan replaced Crash Morgan on drums, and the group played themselves in the movie Cocktail (1988). In 1990 came their fourth album, Rock and Sway.

Seven years after he left Messenjah, Blackwood recorded the independent hit Unforeign Dub. In 1999 Messenjah released the CD, Catch De Vibe.

Albums/CDs:

Rock You High	Wea 25-02021	1982
Root Up (EP)	Wea 25-97870	1983
Jam Session (EP)	Wea 25-95610	1984
Night Rider (EP)	VRI-00100	1986
Cool Operator	VRI VLP-001	1987
Rock & Sway	KUP KCLP-100	1990
Cool But Deadly	Musimart MRCD-1152	1994
Catch Da Vibe	Messenjah MJH 1426	1999

Megan Metcalfe

The daughter of radio personality/columnist Joy Metcalfe, Megan began writing songs and playing in cafes and festivals in her hometown of Vancouver when she was a teenager. In 1982 she won the Vancouver Amateur Talent Contest.

A founding member of the Pacific Songwriters Association, it was not until September 1991 when she received a standing ovation at Seattle's Bumbershoot Festival was she convinced that singing could be a career.

In 1995 she recorded the independent album, Love Is An Outlaw, which EMI re-released as Megan Metcalff in February 1996. Produced by Robbie Steininger (Sue Medley), the songs ranged from a reaction to a news story about a senseless death in South Africa in The Marrow and The Bone, to Truehearts that dealt with honesty in a relationship. The first single, Starbird Road, showcased Megan's poetically nostlagic mood.

Singles:

Starbird Road	EMI 36900	1996
Truehearts	EMI 36900	1996
Let It Rain	EMI 36900	1996

Albums/CDs:

Love Is An Outlaw	Stonecutter 648	1995
Megan Metcalfe	EMI 36900	1996

Mighty Pope

Born Earl Heedram in Jamaica, Mighty Pope grew up singing in church choirs, but after graduating from high school in Toronto, he lost interest in music and became an accountant. In 1966 he returned to singing when some of his friends encouraged him to sing on stage. For the next twelve years he worked hard at perfecting his disco act, and adopted Pope as his first stage name, then Mighty Pope. He received his big break in the late 1970s when he was asked to open for Natalie Cole at Ontario Place. His first hit was, If You Want a Love Affair in 1976, followed by the Top 20 hit, Heaven on the Seventh Floor in 1977.

Singles:

If You Want a Love Affair	RCA PB-50250	1976
Heaven on the Seventh Floor	RCA PB-50380	1977
Can't Get By Without You	RCA PB-50411	1977
Sweet Blindness		1979/80

Album:

Mighty Pope	RCA KKKL1-0257	1977

Lynn Miles

Born on September 29, 1958 in Sweetsburg, Quebec, Lynn Miles first studied the violin, flute, piano and voice as a child. She started writing songs when she was ten years old.

A gifted guitarist and pianist, she has written over four hundred songs which range from folk and pop to country. Her early influences include Carole King, Jackson Browne and The Eagles.

While she was in high school she started performing in public.

In 1987 she recorded her self-titled debut album on Snowy River Records. Three years later came her sophomore effort, Chalk This One Up To The Moon.

Lynn has appeared on various CBC radio shows such as Swinging On A Star, Simply Folk, Morningside, The Entertainers, and Musical Friends, and performed at the National Arts Centre in Ottawa, Harbourfront in Toronto, Railway Club in Vancouver, and The Frostbite Music Festival in Whitehorse, up as well as various folk festivals across the country.

Outside Canada she has performed at New York's The Speakeasy, Nashville's Bluebird Cafe and the Southeast Alaska State Fair, and the Bermuda Folk Club, in addition to venues in Portugal, Spain, France, Germany and Seville, Spain.

After recording her first two albums on Snowy River, *Lynn Miles*, *Chalk This One Up To The Moon*, she switched to Philo Records with, *Slightly Haunted*, *Night In A Strange Town* and *Unravel*, Truth North.

Albums/CDs:

Lynn Miles	Snowy River SRR S06	1987
Chalk This One Up To The Moon	Snowy River SRR S30	1990
Slightly Haunted	Philo 1190	1996
Night In A Strange Town	Philo 1215	1998
Unravel	True North TND 264	2001
Love Sweet Love	True North TND 353	
Black Flowers	True North TND 531	2009
Fall For Beauty	True North TND 533	2009

Alan Mills

He was born Albert Miller on September 7, 1913 in Lachine, Quebec. In 1935 he began his singing career when he joined the John Goss London Singers, a folk group that toured North America. When he left he went to work as a reporter at the now-defunct Montreal Herald, where he was a police reporter in his teens, and The Montreal Gazette.

In 1944 he left journalism, changed his name to Alan Mills, and combined a singing career with acting and radio. Completely bilingual, he often participated in French radio productions.

He hosted a weekly children's show on CBC radio, Folk Songs For Young Folk in 1947 and from 1952 to 1955 on Songs de Chez Nous with singer and folklorist Helene Baillargeon.

On stage, he was accompanied by Gilbert Lacombe on guitar, who also appeared with him on several of his recordings He also wrote his own songs, one of which was the popular I Know An Old Lady Who Swallowed A Fly in 1951, which humorously described the fate of a woman who ingested everything from a spider to a horse in order to rid herself of the fly. In 1964 it was sung by Burl Ives on the soundtrack of a National Film Board production of the same name.

Mills continued to act in both English and French radio dramas and TV commercials in Montreal. He wrote the play, Ti-Jean and the Devil, which premiered on CBC radio on June 21, 1961.

His recordings were on Folkways, RCA and Dominion and he wrote the accompanying booklet to the 1967 nine-volume album set, Canadian Folk Songs: A Centinnial Celebration. He was made a Member of the Order of Canada in 1974.

Mills died of cancer on June 14, 1977.

Singles:

The Ballad Of Bordeaux Jail	Capri 958
D'ou viens-tu Bergere? (78)	Dominion 7001
Mon beau sapin (78)	Dominion 7002
Fais dodo Cola (78)	Dominion 7003
Widdicombe Fair (78)	RCA 56-0044
The Keeper (78)	RCA 56-0051
The Kelligrew's Soiree (78)	RCA 56-0058
I Know An Old Lady	Dominion 45-37
Kemo-Kemo (w/Gilbert Lacombe)	Dominion 45-38

Albums/CDs:

Songs By Alan Mills	RCI 21	1950
Alan Mills, Folk Singer	RCI 81-84	1952
Folk Songs of French Canada	Folkways FW-6929	1952
Folk Songs of Newfoundland	Folkways FW-6831	1953
Songs of The Maritimes	RCI 102	1954
Duets And Songs of French Canada (W/Helene Baillargeon)	Folkways FW-6918	1955
Folk Songs of Acadia	Folkways FW-6973	1956
French Songs For Children	Folkways FW-7018	1956
Folk Songs For Youngfolk I	Folkways FC-7021	1956
Folk Songs For Youngfolk Ii	Folkways FC-7022	1956
Raasche And Alan Mills Sing Jewish Folk Songs	Folkways FW-8711	1956
Songs of The Maritimes	Folkways FW-8744	1957
Favorite Songs of Newfoundland	Folkways FW-8771	1957
Canada's Story In Song	Folkways FW-3000	1960
Songs, Fiddle Tunes and Folk Tales From Canada	Folkways FG-3532	1961
14 Numbers, Letters And Animals Songs For The Very Young	Folkways FC-7545	1972

Frank Mills

Born on June 27, 1942 in Verdun, Quebec, Frank Mills grew up in Montreal. By the time he was four years old he could play the piano by ear, and in high school he played the trombone. After graduation he went to McGill University where he studied medicine. However, he gave it up all for a music career in 1965. For the next two years he sold industrial gases and real estate until he was invited to join The Sirocco Singers who broke up after three months. From 1968 to 1970 he was a member of The Five Bells.

In September, 1971 he released his first solo album, *Seven of My Songs* (Plus Some Others). The following year he had a big hit with the song, Love Me Love Me Love, from his second album, *Reflections of My Childhood*. Following its success, Frank went through a period of seven long, lean years, but continued to write and record.

One of the tunes, Music Box Dancer was first recorded in 1973 but Polydor Records shelved it. It was finally released in 1978 after Dave Watts of CFRA radio in Ottawa convinced Mills that it was a hit, based on his listeners' response for airplay.

Originally inspired by his daughter Nancy who wanted her jewelery box fixed, Music Box Dancer eventually earned a place in the millionaires club, based on one million air plays. It was a hit in twenty-six countries and it also helped earn him International Artist of the Year in Japan in 1979. Music Box Dancer reached #3 on Billboard's Hot 100 in 1979 and was certified a million seller on March 29, 1979.

In 1992 he and John Loweth, Mills' sheet music publisher, formed Music Box Dancer Ltd. Mills retired from performing in December 2000.

Singles:

Love Me Love Me Love	Polydor 2065-076	1972
Poor Little Fool	Polydor 2065-117	1972
Sunshine Morning	Polydor 2065-136	1972
Reflections Of My Childhood	Polydor 2065-136	1972
How Can I Be Sure	Polydor 2065-175	1973
When Summer Is Gone	Attic AT 138	1976
Look At Me Real	Attic AT 131	1976
Music Box Dancer	Polydor 2065-392	1979
Peter Piper	Polydor PD-2002	1979
Most People Are Nice		1979
Breakaway		1980
Happy Song		1981
Plaisir d'amour	Capitol 72869	1981

Prelude To Romance	Capitol 72873	1981
Rondo In America	Capitol 72908	1982
Heart of the City	Capitol SPRO-318	1986
Seascapes	Capitol SPRO-341	1986

Albums/CDs:

Seven of My Songs	Polydor 2424-030	1971
Reflections of My Childhood	Polydor 2424-060	1972
Frank Mills	Sonogram LSG 72005	1974
(Reissued In 1978 As The Poet and I - Pol 2424-170)Images D'un Bistro	Sonogram LSG-72001	1975
Look At Me Real	Attic LAT 1009	1976
Sunday Morning Suite	Polydor PD1-6225	1978
The Frank Mills Album	Polydor PD1-6305	1980
Prelude To Romance	Capitol ST-6488	1981
Rondo	Capitol ST 6496	1982
Music Box Dancer	Capitol ST 6501	1983
A Special Christmas	Capitol ST 6506	1983
Traveller	Capitol ST 12388	1984
Transitions	Capitol ST 6548	1986
Over 60 Minutes With	Capitol 46889	1987
My Piano	Capitol C1-91077	1988
Together Through The Years	Capitol S2-80004	1989
Gather Round The Piano	Capitol 80015	1991
Christmas With Frank Mills & Friends	Capitol 80021	1992
Homeward	Music Box MB4 7003	1994
Best Of Frank Mills:Happy Piano	Music Box MB4 7005	1994
A Traditional Christmas	Music Box MB4 7007	1995
25 Years Of Piano Music	Music Box MB4 7010	1996
Goodnight My Love	Music Box MB4 7012	1996
Frank Mills Goes To The Movies	EMI 557492	1997
Canada	Music Box MB4 7018	1997

Minglewood Band

Paul Dunn (backup vocals)
Paul Hann (bass guitar, violin, backup vocals)
Mark McMillan (lead guitar)
Matt Minglewood (lead vocals, guitar)
Enver Sampson Jr. (backup vocals)
Bob Woods (drums, percussion)

The history of the Minglewood Band goes back to the late 1960s when Matt Minglewood joined Caper Sam Moon in the band Moon, Minglewood and The

Universal Power. When they broke up, Matt went on to form his own band. In 1976 they released their self-titled independent album. Three years later, they signed to RCA Records.

Enver Sampson Jr. who joined the band in the early 1970s died in a motorcycle accident in 1985. By the mid-1980s the Minglewood Band had disbanded. Matt went on to have a solo career on Savannah Records. In 1986 the label released the single, Far Side of Town, followed by another, You're Not Drinking Enough from his debut album, The Promise (1988).

Singles:

Ain't What It Used To Be	RCA PB-50528	1979
Whiz Kid	RCA JB-50545	1979
Counting On You		1980
Me And My Baby	RCA PB-50585	1980
Rocket Fuel		1981
Highway To Your Heart	RCA PB-50634	1981
I'm Gonna Forgive You Again		1981
Me And The Boys	Savannah SRS-835	1985
Runaway (Matt Minglewood)	Savannah PRO 611	1988
Some Day I'm Gonna Ride In A Cadillac (Matt Minglewood)	Savannah PRO 629	1988

Albums/CDs:

Minglewood Band	Solar SAR 2010	1976
Minglewood Band	RCA KKL1-0325	1979
Moving	RCA KKL1-0370	1980
Smokers - Best Of	RCA KKL1-0472	1982
Out On A Limb	RCA KKL1-0415	1983
M5	CBS Records	1985
Me And The Boys	Savannah SRL 9825	1985
The Promise (Matt Minglewood)	Savannah SRL 9830	1988
The Best Of The Minglewood Band	BMG 10708	1992
The Legendary First Album	AtlanticA MBCD	1993
Drivin' Wheel (Matt Minglewood)	Norton Nort 99-1	1999

Joni Mitchell

Born Roberta Joan Anderson in Fort McLeod, Alberta (near Lethbridge) on November 7, 1943, and raised in Saskatoon, Saskatchewan, she studied piano as a child. She later learned the ukelele and guitar, and started singing when she had contracted polio at the age of nine.

While studying at the Alberta College of Art, she made her professional debut at The Depression, a local coffeehouse in Calgary in 1963. In 1964 she married folksinger Chuck Mitchell, but their marriage was short-lived. Joni moved to Toronto where she performed at Yorkville's Penny Farthing.

During this time, American folksinger Tom Rush began singing her songs, such as Urge for Going and The Circle Game, and Mitchell started to become famous.

She moved to Greenwich Village in New York in 1966 and, two years later, settled in Los Angeles. In 1968 Reprise Records released her self-titled debut album, which was re-titled *Song for a Seagull* for its U.S. release.

By the time her album *Blue* was released she had gone from being the pop star of such songs as Big Yellow Taxi and Woodstock to a more introspective singer-songwriter. By 1979 when Asylum Records released Minglus, Joni's music had matured.

During the 1980s she released four albums, including the political Dog Eat Dog on Geffen. She also took over creative control of her recordings, which featured her own paintings on the covers.

In the 1990s her recordings consisted of two compilations, Hits and Misses, which represented some of Joni's best work as a singer/songwriter.

She has been awarded many honors, including the Century Award from Billboard Magazine in 1995, and both Sweden's Polar Music Prize and induction into the Rock and Roll Hall of Fame in 1997. In 2007 Big Yello Taxi, Both Sides Now, Help Me, Woodstock, and You Turn Me On I'm A Radio were inducted into Canadian Songwriters Hall of Fame in 2007.

Singles:

Big Yellow Taxi	Reprise 0906	1970
Carey	Reprise 1029	1971
California	Reprise 1049	1971
You Turn Me On (I'm A Radio)	Asylum AS 11010	1972
Raised On Robbery	Asylum AS 11029	1974
Help Me	Asylum AS 11034	1974
Free Man In Paris	Asylum AS 11041	1974
Big Yellow Taxi (live version)	Asylum E 45221	1975
Carey/Jericho	Asylum E 45244	1975
In France They Kiss On Main Street	Asylum AS E 45298	1976
Coyote	Asylum E 45377	1976
Jericho	Asylum E 45467	1977
My Secret Place	Geffen92-78877	1988
Come In From The Cold	Geffen24302	1991
How Do You Do Stop	Reprise 45786	1994
Sex Kills	Reprise 45786	1994
Crazy Cries Of Love	Reprise 46451	1998
Both Sides Now	Reprise 47620	2000

Albums/CDs:

Joni Mitchell	Reprise RS 6293	1968
(Song to a Seagull – U.S. Only)		
Clouds	Reprise RS 6341	1969
Ladies of the Canyon	Reprise RS 6376	1971
Blue	Reprise MS 2038	1971
For the Roses	Asylum SD-5057	1972
Court and Spark	Asylum 7ES-001	1974
Miles of Aisles	Asylum AB-202	1974
The Hissing of The Summer Lawns	Asylum 7ES-1051	1975
Hejira	Asylum 7ES-1087	1976
Don Juan's Reckless Daughter	Asylum BB-101	1977
Mingus	Asylum X5E-505	1979
Shadows and Light	Asylum 2XBB 704	1980
Wild Things Run Fast	GeffenXGHS 2019	1982
Dog Eat Dog	GeffenXGHS 24074	1985
Chalk Mark in a Rain Storm	GeffenXGHS 24172	1988
Night Ride Home	Geffen24302	1991
Turbulent Indigo	Reprise 45786	1994
Taming the Tiger	Reprise 46451	1998
Both Sides Now	Reprise 47620	2000
Travelogue	Nonesuch 798172	2002
Shine	Hear Music 30457	2007

Kim Mitchell

Born on July 10, 1952 in Sarnia, Ontario, Kim Mitchell started out as leader, singer/songwriter and guitarist for the art rock band Max Webster. When he was five years old, his father bought him his first guitar. Growing up in his hometown his musical influences were Jimi Hendrix and Eric Clapton.

In 1984 he released his debut album, Akimbo Logo which went double platinum in Canada (over 200,000 copies). From it came the hit single Go For Soda, which went Top Five in the summer of 1984.

It was endorsed by the 60,000-member-strong organization, Mothers Against Drunk Driving (or Madd) in the United States as its 1985 summer theme. Written by Mitchell and lyricist Pye Dubois, it was not meant to be an anti-alcohol statement. However, the chorus was perfect for Madd which said, "Might as well go for soda/Nobody hurts and nobody cries/Go for soda/Nobody drowns and nobody dies."

By 1986 Mitchell continued to enjoy success with Patio Lanterns, the first of three hits from the album, Shakin' Like A Human Being. That same year, the magazine, Music Express honored him with the title Working Class Hero.

The Kingswood Music Theatre north of Toronto awarded Kim with the first ever Platinum Ticket Award in 1988 to celebrate 100,000 tickets sold over a five year period.

Mitchell continued to record and perform into the 1990s. In 1999 came the CD, *Kimosabe*, his first in five years.

Singles:

Go For Soda	Alert BDS-502	1984
All We Are	Alert BDS-503	1984
Patio Lanterns	Alert BDS-514	1986
Alana Loves Me	Alert BDS-515	1986
Easy To Love	Alert BDS-516	1987
In Your Arms	Alert BDS-520	1987
Rock 'n' Roll Duty		1989
Rockland Wonderland	Alert DPRO-003	1989
Lost Lovers Found	Alert Z1-81010	1990
All We Are (Live)	Alert Z1-81010	1990
Expedition Sailor	Alert Z1-81010	1990
I Am A Wild Party	Alert Z1-81010	1990
Find The Will	Alert Z2-81019	1992
America	Alert Z2-81019	1992
Pure As Gold	Alert Z2-81019	1992
Some Folks	Alert Z2-81019	1992
Acrimony	Alert Z2-81024	1994
The U.S. of Ache	Alert Z2-81024	1994
Kimosabe	Chinook 99057	1999

Albums/CDs:

Kim Mitchell	Anthem ANM-1-5001	1982
Akimbo Alogo	Alert BD-101	1984
Shakin' Like a Human Being	Alert BD4-1004	1986
Rockland	Alert Z1-81010	1989
I Am a Wild Party	Alert Z2-81015	1990
Aural Fixations	Alert Z2-81019	1992
Itch	Alert Z2-81024	1994
Kimosabe	Chinook 99057	1999

Mitsou

Born Mitsou Gelinas on September 1, 1970 in Montreal, this pop siren captured audiences in her native Quebec with her hit, Bye Bye Mon Cowboy in 1989. A year earlier, she received the Felix Award, Quebec's equivalent of the Juno Awards, for Most Promising Artist.

Mitsou comes from one of Quebec's most famous families. Her grandfather was the renowned writer/actor Gratien Gelinas and her father, Alain Gelinas is also an actor. At 13 she concentrated on acting and appeared in TV ads, French theatrical productions in arts school and had a role in a French TV series. While in her teens she also yearned to start her own rock band. She met Pierre Gendron who would later become her future manager.

The success of Bye Bye Mon Cowboy in 1988 made her a French superstar in North America and in Europe. At 18 her image as a sex kitten a la Madonna was innocent and stunning. It didn't matter that she sang in French, or was the first artist to travel cross Canada to be accepted in her first language.

In 1991 the release of the video for Dis-Moi, Dis-Moi (Tell Me, Tell Me) featured nudity. The way it presented the human body as a work of art was provocative. The controversy over the song led to a multi-million dollar deal with Disney's Hollywood Records.

In 1992 she recorded her first English language album, *Heading West* and from it was the single, Deep Kiss. She co-wrote the title song with Cyndi Lauper. Her second English album, *Tempted* came out in 1993. After a five year hiatus following the release of Ya Ya (1994), she returned with *Generation* in 1999.

Singles:
Rock 'n Roll Is Back Again	Trema 410.132	1980
Bye Bye Mon Cowboy	ISBA 519	1988
La Corrida	ISBA 545	1989
Les Chinois	ISBA 550	1989
Mademoiselle Anne	ISBA NK-563	1990
Dis-Moi, Dis-Moi	ISBA Cs	1991
Lettre a un cowboy	ISBA NK-636	1991
A Funny Place (The World Is)	ISBA ISCD 2025	1991
Deep Kiss	TOX 1001Cs	1992
Heading West	TOX 0001	1992
Everybody Say Love	TOX 0001	1993
Loving Me Is Not A Sin	TOX 0001	1994
Father Angel	AGEK 2118	1994
Le YaYa	AGEK 2118	1994/95
J'ai Toujours	AGEK 2118	1995
Envie D'Aimer	AGEK 2118	1995
Ouvre-moi	GEN2-1135	1999

Albums/CDs:
El Mundo	ISBA ISCD 2015	1988
Terre Des Hommes	ISBA ISCD 2025	1990
Heading West	ISBA/TOX 0001	1992
Tempted	AGEK 2117	1993
Ya Ya	AGEK 2118	1994
Generation	GEN2-1135	1999

Jackie Mittoo

Born in Montego Bay, Jamaica on March 3, 1948, Jackie Mittoo began his music career in his teens in Kingston, Jamaica where he worked with such groups as The Rivals, The Sheiks, and The Skatalites. He was a major figure at Coxsone Dodd's Jamaician Record Manufacturing Co., Studio One, where he was a member of several studio groups such as The Soul Vendors, Sound Dimenson, The Invaders, Brentford All Stars, and New Establishment. While working there he also backed up such reggae luminaries as Bob Marley and The Wailers, Jimmy Cliff, The Heptones, Delroy Wilson and Alton Ellis among others. Before moving to Toronto in 1969, he played on Johnny Nash's two American hits, Hold Me Tight and Cupid.

During his stay in Canada he continued to work in Jamaica. In 1971, he had his only major chart success as a solo artist with the instrumental hit, Wishbone. In 1985 he was inducted into the Black Music Association of Canada's Hall of Fame.

Although he made only three albums in Canada, he did make other albums outside Canada that were distributed by Coxson (IN London- CSL 8009; Evening Time CSL 8012), Third World (THE Keyboard King - TWS 501; Hot Blood - TWS 912; In Cold Blood - TWS 931), Showcase (Studio One - SOL 0130), and Wackie's (Wild Jockey - W 2749). Mittoo's recordings are also available on various compilations distributed by Heartbeat.

He died of cancer in Toronto on December 16, 1990. In 1995 the two-CD set, A Tribute To Jackie Mittoo (Heartbeat HB-189/190) featured the best of the artist's recordings.

Single:

Wishbone/Soul Bird	Summus 2502	1971

Albums/CDs:

Wishbone	Summus SUS-50002	1971
Reggae Magic	CTL 477-5164	1972
Let's Put It All Together	CTLS 5189/UALA 442G	1975
Jackie Mittoo	UA UALA 804R	1978

The Moffatts

Bob Moffatt (vocals, congas, drums)
Clint Moffatt (vocals, bass, percussion)
Dave Moffatt (vocals, keyboards)
Scott Moffatt (vocals, electric and acoustic guitars)

The Moffatts are four brothers from Victoria, British Columbia who started as an opening act for Darlana, the family's country act.

Scott is the oldest, while Clint, Dave and Bob are triplets. They began singing the national anthem at various sports and political events.

Their first big break came when Ralph Emery, then host of The Nashville Network's Nashville Now, hired them to appear on an irregular basis. Their exposure on national television helped them to secure a recording contract with Polydor, who released their self-titled debut album in 1995.

Their appearances on Nashville Now resulted in Moffatmania across America. After the release of The Moffatts, they were busy promoting their Caterpillar Crawl line dance tape on The Nashville Network, Country Music Televison, Nickelodeon, and The Cartoon Network. They also appeared on Sally Jessy Raphael, Music City Tonight, The Tonight Show, and Live With Regis and Kathy Lee Gifford.

By the summer of 1998 the Moffatts had changed musical direction, and were now signed to EMI, who released Chapter 1: A New Beginning. Moffatmania continued to follow them with the release of such hits as I'll Be There For You and Miss You Like Crazy.

Singles:

When God Made You	POL 527373	1995
Caterpillar Crawl	POL 527373	1995
I'll Be There For You	EMI 95169	1998
Miss You Like Crazy	EMI 95169	1998
Girl of My Dreams	EMI 95169	1999
Until You Loved Me	EMI 95169	1999
Bang Bang Boom	EMI 89155	2000

Albums/CDs:

The Moffatts	Polydor 527373	1995
Chapter 1: A New Beginning	EMI 95169	1998
Submodalities	EMI 85692	2000

Moist

David Usher (vocals)
Mark Makoway (guitar)
Jeff Pearce (bass)
Paul Wilcox (drums)
Kevin Young (keyboards)

This five-man band formed in Vancouver, British Columbia in 1993. David Usher, Mark Makowy, Jeff Pearce and Kevin Young are from Kingston, Ontario, while Paul Wilcox is from Vancouver.

Moist started out as an independent band who recorded their first independent, self-titled cassette in 1993. They later signed a deal with EMI Music Publishing and recorded their debut CD, *Silver*, which included the first hit and video, Push that became a national hit thanks to the support of MuchMusic.

After signing to EMI Music Canada in 1994, Silver was re-released and sold three times platinum (300,000).

In 1996 the group moved to Montreal, and later that same year, EMI released their sophomore CD, *Creature*.

Usher released the solo effort, Little Songs (1998) featuring the single, Forestfire. His second, Morning Orbit (EMI 276832) came out in 2001.

EMI released the group's third album, *Mercedes Five and Dime* in 1999 and *Machine Punch Through: singles* in 2001.

Singles:
Push	EMI 229608	1993/94
Silver	EMI 229608	1994
Believe Me	EMI 229608	1994/95
Machine Punch Through	EMI 229608	1995
Leave it Alone	EMI 236188	1996
Resurrection	EMI 236188	1996/97
Tangerine	EMI 236188	1997
Breathe	EMI 962952	1999
Underground	EMI 962952	1999

Albums/CDs:
Silver	EMI 229608	1994
Creature	EMI 236188	1996
Mercedes Five and Dime	EMI 962952	1999
Machine Punch Through: singles	EMI 345422	2001

The Mongrels

Joey Gregorash (lead vocals, drums)
John Hart (bass)
John MacInnis (rhythm guitar)
Jeff Marrin (lead vocals)
John Nykon (lead guitar)

This Winnipeg group began as an instrumental group called The Wellingtons in 1964 with Joey Gregorash, John Brennan, John Nykon, and Peter Rutherford. Gregorash changed their name to The Mongrels, after his favorite dog, later that same year. All but Joey Gregorash remained in the group when the other original members left between 1965-67. The new additions were Larry Rasmussen on drums, Duncan Wilson on lead guitar, Mark Hastings on bass, and Garth Nosworthy on bass.

In 1968, Gregorash left to become a TV host and later went on to have a successful solo career in the 1970s and 1980s. He was replaced by Alan Schick. The rest of the group included Rasmussen, Wilson, and Nosworthy. With their new lead singer, they recorded four singles for Franklin Records, and one on RCA Victor. Their second single, My Woman was written and produced by Randy Bachman, and another single, Funny Day made it on the "Rate a Record" segment on Dick Clark's American Bandstand.

The Mongrels broke up in the early 1970s. Alan Schick had some success with the single, Lucy Lucy Lucy (MCA 40144) in 1973/74. A second single, Soul Deep/Summer Song (MCA 40254 – 1974) was not a hit. Both came from the album, Lucy Lucy Lucy (MCA 361 – 1973).

Singles:

Sitting In The Station	Franklin 607	1968
My Woman	Franklin 619	1968
Funny Day	Franklin 624	1969
Do You Know Your Mother	Franklin 632	1969
Ivy In Her Eyes	RCA 75-1036	1970

Monkey House

Don Breithaupt (lead vocals, keyboards)
Rikki Rumball (vocals)

Monkey House began as a studio project at Marigold Productions in Mississauga in 1991 when Don Breithaupt was writing songs for other artists. He decided it was time to record some of his own songs, so he and Rikki became the Toronto based duo named after Kurt Vonnegut's book, Welcome To The Monkey House. Their debut CD, *Welcome To The Club* on Aquarius/EMI, featuring Lazy Nina, was released in 1992.

Breithaupt was born on April 8, 1961 in Sault Ste. Marie and raised in Mississauga. He studied composition at Berklee College of Music in Boston, and received a Bachelor of Arts (Honors) degree in English and Film Studies from Queen's University.

In the 1980s he began writing songs in collaboration with other Toronto based songwriters. Among the artists who have recorded his songs include Debbie Johnson, Carol Medina, Aashna, and The Stampeders. Don has also co-produced Rumball's debut album, Strange Girl (1996). That same year, St. Martin' Press published, Precious and Few: Pop Music In The Early Seventies, which he wrote with his brother Jeff. Monkey House's sophomore CD, *True Winter* came out in 1998.

Singles:

Big Money	Aqua 2569	1992/93
Lazy Nina	Aqua 2569	1993
A Matter of Moments	Aqua 2569	1993/94
Just Like Me	Aqua 2569	1994
Road Movie	MGOCD 00010	1998

Albums/CDs:

Welcome To The Club	Aquarius 2569	1992
True Winter	Mar MGOCD 00010	1998

Mae Moore

Born in Brandon, Manitoba and raised in Southwestern Ontario, Mae Moore grew up listening to Bob Dylan, Crosby, Stills, Nash and Young and Joni Mitchell. While working in the tobacco fields of Ontario she never wanted a job as a singer, only as a songwriter.

Not until she moved to Vancouver in 1981 did she play acoustic guitar and dulcimer in a trio and later in a group called Foreign Legion. In the mid-1980s she met songwriter John Dexter and together he and Mae wrote some songs together, one of which later became Heaven In Your Eyes. She is credited as a co-writer on the song with Dexter and Mike Reno and Paul Dean of Loverboy.

Living in Vancouver she worked in bakeries, stores and factories by day, while honing her craft as a singer/songwriter by night. She became friends with Barney Bentall and his lead guitarist Colin Nairn and Geoff Kelly from Spirit of the West.

Through their support she was able to secure a recording contract with CBS Records (now Sony Music). Kelly and Nairn agreed to produce her debut album, Oceanview Motel, which came out in 1990.

She was dropped by the label after two more albums, *Boehemia* and *Dragonfly*, but returned on Jann Arden's Big Hip Records, distributed by Universal Music, in

1999 with the release of a self-titled effort. Epic released a greatest hits collection called Collected Works 1989-1999 in 2000.

Singles:

I'll Watch Over You	Epic BEK 80155	1990
Where Loneliness Lives	Epic BEK 80155	1991
Red Clay Hills	Epic BEK 80155	1991
Bohemia	Epic EK 80174	1992
Because Of Love	Epic EK 80174	1993
Coat of Shame	Epic EK 80174	1993
The Wish	Epic EK 80174	1993
Genuine	Epic EK 80222	1995
Watermark	Epic EK 80222	1995
Love Won't Find Us Here	Epic EK 80222	1996
Deep Water	Virgin 44908	1997/98
Free To Love Me (Warm Song)	Big Hip 90378	1999

Albums/CDs:

Oceanview Motel	Epic BEK 80155	1990
Bohemia	Epic EK 80174	1992
Dragonfly	Epic EK 80222	1995
Mae Moore	Big Hip 90378	1999
Collected Works 1989-1999	Epic EK 80562	2000

Moran

Moran (or John Moran) is a singer/songwriter from Dundee, Scotland who grew up with aspirations to become a rock singer. He started singing under the name of Johnny Hudson, and later formed his own group, The Poor Souls. He also hosted a thirteen-week TV show called Teen Beat. When the show finished, he came to Canada with his parents.

Settling in Toronto, Moran wanted to continue his interest in music and he began looking for a Canadian version of The Poor Souls. Once they were together, they toured between Kapsukasing and Welland, Ontario. After two years the members of the band quit, and Moran went solo.

He began writing his own songs, one of which became The Beatles' Thing, which was his first hit single on Columbia Records.

After two more singles and one album for the label, Moran was never heard from again.

Singles:

The Beatles' Thing	Col C4-3082	1973
Lady Loves Me	Col C4-3082	1973
Come Join Me	Col C4-4018	1973
Falling In Love Again	Col C4-4051	1974

Album:

Come Join Me	Col ES 90231	1973

Alanis Morissette

Born in Ottawa, Ontario on June 1, 1974, Alanis Morissette first wanted to be singer when she was three years old. By the time she was nine she was already writing her own songs, and at ten she was on the TV show, You Can't Do That On Television. In 1987 Rich Dodson and Lindsay Morgan co-produced her first hit single on Lamour Records, Fate Stay With Me/Find The Right Man.

In 1989 she was introduced to John Alexander, then Director of MCA Records, by Leslie Howe of the Ottawa group One To One. When she heard Walk Away on a demo tape, it impressed Alexander enough to sign her. Howe and Alanis co-wrote all the songs on her self-titled debut album in 1991. The video of her first single, Too Hot was filmed in Los Angeles. Alanis became one of the top dance acts of the early 1990s with her other songs, including An Emotion Away and No Apologies.

Tired of being a pop/dance star, she began to write songs that were more introspective. She now became an alternative artist and was now using her last name as part of her new image. Signed to Madonna's Maverick label, Morissette's debut album, Jagged Little Pill came out in June 1995. Its success was unprecedented for an album in Canada, and at the 1997 Juno Awards she was one of three artists honored with an International Achievement Award. The other two were Celine Dion and Shania Twain.

Early in 1998 her song, Uninvited was featured on the soundtrack of the film, City of Angels. On November 8, 1998 her sophomore Maverick album, *Supposed Former Infatuation Junkie* was released.

Singles:

Fate Stay With Me	Lamour LMR-10-12	1987
Too Hot	MCA 10253	1991
Feel Your Love	MCA 10253	1991
Walk Away	MCA 10253	1991/92

Plastic	MCA 10253	1992
An Emotion Away	MCA 10731	1992/93
Real World	MCA 10731	1993
No Apologies	MCA 10731	1993
Change (Is Never Waste of Time)	MCA 10731	1993
You Oughta Know	Maverick 45901	1995
Hand In My Pocket	Maverick 45901	1995/96
Ironic	Maverick 45901	1996
Ironic (EP)	Maverick 43650	1996
Ironic (CD/S)	Maverick 43050	1996
You Learn	Maverick 45901	1996
You Learn (CD/S)	Maverick 17644	1996
Hand Over Feet	Maverick 45901	1996
Uninvited	War/REP 46867	1998
Thank U	Maverick 47094	1998
Unsent	Maverick 47094	1999
So Pure (CD/S)	Maverick 16967	1999
That I Would Be Good	Maverick 47589	1999/00
Hands Clean	Warner CD 16708	2002

Albums/CDs:

Alanis	MCA 10253	1991
Now is the Time	MCA 10731	1992
Jagged Little Pill	Maverick 45901	1995
Thank U (EP)	Maverick 44572	1998
Supposed Former Infatuation Junkie	Maverick 47094	1998
So Pure (EP)	Maverick 44704	1999
MTV Unplugged	Maverick 47589	1999

Morse Code Transmission

Joceyln Julien (electric guitars)
Raymond Roy (drums)
Christian Simard (lead vocals, keyboards)
Michel Vallee (bass guitar)

The history of Morse Code Transmission began in 1967 when the quartet from Quebec was first known as Les Maitres (The Masters). Founded by Michel Vallee and Raymond Roy, they played the club circuit in Quebec. They were a cover band who sang songs by The Beatles, The Bee Gees, Tom Jones, Robert Charlebois, Peter and Gordon and Claude Leveillee.

Les Maitres recorded three singles without success. Although they were French, they sang in English. By the early 1970s they had changed their name to

Morse Code Transmission. They also signed a record contract with RCA. The label released their self-titled debut album, and single, *Oh Lord*, in 1971.

Produced by Bill Misener of Sun Bar Productions, the French group did not know English well enough to write lyrics. They used the talents of Misener, Graeme Box, John de Nottbeck and the late Stan Rogers.

Morse Code Transmission gave its final performance on October 31, 1990 at the Anglicane in Levis near Quebec City.

Singles:

Un grand amour (Les Maitres)	RCA 75-5037	1969
Une nuit avec toi (Les Maitres)	RCA 75-5056	1970
Tu le sauras demain	RCA 75-5063	1970
Oh Lord	RCA 75-1066	1971
Cold Society	RCA SPCS-45-116	1972
Demain tout va changer	Morse Code 7801	1974
Cocktail	Capitol 72760	1975
Punch	Capitol 72770	1975
Qu'est-ce-que t'as compris	Capitol 85116	1976
L'eau tonne	Capitol 85127	1976
Qu'est-ce-que t'es v'nu faire ici	Capitol 85128	1976
Chevalier d'un regne	Capitol 85139	1977
Je suis le meme	Capitol 85147	1977
Superstar	Celsius 728	1982
Still On My Mind	Aquarius 6006	1983

Albums/CDs:

Morse Code Transmission	RCA Vsp-4575	1971
Morse Code Transmission Ii	RCA Vsp-6092	1972
La Marche Des Hommes	Capitol ST 70038	1975
Procreation	Capitol ST 70046	1976
Je Suis Le Temps	Capitol ST-70051	1977
Les Grands Succes De Morse Code	Capitol ST-70063	1978
Code Breaker	Aquarius AQR 536	1983

Motherlode

Steve Kennedy (tenor sax, harmonica)
Ken Marco (guitar)
William "Smitty" Smith (keyboards)
Wayne "Stoney" Stone (drums)

This quartet from London, Ontario began playing together in 1968 as part of Grant Smith and The Power, a nine-piece soul band from Toronto. (see Grant Smith And The Power) Steve, Ken, William and Wayne grew tired of playing hits by other artists and left the group in 1969 to form Motherlode.

Steve Kennedy from Windsor, Ontario began playing guitar and later studied the saxophone under the direction of noted saxophonist Bill Sparling. In 1965 he formed a group called The Silhouettes with Doug Riley (Dr. Music), Terry Bush, Howard Glen, and Fred Theriault. After some personnel changes, they called themselves Eric Mercury, Dianne Brooks and The Soul Searchers. They disbanded in 1968. After playing in other groups, Kennedy went to the Image Club in London, Ontario and convinced Marco, Stone and Smith to form Motherlode.

Ken Marco began playing in various local groups in his native Brantford. At 17 he toured with the Bar-Kays in northern Ontario. He later moved to Chicago and joined the Upset. He returned to Canada and played lead guitar for Grant Smith and The Power.

William "Smitty" Smith is the only non-Canadian member. Born in Belleville, Virginia, he began his musical career with the Belltones when he was nine years old. He emigrated to Canada in 1964 and played with the Soul Searchers, David Clayton-Thomas, Grant Smith and The Power and Lenny Breau. Smith died in Los Angeles on November 28, 1997 of a heart attack.

Wayne "Stoney" Stone hails from London, Ontario and started taking drum lessons when he was 11. At 18 he played with various local rock group. After graduating from high school he moved to Toronto and became the drummer for Grant Smith and the Power.

As Grant Smith and The Power they enjoyed success with a cover version of The Spencer Davis Group's Keep On Running in 1968.

In 1969 producer Mort Ross was impressed enough to sign the band to a contract with Revolver/Compo in Canada and Buddah in the U.S. When I Die, the first single, came out in the summer of 1969.

At the end of 1971, Motherlode disbanded. In 2011, When I Die was inducted into the Canadian Songwriters Hall of Fame.

Singles:

When I Die	Revolver 002	1969
Memories Of A Broken Promise	Revolver 004	1969
Dear Old Daddy Bill	Revolver 005	1970
Whippoorwill	Revolver 008	1970
All That's Necessary	Revolver 011	1971

Albums/CDs:

When I Die	Revolver RLPS 501	1969
Tapped Out	Revolver RLPS 502	1970
When I Die/Tapped Out	Pace 007	1995

Mother Tucker's Yellow Duck

Pat Caldwell (mouth harp, vocals)
Charles Faulkner (bass)
Roger Law (guitar) Replaced by Les Law
Hugh Lockhead (drums)
Donny Mc Dougall (guitar, vocals)

Formed by Hugh Lockwood and Roger Law in 1967, this quintet from the west coast had its first hit, One Ring Jane on London Records in the spring of 1969. Pat Caldwell was responsible for coming up with the group's name. After they broke up in 1971, Donny Mc Dougall joined The Guess Who in 1972.

Singles:
One Ring Jane	Duck 2	1969
I/Funny Feeling	Duck 1	1969
Starting A New Day	Capitol 72614	1970

Albums/CDs:
Home Grown Stuff	Capitol 6304	1969
Starting A New Day	Capitol 6352	1970

Moxy Fruvous

Michael Ford (guitar, percussion, vocals)
Murray Foster (bass, guitar, vocals)
Jean Ghomeshi (drums, percussion, vocals)
David Matheson (guitar, accordion, vocals)

This quasi-a capella group began as street buskers on the streets of Toronto's Harbourfront in 1990. It was not until February, 1992 that they decided to pursue music as a career.

In 1992 they released an independent cassette of six songs. One of them, *King of Spain* became their first video which was shot outside of the Bloor Cinema in Toronto. The song is a fable about a dethroned European monarch who is now working in Toronto for minimum wage. David Matheson is responsible for giving it a Brazilian beat.

Their music is often hard to define because their songs are drawn from various influences, from Barbershop singing of the late 19th century to the Broadway musicals of the 1920s, 1930s and 1940s. Another is jazz.

Signed to Warner Music, Moxy Fruvous's debut album *Bargainville* was released early in 1993. It contained King of Spain and Stuck In The 90s, the first single.

Individually, Ghomeshi and Matheson are baritones, Ford's a tenor and Foster's a bass. Together, they make one diverse musical group. Their subsequent releases continued to show the group's musical growth.

Singles:
King of Spain	Wea 93134	1992
Stuck In The 90s	Wea 93134	1993
My Baby Loves A Bunch of Authors	Wea 93134	1993
Fell In Love	Wea 93134	1994
I Will Hold On	TND 0182	1999

Albums/CDs:
Bargainville	Wea 93134	1993
Wood	Wea 10616	1995
The B Album (EP)	Wea 15223	1996
Live Noise	Wea 23269	1998
Thornhill	True North TND 0182	1999

Moxy

Buddy Caine
Earl Johnson
Terry Juric
Buzz Sherman
Bill Wade

Moxy evolved from Leigh Ashford in late 1974, and was comprised of Buzz Sherman, Terry Juric, Buddy Caine, Earl Johnson, and Bill Wade. Their first three albums, Moxy, Moxy II, and Ridin' High featured an amalgam of simple, straight-forward lyrics underscored by simple guitar licks. Before each concert, a tape made by Wade introduced the band: "Someone once said that he who makes the loudest noise always gets heard first." Then there would be the sound of a jet and a phased sonic boom followed by, Ladies And Gentlemen, Will You Please Welcome Moxy!

The group went through other personnel changes. By the release of Under The Lights in 1978 both Wade and Sherman had left, and were replaced by Danny Bilan and Michael Rynoski respectively. Sherman who left to start his own group, Buzzsaw, died in a motorcycle accident on June 16, 1983. In 1984 the independent Ahed label released A Tribute To Buzz Sherman. Bill Wade died of cancer on July 27, 2001.

Other members of the group included Woody West, who had replaced Johnson, and Doug MacAskill who replaced West. In 2001 the lineup was comprised of Kim Hunt, Earl Johnson, Bud Caine, Brian Maxim, and Jim Samson.

Singles:

Can't You See I'm A Star/ Out of the Darkness	Yorkville 45105	1974
Take It or Leave It	POL 2065-318	1976
Cause There's Another	POL 2065-340	1977
Sing To Me	POL 2065-387	1978
Sailor's Delight	POL 2065-394	1978
Ridin' High/Change In My Life	Ahed AH 1010	1984

Albums/CDs:

Moxy	Polydor 2490-132	1976
Moxy II	Polydor 2480-372	1976
Take It or Leave It	Polydor 2480-	1977
Ridin' High	Polydor 2480-402	1977
Under The Lights	Polydor 2480-460	1978
A Tribute To Buzz Shearman	Ahed AZ-8277	1984
Self Destruction	Pacemaker 001	1994
Moxy (CD-R)	Pacemaker 016	1996
Moxy II (CD-R)	Pacemaker 017	1996
Moxy V	Pacemaker Make-1	2000

Anne Murray

Anne Murray was born in Springhill, Nova Scotia on June 20, 1945. She was English Canada's first international female singing star. Since 1970 she has sold over 22 million albums earned four Grammys and almost 30 Junos. In 1980 the Canadian Recording Industry Association honoured her as the female recording artist of the decade.

Growing up her parents encouraged her to take piano and vocal lessons. She made her first TV appearance on Moncton, New Brunswick's CKCW-TV's Supper Club where she sang Moon River. Her first professional audition was in 1964 for the CBC-TV show, Singalong Jubilee, where she met her future husband, Bill Langstroth, whom she married in 1975 on her 30th birthday. Anne ended up being a regular on CBC-TV's Let's Go.

Brian Ahern, musical director of Singalong Jubilee, later invited Anne to record an album for Arc Records and in 1968, *What About Me* was released. Anne's first major hit on Capitol Records was Gene McLellan's Snowbird, which sold over one million copies and made her the first female artist from Canada to receive a gold record, when she appeared on The Merv Griffin Show in November 1970.

Since the early 1970s Anne Murray has received many other honors, including chairperson of the Toronto Save The Children Fund from 1978-1980, and a star on Hollywood's famous Walkway of Stars.

Anne returned to EMI with the release of her CD, *Croonin'* in 1993. A year later came a box set honoring her work as one of our premier songstresses. In 1997 there was *An Intimate Evening With Anne Murray...Live*, which was also a CBC-TV special of the same name. Her next two albums were *What A Wonderful World* (1999) and *What A Wonderful Christmas* (2001). Two of her singles are million sellers: Snowbird on November 16, 1970 and You Needed Me on October 26, 1978.

Singles:

Title	Label/Number	Year
Paths of Victory	Yorkville 45021	1968
It's All Over	Yorkville 45023	1968
Thirsty Boots	Capitol 72592	1969
Bidin' My Time	Capitol 72604	1970
Snowbird/Rain	Capitol 72623	1970
Snowbird/Just Bidin' My Time	Capitol 2738	1970
Sing Hi, Sing Low	Capitol 72631	1970
A Stranger In My Place	Capitol 72637	1971
It Takes Time	Capitol 72642	1971
Talk It Over In The Morning	Capitol 72649	1971
I Say A Little Prayer/By The Time I Get To Phoenix (with Glen Campbell)	Capitol 3200	1971
Cotton Jenny	Capitol 72657	1972
Robbie's Song For Jesus	Capitol 72668	1972
Danny's Song	Capitol 72682	1972/73
What About Me	Capitol 72700	1973
Send A Little Love My Way	Capitol 72704	1973
Love Song	Capitol 72714	1973/74
He Thinks I Still Care	Capitol 3867	1974
Son Of A Rotten Gambler	Capitol 72737	1974
You Won't See Me	Capitol 72727	1974
Just One Look	Capitol 72737	1974
Day Tripper	Capitol 4000	1974/75
Uproar	Capitol 4025	1975
Sunday Sunrise	Capitol 4142	1975
The Call	Capitol 4207	1976
Golden Oldie	Capitol 4265	1976
Things	Capitol 4329	1976
Sunday School To Broadway	Capitol 4375	1977

Walk Right Back	Capitol 4527	1978
You Needed Me	Capitol 4574	1978
Hey Daddy	Capitol 72801	1978/79
I Just Fall in Love Again	Capitol 4675	1979
Shadows In The Moonlight	Capitol 4716	1979
Broken Hearted Me	Capitol 4773	1979
Daydream Believer	Capitol 4813	1979
Lucky Me	Capitol 4848	1980
I'm Happy Just to Dance With You	Capitol 4878	1980
Could I Have This Dance	Capitol 4920	1980
Blessed Are The Believers	Capitol 4987	1981
We Don't Have To Hold Out	Capitol 5013	1981
It's All I Can Do	Capitol 5023	1981
Christmas Medley	Capitol SPRO 9723	1981
Song For The Mira	Capitol 72910	1982
Another Sleepless Night	Capitol 5083	1982
Hey Baby!	Capitol 5145	1982
Somebody's Always Saying Goodbye	Capitol 5183	1982/83
A Little Good News	Capitol 5264	1983
That's Not The Way	Capitol 5305	1984
Just Another Woman In Love	Capitol 5344	1984
Nobody Loves Me Like You Do	Capitol 5401	1984
I Don't Think I'm Ready For You	Capitol 5472	1985
Time Don't Run Out On Me	Capitol 86436	1985
Now and Forever (You And Me)	Capitol 5547	1986
Who's Leaving Who	Capitol 5576	1986
My Life's A Dance	Capitol 73002	1986
Are You Still In Love With Me	Capitol 44005	1987
Anyone Can Do The Heartbreak	Capitol 44053	1987
On And On	Capitol 5655	1987
Perfect Strangers (with Doug Mallory)	Capitol 44134	1988
Flying On Your Own	Capitol 44219	1988
Slow Passin' Time	Capitol 44272	1988/89
Who But You	Capitol 44341	1989
If I Ever Fall In Love Again (w/Kenny Rogers)	Capitol 44432	1989
Feed This Fire	Capitol 94102	1990
Bluebird	Capitol 94102	1990/91
New Way Out	Capitol 94102	1991
Everyday	Capitol 96310	1991
I Can See Arkansas	Capitol 96310	1992
Make Love To Me	Capitol 27012	1993
The Wayward Wind	Capitol 27012	1994
Over You	EMI 31158	1994/95
What Would it Take	EMI 36501	1996
That's What My Love Is For (w/Aaron Neville)	EMI 36501	1996/97
That's the Way It Goes	EMI 36501	1997

Somebody's Always Saying Goodbye	EMI 59694	1997
Let There Be Love (w/Dawn Langstroth)	EMI 20932	1999
What a Wonderful World	EMI 20932	2000

Albums/CDs:

What About Me	ARC As-782	1968
This Way Is My Way	Capitol ST 6330	1969
Honey, Wheat, & Laughter	Capitol ST 6350	1970
Straight, Clean & Simple	Capitol ST 6359	1971
Talk It Over In The Morning	Capitol ST 6366	1971
Anne Murray/Glen Campbell	Capitol SW 869	1971
Annie	Capitol ST 6376	1972
Danny's Song	Capitol ST 6393	1973
A Love Song	Capitol ST 6409	1974
Country	Capitol ST 6425	1974
Highly Prized Possession	Capitol ST 6428	1974
Together	Capitol ST 11433	1975
Keeping In Touch	Capitol ST 11559	1976
There's A Hippo In My Tub	Capitol ST 6454	1977
Let's Keep It That Way	Capitol ST 11743	1978
New Kind of Feeling	Capitol SW 11849	1979
I'll Always Love You	Capitol S00-12012	1979
A Country Collection	Capitol ST-12039	1980
Somebody's Waiting	Capitol SOO-12064	1980
Greatest Hits	Capitol Soo-12110	1980
Where Do You Go When You Dream	Capitol S00-12144	1981
Christmas Wishes	Capitol SB-16232	1981
Hottest Night of the Year	Capitol ST-12225	1982
A Little Good News	Capitol ST-12301	1983
Heart Over Mind	Capitol SJ-12363	1984
Something To Talk About	Capitol SJ-12466	1986
Harmony	Capitol ST-12562	1987
Country Hits	Capitol CDP7-46487	1987
As I Am	Capitol C1-48764	1988
Christmas	Capitol C1-90886	1988
Greatest Hits Volume Ii	Capitol 92072	1989
You Will	Capitol 94102	1990
Yes I Do	Capitol 96310	1991
Fifteen of The Best	Capitol 95954	1992
Croonin'	Capitol 27012	1993
The Best of...So Far	EMI 31158	1994
Now And Forever (Box Set)	EMI 31159	1994
The Best of the Season	EMI 31145	1994
Anne Murray	EMI 36501	1996
An Intimate Evening With (Live)	EMI 59694	1997
The Signature Series Volume 1	EMI 95407	1998
The Signature Series Volume 2	EMI 95408	1998
The Signature Series Volume 3	EMI 95409	1998
What a Wonderful World	EMI 20932	1999
What a Wonderful Christmas	EMI 34203	2001

Bruce Murray

Bruce Murray was born in Springhill, Nova Scotia on April 11, 1952. As Anne Murray's younger brother, he carried on the family's musical tradition. He took piano lessons as a boy and within six months he was a church organist. At age eleven he studied voice with Karen Mills, to whom he dedicated his self-titled debut album, released by Quality Records in 1976.

After the release of the album's second single, We're All Alone, he toured with Olivia Newton-John, Tanya Tucker and actor/comedian Dom DeLuise.

Bruce later appeared at the Troubadour in Los Angeles, and made a number of guest appearances on such TV shows as Juliette, City Lights, The Juno Awards, 90 Minutes Live, and The Bobby Vinton Show.

In addition to three singles and one album on CBS Records, he also had an album on Capitol. Today his singing career is limited to background vocals on his sister's recordings.

Singles:

Belle of the Ball	Quality 2188X	1975
We're All Alone	Quality Q2223X	1977
Could it be Love I Found Tonight	CBS C4-4172	1977
Who, What, When, Where, Why	CBS	1978
In the Still of the Night	CBS	1979
From Now On	Capitol 72885	1982

Albums/CDs:

Bruce Murray	Quality SV 1920	1976
There's Always a Goodbye	CBS PCC-80015	1979
Two Hearts	Capitol ST 6512	1984

Alannah Myles

Alannah was born in Toronto on December 25, 1958 to Shelagh and William Byles With her father a former broadcaster she grew up listening to radio in Toronto. She later moved to Buckhorn, Ontario (north of Peterborough). She wanted to be a singer since she was five-years old. At eleven she started playing the guitar. She started honing her craft in the mid-1980s. She changed her last name to Myles and started projecting the image of a sexy pop star with her powerful voice and stage persona. By the time she was nineteen she was performing in various clubs in and around Toronto.

In 1980 she met singer/songwriter Christopher Ward who introduced her to Bessie Smith, Billie Holiday and Patsy Cline. Four years later, Myles and Ward met David Tyson, a songwriter who had written for Joe Cocker and Donna Summer.

Together they wrote the songs that ended up on Alannah Myles' self-titled debut album on Atlantic Records. When it was released in 1989, it went on to sell more than five million copies and held the record for being the biggest selling debut album by a Canadian artist.

Black Velvet, the second single released from the album, went to number one on Billboard's Hot 100 on March 24, 1990 where it stayed for two weeks. It was certified a million seller on March 20, 1990.

In 1992, Song Instead of a Kiss from Rockinghorse went to number one in RPM.

Alannah's subsequent releases, *A-Lan-Nah* and *Arival*, did not do as well as her debut album. In 1998 the album, *Very Best of Alannah Myles* was released.

Singles:

Love Is	Atlantic 78 89187	1989
Black Velvet	Atlantic 78 88387	1989
Still Got This Thing	Atlantic 81956	1990
Lover of Mine	Atlantic 81956	1990
Song Instead of A Kiss	Atlantic 82402	1992
Tumbleweed	Atlantic 82402	1992
Our World Our Times	Atlantic 82402	1993
Livin' on a Memory	Atlantic 82402	1993
Sonny Say You Will	Atlantic 82402	1993
Family Secret	Atlantic 82842	1995
Blow Wind Blow	Atlantic 82842	1996
Bad 4 You	ARK21 8-23002	1997

Albums/CDs:

Alannah Myles	Atlantic 81956	1989
Rockinghorse	Atlantic 82402	1992
A-Lan-Nah	Atlantic 82842	1995
Arival	ARK21 8-23002	1997
Very Best of Alannah Myles	ARK21 80925	1998

Myles & Lenny

Myles Cohen   (lead vocals, guitars)
Lenny Solomon (violins, viola, mandolin)

Myles was born in Montreal and had been writing music since he was 13. A self-taught guitarist he began playing with bands around Toronto while still in his teens. The son of Stanley Solomon, the Toronto Symphony Orchestra's principal violist, Lenny began studying the piano at age six and playing the violin at seven. He later studied music at McGill University in Montreal, and has played violin in the National Youth Orchestra. The latter was a featured soloist on albums by Flying Circus and Luke Gibson.

The two first met while attending high school in Toronto. When they discovered their musical styles were compatible, they decided to become a duo in 1969. Based in Toronto, they were part of the Canadian music scene for seven years.

Their first real engagement was the 1969 Mariposa Songwriters Conference where the duo learned to grow professionally and musically.

A year's contract with GRT Records in 1972 allowed them to make their very first record, *Time To Know Your Friends*. Two years later they joined Columbia where they experienced major success.

On tour to promote their self-titled debut album in 1974 were three backup musicians: Ivan Boudreau on bass, Bill MacKay on drums and Rick Doyle on guitar.

With each passing year they were together, they began to experience musical differences. On June 2, 1976 Myles dissolved his partnership with Lenny. Myles formed his own band named after himself, which later became known as Ambush. They were together from November 1976 to April 1977.

In 1978 Myles went solo and signed with the Toronto independent label, Change Records. His debut album, *Take A Ride With Me* and single, a remake of the old Myles & Lenny hit Hold On Lovers, were released that same year. He also recorded Holiday, which was a bigger hit for The Bee Gees in 1967.

Lenny Solomon went on to form a jazz quintet named after himself. His jazz recordings include After You've Gone (Bay Cities BCD 2005 - 1992) and The Gershwin Sessions (Jazz Inspiration 9309- 1995).

By Myles & Lenny
Singles:

Time To Know Your Friends	GRT 1230-28	1972
Can You Give It All To Me	Columbia C4-4069	1974/75
Hold On Lovers	CBS C4-4091	1975
I Care Enough	CBS C4-4114	1976
Holding Out Too Long	CBS	1978

Albums/CDs:

Myles And Lenny	Columbia KC 33366	1975
It Isn't The Same		1975

By Myles Cohen
Singles:

Hold On Lovers	Change CH 45002	1978
Holding Out Too Long	Change CH 45008	1978
Dirty Business	Change CH 45012	1979
Start All Over Again	Change CH 45021	1979
Holiday	Change	1979
Jamaica	Change	1979

Albums/CDs:

Take A Ride With Me	Change CLP 8002	1978
Start All Over Again	Change CLP 8005	1979
Myles High	Change CLP 8012	1980

The Mynah Birds

Ritchie Grand (drums)
Ricky James Matthews (vocals)
Bruce Palmer (guitar)
John Yachimak (rhythm guitar)
Neil Young (guitar)

Fronted by Ricky James Matthews, The Mynah Birds started in Toronto in 1965. Bruce Palmer had left Jack London and The Sparrows to join the group.

In 1965 The Mynah Birds recorded one single on Columbia Records, The Mynah Bird Hop. By the end of March 1966 they had broken up.

Neil Young and Bruce Palmer went on to become members of Buffalo Springfield, while Young became a member of Crosby, Stills, Nash and Young before going solo in 1970. Ricky Matthews changed his name to Rick James and became one of the progenitors of punk funk.

Single:

The Mynah Bird Hop	Columbia C4-2650	1965

Bif Naked

Born in 1971 in New Delhi, India, Bif Naked was adopted by two American missionaries who ended up settling in Winnipeg, Manitoba. At 17 she was performing on stage as a member of the group Jungle Milk. Clad only in her lingerie, she sang a combination of rap and Doris Day songs. She then toured with Gorilla Gorilla, an underground band, and fronted two other groups, Chrome Dog and G-Force Guitar Band. Tired of singing in all-male bands she wanted to create a sound and style all her own. In 1994 she recorded the EP, Four Songs And A Poem, which was released on Plum Records. That same year came her self-titled debut album, featuring Daddy's Getting Married. Four years later, Aquarius released, *I Bificus*, which included the popular Spaceman. Her song, We're Not Gonna Take It was included on the soundtrack of the film, Ready To Rumble (2000) and she made her film debut in the LS Entertainment film, Lunch With Charles (2001).

Singles:

Daddy's Getting Married	Plum Records 4006	1994
Never	Plum Records 4006	1995
Chotee	Aquarius 00584	1998
Spaceman	Aquarius 00584	1998
Lucky	Aquarius 00584	1998
Moment of Weakness	Aquarius 00584	1999
Lucky	Aquarius 00584	1999
We're Not Gonna Take It	Warner 92914	2000
I Love Myself Today	LAVA/Atlantic 83509	2001

Albums/CDs:

Four Songs & A Poem (Ep)	Plum Records 4005	1994
Bif Naked	Plum Records 4006	1994
I Bificus	Aquarius 00584	1998
Another Five Songs & A Poem (Ep)	Warner 92914	2000
Purge	Lava/Atlantic 83509	2001

Nash the Slash

Nash the Slash, whose real name is Jeff Plewman, was a member of the Toronto rock band FM from 1976 to 1978. As the most famous member of the trio, he wore bandages to disguise his face. Born and raised in Toronto, he was a classically trained violinist. When he left FM, he lived in England where he did a few punk shows, worked on Gary Numans' Dance album, and created the electronic sound effects used for the film, The Kidnapping of the President. He also wrote scores for the film Road Kill, and some National Film Board productions.

He has made several solo recordings on Cut-Throat Records, notably And You Thought You Were Normal, Decomposing, and Thrash, and the soundtrack to the classic silent film, Nosferatu (2001).

He retired in 2012 and died at 66 on May 12, 2014.

Singles:

Dead Man's Curve	CUT 3/WRC3-1173	1980
1984 (12")	Quality QDC 301	1984

Albums/CDs:

Bedside Companion (Ep)	Cut-Throat CUT-1	1978
Dreams And Nightmares	Cut-Throat CUT-2	1978
Children Of The Night	Virgin VL 2212	1981
Decomposing	Cut-Throat CUT-5	1982
And You Thought You Were Normal	Cut-Throat CUT-6	1982
American Bandages	Quality Sv 2132	1984
Thrash	Cut-Throat 3 CD	1999

National Velvet

Maria Del Mar (lead vocals)
Mark Crossley (guitar)
Garry Flint (drums)
Mark Storm (bass) Replaced by Darrell Flint

This Toronto group was led by lead vocalist and principal songwriter Maria Del Mar who formed her first band, Fatal K.O. as a teenager. She later went to Montreal and then Toronto where she realized her dream of becoming a singer. After meeting Mark Storm, it was the beginning of what eventually became National Velvet in 1984.

Storm also had a dream of being a rock singer. He rented a bass guitar and began writing songs. The rest of the group came from such punk rock bands as Sylum, United State, and Blank Generation.

In 1986 they recorded a self-titled four song EP that was released independently. Over the next nine years, they recorded for Intrepid, Capitol and BMG.

With the release of their CD, *Wildseed* in 1995, the lineup of the group was comprised of Del Mar, Crossley, Garry Flint, along with Darrell Flint and Tim Welch.

Singles:

Pacifist At Risk	Intrepid N1-90336	1987
Flesh Under Skin		1988
68 Hours (12")		1988
Bam Bam	Intrepid N1-90336	1988/89
Shine On	Cap 93939	1990
Sex Gorilla	Cap 93939	1990

Albums/CDs:

National Velvet	ENV 8609-001/2	1986
National Velvet	Intrepid N1-90336	1988
Courage	Capitol 93939	1990
Wildseed	BMG 51002	1995

Rick Neufeld

Rick Neufeld was born in 1947 and raised in the Mennonite farming community of Boissevain in Manitoba. After studying architecture at the University of Manitoba and travelling throughout Europe and North America, he decided to concentrate on a new career as a singer/songwriter. He began playing at coffeehouses throughout Canada, and performed at many folk festivals. In the early 1970s he hosted his own CBC-TV series called The Songsingers, and later he co-hosted, with Colleen Peterson, On The Road on CBC-TV.

His best known songs are Moody Manitoba Morning, which was recorded by The Five Bells in 1969, and Country Princess.

He recorded his debut album, *Hiway Child* in 1971. His other albums are *Prairie Dog* and *Manitoba Songs*.

In 1980 he stopped performing and became a tour bus driver for Graham Shaw, a singer/songwriter from Winnipeg who needed a bus for his eastern tour. While driving Bruce Cockburn on one of his tours, Neufeld decided that he liked the road enough to do it for a living. Nicknamed "The Noof," he has driven for Streetheart, Harlequin, Red Rider, Glass Tiger, Kim Mitchell, Anne Murray, Colin James, and Prairie Oyster among others.

Singles:

Moody Manitoba Morning	Warner Bros 5025	1970
Country Princess	Astra AS 1001	1971
Sing (A Christmas Song)	Astra AS 4531	1972
A Most Amazing Lady	RCA PB-50062	1975
A Love Worth Living For	RCA KPBO 0039	

Albums/CDs:

Hiway Child	Astra AS 1001	1971
Prairie Dog	RCA	1975
Manitoba Songs		1978

Night Sun

Les Casson (congas, bodhran, percussion, background vocals)
Chris Coleman (mandolin, clarinet, Irish flute, tin whistles, background vocals)
Bonnie Dawson (accordion, acoustic guitar, background vocals)
Ellen Hamilton (lead vocal, acoustic guitar, banjo)
Adam Hodge (bass, background vocals)

Night Sun started in 1990 in the Inuit town of Iqualuit in the Northwest Territories (now Nunavut), with Ellen Hamilton, Bob Longworth, and brothers Chris and Erik Coleman. They released their self-titled independent debut album in 1991.

After the release of their second CD, Calling, Ellen Hamilton and Chris Coleman moved to Kingston in 1995 where they were joined by Les Casson, Bonnie Dawson, and Alec Barken. Adam Hodge replaced Barken in 1997. Les hails from Fonthill, Ontario, while the rest of the group is from Kingston, Ontario.

In 1996, Ellen Hamilton won Ontario's Songs from the Heart songwriting competition for Damn This Wind, the opening track on *Calling*. She also received the Ontario Council of Folk Festivals' songwriting award that same year.

During the last four years they have established themselves as one of Canada's top folk acts, and have played at many folk music festivals across Canada and the United States, notably the Winnipeg Folk Festival, Owen Sound's Summerfolk, Inuvik's Great Northern Arts Festival, Ottawa Folk Festival, Iqualuit's Tooniq Tyme, Sunfest in London, Ontario, and the All Folks Festival in Kingston. In 1998 they participated in the Canada Day Closing Ceremonies in Ottawa.

Albums/CDs:

Night Sun	Night Sun NSCD 001	1991
Calling	Night Sun NSCD 002	1993
Home	Night Sun NSCD 004	1997
One Moment Of Grace	Night Sun NSCD 005	1999
Drive	Night Sun NSCD 006	2004

Noah

Paul Clapper (vocals, keyboards) Replaced by Ron Neilson (1972)
Barry "Buzz" Vandersel (lead vocals, bass)
Marinus Vandertogt (guitar, background vocals)
Peter Vandertogt (drums)

This Trenton, Ontario group began as Tyme And A Half in 1968.

They were comprised of Paul Clapper, Barry Vandersel, and Marinus and Peter Vandertogt. Their first two Singles:, It's Been A Long Time and Cassandra were released on the Nimbus Nine label.

In 1970 they changed their name to Noah because they needed a name to go along with their new sound. They were no longer playing AM radio material but songs with a heavier rock sound. RCA Victor released their self-titled album that same year. Their next album, on Dunhill Records, was *Peaceman's Farm* (1972). The title track helped popularize the band's music.

That same year, Clapper left and was replaced by Ron Neilson on guitar. The next major change came in 1975 when Barry Vandersel suddenly died and the group broke up. Ron Neilson is a member of the showband, The Neilsons, who played gospel music in churches as well as country music. In 1995 their first, self-titled CD was released.

By Tyme And A Half
Singles:

It's Been A Long Time	Nimbus Nine 9008	1969
Cassandra	Nimbus Nine 9011	1969

By Noah
Singles:

Summer Sun	Dunhill	1971
Peaceman's Farm	Dunhill 4308	1972

Albums/CDs:

Noah	RCA LSP 4432	1970
Peaceman's Farm	RCA DSX 50117	1972

The Nocturnals

Carl Ericson (sax)
Wayne Evans (bass)
Ron Henshel (lead guitar)
Bill McBeth (lead vocals, drums)
Roger Skinner (sax)
Chad Thorpe (organ)

The Nocturnals started in 1958 in Haney, British Columbia. The original group played country music at Eagles clubs and Legion halls. As the older members left the group, they switched to rock and roll. The lineup, which remained the same for almost ten years, consisted of Ron Henshel, Chad Thorpe, Bill McBeth, Carl Ericson and Wayne Evans. With the addition of Roger Skinner in 1964-65, the Vancouver-based band had expanded to six members.

Their first hit was, Because You're Gone, on Regency Records in the summer of 1965. They also recorded on Trans-World and Embassy.

They were the only west coast group to appear at Expo 67. They gradually changed their sound again, this time to rhythm and blues.

The Nocturnals broke up in 1968. Evans joined The Missing Links, an east coast band; McBeth became a member of Canada which later became Scrubbaloe Caine, Ericson switched to playing country, while Thorpe became a marine biologist and Henshel, a postman.

Singles:

Because You're Gone	Regency 959	1965
This Ain't Love	Regency 964	1966
Ain't No Big Thing	Trans-World 1669	1967
Lovin' Blues	Trans-World 1681	1967
Detroit	Embassy	1967

Don Norman and The Other Four

Gary Comeau (lead guitar, background vocals)
Brian Dewhurst (drums)
Ron Greene (rhythm guitar, keyboards, backing vocals)
Bill Helman (bass, background vocals)
Don Norman (lead vocals, rhythm guitar)

The history of Don Norman and The Other Four began on Sparks Street in Ottawa in the late summer of 1965, when Gary Comeau, Ron Greene, Bill Helman and Paul Huot met. Don Norman was invited to join during a chance meeting between Gary and Ron. It was during this time that Paul declined to join the group. With the addition of Brian Dewhurst, the band first called themselves Don Norman and The Esquires. Since another Ottawa group was called The Esquires, they were taken to court over the use of the name. Norman signed an out-of-court settlement that ordered he discontinue the name "Esquires".

Gary Comeau suggested they call themselves Don Norman and The Other Four. John Matthews was then added as second lead vocalist and sax player. They were managed by John Pozer, a local radio and televisin personality.

They made their first single in the spring of 1966 at the RCA Victor Studios in Toronto. It was All Of My Life, written by Don Norman. The B side was The Bounce, a song originally recorded by The Olympics in 1963. All Of My Life and

The Bounce were re-recorded in French as Je T'ai Cherche and Le Bounce respectively, and released on the Sol Pege label.

In the summer of 1966, Comeau left to join The Townsmen, another Ottawa group. He was replaced by Art Kirkby on guitar and flute.

Early in 1967, they made their second single, Low Man, another Norman original at Stereo Sound Studios in Montreal. It was released on the Sir John A label, which was distributed by RCA.

That same year, the group lost Bill Helman, Brian Dewhurst and John Matthews. They were replaced by John Winskell on lead guitar and background vocals, Rick Paradis on lead vocals, and John "Skip" Layton on drums. They played together until they disbanded in the summer of 1967.

Singles:
All Of My Life/Le Bounce	Barry 3419/MGM 13562	1966
Low Man	Sir John A RG-1015	1966
Your Place In My Heart	Sir John A RG-1019	1967
Low Man	Sir John A 3	1967

Tom Northcott

Born in Vancouver on August 29, 1943, Tom Northcott primary musical influence was his father who was a cellist and singer.

Tom was first in a band called the Kerrisdale Kiwanas Boys Band in which he played the trumpet. He later taught himself how to play the guitar.

In 1958 he learned the three chords necessary to play The Everly Brothers' Bye Bye Love and George Hamilton IV's If You Don't Know, I Ain't Gonna Tell You in a talent contest where he came in second.

He later started singing Hank Snow songs and later honed his skills as a entertainer in the revue, The Talentaires, sponsored by a branch of the Legion.

Between 1964 and 1966, Tom was the star of the CBC TV show, Let's Go, and sang with CKLG's Vancouver Playboys. During the summer of 1965 they toured together.

In 1965 Northcott recorded the single, She Loves Me, She Loves Me Not/I'll Cry Tomorrow, on his own Syndrome label, with the Vancouver Playboys singing backup. Another single released in late 1965, Just Don't backed by Let Me Know was by The Tom Northcott Trio. On Goin' Down, the next single, Tom was backed by The Eternal Triangle which was comprised of Howie Vickers (The Collectors & Chilliwack) and Susan Pesklevitz (The Poppy Family)

When he left Let's Go in 1966, he had formed his own trio, which, besides himself, was made up of Rick Enns on bass, and Mike "Kat" Hendrikse on drums. They were together for less than a year.

Enns joined The United Empire Loyalists, who had one single, No No No (1967).

After the release of Sunny Goodge Street during the summer of 1967, Northcott signed with Warner. One of his hits with the label was The Rainmaker in 1969/70, which used five percussionists and a string section. During this time he had also started his own production facility, Studio 3, where he produced such acts as Crosstown Bus, The Irish Rovers and Anne Attenborrow.

Northcott retired from the music business after the the release of The Last Thing On My Mind on Warner Brothers in 1972. He sold his studio to become a fisherman. He only returned to the studio to record Born To Boogie on his Fifi Laflamme label, and The Canada Song about the constitutional debate in Canada in 1981. In 1983 he studied to become a lawyer. After graduation he took up writing songs again. In 1993 he released So You Thought You Heard It All in 1993, and in 1997 the *Joyful Songs of Leonard Cohen*.

Today, he lives in Vancouver.

By The Tom Northcott Trio
Singles:

Just Don't	Syndrome 1001	1965
She Loves Me	Syndrome 1002	1966
Goin' Down	Syndrome 1007	1966

By Tom Northcott
Singles:

Sunny Goodge Street	New Syndrome 18	1967
1941	Warner Bros 7160	1968
Girl From The North Country	Warner Bros 7221	1968
Make Me An Island	Warner Bros 7283	1969
The Rainmaker	Warner Bros 7330	1969/70
Crazy Jane	New Syndrome 106	1970
I Think It's Gonna Rain Today	UNI 55262	1970/71
Spaceship Races	UNI 55262	1971
The Last Thing On My Mind	Warner Bros CW4016	1972
The Trouble With Love	Axe	1990

Albums/CDs:

The Best Of Tom Northcott	Warner Bros WS 1859	1970
Upside Downside	UNI 73108	1971
The Best Of Tom Northcott 1964-1971	Neptoon	1990
So You Thought You Heard It All	Full Circle CD 1	1993
Joyful Songs of Leonard Cohen	Full Circle CD 2	1997

Northern Lights

For the first time in Canadian history, an all-star lineup of Canadian artists gathered together under one roof to record, Tears Are Not Enough (Columbia 7BEN-7073 - 1985) for Ethiopian famine relief. David Foster wrote the music, while Bryan Adams and his songwriting partner Jim Vallance wrote the lyrics. Rachel Paiement (of Cano fame) wrote the French translation of the words. Paul Hyde of the Payola$ christened the song. The video of Tears Are Not Enough was directed by Stephen Surjik. It was filmed in Toronto on February 10, 1986.

It was Canada's answer to British pop star Bob Geldof's Band Aid benefit recording of Do They Know It's Christmas? and the American relief recording We Are The World by USA For Africa.

The following Canadians participated in "Tears Are Not Enough":

Bryan Adams
Paul Anka
Carroll Baker
Veronique Beliveau
Doug Bennett
    (*of Doug & The Slugs*)
Salome Bey
Liona Boyd
John Candy
    (*actor/comedian*)
Robert Charlebois
Tom Cochrane
Bruce Cockburn
Burton Cummings
Lisa Dal Bello
Claude Dubois
Rik Emmett
    (*of Triumph*)
Wayne Gretzky
    (*Canadian hockey's 'The Great One'*)
Corey Hart
Ronnie Hawkins

Dan Hill
Honeymoon Suite
Tommy Hunter
Paul Hyde
    (*of The Payola$*)
Martha Johnson
    (*of Martha & The Muffins*)
Geddy Lee
    (*of Rush*)
Eugene Levy
    (*actor/comedian*)
Gordon Lightfoot
Murray McLauchlan
Frank Mills
Joni Mitchell
Kim Mitchell
Anne Murray
Bruce Murray
Aldo Nova
Catherine O'Hara
    (*actress/comedienne*)

Oscar Petersen
Carole Pope
  (of Rough Trade)
Lorraine Segato
  (of The Parachute Club)
Paul Shaffer
  (Music director of NBC's
  'Late Night with David Letterman)

Graham Shaw
Jane Siberry
Liberty Silver
Wayne St. John
Ian Thomas
Jim Vallance
Neil Young
Alfie Zappacosta

The Northern Pikes

Merl Bryck (vocals, guitar)
Rob Esch (drums) Replaced by Don Schmid
Bryan Potvin (vocals, guitar)
Jay Sembo (vocals, bass)

From Saskatoon, The Northern Pikes evolved in March 1984 from other Saskatchewan groups. Jay Semko was in The Idols and Seventeen Envelope; Merl Bryck in The Idols; Glen Holingshead in the Idols and Dash Riprock & The Boulders; Brian Potvin in Doris Daye, and Al Edgar in Doris Daye and Seventeen Envelope.

After recording a self-titled six song EP produced by the band and Mitch Barnett, the group's lineup changed to include Jay Semko, Merl Bryck, Glen Holingshead, and Bryan Potvin. In June 1984 they added drummer Rob Esch.

Their distinctive style of upbeat pop music made them a popular rock band through five studio albums and a live set. The lineup of the group from 1985 to 1987 included Esch, Potvin, Bryck, and Semko.

By the release of their album, *Big Blue Sky* in 1987, Don Schmid had replaced Esch.

The Northern Pikes broke up in 1993. Jay Semko recorded the solo album, *Mouse* (Iron Music Group – 651004 – 1995), which included the singles Strawberry Girl, Times Change, and Mouse in a Hole.

In 2000, the group reunited, and Bryan Potvin's solo album, *Heartbreakthrough* (Universal – 421992) was released.

Singles:
Teenland	Virgin VS 1379	1987
Things I Do For Money	Virgin VS 1397	1987
Wait for Me	Virgin VS 1441	1988

One Good Reason	Virgin VS	1988
Hopes Go Astray	Virgin VS 1458	1989
Let's Pretend	Virgin VS 1478	1989
She Ain't Pretty	Virgin VL 3084	1990
Girl With A Problem	Virgin VL 3084	1990
Kiss Me You Fool	Virgin VL 3084	1990/91
Dream Away	Virgin VL 3084	1991
Everyone's A Hero	Virgin PROMO	1992
Twister	Virgin 86501	1992
Believe	Virgin 86501	1993
Everything	Virgin 86501	1993
Worlds Away	Virgin 86501	1993

Albums/CDs:

Northern Pikes	B&R WRC1-3447	1984
Scene In North America	B&R WRC1-4137	1985
Big Blue Sky	Virgin VL 3001	1987
Secrets Of The Alibi	Virgin VL 3041	1988
Snow In June	Virgin VL 3084	1990
Neptune	Virgin 86501	1992
Gig (Greatest Hits Live)	Virgin 39191	1993
Hits & Assorted Secrets 1984-1993	Virgin 482192	1999

The Nylons

Ralph Cole Replaced by Arnold Robinson (1981)
Marc Connors
Paul Cooper Replaced by Micah Barnes (1990); Gavin Hope (1994); Mark Cassius Ferguson (1998)
Claude Morrison
Billy Newton-Davis Replaced by Garth Mosbaugh (1994)
Denis Simpson Replaced by Ralph Cole (1979)

This a cappella quartet from Toronto has been together since 1979. All four original members, Marc Connors, Paul Cooper, Claude Morrison and Denis Simpson, were part of the Toronto theatre scene who would sing together at parties thrown by fellow actors. After they were invited to sing at a cabaret where they ended up staying for six weeks, The Nylons were born.

During the next two years the group went through the first of several personnel changes. First to leave in April 1979 was Simpson. He was replaced by Ralph Cole who left in November 1980. Arnold Robinson joined the three original members in March 1981.

After establishing themselves on the club circuit, they caught the attention of

Attic Records who signed them to a record contract in 1981. They recorded cover versions of old rock classics such as Silhouettes by The Rays, The Lion Sleeps Tonight by The Tokens, and One Fine Day by The Chiffons.

International recognition followed six years later when Attic released the album, *Happy Together* and the single, Kiss Him Goodbye, a revival of Steam's 1969 smash, Na Na Hey Hey Kiss Him Goodbye. In 1986 they won the best singer award at the 15th Annual Tokyo Music Festival for the song Up The Ladder To The Roof, the old Supremes hit.

They opened for such acts as Pointer Sisters and Hall and Oates before headlining their own U.S. tour in 1987.

Paul Cooper decided to leave the group in 1990. He was replaced by Micah Barnes, who convinced the a capella group to sing cover songs by Prince and Labelle. On March 25, 1991 Connors died of viral pneumonia at age 43. Billy Newton-Davis, a three-time Juno Award-winning vocalist for his albums, Love Is A Contact Sport and Spellbound, became part of the group's new sound when he joined the group in 1991. In 1992 they signed with BMG Music and released the album, *Live To Love*.

In 1994 there were more personnel changes. Newton-Davis left and was replaced by Garth Mosbaugh, and Barnes was replaced by Gavin Hope from the Calgary-based group, The Earthtones.

Later that same year, BMG released the two albums, *Because* and *Harmony: The Christmas Songs*, which featured Claude Morrison's original song, What Does Christmas Mean To Me.

During the fall of 1998, Hope left to star in the Toronto production of Rent, and was replaced by Mark Cassius Ferguson.

Singles:

The Lion Sleeps Tonight	Attic AT 268	1982
Silhouettes	Attic AT 279	1983
Up The Ladder To The Roof	Attic AT 283	1983
That Kind of Man	Attic AT 290	1983
Take Me To Your Heart	Attic AT 314	1984
Perpetual Emotion		1984
Stepping Stone	Attic AT 306	1984
Combat Zone	Attic AT 324	1984
Kiss Him Goodbye	Attic AT 348	1987
Kiss Him Goodbye	Open Air 0022	1987
Happy Together	Open Air 0024	1987
Chain Gang		1987
Dance of Love	Attic AT 364	1988
Wildfire	Attic AT 388	1989
Drift Away		1989
Busy Tonight		1990

Call My Name		1991
One Fine Day		1991
Don't Look Any Further	Scotti/SCB 75255	1992
Time of the Season	Scotti/SCB 75435	1994
Love T.K.O.	Scotti/SCB 75435	1994/95
Just When I Needed You	Scotti/SCB 75435	1995
God Only Knows	Scotti/SCB 5499	1996
Smalltown Boy	Scotti/SCB 5499	1996
I Can't Go For That	Shoreline/SEL 14009	1997

Albums/CDs:

The Nylons	Attic LAT 1125	1982
One Size Fits All	Attic LAT 1152	1982
Seamless	Attic LAT 1190	1984
Happy Together	Attic LAT 1233	1987
Rockapella	Attic LAT 1254	1989
Four on the Floor	Attic ACD 1301	1991
Live to Love	Scotti SCB 75255	1992
Because	Scotti SCB 75435	1994
Harmony: The Christmas Songs	Scotti SCB 724462	1994
Run for Cover	Scotti SCB 5499	1996
Illustrious: A Collection of Classic Hits	Attic ACDM 1375	1996
Fabric of Life	Shoreline/SEL 14009	1997
Play on	Linus 207131	2002
Skin Tight	Linus 270134	2011

Ocean

Janice Brown (lead guitar)
Greg Brown (vocals, keyboards)
Jeff Jones (bass, vocals)
Chuck Slater (drums)
Dave Tamblyn (guitar)

Ocean started in Toronto in 1969. Signed to Yorkville Records, their first hit, and only million selling single, was Put Your Hand In The Hand, written by Gene MacLellan. In the U.S. they were on the Kama Sutra label.

The original lineup of the group was comprised of Janice and Greg Brown, Jeff Jones, Chuck Slater, and Dave Tamblyn. In 1973 Slater was replaced by Paul Kraussen.

After two albums, *Put Your Hand in the Hand* and *One More Chance*, the group broke up in 1975.

Jones went on to work as a session musician and actor, and in 2000 Bullseye Records released his debut solo album, *Magic Words*.

Singles:

Put Your Hand in the Hand	Yorkville 45033	1971
Deep Enough for Me	Yorkville 45035	1971
We've Got a Dream	Yorkville 45039	1971
Make the Sun Shine	Yorkville 45057	1972
One More Chance	Yorkville 45062	1972
I Have a Following	Yorkville 45078	1973

Albums/CDs:

Put Your Hand in the Hand	Yorkville YVS 33005	1971
One More Chance	Kama Sutra 2064	1972

Octavian

Daryl Alguire (lead vocals)
Warren Barbour (guitar)
Kirk Darrow (drums)
Bill Gavreau (lead guitar)
Ray Lessard (bass)
Rob McDonald (keyboards)
John Pulkinen (lead vocals)

This Ottawa septet has been together since 1969 when they were all in high school and known as Octavius. Their first engagement was at Green Door Chaudiero Club before an audience of members of Satan's Choice. The name of the group changed to "Octavian" when it was misspelled on a marquee at the Woodstock Ontario Rock Club.

They toured throughout eastern Ontario and upper New York State, and played covers of hits by The Hollies, The Association, Crosby, Stills, Nash and Young, The Beach Boys and The Beatles.

Although each member played part-time while holding down other jobs, it took six years before the group was signed to MCA Records and they could play on the road full time.

Their first single release was Good Feeling (To Know) in the fall of 1974. It failed to crack the Top 10. Their second, Round and Round fared better when it came out in 1975. That same year they also drew a sell-out crowd at the Forum in Ontario Place.

Mismanagement and communication problems with their record company forced an end to Octavian in late 1979.

Singles:
Good Feeling (To Know)	MCA 40319	1974
Round and Round	MCA 40399	1975
Hold Me, Touch Me	MCA 40454	1975/76
You Can't Do That	MCA 40530	1976
Some Kinda People		1975
Can't Stop Myself From Lovin' You	MCA 40704	1979

Album:
Simple Kinda People	MCA 2168	1975

The Odds

Paul Brennan (drums) Replaced by Pat Steward
Steven Drake (guitar, vocals)
Doug Elliot (bass)
Craig Northey (vocals, guitar)

This Vancouver-based quartet began as a cover band called Dawn Patrol in the early 1980s. They played songs from The Beatles and BTO to Terry Jacks' Seasons In The Sun.

In 1987 they began playing original material and changed their name to The Odds. Disappointed by the poor response to their music from the Canadian Music Industry, they moved to Los Angeles where they played at Coconut Teasers, a local nightclub. It led to a contract with Zoo Records in Los Angeles, and a tour with Warren Zevon.

Neapolitan, the first album by The Odds was released in 1991. From it came the single, Wendy Under The Stars.

Two years later, their second album, *Bedbugs* was released. The first single, Heterosexual Man sparked controversy because of its suggestive lyrics. Its accompanying video featured The Odds in drag, and The Kids In The Hall, a Toronto comedy troupe, as crazy drunks.

With the release of Good Weird Feeling in January 1995, Pat Steward had joined as their new drummer.

In between this and their next album, Nest, released in November 1996, Drake had engineered, produced and mixed 54-40's

Trusted By Millions, while the rest of the group worked on the soundtrack for the film, Kids In The Hall: Brain Candy (1996).

Singles:

Love Is The Subject	Zoo ZP17028/Zoo 11013	1991/92
King Of The Heap	Zoo 11013	1992
Wendy Under The Stars	Zoo 11013	1992
Good Weird Feeling (CD/S)	Elektra 61848	1992
Heterosexual Man	Zoo 11053	1993
It Falls Apart	Zoo 11053	1993
Jack Hammer	Zoo 11053	1994
Yes (Means It's Hard To Say No)		1994
Truth Untold	Wea 98980	1995
Eat My Brain	Wea 98980	1995
Someone Who's Cool	Wea 16618	1996
Make You Mad	Wea 16618	1997

Albums/CDs:

Neopolitan	Zoo 11013	1991
Bedbugs	Zoo 11053	1993
Good Weird Feeling	Wea 98980	1995
Nest	Wea 16618	1996

Offenbach

Gerry Boulet (lead vocals)
Johnny Gravel (lead guitar)
Michael Lamonthe Jr. (bass) Replaced by Norman Kerr (1977/78)
Breen LeBoeuf (added in 1979)
Wezo (Real name: Roger Belval) (drums) Replaced by Pierre Lavoie (1977/78), Robert Harrison (1979-1982)
John McVale (added in 1979)
Jean Millaire (guitar)

Formed in 1969 this Montreal blues/rock band's strength was Boulet's voice that one Toronto music critic described as sheer throat-ripping volume that has no equal anywhere. The original three members (Boulet, Lamonthe, and Belval) played in a group called Les Gants Blancs. They were one of the original bands in the province of Quebec to emerge after the heyday of American imitators Les Classels, Les Houlops and Les Sultans.

In the early 1970s rock music in Quebec was considered almost sacrilegious. Still, the group played, A Mass for the Dead, live at St. Joseph's Oratory in Montreal. Their performance helped give the group much needed publicity and it led to a recording contract with the independent Barclay label. Their debut French album in 1972 was called Offenbach Soap Opera.

They released their first English album, *Never Too Tender* (A&M Records) in 1977. That same year they became the top blues/rock group in Quebec.

Bassist Lamonthe and drummer Wezo left the group in 1977, and were replaced by Kerr and Lavoie respectively. Both Kerr and Milliare left in 1978. The former joined a jazz rock group, while the latter joined Francois Guy. In 1979, Breen LeBoeuf and John McVale were added.

Two years later, the group took a year off, and in 1982, they were back on tour in Quebec. During this time, drummer Robert Harrison left the band. He was replaced by Paul Martel.

In 1984, Gerry Boulet recorded a solo album called, *Presque 40 Ans De Blues*.

Offenbach broke up in 1986. Their last album, *Le Dernier Show* (1986) was recorded at the Montreal Forum on November 1, 1985.

Gerry Boulet went on to have a brief but successful solo career. His first album after Offenbach disbanded was *Rendezvour*, which was well received when it came out in late 1988. About this time he learned that he had colon cancer. He died on July 16, 1990.

Singles:

Caline de blues	Barclay 61821	1972
Domine Jesus Christ	Barclay 60238	1972
Memento (w/Yvon Hubert)	COGITO 002	1972
Caline de doux	Barclay 60254	1973
Quebec Rock	DERAM 571	1975
Never Too Tender	A&M 434	1976
High Down	A&M 438	1976
Chu un rocker	A&M 444	1977
Sad Song	A&M 449	1977
La Voix que j'ai	A&M 451	1977
Mes blues passent pu dans porte	KD-9050	1978
Ayoye	KD-9060	1979
Caline de blues	SS-6000	1979
Rock Bottom	SS-6002	1980
Ride Ride Ride	SS-6003	1980
Ouvre-moi ta porte	SS-6004	1981
Le bar-salon des deux toxons	SS-6006	1982
Prends pas tout mon amour	CBS C5-4336	1983
Le juge et l'assassin	CBS C5-4344	1983
Zimbabwe	CBS C5-4350	1983
Seulement qu'une aventure	CBS C5-7078	1985
La Louve	CBS C5-7107	1985

Albums/CDs:

Offenbach Soap Opera	Barclay 80137	1971
Saint-Chrone De Neant	Barclay 80153	1972
Tabarnac	Deram/LonAdef-117/118	1974

Les Grand Succes De	Barclay 75020	1975
Never Too Tender	A&M Sp 9025	1976
Offenbach	A&M Sp 9027	1977
Traversion	KD-963	1978
En Fusion	SS-1701	1979
Rock Bottom	SS-1702	1980
Coup De Foudre	SS-1704	1981
Tonnedebrick	CBS Pfc-80077	1983
A Fond D'train Live	CBS Gfc-80086	1983
Rockorama	CBS Pfc-80103	1985
Le Dernier Show	CBS Gfc-80109	1985

Mary Margaret O'hara

Born and raised in the suburb of Islington in Toronto, Mary Margaret O'Hara was exposed to music by her father who sang scat when he wasn't working on the railway, and by her mother who liked to write songs.

A graduate of the Ontario College of Art in Toronto, Mary Margaret has had extensive experience in the visual arts, and she has acted in Second City's touring company with the late John Candy and Eugene Levy.

In 1977 she joined Songship, a uniquely innovative band. By 1981 this four-man group had changed their name to the Go Deo Chorus and developed a following in O'Hara's hometown. When they made their last appearance in July 1983, she was approached by Virgin Records to make an album.

What made her music unique was the layered harmonies of her music that transcended the average pop song. She recorded her album in Monmouth, Wales at the Rockfield Studio, where she worked with engineer Paul Cobbold, legendary folk producer Joe Boyd, and Eno-collaborator Michael Brook. Entitled, *Miss America*, it was not released until 1988. It was reissued on CD in 1996 (Virgin 86126).

She also wrote the songs for, and starred in, the film, Apartment Hunting (2001).

Single:
Body In Trouble	1989

Albums/CDs:
Miss America	Virgin VL-2559	1988
Miss America (Reissue)	Virgin CD 86126	1996

One to One

Leslie Howe (instrumentalist)
Louise Reny (lead vocals)

The Ottawa duo One To One was comprised of Leslie Howe and Louise Reny. Louise had aspirations to be a singer ever since she was six years old when her parents bought her a record player and she sang along to the Osmonds and The Jackson Five. As a teenager she sang along when her older brother played Elton John songs on the piano. When she was in the tenth grade she became the lead singer in a group called Mainstream.

Leslie Howe started playing the guitar at age twelve and was in a rival band until he joined Louise in Mainstream. From 1975 to 1983 they played 70s hard rock and opened for The Beach Boys and Julian Lennon. They also established themselves as far as British Columbia.

Both Leslie and Louise wrote original material for the band. When they wanted to get away from the Led Zeppelin style of playing the other members left, and the duo became One To One.

By late 1984 they had recorded some demo tapes, one of which was their first hit single, There Was A Time. When no company in Canada expressed interest in their music, they relocated to England and then Germany where they recorded their first album at Union Studios. They later signed to Bonaire Records, which was picked up in Canada by Wea Music of Canada (now Warner Music) in late 1985.

In March 1986 their first album, Forward Your Emotions, was released. It included their second single, Angel In My Pocket, which gave them their big break.

Between their first and second albums, Leslie started his own label, Ghetto Records where he produced Mr. Bones and Alanis Morissette. In 1992 A&M Records released the duo's second and last album, Imagine It.

By 1994 Louise and Leslie added guitarist Mike Goyette, bassist Tim Dupont and drummer Andrew Lamarche to form the group, Sal's Birdland. That same year, their debut album, *So Very Happy* (GRD 10121), was independently released on Ghetto Records. Their second album, *Nude Photos Inside* (Discovery 12081), was distributed by Warner Music Canada in September 1995. The first single was Love is Groovy.

Another name change in 1996 to Artificial Joy Club resulted in a recording contract with Interscope/Universal, who released their debut CD, Melt (Interscope 90125) in July 1997. Sick and Beautiful was the first single.

Singles:

There Was A Time (12")	Wea 25-88570	1985
There Was A Time	Wea 25-88577	1985
Angel In My Pocket	Wea 92-87397	1986
Angel In My Pocket (12")	Wea 25-86210	1986
Black On White	Wea 25-85787	1986
Hold Me Now	Wea BON 12127	1987/88
Love Child	Wea BON 22127	1989
Love Child (12")	Wea PRO 639	1989
Do You Believe	Wea BON 22137	1989
We've Got The Power	Wea BON	1989
Peace Of Mind (Love Goes On)	A&M 5364	1992
Memory Lane	A&M 5364	1992
Friends	A&M 5364	1992

Albums/CDs:

Forward Your Emotions	Wea Bon 25-25811	1986
Imagine It	A&M 5364	1992

The Original Caste

Graham Bruce (vocals, bass)
Peter Brown (drums) Replaced by Joseph Cavender
Bruce Innes (vocals, lead guitar)
Dixie Lee Stone (lead vocals)
Bliss Mackie (vocals, rhythm guitar)

The history of this Calgary group goes back to 1965 when Bruce Innis, Graham Bruce and Bliss Mackie were in the Bruce Innis Trio.

When Dixie Lee Stone (later Dixie Lee Innes) joined in 1966, they became The North Country Singers. They remained a four piece group until 1968 when Peter Brown became a member. He was later replaced by Joseph Cavender in 1970.

The name of the group changed to The Original Caste in 1968, when they recorded I Can't Make It Anymore on Dot Records.

Their biggest hit was One Tin Soldier, released in November 1969. A year later, their self-titled debut album came out.

By the release of their second album, Back Home, on Tommy Banks' Century II label, the lineup of the group had changed to Bruce and Dixie Lee Innis on lead vocals, Gary Carlson on bass, and Tommy Doran on drums.

They broke up in 1975. Dixie Lee Innes's solo material includes the Singles:,

Black Paper Roses (Bell 1972), Queen of Colby, Kansas (PLP 457705 - 1977), and Watch Me Fly (PLP R 6302 - 1977), and the albums, Dixie Lee Innes (Bell 6074 - 1972) and Chinook (PLP R 62941 - 1977). Today, she lives in British Columbia, while Bruce runs his own studio called Big Woody in Hailey, Idaho. He has also recorded on his own, including the album, Bruce Innes (CenturyII ST 17002 - 1974), and the single, The Fat Girl and the Midget (CenturyII 1512 - 1974).

Singles:

I Can't Make It Anymore	Dot 17071	1968
One Tin Soldier	Bell TA 186	1969
Mr. Monday	Bell TA 192	1970
Country Song	Bell TA 197	1970
Nothing Can Touch Me	Bell TA 197	1970
Ain't That Tellin' You People	Bell TA 204	1970
Sault Ste. Marie	Bell TA 211	1971
When Love Is Near	Bell TA 211	1971
One Tin Soldier	Bell GT 49	1973
Overdose of the Blues	CenturyII 1501	1973
We Will Live Together	CenturyII 1507	1974
Slide Up Under My Shoulder	CenturyII 1515	1974

Albums/CDs:

One Tin Soldier	Bell TA 5003	1970
Back Home	CenturyII ST 17001	1974

Our Lady Peace

Chris Eacrett (bass)
Raine Maida (lead vocals)
Jeremy Taggart (drums)
Mike Turner (guitars)

From Toronto, Ontario, Our Lady Peace arrived at its name from a poem written by Mark Van Doren in 1943. Like the mood and the character in the poem, the group's music is darkly optimistic.

The diversity of musical influences among the group's four members: Raine Maida for East Indian artist Sheila Chandra and Sinead O'Connor; Chris Eacrett for Rage Against The Machine, Living Colour, and Sting; Mike Turner for The Sex Pistols, Boomtown Rats and The Jam, and Jeremy Taggart's for music that was jazz-influenced.

Formed in 1992 after Maida answered Turner's ad for a guitarist in NOW

Magazine. Two years later, Epic Records released their debut album, *Naveed*, named after a Middle Eastern term that means bearer of good news.

By the release of their sophomore effort, Clumsy, in 1997, Duncan Coutts had replaced Eacrett.

Singles:

Needle and The Damage Done	CBS Z2K80199	1994
Starseed	Epic EK 80191	1994
Listen	Epic EK 80191	1994
The Birdman	Epic EK 80191	1994
Hope	Epic EK 80191	1994/95
Naveed	Epic EK 80191	1995
Supersatellite	Epic EK 80191	1995
Julia	Epic EK 80191	1995
Superman's Dead	Columbia CK 80242	1996/97
Clumsy	Columbia CK 80242	1997
Automatic Flowers	Columbia CK 80242	1997
Carnival	Columbia CK 80242	1997/98
4AM	Columbia CK 80242	1998
One Man Army	Columbia CK 63707	1999
Thief	Columbia CK 63707	2000
Life	Columbia CK 80598	2001
In Repair	Columbia CK 80598	2001

Albums/CDs:

Naveed	Epic EK 80191	1994
Clumsy	Columbia CK 80242	1997
Happiness...Is Not A Fish That You Can Catch	Columbia CK 63707	1999
Spiritual Machines	Columbia CK 80598	2000

Michel Pagliaro

Michel Pagliaro was born on November 9, 1948 in Lajeunesse, Quebec. He began playing the guitar at age eleven, and had mastered the instrument when he was only fifteen. Eager to join in a rock band, he started playing with Montreal's Les Stringmen, Les Bluebirds and Les Merseys. By his eighteenth birthday he had organized his first group, Les Chancelliers, whose first hit was Personne on Miracle Records. After recording six more singles and two albums with the group, he left to pursue a solo career.

In 1970 he started recording for CHUM's Much Records and released his first hit single in English, Give Us One More Chance. Three years later he had a huge hit with J'entends Frapper, which became the biggest selling single in the history of the Quebec industry. Its impact in English Canada was felt in Kingston where it became number one at both CKWS 960 (now CFFX) and CKLC 1380.

For the next two years he played with a group who called themselves les Rockers. By 1975 Pagliaro had switched to Columbia Records where he scored a big hit with What The Hell I Got.

In the 1980s Michel worked with French recording artist Jacques Higelin on his albums Aie! and Live a Bercy, while continuing to record his own material. Two songs, Les bombes and Dangereux, were hits only in Quebec.

For most of the 1990s Pagliaro spent a lot of time writing new songs. In July 1992, he took part in Montreal's 350th Anniversary celebrations. Audiogram released the two CD set, *Hit Parade*, a compilation of his older material in 1996, and Star/Select, the CD *Goodbye Rain* in 1998, which included five previously unreleased songs.

As The Chanceliers
Singles:

Personne	Miracle 1304	1966
Qu'attends tu de moi	Fantastic 3620	1966
Le P'tit Poppy	Citatiion 9014	1966
Toi Jeune Fille	Citatiion 9020	1967
Oogum Boogum	Citatiion 9022	1967
Noel Blanc	Citatiion 9030	1967
A Paris la nuit	Citatiion 9031	1967

Albums/CDs:

Les Chanceliers	Citatiion CN 16010	1967
Rock'n Roll	Citatiion C 298 5	1969

As Michel Pagliaro
singles

Comme d'Habitude	DSP 8625	1966
Spooky	DSP 8628	1968
Tous les arbres sont en fleurs	Citatiion 9053	1968
Ton non imprime dans mon coeur	DSP 8636	1968
Hey Jude	DSP 8641	1968
Le petit enfant saint	DSP 8644	1968
Que le monde est beau	Spectrum1	1969
A t'aimer	Spectrum5	1969
C'est l'ete	Spectrum7	1969
Pour toi Pour toi	Spectrum12	1969
Delta Boy (w/Nanette Workman)	Spectrum14	1970
L'amour est la	Spectrum21	1970
J'ai marche pour une nation	Spectrum24	1970
Walking Across The Nation	Hipp 87204	1970
Give Us One More Chance	Much 1001	1970

We're Dancing	Much 1002	1971
M'lady	AMI 801	1971
Lovin' You Ain't Easy	Much 1010	1971
Pagliaro	AMI 802	1972
Rainshowers	Much 1013	1972
J'entends Frapper	RCA 75 5144	1972
Revolution	Much 1015	1972
Some Sing, Some Dance	Much 1017	1972
Run Along Baby	Much 1023	1973
Northern Star	Much 1027	1973
Fou de toi	RCA 75 5154	1973
Little Queenie	RCA KPBO 50025	1973
Faut tout donner	RCA KMBO 5031	1973
Killing Time	RCA KPBO 50033	1973
Fievre des tropiques	RCA KPBO 50040	1974
Sure, Maybe	Much CH 1027	1974
What The Hell I Got	CBS C4 4107	1975
Dans le peau	CBS C4 4110	1975
Walking The Dog	CBS C4 4116	1975
Ca va brasser	RCA PB 50095	1975
Nobody/Louise	CBS C4 4124	1975
Emeute dans la prison	CBS C4 4139	1976
Last Night	CBS C4 4146	1976
Happy	CBS C4 4151	1976
I Don't Believe It's You	CBS C4 4116	1976
Dock of the Bay	CBS C4 4154	1977
Time Race	CBS C4 4159	1977
Happy Together	CBS C4 4166	1977
Gloire a nous	CBS C4 4178	1977
T'es pas tout seul a soir	Martin 10733	1978
Spider Woman	Poison 5008	1978
Le petit train	Martin 10744	1979
Travailler	TC 10	1981
Romantique	TC 11	1981
Quand on fait l'amour	TC 13	1982
Cadillac	TC 14	1982
Body, Mind and Soul	BBR 2002 MU 110	1984
Les bombes	AQ 6030	1987
L'espion	Alert 531	1989
Coup de coeur	Alert 535	1989
Heros	Alert 536	1989
Sous pein d'amour	Audiogram 5084	1989
Une vie a vivre	Audiogram 5096	1990

Albums/CDs:

Pag	Spectrum103	1970
Pagliaro	PAX 6604	1971
Pagliaro	Much CHLP 5001	1972
Pagliaro Live	RCA KXL 2 5000	1973

Rockers	RCA KPL1 0042	1974
Pagliaro	RCA KPL1 0075	1974
Pagliaro	CBS KC 33901	1975
Pagliaro Aujourd'hui	CBS PFS 90384	1977
Time Race	Columbia PES 90408	1977
Pagliaro Rock 'N R0ll	Martin M 16208	1978
Bamboo	TCM 1005	1981
Rock Avec Peg	K TEL KF 200	1982
Pagliaro Avant	Aquarius 547	1987
Sous Peine D'amour	Alert 281009	1988
Hit Parade	Audiogram 10087	1996
Goodbye Rain	Disque 9600	1998

Painter

Barry Allen (rhythm guitar, vocals)
Doran Beattie (lead vocals)
Bob Ego (drums)
Dan Lowe (lead guitar)
Wayne Morice (bass, vocals)

The Calgary group 49th Parallel became known as Painter in 1970. Barry Allen, who had several hits on Capitol Records such as Lovedrops, joined the group, along with Bob Ego and Wayne Morice.

That same year, they recorded the single Daybreak on the Molten 3 label. Two years later, came their second, Country Man, on London Records. By 1973 they had switched to Elektra Records and had national exposure with the hit, West Coast Woman. Their only album also came out.

In 1974 Painter went through another change in personnel, and became known as Hammersmith.

Singles:
Daybreak	Molten 3	1970
Country Man	LondonM. 17444	1972
West Coast Woman	Elektra 45862	1973
Goin' Home To Rock 'n Roll	Elektra 45873	1973/74
Song For Sunshine	Elektra 45886	1974

Albums:
Painter	Elektra EKS 75071	1973

The Parachute Club

Keith Brownstone (guitar)
Billy Bryans (drums, percussion)
Lauri Conger (keyboards, synthesizer, vocals)
Margo Davidson (saxophone, percussion, vocals)
Dave Gray (rhythm guitar)
Julie Masi (percussion, vocals)
Lorraine Segato (vocals, guitar, percussion)
Steve Webster (bass)

The history of The Parachute Club goes back to 1977 when Lorraine Segato met Billy Bryans. Both were members of Mama Quilla II, a seven-piece rock and roll band, and V which was comprised of prominent reggae, pop, and funk musicians who played in and around Toronto in 1981–82.

When neither of these two groups were unable to perform at the opening night party of the 1982 Toronto Film Festival, Lorraine and Billy organized The Parachute Club. The name came from a postcard entitled, "Drummer monkey and parachutist" from close friend and fellow member Lauri Conger.

Conger's contribution to the group is her extensive training in mime. She portrayed the mime clown, Sam in the group's videos for Rise Up and Boy's Club.

The fourth member of the group was Margo Davidson who played with Gary O and Craig Russell.

Julie Masi joined The Parachute Club in December, 1982. Raised in Winnipeg, Manitoba, she performed in many of the city's studios and clubs. When she moved to Toronto she worked with Kerr Whitely and The Paradise Revue, and the Cuban Fence Climbers.

On rhythm guitar was Dave Gray who was recruited to play on The Parachute Club's debut album, *Rise Up* in 1983. He had played with several of Toronto's blues and rock bands and was a master of guitar stylings. After working on the group's debut album, he was asked to stay.

In the spring of 1984, Keith Brownstone became the eighth and newest member. He had played funk and reggae in the bands R.Z. Jackson and David Bendeth.

After a string of hit Singles:, the group broke up in 1988. Lorraine Segato went on to pursue a solo career. She recorded Good Medicine, her first single in 1989, and in 1990 came her debut album, *Phoenix* (Warner 71202) which produced the hits, Stealin' Fire and Givin' It All We Got. Her second solo release, *Luminous City* (True North TNSD 0164) came out in 1998.

Singles:

Rise Up	Current/WAKE 3	1983
Rise Up (12")	RCA WASH 2	1983
Sexual Intelligence (12")	RCA JD 7095	1984
Alienation	Current WAKE 5	1984
Boy's Club	Current WAKE 6	1984
At the Feet of the Moon	RCA PB 50801	1985
Act of an Innocent	RCA PB 50814	1985
Innuendo	RCA PB 50839	1985
Love is Fire	RCA PB 50890	1986
Love is Fire (12")	RCA 5952 1 RD	1986
Love and Compassion	RCA PB 50912	1987
Walk to the Rhythm	RCA PB 50927	1987
Walk to the Rhythm (12")	Current KD 10016	1987
Big Big World	RCA PB 50978	1988

Albums/CDs:

The Parachute Club	Current WAVE 2	1983
At the Feet of the Moon	RCA KKL1 0553	1984
Moving Thru the Moonlight	RCA KKL1 9003	1985
National Velvet (EP)	ENV 8609 001	1986
Small VictorIES	RCA KKL1 0573	1986
Wild Zone: The Essential Parachute Club	RCA 17284	1992
Rise UP '92 (EP)	RCA JD 51074	1992

Paradox

Francois Cossette (vocals, lead guitar) Added in 1988
Sylvain Cossette (vocals, guitar)
Jean Francois Houle (vocals, bass)
Denis Lavigne (vocals, drums)

This Montreal-based group started out as a trio in late 1984 in Grand Mere, Quebec as a cover band. Denis and Jean Francois's vivid imagination and technical wizardry, combined with Sylvain's vocal stylings earned them a reputation as one of Eastern Canada's premiere live acts.

In June, 1988 they received the Canadian Factor Award which became a stepping stone to recording their debut album. That fall they signed a contract with MCA Music America.

About this time Francois Cossette, Sylvain's younger brother joined the group as lead guitarist to make it a quartet.

Their first hit single was Waterline in 1989 from their self-titled debut album.

In the 1991 they had success with their second album, *Obvious Puzzle*, and its first single, Kiss Me On The Lips.

By the middle of the 1990s, the group had broken up and Sylvain Cossette went on to have a solo career. His first two albums were Comme L'ocean (1994) and Blanc (1997).

Singles:
Waterline	MCA 42306	1989
Another Day	MCA 42306	1989
Catch Me In The Act	MCA 42306	1990
Kiss Me On The Lips	MCA 10337	1991

Albums/CDs:
Paradox	MCA 42306	1989
Obvious Puzzle	MCA 10337	1991

Partland Brothers

Chris Partland (vocals, guitar)
G.P. Partland (vocals, percussion)

The Partland Brothers grew up in Colgan, a small rural community north of Toronto. Inspired by The Beatles, their mother took them to see the film, A Hard Day's Night. From that experience they knew music was going to be their career.

G.P. and Chris were first members of the Toronto bar band Oliver Heavyside in 1979. In 1983 they won the Homegrown contest sponsored by Toronto radio station Q107. When they split up in the late 1980s, impresario James Martin encouraged Chris and his brother to become a duo.

In 1987 they signed a record contract with Capitol Records. Their first album, *Electric Honey* contained an upbeat collection of light pop tunes. The first single, Soul City was a Top 30 hit on Billboard's Hot 100 in June of 1987.

Their second album, Between Worlds came out in 1990. It produced the single Honest Man.

Three years later, the Partland Brothers were on a new label, Kinetic Records. Their debut, Part Land, Part Water was released in 1993. Produced by Ken Greer at Metalworks Studio in Mississauga, the first single was Lift Me Up.

Singles:
Soul City	Capitol B 73005	1986
Soul City (12")	Capitol SPRO 314	1986
One Chance	Capitol B 73033	1990

Honest Man	Capitol C4 93394	1990
Untouched	Capitol C4 93394	1990
Christmas Day	CGP1	1991
Lift Me Up	Kinetic/Demon 912	1993
Fields	Kinetic/Demon 912	1993
Under The Moonlight	Kinetic/Demon 912	1993

Albums/CDs:

Electric Honey	Capitol ST 6543	1986
Between Worlds	Capitol C2 93394	1990
Part Land, Part Water	Kinetic/Demon 912	1993

A Passing Fancy

Rick Mann (bass)
Brian Price (organ, harmonica, vocals)
Phil Seon (lead guitar)
Jay Telfer (lead vocals, rhythm guitar)
Louis Pratile (drums) Replaced by Steve Wilson

This rhythm and blues group from Toronto, Ontario started in the summer of 1965 as The Dimensions with Jay Telfer, Rick Mann, Phil Seon, Brian Price and Greg Hershitt. Later that same year they changed their name to A Passing Fancy, and went through a number of personnel changes. Hershitt had left and Louis Pratile had joined the group, but only briefly. By October 1966 Steve Wilson had replaced Pratile as the group's new drummer.

For ten months they were managed by Bernie Finkelstein, who went to look after The Paupers, Kensington Market, Johns Mills Cockell, Bruce Cockburn and Murray McLauchlan.

During Canada's centennial year the band played at the Canadian National Exhibition in Toronto where they signed 3,000 autographs.

They also played in London, Owen Sound, and Brockville.

Signed to Columbia Records, their first hit was I'm Losing Tonight, written by Jay Telfer, in 1967. After three more singles with Columbia, the original group broke up in May 1968.

Later that same year, there was a second group comprised of Fergus Hambleton on organ, Ron Cameron on guitar and lead vocals, Danny Troutman on bass, Wally Cameron on drums, and Brian Smith on rhythm guitar. Boo Records also released the album, A Passing Fancy, containing the group's old hits and new songs, one of which included the single, Islands.

At the time the group broke up in 1969, their lineup consisted of Glen Brown on vocals, Stan Lemon on lead guitar, Brian Maxim on bass, Ray Novack on organ, and Robin Boers, formerly with The Ugly Ducklings, on drums.

Singles:
I'm Losing Tonight	Columbia C4 2729	1967
I Believe In Sunshine	Columbia C4 2767	1967
People In Me	Columbia C4 2772	1967/68
Islands	Boo 684	1968

Album:
A Passing Fancy	Boo BST 6801	1968

The Paupers

Chuck Beale (lead guitar)
Denny Gerard (bass guitar) Replaced by Brad Campbell (1968)
Bill (Marion) Misener (guitar) Replaced by Adam Mitchell (1965)
Ronn (Skip) Prokop (lead vocals) (1965 68)

Formed in Toronto in 1964, The Paupers started out as a pop band with such hits as Never Send You Flowers and If I Told My Baby on Red Leaf Records. They were comprised of Ronn (Skip) Prokop, Chuck Beal, Denny Gerrard and Bill Marion (aka Bill Misener), who was replaced by Adam Mitchell in 1965. Mitchell was instrumental in changing the group's sound to folk/rock.

Managed by Bernie Finkelstein, they went to New York where they played at the Cafe Au Go Go. It was there the group met Albert Grossman, who was already managing Bob Dylan and Peter, Paul and Mary. Grossman was so impressed by The Paupers that he eventually became their new manager. He also took them to New York where they recorded their first album, *Magic People*, which was released on Verve in 1967.

In 1968 Brad Campbell, formerly with the group, The Last Words, replaced Gerrard. Later that same year, Prokop left to work as a session drummer. He had already played on Peter, Paul and Mary's 1967 hit, I Dig Rock and Roll Music. Prokop later co founded Lighthouse with Ralph Cole and Paul Hoffert.

By the end of 1968, Campbell left to join Janis Joplin's Full Tilt Boogie Band. Misener and Mitchell continued with The Paupers until 1969. Both recorded solo material; Misener had a minor hit with Little Ole Rock and Roll Band in 1972, while Mitchell failed to succeed with such songs as Fool For Love (1979) and Dancing Round and Round (1980).

Singles:

Never Send You Flowers	Red Leaf 65002	1965
If I Told My Baby	Red Leaf 65003	1965
For What I Am	Roman 1103	1965
Long Tall Sally	Roman 1111	1966
If I Call You By Some Name	Verve Folkways 5033	1966/67
Simple Deed	Verve Folkways 5043	1967
One Rainy Day	Verve Folkways	1967
Magic People	Verve Folkways 5062	1967
Think I Care	Verve Folkways 5074	1967
Cairo Hotel	Verve Folkways	1968

Albums/CDs:

Magic People	Verve Forecast 3026	1967
Ellis Island	Verve Forecast 3051	1968

The Payola$

Paul Hyde (vocals)
Bob Rock (vocals)
Chris Taylor (drums)
Larry Wilkins (bass)

The origins of this four-man band from Vancouver go back to 1979 when they were struggling to be heard.

Singer/songwriter Hyde was born in England and emigrated with his family to Victoria, B.C. when he was 15. Rock is a native of Victoria who befriended Hyde and later formed the Payola$.

They recorded the single, China Boys on their own Slophouse label. It led to a contract with A&M Records.

Despite a record label, they continued to be uncomfortable on stage as performers because they felt the audience did not understand them.

In 1982 the release of Soldier established them on Canadian radio. Three years later, A&M dropped the group and they broke up.

Rock and Hyde continued to record together as a duo until Paul Hyde left to go solo. Bob Rock later formed the heavy rock band Rockhead in Vancouver. (see Rockhead)

By Paul Hyde & Payolas
Singles:

China Boys	A&M AM	1979
Eyes of A Stranger	A&M AM 576	1982

Soldier	A&M AM 1747	1982
Where Is This Love	A&M AM 635	1983
I'll Find Another You (Who Can Do It Right)	A&M AM	1983
Never Said I Loved You (w/Carole Pope)	A&M AM 623	1983
Stuck In The Rain	A&M AM 677	1985
You're The Only Love	A&M AM 682	1985
Here's The World	A&M AM 692	1985
It Must Be Love	A&M AM 2761	1986

Albums/CDs:

In A Place Like This	A&M SP 9052	1981
No Stranger To Danger	A&M SP 9070	1982
Hammer On A Drum	A&M SP 4958	1983
Here's The World For Ya	A&M SP 5025	1985
Between A Rock And A Hyde Place: The Best of The Payola$	A&M SP 9134	1993

By Paul Hyde
Singles:

America Is Sexy (12")	Capitol C1 75246	1989
America Is Sexy	Capitol B 73095	1989
What Am I Supposed To Do	Capitol B 73103	1989

Album:

Turtle Island	Capitol C1 92414	1989

By Rock & Hyde
Singles:

Dirty Water	Capitol 73019	1987
I Will	Capitol 73027	1987

Album:

Under The Volcano	Capitol ST 6555	1987

Pear of Pied Pumkin

Joe Mock (guitar, vocals)
Rick Scott (dulcimer, vocals)
Shari Ulrich (guitar, vocals)

Formed in 1974, they started out as the Pied Pumkin String Ensemble comprised of Joe Mock, Rick Scott and Shari Ulrich. Scott, born in San Antonio, Texas, moved to Canada in the late 1960s and was a member of The Lotus Eaters, while Regina born Mock was a member of his own band, Mock Duck in Vancouver and

Ulrich had moved to Vancouver in 1972 from California. Their self-titled debut album was released in 1974 on their own Squash record label. In 1976 Ulrich left to join Valdy's Hometown Band, and Mock and Scott became Pied Pear for the next six years. Ulrich went on to have a successful solo career in 1978, and Mock moved to Tokyo, then Paris where he lives today.

Scott turned to acting and appeared in the stage productions of Ann Mortifie's Reflections on Crooked Walking, John Lazarus' The Late Blumer, Barnum and Angry Housewives as Wally the Weatherman. He then formed The Rick Scott Band in 1985 with Harris Van Berkel, Andy Graffiti and Connie Lebeau. Since 1990 Scott has been a children's entertainer who has performed in schools, theatres and festivals across Canada, the United States, Asia and Australia.

He has also been a spokesperson for the Down Syndrome Research Foundation. In the early 1980s, he founded the Children's CBC TV series, Switchback, and was a regular on Fred Penner's Place on CBC TV.

Scott reunited with Mock and Ulrich in 1989. The Lost Squash Tapes, recorded in 1976, was released that same year. They have since reunited again and toured across Canada in support of their album, Plucking Devine: Selected Recordings 1974 80. Scott's own recordings include You Better Dancing (Jester Records Jest OO1 1985), The Electric Snowshoe (Jester OO2 1989), Rick Around The Rock (Jester OO3 1992), and Philharmonic Fool (Jester OO4 1995).

Albums/CDs:

Pied Pumkin String Ensemble	Squash Records #1	1974
Pied Pumkin Allah Mode	Squash Records #2	1976
Pied Who? Pied What?	Squash Records #3	1977
Pied Pear	Squash Records #4	1980
Pied Pear Elementary	Squash Records #5	1981
The Lost Squash Tapes	Squash Records #6	1989
Plucking Devine	Squash Cd #6	1998
Pied Alive	Jester Records 005	2000

Pepper Tree

Tim Garagan (vocals)
Ritchie Richmond (guitar)
Lenny Brennan (bass)

The Pepper Tree was formed in Nova Scotia in 1967. The original members of the group were Tim Garagan from Friends Of The Family and guitarist Ritchie Richmond and bassist Lenny Brennan, to members of Lost Children. In 1969 they signeo Capitol Records. Their best known hit was Mr. Pride in 1970. Their only album, *You're My People*, came out in 1971.

By the end of the 1970s they broke up. In 1991 they reunited with Garagan as the only original member.

Singles:
Everywhere	Capitol 72612	1970
Mr. Pride	Capitol 72612	1970
Try	Capitol 72640	1971
You're My People	Capitol 72650	1971
Love is a Railroad	Capitol 72666	1972
Midnight Lady	Capitol 72690	1973

Album:
You're My People	Capitol ST 6364	1971

Percy and The Teardrops

Joe Brady (bass)
Bob Cook (keyboards)
Paul LaPlante (lead guitar)
Brian Maxwell (lead vocals)
Tom Revill (drums)

Formed in 1971 in Kingston, Ontario, Percy and The Teardrops specialized in classic rock and roll, much like Sha Na Na, their American counterpart. The original group was comprised of Tom Revill, aka Percy Moran, Bob Cook, Paul LaPlante, Joe Brady, and Brian Maxwell. Other members included Boppin' Bobby Nelson, Chris Harvey, S. J. Lawrence, Greg Travers, Jan Turney, Bob Metcalfe, J.J. Golden, and Bernie Smith.

In 1980 they recorded their only album, *Almost Live*, on their own Drop label, recorded at Marc Sound in Ottawa. They broke up in 1986.

Album:
Almost Live	Drop BWS 1001	1980

Perth County Conspiracy

Michael Butler (bass)
Richard Keelan (guitar, vocals)
Cedric Smith (guitar, vocals)

Inspired by the Chicago seven trial definition of a conspiracy as two or more people in the same place breathing together, this trio from Stratford, Ontario was formed in 1969 by Cedric Smith and Richard Keelan. Stratford is in Perth County.

As the principal songwriters of the group, their music mixed the words of Dylan Thomas, William Shakespeare, British poet Christopher Logue with gentle and satirical lyrics about love, freedom and peace.

They recorded for Columbia Records. Their first two albums were called *The Perth County Conspiracy Does Not Exist* (1970) and *Perth County Live* (1972).

Their first single, You've Got To Know was an edited version from the album, Perth County Conspiracy Does Not Exist. Its flip side, also from the same album, was called Keeper Of The Key.

The Perth County Conspiracy recorded a live album called Break Out In Berlin which was released in 1976. Cedric Smith and Terry Jones collaborated on one record together, Ten Lost Years-And Then Some in 1977.

With the breakup of the group in the late 1970s, Cedric Smith turned to acting. His most notable role was Alec King in the CBC TV series, Road To Avonlea.

Singles:
You've Got To Know	Columbia C4 2963	1971
Uncle Jed	Columbia C4 3010	1971/72

Albums/CDs:
Perth County Conspiracy Does Not Exist	Columbia ELS 375	1970
Alive	Columbia ES 90036	1971
Break Out In Berlin	Rumour V	1976
Ten Lost Years And Then Some	Rumour VI	1977

Colleen Peterson

Born in Peterborough, Ontario on November 14, 1950, Colleen Peterson started playing when she bought her first guitar with Lucky Green stamps at age thirteen. While still a teenager she moved to Ottawa, where she performed as a folk singer and also as lead vocalist in various rock bands. While the folk trio Three's A Crowd was playing in Ottawa, Colleen was invited to fill in for Donna Warner as their new lead singer, and later became a full-fledged member.

In 1970 she moved to Kingston and with singer Mark Haines became half of the duo Spriggs and Bringle. They toured Canada and the United States for the next four years.

Beginning To Feel Like Home, her first album for Capitol Records in 1976, contained her signature song, Souvenirs. She made two more albums with the label, *Colleen* and *Takin' My Boots Off.*

Between 1976 and 1995 she had a string of hit singles on RPM Weekly's national country chart. They included I Had It All, Weather The Storm, and Mr. Conductor.

The 1980s saw her perform at the Mariposa Folk Festival and Expo 86. In 1993 she joined Sylvia Tyson, Cindy Church and Caitlin Hanford to form the group Quartette.

Colleen Peterson died of ovarian cancer on October 9, 1996.

Albums/CDs:

Beginning To Feel Like Home	Capitol ST 11567	1976
Colleen	Capitol ST 11714	1977
Takin' My Boots Off	Capitol ST 11835	1978
Basic Facts	Book Shop BSR 766	1988
Let Me Down Easy	Inter CDI 9102	1991
Beginning To Feel Like Home	EMI 30656	1994
Whatever Goes Around Comes Around	EMI 33362	1995

Photograph

Andy Forgie (lead vocals)
John Paul Murphy (drums, percussion)
Mark Rashotte (6 & 12 string guitars)
Mark Wilkins (bass guitar, vocals)

The history of this Belleville group goes back to 1968 when Andy Forgie, Mark Roshotte and John Paul Murphy practiced in the basement of St. Michael's Church. With the addition of a fourth member, Tom Ward, they performed under the name The Fog. They later changed their name to Creed.

In 1974 Ward left and was replaced by Mark Wilkins, and in 1976 Creed recorded their only single, Westminster Abbey (Skyline CE 1007).

As Creed they shared the same stage with April Wine, The Stampeders, Edward Bear, Tom Cochrane and Red Rider, and Loverboy's Paul Dean. Tired of playing cover tunes by Tommy James and others, they became The Elevators and started using original material in their act.

In the fall of 1980 Cochrane was able to clinch a record deal with Capitol Records for the Belleville group. However, they had to change their name again in order to avoid a lawsuit from a group in Boston who had the same name, so they became Photograph.

Capitol released their self-titled debut album in 1981, featuring the hit singles The Last Dance, Sarah, and Blow Away.

In the early 1980s they changed their name to 98.6, and broke up in 1984. The group recorded the single, She's A Romantic (Access AC 22284) under the name Restless Hearts later that same year. They have reunited as Photograph since then for the occasional charity event and community festival. Today, Forgie is a children's entertainer and composer.

Singles:
The Last Dance	Capitol 72835	1981
Blow Away	Capitol 72854	1981
Sarah	Capitol 72862	1981

Album:
Photograph	Capitol ST 6480	1981

Pinky

Pinky, who was born Victor Dauvin in Sackville, New Brunswick, was the original lead singer for Lighthouse. He had previously played in The Stitch In Tyme. He recorded three singles for United Artists which were all released in 1972.

Singles:
Tell Me Who	United Artists 50909	1972
Don't Send Someone	United Artists 50944	1972
Cheatin' Mistreatin'	United Artists 50986	1972

Platinum Blonde

Sergio Galli (guitar)
Mark Holmes (lead vocals)
Kenny MacLean (bass)
Chris Steffer (percussion)

Platinum Blonde was formed in Toronto in 1982 by lead vocalist Mark Holmes. Named after the group's hairstyles, they were one of Canada's major pop groups in the mid 1980s. Signed to Columbia Records, their debut album, Standing In The Dark was released in 1983. Their second album, Alien Shores, was a watershed album for the group, which went on to sell quintuple platinum.

In 1985 Kenny McLean was added to the group, and two years later Chris Steffler was replaced by Sascha Tukatsch.

By 1990 the group became known as The Blondes, who broke up later that same year. Kenny McLean went on to record the album, Don't Look Back (Justin JEC 0001 1990), while Mark Holmes became a member of the group Breed in the fall of 1992.

Singles:

Not in Love	Columbia C4 7044	1983
Doesn't Really Matter	Columbia C4 4351	1984
Standing in the Dark	Columbia C4 7000	1984
Sad Sad Rain	Columbia C4 7026	1984
Not in Love	Columbia C4 7044	1985
Crying Over You	Columbia C4 7085	1985
Situation Critical	Columbia C4 7120	1985
Hungry Eyes	Columbia C4 1149	1986
Somebody Somewhere	Columbia C4 7127	1986
Pere Noel	Columbia C4 7195	1986
Contact	Epic E4 3017	1987
Connect Me	Epic E4 3025	1988
Fire	Columbia 34 7717	1988
If You Go This Time	Epic E4 3048	1988
Yeah Yeah Yeah (The Blondes)	Justin JD 0002	1990
Tara (The Blondes)	Justin JD 0002	1990

Albums/CDs:

Platinum Blonde	Columbia CEP 80084	1982
Standing in the Dark	Columbia PCC 80090	1983
Alien Shores	Columbia PCC 80105	1985
Contact	Epic FE 40949	1987
Yeah Yeah Yeah (Blondes)	Justin JD 0002	1990
Seven Year Itch: 1982–89	Columbia TVK 24054	1999

The Pointed Sticks

Tony Bardach (sax)   Replaced by John Farano (1980)
Nick Jones (vocals)
Ken Montgomery (drums) Nickname: Dimwit
Bill Napier Hemy (guitar)
Gord Nicoll (keyboards) Nickname: Dash Ham
Scott Watson (bass)

Formed in 1978 in suburban Vancouver, B.C., the Pointed Sticks began as a group that won a Battle of the Bands contest on the CBC network's Great Canadian Gold Rush. The group's name came from a Monty Python skit. They made their debut in Vancouver on August 23, 1978. Nick Jones and Gord Nicoll were the principle songwriters of the group.

They became the first Canadian group to sign with England's Stiff Records. In the U.S. they developed a following at two clubs, San Francisco's Deaf Club and Los Angeles's Starwood.

In 1980 they released three singles on the Vancouver-based Quintessence label, which included their three singles What Do You Want Me To Do?, Lies, and The Real Thing. By the end of the year saxophonist John Farano replaced Tony Bardach and bassist Scott Watson was added to make the group a sextet.

The Pointed Sticks broke up in June 1981. Zulu Records in Vancouver released the CD retrospective, Part Of The Noise, In 1995.

Singles:
What Do You Want Me To Do?	Quintessence QS 101	1980
The Real Thing	Quintessence QS 103	1980
Lies	Quintessence QS 104	1980

Albums/CDs:
Perfect Youth	Quintessence QLP 002	1980
Part of The Noise	Zulu 15 2	1995

The Poppy Family

Susan Jacks (vocals, Petersen's bean pod)
Terry Jacks (vocals, guitar)
Craig Mc Caw (guitar, sitar)
Satwant Singh (tablas, bongos, percussion)

The husband and wife team of Susan and Terry Jacks started recording together in the fall of 1967 with the song, Beyond The Clouds. It was not until their third single, Which Way You Goin' Billy? that they achieved national success in 1969. A year later, it became a big hit in the United States and sold two million copies.

Susan and Terry Jacks first played together in a group called Powerline. She was a vocalist, while he played guitar. With guitarist Craig Mc Caw, they formed a new group, Winkin' Blinkin' and Nod which later became The Poppy Family. On June 22, 1970, *Which Way You Goin' Billy?* was certified a million seller.

One of The Poppy Family's hits, No Good To Cry was first recorded in 1967 by The Wildweeds, an American group. Another, That's Where I Went Wrong went to the top of the French charts in Quebec as Le Bateau du Bonheur, in the fall of 1970.

In 1973, The Poppy Family broke up. Both Susan and Terry Jacks went on to have successful solo careers. (see The Chessmen, Susan Jacks, Terry Jacks)

Singles:
Beyond The Clouds	London M.17364	1968
What Can The Matter Be	London M.17369	1969
Which Way You Goin' Billy?	London M.17373	1969
That's Where I Went Wrong	London M.139	1970
I Was Wondering	London M.148	1971
Where Evil Grows	London M.148	1971
I'll See You There		1971
No Good To Cry	London M.164	1971
Good Friends	LondonM.172	1972

Albums/CDs:
That's Where I Went Wrong (Which Way You Goin' Billy? In 1970)	Londonps 568	1969
Which Way You Goin' Billy? (The Poppy Family In The U.S.)	Londonps 574	1970
Poppy Seeds	Londonps 599	1971
The World of Terry Jacks & The Poppy Family	Gold/Lond0n SPA 160	1976
The World of Susan Jacks & The Poppy Family	Gold/London SPA 161	1976
The Poppy Family's Greatest Hits	A&M 69998	1989
A Good Thing Lost 1968 1973	March 80304	1996

Powder Blues Band

Gordie Bertram (sax)
Mark Hasselbach (trumpet)
Wayne Kozak (sax)
Jack Lavin (bass)
Tom Lavin (guitar)
Duris Maxwell (drums)
Willie Mc Calder (keyboards)
David Woodward (sax)

This Vancouver blues band was founded in 1978 by Chicago-born guitarist Tom Lavin, his brother Jack and Mc Calder. All eight members came from other groups: Tom used to be with Prism, Jack with Teen Angel, Mc Calder with Willie and The Walkers, Maxwell with Doucette and Skylark, Woodward with Downchild, Kozak with Cobra, Prism and Denise Mc Cann, Bertram with Foreman Byrnes, and Hasselbach with the jazz group, Airbrush.

The band's musical influences go back to the early 1960s with blues and R&B standards. Their first big break came at a music store called the A&B in Vancouver when the store manager sold all copies of the group's album, *Uncut* in two days. When a CFOX deejay started playing their music, demand for the group increased and they eventually signed a contract with RCA Records. Their first single was Doin' It Right in 1980.

They later recorded for other labels and in 1993 recorded an album of all new material called Let's Get Loose. In 1997, their 1981 taped concert with blues legend Lowell Fulsom at Vancouver's Blue Wave Club was released by Stony Plain (Lowell Fulsom Stony PlainSPCD 1233). The Powder Blues Band celebrated twenty years together in 1998, and in 2001 an all-new album called *Swingin' the Blues* was released on the Peerless label.

Singles:

Doin' it Right	RCA PB 50562	1980
Boppin' with the Blues	RCA PB 50580	1980
What've I Been Drinking	RCA PB 50589	1980
Thirsty Ears	Liberty 1423	1981
Hear that Guitar Ring	RCA PB 50613	1981
Lovin' Kissin' & Huggin'	Cap 77003	1981
Joy Ridin'	Liberty 77005	1981
Jump Up	Liberty 77010	1982
I'm on the Road Again	Blue Wave BW R007	1985

Albums/CDs:

Uncut	Blue Wave 1179	1979
Uncut	RCA KKL1 0365	1980

Thirsty Ears	Liberty LT 1105	1981
Party Line	Liberty LT 51136	1982
Red Hot/True Blue	RCA KXL2 0518	1983
Live At Montreux	Blue Wave BWR 007	1985
First Decade Greatest Hits	Wea CD 71359	1990
Let's Get Loose	Wea CD 92488	1993
Swinging the Blues	Peerless 52001	2001

Peter Pringle

Peter Pringle was born on September 7, 1955 in Halifax, Nova Scotia. He first became involved with music when he was growing up in Toronto where he studied classical piano and sang with the Canadian Opera Company. His career in opera came to an end when he turned 13 and his voice changed from a soprano to a baritone. He later studied Indian music with Ravi Shankar.

His first hit was Gonna Get A Lady on Reprise Records in 1976.

Three years later, he headlined his own CTV network special, and in 1981 recorded his first French album, *Magicien*. In 1992 he toured in the title role of Noel Coward in the stage production of Coward: A Portrait which drew rave reviews.

Today, Pringle lives in Quebec where he has rediscovered Soviet inventor Lev Serggeyvich Termin's theremin, which has been hailed as the granddaddy of electronic music. In 1998, Peter attended a trade show in Toronto where he showed off his Hoffman theremin, which was played on many soundtracks of such classic films as Spellbound, The Thing, and The Day the Earth Stood Tall.

Singles:
Gonna Get a Lady	Reprise 1359	1976
You Really Got Me Needing You Now	Warner Bros 8456	1977
Let Me Love You	Warner Bros 0021	1977/78
Outside and Inside	Phono PH 403	1979
I Could Have Been a Sailor	A&M AM 506	1980
It Just Occurred To Me	A&M AM 524	1981
Stranger	A&M AM 544	1981
Hold On to the Night	A&M AM 532	1981
Why Did I Wait So Long	A&M AM 583	1982
Fantasies in Your Eyes	A&M AM 632	1983
Souris Moi	A&M AM 665	1984

Albums/CDs:
Peter Pringle	Warner Bros MS 2243	1975
Magicien	A&M SP 90581	1981
Rain Upon the Sea	A&M SP 9054	1981

Fifth Avenue Blue	A&M SP 9072	1982
Pour Une Femme	A&M SP 9073	1982
Souris Moi	A&M SP 9098	1984
Fantasies	A&M SP 9101	1984
Chansons D'amour	A&M SP 9121	1985
Portraitd'un ADIEU	Polydor PTF 1 7014	1985
Pauvre Casanova	Kebec Disc KD 631	1986
Noel Coward: A Portrait	Aquarius AQR 543	1987
Le Jeu D'amour	Morin PGMCD 1303	1991

Prism

Ab Bryant (bass) Replaced by Al Harlow
Rodney Higgs (drums, keyboards) Replaced by Rocket Norton
Tom Lavin (rhythm guitar, vocals)
Lindsay Mitchell (lead guitar, vocals)
Ron Tabak (lead vocals) Replaced by Henry Small

The origins of Prism go back to the late 1960s when Jeff Edington, Lindsay Mitchell, Rocket Norton and Steve Whalley were in The Seeds of Time. They recorded two Singles:, My Hometown and Cryin' The Blues, both on Coast Records. After some personnel changes they became Stanley Screamer in July 1976. Less than a year later, they became Prism, and were comprised of Ron Tabak, Lindsay Mitchell, Tom Lavin, John Hall, Ab Bryant, Rodney Higgs, Bruce Fairbairn and Tom Keenlyside. Signed to the now defunct GRT label, they recorded several albums for the label including *Prism*, *See Forever Eyes*, and *Armageddon* before switching to Capitol.

In 1978 Lavin left to start The Powder Blues Band, Bryant, who later became a member of The Headpins and Chilliwack, was replaced by Al Harlow, and Rodney Higgs, who was really songwriter Jim Vallance, also left in 1978 and was replaced by Norton. Tabak, who left in 1981, died in December 1984 after being struck by a car while riding his bicycle in Vancouver. Henry Small, who was previously in Scrubbaloe Caine and Small Wonder, had replaced him.

There were more personnel changes into the 1990s, and their most current release was the CD, Jericho, in 1993. Their lineup then was comprised of Darcy (lead vocals), Andy Lorimer (keyboards and vocals), Norton, Mitchell, and Harlow. They are still touring today. A CD of *The Seeds of Time* was released in 1992 by Eternal Enterprises Music (The Immortal Seeds of Time EEM 001).

By Seeds of Time
Album:

The Immortal	EEM 001	1992

By Prism
Singles:

Spaceship Superstar	GRT 1230 138	1977
Take Me To The Captain	GRT 1230 141	1977/78
Take Me Away	GRT 1230 157	1978
Flyin'	GRT 1230 156	1978
You're Like The Wind	GRT 1230 165	1979
Armageddon	Magnum 1242 8802	1979
Virginia	Magnum 1242 8804	1979
You Walked Away Again	Magnum 1242	1979/80
American Music	Capitol 72834	1980
Night To Remember	Capitol 72822	1980
Young And Restless	Capitol 72829	1980
Cover Girl	Capitol 72840	1980/81
Don't Let Him Know	Capitol 72867	1981

Albums/CDs:

Prism	EMI INS 3014	1977
See Forever Eyes	GRT 9230 1075	1978
Armageddon	Magnum 9242 2001	1979
Young and Restless	Capitol ST 12072	1980
Small Change	Capitol ST 12184	1981
Beat Street	Capitol ST 12226	1983
All The Best From Prism	Capitol ST 6477	1985
Over 60 MinuteS With	Capitol 91173	1988
Jericho	Spinner SPJ 612	1993

The Prowlers

Carl Ashley (drums)
Fred Bennett (lead guitar)
Carl Ries (sax)
Larry Tillyer (bass)
Les Vogt (vocals, rhythm guitar)

In 1958, The Prowlers were one of the early rockabilly bands in Vancouver. Led by Les Vogt (pronounced "vote"), they were, at first, a band who just played together in a member's basement. They were later invited to appear on a local radio program hosted by Jack Cullen, who arranged for them to play live over the on air phone line. They recorded two singles on Aragon Records: Rock Me Baby and Get A Move On Baby. When they broke up in 1959–60, Vogt recorded the single, Gonna Sit Right Down and Cry Over You (Jaguar 1001), which was a local hit in 1962. He left the performing side of the business that same year.

Singles:
Rock Me Baby	Aragon 302	1958
Get a Move on Baby	Aragon 303	1959

The Pukka Orchestra

Neil Chapman (lead guitar)
Tony Duggan Smith (rhythm guitar)
Graeme Williamson (vocals)

Formed in 1979 in Toronto, the name pukka (pronounced puck a) comes from a Hindu word meaning first rate, permanent, genuine. The Pukka Orchestra offered a unique musical style of folk rock. They were a regular club attraction in Toronto.

Signed to Solid Gold Records, their self-titled debut album came out in 1984. It contained a wide range of material from the headlong rush of Power Cut to the melodic Might As Well Be On Mars.

The group's first single, Listen to the Music was a cover version of the Tom Robinson/Peter Gabriel song, which was originally entitled Atmospherics.

Singles:
Listen To The Radio	Solid Gold SGS 751	1984
Cherry Beach Express	Solid Gold SGS 756	1984
Might As Well Be On Mars	Solid Gold SGS 758	1984/85

Albums/CDs:
The Pukka Orchestra	Solid Gold SGR 1022	1984
The Palace Of Memory (EP)	Major Label 12 PUK 010	1987

Pure

Jordy Birch (lead vocals)
Leigh Grant (drums) Replaced by Jim Hobbs
Dave Hadley (bass)
Mark Henning (keyboards)
Todd Simko (guitar)

This quintet from Vancouver, B.C. began first as After All and Grin Factory which were comprised of four members. With the addition of bassist Dave Hadley they changed their name to Pure.

They self produced and recorded a few songs on tape which were enthusiastically received at a music conference in Vancouver in February, 1991. This led to a contract with Reprise/Warner.

On May 30, 1992 a seven inch green vinyl single, Greedy/Laughing Like A Fiend was released. It was followed a month later by a four song EP entitled Greed.

The song Greedy was featured in the Paramount film Cool World (1992) directed by Ralph Bakshi of Fritz The Cat fame.

Pureafunalia, the group's debut album on Reprise came out on September 15, 1992. The group started their own production company and label called Shag in 1995. By the release of *Feverish* (1998), they were comprised of four members and had a new drummer, Jim Hobbs.

Singles:

Blast	Mammoth MR1502	1992
Blast	Pro CD 5947	1992
Spiritual Pollution	Mammoth MR1502	1993
Blissful Kiss	Reprise CDW45038	1993
Pure	Reprise CDW45038	1993
Chocolate Bar	Mammoth 980181	1998
Feverish	Mammoth 980181	1998

Albums/CDs:

Greed (Ep)	Reprise 45003	1992
Pureafunalia	Mammoth MR 1502	1992
Generation 6 Pack	Reprise CDW45038	1994
Extra Purrestrial (Ep)	Shag 2001	1995
Generation 6 Pack (Cd R)	Mammoth 92731	1996
Feverish	Mammoth 980181	1998

The Pursuit of Happiness

Kris Abbott (guitar, vocals)
Moe Berg (guitar, vocals)
Brad Barker (bass, vocals)
Dave Gilbey (drums)
Susan Murumets (vocals)
Rachel Oldfield (vocals)
Johnny Sinclair (bass, vocals)

The Pursuit of Happiness (TPOH) was one group that went through a number of personnel changes from its inception in 1985. By the time their third album came out in 1993, Moe Berg and Dave Gilbey were the only original members left. Johnny Sinclair was the original bass player. He, Berg and Gilbey were joined by two backup singers, Tam and Tasha Amabile who hailed from Saskatoon, Saskatchewan. They left in 1989.

After the band's album One Sided Story came out in 1990, they lost Susan Murumets. The fourth female voice to leave was Leslie Stanwyck, who joined Sinclair to form the group, Universal Honey.

Moe Berg was a veteran of several Edmonton bands such as Modern Minds, Troc '59 and Face Crime. Dave Gilbey played with Berg in some of them, while Johnny Sinclair came from Saskatoon, Sask. The Amabile sisters had fronted a Winnipeg band called Dash and The Dots.

In 1986 TPOH made a video of the song, I'm An Adult Now which was filmed on Queen Street West in Toronto. Its exposure on MuchMusic helped them achieve success throughout the rest of Canada.

The Toronto-based group had several hits between 1987 and 1990. In 1992 they signed with Mercury/Polygram. Their first album, *The Downward Road* released in 1993, was produced by Ed Stasium in Los Angeles.

After touring to promote their album, *The Wonderful World Of* in 1996 97, Moe Berg released his first solo effort, *The Summer's Over* (1997, Iron Music Group 651021)

Singles:

I'm An Adult Now	Independent	1986
I'm An Adult Now	Wea 25 83877	1987
I'm An Adult Now (12")	Wea 25 83870	1987
Killed By Love	Chrysalis 45018	1987
Killed By Love (12")	Swell Slxd 001	1988
Hard To Laugh	Chrysalis 8846	1988
Beautiful White	Chrysalis 45081	1989
She's So Young	Chrysalis 45016	1989
Two Girls In One	Chrysalis Vk 41757	1990
New Language	Chrysalis VK 41757	1990
Cigarette Dangles	Mercury512972	1993
I'm Ashamed of Myself	Mercury512972	1993
Pressing Lips	Mercury512972	1993
Gretzy Rocks	Iron Music Group 51003	1995
Young And In Love	Iron Music Group 51003	1995
Kalendar	Iron Music Group 51003	1995/96
I Should Know	Iron Music Group 51003	1996
She's The Devil	Iron Music Group 51003	1996
Carmalina	Iron Music Group 51010	1997

Albums/CDs:
Love Junk	Chrysalis CHS 41675	1988
One Sided Story	Chrysalis VK 41757	1990
The Downward Road	Mercury512972	1993
Where's the Bone	Iron Music Group 51003	1995
Wonderful World Of	Iron Music Group 51010	1996

Rain

Phyllis Brown (lead vocals, piano)
Charley Hall (organ)
Ron Hiller (lead vocals, piano)
Bill McLaughlin (guitar)
Chris Woroch (drums)

Rain formed in Kitchener, Ontario in 1969. Fronted by Phyllis Brown (aka Phyllis Boltz), their first single was, Out Of My Mind on London Records. They later made one album and one single for Greg Hambleton's Axe Record label. Rain broke up in 1973. Phyllis became Charity Brown and had a string of hits on A&M Records.

Singles:
Out of My Mind	London17410	1971
Stop Me From Believing	Axe 1	1972
Find Your Love	Axe 5	1972
Make Me	Axe 9	1972

Album:
The Rain Album	Axe Axs 501	1972

The Rankins

Cookie Rankin (vocals)
Heather Rankin (vocals)
Jimmy Rankin (vocals)
John Morris Rankin (piano, fiddle)
Raylene Rankin (vocals)

From Mabou, Cape Breton, The Rankins began playing music in their family home where neighbors gathered every third weekend for a party or ceilidh, as it is known in Gaelic. With their father on violin and mother on piano, the eldest Rankin children learned Celtic dance steps and songs. As they grew up and left the family fold, the younger ones replaced them.

In 1989, Cookie, Heather, Raylene, Jimmy, and John Morris Rankin played at local weddings and dances. Eventually they were encouraged to perform at various folk festivals, and they became The Rankin Family. Raylene, who had graduated with a law degree from Dalhousie University, handled most of their bookings, while their mother looked after mail orders for their two independent cassettes, *The Rankin Family*, and, *Fare Thee Well Love*. They made their national TV debut on CBC's On The Road Again with host Wayne Rostad, and performed at the Glen Echo Folk Festival and Winnipeg Folk Festival.

In September 1990, the CBC network televised their appearance at the Beddeck and Winnipeg festivals for a one-hour TV special called, Here Come The Rankins.

After signing with EMI in 1992, their independent cassettes were re-released, and the following year came their major label debut, North Country. With each subsequent release, the group has built up a loyal following and in the wake of their success other groups and artists like MacKeel, Natalie MacMaster, Ashley MacIsaac, and Great Big Sea have emerged to various degrees of success.

In the fall of 1998, Raylene Rankin left and they became known as The Rankins. They broke up in 1999. John Morris Rankin died on January 16, 2000.

Jimmy Rankin released his first solo album, *Song Dog* (Song Dog 70528) in 2001.

Singles:

Mo Run Geal, Dileas	EMI 99995	1989
Orangedale Whistle	EMI 99996	1992
Fare Thee Well Love	EMI 99996	1992/93
Gillis Mountain	EMI 99996	1993
Rise Again	EMI 80683	1993
North Country	EMI 80683	1993/94
Borders And Time	EMI 80683	1994
Tramp Miner	EMI 80683	1994
Lisa Brown	EMI 80683	1994
Turn That Boat Around	EMI 80683	1994/95
The Grey Dusk of Eve	EMI 82013	1995
You Feel The Same Way Too	EMI 832348	1995
The River	EMI 832348	1995/96
Forty Days And Nights	EMI 832348	1996
Roving Gypsy Boy	EMI 52969	1996/97
Movin' On	EMI 21203	1998
Maybe You're Right	EMI 21203	1998
Let It Go	EMI 21203	1998

Albums/CDs:

The Rankin Family	EMI 99995	1989
Fare Thee Well Love	EMI 99996	1990
North Country	EMI 80683	1993
Endless Seasons	EMI 832348	1995
Grey Dusk of Eve (EP)	EMI 82013	1995
Collection	EMI 52969	1996
Uprooted	EMI 21203	1998

Gary Rasberry

Gary Rasberry is an artist, educator and singer based in Kingston, Ontario. In 2011 Idea Manufactory Press published his first book of poetry called *As Though it Could be Otherwise*. Two years later, Hidden Brook Press published, *More Naked Than Ever*.

Before recording two solo albums, *What's The Big Idea* and *The Very Next Day*, he was a member of the folk group, Fireweed, Who released a self-titled album in 1999 that was recorded in Kingston, Ontario.

What's The Big Idea contained songs recorded at a school in Yarker, Ontario. It was nominated for a Juno as Children's Album of the Year in 2014.

The Very Next Day, his second album was made with Dave Clark of The Rheostatics and The Woodshed Orchestra, a nine-piece band from Toronto, Ontario.

Albums/CDs:

What's The Big Idea?	Razzletone	2013
The Very Next Day	Razzletone 032970	2014

Rawlins Cross

Brian Bourne (bass, Chapman Stick, background vocals)
Ian McKinnon (highland bagpipe, trumpet, tin whistles, background vocals)
Dave Panting (guitars, mandolin, lead and background vocals)
Geoff Panting (keyboards, button accordions, lead and background vocals)
Pamela Paton (drums)
Derek Pelley (background vocals)
Tom Roach (drums, percussion)
Lorne Taylor (bass)

This folk group is comprised of brothers Dave and Geoff Panting and Ian McKinnon. Originally, they wanted to call themselves The Open Road but it was already taken. Formed in 1988, they chose Rawlins Cross, after an area in their hometown of St. John's, Newfoundland where several major streets converged.

With the addition of drummer Pamela Paton and bassist Lorne Taylor, the band's sound changed to Celtic Rock in 1989. They toured western Newfoundland and Nova Scotia where their mix of musical styles was praised by both critics and fans.

Dave and Geoff, the chief songwriters of the group, were former members of Figgy Duff. Geoff also co wrote and produced the theme for the CBC TV show, *Codco*. McKinnon from Port Hawkesbury had performed and competed in concerts and bagpipe competitions in Scotland, England, the United States and Canada, hosted the 1983 CBC documentary International Gathering of the Clans, and played Angus The Piper in the 1987 CBC TV movie, Island Love Song.

In January 1989 Rawlins Cross was featured on the MuchMusic special, Rock On The Rock. Later that same year, their debut album, *A Turn of the Wheel* was released on the Stony Plain label.

With the release of their second album, *Crossing the Border* (1991), McKinnon had set up his own label, Ground Swell Records, to insure the group's recordings were properly marketed, and to foster unknown acts of other East Coast artists like The Rose Vaughn Trio, John Campbelljohn, Saltwater Rose, Teresa Doyle and Blackpool.

Before their next album, *Reel 'N Roll* came out, the group went through a personnel change; Brian Brown replaced Taylor, and Howie Southwood replaced Paton. They also added a sixth member, Joey Kitson on lead and backing vocals and harmonica.

With their subsequent albums, including *Living River, Celtic Instrumentals*, and *Make it on Time*, Rawlins Cross continued to epitomize the best in Canadian Celtic Rock, by fusing various styles of Celtic folk music with more progressive sounds.

Albums/CDs:

A Turn of the Wheel	Groundswell 10422	1989
Crossing the Border	Groundswell 10423	1992
Reel 'N Roll	Groundswell 10104	1993
Living River	Groundswell 13666	1996
Celtic Instrumentals	Groundswell 18143	1997
Make it on Time	Groundswell 23101	1998

Ginette Reno

Born on April 28, 1946 in Montreal, Ginette Reno started singing when she was two years old. At four she listened to records in those little booths where you could sit and listen. On Fridays she sang at one of the local banks as the Piaf of Market Street.

From the age of five she was determined her career was going to be a singer and an actress. When she was eight she sang at a church wedding and made $22.00.

One of the local radio stations was CKVL, who had an amateur show on Saturday mornings, and sometimes they would let her sing the English songs she knew by heart.

She started singing in clubs at thirteen, and often would fall asleep in school because she didn't get home until three or four in the morning. When she was in grade nine, she quit school and later won a local talent contest. The prize was $40.00 to do twenty-two shows for a week in a nightclub. When audiences responded in kind to her singing, she ended up staying longer than a week, and she started working 52 weeks a year in nightclubs.

In 1962 she recorded her first single, J'aime Guy on Apex Records. During the next five years she had several hits in Quebec.

She switched to the Grand Prix label in 1967 and success continued to follow. Two years later, she recorded her English single for Parrot, Every Day Working Man, but it was not a hit in English Canada.

During the early 1970s she sang with Roger Whittaker on British television and performed with a seventy-voice choir and a symphony orchestra at the Place des Arts.

In the mid 1970s she studied acting at Lee Strasberg's Academy of Dramatic Arts in California.

From 1977 to 1998 she returned to recording only in French, and also acted in such acclaimed movies as Leolo (1992) which was a hit at both the Cannes Film Festival in France and The Toronto Film Festival. In 1998 she recorded her first English album in over twenty years, *Love is All*.

Singles:

J'aime Guy	Apex 13257	1962
Roger	Apex 13276	1963
Bobby	Apex 13292	1963
Tou peut recommencer	Apex 13309	1963
Le petit voisin	Apex 13329	1964

Seize ans	Apex 13352	1964
Tous vivras toujours dans mon couer	Apex 13372	1964
Si je pouvais vivre avec toi	Apex 13394	1965
Les yeux fermes	Apex 13414	1965
Je vivrai seule	Apex 13427	1965
Une nuit encore	Apex 13440	1966
Les jeux d'ete	Apex 13449	1966
Chere maman	Apex 13458	1966
Au revoir	Apex 13471	1967
Quelqu'un a aimer	Apex 13486	1967
Ma roue de fortune	Apex 13496	1967
La derniere valse	Grand Prix 5301	1967
Le lecon d'amour	Grand Prix 5305	1968
Non, c'est rien	Grand Prix	1968
Le chemin de San Jose	Grand Prix 5311	1968
Tu m'as donne la vie	Grand Prix 5315	1968
Les enfants oublies	Grand Prix 5318	1968
C'est mon coeur qui chante clair	Grand Prix 5323	1969
Le sable et la mer(w/J.Boulanger)	Grand Prix 5324	1969
Don't Let Me Be Misunderstood/ Everything That I Am	Parrot 40043	1969
Crowded By Emptiness	Parrot 40050	1970
Reste pres de moi	Grand Prix 5333	1970
Beautiful Second Hand Man	Parrot 40053	1970
La grande vie	Grand Prix 5337	1970
Aimer le si fort	Grand Prix 5338	1970
So Let Our Love Begin	Parrot 40061	1971
I've Got To Have You	Parrot 40063	1971
Nous n'aimerons jamais assez la vie	Grand Prix 5343	1971
L'amour est un carousel	Grand Prix 5344	1971
Choisi l'ombre ou le soleil	Grand Prix 5345	1971
Je m'en vais	Grand Prix 5346	1972
Fallin' In Love Again	Parrot 40068	1972
Dans la vie tout	Grand Prix 5347	1972
Can't Get Hurt Anymore	Parrot 383	1972
Here Comes The Heartache	Coral 62400	1973
Everyday Working Man	Parrot 2545	1973
I'll Bring You Apples	Parrot 2550	1974
Des croissants de soleil	Trans-World 119	1974
Light Of Love	Parrot 2558	1974
T'es Mon Amour (w/J.P. Ferland)	LondonL.2562	1974
Des Croissants De Soleil Reparti	Trans-World 900	1975
Je t'ai fait une chanson	Trans-World 901	1975
Un peu plus loin	Trans-World 906	1975
Mere d'une fille	Trans-World 917	1976
Ma chanson, c'est toi	Melon Miel MM 1	1977
Trying To Find A Way	Honey Dew HD 101	1977
La vie	Melon Miel MM 2	1977
But I Am The Woman	Honey Dew HDX 1	1978
I'll Never Find Another You	Honey Dew HD 102	1978

Un jour mon prince viendra	Melon Miel MM 3	1978
Toi le poete	Melon Miel MM 4	1979
Je ne suis qu'une chanson	Melon Miel MM 5	1980
Ca va mieux	Melon Miel MM 6	1980
Quand on se donne	Melon Miel MM 7	1981
Seule	Melon Miel MM 8	1981
Ma mere chantait	Melon Miel MM 9	1982
A quoi resemble le bon Dieu	Melon Miel MM 10	1982
La quete	Melon Miel MM 11	1983
Un homme ca tient chaud	Melon Miel MM 13	1983
Une femme sentimentale	Melon Miel MM 14	1984
Un coeur	Triangle 45 111	1984
C'est beaucoup mieux comme ca	Melon Miel MM 15	1984
Paris Quebec	Melon Miel MM 17	1986
De plus en plus fragile	Melon Miel MM 18	1986
Merci la vie	Melon Miel MM 20	1986
Au premier rang	Melon Miel MM 21	1987
Quand ca balance	Festival De Jazz 2500	1987
N'me laisse pas m'en aller	Melon Miel MM 22	1987
La deuxieme voix	Melon Miel MM 23	1988
Comment de dire	Melon Miel MM 26	1989
Je suis la femme	Melon Miel MM 27	1989
La prochaine fois que j'aurai 20 ans	Melon Miel MM 28	1990
Vie privee	Melon Miel MM 29	1991
L'essentiel (CD/S)	Melon Miel MM 30	1991
Y'va des enfants (CD/S)	Melon Miel MM 31	1992
Tu m'fais voir des etoiles	Melon Miel MM 514	1997

Albums/CDs:

Ginette Reno	Apex ALF 1555	1962
Ginette Reno: Formidable	Apex ALF 1568	1964
Ginette En Amour	Apex ALF 1580	1965
Le Monde De Ginette Reno	Apex ALF 1589	1966
En Spectacle A La Casa Loma	Apex ALF 1595	1966
Quelqu'un A Aimer	Apex ALF 1597	1967
Les Grand Succes D'une Vedette	Apex ALF 71802	1968
Ginette Reno, Collection No.1	Lero LS 773	1968
Ginette Reno, Collection No.2	Lero LS 774	1968
Ginette Reno	Grand Prix GPS 3301	1969
A La Comedie Canadienne 1969	Grand Prix GPS 3304	1969
Ginette Reno	Grand Prix GPS 3307	1969
Ginette Reno	Parrot PAS 71032	1970
Noel Avec Ginette Reno	Grand Prix GPS 3312	1970
Beautiful Second Hand Man	Parrot PAS 71045	1971
Touching Me Touching You	Parrot PAS 71058	1972
Aimez Le Si Fort	Grand Prix GPS 3310	1971
A La Comedie Canadienne, A Quichet Ferme	Grand Prix GPS 1399	1971
Ombres Et Soleil	Grand Prix GPS 3314	1973
Album Souvenir	Grand Prix SGPS 1	1973
Aimons Nous	Trans-World TWK 6507	1974

The Best of Ginette Reno	Parrot PAS 71074	1975
Trying To Find A Way	Honey Dew HD 1000	1979
Je Ne Suis Qu'une Chanson	Melon Miel MM 502	1980
Quand on Se Donne	Melon Miel MM 503	1981
Boucherville Et Paris 1982	Melon Miel MM 505	1982
Souvenirs Tendres	Melon Miel MM 506	1983
Ginette Reno	Melon Miel MM 507	1984
La Course Au Bonheur	Triangle TR 1401	1984
Ginette Reno/Michel Legrand	Festival De Jazz Fj 10	1985
Si Ca Vous Chante	Melon Miel MM 508	1986
Ne M'en Veut Pas	Melon Miel MM 509	1988
Ma Vie En 20 Chansons	Melon Miel MM 510	1990
L'essentiel	Melon Miel MM 511	1991
En Concert	Melon Miel MM 512	1993
Versions Reno	Melon Miel MM 513	1995
La Chanteuse	Melon Miel MM 514	1997
Love Is All	Attic ACD 1513	1998
Un Peu Plus Haut Le Nouveau Spectacle	Melon Miel 515	1999
Un Grand Noel D'amour	Melon Miel 516	2000

The Rheostatics

Dave Bidini (rhythm guitar, vox)
Dave Clark (drums, vox) Replaced by Don Kerr
Martin Tielli (lead guitar, vox)
Tim Vesely (bass, vox)

The Rheostatics started out as a trio in Etobicoke, Ontario in 1980 when Dave Bidini, Dave Clark and Tim Vesely were still in high school. At first they wanted to call themselves The New Originals, but ended up with rheostatic, when they confused the former with a rheostat. Martin Tielli joined the group in 1986.

In 1987 they came out with their Greatest Hits album, which was released independently.

During the early 1990s they made two critically acclaimed albums, *Melville* and *Whale Music*. The former included Horses, a song Neil Peart of Rush considered a masterpiece in Canadian folklore, while the latter became the soundtrack of the film of the same name, based on Paul Quarrington's novel. The soundtrack also included Claire, a song from their 1994 album, *Introducing Happiness*. They also wrote a 40-minute piece of music in honor of the Group of Seven's 75th Anniversary in 1995.

The only personnel change in the history of The Rheostatics came in 1996 when Dave Clark left, and was replaced by Don Kerr.

In 1998 the group released their ninth album, *The Nightlines Sessions*, a continuous collage of previously unreleased songs, jams and skits that were originally recorded for the final broadcast of CBC Radio's Nightlines program, hosted by David Wisdom. That same year, McClelland and Stewart published Bidini's tome, *On a Cold Road*, which was written during the group's 1996/97 tour with The Tragically Hip. Martin Tielli released a solo album, *We Didn't Even Suspect That He Was the Poppy Salesman* (Sixth Shooter 391051) in 2001.

Singles:
Soul Glue	Sire/WAR 45564	1992
Shaved Head	Sire/WAR 45564	1992
Claire	Sire/WAR 45670	1994
Bad Time To Be Poor	CARD 1039	1996

Albums/CDs:
Greatest Hits	X Records XR 87002	1987
Melville	Intrepid 0004	1991
Whale Music	Sire/War 45564	1992
Introducing Happiness	Sire/War 45670	1994
Music Inspired By the Group of 7	Gsmc 006	1995
The Blue Hysteria	Card 1039	1996
Double Live	Drog 041	1997
The Nightlines Sessions	Drog 055	1998
The Story of Harmelodia	Perimeter 030003	1999
Night of the Shooting Stars	Perimeter 509642	2001

Riverson

Rayburn Blake (guitar)
Brian Edwards (bass, vocals)
Franki Hart (acoustic guitar)

From Montreal, Riverson was made up of two members of Mashmakhan, Rayburn Blake and Brian Edwards, and Franki Hart, formerly with the group Freedom (aka Freedom North). The addition of Graham Lear complemented the group's live appearances. He was later replaced by Michael Burman, when Lear left to play with Gino Vannelli. Riverson recorded for Columbia Records. Their first single, Clear Night was released in 1972. There were two more singles and an album before the group split up in 1974.

Singles:
Clear Night	Columbia C4 3077	1972/73

| Eleanor Rigby | Columbia C4 3093 | 1973 |
| Sittin' Waitin' | Columbia C4 4003 | 1973 |

Album:

| Riverson | Columbia ES 90136 | 1973 |

Robbie Robertson

He was born Jaime Robbie Robertson in Toronto on July 5, 1943. His mother, a Mohawk descendant, was raised on the Six Nations Reservation near Brantford, Ontario. While visiting there as a young boy, he learned to play the guitar. As a teenager he played in various groups such as Little Caesar and the Consuls, Robbie and The Robots, and Thumper and The Trambones.

In 1960 he joined The Hawks, which also included future Band members Levon Helm, Rick Danko, Richard Manuel, and Garth Hudson.

Five years later, Robertson and Helm toured with Bob Dylan as part of his backup group at Forest Hills, New York, and at the Hollywood Bowl. Dylan and The Hawks then toured the United States, Australia, Great Britain and Europe. Robertson appeared on Dylan's *Blonde on Blonde* album in 1966. The following year, Dylan and The Hawks recorded the bootleg album, *Great White Wonder* in a West Saugerties, New York basement, which Columbia Records officially released as The Basement Tapes in 1975.

The Hawks changed their name to The Band in 1968, and for the next eight years they established themselves as one of Canada's best known bands.
Robertson's contribution to the group was his unique mix of white gospel, bluegrass and 19th century parlor music with country and rock. His images deftly captured the spirit of America.He wrote The Night They Drove Old Dixie Down which was certified a million seller for Joan Baez on October 22, 1971.

It was originally the flipside to The Band's 1969 Capitol single, Up On Cripple Creek.

In 1978, he contributed new songs to director Martin Scorsese's film of The Band's farewell concert, The Last Waltz. This experience led Robertson to concentrate on composing music for other films, such as Carny (which he also acted and co wrote the screenplay), Raging Bull, The King of Comedy, The Color of Money and Jimmy Hollywood.

Robertson's self-titled debut album on Geffen Records came out in 1987, and featured songs based on his native roots. After Storyville (1991), he worked on the soundtrack for the six hour documentary, The Native Americans, which was released on CD as *Music for the Native Americans* (1994). *Contact From the Underworld of Red Boy* (1998) was another foray into the artist's native roots, and featured a number of American Indian performers. In 2003 he was honoured with a star on Canada's Walk Of Fame in 2003. He is active today as a film and TV composer.

Singles:

Showdown At Big Sky	Geffen92 81757	1987/88
Showdown At Big Sky (12")	Geffen92 07960	1988
Somewhere Down The Crazy River	Geffen92 81117	1988
Christmas Must Be Tonight	A&M 17081	1988
What About Now	Geffen24303	1991
Go Back To Your Woods	Geffen24303	1991/92
Shake This Town	Geffen24303	1992
Bad Intentions	Atlantic 23070	1994
Skin Walker	EMI 28295	1994
Mahk Jchi (Heartbeat Drum Song)	EMI 28295	1994/95
Mahk Jchi (Heartbeat Drum Song)(12")	Cap SPRO 79510	1995
Ghost Dance	EMI 28295	1995
Crazy Love		1996
Unbound	EMI 54243	1998

Albums/CDs:

Robbie Robertson	Geffen XGHS 24160	1987
Storyville	Geffen GEFD 24303	1991
Music for the Native Americans	EMI 28295	1994
Contact From the Underworld of Redboy	EMI 54243	1998

Alys Robi

Born on February 3, 1923 in Quebec City, Alys Robi's musical career started at the young age of seven when she sang on radio station CHRC, and in the revue, Ten Nights In A Bar Room at the Capitol Theatre.

She won several amateur contests, and was a finalist in 1932 at a major amateur competition hosted by Major Bowes. At thirteen she sang at another Quebec radio station, CKAC, and worked with the Madame Rose Ouellette National Theatre Troupe.

In 1942 while performing at The Esquire Club she met CBC producer Morris Davis, who invited Robi to appear on the network shows hosted by Lucio Agostini and Allan McIver.

Her first of more than thirty singles with RCA Victor was Beguine backed by Le tram for RCA Victor in 1942.

She became well known in New York, Hollywood, Paris, Rio de Janeiro, and Mexico, and appeared on BBC television. Her career suddenly stopped in 1948 when she became mentally ill. In 1952 she resumed her career and was a success in Montreal's piano bars and cabarets and other parts of Quebec.

In 1980 she wrote her first of two autobiographies, *Ma Carriere, Ma Vie*. Her second, *Long Cri dans la nuit: Cinq annees a l'Asile*, in 1990, dealt with her mental illness. A film about her life, *Alys Robi: The Broken Dream* (1994) starred Joelle Morin in the title role. She died in Montreal on May 28, 2011.

Singles:

Title	Catalog	Year
Beguine	RCA 56 5111	1942
Tico Tico	RCA 56 5112	1942
La route enchante	RCA 56 5113	1943
Rhum et Coca Cola	RCA 56 5114	1944
Bresil	RCA 56 5115	1944
Besame mucho	RCA 56 5116	1944
Laura	RCA 56 5117	1944
Lorsque tu reviendras	RCA 56 5118	1944
Adios Muchacho	RCA 56 5119	1944
Ca atomique t' y	RCA 56 5122	1945
Le bonheur n'est qu'un reve	RCA 56 5124	1945
Cachita	RCA 56 5126	1945
Viens tout pres de moi	RCA 56 5127	1945
Sans tes caresses	RCA 56 5128	1945
Mon chant d'amour	RCA 56 5129	1946
Dans un petit baiser	RCA 56 5130	1946
Jalousie	RCA 56 5131	1946
La gypsy	RCA 56 5132	1946
Nuit et jour	RCA 56 5133	1946
Chaque nuit	RCA 56 5134	1947
Tu verras	RCA 56 5137	1947
Sonata	RCA 56 5140	1947
Je vous aime	RCA 56 5144	1948
Dis moi que tu'm'aimes	RCA 56 5145	1948
Mon coeur n'appartient qu'a toi	RCA 56 5151	1948
Ballerina	RCA 56 5154	1949
La danseuse est creole	RCA 56 5158	1949
La vie en rose	RCA 56 5160	1949
C'est Noel	Quality 210	1957
Anna	Quality 211	1958
Je prie pour notre amour	Rusticana 314	1966
Laissez moi encore chanter	Saisons SNS 6615	1989

Albums/CDs:

Les Succes D'alys Robi	RCA GALA CGP 101	1962
Ma Carriere, Ma Chansons	TCM 1002	1980
Laissez Moi Encore Chanter	Saisons SNS 90019	1989

Garnet Rogers

Garnet Rogers was born on May 3, 1955 in Hamilton, Ontario. Growing up he was exposed to country music broadcasts of the Grand Ol' Opry and often sang in harmony with his older brother Stan. Like his older brother, Garnet started with the ukelele but gave it up to learn the flute, violin and guitar. Barely out of high school, he joined his brother on the road and later served as accompanist and arranger on all of his late brother's recordings. After Stan's death, Garnet toured with Scottish singer Archie Fisher, and began recording on his own Snow Goose Songs label.

The younger Rogers' self-titled debut album came out in 1984. Until 1989 all of his recordings featured his own instrumentals and songs by other Canadian songwriters such as Willie P. Bennett, Roy Forbes, Connie Kaldor, James Keelaghan, Doug McArthur, and Ian Tamblyn.

Today, he is an established singer/songwriter in his own right and has headlined concerts at Wolf Trap, Lincoln Centre, and Art Park. He has also performed with Mary Chapin Carpenter, Billy Bragg, and Ferron.

Albums/CDs:

Garnet Rogers	Snow Goose Songs SGS 1111	1984
Off The Map	Snow Goose Songs SGS 1112	1986
The Outside Track	Snow Goose Songs SGS 1113	1986
Speaking Softly In The Dark	Snow Goose Songs SGS 1115	1988
Small Victories	Snow Goose Songs SGS 1117	1990
At A High Window	Snow Goose Songs SGS 1121	1991
Summer Lightning Live	Snow Goose Songs SGS 1123	1994
Night Drive	Snow Goose Songs SGS 1125	1996
Sparrow's Wing	Snow Goose Songs SGS 1127	1999

Stan Rogers

He was born Stan Allison Rogers in Hamilton, Ontario on November 29, 1949. As a child growing up he often visited his grandparents' home in Hazil Hill, Nova Scotia where he sat and listened to his parents, grandparents, aunts and uncles as they sang the songs of Hank Snow, Hank Williams, and Jimmie Rodgers (The Singing Brakeman).

In his mid teens he played in various rock groups, such as Predator and Stanley and The Livingstones. When he discovered the historical significance of the Canadian folk song, he switched to singing folk music. He made his debut at The Ebony Night, a folk club owned by painter Bill Powell, in 1963.

With bluegrass guitarist Nigel Russell and female singer Terri Olenick, Stan formed the trio, The Hobbits, named after J.R.R. Tolkien's Lord of the Ring trilogy. When they split up in 1969, Stan and Nigel continued to play together.

During this time, Stan began to write his own songs and in 1970 he was offered a chance to record a Christmas single for RCA, Here's To You, Santa Claus. Disillusioned by the company executives who felt he should sing novelty songs, he went to university where he studied to be a teacher. When Gordon Lightfoot invited him to sit in on the final mixing of his album, *Sit Down, Young Stranger*, Stan was convinced more than ever that he wanted to be a singer.

In 1972 he moved to London, Ontario where he sang at Smale's Pace Folk Club which was then one of the top folk clubs in Canada.

A year later, he recorded a three song EP on the CBC's transcription label: Three Pennies, Past Fifty and Guysborough Train. Stan also began appearing at folk festivals across Canada, where he was joined by his younger brother Garnet on fiddle, flute and electric guitar, and bassist Jim Ogilvie.

Stan recorded his first album, *Fogarty's Cove*, in 1976, which was a collection of songs influenced by his many trips to Nova Scotia. It was also a collaborative effort with poet Bill Howell, whom he worked with on the CBC radio show, Anecdote. While working on this album, Stan honed his skills as a songwriter whose ideas came from the plight of the working man. His later albums included historical songs (Man With The Blue Dolphin), political songs (The Mary Ellen Carter) and comic songs (Garnett's Home Made Beer, a take off on Barrett's Privateers written by folksinger Ian Robb).

By the early 1980s Rogers had become a prominent figure in Canada's contemporary folk music scene. On June 2, 1983 he died along with the other passengers of Flight 797 when it crash landed in Cincinatti, Ohio. In 1989, the CBC aired the documentary, *One Warm Line*, about the life of Stan Rogers. Four years later came the first posthumous release, Home In Halifax, a live concert taped by the CBC in 1982. There have also been two tribute albums, *Remembering Stan Rogers Vol. I* (1995), *Remembering Stan Rogers Vol II* (1996), and a collection of live material, *From Coffee House To Concert Hall* (1999).

Single:
Here's to You, Santa Claus	RCA 57 1056	1970

Albums/CDs:
Fogarty's Cove	Barnswallow BS 1001	1976
Turnaround	Fogarty Cove Music FCM 001	1978
Between the Breaks	Fogarty Cove Music FCM 002	1979
Northwest Passage	Fogarty Cove Music FCM 004	1980
For the Family	Folk Traditionr 002	1982
From Fresh Water	Chm 001	1984
Home in Halifax	Fogarty Cove Music FCM 010	1993
From Coffee House to Concert Hall	Fogarty Cove Music FCM 012	1999

Vladymir Rogov

Born in Hanover, West Germany on May 10, 1948 to Russian parents, Vladymir Rogov is a self-taught guitarist. In 1959 he moved with his parents to England where he went to school. While there he was exposed to Gilbert and Sullivan. He also joined a band called The Red Earth, and later wrote songs for producer Mickie Most.

In 1975 he moved to Toronto, Ontario where he became involved in a group called New World. He also taught design at the Ontario College of Art and other community colleges.

Signed to Change Records, he recorded the single, All Around The World in 1978. There was also the album, *Love is a Killer*. In 1981 he recorded as Arkitex, a name inspired by author Ayn Rand.

Since 1984 Rogov has lived in California where he runs his own company, Rogov International Design.

By Vlaydmir Rogov
Singles:
All Around The World	Change	1978
There's A Woman In That Child	Change CH 45024	1979

Album:
Love Is A Killer	Change Clp 8011	1980

By Arkitex
Single:
Throwing My Heart To The Wind	Rio 742	1981

Album:
Arkitex	Rio 1023	1981

Rough Trade

John Cessine (percussion)
Marv Kanarek (percussion)
Carole Pope (vocals)
Happy Roderman (bass)
Sharon Smith (piano)
Kevan Staples (guitar)

The origins of Rough Trade go back to 1968 when Carole and Kevan began singing as a folk duo in Yorkville. A year later they formed a band called O and appeared in the film, Osaka '70.

In 1971 they worked as The Bullwhip Brothers, and three years later they became Rough Trade.

Pope's leather outfit brought female sexuality to Canadian rock. Lorraine Segato of Parachute Club, another Canadian group, described Pope's new look as breaking new ground in the politics of sexuality. In 1985 Rough Trade made their last album together.

Singles:
Fashion Victim	True North TN4 157	1980/81
High School Confidential	True North TN4 159	1981
All Touch	True North TN4 165	1982
Crimes Of Passion	True North TN4 175	1983
Territorial	True North TN4 187	1983
Sexual Outlaw	True North TN4 192	1984
On The Line	True North TN4 194	1984/85

Albums/CDs:
Rough Trade Live!	Umbrella UMB DD1	1976
Avoid Freud	True North TN43	1981
For Those Who Think Young	True North TN48	1982

Shaking The Foundations	True North TN50	1982
Weapons	True North TN55	1983
O Tempora! O Mores!	True North TN58	1984
Best of Birds Of A Feather	True North TN64	1985

The Rover Boys

Billy Albert (lead vocals)
Larry Amato (first tenor)
Al Osten (bass)
Doug Wells (second tenor)

The Rover Boys started in Toronto in 1950 as a vocal trio. Four years later they were discovered by disc jockey Bill Silbert who helped them get a recording contract with Coral Records. After only one single release in 1954, the group switched to ABC Paramount, where they backed up Paul Anka, who was also with the label in the United States. At ABC Paramount they had four Singles:, one of which, *Graduation Day*, was a top twenty hit on Billboard's Top 100 in 1956.

Singles:
Show Me	Coral 61271	1954
Love Me Again	ABC PAR 9659	1955
My Queen	ABC PAR 9678	1956
Graduation Day	ABC PAR 9700	1956
From a School Ring to a Wedding Ring	ABC PAR 9732	1956

Craig Ruhnke

Craig Ruhnke's musical career began in the late 1960s when he was a member of the Groovin' Company. The Toronto-based singer/songwriter then worked at Don Valley Music, Wea's publishing arm, where one of his songs, I'll Always Love You was recorded by Pinky (Lighthouse).

In 1974 Ruhnke recorded his first song for the label, My World. By the summer of that same year, he had switched over to United Artists who released his first Top 10 hit, Summer Girl.

During the 1980s he recorded for A&M, Sefel Records, and his own label, Pinnacle.

Singles:

My World	Reprise CR 4022	1974
Summer Girl	United ArtistsUAXW 453	1974
Sweet Feelin'	United ArtistsUAXW 567	1974
I Need My Woman	United ArtistsUAXW 612	1975
Summer Love	United ArtistsUAXW 814	1975
Surfin' All Summer Song	United ArtistsUAXW 663	1975
It's Too Good to Know	United ArtistsUAXW 749	1976
Why Don't You Come Up and See Me	United ArtistsUAXW 857	1976
Wear My Love (Craig Ruhnke Band)	Polydor 2065 389	1978
It's Time to Fall in Love	Polydor 2065 400	1979
The First Time	A&M AM 477	1979
I Need You to Be There	A&M AM 486	1979
You're a Heartbreaker	A&M AM 498	1980
Heartache	A&M AM 509	1980
I Can't Live Without Your Love	A&M AM 527	1981
Reach Out (Craig Runkey)	A&M AM 536	1981
Baby Blue	Sefel Records 45 010	1982
You're So Beautiful	A&M AM 642	1984
Give Me the Night Time	A&M AM 666	1984
Lovin' Eyes	Pinnacle WRC3 3880	1985

Albums/CDs:

Sweet Feelings	United ArtistsUALA 415G	1975
Hot Spell	United ArtistsUALA 641G	1976
Craig Ruhnke Band	A&M Records 1A	1979
Just Like the Old Times	Sefel Records SEF 1006	1982
Keep the Flame	A&M Records SP 9102	1984

Rush

Geddy Lee (bass, vocals)
Alex Lifeson (lead guitar)
John Rutsey (percussion)

The origins of this Toronto group go back to the spring of 1968 when Alex Lifeson, the son of Yugoslavian parents, and John Rutsey played in a group called The Projection, who later broke up that summer.

With Jeff Jones on bass and lead vocals, John and Alex formed another group which, at the suggestion of John's older brother, Bill, became Rush. They played at the Coff In, a drop in centre in Toronto. When Jeff left to join the band, Lactic Acid, Geddy Lee replaced him.

In September 1968, Rush's repertoire included six songs by Cream, along with covers of Jimi Hendrix, The Who, Jeff Beck, The Rolling Stones, and Elvis Presley's Jailhouse Rock, sung in Yugoslavian.

During this time, Rush started writing their own songs, one of which was Losing Again.

On Christmas Day 1968 keyboardist Lindy Young became the fourth member. In May 1969 Geddy Lee was forced out of the band and their name changed to Hadrian. Joe Perna also joined on bass and vocals.

Lee started Ogilvie, a rhythm and blues group, renamed Judd. Hadrian broke up when Lindy left to join Judd until they disbanded in September 1969.

With Alex and John groupless, they became impressed by the first Led Zeppelin album. With Lee, they reformed Rush. But this time they were going to play heavy rock. The change received a mixed reaction from their fans. Unable to support themselves full time with their music, they each took on day jobs.

In February 1971 guitarist Mitch Bossi became the fourth member, and the group became regulars at Toronto's Abbey Road pub.

They also made some amateur recordings in each other's basements and at various shows.

Their first professional recording session was at Eastern Sound Studios, Toronto in 1973, where they recorded their first, and only cover version of an old song, Buddy Holly's Not Fade Away.

In 1974 Rush released their self-titled debut album on Moon Records. That same year, Rutsey left the group and was replaced by Neil Peart, a former member of the St. Catharines' band Hush, who joined the group on their first full time U.S. tour. They also taped an episode for the ABC TV In Concert series, which aired on December 6, 1974.

Since their inception they have become Canada's power pop trio and have attracted a loyal fan base internationally. Their early albums, *Fly by Night* and *Caress of Steel*, were inspired by J.R.R. Tolkien's Lord of the Rings.

In the mid to late 1990s, the members of the group took on separate projects. Peart, with the help of Cathy Rich, the daughter of the late jazz drummer, released the tribute album, *Burning for Buddy* (1994), while Lifeson recorded his first solo album, *Victor* (1996) and Geddy Lee, *My Favorite Headache* (2000).

The group was honored with its own star on Canada's Walk of Fame in Toronto.

Singles:

Not Fade Away	Moon 001	1973
Lakeside Park	Mercury73737	1975
In The Mood	Mercury73647	1975
Fly By Night	Mercury73681	1975

Return of the Prince	Mercury 73728	1975
Lessons	Mercury 73803	1976
Closer To The Heart	Anthem ANS 004	1977
Circumstances	Anthem ANS 009	1978
Spirit Of The Radio	Anthem ANS 017	1980
Entre Nous	Anthem ANS 021	1980
Limelight	Anthem ANS 031	1981
Tom Sawyer	Anthem ANS 034	1981
Closer To The Heart (Live)	Anthem ANS 039	1981
New World Man	Anthem ANS 046	1982
Subdivisions	Anthem ANS 048	1983
The Body Electric	Anthem ANS 059	1984
Mystic Rhythms	Anthem ANS 069	1985
The Big Money (12")	Anthem APE 029	1985/86
Time Stand Still (12")	Anthem SPE 038	1987
Lock & Key (12")	Anthem SPE 039	1987
Marathon (Live) (12")	Anthem PRO 1	1989
Show Don't Tell	Anthem ANK 1059	1990
The Pass	Anthem ANK 1059	1990
Superconductor	Anthem ANK 1059	1990
Dreamline	Anthem ANK 1064	1991
Roll The Bones	Anthem ANK 1064	1991
Ghost Of A Chance	Anthem ANK 1064	1992
Stick It Out	Anthem ANK 1067	1993
Nobody's Hero	Anthem ANK 1067	1994
Test For Echo	Anthem ANK 1073	1996
Half The World	Anthem ANK 1073	1996/97
Driven	Anthem ANK 1073	1997
Spirit of the Radio	Anthem AND3 1092	1998/99

Albums/CDs:

Rush	Moon MN 100	1974
Fly By Night	Mercury SRM1 1023	1975
Caress Of Steel	Mercury SRM1 1046	1975
2112	Mercury SRM1 1079	1976
All The World's A Stage	Mercury SRM2 7508	1976
A Farewell To Kings	Anthem ANR 1 1010	1977
Archives	Anthem ANR 3 1013	1978
Hemispheres	Anthem ANR 1 1015	1979
Permanent Waves	Anthem ANR 1 1021	1980
Moving Pictures	Anthem ANR 1 1030	1981
Exit...Stage Left	Anthem ANR 4 1035	1981
Signals	Anthem ANR 1 1038	1982
Grace Under Pressure	Anthem ANR 1 1045	1984
Power Windows	Anthem ANR 1 1049	1985
Hold Your Fire	Anthem ANR 1 1051	1987
Presto	Anthem ANK 1059	1989
A Show of Hands	Anthem A1 1055	1989
Chronicles	Anthem AN2K 1060	1990

Roll The Bones	Anthem Ank 1064	1991
Counterparts	Anthem Ank 1067	1993
Test For Echo	Anthem ANK 1073	1996
Retrospective I (1974 1980)	Anthem ANSSD 1087	1997
Retrospective Ii (1981 1987)	Anthem ANSSD 1088	1997
Different Stages – Live	Anthem AND3 1092	1998
Vapor Trails	Anthem 510962	2002
Rush in Rio	Anthem 520002	2003
Feedback	Anthem 520012	2004
Replay X 3	Anthem 520079	2006
Snakes & Arrows	Anthem 520122	2007
Snakes & Arrows Live	Anthem 520492	2008
Grace Under Pressure	Mercury325202	2009
Live In Cleveland	Anthem 521612	2011
Clockwork Angels	Anthem 521722	2012
Clockwork Angels Tour	Anthem 522222	2013

Ryan's Fancy

Fergus O'Bryne (vocals, guitar, bodhran, banjo)
Dermot O'Reilly   (vocals, guitar, tambourine, mandolin)
Denis Ryan (vocals, tin whistle)

Originally from Ireland, Denis Ryan, Dermot O'Reilly and Fergus O'Bryne eventually ended up playing together in the group, Sullivan's Gypsies who later changed their name to Ryan's Fancy in 1971.

From Dublin, O'Bryne settled in Toronto when he arrived in 1967. He was a classically trained pianist, noted banjo player, and was adept on both the six and twelve string guitars, mandolin, and Irish drum or bodhran. O'Reilly, whose musical career began in his father's minstrel shows at age twelve. He had a brief career as a rock and roll musician before he switched to folk, and arrived in Canada in 1968, where he settled in Hamilton, Ontario. Ryan was born in Newport, Tipperary and was best known for his rendition of Danny Boy. He came to Canada in 1969 to study medicine, but ended up playing in a pub by night and driving a truck by day.

All three were involved in Irish folk groups when they all met as members of Sullivan's Gypsies. Their first album, *Ryan's Fancy Sung By Sullivan's Gypsies* was released independently. They later recorded on the Audat and Boot labels.

The group was featured in three TV series: Ryan's Fancy, Tommy Makem and

Ryan's Fancy, and Canadian Express. They also starred and sang in the CBC TV movie Pirate's Gold in 1980.

Ryan's Fancy broke up in 1987. Fergus went on to become a schoolteacher, Denis became a stockbroker and a founding member of Highland Breweries in Cape Breton, and Dermot pursued a career as a troubadour/folksinger.

In 1991, Denis recorded the solo CD, *Mist Covered Mountains* on the independent Brookes Diamond label (DRCD 228).

Single:
Mist Upon A Morning Boot   1979/80

Albums/CDs:
Sullivan's Gypsies	Harmony KHE 90176	1970
An Irish Night At The Black Knight	Marathon MS 2105	1970
Dark Island	Audat 477 9001	1971
Looking Back	Audat 477 9015	1972
Newfoundland Drinking Songs	Audat 477 9024	1973
Times To Remember	Audat 477 9047	1973
Ryan's Fancy Live	Audat 477 9085	1975
Brand New Songs	RCA KXL1 0202	1977
A Time With Ryan's Fancy	Boot Bos 7197	1979
Sea People	Boot BOS 7212	1980
Dance Around This One	Boot BOS 7217	1981
Irish Love Songs	Boot BOS 7232	1982

Saga

Ian Crichton (guitar)
Jim Crichton (bass)
Jim Gilmour (keyboards)
Steve Negus (drums)
Michael Sadler (vocals)

Formed from the nucleus of Fludd (Jim Crichton, Steve Negus, Peter Rachon) and ex members of Truck (Michael Sadler) and Kickback (Ian Crichton), Saga's progressive rock sound distinguished them as a unique act with keyboards being used for orchestration rather than the traditional piano and organ.

They started out in Toronto in 1977 as a trio called Pockets, comprised of Jim Crichton, Sadler and Negus. When Jim's brother, Ian, and Gilmour joined they became known as Saga. In the mid 80s, Gilmour and Negus left and the group continued as a trio.

With the release of their album, *Security of Illusion* in 1993, the group had returned to its original lineup. The songs for Steel Umbrellas (1994) were originally used in the syndicated TV series, Cobra. Their subsequent albums included the live album, *Detours* (1998), which included songs taken from their shows in Germany, Austria and France, and *House of Cards* (2001), a continuation of the group's growth as an innovative rock band.

Singles:

How Long	Maze MS 808	1978
It's Time (Chapter Three)	Polydor 2065.419	1980
Compromise	Maze MS 801	1980
See Them Smile	Polydor 2065 422	1980
Don't Be Late	Maze MS 802	1981
Wind Him Up	Maze MS 804	1982
On The Loose	Maze MS 808	1982
The Flyer	Maze MS 809	1983
Scratching The Surface	Maze MS 810	1984
What Do I Know	Maze MS 811	1985
What Do I Know (12")	Por RAS 2150	1985
Misbehaviour	Maze MS 812	1985
Only Time Will Tell	A&M AMS 111	1986

Albums/CDs:

Images at Twilight	Polydor 2424 202	1979
Silent Knight	Maze ML 8003	1980
Worlds Apart	Maze ML 8004	1981
In Transit	Maze ML 8006	1982
Heads or Tales	Maze ML 8007	1983
Behaviour	Maze ML 8010	1985
Wildest Dreams	Bonaire Amd 1100	1987
Beginner's Guide to Throwing Shapes	Bonaire 210367	1989
The Works	Bonaire 354333	1991
All the Best 1978 1993	Quality QCD 2033	1993
Security of Illusion	Avalanche AVR 001	1993
Steel Umbrellas	Polydor 523054	1994
Very Best of		1994
Generation 13	Bonaire BNA 0014	1995
Pleasure & The Pain	Bonaire BNA 0016	1997
Phase One (Ep)	H Art Musik 18012	1997
How Do I Look	Steamhammer SPV 52692	1998
Detours Live	Steamhammer SPV 18002	1998
Defining Moments Volume One	True North TND 199	1998
Full Circle	Steamhammer SPV 21462	1999
House of Cards	True North TND 229	2001

Buffy Sainte Marie

Buffy Sainte Marie was born on February 20, 1942 on the Piapot Reserve at Craven, Saskatchewan. Orphaned when she was only a few months old, she was later adopted by Winifred Kendrick Saint Marie. Her adoptive parents were part Micmac. They moved Buffy to Wakefield, Massachusetts where she became a U.S. citizen. Growing up she taught herself to play the piano and, later in her teens, the guitar.

She attended the University of Massachusetts and it was there she started her career as a folksinger. In 1963 she received a degree in philosophy. She also went to New York where she performed at the Gaslight Cafe in Greenwich Village. The New York Times hailed her as a promising new talent and she continued to play at other Village nightspots.

Herbert S. Gart, a New York talent agent, helped her sign her first recording contract with the Vanguard Recording Society. In 1964 her debut album, It's My Way was released.

In 1965 she made her first appearance at New York's Carnegie Hall, the Newport Folk Festival and Royal Albert Hall in London. Other artists such as Neil Diamond (Until It's Time For You To Go), and Glen Campbell (Universal Soldier) have recorded her material.

In 1982, Buffy won an Oscar as co writer of Up Where We Belong, from the film, An Officer And A Gentleman (Paramount Pictures). After a 14 year absence, she released her 14th album, Coincidence and Likely Stories in 1992. She has appeared as a regular on the children's series, Sesame Street, and earned a Doctorate in Fine Arts from the University of Massachusetts. She holds dual citizenship papers for both Canada and the United States. In 1999 she was honoured with a star on Canada's Walk of Fame in Toronto. Universal Soldier was inducted into the Canadian Songwriters Hall of Fame in 2005.

Singles:

Circle Game	Vanguard 35108	1970
I'm Gonna Be A Country Girl Again	Vanguard 35148	1972
Mister Can't You See	Vanguard 35151	1972
He's An Indian Cowboy In The Rodeo	Vanguard 35156	1972
Can't Believe The Feelin'	MCA 40193	1974
I Can't Take It	MCA 40286	1974
Nobody Will Ever Know It's Real But You	MCA 40368	1975
All Around The World	MCA 40413	1975
Starwalker	ABC 1022 12183	1976
Fallen Angels	EMI 221920	1992

The Big Ones Get Away	EMI 221920	1992
Darling Don't Cry	EMI E235059	1996
Until It's Time For You To Go	EMI E235059	1996

Albums/CDs:

It's My Way	Vanguard VRS 9142	1964
Many a Mile	Vanguard VSD 79171	1965
Little Wheel and Spin	Vanguard VSD 79211	1966
Fire And Fleet and Candlelight	Vanguard VSD 79250	1967
I'm Gonna Be a Country Girl Again	Vanguard VSD 79280	1968
Illuminations	Vanguard VSD 79300	1969
The Best of Buffy Sainte Marie, Vol I	Vanguard 3/4	1970
She Used to Wanna Be a Ballerina	Vanguard VSD 79311	1971
Moonshot	Vanguard VSD 79312	1972
Quiet Places	Vanguard VSD 79330	1973
Native North American Child: An Odyssey	Vanguard VSD 79340	1974
Buffy	MCA 405	1974
Changing Woman	MCA 451	1975
Sweet America	ABC 9022 929	1976
Coincidence and Likely Stories	EMI 221920	1992
Up Where We Belong	EMI 235059	1996
Singing Sam		1998
Cry With the Eagle		1999
Canada, Oh Canada		2001
Best Of Vanguard Years		2008
Running For the Drum	Cinefocus 214758	2008
Power in the Blood	True North TND 603	2015

The Sands of Time

Eric Baragar (vocals, guitar)
Tim Campbell (vocals, guitar)
Dave Conley (vocals, keyboards)
Michael Goettler (vocals, bass)
Steve Smith (vocals, drums)

Formed in 1966, this Belleville, Ontario group began as Ken and The Continentals with Tim Campbell, Eric and Dennis Baragar, Al O'Hara, Ted Elvins and Ken Williams. Williams later became their manager and renamed the band, The Sands of Time. They performed at Man and His World at Exp '67, and were the youngest band in Canada to tour the east coast. In 1969 they played at the Canadian National Exhibition in Toronto and toured the west coast.

Vernon Martin replaced Elvins on lead vocals and their sound was a musical blend of rhythm and blues and British rock. The rest of the band was comprised of the Eric and Dennis Baragar, Goettler, Campbell and O'Hara. Dennis, Martin, and O'Hara later left and the group became a five-man band, with the addition of Dave Conley and Steve Smith.

In 1970 they recorded their only hit, I've Got A Feeling and, a year later, they moved to Toronto. After recording an album that was never released, they returned to Belleville. Conley stayed in Toronto, while the rest of the band broke up.

Eric Baragar pursued a solo career, and later started Sands of Time II with Goettler,

Trevor Burt on guitar and vocals, Doug Leal on drums, and Brent Bailey on keyboards. They, too, broke up after a few months. In 1977 most of the original members of The Sands of Time formed a new group called, Bentwood Rocker.

Singles:
I've Got A Feeling	MTCC MT 1004	1970
I've Got A Feeling (U.S.)	National General NGR 11	1971

Satan and the D Men

Wayne Falconer (vocals, guitar)
Wayne Cardinal (bass)
John Karwacki (drums)
Russell Percy (keyboards)
Terry Styles (rhythm guitar)

Formed in 1965 in Keewatin Kenora, Ontario, Satan and The D Men were a rock band who recorded one single, She'll Lie, on Eagle Records. They moved to Winnipeg, Manitoba in 1968, and two years later they broke up. From 1985 to 1997 the group reunited in Kenora.

Wayne Faulconer was a member of the Jarvis Street Revue from 1970 1974. Today, he fronts The Wayne Faulconer Band in Thunder Bay, Ontario. They have made two independent CDs, *Band's Gotta Do What A Band's Gotta Do* (1997), and *Shivers, Quivers & Quakes* (1998).

Single:
She'll Lie	Eagle 112	1965

The Sceptres

Ron Dykhof (lead vocals, electric piano)
Bill Garry (Ott) (bass, background vocals)
Tim Hewlings (guitar, background vocals)
(W.F.) Tyler William (drums, background vocals)

Montreal's The Sceptres started in September 1964. The original lineup of the group was comprised of (W.F.) Tyler William, who went to high school in Kingston and played in two groups, The Monarchs and Bob McCord and The Vibrations; Ron Dykhof, Bill Garry (Ott), and Tim Hewlings. They recorded and performed in both English and French.

In November 1965 they recorded their first hit single, It's All Over Now on the Fi Sound label at RCA's Montreal studios. During the summer of 1966, Dykhof left and was replaced by Marty Butler, who had previously been a member of The Ray Mart Trio. After another single in English, Can't Get You Off My Mind, the group recorded their first French single with Butler called, Enfin Seul Ensemble/Et Maintenant (1967). That same year they returned to RCA for I Never Had A Love Like That, which was a number one hit at radio station CFRA in Ottawa on September 1, 1967.

In 1968 the group recorded for Polydor where they had two hits: Juicy Morning and Good Morning New Day.

The Sceptres stage act included songs by Jay and The Americans, The Happenings, Gene Pitney, The Four Seasons and Roy Orbison. They were popular at the Tiki Club in Brockville, Le Coq d'Or in Toronto, and were the first rock group to play at Place des Arts in Montreal. They broke up in 1969.

Butler went on to have a successful solo career as a singer/songwriter until he died in 1996, Ott has held various executive positions in the Canadian recording industry, Hewlings is a studio musician who owns his own acoustical consulting and technical services business in Montreal, and Tyler operates his own chartered accountant firm in Ottawa.

Singles:

It's All Over Now	Fi Sound FSS 101	1965
Can't Get You Off My Mind	Allied FSS 104	1966
Enfin Seul Ensemble	Alliance AF 502	1967
I Never Had A Love Like That	RCA 57 3436	1967
Moi Je Pense Toujours A Toi	RCA 57 5778	1967
Something's Coming Along	Allied AR 6353	1968
Juicy Morning	Polydor 540.004	1968
Good Morning New Day	Polydor 540.010	1969

Eddie Schwartz

Born on December 22, 1949 in Toronto, Eddie Schwartz has been writing songs since he was 11 years old. His first big success as a songwriter was the 1980 hit, Hit Me With Your Best Shot which was recorded by Pat Benatar. Others who have recorded his songs include The Doobie Brothers (The Doctor), Joe Cocker (Two Wrongs), Paul Carrack (Don't Shed A Tear) and Gowan (All The Girls In The World).

In 1976 Eddie was a guitarist in Charity Brown's backup band. Three years later he signed a contract with Infinity Records but the label folded before anything was released.

Early in 1980 he released his debut single, Two Hearts Full of Love on Atco Records. Other hits followed but his success as a songwriter overshadowed any talent he had as a singer. His songs have been recorded by more than 100 artists in 60 countries. Today, he continues to write and produce songs.

Singles:

Two Hearts Full Of Love	A&M AM	1980
Does A Fool Ever Learn	A&M AM 511	1981
Heart On Fire	A&M AM 546	1981
All Our Tomorrows	A&M AM 559	1982
Over The Line	A&M AM 567	1982
Spirit Of The Night	A&M AM 577	1982
Don't Come To Me	Wea 25 92557	1984
Strike	Wea 25 96227	1984
Bourbon Street	SelectMHRCD0022	1995
Every Road I Take	SelectMHRCD0022	1995

Albums/CDs:

Schwartz	A&M SP 9047	1980
No Refuge	A&M SP 9056	1981
Public Life	Wea 25 03411	1983
Tour De Schwartz	Select MHRCD0022	1995

Jack Scott

Born Jack Scafone in Windsor, Ontario on January 28, 1936, he moved to Detroit, Michigan in his teens with his New York born father and Italian mother, who later taught the young Jack how to play the guitar. He started singing in high school with his brother Jerry in the country and western band, The Southern Drifters. When a local deejay in Detroit heard Jack at a high school dance, he was invited to make some demos (demonstration records). Response to Jack's songs led to a recording contract at ABC Paramount in 1957. His first two hits with the label were Baby She's Gone and Two Timin' Woman. Backing him up were Stan Getz and The Tom Cats (David Rohiller on lead guitar and cousin Dominic Scafone on drums).

A year later, he signed with Carlton Records. A new group from Windsor, The Chantones became his new backup group. They would sing on all of his hits but Burning Bridges. (see The Chantones)

Scott's biggest hit at Carlton was My True Love in 1958, the same year he was drafted into the army. Discharged in 1959, he began recording for a new label, Top Rank, and had a Top 5 hit with What In The World's Come Over You.

In 1961 he signed to Capitol Records. Three years later, they released a greatest hits album called *Burning Bridges and More of the All Time Great Hits of Jack Scott*. By the mid 1960s, Scott's career began to fade. He was signed to three different labels (ABC Paramount, GRT and Jubilee) before switching from rock to country in 1974. Capitol released a CD of the artist's best in their "Collectors Series" in 1990.

Singles:

Before The Bird Flies	ABC 10843	1957
Baby, She's Gone	ABC PAR 9818	1957
Two Timin' Woman	ABC PAR 9860	1957
Leroy/My True Love	Carlton 462	1958
Geraldine	Carlton 483	1958
Goodbye Baby/Save My Soul	Carlton 493	1958
I Never Felt Like This	Carlton 504	1959
The Way I Walk	Carlton 514	1959
There Comes A Time	Carlton 519	1959
What Am I Living For	Guaranteed 209	1960
Go Wild Little Sadie	Guaranteed	1960
What In The World's Come Over You	Top Rank 2028	1960
Burning Bridges	Top Rank 2041	1960
Oh, Little One	Top Rank 2041	1960
It Only Happened Yesterday/Cool Water	Top Rank 2055	1960
Patsy	Top Rank 2075	1960
Is There Something On Your Mind	Top Rank 2093	1961
A Little Feeling (Called Love)	Capitol 4554	1961
My Dream Come True	Capitol 4597	1961
Steps 1 And 2	Capitol 4637	1961
Sad Story	Capitol 4796	1962
Part Where I Cry	Capitol 4738	1962
Cry Cry Cry	Capitol 4689	1962
If Only	Capitol 4855	1962
Strangers	Capitol 4903	1963
All I See Is Blue	Capitol 4955	1963
There's Trouble Brewin'	Groove 0027	1963
Jingle Bells Slide	Groove 0027	1963
I Knew You First	Groove 0031	1964
Thou Shalt Not Steal	Groove 0042	1964

Flakey John	Groove 0049	1964
What A Wonderful Night Out	Groove 0037	1964
I Don't Believe In Tea Leaves	RCA 8505	1965
Don't Hush The Laughter	RCA 8724	1965
Looking For Linda	RCA 8685	1965
Before The Bird Flies	ABC 10843	1966
My Special Angel	Jubilee 5606	1967

Albums/CDs:

Presenting Jack Scott (EP)	Carlton 1070/1071	1958
Jack Scott	Carlton 12 107	1958
Jack Scott Sings (Ep)	Carlton 1072	1959
What Am I Living For	Carlton 12 122	1960
Jack Scott (Ep)	Top Rank1001	1960
I Remember Hank Williams	Top Rank319/619	1960
The Spirit Moves Me	Top Rank348	1961
What In The World's Come Over You	Top Rank626	1961
Burning Bridges	Capitol St 2035	1964
Collector's Series	Capitol 793192	1990

Scrubbaloe Caine

Paul Dean (lead and slide guitar)
Al Foreman (keyboards, harmonica, lead vocals)
Jim Harmata (lead guitar)
Jim Kale (bass, vocals) Replaced by Greg Stefaniuk (1974)
Bill McBeth (drums, percussion, vocals)
Henry Small (electric violin, lead vocals) (1972 1975)

Formed in Vancouver in 1972, Scrubbaloe Caine evolved out of two groups, Canada and Cannonball. Paul Dean, Al Foreman, Jim Harmata, Henry Small, and Bill McBeth had worked together in the Trials Of Jayson Hoover. McBeth had also been a member of The Nocturnals. When Cannonball played at The Fireplace Club in Winnipeg, they ended staying there as the house band. It was during this time that Jim Kale, formerly of The Guess Who, joined Cannonball and the group changed their name to Scrubbaloe Caine. Signed to RCA, their first hit was Feelin' Good On Sunday from the album, *Round One*. In 1974, Kale left and was replaced by Greg Stefaniuk. Small also left to start his own group, Small Wonder, in Toronto in 1975. Scrubbaloe Caine broke up in the late 1970s.

Singles:

Feelin' Good On Sunday	RCA 0148	1973
I'm A Dreamer	RCA PB 10041	1974
Travellin'	APBO 0241	1974
Feelin' Down	Amherst AMC 601	1976

Album:

Round One	RCA APL1 0263	1973

Shadowy Men on a Shadowy Planet

Brian Connelly (guitar)
Reid Diamond (bass)
Don Pyle (drums)

Formed in October 1984 in Toronto, Shadowy Men on a Shadowy Planet was an instrumental rock band whose live shows often revolved around themes, such as Laser Men, Fourteen In Dog Years, and Dark Side of the Moon. The group did not tour Canada until 1986. They composed the score for CBC TV show, The Kids in the Hall from 1989 to 1994. Shadowy Men on a Shadowy Planet dissolved in 1995. Brian Connelly joined the Heatseekers, who contributed to one side of a seven-inch single before they broke up. Don Pyle and Reid Diamond formed the group Phono Comb, who recorded on the Chicago label Quarterstick in 1996. He died of cancer on February 17, 2001.

Singles:

Love Without Words	Jet Pac	c1985
Wow Flutter Hiss	Jet Pac	c1986
Schlaggers!	Jet Pac	cc1987
Live With Extra Bread & Cheese	Jet Pac	1987
Explosion of Taste	Jet Pac	1988
Dog and Squeegie	Estrus Records	1993
Take Outs	Derivative Records	1993

Albums/CDs:

Four Song EP	WRC3 4435	1986
OUR Weapons ARE USELESS (EP)	ACS 5033	1987

Good Cop Bad Cop (EP)	WRC3 4996	1987
Savvy Show Stoppers	Cargo 09	1990
Six Song EP (Red vinyl)	IPU 19	1991
Tired Of Waking Up Tired/ Alouette (Green Vinyl)	Cargo CAR 702	1991
Dim The Lights, Chill The Ham	Cargo CAR 014	1991
Sport Fishin'	Cargo CAR 017	1993
It's A Wonderful Record (w/Moto) (Christmas EP white vinyl)	JET PAC 712A	1994

Sheriff

Freddy Curci (vocals)
Steve De Marchi (guitar)
Rob Elliott (drums)
Wolf Hassel (bass)
Arnold Lanni (keyboards)

Sheriff, a six-man band from Toronto, Ontario, formed in early 1979. In 1983 after four years of touring they signed with Capitol Records. Their biggest hit, When I'm With You (1983), was re released in 1989 by Capitol, when it reached number one on Billboard's Hot 100 chart on February 4, 1989 for one week. The first time in Canadian music history where a group had a number one hit after disbanding in the United States. They refused to get together because they all had moved on with their careers: Arnold Lanni and Wolf Hassel formed Frozen Ghost in 1985, while Freddy Curci and Steve De Marchi started Alias. Curci also had brief success on his own as a solo performer.

Singles:
You Remind Me	Capitol 72889	1982
You Remind Me (12")	Capitol SPRO 211	1982
When I'm With You	Capitol 72901/5199	1983
Mama's Baby	Capitol 72906	1983
When I'm With You	Capitol 72901	1989

Albums/CDs:
Sheriff	Capitol ST 12227	1983
Sheriff Live (EP)	Capitol SPRO 232	1983

Jane Siberry

Jane Siberry was born in Toronto on October 12, 1955. As a child she played the piano. In her teens she started playing the guitar. While studying biology at the University of Guelph she began performing as a folksinger. With Wendy Davis she formed the acoustic duo Java Jive, accompanied by bassist John Switzer. When they split up, Siberry continued to hone her craft as a songwriter, and in 1981 her self-titled independent debut album was released.

Her songs have ranged from the surreal poetry of her debut album, the simplicity of life in Map of the World on *No Borders Here*, the dramatic and visually exciting Vladimir Vladimir on *The Speckless Sky*, the optimism in *Bound by the Beauty*, to the more metaphorical songs on *Maria*. Her songe, Mimi on the Beach, was released in 1985 was seven and a half minutes long and told about a woman floating on a pink surfboard.

Some of her songs have also appeared on the soundtracks of several movies, notably Sleeping in The Devil's Bed in Until the End of the World (1991), Call Me and Slow Tango in Far Away So Close (1993), and It Can't Rain All The Time in The Crow (1994).

In 1996 she started her own company called Sheeba Productions. Through Sheeba she has released her own CDs and published three books. Her CDs, including: *Hush* (2000) and *City* (2001). Her books included: *Swan* (1998), *One Room Schoolhouse* (1999) and *New Year's Baby* (2000).

Singles:

You Don't Need	Duke StreetDSR 31006	1984
Mimi on the Beach	Duke StreetDSR 91007	1984
Mimi on the Beach (12")	Open Air OA 17338	1984
I Muse Aloud	Duke StreetDSR 31006	1984
The Waitress	Duke StreetDSR 71007	1984
One More Colour	Duke StreetDSR 71019	1985
Bound by the Beauty	Duke StreetDSRD 8933	1989
Everything Reminds Me of My Dog	Duke StreetDSR	1989
Hockey Song	Duke StreetDSR 81058	1990
Life is the Red Wagon	Duke StreetDSR 31058	1990
Calling All Angels (w/k.d. lang)	Reprise 26707	1992
Sail Across the Water	Warner 26824	1993
Temple	Warner 26824	1994
It Can't Rain All the Time	Warner 26824	1994
Love is Everything	Warner 26824	1994
Lovin' Cup (CD/S)	Warner 12 17742	1995
An Angel Stepped Down	KOCH 79390	1996

Albums/CDs:

Jane Siberry	Street SR 002	1981
Jane Siberry (EP)	Duke StreetDSR 12018	1984
No Borders Here	Duke StreetDSR 31006	1984
The Speckless Sky	Duke StreetDSR 31019	1985
The Walking	Duke StreetDSR 31040	1987
Bound by the Beauty	Duke StreetDSR 31058	1989
When I Was a Boy	Warner 26824	1993
A Collection 1984 1989	Duke StreetDSR 31093	1994
Maria	Reprise 45915	1995
Teenager	KOCH 79390	1996
A Day in the Life	Sheeba 0002	1997
Tree	Sheeba 0006	1999
Lips	Sheeba 0007	1999
New York Trilogy (Box Set)	Sheeba	1999
Child: Music for the Christmas	Sheeba 3219	1999
Hush	Sheeba 0008	2000
City	Sheeba 0010	2001

Les Sinners

Jay Boivin (guitar)
Francois Guy (vocals, guitar)
Georges Marchand (guitar)
Louis Parizeau (drums)
Charles Prevost Linton (bass, vocals)

Les Sinners organized in the summer of 1965 in Montreal with Jay Boivin, Francois Guy, Georges Marchand, Louis Parizeau, and Charles Prevost Linton. A year later, they went through a major personnel change when Boivin was replaced by Ricky Johnson, who, in turn was replaced in 1967 by Jean Guy "Arthur" Cossette from Les Jaquars. Marchand also left in 1966 to join Les Merseys.

The group's first single on London Records was Elle est revenue, and later recorded a cover version of The Beatles' Penny Lane on Jupiter Records.

In 1968 the group dissolved and Guy started the group, La Revolution Francais, with two former members of Les Sinners (Cossette and Marchand) and Richard Tate and Angelo Finaldi.

Les Sinners returned with a new lineup in 1970 and recorded sevral singles such as Je Chante on RCA. They broke up in 1976.

Singles:

Elle est revenue	LondonFC 734	1966
Hymne a Zoe	LondonFC 743	1966
La troisieme fuite de Mohamed'z'Ali	LondonFC 749	1966
Penny Lane	Jupiter 1088	1967
Ne reste pas sous la pluie	Jupiter 1099	1967
Tard il se fait tard	Jupiter 1132	1968
Go Go Trudeau	Jupiter 1138	1968
Les hippies du quartier	Jupiter 1149	1968
Quebecois	Jupiter	1968
La place	Jupiter 2000	1969
La ballade du bucheron	Canusa C 364	1969
Ma belle amie	R&B 604	1970
Hey Hey Rock and Roll	RCA 75 5054	1970
Je chante	RCA 75 5064	1970
Quebec nous t'aimons	Trans-World TW 69	1971
Jungle	Trans-World TW 77	1971
Messiers les jures	Matrice CT 38340	1972
Des gens ben corrects	Campus 6013	1972
On sera bien cheznous	Campus 6023	1972
Viens avec moi	Union 3502	1973
Ca finit toujours par l'amour	Union 3511	1974
Douce folie	Union 3515	1974
Quel epouantail	Celebration CEL 2131	1975
Agnes Sorel	Celebration CEL 2137	1975
Springbed Boogie	Celebration CEL 2138	1976

Albums/CDs:

Sinners: Sinerisme	Rusticana CKL 1243	1967
Les Sinners	Jupiter JDY 7009	1968
Vox Populi	Jupiter YDS 8015	1968
Les Sinners Chantent 24 Succes	Jupiter JPL 11022	1968
Sinners	Trans-World TWF 6801	1971
Sinners	Celebration CEL 1904	1975
LE Chemin De Croix De Jos Roy	CBS PFS 90383	1976
Les Sinners	Merite 22 908	1991

Skydiggers

Peter Cash (vocals, guitar)
Josh Finlayson (guitar)
Andy Maize (vocals)
Ronnie Von Johnnie (bass)
Wayne Stokes (drums)

The Toronto based Skydiggers started in the winter of 1987–88 when Andy Maize, Peter Cash and Josh Finlayson first played together. Andrew Cash, Peter's older brother and a recording artist in his own right, gave the group its name. Their critically acclaimed, self-titled debut album was released in 1989.

In 1991 Wayne Stokes and Ronnie Von Johnnie joined the group. Stokes left in 1992 after The Skydiggers finished recording their album, Restless. Another change in the group came in 1996 when Peter Cash left. Bassist Ron Macey, drummer Gavin Brown, and guitarist/vocalist Paul MacLeod joined in late 1997. Brown was later replaced by Joel Anderson in 1998.

By the release of their fifth album, Desmond's Hip City (1997), they had established their own label, Hip City Records, distributed by Dave's Records of Guelph (Drog). Still Restless The Lost Tapes (1999) was a reissue of their 1992 album *Restless* from an alternate 1991 session which included three extra tracks, including a version of Good King Wenceslas. Their next album, *Here and Back* (2000) was a live set featuring performances from their annual holiday shows at The Horseshoe Tavern in Toronto in December 1999 and The Sidetrack Cafe in Edmonton in January 1998.

Singles:

We Don't Talk Anymore	Sky 11847	1990
Monday Morning	Sky 11847	1990
I Will Give You Everything	Sky 11847	1991
A Penny More	FRE 00102	1992
Feel You Closer	FRE 00102	1992/93
Slow Burning Fire	FRE 00102	1993
I'm Wondering	FRE 00106	1993
80 Odd Hours	FRE 00106	1994
Mr. Soul	CBS Z2K80199	1994
What Do You See	Wea 10618	1995
You've Got a Lot of Nerve	Wea 10618	1995/96
It's a Pity	Wea 10618	1996

Albums/CDs:

The Skydiggers	Sky 11847	1989
The Skydiggers	Enigma 73555	1990
Restless	FRE 00102	1992
Just Over This Mountain	FRE 00106	1993
Road Radio	Wea 10618	1995
Desmond's Hip City	Drog 00372	1997
Still Restless The Lost Tapes	Drog 069	1999
Here and Back Live	HCR001	2000

Skylark

B.J. Cook (lead vocals)
David Foster (keyboards)
Donny Gerard (lead vocals)
Carl Graves (percussion)
Duris Maxwell (drums) Replaced by Brian Hilton
Norman Mc Pherson (lead guitar) Replaced by Allan Mix
Steven Pugsley (bass)

The history of this Vancouver-based group goes back to 1969 when Brian Hilton, Steve Pugsley, B.J. Cook, and David Foster played together in The Hawks. In 1971, B.J. decided she wanted to be in her own group which became known as Skylark. The original group was comprised of Flip Aroliano, Joani Taylor, and B.J. on vocals; Michael "Kat" Hendricks on drums, Doug Edwards on lead and rhythm guitar, Foster on keyboards and Pugsley on bass.

By the time the group went into the studio to record their self-titled debut album on Capitol, the lineup changed to include Donny Gerard and Carolyn Cook on vocals and Duris Maxwell on drums.

During this time Skylark became one of the first integrated groups.

In 1972 Pugsley, Edwards and Carolyn Cook left. The nucleus of the group consisted of Foster, Carl Graves, who was added on vocals, B.J. Cook, Donny Gerard, and Brian Hilton, who replaced Maxwell.

Their biggest hit was Wildflower, written by Vancouver studio musician Doug Edwards and Victoria policeman Dave Richardson.

Gerrard's smooth vocals made it one of the top hits of 1973 in both the United States and Canada.

After the release of their second album, Skylark 2, the group disbanded. The last lineup of the group included Bobby Taylor, B.J. Cook, Gerard, Graves, and Pugsley.

Gerard went on to have minor success with Words Are Impossible in 1976. Graves had two hits in 1975 with Baby, Hang Up The Phone and Hey Radio. Maxwell became a member of The Powder Blues Band. Foster went on to become a successful recording artist and producer. In 2011 Wildflower was inducted into The Canadian Songwriters Hall of Fame.

Singles:

What Would I do Without You	Capitol 3378	1972
Wildflower	Capitol 3511	1973

| I'll Have to Go Away | Capitol 3661 | 1973 |
| Words (Are Impossible) | Greedy 101 | 1974 |

Albums/CDs:

Skylark	Capitol ST 11048	1972
Skylark 2	Capitol ST 11256	1974
Wildflower: Golden Classics	Collectables 5800	1996

Amy Sky

Amy Sky (nee Shiner) was born in Toronto on September 24, 1960.

After earning a degree in theory and composition from the University of Toronto, she toured with Ronnie Hawkins' backup band. She then left for Los Angeles where she honed her craft as a songwriter while working first at MCA Music, then Warner/Chappell in 1986. Eager to record to her own songs, she moved back to Toronto with her husband, singer/songwriter Marc Jordan.

In 1996 Iron Music Group released her debut album, Cool Rain.

That same year, she starred David Cassidy in the Toronto production of Blood Brothers. Her sophomore effort, Burnt By The Sun, came out in 1998, followed by Phenomenal Woman in 2000.

Singles:

Don't Leave Me Alone	IMG 51005	1996
I Will Take Care of You	IMG 51005	1996
Til You Love Somebody	IMG 51005	1997
If My Heart Had Wings	IMG 51005	1997
Love Pain and the Whole Damn Thing	IMG 51027	1998
Waterfall	IMG 51027	1998
Heaven (Opened Up Its Doors)	IMG 51027	1999
Ordinary Miracles	IMG 51027	1999/00

Albums/CDs:

Cool Rain	IMG 51005	1996
Burnt by the Sun	IMG 51027	1998
Phenomenal Woman	Latta LP002	2000

Sloan

Jay Ferguson (guitar, vocals)
Chris Murphy (bass, vocals, erased guitar)
Patrick Pentland (guitar, vocals, bass)
Andrew Scott (drums, vocals, guitar)

Sloan first organized in early 1991 in their hometown of Halifax, Nova Scotia. Jay Ferguson and Chris Murphy first played together in a punk band called Kearney Lake Road. Andrew Scott and Murphy both attended The Nova Scotia College of Art and Design, while Ferguson and Patrick Pentland both earned degrees in history.

The name of the band came from a nickname of a girl they knew in Halifax, and their first show was in April 1991. By the end of the year they had saved up enough money to record a few songs that became the Peppermint EP, released in October 1992.

Their first full-length album, *Twice Removed* came out in 1994 and established the band's distinctive rock sound that has earned them a loyal following of fans.

In 1995 the group went on hiatus, contrary to rumours on the internet that they had broken up. They returned the following year with their own label, murderecords, and a new album, *One Chord to Another*. The label had a roster that included Jale, Thrush Hermit, and The Super Friendz.

With each subsequent release, the band proved that the magic was still there, and they are still active today.

Singles:

Underwhelmed	Murder CD001/DGCD 24498	1992
Sugartune	Murder CD001/DGCD 24498	1993
500 Up	Murder DGCD 24498	1993
Coax Me	MCA DGCD 24711	1994
People of the Sky	MCA DGCD 24711	1994/95
Stood Up	MCA DGCD 24711	1995
The Good in Everyone	Murder SD23	1996
Everything You've Done Wrong	Murder SD23	1996
The Lines You Amend	Murder SD23	1997
Money City Maniacs	Murder SD036	1998
She Says What She Means	Murder SD036	1998
Keep on Thinkin'	Murder SDO36	1999
If it Feels Good, Do It	Murder 88102	2001

Albums/CDs:

Peppermint (EP)	Murder CD 001	1992
Smeared	Murder DGCD 24498	1992
Twice Removed	MCA DGCD 24711	1994
One Chord to Another	Murder SD23	1996
Navy Blues	Murder SD036	1998
4 Nights at the Palais Royale	Murder D2 39	1999
Between the Bridges	Murder 22034	1999
Pretty Together	Murder 88102	2001
Double Cross	Murder 050	2011
Commonwealth	Murder 058	2014

Grant Smith and The Power

Brian Ayers (sax)
Michael Harrison (bass)
Steve Kennedy (sax)
Kenny Marco (guitar)
Ralph Miller (trumpet)
Jon Palma (guitar)
Grant Smith (vocals)
William Smith (organ)
Val Stevens (organ)
Wayne Stone (drums)

Based in Toronto, Ontario, Grant Smith and The Power formed in Toronto in January 1967. On stage, Smith wore a light blue or olive green suit, while the rest of the group dressed in bright orange. The original lineup was comprised of Ralph Miller, Brian Ayers, Charlie Miller, Wayne Stone, Val Stevens, Mike Harrison, Jim Pauley, and Grant Smith. They became well known for their rhythm and blues sound at The In Crowd, a club in Yorkville Village.

In the fall of 1967 after some personnel changes, they recorded their first single, Keep on Running, a remake of the Spencer Davis hit from 1966. Released in 1968, it was the title track from the album of the same name, produced by John Irvine (McKenna Mendelson Mainline, A Passing Fancy).

Before the group broke up at the end of 1968, they recorded the single, Thinkin' of You for MGM. Kenny Marco, William Smith, Steve Kennedy, and Wayne Stone went on to form Motherlode.

Singles:

Keep on Running	Boo 681	1968
Thinkin' of You	MGM 13979X	1968

Albums/CDs:

Keep on Running	Boo BST 6802	1968

Laura Smith

Born and raised in London, Ontario, Laura Smith was a gifted and sensitive child who loved horses, dance, and poetry. When a friend took her to meet poet Margaret Avison at the University of Western Ontario, Laura showed her her poetry, and Avison became her mentor.

In the mid 70s, Smith started writing and singing her own material. She also worked as a secretary in her hometown, where she took an interest in the local jazz and folk scene.

She then moved to Toronto in the 1970s where she studied at the Royal Conservatory of Music. In 1984 she met Paul Crawford, a lighthouse keeper from St. Paul's Island, Nova Scotia. She moved to be with him, because he believed in her music and completely supported her. When that relationship ended, she moved to Halifax.

After recording Elemental on CBC Variety Recordings, her career started to take off. Among the artists she opened for included John Prine, Richard Thompson and Odetta. She also performed at music festivals across Canada and in Seattle, Washington.

In 1994 Atlantica Music released her sophomore effort, Between The Earth And My Soul. She then signed with Universal Music, who released her label debut, It's A Personal Thing in 1997.

Singles:

My Bonny	AtlanticA 50235	1995
Four Letter Word (For Lonesome)	AtlanticA 50235	1996
It's A Personal Thing	UNIV UMSD 81033	1997
I Didn't Dream	UNIV UMSD 81033	1997

Albums/CDs:

Elemental	CBC VR 1001	1989
Between The Earth And My Soul	AtlanticA 50235	1994
It's A Personal Thing	Universal UMSD 81033	1997
Vanity Pressed: A Collection	Universal UMSD 81099	1998
Everything Is Moving	Borealis BCD 224	2013

The Smugglers

K. Beezely (bass, background vocals)
David Carswell (guitar, mandolin, organ)
Bryce Dunn (drums, tambourine)
Grant Lawrence (vocals, tambourine, maracas)
Nicholas Thomas (guitar, background vocals)

The genesis of this Vancouver-based group began at Hillside Secondary School in 1990 where Nicholas Thomas, David Carswell and Grant Lawrence formed The Smugglers. That same year, they were invited to join the Young Fresh Fellows on a tour of northwestern United States, which led to an engagement at a Boise, Idaho nightclub. On another tour of the northwestern United States, they met Nardwuar the Human Serviette of Scratch Records. He was responsible for the group's first single, Up and Down/Seattle Bound, which he put on his own label, Nardwuar Records.

Beez joined the group in 1991, while Bryce Dunn in 1992. For four years they entertained at various clubs, church halls and pubs in West Vancouver.

Their subsequent releases on vinyl in Germany and Spain established them as an international group, while their releases on Mint Records in Canada and Lookout Records in the U.S. have helped them attract a loyal following.

The Smugglers maintained the same lineup until the release of Growing Up Smuggler in 1998, when it included John Collins on bass and Danny Frazio on drums, in addition to Lawrence, Carswell, and Thomas.

Singles:

Up and Down	Nardwuar/Cleo 2	1990
Atlanta Whiskey Flats (12")	Trade Mark Of Quality (no #)	1992
At Germany (Germany)	Screaming Apple Scap 017	1992

Albums/CDs:

At Marineland (10")	Nardwuar/CLEO 3	1991
In The Hall Of Fame: All Time Great Golds	Popllama	1993
Wet Pants Club (EP)(Spain)	Radiation Records (no #)	1993
Wet Pants Club (EP)(Canada)	Rare 004	1994
Party Party Party Pooper (EP)	Mint MRS 007	1994
Selling The Sizzle	Mint MRD 016	1995
Buddy Holly Convention	Mint MRD 028	1998
Growing Up Smuggler	Mint 1+2	1998
Rosie	Mint MRD 036	2000

Snow

Born Darrin O'Brien on October 30, 1969 in the Toronto, Ontario suburb of North York, Snow learned his Jamaican DJ style rap from his friends. His Jamaican-born patron Prince gave him his stage name because he was white and came from Canada.

On his debut album, 12 Inches Of Snow (1992) his songs dealt with his experiences as a criminal, such as Lonely Monday Morning and Informer, the album's first single, which became a huge hit in Canada and the United States, where it spent seven weeks at number one on Billboard's Hot 100 in 1993. In May, 1993 Warner released Girl, I've Been Hurt as the second single.

MurderLove followed in 1995 but it was not well received. In 1997 came *The Greatest Hits of Snow*, followed by *Mind on the Moon* in 2000.

Singles:

Informer	EWA 92207	1992/93
Girl, I've Been Hurt	EWA 92207	1993
Runway	EWA 92207	1993
Anything for You	EW 66155	1995
Murder Love	EWA 61737	1995
Everybody Wants to be Like You	Virgin 5861629	2000

Albums/CDs:

12 Inches of Snow	EWA 92207	1992
Murder Love	EWA 61737	1995
The Greatest Hits of Snow	EWA 62075	1997
Mind on the Moon	Virgin 27778	2000

Gino Soccio

Born in Verdun, a suburb of Montreal, on September 9, 1955, Gino Soccio learned the piano from a group of nuns when he was eight years old. He was able to learn pieces of music in five minutes because he had an ear for music.

In the late 1970s he was involved in a disco project called Kebekelektrik which allowed him to use his skills as a multi-instrumentalist. He also produced albums by Karen Silver and Montreal's Witch Queen.

Under his own name, Gino recorded his first album, *Outline* in 1979, which was released internationally in Europe and South America where it was a big seller.

In 1980 came his second album, *S Beat* which was recorded in Studio St.

Charles in Montreal, the first of three released on the Celebration label. A greatest hits package followed in 1990 on Unidisc.

Singles:

Sauve qui peut	Montreco 5001	1977
Dancer	Celebration CEL 2329	1979
Dance To Dance	Celebration CEL 2340	1979
Les Visiteurs	Celebration CEL 2291	1979/80
Fake	Skyline 027	1980
Heart Breaker	Celebration CEL 2379	1980
Closer	Celebration CEL 2391	1981
It's Alright	Celebration CEL 2413	1982
Remember	Celebration CEL 2422	1982
Closer	Celebration CEL 2427	1983
Turn It Around	Celebration CEL 2440	1984
Out of My Life	Celebration CEL 2452	1984
Human Nature	Celebration CEL 2459	1985
Camouflage	Celebration CEL 2466	1985
Love The One You're With	Broken Records 7001	1988

Albums/CDs:

Kebekelectrik	Direction DLP 10023	1977
Outline	War RFC 3309	1979
S Beat	Celebration CEL 2066	1980
Closer	Celebration CEL	1981
Face To Face (EP)	Celebration CEL 2114	1982
Remember	Celebration CEL 2134	1984
Greatest Hits	Unidisc K2 8012	1990

Jack London and The Sparrow

Art Ayre (piano, organ, harmonium)
Dennis Edmonton (vocals, lead guitar)
Jerry Edmonton (vocals, drums, harmonica)
John Kay (harmonica, vocals)
Jack London (lead vocals)
Goldie Mc John (keyboards)
Nick St. Nicholas (vocals, bass)

The origins of this Oshawa, Ontario group began in 1964 when Dave Marden came to Canada from England after the start of the British Invasion. Changing his name to Jack London after the famous novelist who wrote The Sea Wolf and Call of the Wild, he was joined by Art Ayre, brothers Dennis and Jerry Edmonton and Nick St. Nicholas to form the quintet, Jack London and The Sparrows.

Signed to Capitol Records, their first hit single was If You Don't Want My Love in February, 1965. The following year, the label released their first album, Presenting Jack London and The Sparrows.

John Kay who came to Canada from Germany in 1958 joined the group on harmonica in 1965. Goldie McJohn also joined on keyboards.

During the summer of 1965, Capitol released the single, Hard Times with the Law under the name The Sparrows.

By 1966 Jack London had left the group and John Kay became the group's new lead singer. Now known as John Kay and the Sparrow, they had one self-titled debut album on Columbia Records.

Changes in the group's personnel and financial problems forced the group to split up in June of 1967. Dennis Edmonton changed his name to Mars Bonfire and had a brief solo career. (see Mars Bonfire)

Nick St. Nicholas joined Time, a Los Angeles group and Kay went on to form Steppenwolf.

By Jack London and The Sparrows
Singles:
If You Don't Want My Love	Capitol 72203	1965
I'll Be the Boy	Capitol 72210	1965
Our Love Has Passed	Capitol 72229	1965

Album:
Presenting Jack London and The Sparrows	Capitol T 6115	1965

By The Sparrows
Single:
Hard Times with The Law	Capitol 72257	1965

By John Kay and The Sparrow
Singles:
Tomorrow's Ship	Columbia 43755	1966
Green Bottle Lover	Columbia 44396	1967
Square Headed People	Columbia 44769	1969

Albums/CDs:
John Kay and The Sparrow	Columbia CS 9758	1969
Best of John Kay and The Sparrow	Columbia CK 53044	1993

Spirit of the West

Vince Ditrich (drums)
J. Knutson (bass)
Geoffrey Kelly (flute, bodhran, guitar)
John Mann (vocals, guitar)
Hugh McMillan (mandolin, bass)
Linda Mc Rae (bass, accordion, vocals)

This Vancouver-based band began in 1983. Their music is rooted in Celtic folk/rock. Founded by John Mann and Geoffrey Kelly, their songs deal with suicide (Roadside Attraction), mentally handicapped (Putting Up with The Joneses), oil spills (Dirty Pool) and the way we're destroying the world (The Wrecking Ball).

The group's first album, *Tripping Up The Stairs* (1986) was produced with the help of fellow Vancouverite Barney Bentall.

They have gone through some personnel changes, the first of which during the summer of 1988 when J. Knutson was replaced by Hugh Mac Millan, whose experience in jazz, country and western and swing bands helped improve the band's sound. Mac Millan later left for a brief time, to be replaced by Daniel Lapp who, in turn, left in 1990 to join the Jarvis Benoit Group in Halifax. Bassist/accordionist Linda Mc Rae was added to the group during Mac Millan's absence. She remained with the group when he returned. Vince Ditrich was added on drums to complement the band's sound in 1990.

McRae left in January 1997 to pursue a solo career. Stony Plain released her debut album, *Flying Jenny* (Stony Plain SPCD 1239) later that same year.

The Spirit of the West recorded Open Heart Symphony (1996) with the Vancouver Symphony Orchestra, but returned to their Celtic and pop/rock roots in 1997 with Weights and Measures.

Singles:

The Crawl	Stony Plain SPS 1045	1986/87
Save This House	Wea 70971	1990
D For Democracy	Wea 74692	1991
Political	Flying Fish 70475/74692	1991
And If Venice Is Sinking	CDN 21/Wea 93642	1993
Five Free Minutes	Wea 93642	1994
Sadness Grows	Wea 93642	1994
6th Floor	Wea 93642	1994
Is This Where I Came In	Wea 93642	1994/95
Tell Me What I Think	Wea 10615	1995
Two Headed	Wea 10615	1995/96

Mildred	Wea 10615	1996
Williamson's Garage	Wea 14600	1996
Soldier's Boy	Wea 19716	1997

Albums/CDs:

Spirit of the West	Triniti	1984
Tripping Up the Stairs	Stony Plain SPL 1098	1986
Labour Day	Stony Plain SPL 1123	1988
Old Material 1984 1986	Stony Plain SPL 1141	1989
Save This House	Wea 70971	1990
Go Figure	Wea 74692	1991
Faithlift	Wea 93642	1993
Two Headed	Wea 10615	1995
Open Heart Symphony	Wea 14600	1996
Weights and Measures	Wea 19716	1997
Hit Parade	Wea 29307	1999

The Spoons

Colin Cripps (guitar)
Gordon Deppe (vocals, guitar)
Sandy Horne (bass)
Rob Preuss (keyboards)
Derrick Ross (drums)

Sandy Horne and Gordon Deppe formed The Spoons while both attended high school in Burlington, Ont. in 1979. Based in Toronto, their pop/rock style of music appealed to mostly teenagers. By the late 1980s they had grown up with their audience and were playing music with a harder edge.

Their debut album, *Stick Figure Neighborhood* (on the independent Ready Records label) was released late in 1981, while their first single, Nova Heart was a hit in 1982.

Four years later, the band went through some personnel changes. They also switched to Anthem Records in the spring of 1986. *Bridges Over Borders*, their label debut, came out in the fall.

The two new members, keyboardist Scott MacDonald and drummer Ian Hendry and the addition of a fifth, guitarist Colin Cripps helped contribute to the group's tougher sound, which was different from their early days as the exponents of romantic electro pop.

Although they never officially broke up, Cripps went on to become a member of Crash Vegas and Junkhouse, while Horne started Dog Won't Bite, whose debut album was *Schplatterfunk* (1993).

Singles:

Nova Heart	Ready SR 201	1982
Arias and Symphonies	Ready SR 271	1982
Smiling in Winter	Ready SR 272	1983
Old Emotions	Ready SR 391	1983
Tell No Lies	Ready SRB 00481	1984
Romantic Traffic	Ready SR 482	1985
When Time Turns Around	Anthem ANS 081	1988
Waterline	Anthem ANS 082	1989

Albums/CDs:

Stick Figure Neighbourhood	Ready LR 012	1981
Arias and Symphonies	Ready LR 027	1982
Talkback	Ready LR 039	1983
Bridges Over Borders	Anthem ANR 1 1050	1986
Vertigo Tango	Anthem ANR 1 1054	1988
Collectible Spoons	MCAD 11186	1994

The Staccatos

Mike Bell (drums, vocals)
Rick Bell (drums, vocals)
Vern Craig (guitar, vocals)
Les Emmerson (lead guitar, vocals)
Ted Gerow (keyboards)
Brian Rading (bass, vocals)

This Ottawa quintet began playing together in 1963. Dean Hagopian, a local radio personality in Ottawa, was the group's first lead singer in 1963–64. At first they were a cover band that played songs by The Four Seasons, The Hollies and The Beach Boys. Les Emmerson replaced Hagopian in 1964.

The original recording group consisted of Rick Bell, Vern Craig, Les Emmerson, and Brian Rading. Their first single on Allied Records was It Ain't Easy in late 1964.

Their next, Small Town Girl was their first on Capitol Records in 1965. In 1967, Half Past Midnight became one of the biggest Canadian Rock singles of the year. It was later recorded by The Stompers, a group from Australia.

In March, 1968 the Staccatos released an album called, *The Five Man Electrical Band*. They officially adopted the latter album's name, in 1969. Their first single under their new name was It Never Rains on Maple Lane, backed by Private Train. The following year, the group recorded Moonshine (Friend of Mine) which was included in the movie, The Moonshine War (1970).

The group's next single was Signs on Lionel Records, which was an instant hit from Windsor, Ontario to Augusta, Georgia and Baton Rouge, Louisiana. Polydor agreed to release the single nationwide in Canada and was certified a million seller on August 30, 1971. The label continued to release more singles such as Absolutely Right, Money Back Guarantee, and I'm A Stranger Here. Signs was later recorded live by Tesla from Sacramento, California on July 2, 1990. It peaked at #8 on Billboard's Hot 100 in 1991.

The Staccatos broke up in 1973. The singles, Werewolf and Johnny Get a Gun were later released to fulfill a contractual obligation. Les Emmerson had success as a solo artist with the hits, Control Of Me (Lion 141, 1972/73), Cry Your Eyes Out (Lion 155, 1973), Cliches (Polydor 14247), and Watching The World Go By (Polydor 14269, 1975).

Emmerson later started two other groups, the Emmerson Electrical Band and Blue Blood. The latter released one single, One Way Life (U Turn Sign) in 1980. Up until the summer of 1998 he was one third of the trio, Cooper, King and Emmerson. Signs was inducted into the Canadian Songwriters Hall of Fame in 2008. Brian Rading died on June 8, 2016.

By The Staccatos
Singles:

It Isn't Easy	Allied 6339	1964
Small Town Girl	Cap 72244	1965
Move to California	Cap 72281	1965
Do You Mind If I Dance With You, Girl	Cap 72281	1965
It's A Long Way Home	Cap 72329	1966
C'Mon Everybody	Cap 72371	1966
Let's Run Away	Cap 72395	1966
Half Past Midnight	Cap 72453	1967
Catch the Love Parade	Cap 72497	1967
Walker Street	Cap 72526	1967
Didn't Know the Time	Cap 2260	1968

Albums/CDs:

Initially The Staccatos	Capitol T 6158	1965
A Wild Pair (w/the Guess Who)	Nimbus NNE100	1968
The Five Man Electrical Band	Capitol T 165	1968

By Five Man Electrical Band
singles

Riverboat	Capitol 2628	1969
It Never Rains on Maple Lane	Capitol 2368	1969
Private Train	Capitol 2368	1969
Lovin' Look	Capitol 2517	1969
Sunrise to Sunset	Capitol 2562	1969
Moonshine (Friend of Mine)	Polydor 2065 030	1970

Hello Melinda Goodbye	Polydor 2065 042	1970
Signs	Polydor 2065 042	1971
Absolutely Right	Polydor 2065 089	1971
Julianna	Polydor 2065 103	1972
Devil and Miss Lucy	Polydor 2065 123	1972
Money Back Guarantee	Polydor 2065 142	1972
I'm a Stranger Here	Lion 149	1973
Baby Wanna Boogie	Lion 160	1973
Werewolf	Polydor 14221	1974
Johnny Get a Gun	Polydor 14263	1975

Albums/CDs:

Goodbyes And Butterflies	Polydor 2424 020	1971
Coming Of Age	Polydor 2424 047	1972
Sweet Paradise	Lion LN 1009	1973
Power of the Five Man Electrical Band	Polydor PD 6029	1975
Absolutely Right	Polydor 523331	1995
First Sparks: The Anthology	Pace 076	2009

The Stampeders

Kim Berly (drums)
Race Berly (vocals)
Rich Dodson (guitar, bass, vocals)
Ronnie King (guitar, bass, vocals)
Van Louis (vocals)
Brendan Lyttle (bass)
Len Roemer (rhythm guitar)

The Stampeders started in Calgary, Alberta in October, 1963 when Rich Dodson, Brendan Lyttle, Len Roemer, and Kim Berly practiced together as The Rebounds. On stage they played music by The Ventures and The Shadows.

Through Mel Shaw, co-producer and talent co-ordinator of Calgary TV's Guys and Dolls, the group gained local exposure. Shaw also became their manager, and changed their name to The Stampeders in December 1964. He also arranged for the group to play regularly at a local Calgary club called The Conquistador in 1965. That same year, two new members were added, Van King and Race Berly, Kim's brother. By the end of 1965, Roemer left, and was replaced by Ronnie King, who had been in another Calgary band, The Paint Brushes.

During a tour of Canada in 1967, they recorded their first single, Morning Magic in Montreal, which was released on MWC, Mel Shaw's own label.

By the end of 1968, Race Berly had left, while Brendan Lyttle and Van King left early in 1969. The Stampeders were now a trio.

In 1970 they recorded their first album, Against The Grain, which included the Singles:, Carry Me and Sweet City Woman. The latter went to #1 on RPM's singles Chart and #8 on Billboard's Hot 100 in 1971. In 1972 they were given Holland's prestigious Edison Award.

The CBC TV network produced a documentary about the group called, A Short Visit To Planet Earth which aired on November 15, 1973. Simulated space effects were used to celebrate the terrestrial landing of Ronnie, Rich and Kim as they sang some of their old hits plus some new songs from their album, *From the Fire*. The show's finale featured the songs Wild Eyes and Johnny Lightning as the audience clapped and cheered along.

By the end of 1976, there were more personnel changes. In 1976 a second drummer and a three man brass and reed section were added. Dodson also left to go solo in December. He was replaced by Doug Macaskill, former lead guitarist with Deja Vu. In 1978 Berly left to go solo. King switched to the guitar and was joined by his brother Roy on bass. The group was now billed as The Stampeders featuring Ronnie King.

By the end of the decade, the group had split up. The three original members live in Calgary. Kim is a carpenter, Ronnie works in television, and Dodson records for Marigold Records. He also has written and published his own material under the name of Sleepy Cat Music. In 1988 he wrote Toronto singer Debbie Johnson's 1988 hit, Just Like Magic.

In 1992 they were reunited on CTV's The Dini Petty Show. In 2011, they recorded their album, *Live at the Mae Wilson in Moose Jaw*, Saskatchewan.

Singles:

House of Shake		1965
You Never Know Until You Cry		1966
Morning Magic	MWC 2001	1967
Be A Woman	MGM 13970	1968
Crosswalk	Melbourne 3314	1969
Carry Me	MWC 1003	1970/71
Sweet City Woman	MWC 1004	1971
Devil You	MWC 1007	1971/72
Monday Morning Choo Choo	MWC 1008	1972
Then Came The White Man	MWC 1008	1972
Wild Eyes	MWC 1009	1972
Johnny Lightning	MWC 1011	1972/73
Oh My Lady	MWC 1012	1973
Minstrel Gypsy	MWC 1013	1973
Running Wild	MWC 1014	1973/74
Me and My Stone	MWC 1015	1974
Ramona	MWC 1016	1974
Hit the Road Jack	MWC 1017	1975

New Orleans	MWC 1018	1975
Playin'in the Band	MWC 1019	1976
Blue eyed Woman (Kim Berly)	MWC	1976
Sweet Love Bandit	MWC 1021	1976
San Diego	MWC 1022	1976

Albums/CDs:

Against the Grain	MWCS 701	1971
Carryin' On	MWCS 702	1972
Rubes, Dudes, And Rowdies	MWCS 704	1973
From the Fire	MWCS 705	1973
New Day	MWCS 706	1974
Backstage Pass	MWCS 707	1975
Steamin'	MWCS 708	1975
Hit the Road	MWCS 709	1976
Platinum	MWCS 710	1977
Ballsy	Apex ATL 1601	1979
Best of The Stampeders	TV INT'L TA 1072	
Stampeders Greatest Hits:		
Canada's Greatest Memories	CGM 101	
Over 60 Minutes With	Aquarius Q2 554	1989
Over 70 Minutes With	Marigold MPL 0005	1998
Over 70 Minutes With Vol II	Marigold MPL 0012	1999
Live at the Mae Wilson	Marigold MPL-11001	2011

Steel River

Rob Cockell (bass)
John Dudgeon (lead vocals)
Tony Dunning (guitar)
Bob Forrester (keyboards)
Ray Angrove (drums) Replaced by Dennis Watson (1980)

This Toronto-based band started playing in 1965 when the four original members performed together in small clubs and high schools. In 1969 they played professionally for the first time as Steel River. Producer Greg Hambleton signed them to his Tuesday label in 1970, and their first hit was Ten Pound Note, from their debut album, Weighin' Heavy. A second album on the Tuesday label, A Better Road was released in 1971.

Steel River disbanded in 1974, but reunited in 1980 to record the album, Armoured Car, which included the singles, Armoured Car and We Want You To Love Us.

Singles:

Ten Pound Note	Tuesday GH 101X	1970
Walk By The River	Tuesday GH 105X	1971
Southbound Train (Stand Up)	Tuesday GH 110X	1971
Mexican Lady	Tuesday GH 113X	1971/72
Just Remember	Axe 14	1974
Armoured Car	Axe 60	1980
We Want You To Love Us	Axe 61	1980

Albums/CDs:

Weighin' Heavy	Tuesday GHL 1000	1970
A Better Road	Tuesday GHL 1003	1971
Armoured Car	Axe AXM 1001	1980

Suzanne Stevens

Born in 1950 in the suburb of Verdun, Montreal, Quebec, Suzanne Stevens was the youngest of eleven children. She studied piano in her teens and had been singing in amateur theatrical productions. In 1972 she took part in a local TV talent search and won her own 13-week TV series.

In 1973 she recorded her first single, Le Soleil on Capitol Records, which was a hit in both Quebec and France.

By early 1974 she made her English singing debut on the Juliette Show, and at the Theatre des Varietes in Montreal.

She also recorded her first English language single for Capitol, Mother Of Us All, followed by House Full Of Women.

Her biggest English hit was Make Me Your Baby in 1976, a remake of Barbara Lewis' 1965 hit.

Her 1976 English album, *Love's the Only Game in Town* included songs written by four different Canadian composers: Sylvia Tyson, Gene MacLellan, Ives Lapierre and Judi Richards.

Singles:

Le Soleil	Capitol 85.084	1973
On quitte le port a 16 ans	Capitol 85.092	1973
Tout va bien	Capitol 85.097	1974
Mother of Us All	Capitol 72729	1974
Lonesome River	Capitol 72738	1974
Comme deux enfants	Capitol 85.099	1974
En Route		1974
Je Ne Vivais Pas Avant Toi	Capitol 85.104	1975

Make Me Your Baby	Capitol 72763	1975/76
Viens t en, viens t'en	Capitol 85.112	1976
Doesn't It Seem Like A Miracle	Capitol 72767	1976
Moi, de la tete aux pieds	Capitol 85.115	1976
L'as Tu Vu Le Soleil	Capitol 85.121	1976
Knowing How Knowing When	Capitol 72773	1976
Pour l'amour	Capitol 85.125	1976
Que tu es loin	Capitol 4366	1976
Apres la pluie, le beau temps	Capitol 85.132	1977
Crazy About You	Capitol 4395	1977
Losing End	Capitol 4503	1977
Fais ta vie	Capitol 85.148	1978
Les nuits sont trop longues	Capitol 85.154	1979
Fais confiance a la'amour	Capitol 85.161	1979
Let It Burn	CBS C5 4231	1979
This Is Love	Tojo 1022	1984

Albums/CDs:

En Route	Capitol ST 70032	1974
Moi De La Tete Aux Pieds	Capitol ST 70039	1975
Love's The Only Game In Town	Capitol ST 6439	1975
Crystal Carriage	Capitol ST 11615	1977
Stardust Lady	Capitol ST 11717	1977
Les Nuits Sont Trop Longues	Capitol ST 70065	1979

Stitch in Tyme

Vicotr (Pinky) Dauvin (drums, vocals)
Grant Fullerton (guitar, vocals)
Donald Morris (bass, vocals)
Bob Murphy (keyboards, vocals)
Bruce Wheaton (guitar, vocals)

Bruce Wheaton, Donald Morris and Victor ("Pinky") Dauvin first played together in The Continentals. Bruce left in 1963 to join The Royal Canadian Air Force, and joined The Vibrasonics while stationed in Camp Borden. When he was posted to Downsview, Ontario, he formed the group Chester and The Rogues, which was changed to Chester and The Unknowns when Wheaton learned that there was a group called The Five Rogues. Chester and The Unknowns appeared on Go Go '66, Robbie Lane's TV show. While still in Toronto, Wheaton left the Air Force and started another band called The Purple Harts. When his high school musician friends in the Nova Scotia band, The Untouchables invited Bruce to join, The

Purple Harts and The Untouchables merged to become The Golden Earring. When they arrived in Toronto in 1966, they changed their name to The Stitch In Tyme. Joining Morris, Wheaton and Dauvin were Grant Fullerton and Bob Murphy.

In 1966 they recorded a cover version of The Beatles' song, Got To Get You Into My Life on Yorkville Records. They performed on CBC's After Four, toured Ontario, Quebec and The Maritimes, and played at the official opening of Expo 67.

They then flew to New York City where they recorded their second single, New Dawn. When they returned to Toronto they performed at the opening of a new coffee house club called The Flick.

The Stitch In Tyme broke up in late 1968. Wheaton put together the band, Rockin' Chair with Scott Cushnie, who would later organize the group Tundra. After Rockin' Chair, Wheaton, Murphy, and Morris formed Soma in Truro, Nova Scotia in 1969. Later that same year, Wheaton left to start Everyday People in Toronto, and in 1974 he moved back to Nova Scotia where he formed Molly Oliver. They broke up in 1986 and reformed in 1999.

Singles:
Dry Your Eyes/Point of View	ARC 1133	1966
Got To Get You Into My Life	Yorkville 45001	1967
New Dawn	Yorkville 45011	1967

Kim Stockwood

Born in St. Johns, Newfoundland on November 11, 1965, Kim Stockwood grew up listening to her father's rock'n roll collection. In 1990 she was working as a copywriter for an ad agency in her hometown when a friend suggested she sing a couple of songs at a local pub.

Over the next two years she sang on weekends and wrote songs with Doug Randall, an acoustic player from St. John's. The response to her work was immediate and it drew attention from the local CBC station.

In 1992 she moved to Toronto where she sang at a local pub's amateur night. Eventually she caught the attention of Mike McCarty from EMI Music Publishing who was impressed enough to get her signed to a songwriting deal. She then went to Nashville and Los Angeles where she honed her craft as a songwriter, and wrote over fifty songs.

Her debut album, *Bonavista*, came out in August 1995. The first single was *She's Not In Love*. Her sophomore album, *12 Years Old* came out in 1999.

Singles:

She's Not In Love	EMI 52356	1995
Enough Love	EMI 52356	1995/96
Jerk	EMI 52356	1996
12 Years Old	EMI 57177	1999
You And Me	EMI 57177	1999
It's A Marshmallow World	EMI 22382	1999

Albums/CDs:

Bonavista	EMI 52356	1995
12 Years Old	EMI 57177	1999

Stonebolt

Danny Atchison (bass)
Brian Lousley (drums)
Roy Roper (guitar)
Jon Webster (keyboards)
David Wills (vocals)

Stonebolt's origins go back to the late 1960s when Roy Roper and Brian Lousley, two North Vancouver schoolmates wanted to start their own band. They listened to records and studied the older bands that came to their school dances. Not long after, bassist Danny Atchison made it a trio. They first called themselves Perth Amboy before they settled on Stonebolt. The addition of Jon Webster and David Wills made the band complete.

Based in Vancouver, they were Canada's answer to The Eagles. It was not until 1977 that their career took off. Walter Stewart, an associate of Johnny Rivers, heard them in Vancouver and signed them to Parachute Records, a subsidiary of Casablanca.

Their self-titled debut album came out in 1978. The first single, Queen of the Night was a modest hit, while the second single, I Will Still Love You was a national hit in Canada. It also peaked at #29 on Billboard's Hot 100.

In 1979 the group's future was in limbo when Parachute Records went bankrupt. A year later, in 1980, they signed with RCA Records who released the albums, *Keep it Alive* and *New Set of Changes*. Stonebolt was unable to duplicate the success of I Will Still Love You.

Singles:

Queen of the Night	Parachute RR 507	1978
I Will Still Love You	Parachute RR 512	1978

Was It You	Parachute RR 522	1978
Love Struck	Parachute RR 522	1980
Don't Ya Hide It	RCA PB 50547	1980
Price of Love	RCA PB 50571	1980
Crying Again Tonite	RCA PB 50591	1980
New Set of Changes	RCA JB 50612	1980

Albums/CDs:

Stonebolt	Parachute RRLP 9006	1978
Stonebolt (EP)	RCA KJL1 7075	1979
Keep it Alive	RCA KKL1 0357	1980
New Set of Changes	RCA KKL1 0380	1980

Strange Advance

Drew Arnott (keyboards, drums, vocals)
Paul Iverson (bass)
Darryl Kromm (vocals, guitar)

Strange Advance formed in Vancouver in 1980. Comprised of Drew Arnott, Darryl Krom and Paul Iverson, their debut album, *Worlds Away* was released in 1982 on Capitol Records, produced by Bruce Fairbairn (Loverboy, Prism). By the release of their second album, *2WO*, in 1985, Iverson had left to become a family man. Down to just the duo of Arnott and Kromm, Strange Advance was able to concentrate more on the rhythm and vocal inflections of their music. The two of them met when they played Strawbs and Bryan Adams cover songs in Vancouver clubs. After the release of their third album, *The Distance Between* in 1988, the duo split up.

Singles:

She Controls Me	Capitol 72896	1983
Kiss In The Dark	Capitol 72907	1983
Worlds Away	Capitol 5232	1983
We Run	Capitol 72960	1985
We Run (12")	Capitol V 75089/SPRO 259	1985
Love Becomes Electric	Capitol 73041	1988
Love Becomes Electric (12")	Capitol SPRO 346	1988

Albums/CDs:

Worlds Away	Capitol ST 12232	1982
2WO	Capitol ST 12349	1985
The Distance Between	Current/Capitol 48550	1988
Over 60 Minutes With	Capitol 46887	1989

Streetheart

Herb Ego (drums, Bombay percussion)
Daryl Gutheil (keyboards, vocals)
John Hannah (guitars, vocals)
Kenny Shields (lead vocals, percussion)
Ken Sinnaeve (bass, sax)

Streetheart, originally based in Regina, Saskatchewan, evolved out of two other groups. Kenny Shields was in Witness Inc. from 1964 to 1970, while Daryl Gutheil and Ken "Spider" Sinneave were in the Saskatoon group Wascana in 1975, who renamed themselves Witness in 1976. Paul Dean and Matt Frenette also joined the group that same year, when they changed their name to Streetheart and moved to Winnipeg. In 1978 Atlantic released their self-titled debut album, with a special edition in red vinyl.

The Scottish group Nazareth was so impressed by Streetheart that they produced their second album, *Under Heaven Over Hell*, which came out in 1979. That same year, Dean and Frenette left to form Loverboy in Calgary, Alberta with Mike Reno.

Over the next five years Streetheart became one of the country's most popular rock bands. One of their best-known hits was Under My Thumb in 1979, a cover version of The Rolling Stones song from their 1966 album, *Aftermath*. Streetheart disbanded in 1984.

Singles:

Title	Label	Year
Look at Me	Atlantic CAT 72002	1978
Here Comes The Night	Atlantic CAT 1502	1979
Under My Thumb	Atlantic CAT 1505	1979
Draggin' You Down	Wea 72009	1980
Joke's On You	Wea 72010	1980
Tin Soldier	Capitol 72842	1980/81
Teenage Rage	Capitol 72849	1981
Action	Wea 72016	1982
What Kind of Love Is This (12")	Capitol SPRO 234	1982
What Kind of Love Is This?	Capitol 72875	1982
One More Time	Capitol 72881	1982
Comin' True	Capitol 72902	1983
Have It Your Way	Capitol 72911	1983
Midnight Love	Capitol 72921	1983

Albums/CDs:

Title	Label	Year
Streetheart (12")	Atlantic EPA 72005	1978
Meanwhile Back In Paris	Atlantic KCA 92002	1978
Under Heaven Over Hell	Atlantic KCA 25001	1979
Under Heaven Over Hell	Atlantic KSD 19228	1979
Quicksand Shoes	Wea 92005	1980

Drugstore Dancer	Capitol ST 6481	1981
Action: Best Of Streetheart	Wea 92010	1981
Streetheart	Capitol ST 6491	1982
Dancing With Danger	Capitol ST 6499	1983
Buried Treasures	Capitol ST 6514	1984
Over 60 Minutes With	Capitol 91599	1989

Streetnoise

Chris Harvey (tenor sax, percussion, vocals)
Ken Mullen (percussion, vocals)
Alex Mumm (Hammond B 3 organ, piano, percussion)
Wayne Scott (bass, vocals)
Larry Stafford (trumpet, percussion, piano, vocals)
Gary Tisdale (drums)
Greg Travers (guitar, vocals)

The origins of Streetnoise from Kingston, Ontario go back to 1969. Their members came from other Kingston bands such as the Ethnic Souls (later the Marshmallow Soup Group), the Torquays, the Varmits, the Challengers, the Sedimentary Rock Band, Belbuekus, the Soul Mine, and the Sound Investment.

The core of Streetnoise was comprised of Ken Mullen, Chris Harvey, Larry Stafford, Gary Tisdale, Greg Travers, Wayne Scott, and Alex Mumm. Other members included guitarist Tim Mavety, organist Bob Metcalfe, drummer Rick "Boog" Scriver, bassist Robin Turcotte, guitarist Jan Turney, trombonist Ian Juby, and singer Ron Ashton.

In 1973 they were offered a recording contract on Revolver Records, but by then they had disbanded. Twenty years later, Larry Stafford brought the group back together for a local high school reunion, and Streetnoise was back. In May, 1997 they released their first independent CD, *Now and Then*. They broke up in 2000.

Album:
Now And Then	Independent (no #)	1997

Stringband

Bob Bossin (banjo)
Terry King (fiddle)
Marie Lynn Hammond (vocals)

Formed in 1971 in Toronto, Stringband began playing campus pubs for little renumeration. On stage their act consisted of an electic mix of Acadic nonsense songs, thirties jazz, bilingual satire, and vintage folk.

The band's roots go back to the radical '60s when Bob Bossin was an anarchist and founding member of the Free University of Toronto, and joined a group of anti-war protestors outside the U.S. consulate in Toronto in May 1969.

Bossin later met Marie Lynn Hammond and the two of them found they liked working together. He gave up his political protests and discovered that he could reach more people through his music. Joined by fiddler Terry King, Stringband became well known in 1970s Yorkville. They each financed their first album, Canadian Sunset, in 1974.

The group's final concert on New Year's Eve in 1977 was billed as "Stringband's Annual Farewell Concert" at Bathurst Street United Church in Toronto. The group's last album, Stringband Live! came out in 1980.

Marie Lynn Hammond released a self-titled solo album on Black Tie Records in 1979. In 1994, Bossin came out with a solo effort, Gabriola VOR1XO on Nick Records, which featured comic, folksy songs in the same vein as Stringband.

Singles:
Dief Will Be Chief Again	Nick 3	1975
I Don't Sleep With Strangers Anymore	Nick 4 1/2	1977

Albums/CDs:
Canadian Sunset	Nick 1	1974
National Melodies	Nick 2	1975
Thanks to the Following	Nick 4	1977
The Maple Leaf Dog	Nick 5	1978
Stringband Live!	Nick 6	1980

Sugar n' Spice

Chuck Gorling (organ, piano)
John MacInnis (rhythm guitar)
Larry Mahler (bass)
Geoff Marrin (male vocals)
Aileen Murphy (vocals)
Kathleen Murphy (vocals)
Maureen Murphy (vocals)
Phil O'Connell (guitar)

Sugar 'n Spice formed in 1967, and made their stage debut on February 9, 1968 in their hometown of Winnipeg. They were comprised of The Murphy Sisters (Kathleen, Maureen, Aileen), Phil O'Connell, Chuck Gorling, Kenn Richard, Larry Mahler, Geoff Marrin and John MacInnis. They opened for The Who in Edmonton and Calgary and appeared on a local TV show, Bob'n The Hits and CBC TV's Let's Go.

Their first single on Franklin Records, Not To Return (1968), was written and produced by Randy Bachman. The group's biggest hit was Cruel War, written by Peter Yarrow of Peter, Paul and Mary fame.

Kathleen Murphy left in 1970 to join The Tweadle Band, while sister Maureen moved to Toronto in November 1971 where she played with Brutus.

In 1972 the group became known as Spice with Laurie Currie (drums, vocals), Bruce Meissner (bass, lead vocals), Aileen Murphy (vocals), and Phil O'Connell (guitar). They broke up in 1974. The Murphy Sisters sang background vocals for The Greaseball Boogie Band (and later when they became Shooter). Aileen and Maureen also sang with Bill Amesbury.

By Sugar 'n Spice
Singles:

Not to Return	Franklin 616	1968
Day By Day	Franklin 620	1968
Cruel War	Franklin 622	1968/69
La Guerre De Se Dechaine	Franklin 625	1969
Something to Believe	Franklin 627	1969
Whisper Girl Shining	Franklin 633	1969
Angeline	Franklin 642	1971

By Spice
Singles:

Sweet Talkin' Woman/ Strawberry Wine	Franklin 646	1972
Just a Little Love	Franklin 647	1972

The Sugar Shoppe

Victor Garber (vocals)
Lee Harris (vocals)
Laurie Hood (piano)
Peter Mann (vocals)

From Toronto, Ontario, The Sugar Shoppe organized in July 1967. All four members came from diverse backgrounds. Peter Mann, acknowledged leader of the group, went to school in Miami and worked as an arranger/writer in New York. It was his arrangement of Bobby Gimby's Canada on Yorkville Records that helped their career takeoff. Lee Harris, one of the female members of the group, had three years of vocal training before she became a member. Her voice contributes to the group's distinctive sound. Laurie Hood, the comedienne of the group, had been playing the piano since she was three. She and Mann created special material for the group's stage act. Victor Garber was a veteran of the stage. The London, Ontario born actor was, at age 15, the youngest member of the University of Toronto's Hart House. Before he joined, he played the coffeehouse circuit, made TV and movie appearances, and worked in the theatre.

The Sugar Shoppe recorded one album for Capitol Records in 1968. Garber has continued to appear on TV and film, notably the Oscar winning Titanic (1997), in which he played the ship's architect, and as Jack Bristow in the ABC TV series, Alias, which premiered in the fall of 2001.

Singles:
Canada	Yorkville YVS 45009	1967
The Attitude	Yorkville YVS 45015	1967
Skip A Long Sam	Capitol 2230	1968
Privilege	Capitol 2326	1968

Album:
The Sugar Shoppe	Capitol St 2959	1968

Sweet Blindness

Bruce Barrow (bass)
Bobby Dupont (lead vocals)
Curtis Lee (lead guitar, lead vocals)
Sonny Milne (drums)
Phil Smith (keyboards)

This Toronto rock and soul band was first known as The Statlers when it was formed in 1967. By mid 1970 they had changed their name to Sweet Blindness. The group's lineup was comprised of Bobby Dupont, vocalist Don Meeker, bassist Ronnie Gant and guitarist Billy Murray. American guitarist Curtis Lee joined in 1974, along with Gabor Szepesi on keyboards and Al Marnie on bass. Szepesi, however, left in September, 1975 and was replaced by former Statler Phil Smith. In 1976 Barrow joined the group when it toured Ontario.

On stage Sweet Blindness played soul and progressive jazz. Their biggest hit was Cowboys to Girls in 1975/76.

Singles:

Cowboys to Girls	Quality 2150	1975/76
Sweet Blindness (Music You Can Ride On)	Quality 2163	1976
National Poddy	Quality 2196	1976
Quebec	Quality 2196	1976
Special Arrangement	Quality 2224	1977
Sunshine Sunshine	Quality 2233	1977

Albums/CDs:

Sweet Blindness	Quality SV 1923	1976
Energize	Quality SV 1943	1977

Syrinx

John Mills Cockell (piano, organ) (born: May 19/43)
Doug Pringle (saxophone)
Malcolm Tomlinson (drums, voice)
Allan Wells (percussion)

The origins of Syrinx go back to the late 1960s when Mills Cockell began experimenting with the Moog and Arp synthesizers. He was one of the first in Canada to use both during live performances. Mills Cockell grew up in Toronto where he attended Malvern Collegiate, and spent two years studying at the Faculty of Music at the University of Toronto. When he left the latter, he studied composition under Dr. Samuel Dolin at the Royal Conservatory of Music. In 1966 John studied electronic music with Gustav Ciamaga at the then new electronic music studio at the Royal Conservatory of Music. He was awarded a Canada Council grant to perform in Vancouver, and in June 1967 received a BMI Student Composer's Award.

In 1968 he performed with a group called Intersystems, and, a year later, with Toronto's Kensington Market and Vancouver's Hydro Electric Streetcar.

Syrinx, which is Greek for panpipes or the vocal box of a bird, evolved in 1970 when Mills Cockell joined forces with Pringle, Wells and Tomlinson. Their music combined Chinese, Balinese, African, North American Indian, Eskimo and ethnic folk in abstract forms. They also created mood music for the Paul Zindel play, Effect of Gamma Rays on Man In The Moon Marigolds, which was directed by Henry Tarvainen and performed at the St. Lawrence Centre For The Arts.

The group split up in 1972. Mills Cockell continued to record on his own. In 1973 he recorded under the name of JFC Heartbeat on the single, Instant Replay. He also recorded four solo albums, *Heartbeat* (True North TN 12 1974); *A Third Testament* (True North TN 17 1974); *Neon Acclerando* (1976), and *Gateway: A New Music Adventure* (1977).

Single:
Tillicum	True North TN 104	1971

Albums/CDs:
Syrinx	True North TN 2	1970
Long Lost Relatives	True North TNX 5	1971

Michael Tarry

He was born Michael Tarry McDermott in Oldham, Lancashire, England on May 18, 1946. Until he was eleven years old, he lived in a neighbourhood in the industrial north of England inhabited by grey skies and soot-stained streets. Life was not easy for an English youngster, so he built hundreds of model airplanes because they represented freedom and escape. He came to Canada with his parents when he was eleven years old.

After playing in various high school bands, he joined The Paytons who backed up Toronto based singer Susan Taylor. The rest of The Paytons included Jeff Smith, Cameron Kinglan, and Danny Petroff who was replaced by Paul Torrance. In 1964 he left The Paytons to concentrate on a solo career. By the late 1960s he had formed The Michael Tarry Group and toured with Bobby Curtola. Five years later, he signed a contract with Columbia Records who released his first single, All That I Love in 1969. It was followed by other singles but no album. In 1970 he fronted a group called Milestone, who also recorded for Columbia. Their only single was called Today/Silent People (Columbia C4 2923).

Continuing to write songs he caught the attention of Reprise Records who signed him in 1973. His first single, Rosalie, was a national hit. It was followed by an album entitled, Memories, and two more Singles:, the title track and Forgotten Man.

In the early 1980s he stopped performing and took a course in broadcasting at Loyalist College. From 1985 to 1995 he worked at CJBQ/CIGL FM in Belleville. Today, he lives in Marmora where he continues to write and record songs in his home studio. One of them, The Marmora Sled Dog Song has been used as the theme of the town's annual sled dog race.

Singles:
All That I Love	Columbia C4 2848	1969
If You Believe	Columbia C4 2863	1969
Neighbours At The Zoo	Columbia C4 2877	1969
What's Your Name	Columbia C4 2878	1969
Sometimes You're Up	Columbia C4 2922	1970
Rosalie	Reprise CR 4017	1973

| Forgotten Man | Reprise CR 4020 | 1973 |
| Memories | Reprise CR 4024 | 1974 |

Album:

| Memories | Reprise RSC 8007 | 1973 |

Bobby Taylor & The Vancouvers

Thomas Chong (guitar)
Wes Henderson (bass)
Robbie King (keyboards)
Ted Lewis (drums)
Edward Patterson (guitar)
Robert "Bobby" Taylor (lead vocals)

This Vancouver-based band established itself on the city's club circuit in the mid 1960s. Their future changed when Diana Ross was in Vancouver with the rest of the Supremes and saw the Canadian group perform. She was so impressed that she set them up with a record deal with Motown's subsidiary label, Gordy Records. The first single by Bobby Taylor and the Vancouvers was Does Your Mama Know About Me in August 1968. After two more hits they broke up. Chong became half of the comedy duo Cheech and Chong. Bobby Taylor is credited for discovering The Jackson Five who became one of Motown's biggest acts of the 1970s.

Singles:

Does Your Mama Know About Me	Gordy 7069	1968
I Am Your Man	Gordy 7073	1968
Malinda	Gordy 7079	1968/69

Albums/CDs:

| Bobby Taylor & The Vancouvers | Gordy 930 | 1968 |
| Taylor Made Soul | Gordy 942 | 1968 |

R. Dean Taylor

R. Dean Taylor was born in Toronto on May 11, 1939. In the early 1960s he played piano and sang with various groups and recorded for Barry Records. When success did not come, he moved to Detroit where he became a ghostwriter for

Motown Records. When the label introduced the subsidiary, Rare Earth, Taylor finally achieved success with Indiana Wants Me, which peaked at #5 on Billboard's Hot 100 in 1970. He had other songs on the Rare Earth label, but nothing equalled the success of Indiana. Late in 1981 he made an unsuccessful comeback with, Let's Talk it Over.

Singles:

At The High School Dance	Barry 3023	1960/61
I'll Remember	Barry 3099	1962
Let's Go Somewhere	Mowtown VIP 25027	1966
Indiana Wants Me	Rare Earth R5013	1970
Ain't it a Sad Thing	Rare Earth R5023	1971
Gotta See Jane	Rare Earth R5004	1971
Candy Apple Red	Rare Earth R5030	1971
Taos New Mexico	Rare Earth R5041	1972
Shadow	Rare Earth R5041	1973
Bonnie	Jane/GRT 1212 1001	1973
There's a Ghost In My House	Mot VIP 25042F	1974
Wipe My Tears Away (with Mandy)	Jane 1212 1002	1974
Walkin' in the Sun	Jane/GRT 1212 1004	1975
We'll Show Them All	Jane/POL 2065 288	1976
Let's Talk it Over		1981/82

Album:

I Think, Therefore, I Am	Rare Earth RS 522	1970

The Tea Party

Jeff Burrows (drums)
Stuart Chatwood (bass)
Jeff Martin (vocals, guitar)

Formed in 1990 in Windsor, Ontario, The Tea Party was founded by Jeff Martin. He first learned to play the guitar by listening to such blues legends as Sonny Williamson and Robert Johnson, and the avant blues/folk sound of poet and guitar legend Roy Harper.

Named after the Boston Tea Party, all three members first played together in high school in their home town. Martin's vocals has been compared to the late Jim Morrison of The Doors.

In 1991 they came out with their first independent CD, which was distributed by Eternal Discs. From it came the first single/video, Let Me Show You the Door.

Two years later, they signed a contract with EMI. Their debut album, *Splendor Solis* was recorded at White Crow Audio in Vermont. The first single was The River.

Their subsequent releases helped build a loyal fan base for the group, and during a tour of Australia, Martin picked up the esraj, one of many scarce instruments he owns. Their CD, *Triptych* (1999) included Daniel Lanois' The Messenger.

Singles:

Let Me Show You the Door	Independent	1991
The River	EMI 89419	1993
Save Me	EMI 89419	1993
A Certain Slant of Light	EMI 89419	1994
Midsummer Day	EMI 89419	1994
Fire in the Head	EMI 32350	1995
The Bazaar	EMI 32350	1995
Sister Awake	EMI 32350	1995
Temptation	EMI 55308	1997
Babylon	EMI 55308	1997/98
Release	EMI 55308	1998
Psychopomp	EMI 55308	1998
Heaven Coming Down	EMI 96545	1999
The Messenger	EMI 96545	2000
Walking Wounded	EMI 27682	2001
Lullaby	EMI 29721	2001
Angels	EMI 29721	2001

Albums/CDs:

The Tea Party	Independent	1991
Splendor Solis	EMI 89419	1993
The Edges of Twilight	EMI 32350	1995
Alahambra (EP)	EMI 37240	1996
Transmission	EMI 55308	1997
Triptych	EMI 96545	1999
Tangents	EMI 27682	2000
Collection	EMI 27682	2000
The Interzone Mantras	EMI 29721	2001

Teaze

Mark Bradac (guitar, background vocals)
Brian Danter (lead vocals, bass)
Mike Kozak (drums)
Chuck Price (guitar, background vocals)

Teaze was organized in 1975 in Windsor, Ontario, when Kozak, Price and Bradac joined Danter to form a group. They played the local club circuit but success at home was hard to achieve. Force One Records released their first album and single in 1976. Not until 1978 when they travelled to Japan did they experience stardom. Their 10-day tour was almost like Beatlemania in the U.S. Teazemania did not happen in Canada. Although they signed a contract with Aquarius Records in 1977, the response to their debut album was negative. Two years later, they moved their base of operations from Windsor to Montreal. Of all their single releases, their only national hit was Sweet Misery in 1978. In 1990 Capitol released a greatest hits collection in their Over 60 Minutes series.

Singles:

Boys Night Out	Forceone FO.001	1976
Sweet Misery	Aquarius AQ 5071	1978
Stay Here	Aquarius AQ 5074	1978
Heartless World	Aquarius AQ 5082	1978
Loose Change	Aquarius AQ 5086	1979
Roses & Chrome	Aquarius AQ 5091	1980
Living On The Edge	Aquarius AQ 5094	1980
That Kind of Girl	Aquarius AQ 5096	1980

Albums/CDs:

Teaze	Forceone FO.7001	1976
On The Loose	Aquarius AQR 516	1978
Tour Of Japan	Aquarius AQR 520	1979
One Night Stands	Aquarius AQR 523	1979
Baby Shots	Aquarius AQR 528	1980
Over 60 Minutes With	CAP 00557	1990

Teenage Head

Frank Kerr (vocals)
Gord Lewis (guitar)
Steve Mahon (guitar)
Nick Stipanitz (bass)

This quartet from Hamilton, Ontario first began playing together in high school. The four are named after a song of the same name by The Flamin' Groovies and were comprised of Frank Kerr, whose real name is Frankie Vernon, Gord Lewis, Steve Mahon, and Nick Stipanitz.

They first gained attention in 1977 in Toronto as part of the punk explosion that included The Diodes among other groups. Teenage Head's notoriety began after they played at the Crash'n Burn Club in Toronto. Success followed them at Max's in New York where they opened for Devo.

In September 1980 Lewis suffered severe spinal injuries from a car crash and did not rejoin the band until March 1981.

Two years later they joined Joan Jett, Madness, and Greg Kihn and Cheap Trick at Nashville's Electric Cowboy Festival.

Their early hits were on the Attic label, although they did record for other labels, such as Fringe and Ahed.

The release of their album, *Endless Party Live* in 1984 saw two new members join the group, guitarist Dave Des Rosches and drummer Jack Pedler. Dave Rave, formerly of The Shakers from Hamilton, joined the group on tour. After the album *Electric Guitar* in 1988, it was seven years before their next release, *Head Disorder*. Frank Kerr died on October 15, 2008.

Singles:

Somethin' on My Mind	Attic AT 220	1980
Let's Shake	Attic AT 229	1980
Some Kinda Fun	Attic AT 249	1982
Let's Go to Hawaii	Attic AT 271	1982
Tornado	MCA 52220	1983
Frantic Romantic	AHED RC 21 1	1986
Everybody Needs Somebody	Fringe FPS 1784	1988

Albums/CDs:

Teenage Head	Epic PEC 90534	1979
Frantic City	Attic LAT 1081	1980
Backwards in Bed With		1981
Some Kinda Fun	Attic LAT 1124	1982
Tornado (EP)	MCA 36001	1983
Endless Party	Ready LR 046	1984
Electric Guitar	Fringe FPL 3064	1988
Head Disorder	Loud Rock 5011	1995

Jay Telfer

Jay Telfer was born on December 22, 1947 in Moose Jaw, Saskatchewan. He moved to Toronto with his parents in 1952.

As a teenager in the early 1960s, he was a member of the folk group, The Voyageurs. In 1965 he was one of the original members of the A Passing Fancy, who were part of the Yorkville music scene. When they broke up in 1968, Jay wrote the theme song for the musical comedy revue, Watch The Birdie, which Sir John A Records released as a single.

He was then involved in the Toronto production of Hair, and with Fergus Hambleton recorded the album, Come Together, in 1969.

In 1970, he joined Doug Barnes to form the duo, God's Yacht, and Steel River recorded Ten Pound Note, written by Telfer.

He moved to Los Angeles in 1975 where he started a new career as screenwriter. Two of his screenplays became the movies, Marjorie My Love and The Boys Revenge.

In 1978 he returned to Toronto where he wrote the teleplay for You've Come A Long Way Katie, and two episodes of the CBC TV series The Great Detective. In the early 1980s he wrote two radio plays that were nominated for an Actra Award, With My Eyes Wide Open and Pony The Dog. He also wrote a third radio play, Mysterious Ways.

Since 1995 Jay has been editor and publisher of The Way Back Times, a newspaper devoted to antiques, in Belleville, Ontario.

Singles:
Watch The Birdie	Sir John A 6	1968
Time Has Tied Me	Axe 15	1974
Anything More Than Your Smile	Axe 18	1974
I Write Your Name (On The Wall Above My Bed)	Axe 21	1975

Albums/CDs:
Time Has Tied Me	Axe AXS 505	1974
Heart Of Aluminum Foil (CS)	GWM 101	1992

Diane Tell

Diane Tell, whose real last name is Fortin, was born in Quebec City on December 24, 1959. She attended the conservatory of music in Val D'Or where she learned how to play the violin. In 1971 she studied at the College Marie de France where she worked as a receptionist in a doctor's office. A year later, she returned to Montreal to study classical guitar.

In 1975 while she worked as a telephone operator in a Montreal hospital, she was invited to record her first album after a deal with RCA fell through. She performed at the Olympic Games in Montreal in 1976, and in October 1977 her self-titled debut album on Polydor Records was released.

Along with other established Quebec acts like Harmonium, Offenbach, and Celine Dion, Diane became one of Quebec's brightest young stars of the early

1980s. She sang in Old Montreal bars for two years until her big break came with the song, L'Eveche. In Old Montreal she was compared to singer Elaine McIllwaine.

In 1981 her album, *En Fleche* sold more than 150,000 copies and she won four Felix Awards, Quebec's equivalent of the Junos. That same year she was a guest on Elton John's TV special and Perry Como's annual Christmas show from Quebec City. The following year she played at the now defunct new wave club, The Edge in Toronto and appeared at the Juno Awards. In 1981 she won the Pop Song of The Year Award for Si J'Etais Un Homme.

During the next decade she starred in La legende de Jimmy and toured France, Switzerland, Germany and Austria with French singer Marilyn Montreuil. In 1996 came the CD, *Desir Plaisir Soupir*.

Singles:
Rendez vous	Polydor 2065.378	1977
Les cinemas bas	Polydor 2065.390	1977
Gilberto	Polydor	1979
Clic	Polydor 43 DJ	1980
Si j'etais un homme	Polydor 2065.442	1981
Miami	Polydor	1981
Souvent, longtemps, enormement	Polydor 2065.465	1982
La falaise	Polydor 2065.474	1982
On a beau	Polydor	1983
Savoir	Polydor 2065.487	1984
Pleure pas pour moi	Polydor 2065.494	1984
Par les temps qui viennent	Polydor 2065.497	1985
Manhattan monotone	Polydor Tell 1	1985
Fairea a nouveau connaissance	Tell 2	1986
J'arrive pas j'arrive	Tell 3	1986
Paradis d'espace	Tell 4	1987
Gilberto 87	Polydor DJ 97	1987
Je pense a toi comme je t'aime	CBS C5 3044	1988
Degriffe moi	CBS C5 3071	1988
Les yuppies	CBS C5 3078	1989
La legende de Jimmy	CBS NK 560	1990

Albums/CDs:
Diane Tell	Polydor 2424.165	1977
Entre Nous	Polydor 2424.203	1979
En Fleche	Polydor 2424.217	1980
Chimeres	Polydor 2424.236	1981
On A Besoin D'amour	Polydor 2424.249	1984
Faire A Nouveau Connaissance	Polydor 829 493 1	1986
Paris Montreal	Polydor 831 493 1	1987
Degriffe Moi	CBS CK 90773	1988
Collection D'or	Columbia WCK 90970	1996
Desir Plaisir Soupir	Columbia CK 91083	1996

13 Engines

John Critchley (vocals, guitar)
Grant Ethier (drums)
Jim Hughes (vocals)
Mike Robbins (guitar)

This band from Toronto, Ontario evolved in 1985 from The Ikons, a group from York University. A year later they changed their name to Thirteen Engines.

They signed a record deal with EMI/Capitol, and in 1987 recorded their first album, *Before Our Time*. It was recorded at the Old Schoolhouse studio near Detroit, the home of the Motor City Five and Ig and The Stooges.

The group's songwriters were Mike Robbins, John Critchley and Jim Hughes. Their songs were a mix of catchy plainsong melodies with serious lyrics about a variety of subjects, such as deformed children in Reptile Boy to the more lighthearted Menefreghista, a Sicilian term for someone who just doesn't care.

Shortly after the release of Conquistador in 1995, Grant Ethier left, and the rest of the group broke up in December 1997. John Critchley released his debut solo album, Crooked Mile (Sound King 901032) in 2000.

Singles:

Beached	Nocturnal	1989
Big Surprise	EMI 96207	1991
King of Saturday Night	EMI 96207	1991
More	EMI 80043	1993
Smoke And Ashes	EMI CD PRO 738	1993
Bred In The Bone	EMI CD PRO 809	1993
Beneath My Hand	EMI 32349	1995
Tailpipe Blues	EMI 32349	1995
Slow	EMI 32349	1996

Albums/CDs:

Before Our Time	Nocturnal Not 1	1987
Bryam Lake Blues	Nocturnal Not 2	1989
A Blur To Me Now	EMI 96207	1991
Ignition (EP)	EMI PRO 711	1993
Perpetual Motion Machine	EMI 80043	1993
Conquistador	EMI 32349	1995
Perfect Largeness: the Nocturnal Years	Nocturnal Not 10	1996

Ian Thomas

Ian Thomas was born in Hamilton, Ontario on July 23, 1950. The son of a Welsh Baptist minister and Scottish mother, he studied classical piano and later worked as an arranger for the Hamilton Symphony Orchestra. While still in his teens, he was a member of the folk trio, Ian, Oliver and Nora that later evolved into the group, Tranquility Base.

In 1971 he left them to work as a producer at the CBC where his credits included The National Fireworks Company for radio and The Barbara McNair Show, Ian Tyson and Music Machine series for television.

Signed to GRT Records, his first hit was Painted Ladies, which was inspired by Ian's days when he played the local bar circuit which was frequented by middle aged ladies wearing heavy make up.

His other hits included Long Long Way, Liars, Right Before Your Eyes and Come The Son.

The 1980s saw Thomas gain international success as a songwriter. On his 1985 album, Add Water, there were two songs that became big hits in Australia for Daryl Braithwaite, former lead singer of the 1970s band The Sherbs: As The Days Go By and All I Do. Another female vocalist named Gina, recorded a French version of As The Days Go By, which was a hit in Quebec in 1989.

Thomas was next in a group called The Boomers who became a sensation in Germany. In 1993 Anthem released the retrospective CD, *Looking Back*, a best of collection.

Singles:

Painted Ladies	GRT 1230 58	1973
Come The Son	GRT 1230 74	1974
Long Long Way	GRT 1230 76	1974
Mother Earth	GRT 1230 89	1975
Julie	GRT 1230 95	1975
The Good Life	GRT 1230 103	1975
Liars	GRT 1230 112	1976
Mary Jane	GRT 1230 118	1976
Right Before Your Eyes	GRT 1230 123	1977
Coming Home	GRT 1230 143	1978
Time Is The Keeper	GRT 1230 169	1979
Pilot	GRT 1230 177	1979
Hold On	Anthem ANS 032	1981
Borrowed Time	Anthem ANS 035	1981
Chains	Anthem ANS 036	1981
I'll Do You Right	Anthem ANS 058	1984

Touch Me	Anthem ANS 070	1985
Levity	Wea 25 77387	1988
Back To Square One	Wea 25 79447	1989

Albums/CDs:

Ian Thomas	GRT 9230 1037	1973
Long Long Way	GRT 9230 1044	1974
Delights	GRT 9230 1054	1975
Calabash	GRT 9230 1063	1976
Still Here	GRT 9230 1067	1978
Glider	GRT 9230 1082	1979
Best of Ian Thomas	Anthem ANR 1 1024	1980
The Runner	Anthem ANR 1 1032	1981
Riders on Dark Horses	Anthem ANR 1 1044	1984
Add Water	Anthem ANR 1 1047	1985
Levity	Wea 55556	1988
Looking Back	Anthem WAGK 1068	1993

Three's a Crowd

Bruce Cockburn (lead guitar, vocals)
Sandy Crawley (guitar, vocals)
Wayne Davis (bass)
Ken Koblun (bass)
Richard Patterson (drums)
Dennis Pendrith (bass)
Colleen Peterson (vocals)
Comrie Smith (bass)
Brent Titcomb (rhythm guitar, comedy, vocals)
Trevor Veitch (lead guitar, vocals)
Donna Warner (vocals, comedy)
David Wiffen (rhythm guitar, vocals)

This trio was one of Canada's first folk/rock groups. Founded in 1964 in Vancouver by Warner, Veitch and Titcomb, they were first known as The Bill Schwartz Quartet, with apologies to Schwartz's absence since he did not exist. They performed in coffeehouses in western Canada for a year then moved to Toronto in 1965. The following year they released their first hit single, Bound To Fly, on Epic Records.

In 1966 singer songwriter David Wiffen and bass guitarist Comrie Smith were added when the trio played at Ottawa's Le Hibou Coffee House. Richard Patterson, who was a member of The Children at the time, also joined on drums. The new group moved to Toronto and played at many coffeehouses throughout

Canada and the northeastern United States. They also performed at the Ontario Pavilion at Expo 67.

When Mama Cass Elliott and Papa Denny Doherty saw them play, the former arranged for Three's A Crowd to record a demo tape in New York. Signed to Dunhill they made two hit Singles:, Bird Without Wings, which was written by Bruce Cockburn, and Let's Get Together.

They later recorded the album, *Christopher's Movie Matinee* in Los Angeles, and the group ended up staying there.

After a tour of the United States, the band drifted apart. Donna Warner left due to illness. When they were offered to tour the college circuit, Wiffen and Patterson returned to Ottawa.

Upon their return, independent TV producer Sid Banks contacted them about appearing on the CBC weekly TV variety series, One More Time, hosted by Broadway star Gilbert Price. Taped in Montreal at the CFCF TV studios, it featured the new lineup of the group: Richard Patterson (drums), David Wiffen (lead vocals, guitar), Bruce Cockburn (guitar and vocals), Colleen Peterson (vocals), Sandy Crawley (guitar and vocals), Wayne Davis (bass), and Dennis Pendrith (bass).

When Bruce Cockburn wanted to leave to pursue a solo career, Three's A Crowd broke up. Although this version of the group never made a record, they did make a video of Cockburn's song, Electrocution Of The Word, which was showcased at the Youth Pavilion of Ottawa's Central Canadian Exhibition.

Wiffen had a brief solo career in the early 1970s, and Patterson went to work with the CBC in Ottawa, and was a member of the country/swing group The Radio Kings. Cockburn and Peterson went on to have successful solo careers from the 1970s on. The former enjoyed success with such hits as Wondering Where the Lions Are and If a Tree Falls, while the latter gained fame with the hit Souvenirs in 1976, which became her signature song. Sandy Crawley was President of the Toronto Actors Union, and Dennis Pendrith was a session player in Toronto. Titcomb made a name as a songwriter with such songs as Sing Hi Sing Lo, People's Park, Lift Your Hearts To The Sun, Bring Back The Love and I Still Wish You The Very Best.

Singles:
Bound To Fly	Epic 5 10073	1966
Honey Machine	Epic 5 10151	1967
Coat of Colours	Dunhill 4120	1968
Bird Without Wings	Dunhill 4120	1968
Let's Get Together	Dunhill 4131	1968

Album:
Christopher's Movie Matinee	Dunhill DS 50030	1968

Thundermug

James Corbett (bass)
Joe De Angelis (vocals)
Bill Durst (lead guitar)
Ed Pranskus (drums)

Formed in 1969 in London, Ontario, Thundermug was named after the chamber pot that used to be under the bed before there was indoor plumbing. Signed to Axe Records, their first hit was a remake of The Kinks' 1964 hit, You Really Got Me. Their second single, Africa was a national hit in Canada in 1972, and was taken from their first album, *Thundermug Strikes*.

The group's original vocalist, Joe De Angelis left in 1975, and they continued as a trio until they broke up in 1978.

In 1991, Durst and Corbett started playing together. With Corey Thompson added on drums, they became a cohesive unit and in 1994 recorded the CD, *Who's Running My World* on the independent Raven Recordings label.

Thompson left in 1996 and was replaced by Justin Burgess who stayed with the group until September 1997, when the group's original drummer, Ed Pranskus rejoined his former bandmates. Their second CD, *Bang the Love Drum* was released in 1997.

Singles:

You Really Got Me	Axe 3	1972
Africa	Axe 4	1972
Orbit	Axe 8	1973
Breaking Up Is Hard To Do	Axe 16	1974
Wanna Be With You	Axe 16	1974
Let's Live Together	Axe 20	1975
Banga Banga	Axe 28	1975
Clap Your Hands and Stamp Your Feet	Axe 33	1976
Old Songs	Axe 39	1976
Who's Running My World	Raven 94712	1994
Blue Water	Raven 94712	1994/95
She Said	Raven 94712	1995
You	Raven 89473	1997
Jerk	Raven 89473	1997

Albums/CDs:

Thundermug Strikes	Axe AXS 502	1972
Orbit	Axe AXS 504	1973
Ta Daa!	Axe AXS 507/509	1974
Who's Running My World	Raven 94712	1994
Bang The Love Drum	Raven 89473	1997

The Tierras

Trish Colter (vocals)
Colina Phillips (vocals)
Jackie Richardson (vocals)
Betty Richardson (vocals)
Brenda Russell (vocals)
Arlene Trotman (vocals)
Nerene Virgin (vocals)

This R&B/pop group from Toronto started in 1964. The first version was comprised of Jackie and Betty Richardson, Colina Phillips, Arlene Trotman, and Trish Colter. Their first single, Foolish Girl, was recorded on the independent Op Art label in 1967.

When Betty left that same year, the group became a trio made up of Nerene Virgin, Colter and Phillips. In 1968 they went to New York to record their second single, Where Does All The Time Go, on Barry Records. They were managed by Al Rain who was also a songwriter and producer. His most recognized song is Travelin' Man, the theme from CBC TV's The Tommy Hunter Show. In 1971, The Tierras broke up.

Singles:

Foolish Girl	Op Art 1003	1967
Where Does All The Time Go	Barry 3491	1968

Ken Tobias

Ken Tobias was born on July 25, 1945 in Saint John, New Brunswick. His professional career began in 1961 while still in high school, when he was lead singer in the folk group, The Ramblers with his brother Tony, Bob Bonnell and Mike Waye (The Bells). They were recorded on the independent album, Dartmouth "Y" Hootenanny: A Collection Of Folk Songs Recorded Live At Dartmouth High School on April 4, 1964. One of the songs from the album, Little Drops of Water was charted locally.

When Ken graduated from high school in 1965, he moved to Halifax, Nova Scotia where he worked as a mechanical draftsman and sang in local coffeehouses. In the spring of 1966 he joined the cast of CBC TV's Singalong Jubilee. His exposure on national television led to his appearance in Ottawa for the annual

Dominion Day celebrations, where he sang This Is The Maritimes, a song written by Ken and his brother Tony.

When he wasn't singing on Singalong Jubilee, he was a member of the rock group, the Badd Cedes in Halifax, and Chapter V in Toronto.

The latter recorded two Singles:, The Sun Is Green and Headshrinker, on Verve Records, and disbanded in December 1966. Ken then returned to Halifax to hone his talent as a singer/songwriter and started his own folk/rock group, The Book of Tobias.

In the fall of 1967, he was invited to join a new group in Montreal called The Crystal Staircase, who recorded two songs written by Tobias but they were never released. In the spring of 1968, they broke up and Ken rejoined the cast of Singalong Jubilee in Halifax. When the season ended, he went to Montreal to concentrate on a solo career.

Ken moved to Hollywood where he met Bill Medley of the Righteous Brothers, who signed him to a recording and publishing deal. His first single on Bell Records, You're Not Even Going To The Fair, entered RPM's Top singles Chart on November 1, 1969. Ken had moved back to Montreal.

By the spring of 1970, Tobias had returned to Hollywood to concentrate on his writing and recording. During this time The Bells had recorded his song, Stay Awhile, which peaked at #1 on RPM's Top singles Chart.

Throughout the 1970s, he had recorded for MGM and Attic Records. His hits included I Just Want To Make Music, Every Bit Of Love, Lover Come Quickly, and Give A Little Love. During the next decade, his creative talents included painting, and writing and producing for film and television. He wrote the score for the 1987 award winning film, Shahira, and the 1991 TV documentary, The Greenpeace Years, which aired on CBC. Today, Ken is still writing and performing.

Singles:

You're Not Even Going To The Fair	Bell 810X	1969
Now I'm In Love	MGM K14273	1971
I'd Like To Know	MGM CB 106X	1971
Dream No. 2	Verve VF 800X	1972
I Just Want To Make Music	Verve MV 10692	1973
Fly Me High	MGM K 14634	1973
On The Other Side	MGM M 14702	1974
Lover Come Quickly	MGM 14723	1974
Lady Luck	Attic AT 106	1975
Run Away With Me	Attic AT 111	1975
Every Bit of Love	Attic AT 118	1976
Give A Little Love	Attic AT 124	1976
Oh Lynda	Attic AT 137	1976

Lovin' Fever	Attic AT 148	1976
Dancer	Attic AT 162	1977
I Don't Want To Be Alone	Attic AT 174	1977/78
New York City	Attic AT 184	1978
Silver Saddle	Attic AT 194	1978
Here You Are Today	Gloo WRC 2821	1983
Crazy For Loving You	CBC LMS 003	1984

Albums/CDs:

Dream #2	MGM/VERVE MV 5085	1972
Magic's In the Music	MGM SE 4917	1973
Every Bit of Love	Attic LAT 1006	1975
Siren Spell	Attic LAT 1013	1977
Street Ballet	Attic LAT 1033	1977
So Far so Good	Attic LAT 1050	1978

Ken Tobias/Friends:

A Kid's Album of Pop Songs	Kiddin' Round KR 79806	1984
Gallery	CBC LM 483	1984

Toronto

Brian Allen (guitar)
Sharon Alton (guitar)
Nick Costello (bass)
Jim Fox (drums)
Scott Kreyer (keyboards)
Holly Woods (vocals) (Real name: Annie Woods)

Named after an Indian word that means "meeting place," Toronto organized in 1979. Holly (Annie) Woods, Jim Fox and Brian Allen were former members of the group Rose. They were joined by Sharon Alton, Nick Costello, and Scott Kreyer. Their debut album on Solid Gold Records, *Lookin' for Trouble*, was produced by Bill Henderson and Brian MacLeod of Chilliwack.

On stage they were one of the loudest rock bands to come out of Canada. Lead by British-born Woods, who grew up in Toronto, she was compared to a young Ann Margret in her Spandex, tiger-striped jump suit. Costello, Fox and Kreyer all hailed from Rochester, N.Y.

After such hits as Even The Score, Your Daddy Don't Know and Get It On Credit, Alton and Allen left in 1983. The band continued as Holly Woods and Toronto, who released the album, *Assault and Flattery* (SGR 1024), which included the hit single, New Romance. They broke up in 1984.

Singles:

Even The Score	Solid Gold SGS 700	1980
Lookin' For Trouble	Solid Gold SGS 701	1980
5035	Solid Gold SGS 702	1980
Still Talkin' Bout Love	Solid Gold SGS 708	1980
Your Daddy Don't Know	Solid Gold SGS 719	1982
Enough Is Enough	Solid Gold SGS 713	1982
Start Tellin' The Truth	Solid Gold SGS 724	1982
Get It On Credit	Solid Gold SGS 732	1982
Girls Night Out	Solid Gold SGS 737	1983
All I Need	Solid Gold SGS 742	1983
Ready To Make Up	Solid Gold SGS 743	1984
New Romance	Solid Gold SGS 753	1984

Albums/CDs:

Lookin' For Trouble	Solid Gold SGR 1000	1980
Head On	Solid Gold SGR 1005	1981
Get It On Credit	Solid Gold SGR 1011	1982
Girls Night Out	Solid Gold SGR 1016	1983
Assault And Flattery	Solid Gold SGR 1024	1984
Greatest Hits	Solid Gold SGR 1021	1984
Greatest Hits (CD R)	CBS VCK 80128	1988

Jerry Toth

Born in Windsor, Ontario on November 15, 1928, Jerry Toth came from a musical family. His father, Carl Toth (who died in 1958), worked as a gypsy fiddler whose gypsy orchestra named after him was prominent in Toronto's Hungarian nightclubs. Jerry's two brothers Rudy and Tony were also accomplished musicians.

Jerry Toth was an accomplished saxophonist, clarinetist, flutist, arranger, composer and producer. He played the alto sax between 1945 and 1953 in such dance bands of Stan Patton, Bobby Gimby, and Trump Davidson.

In 1953 Toth studied woodwinds in Los Angeles with Dale Eisenhuth. He then returned to Toronto where he worked with saxophonist Roy Smith in a local jazz band. From 1956 to 1974 Toth was a member of Phil Nimmons' jazz bands.

From 1954 he began playing in CBC orchestras under the direction of Jack Kane. Toth was music director for the CBC's Parade, Mallets and Brass and The Hit Parade.

During the mid 1960s he began writing and producing jingles with his brother Rudy, and served as audio consultant for many TV productions.

In 1967 he wrote the musical score for the film, A Place To Stand which was first shown to the public at Expo 67 in Montreal. At the 1968 Academy Awards it won in the Best Short Subjects (Live Action) category.

His recording career started in 1969 with The Music of Jerry Toth on the Canadian Talent Library label. He recorded other albums into the late 1970s. Between 1970 and 1990 he also recorded as a soloist with Phil Nimmons and as a member of the Boss Brass.

Jerry Toth died on March 31, 1999.

Singles:
A Rock Madrigal For Mehitabel (Jerry Toth Singers)	CTL 477 827	1972
Moment of Love (Jerry Toth Singers)	WAR CW 4001	1972

Albums/CDs:
The Music of Jerry Toth	CTL 477 5116	1969
Moment of Love	Warner WSC.9008	1972
The Twelve Sides Of	CTL 477 5171	1972
The Classic Jerry Toth	CTLS 5201/UALA 666G	1976

Toulouse

Heather Gauthier (vocals)
Judi Richards (vocals)
Lorri Zimmerman (vocals)

Toulouse was a female trio from Montreal, formed by Judi Richards, a native of Toronto, in 1976. She was joined by sisters Heather and Mari Lou Gauthier. Mari Lou was replaced at the end of 1976 by Laura Niedzielski Zimmerman, and her sister Heather by Liette Lomez in 1979. They were comfortable singing in both English and French, and recorded in both languages. Their first album, *Export* (1976) was their only English album. In 1986 Toulouse broke up.

Singles:
Lindberg	Magique 3803	1976
On a rien a perdre	Magique 3804	1976
It Always Happens This Way	Magique MAG 10	1977
A.P.B.	Magique MAG 11	1977
365 jours d'amour	Magique 3806	1977
Tonight I Feel Like Dancing	Magique 3808	1977
What Would My Mama Say	Magique 3810	1977/78
Prends moi, je veux t'aimer	Magique 3811	1978
Don't Play With My Heart	Magique 3813	1978
Comme la lumiere	Magique 3814	1978

Funky Station	Magique 3815	1979
Je n'ai jamais pense	Magique 3817	1979
Tout bas, tout doux	CBS C5 4236	1979
Boogie Man	CBS C5 4242	1980
11 A.M. n'Rainin'	CBS C5 4251	1980
Rock My Love	CBS	1980
Tendre doux	CBS C5 4279	1981
Que c'est que c'est (w/Robert Charlebois)	CBS C5 4287	1981
C'est toujours comme ca l'amour	CBS C5 4293	1982
Mont Royal	CBS C5 4588	1982
Miss Pacman	Kebec Disc KD 9209	1983
Le seul homme	Kebec Disc KD 9218	1983
Dites Ciao	Kebec Disc KD 9292	1985
It Always Happens This Way		1977

Albums/CDs:

Export	Magique 7603	1976
Potion Magique: Boule Noire Et Toulouse	Magique 7604	1976
Taxi Pour Une Nuit Blanche	Magique 7605	1978
Dangerous Ladies	CBS PFC 80036	1979
Trois Dimensions	CBS PFC 80053	1981

The Townsmen

Paul Huot (drums, vocals)
Andre Legault (guitar, vocals)
Wayne Leslie (bass, vocals)
Dave Milliken (lead guitar)
Frank Morrison (lead singer)

The history of The Townsmen goes back to the early 1960s in Ottawa when Frank Morrison, Dave Milliken and Wayne Leslie were The Darnells. In 1965, they changed their name to The Townsmen when they added two new members, ex Esquire Paul Huot and Andy Legault. Signed to the Regency label, their first hit was I'm Such A Dreamer in 1965. They toured Canada where they opened for The Rascals, The McCoys, The Turtles and Gary Lewis and The Playboys. In 1966 Andre Legault left, and two new members were added; Buddy Stanton on piano and vocals, and John Bocho on guitar and vocals. Huot left in 1967 and later played in The Interpretation and Canada Goose, two other Ottawa groups. The Townsmen disbanded in 1969.

Singles:

I'm Such a Dreamer	Regency963	1965
Funny How Love Can Be	Regency970	1966
The Lion Sleeps Tonight	Regency973	1966
He's in Town	Regency975	1967
We're Doin' Fine	Regency973	1967
Heaven in The Middle of Town	Regency970	1968
Rockin' Chair	POL 540 008	1968
I Can't Find My Way Home	Ottawa OR 4201	1969
Winds Blowin' Diamonds Tonite	Ottawa OR 4210	1969

The Tracically Hip

Bobby Baker (guitar)
Gordon Downie (vocals)
Johnny Fay (drums)
Paul Langlois (guitar)
Gord Sinclair (bass)

Formed in 1986, this Kingston-based band took its name from ex-Monkees Michael Nesmith's Elephant Parts video. Three quarters of the band had graduated with degrees in various disciplines: Gord Sinclair in history, Gord Downie in political science and film, and Bobby Baker in art. Johnny Fay wanted a career in music, and with the addition of Paul Langlois the group was born.

They played the local clubs and toured across Canada from Montreal to Vancouver. Their brand of rock became popular and it captured the attention of MCA Records President Bruce Dickinson, who signed the band after seeing them perform at Toronto's Horseshoe Tavern.

Their many hits included Blow at High Dough, Courage, Locked in the Trunk of a Car, and their signature song, New Orleans is Sinking.

On stage it's Downie's strong vocals, in harmony with the searing guitars and strong rhythms of the rest of the band that contribute to their overall, unique sound. The progression of their music has matured from album to album, while their live appearances show the growth of one of Canada's enduring rock groups. Their popularity has extended internationally to such countries as Holland, Belgium, Australia, and the United States.

In 2001, Gord Downie released his first solo album, *Coke Machine Glow* (Wiener Art Records 422112).

Encyclopedia of Rock, Pop & Folk Music in Canada

Singles:

Smalltown Bringdown	MCA 37330	1987
Blow at High Dough	MCA 6310	1989
New Orleans is Sinking	MCA 6310	1989
Boots or Hearts	MCA 6310	1990
38 Years Old	MCA 6310	1990
Little Bones	MCA 10173	1991
Three Pistols	MCA 10173	1991
Twist My Arm	MCA 10173	1991
Long Time Running	MCA 10173	1991
On the Verge	MCA 10173	1991
Locked in a Trunk of A Car	MCA 10700	1992
Courage	MCA 10700	1993
At the Hundredth Meridian	MCA 10700	1993
Looking For a Place to Happen	MCA 10700	1993
Grace, Too	MCA 11140	1994
Greasy Jungle	MCA 11140	1994
Nautical Disaster	MCA 11140	1995
So Hard Done By	MCA 11140	1995
Scared	MCA 11140	1995
Thugs	MCA 11140	1995
Ahead by a Century	MCA 81011	1996
Gift Shop	MCA 81011	1996
700 Ft. Ceiling	MCA 81011	1996
Flamenco	MCA 81011	1996
Springtime in Vienna	MCA 81055	1997
Phantom Power	MCA 81083	1998
Fireworks	MCA 81083	1998
Something On	MCA 81083	1999
Bobcaygeon	MCA 81083	1999
My Music @ Work	Universal 157874	2000
Lake Fever	Universal 157874	2000

Albums/CDs:

The Tragically Hip (Ep)	RCA Kzl1 0590	1987
The Tragically Hip (Ep)	MCA 37330	1987
Up to Here	MCA 6310	1989
Road Apples	MCA 10173	1991
Fully Completely	MCA 10700	1992
Day For Night	MCA 11140	1994
Trouble at the Henhouse	MCA 81011	1996
Live Between Us	MCA 81055	1997
Phantom Power	MCA 81083	1998
Music @ Work	Universal 157874	2000
In Between Evolution	Universal 863211	2004
Yer Favourites	Universal 884291	2006
World Container	Universal 705589	2006
We are the Same	Universal 700833	2009
From The Vault Vol 4	Universal 701147	2009
Now for Plan A	Universal 717336	2012
Man Machine Poem	Universal 765442	2016

Tranquility Base

Steve Hagg (bass)
Nora Hutchinson (vocals)
Oliver MacLeod (guitar)
Ron Parks (drums)
Ian Thomas (vocals, guitar)
Nancy Ward (keyboards)

Tranquility Base started in Hamilton, Ontario in 1969. They were your average pop group that went through several personnel changes. Ian Thomas was in the group when they were signed with RCA and had minor success with the hit, If You're Lookin'. He left at the end of 1971 to go solo. Other members of the group included Stan Rogers, Lorence Hud, Franki Hart (Freedom and Riverson), and Mike Oberle, who started the roadhouse band at the Lulu's nightclub in Kitchener, Ontario. In 1973 Tranquility Base recorded The Future and The Past, Kingston, Ontario's Official Tercentenary Song. Two years later, the group disbanded.

Singles:
If You're Lookin'	RCA 74 0330	1970
In The Rain/Day Is Over	RCA 75 1033	1972
The Future And The Past	AMK 3	1973

The Travellers

Simone Cook (vocals)
Sid Dolgay (mandocello)
Pam Fernie (vocals)
Jerry Goodis (vocals)
Jerry Gray (banjo, lead singer)
Helen Gray (vocals)
Aileen Lawrence (vocals)
Joe Lawrence Hampson (bass)
Marty Meslin (vocals)
Ted Roberts (guitar)
Oscar Ross (vocals)
Don Vickery (drums)
Ray Woodley (guitar)

Formed in the summer of 1953, The Travellers were one of Canada's best-known folk singing groups. The founding members were Jerry Gray, Sid Dolgay, Helen Gray, Jerry Goodis, and Oscar Ross. They made their TV debut in 1954 on CBC's

Haunted House, and were finalists on Pick The Stars on the same network.

Helen Gray left in 1954 and was replaced by Simone (Johnston) Cook, who, in turn, left in 1969 was replaced by Pam Fernie, formerly with The Courriers, who stayed until 1974. Other members of the group included Aileen Ahern, Marty Meslin, Ted Roberts, Joe Lawrence Hampson, Don Vickery, and Ray Woodley.

From the mid 1950s to the early 1960s, they entertained audiences with their simple melodies. They headlined the first Mariposa Folk Festival in 1961, and toured Russia as part of A Musical Tour of Canada the following year. In 1964 they played before Queen Elizabeth II and Prince Philip at a Royal Command Performance in Charlottetown.

During Canada's Centennial Year, the group played 135 concerts across the country, toured several army bases, and performed at Expo 67. The 1970s saw them entertain at Expo 70 in Osaka, Japan, and Canadian Armed Forces in Cyprus with Harry Belafonte, Oscar Brand, Anne Murray, Gordon Lightfoot, Oscar Peterson, Judy Collins and Catherine McKinnon.

The Travellers celebrated their 40th anniversary on October 3, 1993 with a concert at the Minkler Auditorium at Seneca College, Toronto. In 1999 Sony Music released the retrospective CD, *This Land is Your Land 1960 1966*. Sid Dolgay died on December 25, 2014 and Jerry Goodis on November 8, 2002.

Albums/CDs:

Across Canada with the Travellers	Hallmark CS 7	1957
Sing Songs of North America	Hallmark CS 9	1959
Quilting Bee	Columbia FS 512	1960
Introducing the Travellers	Columbia BN 26013	1961
Making Hay	Columbia FL 288	1962
The Travellers on Tour	Columbia FS 545	1962
Something to Sing About	Columbia FS 610	1963
We're On Our Way Again	Columbia EL 103	1964
The Travellers Still Travelling	Harmony HES 6003	1966
This Land	Arc AS 250	1967
A Century of Song	Arc AS 261	1967
The Travellers Applaud Canada	Arc AS 268	1968
The Travellers Sing For Kids	Caedmon Ml700	1970
The Travellers	CBC LM 82	1970
Merry Go Round	Elephant LFN 80 03	1980
This Land is Your Land 1960 1966	Columbia ZK 80388	1999

Triumph

Rik Emmett (guitar)
Mike Levine (bass)
Gil Moore (vocals, drums)
Rick Santers (guitar)
Phil X (guitar)

Formed in mid 1975 in Toronto, this trio of heavy metal rockers first established themselves on the city's club circuit. Emmett was a former student at Humber College, while Moore worked in a local unknown group and operated a small booking agency. Levine worked with Emmett and Moore to come up with a sound that would make them unique. It was not until they recorded a remake of Joe Walsh's Rocky Mountain Way that Triumph was noticed back home. They had established themselves in Texas in the mid 1970s.

The group headlined their own show at Toronto's Massey Hall in 1978. They continued to have commercial success on the charts until 1987 when Rik Emmett left. The group later broke up.

In 1992 the two original members, Mike Levine and Gil Moore reunited to form a new version Triumph with guitarists Rick Santers and Phil X. That same year, Virgin released their CD, *Edge of Excess*. They also had their first Top 40 hit, Trouble Maker, from the soundtrack of the film Hellraiser III: Hell On Earth (1992).

Singles:

Hobo	Attic AT 115	1975
24 Hours a Day	Attic AT 136	1976
What's Another Day of Rock and Roll	Attic AT 149	1976
Rocky Mountain Way	Attic AT 173	1978
Hold On	Attic AT 203	1979
Lay It on The Line	Attic AT 213	1979/80
I Can Survive	Attic AT 222	1980
American Girls	Attic AT 230	1980
Magic Power	Attic AT 248	1981
Say Goodbye	Attic AT 257	1982
A World of Fantasy	Attic AT 281	1983
All the Way	POL PDS 2225	1983
A World of Fantasy (12")	POL PDSX 2213	1983
Spellbound (12")	MCA TR 2	1984

Somebody's Out There	MCA 52898	1986
Just One Night	MCA 53014	1987
Let The Light (Shine On Me)	MCA 8738	1987
Never Say Never	MCA 53241	1988
Troublemaker	Virgin TRCD 00120	1992
Child of The City	Virgin TRCD 00120	1992/93
Somewhere Tonight	Virgin TRCD 00120	1993

Albums/CDs:

Triumph	Attic LAT 1012	1976
Rock and Roll Machine	Attic LAT 1036	1977
Just a Game	Attic LAT 1061	1979
Progressions of Power	Attic LAT 1083	1980
Allied Forces	Attic LAT 1122	1981
Never Surrender	Attic LAT 1150	1983
Thunder Seven	MCA 5537	1984
Stages	MCA 2 8020	1985
The Sport of Kings	MCA 4786	1986
Classics: Greatest Hits	MCA 42283/6211	1989
Edge of Excess	Virgin TRCD 00120	1992
King Biscuit Flower Hour: Allied Forces Tour 1981	KBT 88014	1995

Domenic Troiano

Born in Modugno, Italy on January 17, 1946, Domenic Troiano came to Canada with his parents when he was three years old. They settled in Toronto where he would later play an important role in the Toronto music scene in the 1960s. Domenic attended East York Collegiate. A self-taught guitarist, Troiano's major influences were Chuck Berry, bluesmen Albert King and B.B. King, and Wes Montgomery.

In December 1962 Domenic joined Robbie Lane's group The Continentals and later convinced him to change their name to The Disciples. In 1964 he played with Ronnie Hawkins, and was a member of the house band at Club Bluenote. Troiano had also joined The Five Rogues, renamed Mandala in 1966, and later Bush when Mandala broke up in 1969.

When Bush dissolved in 1971, Troiano began recording as a solo artist for Mercury. A year later his self-titled debut album was released, followed by *Tricky* in 1973. During this time he played with the James Gang and in 1974–75 he was a member of The Guess Who. In the late 1970s he formed his own band and recorded for Capitol Records. His hit singles included It's You and We All Need Love.

In the 1980s he began writing music for film and television. He has written the music for such shows as Night Heat (CTV/CBS), Diamonds and Pop Cops (both on CBS), Airwaves (CBC), Cop Talk (Tribune Network), Counter Strike (USA Network) and Secret Service and True Blue (both NBC). The list of TV movies included The Playground for Ray Bradbury Theatre, Republic Pictures' The Swordsman, and While My Pretty One Sleeps for the USA Family Channel.

Other artists he has either written or produced include Shawne Jackson (on her hit, Just As Bad As You), Kilowatt, and Patria, on Troiano's own label, Black Market Records.

He was inducted into the Juno Hall of Fame in 1996. He died on May 25, 2005.

Singles:

The Wear and The Tear On My Mind	MercuryM.73312	1972
Try	MercuryM.73342	1972
Savour The Flavour	Capitol 72792	1977
Here Before My Time (Domenic Troiano Band)	Capitol 72795	1978
Maybe the Next Time (Domenic Troiano Band)	Capitol 72800	1978
Your Past (Is A Part of You)	Capitol 72810	1979
It's You (Troiano)	Capitol 72816	1979
We All Need Love (Troiano)	Capitol 72804	1979

Albums/CDs:

Domenic Troiano	Mercury SRM 1 639	1972
Tricky	Mercury SRM 1 670	1973
Burnin' At the Stake	Capitol ST 11665	1977
The Joke's on Me	Capitol SW 11772	1978
Fret Fever	Capitol ST 11932	1979
Changing of the Guard	EL Mocambo 762	1980
Night Heat (W/Roy Kenner)(12")	A&M Am 23044	1986
Live At Thunder Sound	Capitol SPRO 11	1986
Triple Play 1976 1980 (Cd R)	EMI 37359	1996
The Toronto Sound (CD R)	Mercury538562	1999

Trooper

Ramon McGuire (vocals)
Brian Smith (lead guitar)
Harry Kalinsky (bass)
Frank Ludwig (piano, keyboards)
Tommy Stewart (drums)

The Vancouver-based group began as Winter's Green in 1967, comprised of Ramon McGuire, Brian Smith, Wayne Gibson, Stu Wilson, and Bruce Rutherford. Their music was heavily influenced by The Doors, but by the early 1970s they had changed to more of a commercial pop sound, and changed their name to Applejacks.

Another name change to Trooper came in 1975 when they signed to Randy Bachman's Legend label. Their first single was Baby Woncha Please Come Home.

There were some personnel changes in 1976: Doni Underhill replaced Kalensky, and Frank Ludwig joined on piano. In 1979, he, too, left and was replaced by Rob Deans.

Throughout the 1970s and 1980s, they had many hits. Their biggest was the ballad Oh, Pretty Lady in 1978.

In 1991, Warner Music released Ten, their last album for the label. Today, they are still touring.

Singles:

Baby Woncha Please Come Home	MCA 40447	1975
General Hand Grenade	MCA 40480	1976
Two For The Show	MCA 40583	1976
Ready	MCA 40659	1976
Santa Maria	MCA 40685	1977
We're Here For A Good Time	MCA 40738	1977
Oh Pretty Lady	MCA 40799	1978
Raise A Little Hell	MCA 40924	1978
Round Round We Go	MCA 40940	1978
The Moment That It Takes	MCA 40968	1979
The Boys In The White Sports Car	MCA 40999	1979
Three Dressed Up As A Nine	MCA 41115	1979
Janine	MCA 41172	1980
Good Clean Fun	MCA 41239	1980
Real Canadians	MCA 41301	1980
Are You Still My Baby	MCA 51010	1980
Just One Kiss		1981
Only a Fool	FLIC PB 13085	1982
Money Talks	RCA PB 50689	1982
Boy with the Beat	Wea 25 75157	1986
The Best Way (To Hold a Man)	Wea PRO CD18 P	1989
American Dream	Wea 74703	1991
Kids in Love	Wea 74703	1991

Albums/CDs:

Trooper	MCA 2149	1975
Two for the Show	MCA 2214	1976
Knock 'Em Dead Kid	MCA 2275	1977
Thick As Thieves	MCA 2377	1978
Flying Colors	MCA 3173	1979
Hot Shots	MCA 5101	1979
Trooper	MCA 5151	1980
Money Talks	RCA AFL1 4318	1982
The Last of the Gypsies	Wea 25 64431	1989
Ten	Wea 74703	1991

Tsufit

Born in Jerusalem, Israel, Tsufit grew up in Kingston, Ontario.

She taught herself the guitar and her music combines comedy with world beat and folk music. In 1997 she released the independent cassette, Broccoli's On Sale at Dominion. She has performed in Cleveland and at several Canadian music festivals, including the Elora Fringe Festival, the Ontario Renaissance Festival, and the Tillsonburg Festival by the Lake. Tsufit writes passionate songs in English and her music is influenced by Gypsy melodies and sultry Middle Eastern rhythms. On her first full length CD, Under the Mediterranean Sky she included some Hebrew Chassidic songs. Today, she is a wife and mother She also coaches business owners to write and perform commercials for their businesses.

Album:
Under The Mediterranean Sky   Sunbird   1999

Shania Twain

Shania Twain was born Eileen Regina Edwards on August 28, 1965 in Windsor, Ontario. Her biological parents separated when she was two years old, and she was raised in Timmins, Ontario by her mother and stepfather, Jerry Twain, who was a full-blooded Ojibway Indian. Eileen was legally adopted and registered as fifty per cent North American Indian, and given the name Shania, which means "I'm On My Way."

Growing up she was exposed to musical theatre, country music and such pop stars as The Mamas and The Papas, The Carpenters, The Supremes, and The Jacksons. As a child Shania was encouraged to sing on stage with local bands. By the time she was eight, she was singing on weekends and appeared on TV and radio. She spent summers working in the bush with her stepfather, who was foreman of a thirteen-man reforestation crew. After graduating from high school, she pursued a singing career full time and performed at various nightclubs.

At twenty-one her life changed dramatically when her mother and step father were killed in a car crash. Shania became a sister and mother to her two younger brothers and sister. To support them she took a job as singer at the Deerhurst resort in Huntsville, Ontario, bought a home, and a family truck.

Shania eventually was able to carry on her dream of a career in country music. Her longtime friend and country singer Mary Bailey became her manager. Signed to Mercury Nashville, Shania's self-titled debut album came out in 1993. With such songs as What Made You Say That and Dance With the One That Brought You, she became popular overseas and earned CMT Europe's Rising Video Star of the Year Award.

Shania met her future producer/husband, Robert John "Mutt" Lange at Nashville's Fan Fair in 1993. Together they wrote all the songs on her next two albums, *The Woman in Me* (1995) and *Come on Over* (1997), both of which have sold over ten million copies each. The former tied Patsy Cline's Greatest Hits as the best selling female album in country music history when it sold six million copies by the spring of 1996.

Her songs have also been featured on various soundtracks. No One Needs to Know was featured in the film, Twister, while You've Got A Way in Notting Hill. In addition to her own TV specials in Canada and the U.S., her songs have been charted on Billboard's Hot 100 and Country singles Charts. She became the spokesperson for Revlon in 1999.

Singles:

Dance With The One That Brought You	Mercury 514422	1993
What Made You Say That	Mercury 514422	1993
You Lay A Whole Lot Of Love On Me	Mercury 514422	1993
Whose Bed Have Your Boots Been Under?	Mercury 522886	1994
Any Man Of Mine	Mercury 522886	1995
The Woman In Me (Needs The Man In You)	Mercury 522886	1995
(If You're Not In For Love) I'm Outta Here	Mercury 522886	1995
You Win My Love	Mercury 522886	1996
No One Needs To Know	Mercury 522886	1996
Home Ain't Where His Heart Is (Anymore)	Mercury 522886	1996
God Bless The Child	Mercury 522886	1996
If It Don't Take Two	Mercury 522886	1997
Love Gets Me Every Time	Mercury 568062	1997
You're Still The One	Mercury 536003	1998
Don't Be Stupid (You Know I Love You)	Mercury 536003	1998
From This Moment On (w/Bryan White)	Mercury 536003	1998
Honey, I'm Home	Mercury 536003	1998
That Don't Impress Me Much	Mercury 536003	1999
Man! I Feel Like A Woman!	Mercury 536003	1999
You've Got A Way	Mercury 170123	1999
Come On Over	Mercury 170123	1999
When	Mercury 170123	2000

Albums/CDs:

Shania Twain	Mercury 514422	1993
The Woman In Me	Mercury 522886	1995
Come on Over	Mercury 536003	1997

Beginnings	Medacy 21646	1998
Come on Over (Remixes)	Mercury 170123	1999
Complete Limelight Sessions	Limelight 8140	2001

The Ugly Ducklings

Dave Bingham (lead vocals)
Glynn Bell (guitar)
Robin Boers (drums)
Roger Mayne (guitar)
John Read (bass)

Named after the story by Hans Christian Anderson, The Ugly Ducklings were one of Toronto's top groups. Formed in 1964, the original group was comprised of Dave Bingham, Roger Mayne and Marty Ranger. For one night only they called themselves The Strolling Bones when they played at Cedarbrae Collegiate in Scarborough, Ontario.

In April 1965 they played in Yorkville Village, and later appeared on two CBC TV shows, Through The Eyes of Tomorrow and In Person. They opened for Sam The Sham, The Rolling Stones, The Beach Boys, The McCoys, Gary Lewis and The Playboys and Wilson Pickett.

Nothin', on the Yorktown label, was their first hit in 1966.

It was followed by such hits as the two sided, 10:30 Train/She Ain't No Use To Me, Just In Case You Wonder, and Gaslight.

In September 1967 Mayne left and was replaced by Mike McKenna, who, in turn, left in the spring of 1968. The Ugly Ducklings split up in December 1968.

Ten years later the group reunited, and, in 1980, Razor Records released their new album, Off The Wall. In 1981 after they played at the El Mocambo in Toronto, they broke up again. They have since reunited for the odd concert.

Singles:

Nothin'	Yorktown 45001	1966
10:30 Train/She Ain't No Use To Me	Yorktown 45002	1966
Just In Case You Wonder	Yorktown 45003	1967
Postman's Fancy (unreleased)	Yorktown 45005	1967
Gaslight	Yorktown 45013	1967
Epilogue	Yorktown 45017	1967
Just Another Rock & Roll Band	Razor	1980

Albums/Cds:

Somewhere Outside	YT 50,0001	1966
Off the Wall	Razor RS002	1980
Somewhere Outside		1982
Too Much, Too Soon	Pace 021	1998
Ducktales	Freeway 001	1998
Somewhere Outside	Unidisc/Agek 2185	1998
The Ugly Ducklings	Unidisc/Agek 2186	1998

Shari Ulrich

Born on October 17, 1951 in San Rafael, California, Shari Ulrich moved to Vancouver in 1972. She played with various folk and rock groups before joining Rick Scott and Joe Mock in The Pear of Pied Pumkin in 1974. Their strong harmonies and distinctive sound made them popular on the folk music circuit.

In 1976 she quit Pied Pumkin to join Valdy's backup group, The Hometown Band. After two years she left to concentrate on a solo career. Her debut album, *Long Nights*, on A&M Records came out in 1980, followed by *One Step Ahead* in 1981. She then recorded for MCA and CBS and her own label, Esther.

In 1989 she met Bill Henderson of Chilliwack fame and Roy Forbes (Bim) for a special one-night concert at Vancouver's Winter Roots Festival. They realized their voices complemented each other and decided to form a trio called UHF or Ulrich, Henderson and Forbes. In 1991 they recorded their self-titled debut album on Tangible Records.

In between performances with Henderson and Forbes, Ulrich recorded another solo album, Every Road in 1990. A year later came a Best Of collection, followed by an album of new material called *A View From Here* in 1998. In 2007 she played with Barney Bentall and Tom Taylor and became part of the trio, Bentall Taylor Ulrich. They have two albums to their credit, *Live at Cates Hill* (2009) and *Tightrope Walk* (2016).

Singles:

Bad Bad Girl	A&M AM 501	1980
Oh Daddy	A&M AM 534	1980
Long Nights	A&M AM 520	1981
Save It	A&M AM 550	1982
She Remembers	A&M AM 578	1982
It's Not Love	CBS/Doremus FZT 80144	1990
Every Road	CBS/Doremus FZT 80144	1990

Albums/CDs:

Long Nights	A&M SP 9046	1980
One Step Ahead	A&M SP 9067	1981
Talk Around Town	MCA 5379	1982
Every Road	CBS/Doremus FZT 80144	1990
Best Of Shari Ulrich	Esther 627	1991
A View From Here	Esther 563	1998
Find Our Way	Esther 1919	2010
The Highbargang	True North TND583	2013
Everywhere I Go	Borealis BCD 228	2014

Valdy

Born Valdemar Horsdal to Danish parents in Ottawa on September 1, 1945, he began playing the guitar as a teenager. He took piano lessons for five years and learned orchestrations from Prof. Robin Wood, the dean of the music school in Victoria. Valdy's early career began in the mid 1960s when he was a member of the London Town Criers (1964 65). He went on to play with The Prodigal Sons in Montreal and later worked as a bassist for country singer Blake Emmons. Moving to the west coast he played bass for various groups in Victoria. In 1972 he decided to go solo. Signing with Haida Records, distributed by A&M, his first single was Rock and Roll Song which was inspired by rambunctious crowd at the Aldergrove Rock Festival in 1968.

By 1976 he had recorded five albums and was second to Gordon Lightfoot in record sales for a Canadian folk singer. In August of that year, Valdy represented Canada at the International Song Festival at Sopot, Poland.

One of the major highlights of his career was his association with The Hometown Band. They recorded one album together called *Valdy and the Hometown Band* in 1977.

In 1978 he recorded, *Hot Rocks*, his folk disco album. The title song referred to nuclear spent fuel, while the rest of the album dealt with other serious subjects.

After leaving A&M in 1982, he recorded for Duke Street, Sloth and Peg Music/Sony. In 1993 came the album, *Heart at Work* followed by Smorgasbord (1997), a collection of eclectic songs. More recently, he has performed with the Victoria Symphony, The Kingston Symphony, The Waterford Blues Band, and J.P. Cormier. He also recorded an album of songs with country singer Gary Fjellgaard called Contenders (2000) for the Stony Plain label. In 2015, Rock and Roll Song was inducted into the Canadian Songwriters Hall of Fame.

Singles:

Rock and Roll Song	Haida HS 101	1972
A Good Song	Haida HS 104	1973
Simple Life (Ode To L.A.)	Haida HS 107	1973
Landscapes	Haida HS 110	1973
Renaissance	A&M AM 377	1974
Yes I Can (Any Way You Want Me)	A&M AM 413	1976
Peter And Lou	A&M AM 418	1977
Hometown Band	A&M AM 432	1977
Dirty Old Man	A&M AM 461	1977
Hot Rocks	A&M AM	1978
Sister I Love You	A&M AM 473	1979
Easy Money	SlothSS 101	1980
Thank God He's A Stranger	SlothSS 103	1981
Movie Scene	SlothSS 110	1981
Leavin' Ain't The Only Way To Go	SlothSS 107	1982
Daddy's Okay	SlothSS-108	1983
It's That Melody	Duke StreetDSR 71010	1985
Sonny's Dream	Duke DSR 81010	1986
Roll Man Roll		1987
Living Next To A Candy Store	Rot REC ROT #1	1988
Hey Mr. Michael Wilson		1990
Double Solitaire	Peg Music PMK 012	1993
Link In A Chain	Peg Music PMK 012	1993
Peace of Mind	Rack-On-Tour 101	1997

Albums/CDs:

Country Man	Haida HL 5101	1972
Landscapes	Haida HL 5104	1973
Family Gathering	A&M SP 9103	1974
Family Gathering (Ep)	A&M 386	1974
See How the Years Have Gone By	A&M SP 4538	1975
Valdy and the Hometown Band	A&M SP 4592	1976
Hot Rocks	A&M SP 9034	1978
Passport: Best of Valdy	A&M SP 9038	1979
1001	Slothsl 1001	1980
Valdy's Kid Record	Sloth SL 1003	1982
Notes from Places	Duke Streetdsr 31010	1985
A Classic Collection	A&M 9147	1988
Heart at Work	Peg Music Pmk 012	1993
Smorgasbard	Rack-On-Tour Rot 101	1997
Contenders (W/Gary Fjellgaard)	Stony Plainspcd 1262	2000
The Milrnnium Collection	Universal 303129	2001
Viva Valdy: Live at Last	Rack-On-Tour 22152	2003
Contenders Two	Stony Plainspcd 1321	2007
Read Between The Lines	Rack-On-Tour 22782	2012

Gino Vannelli

Born in Montreal on June 16, 1952, Gino Vannelli was first exposed to music from his father Russ who played in the bands of Bix Belair and Maynard Ferguson. As a youth growing up, the young Gino learned to play the drums. He along with his two brothers, Joe and Ross, listened to Latin bands and went across the border to the United States where they bought R&B records. He later studied theory at McGill University where he formed a rhythm and blues band with his older brother Joe. Another brother, Ross joined his two siblings in the late 1970s. Gino was one of the few white singers to appear on the syndicated TV show, Soul Train.

His recording career goes back to 1970 when he recorded under the name of Vann Elli on RCA. After one single, Gina Bold, he was released from his contract. In 1973, he went to New York where he met Herb Alpert, co-founder of A&M Records, who signed him to the label. The first single to gain national attention in both Canada and the United States was People Gotta Move, which turned out to be the first of several hits between 1974 and 1979. He has since recorded for Arista, Mercury and Polydor.

One of his most successful albums was *Brother to Brother* in 1979, which featured a symphonic suite performed by the Royal Philharmonic Orchestra. In 1995 he switched from pop to jazz with the release of *Yonder Tree*.

Singles:

Gina Bold	RCA Victor 1019	1970
Granny Goodbye	A&M AM 1449	1973
There's No Time	A&M AM 1467	1973
Crazy Life	A&M AM 2536	1973
People Gotta Move	A&M AM 372/1614	1974
Powerful People	A&M AM 1652	1975
Mama Coco	A&M AM 1760	1975
Love Me Now	A&M AM 1732	1975
Keep On Walkin'	A&M AM 1790	1976
Love Of My Life	A&M AM 1861	1976
Fly Into The Night	A&M AM 1911	1976
One Night With You	A&M AM 2025	1977
Feel The Fire	A&M AM 2002	1977
I Just Wanna Stop	A&M AM 2072	1978
Wheels Of Life	A&M AM 2114	1979
River Must Flow	A&M AM 2133	1979
Living Inside Myself	Arista ASO 588	1981
Nightwalker	Arista ASO 613	1981
The Longer You Wait	Arista ASO 664	1982

Black Cars	Polydor PDS 2279	1985
Black Cars (12")	Polydor DJP 151	1985
Hurts To Be In Love (12")	Polydor DJP 163	1985
Hurts To Be In Love	Polydor PDS 2284	1985
Just A Motion Away	Polydor PDS 2289	1985
Wild Horses	Polydor PDS 2298	1987
In The Name Of Money	Polydor PDS 2303	1987
Persona Non Grata	Polydor PDS 2311	1987
The Time Of Day	Polygram 843639	1990
Inconsolable Man	Polygram 843639	1991
Cry Of Love	Polygram 843639	1991
If I Should Lose This Love	Polygram 843639	1991
Living Inside Myself	Polygram 513039	1992
I Die A Little More Each Day	Mercury 742057	1995

Albums/CDs:

Crazy Life	A&M SP 4395	1973
Powerful People (re titled People Gotta Move)	A&M SP 3630	1974
Storm At Sunup	A&M SP 4533	1975
Gist Of Gemini	A&M SP 4596	1976
A Pauper In Paradise	A&M SP 4664	1977
Brother To Brother	A&M SP 4722	1978
Best Of Gino Vannelli	A&M SP 9043	1980
Nightwalker	Arista AL 9539	1981
Black Cars	Polydor PDS 1 6415	1985
Big Dreamers Never Sleep	Polydor PDS 831 608 1	1987
Inconsolable Man	Polygram 843639	1990
Live In Montreal	Polygram 513039	1992
25th Anniversary Classics	A&M AM 2505	1995
Yonder Tree	Mercury 742057	1995
Slow Love	Polygram 57441	1998
Canto	BMG 881012	2002
Live In La	Sonore SRG 012	2014

Denny Vaughan

He was born Dennis Vaughan on December 20, 1922. In his teens he performed on radio station CFRB in Toronto. He studied at the University of Toronto, then toured Europe with The Army Show during World War II. He was also a member of the Allied Expeditionary Force under the direction of Bob Farnon.

Between 1945 and 1949 he sang, arranged and recorded with the British dance bands of Carroll Gibbons, George Melachrino, Cyril Stapleton, and Geraldo. Vaughan also became one of England's top male vocalists, where he became known as "the English Sinatra."

He was also a guest on Farnon's BBC show, Journey into Melody. Two years later, Denny moved to New York where he worked as an arranger for Eddie Fisher, Ezio Pinza and Kate Smith.

Vaughan returned to Toronto in 1952, and two years later he starred on his first CBC radio show, aptly titled, The Denny Vaughan Show, which ran until 1957. He was also heard coast to coast weekdays on the Players programs on the same network.

His most successful recording was the single, Walk Hand In Hand on Spiral Records in 1956, written by Johnny Cowell. He also recorded an album for Coral in 1958.

In 1959 he was appointed maestro of the Queen Elizabeth Hotel Orchestra in at the opening of the Salle Bonaventure in Montreal, where he stayed until 1963.

Vaughn then resumed his recording career and made some albums for the Canadian Talent Library, including *Denny Vaughan*, *Girls I Knew*, and *Denny Vaughan and His Orchestra*.

From 1967 to 1972 he worked in Hollywood as a bandleader and choral director on such TV shows as The Smothers Brothers Show and The Glen Campbell Goodtime Hour. He died in Montreal on October 2, 1972.

Singles:

Walk Hand In Hand	Spiral S 07	1956
Walk Hand In Hand (U.S.)	Kapp K 143	1956

Albums/CDs:

Denny Vaughn	Coral 56038	1958
Denny Vaughn and His Queen Elizabeth Hotel Orchestra	CTL S 5018	1963
Denny Vaughn	CTL S 5048	1964
Girls I Knew	CTL 5092/CAS 2358	1967
Denny Vaughn & His Orchestra	CTL S 5119	1969
Pot Pourri Continental	RCA PCS 1002	

Roch Voisine

Roch Voisine was born on March 26, 1963 in St. Basile, New Brunswick. As the eldest of three children born to Real and Zeland Voisine, Roch was a gifted athlete who, at 12 years of age, wanted to be a professional hockey player. But his career plans all changed when he was sidelined by a serious knee injury when he was eighteen, a pursuit he continued when he attended the University of Ottawa where he studied for a degree in physiotherapy.

He hosted the TV variety show, Top jeunesse for Television Quatre Saison in 1986, and played Danny Ross in the CBC TV series, He Shoots, He Scores.

In 1989 he teamed up with his friend, Stephane Lessard to write the romantic ballad Helene, a song inspired by the latter's breakup with a girlfriend. The song was a success in Quebec and in France, where it sold over a million copies.

Voisine returned to the small screen in the 1992 made for pay TV movie, Armin And Bullik.

Known by his fans as "Le Beau Roch," Voisine's first all English album, *I Will Always Be There* was released in 1993.

His popularity continued in 1996 with the release of *Kissing Rain*, and he continued to perform and record in both English and French.

Singles:

My Calgary	Roch Voisine 1001	1987
Las bas dans l'ombre	Star 3058	1989
Helene	Star STR 3061	1989/90
La bercuse du petit diable	Star STR 3086	1990
Pretty Face	Star STR 8026	1990
A Fishing Day	Star STR 8026	1991
On The Outside	Star STR 8026	1991
Waiting	Star STR 8026	1991
La legende de oochigeas	Star STR 8026	1992
L'idole	Star STR 8026	1993
Oochigeas (Indian Song)	Star STR 8026	1993
I Will Always Be There	Star STR 8056	1993
J'entends Frapper	Star STR 8063	1994
Lost Without You	Star STR 8056	1994
There's No Easy Way	Star STR 8056	1994
Shout Out Loud	Star STR 8056	1994
Am I Wrong	Star STR 8056	1994
She Picked On Me	Star STR 8056	1994/95
For Adam's Sake	Star STR 8056	1995
Heaven Or Hell	Star STR 8056	1995
Mylady Mio Segrato (CD/S)	Star STR 3141	1995
Kissing Rain	BMG 143978	1996/97
Deliver Me	BMG 143978	1997
Je resterai la	RV INT. 2300	1999

Albums/CDs:

Roch Voisine	Roch Voisine RV 101	1987
Roch Voisine	Roch Voisine 20 101	1987
Helene	Star STR 8014	1989
Double	Star STR 8023	1990
Roch Voisine	Star STR 8026	1991
I'll Always Be There	Star STR 8056	1993

Coup De Tete	Star STR 8063	1994
Kissing Rain	BMG 43978	1996
Chaque Feu	RV 2300	1999
Christmas Is Calling	RV 80398	2000
L'album De Noel	RV 2302	2000

The Waltons

Jason Walton Plumb (vocals, acoustic guitar)
David Cooney (drums)
Keith Nakonechy (vocals, bass guitar)

This acoustic pop trio from Regina organized in 1987. After playing various clubs in western Canada they decided it was time to break into the Toronto music scene. They began playing regularly and toured across Canada with The Pursuit of Happiness, The Barenaked Ladies, The Northern Pikes, and The Tragically Hip.

During their live shows, The Waltons honed their material and soon began to develop a loyal following with fans. They released two independent cassettes, *89 Demonstrations* and *Demo Sandwich*, and two MuchMusic/Videofact funded videos of Old and Alone Again.

In 1992 the trio released their debut album, *Lik My Trakter* which included songs about sarcasm (Colder Than You), angst (Don't Let It Slide), defiance (A Fine Line) and the innocence of youth (Naked Rain). Their subsequent albums on Wea included *Cock's Crow* in 1995 and *Empire Hotel* in 1998.

Singles:

Colder Than You	Wea 91951	1992/93
In The Meantime	Wea 91951	1993
The Naked Rain	Wea 91951	1993
I Could Care Less	Wea 91951	1994
Simple Brain	Wea 96143	1994
End of the World	Wea 99435	1995
Wascana	Wea 99435	1995
Michelangelo's Tummy	Wea 99435	1995
Beats The Hell Out Of Me	Wea 21388	1998

Albums/CDs:

Lik My Trakter	Wea 91951	1992
Simple Brain (Ep)	Wea 96143	1994
Cock's Crow	Wea 99435	1995
Empire Hotel	Wea 21388	1998

Christopher Ward

Born in Toronto, Ontario on July 28, 1949, Christopher Ward began singing and playing guitar while attending Trent University in Peterborough, Ontario, where he co-founded the campus radio station with songwriter and film producer Stephen Stohn.

In 1975 Ward signed a recording contract with Warner Music and enjoyed a brief solo career with such songs as Lost In A Love Song and Once In A Long Time. During the 1980s he was a deejay at MuchMusic, Canada's first all video station.

He continued to write songs and in the late 1980s launched the career of Alannah Myles. He and Toronto based songwriter/producer Dave Tyson collaborated on such songs as Love Is and Black Velvet, on her self-titled debut album.

Ward recorded two singles on Attic Records in 1987, Just Like Me and What Kind of Love. Today he is in a songwriter in Los Angeles.

Singles:

Lost In A Love Song	Warner Bros CW 4033	1976
Once In A Long Time	Warner Bros CW 4034	1977
Maybe Your Heart	Warner Bros CW 4036	1978
Imagine A Song	Warner Bros CW 72000	1978
No Time To Cry	Warner Bros CW 5501	1979
So Long Baby Jane	House of Lords2007	1981
Heartbreakin' Beauty	House of Lords2009	1981
Time Stands Still	House of Lords2010	1982
Words On The Wire	House of Lords2014	1982
Just Like Me	Attic AT 356	1987
What Kind of Love	Attic AT 362	1987

Albums/CDs:

SPARK OF DESire	Warner Bros KWSC 92000	1978
Christopher Ward (Ep)	Mint 102	1987
Time Stands Still	House of Lords10004	1981

The Watchmen

Danny Greaves (vocals)
Sammy Kohn (drums)
Peter Loewen (bass)
Joey Serlin (guitar)

This Winnipeg quartet began playing together in 1988. After four years of performing in clubs, they finally released their debut album, *Maclaren Furnace Room* in the fall of 1992. Released independently in 1992, it included, Run and Hide which stirred up controversy because it dealt with violence towards women.

In 1994, MCA released their major label debut, *In the Trees*, which featured songs that had stronger lyrics and more intricate musical collaborations.

With their third, *Brand New Day* in 1996, the group experimented with different types of music as evidenced by the first single, Incarnate which combined talk/rap with a soft melodic hook. Their fourth album, *Silent Radar*, was released by EMI in 1998.

By the release of their fifth album, *Slomotion* (2001), bassist Peter Loewen had left and was replaced by Ken Tizzard, and the group had become a trio with the exit of drummer Sammy Kohn.

Singles:

Run and Hide	MCA 10697	1992
Cracked	MCA 10697	1992
Must to be Free	MCA 10697	1993
The Boneyard Tree	MCA 11105	1994
Wiser	MCA 11105	1994
All Uncovered	MCA 11105	1994/95
Lusitania	MCA 11105	1995
Incarnate (CD/S)	MCA 9618	1996
Incarnate	MCA 81009	1996
Shut Up	MCA 81009	1996
Zoom	MCA 81009	1996/97
Stereo	EMI 59031	1998
Any Day Now	EMI 59031	1998
Say Something	EMI 59031	1998/99
Brighter Hell	EMI 59031	1999
Absolutely Anytime	EMI DPRO 2168	2001

Albums/CDs:

Mclaren Furnace Room	MCA 10697	1992
In the Trees	MCA 11105	1994
Brand New Day	MCA 81009	1996
Silent Radar	EMI 59031	1998
Slomotion	EMI 524575	2001

Wednesday

Randy Begg (drums, guitar, vocals)
John (Jose) Dufek (bass, harp, vocals)
Mike O'Neil (guitary, harp, vocals)
Paul Andrew Smith (guitar, keyboards, vocals)

This Oshawa group gained instant fame in the fall of 1973 with a version of Last Kiss, which was originally released in 1964 by J. Frank Wilson and the Cavaliers. After Wednesday had made the record, John Driscoll, the band's producer, took it to 680 CFTR in Toronto. Its immediate response on Canadian radio made the group an overnight success. Late in 1973 it was added to Billboard's Hot 100 where it peaked at #34. Some of the group's other hits were versions of other rock and roll classics such as Mark Dinning's Teen Angel, Bobby Vinton's Roses Are Red, and Dion's Ruby Baby.

Singles:
Last Kiss	Ampes 1325	1973
Teen Angel	Ampes 1355	1974
Roses are Red	Ampes 1362	1974
Fly Away	Ampes 1365	1975
Here Today, Gone Tomorrow	Skyline Sky 001X	1975
She's a Woman	Ampes AC 1370	1975
Loving You Baby	Skyline Sky 003X	1976
Doing the Best That I Can	Skyline Sky 006X	1976
Ruby Baby	Skyline Sky 011X	1976
Ride Me (Wenzday)	Skyline Sky 014X	1977
Now You're a Lady	Skyline Sky 016X	1977
Elenore (Wenzday)		1981

Albums/CDs:
Last Kiss	Ampes AC 10152	1974
Loving You Baby	Skyline Sky 10160	1976
Nearly Made It (Wenzday)	Skyline Sky 10164	1977

The Weeknd

This Scarborough, Ontario native earned the nickname "The Weeknd" after never coming home when he left with friends. Originally spelt as weekend, it was changed to avoid a copyright issue with a Canadian band with the same name. He was born Abel Tesfayeon February 16, 1990. At 17 he dropped out of school and developed a fan base with self-released albums *Thursday*, *Echoes Of Silence*, and *House of Balloons* in 2011. In 2012 Cash Money released Drake's Crew Love with Weeknd. Monkey Puzzle released Elastic Heart by Sia with Diplo and The Weeknd. Republic Records released his debut album, *Trilogy* in 2012. This was followed by *Kiss Land* in 2013 In 2014, his song, Earned It, was featured on the soundtrack of the film, Fifty Shades of Grey. It was nominated for Best Song. In 2015 his second album, Beauty Behind The Madness was released.

Singles:

Crew Love	Cash Money USCM 00056	2012
Elastic Heart	Monkey Puzzle USRC 00976	2013
Earned It	Republic USUG 401951	2015
Where You Belong	Republic USUG 500008	2015
The Hills	Republic USUG 500738	2015
Can't Feel My Face	Republic USUG 500741	2015
Often	Republic USUG 401324	2015
Real Life	Republic USUG 500914	2015
Tell Your Friends	Republic USUG 500918	2015
Prisoner	Republic USUG 500932	2015
Acquainted	Republic USUG 500920	2015
Losers	Republic USUG 500916	2015
Dark Times	Republic USUG 500930	2015
In The Night	Republic USUG 500951	2015

Albums/CDs:

Trilogy	Republic 719793	2012
Kiss Land	Republic 751447	2013
Beauty Behind the Madness	Republic 750330	2015

Weeping Tile

Mary Harmer (bass, vocals) Replaced by Rebecca Gould
Sarah Harmer (guitar, vocals)
Camille Giroux (drums, vocals)
Luther Wright (guitar, vocals)

Singer/songwriter Sarah Harmer began performing in Toronto as a member of The Saddletramps. She moved to Kingston in 1993 where she started Weeping Tile. Luther Wright, who was a founding member of The Mugworts, joined in 1994, while Camille Giroux in 1995. Sarah's older sister Mary left in 1996 and was replaced by Rebecca Gould.

After the independent Eepee in 1994, they signed to Warner Music, who released their debut album, *Cold Snap*, in 1995. Their second album, *Valentino*, came out in 1997. After touring to promote that album, the group went on a hiatus.

Luther Wright continued to play and record in another Kingston group, Luther Wright and The Wrongs, who have released three CDs, *High or Hurtin'* (1997) and *Luther Wright & The Wrongs* (1999) and *Rebuild the Wall Part 1* (Universal 37652 2001). Sarah Harmer recorded Songs For Clem (1999), a collection of songs in tribute to her father, and You Were Here (Universal 596452 2000).

Singles:
U.F.O. Rosie	Wea 12383	1995
South of Me	Wea 19928	1997
Old Perfume	Wea 19928	1997

Albums/CDs:
Eepee (EP)	Wea 11279	1994
Cold Snap	Wea 12383	1995
Valentino	Wea 19928	1997

Moxie Whitney

Born Moxam Whitney in Brockville, Ontario on June 2, 1919, he started the playing the piano as a child. At seventeen he was leader and guitarist of the Pacific Swingsters, an Hawaiian group at a Toronto theatre. He later played for bandleader Stanley St. John among others and was a trumpeter in the Royal Canadian Air Force during World War II.

In 1946 he formed his own band which played at the Granite Club, and he started playing at various hotels and resorts across Canada, such as the Chateau Lake Louise, the Banff Springs Hotel, The Royal York in Toronto, and Royal Canadian in Honolulu. He also served as a hotelier in Grand Cayman Island and the Bahamas. By 1975 he was back in Canada and, a year later, was bandleader at the Chateau Laurier Hotel in Ottawa.

After singing with Mart Kenney and Jack Kaufman, Roy Roberts became Whitney's band vocalist from 1955 to 1957 and again from 1960. Roberts briefly led his own orchestra before retiring from music to spend more time with his family, and died in September 1983. Moxie Whitney died on July 21, 1989.

Albums/CDs:
Moxie Whitney & His Orchestra	CTL M1034/S 5034	1963
Dancing Around The World	ARC 668	1965
At The Imperial Room	Harmony HES 6009	

Banff
Moxie Whitney & His Big Band

Harmony HES 6011
RCA KXL1 0245

Wide Mouth Mason

Safwan Javed (drums)
Earl Pereira (bass)
Shawn Verreault (vocals, guitar)

This blues/rock trio from Saskatoon, Saskatchewan is comprised of Safwan Javed, Earl Pereira, and Shawn Verreault. Verreault and Javed had known each other since elementary school where they played Wipeout at school assemblies. Pereira met Verreault when the two were in high school.

In late 1995 after Pereira and Javed had graduated from university, they started Wide Mouth Mason with Verreault. They toured the Prairies and in 1996 recorded and distributed their independent cassette, *The Nazarene*, which they made in a shed studio called Brown Sound, owned by Carson Cole, a former pig and chicken farmer.

When Big Sugar's Gordie Johnson and Paul Brennan first heard the group, they wanted Wide Mouth Mason as the opening act on their Canadian tour in late 1996. They were also signed by Warner Music on the strength of a live tape sent by the band's co-manager, Norman Sharpe. The label re-released their independent cassette in February 1997. Two years later came their sophomore release, *Where I Started*, followed by Stew (2000).

Singles:
Midnight Rain	Wea 17328	1997
My Old Self	Wea 17328	1997
This Mourning	Wea 17328	1997/98
Why	Wea 26739	1999
Companion (Lay Me Down)	Wea 26739	1999
Sugarcane	Wea 26739	1999
Smile	Wea 83774	2000

Albums/CDs:
Wide Mouth Mason	Wea 17328	1997
Where I Started	Wea 26739	1999
Stew	Wea 83774	2000

David Wiffen

David Wiffen was born on March 11, 1942 in Redhill, Surrey, England. While in his teens he came to Canada and settled in Toronto. He later hitchhiked across Canada and ended up in Calgary where he briefly managed a coffeehouse called The Depression.

In 1965 he was invited to play with other artists at the Bunk House folk club in Vancouver, which was also going to be recorded for an album. David was the only one who showed up. The recording session ended up being a solo album for Wiffen called, Live at the Bunkhose.

His interest in rock and roll led him to the west coast where he played with The Pacers from northern British Columbia. When they were offered a record deal in Montreal, Wiffen followed them east. The deal, however, fell through and he went to Ottawa.

Now based in Canada's capital, he joined its first folk/rock band, The Children. In addition to Wiffen, it was comprised of Bill Hawkins, Bruce Cockburn, Sneezy Waters, Neville Wells, Sandy Crawley, and Richard Patterson, formerly of The Esquires.

Late 1966 the Vancouver folk trio Three's A Crowd played in Ottawa at the Le Hibou Coffee House. During their visit they met Wiffen, who knew them from his days as manager of The Depression in Calgary.

Since folk music was on its way out, the trio decided to add electric instruments and drums to sound more like the new folk rock sound coming from such American groups as The Lovin' Spoonful. They asked Wiffen to join as lead male vocalist and rhythm guitarist. In addition to him, they added Comrie Smith of Toronto on bass, and Richard Patterson, who was then with The Children, on drums. The expanded version of Three's A Crowd played at various coffeehouses in Canada and the northeastern United States. They were also offered to play the Ontario Pavilion at Expo 67.

When Three's A Crowd played at the Bitter End, a folk club in New York, Wiffen was spotted by a talent scout and ended up being signed to a solo contract with Fantasy Records. His self-titled debut album came out in 1971. It produced two-sided hit single, One Step and More Often Than Not, which has also been recorded by Ian and Sylvia, Jerry Jeff Walker, Eric Anderson, Bill Hughes among others. In 1973 United Artists released Wiffen's album, Coast To Coast Fever which was nominated for a Juno Award.

Until 1985 he had seldom performed in public. His career was interrupted by a battle with alcoholism, drugs and periods of depression. He worked for a messenger service where he delivered envelopes and parcels by car, drove a limousine, and was a driver for Para Trans, a transportation company that served people with disabilities. While working with Para Trans, he injured his back which was later corrected by an operation. During his recovery he found an artistic outlet in painting, sculpture and poetry.

Two volumes of his poetry and other writings have been published. They are *Anthos, Volume 2, Nos. 1 and 2*, and *Wastelands, Vol 1 No. 1*. In 1991 he created a series of paintings and sculptures called Vernissage.

EMI Music Canada reissued his album, Coast To Coast Fever in 1994, and five years later came an album of new material, *South of Somewhere*. Today, Wiffen lives in Ottawa.

Singles:
One Step	Fantasy656	1971
More Often Than Not	Fantasy656	1971

Albums/CDs:
At The Bunkhouse Coffeehouse	International STB 2334	1965
David Wiffen	Fantasy8411	1971
Coast to Coast Fever	United ArtistsUALA 172	1973
Coast to Coast Fever (CD R)	Emi 26707	1994
South of Somewhere	SOS 0449	1998
South of Somewhere	True North TND 186	1999
Songs from the Lost & Found	True North TND 602	2015

David Wilcox

David Wilcox was born in Montreal on July 13, 1949. He was raised by his mother and her family, who were from the province of Moravia in what used to be Czechoslovakia. When he was six or seven years old, David discovered Elvis Presley and wanted to learn the guitar. While in high school he learned to play other instruments, including trumpet, clarinet and flute. Until he was twenty, he was a folk purist. When he was introduced to the blues by bluesman Bukka White, David learned a lot about the guitar. He later bought a pawn ticket for a Fender telecaster from a friend, and not long after he was invited to replace Amos Garrett in Ian and Sylvia's backup band, whom Wilcox toured and recorded. He then joined The Rhythm Rockets until he left to form The David Wilcox Band, and then The Teddy Bears, who played a mix of various styles of music from Big Bands to Rhythm and Blues.

In 1980, the independent label Freedom Records released Wilcox's debut album, *Out of the Woods*, which he had recorded two years earlier. It was picked up by Capitol when he signed with the label. His debut album, *My Eyes Keep Me in Trouble*, was released in August 1983.

Throughout the 1980s and early 1990s, he had such hits as *Breakfast at the Circus* and *The Natural Edge*. By 2000, he had signed to Stony Plain, who released the CD, *Rhythm of Love*, which featured on backup, such singers as Sarah Harmer, Suzie Vinnick, Colin Cripps and Ian Thornley from Big Wreck, ex Shuffle Demon Richard Underhill, and The Band's Richard Bell.

Singles:

Just This Side of Heaven	Capitol 72924	1983
The Grind	Capitol SPRO 256	1984
Blood Money (12")	Capitol SPRO 279	1985
Breakfast at the Circus	Capitol B 73050	1988
Fire in My Bones	Capitol SPRO	1988
Layin' Pipe	Capitol B 73055	1988
Layin' Pipe (12")	Capitol SPRO 347	1988
Between the Lines	Capitol B 73061	1988
Bless the World	Emi 26700	1993
Ecstasy	Emi 26700	1993
Truth and Fiction	Emi 34633	1996
I am the Motor	Emi 833139	1997

Albums/CDs:

Out of the Woods	Freedom FR 010	1980
My Eyes Keep Me in Trouble	Capitol ST 6503	1983
Bad Reputation	Capitol ST 6513	1984
The Best of David Wilcox	Capitol ST 6522	1985
Breakfast at the Circus	Capitol ST 4855	1987
The Natural Edge	Capitol 92464	1989
Over 60 Minutes With	Capitol 46888	1990
Collected Works 1977 1993	Emi 26700	1993
Thirteen Songs	Emi 34633	1996
Nightshift Watchman	Koch 7921d	1996
Greatest Hits Too	Emi 833139	1997
Rhythm of Love	Stony Plain 1271	2000
Rockin' the Boogie	Stony Plain 1283	2002

Wild Strawberries

Ken Harrison (vocals, keyboards, synthesizers, accordion, organ)
Roberta Carter Harrison (vocals)

Named after the 1957 Ingmar Bergman film of the same name, Toronto-based Wild Strawberries is comprised of husband and wife, Ken and Roberta Carter

Harrison. They first met when they studied medicine at the University of Toronto after moving from their hometown of Cambridge, Ontario.

Ken and Roberta first sang in the band, Myrrh Street Bleeding. In 1989 the duo recorded the independent cassette, *Carving Wooden Spectacles*. It was followed by their first album, *Grace*, which featured the song, Life Sized Marilyn Monroe.

In 1994 A&M Records released the album, *Bet You Think I'm Lonely*. Nettwerk Records put out their next two, *Heroine* (1995) and *Quiver* (1998), while Universal Music their fourth CD, *Twist* (2000).

Singles:
Crying Shame	A&M 5009	1993
Bet You Think I'm Lonely	A&M 5009	1994
Mannequin	A&M 5009	1995
Fall	Nettwerk 30099	1995
I Don't Want to Think About It	Nettwerk 30099	1996
Heroine	Nettwerk 30099	1996
Trampoline	Nettwerk 30119	1998
Pretty Lip	Nettwerk 30119	1998
Wrong to Let You Go	Wea 38141	1999
Wish	Universal 422012	2000

Albums/CDs:
Bet You Think I'm Lonely	A&M 5009	1994
Heroine	Nettwerk 30099	1995
Quiver	Nettwerk 30119	1998
Twist	Universal 422012	2000
Formative Years	Maple WW2HA	2005
Project	Wild Straw U2WERO	2013

Willie and The Walkers

Bill Hardie (guitar)
Roland Hardie (drums)
Willie Mac Calder (vocals, keyboards)
Dennis Petruk (guitar)

Formed in 1963, Willie and The Walkers were a quartet with matching guitars that were bought at Harmony Kids, a music store in their home town of Edmonton, Alberta. In the mid 1960s they opened for many acts, including The Guess Who featuring lead singer Burton Cummings, Dino, Desi & Billy, Paul Revere and The Raiders and Cream.

Willie and The Walkers recorded in Clovis, New Mexico with Norman Petty,

Buddy Holly's former manager and producer. By 1967 they had signed with Capitol Records. Their first single was Diamonds and Gold. It was followed by Alone In My Room. The original group split up in the early 1970s. Willie Mac Calder went on to join The Powder Blues Band.

Twenty-five years after they first played together, the original members reunited for Edmonton's First Annual Rock and Roll Reunion in 1988. They were suddenly in demand again. However, the pressure and demands of touring took their toll on the band, and there were some personnel changes.

Dennis Petruk's brother Nick replaced Roland Hardie on drums. There were three new additions: Rick Francis on vocals, R. J. Smarton on keyboards, and guitarist Sam Paladino. They are now known as The Walkers.

Singles:
Diamonds And Gold	Capitol 72456	1967
My Friend	Capitol 72485	1967
Alone In My Room	Capitol 72516	1967/68

Jesse Winchester

Born in Bossier City, Louisiana on May 17, 1944, Jesse Winchester came to Canada in 1967 as a conscientious objector to the Vietnam War. He became a Canadian citizen in 1973 and settled in Montreal with his French Canadian wife and three children. Since his self-titled debut album came out on Bearsville Records in 1970, he has become one of North America's most respected songwriters.

Among those who have recorded his songs include Emmylou Harris, Nicolette Larson, Don Williams, Jimmy Buffett, Joan Baez, The Everly Brothers, Colleen Peterson, Ronnie Hawkins, Lynn Anderson, Brenda Lee, Glen Campbell, Anne Murray, Reba McEntire, The Mavericks, and Wynona. In 1999, Attic released the CD, *Gentlemen of Leisure*.

He died of bladder cancer on April 11, 2014.

Singles:
Yankee Lady	Bearsville BSV 3619	1970
Isn't That So	Bearsville BSV 3601	1973
Snow	Bearsville BSV 3619	1973/74
Third Rate Romance	Bearsville BSV 3645	1974
Let The Rough Side Drag	Bearsville BSV 3814	1976

Everybody Knows But Me	Bearsville BSS 0314	1976
Nothing But A Breeze	Bearsville BSS 0318	1977
Rhumba Man	Bearsville BSS 0320	1977
Sassy	Bearsville BSS 0332	1978
A Touch On The Rainy Side	Bearsville BSV 3888	1978
Sure Enough	Bearsville BSV 3904	1981
Baby Blue	Bearsville BSV 3904	1981
Say What	Bearsville BSS 49711	1981
Want To Mean Something	Attic AT 386	1989

Albums/CDs:

Jesse Winchester	Bearsville BR 2012	1970
Third Down, 110 To Go	Bearsville BR 2102	1972
Learn To Love It	Bearsville BR 6953	1974
Let The Rough Side Drag	Bearsville BR 6964	1976
Nothing But A Breeze	Bearsville BR 6968	1977
A Touch On The Rainy Side	Bearsville BRK 6984	1978
Talk Memphis	Bearsville XBR 6989	1981
Humour Me	Attic LAT 1252	1988
The Best Of	Rhino 70085	1989
Gentleman Of Leisure	Attic ACD 1539	1999

Witness Inc.

Allan Ayers (bass guitar)
Les Bateman (organ, electric piano)
Ed Clynton (guitar)
Craig Kaleal (drums)
Kenny Shields (vocals)

The motivating force behind this quintet from Saskatoon, Saskatchewan is vocalist Kenny Shields. With an exciting stage show and a contract with Apex Records, they built up a following wherever they played. Their first hit on the label was I'll Forget Her Tomorrow. It was a big hit in the Prairie Provinces and Manitoba. They also were a smash stage act who had conquered Western Canada by the summer of 1967.

In the fall of that same year, Jezebel was released as their followup single. Although it had failed to have any impact in Toronto, it sold well out west.

The year 1968 saw the band finally achieve success in Ontario, except in Toronto, with their hit, Harlem Lady. It was also a hit in the Maritime provinces.

Their fourth hit, Visions of Vanessa was released in 1968 but it failed to reach an audience in the Toronto market. It finally happened, however, in 1969 with So

Come With Me.

On stage, Witness played their own material as well as The Moody Blues, The Small Faces, and Blood Sweat and Tears.

Singles:

I'll Forget Her Tomorrow	Apex 77044	1967
Jezebel	Apex 77063	1967
Harlem Lady	Apex 77077	1968
Visions of Vanessa	Apex 77087	1968
So Come With Me	Apex 77093	1969

Priscilla Wright

Born in London, Ontario, Priscilla Wright was the youngest Canadian performer to have a hit in both the United States and Canada with Man In The Raincoat on Unique Records. Written by Warwick Webster, she was backed up by her father and manager Don Wright and The Septette. It went on to sell half a million copies, and peaked at #16 on Billboard's Hot 100 in 1955. Cashbox also named her the Most Promising Female Vocalist of the year.

The popularity of Man In The Raincoat brought her appearances on The Ed Sullivan Show, the CBC network, and with Elvis Presley in the movie short, *A Day in the Life of a Pop Star*.

Since she was still a young teenager, her parents decided to pull their daughter out of the limelight so she would have a normal childhood and finish her education.

By the mid 1980s, Priscilla had returned to performing across Canada and abroad, and was a featured vocalist in the Moxie Whitney Big Band, and The National Press and Allied Workers' Jazz Band.

She became the first female vocalist in Canada to re-record one of her hits and see it reach the Top Ten, when Man In The Raincoat entered RPM's Adult Contemporary chart in 1988 where it peaked at #8.

In 1992, Attic Records released the album, *When You Love Somebody*, and, three years later came, *The Singer and The Song*, an album of jazz and pop standards.

Today, she performs with The Bill Jupp Band and has recorded with Mart Kenney, in addition to continuing her solo career.

Singles:

Man in the Raincoat	Unique 303	1955
Man in the Raincoat	Sparton134	1955
Me and My Bestest Feller	Sparton442	1957
Say You'll Stay Forever	Paylode PL 1993	1985
Heartbeat	Paylode PL 1990	1985
Words on the Wire	Comstock 1801	1986
Man in the Raincoat	Tembo TS 8802	1988
We Rise Again	Musbr DRCD 90001	1990
Midnight Man	Attic ACD 1339	1993
Woman's Intuition	Attic ACD 1339	1993

Albums/CDs:

When You Love Somebody	Attic ACD 1339	1992
The Singer and The Song	Radioland Racd 10003	1995

Neil Young

Born on November 12, 1945 in Toronto, Ontario, Neil Young was one of the first Canadian artists to make it big in the United States. He first became interested in music in 1958 when his father bought him an ukelele for Christmas. Later when his parents separated, Neil moved with his mother to Winnipeg where he learned to play the banjo and guitar.

At Kelvin High in the early 1960s he played in a group called The Squires. In the fall of 1962 he dropped out of school to play music full time. His musical influences included Elvis Presley, The Ventures, The Shadows, The Beatles and Bob Dylan.

Neil began writing his own songs in 1964. He moved back to Toronto where he joined The Mynah Birds. They broke up after a making the single, The Mynah Bird Hop, on Columbia Records.

He then joined Bruce Palmer and relocated to Los Angeles where met Stephen Stills and Richie Furay to form Buffalo Springfield.

For the next two years Young was a member of Buffalo Springfield. When they broke up in 1968, Neil decided to go solo and formed his own backup group called The Rockets, later renamed Crazy Horse. They were comprised of Danny Whitten on lead guitar, Billy Talbot on bass, and Ralph Molina on drums. Nils Lofgren and Frank Sampredo joined later on organ and rhythm guitar respectively.

In August, 1969 he joined Crosby, Stills, and Nash at Woodstock. From 1970 he established himself as one of the nation's top performers. He wrote the soundtracks for such movies as The Landlord (1970) and The Strawberry Statement (1970). His hit single, Heart of Gold, peaked at number one on

Billboard's Hot 100 on March 18, 1972. On April 21, 1972 it was certified a million seller by RIAA.

In November, 1975 he recorded the album, *Zuma* with a reformed Crazy Horse, and was a guest performer in director Martin Scorsese's documentary of the The Band's final concert, The Last Waltz in 1978.

Today, Neil Young continues to be successful as a mainstream pop troubadour. In 1995 he was inducted into the Rock and Roll Hall of Fame.

Singles:

Sugar Mountain	Reprise 0911	1968
Cinnamon Girl	Reprise 0911	1970
Only Love Can Break Your Heart	Reprise 0958	1970
Oh Lonesome Me	Reprise 0898	1971
When You Dance I Can Really Love	Reprise 0992	1971
Going To The Country	Ampes 4000	1971
Heart Of Gold	Reprise RPS 1065	1972
Old Man	Reprise RPS 1084	1972
War Song	Reprise RPS 1099	1972
Time Fades Away	Reprise RPS 1184	1973
Walk On	Reprise RPS 1209	1974
Lookin' For A Love	Reprise RPS 1344	1976
Drive Back	Reprise RPS 1350	1976
Hey Babe	Reprise RPS 1390	1977
Like A Hurricane	Reprise RPS 1391	1977
Bite The Bullet	Reprise RPS 1392	1977
Sugar Mountain	Reprise RPS 1393	1977
Comes A Time	Reprise RPS 1395	1978
Four Strong Winds	Reprise RPS 1396	1978
Hey Hey My My (Into The Black)	Reprise 49031	1979
Hawks and Doves	Reprise 49555	1980
Southern Pacific	Reprise 49870	1981
Sample and Hold (12")	Geffen92 01050	1982
Little Thing Called Love	Geffen92 98877	1983
Computer Age	GeffenXGHS 2018	1983
Wonderin' (with The Shocking Pinks)	Geffen92 95747	1983
Are There Anymore Real Cowboys? (with Willie Nelson)	Columbia 38 05566	1985
Get Back To The Country	Geffen92 88837	1985
Touch The Night	GeffenXGHS 24109	1986
People On The Streets	GeffenXGHS 24109	1986
Weight Of The World	Geffen928623 7	1986
Ten Men Workin'	Reprise 92 79087	1988
This Note's For You	Reprise 92 57914	1988
Needle and The Damage Done	Reprise 1393	1989
Rockin' In The Free World	SIL/FID 7 22776 A	1989
Mansion On The Hill	Reprise CDW26315	1990
Over And Over	Reprise CDW26315	1990
Cinnamon Girl	Reprise CDW26671	1991
War of Man	Reprise CDW45057	1992

Harvest Moon	Reprise CDW45057	1992
Unknown Legend	Reprise CDW45057	1993
From Hank to Hendrix	Reprise CDW45057	1993
Long May You Run	Reprise CDW45057	1993
Philadelphia	Epic EK 57624	1993
All Along The Watchtower	Columbia C2K53230	1993
Sleeps With Angels	Reprise CDW45749	1994
Change Your Mind	Reprise CDW45749	1994
Piece Of Crap	Reprise CDW45749	1994
Prime of Life	Reprise CDW45749	1995
Downtown	Reprise CDW45934	1995
Peace and Love	Reprise CDW45934	1995
Dead Man	Reprise CDW46171	1996
Big Time	Reprise CDW46291	1996
This Town	Reprise CDW46291	1996
Razor Love	Reprise CDW 47305	2000
Fool For Your Love/ All Along The Watchtower	Reprise 100507	2001

Albums/CDs:

Neil Young	Reprise RS 6317	1968
Everybody Knows This Is Nowhere	Reprise RS 6349	1969
After The Goldsrush	Reprise RS 6383	1970
Harvest	Reprise 2032	1972
Journey Through The Past	Warner Bros 2XS 6480	1972
Time Fades Away	Reprise MS 2151	1973
On The Beach	Reprise MS 2180	1974
Tonight's The Night	Reprise MS 2221	1975
Zuma	Reprise MS 2242	1975
Decade	Reprise MS 2257	1977
American Stars And Bars	Reprise KMS 2261	1977
Comes A Time	Reprise MSK 2266	1978
Rust Never Sleeps	Reprise XHS 2295	1979
Live Rust	Reprise 2CRS 2296	1979
Hawks And Doves	Reprise XHS 2297	1980
Re Ac Tor	Reprise XHS 2304	1981
Everybody's Rockin'	Geffen XGHS 4013	1983
Trans	Geffen XGHS 2018	1983
Old Ways	Geffen XGHS 24068	1985
Landing On Water	Geffen XGHS 24109	1986
Life	Geffen XGHS 24154	1987
This Note's For You	Reprise 57191	1988
Freedom	Reprise 92 58991	1989
Ragged Glory	Reprise CD26315	1990
Weld	Reprise CD26671	1991
Harvest Moon	Reprise CDW45057	1992
Lucky Thirteen	Geffen MD24452	1993
Unplugged	Reprise CDW45310	1993
Sleeps With Angels	Reprise CDW45749	1994
Mirror Ball	Reprise CDW45934	1995

Music From & Inspired By The Motion Picture Dead Man	Reprise CDW46171	1996
Broken Arrow	Reprise CDW46291	1996
Year Of The Horse	Reprise CDW46652	1997
Silver & Gold	Reprise CDW47305	2000
Road Rock Volume 1	Reprise CDW48036	2000
Are You Passionate	Reprise 948111	2002
Prairie Wind	CDW 495932	2005
Living With Ar	Reprise 432652	2006
Live At The Fillmore East	Reprise 293684	2006
Chrome Dreams Ii	Reprise 311932	
Massey Hall-1971	Reprise 43328	2007
Live At Canterbury House 1968	Reprise 5512563	2008
Dreamin' Man Live '92	Reprise 511277	2009
Le Noise	Reprise 96186l	2010
Interrnational Harvesters	Reprise 526520	2011
Psychedelic Pill	Reprise 531980	2012
Archives Vol 1 1963-1972	Warner 494975	2012
Live At The Cellar	Reprise 535854	2013
Storytone	Warner 546105	2014
A Letter Home	Reprise 493999	2014
Archives Vol 2 Vinyl Box Set	Reprise 535704	2014
Document	Blue Line 154479	2015
Blur Note Café	Reprise 550219	2015

Yukon

Bob Becker (keyboards)
Wayne Dietrich (bass)
Tom Hishon (drums) Replaced by Ed Miller
Mike Lehman (vocals)
Bill Mononen (guitars)
Ted Zawadski (guitars)

Yukon started out in Kitchener, Ontario in 1965 as a trio comprised of Mike Lehman, Tom Hishon, and Ted Zawadski. They went under various names for the first two years, such as The Fifth Dimension, The Prophet, and The Chase.

In 1967 they added Gino Wojek, who was briefly a member of Copper Penny, Wayne Dietrich, Bob Becker, and Ed Miller replaced Hishon on drums. He rejoined the group in 1969 when they changed their name to Your Favorite Thing. The rest of the lineup was comprised of Zawadski, Dietrich, Beckr, and Bill Monomen. They changed their name to Yukon in 1971.

They began backing up other rock stars who came to Kitchener. One of them,

Freddy Cannon, was instrumental in getting the group signed to Sussex Records. Their first single, Understanding Is Sorrow was released in 1971. They had three other singles with the label, and played with April Wine, Lighthouse, and Crowbar.

Yukon broke up at the end of 1973. Mike Lehman had minor success with the singles (Something's Burning) I'm On Fire (Rubber Bullet 101 1975) and Someday (Can't Stop Myself From Loving You) (Axe 47 1977).

Singles:
Understanding is Sorrow	Sussex 220	1971
A Message	Sussex 228	1972
Fallen Angel	Sussex 249	1973
Flying Machine	Sussex 258	1973

Zon

Howard Helm (keyboards)
Kim Hunt (drums)
Brian Miller (guitar)
Jim Sampson (bass)
Denton Young (vocals)

This five-piece Toronto-based band began recording together in 1978 when they signed to a major multi-national label. Just when they were about to hit it big, the label dropped the group after only two albums, *Astral Projector* (1978) and *Worried About The Boys* (1980). Despite what happened they decided to stay together and work on their next album. They also continued playing which led to changes in the stage act. During this time they caught the attention of Falcon Records, a Canadian Independent label distributed by A&M Records. They signed them in late 1980, and released their first single, For You in 1981. (see Harlequin and Streetheart)

Singles:
Melody	Epic E4 4177	1978
Talkin' About	Epic E4 4189	1978
Sweet Jane	Falcon FAS 1005	1980
For You	Falcon FAS 1006	1981

Albums/CDs:
Astral Projector	Epic PEC 90442	1978
Back Down to Earth	Epic PEC 80026	1979
I'm Worried About the Boys	Falcon FAL 80,003	1980

A Short Bio of Rick Jackson

From Kingston, Ontario, Mr. Jackson is an author, film critic and broadcaster. He grew up on army bases and became interested in collecting music charts from CFNB in Fredericton, New Brunswick.

Even though he never learned to play a musical instrument, he became interested in the information side of the music world. Before going in 1973 to Loyalist College in Belleville, Ontario to take a radio course he already had an encyclopedic knowledge of rock and roll. Beginning in 1973, he started interviewing members of Canadian groups. This eventually led to the first edition of The Encyclopedia of Rock, Pop & Folk Music in Canada published in 1994. While taking a journalism course in 1976 at the University of Waterloo, he interviewed Bobby Vee and Del Shannon and in Kingston, Ontario he interviewed, Buddy Knox. In 1997 he began interviewing more Canadian musicians and groups on his Kingston radio show entitled "Artists and Music of the 20th Century" at CFRC.

Favourable response to the first edition of, *The Encyclopedia of Rock, Pop & Folk Music in Canada* made it possible for him to expand, correct and update the vast quantity of data for the second edition.

He is also the author of the, *Encyclopedia of Canadian Country Music* published in 1996. In 1983 he self-published a volume of movie reviews entitled "At the Movies". Rex Reed, then film critic for The New York Post wrote: "Your love of movies is reflected in your opinions." You can find his film review blog established in 2005 at: www.jacksonfilm.blogspot.ca

CPSIA information can be obtained
at www.ICGtesting.com
Printed in the USA
LVOW03s0045101216
516540LV00002B/2/P